Analyzing
Social Behavior:
Behavior Analysis
and the
Social Sciences

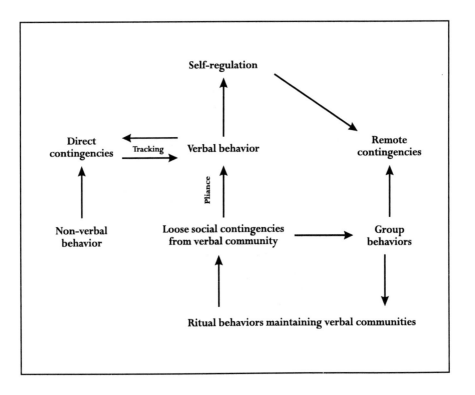

Analyzing Social Behavior: Behavior Analysis and the Social Sciences

Bernard Guerin
University of Waikato

4

Analyzing social behavior: Behavior analysis and the social sciences / by Bernard
Guerin.

399 pp. Paperback. ISBN 1-878978-13-6

Hardback. ISBN 1-878978-14-4

Includes bibliographies and index.

© 1994 CONTEXT PRESS
933 Gear Street, Reno, NV 89503-2729

Printed in the United States of America

Table of Contents

Preface 11

Part I:
The Principles of Behavior Analysis

Chapter 1. Introduction to behavior analysis 15

Chapter 2. The components of behavior analysis 23
  2.1. Antecedent conditions and stimulus contexts................. 23
    Stimulus generalization 24
    Discrimination and perception 25
    Attending to stimuli... 26
    Establishing operations and motivative variables............. 29
    Information, signals and signs 30
  2.2. Behaviors and responses 31
    Response classes and operants.. 31
    Strengthening of response classes...................................... 33
    The natural selection of response classes 34
    Response-induced responses... 36
  2.3. Consequences 37
    General points 37
    Types of consequences 41
    Scheduling of consequences... 51
  2.4. Contingency history 53

Chapter 3. Combining contingencies 55
  3.1. Layers of contingencies.. 55
    Two-term contingencies 55
    Three-term contingencies 58
    Four-term contingencies 62
    Stimulus equivalence classes 63
  3.2. Multiple contingencies 67
    Choices between contingencies 69

Arranging contingencies between multiple responses 71
Restricting contingencies 73
Extinction of contingencies 74
Addition of new contingencies 75
How one contingency can mysteriously
affect another 76
3.3. Analyzing social contingencies 78
What is special about social behavior? 78
Properties of social behavior 80

Part II:
Social Contingencies Without a Verbal Community

Chapter 4. Social discriminations 85
4.1. Conspecifics as stimulus contexts 85
Social versus nonsocial discrimination 86
Discriminative cues 87
4.2. Generalized discriminations provided
by other people 88
Social compliance 89
Verbal behavior 90
Social facilitation 92
Imitation 94
Observational learning 95
Social comparison and auditing 96
Gestures 97
Common points 99

Chapter 5. Social consequences 101
5.1. Properties of social consequences 101
Types of social consequences 101
The dynamic scheduling of social contingencies 103
Verbal control of social consequences 104
5.2. Group contingencies and the allocation
of consequences 105
Contingencies applied to a whole group 105

The "structure" of group contingencies 107
Discrimination in groups 109
Large groups 110
Using group contingencies in practice 112
5.3. The hidden consequences in traditional
     social psychology 112
The manipulations of consequences 113
Anonymity and evaluation 118
The inherent consequences of being in a group 120
Conclusions 121

Chapter 6. Social behaviors and social interaction 125
6.1. Advantages of group behavior 126
6.2. Cooperation 126
6.3. Competition 130
6.4. Helping behavior 132
6.5. Sharing 133
6.6. Social skills and social interaction patterns 134
6.7. Experimental studies of longer term
     social interactions 136
6.8. Verbal behavior, metacontingencies,
     and interlocking social behaviors 136

Part III:
Social Contingencies with a Verbal Community

Chapter 7. Verbal behavior and language use 143
7.1. Principles of linguistic verbal behavior 143
7.2. Types of verbal behavior 146
7.3. Audience control of verbal behavior 149
Verbal conditioning 149
Audience selection of behavior 151
7.4. Instructions and verbally controlled behavior 153
7.5. Correspondence between saying and doing 157
The relations between saying and doing 157
Training correspondence 158

7.6. Verbal behavior and self-regulation 160
7.7. Social compliance and self-regulation 161
7.8. Other linguistic verbal behaviors 164

Chapter 8. Social cognition and behavior analysis 165
8.1. Cognitive psychology and behavior analysis 165
Background to cognition 165
Behavior analysis and the cognitive phenomena 168
8.2. Some private events 175
Anticipation 176
Intention 176
8.3. Thinking 177
8.4. Self events 178
What is the "self"? 179
Self-reporting of behavior 180
Self-reinforcement 184
Self-control 185
Self-reference and self-attribution 186
8.5. Affect and emotion 187
8.6. Intrinsic motivation 187
8.7. Creativity 189
8.8. Decision making and choice 189
A behavioral model of choice 190
Verbal behavior and decision making.......................... 191
8.9. Zen and the art of
contingency-governed behavior 194

Chapter 9. Verbal communities 197
9.1. Conceptions of verbal communities............................ 198
Social science conceptions of community..................... 198
Sociolinguistic speech communities 202
Self-categorization and social identity theories 205
"Community" in community psychology 207
The "stranger" in sociology 209
9.2. Social behavior as discriminative
context and consequence 210

9.3. Behaviors maintaining a community 211
  Languages and paralanguages 212
  Totems, taboos and rituals 213
  Money and commodity exchange 219
  Verbally controlled behavior: Bureaucracy,
    law and rationality 222
9.4. The evolution of verbal communities 227
  Historical 227
  The life of communities over time 228

Chapter 10. Behaviors maintained by a verbal community ... 231
  10.1. Attributions and social attributions 232
  10.2. The social construction of knowledge 235
  10.3. Attitudes and attitude change 236
    Attitudes and verbal behavior 236
    Attitude change 241
    The theory of reasoned action 243
  10.4. Impersonal trust 245
  10.5. Social support, weak ties and social networks 246
  10.6. Social remembering 247
  10.7. Music and writing 248
  10.8. Rumours 251
  10.9. Modernity, mass media and
    computer communication 252

Part IV:
Applying Behavior Analysis

Chapter 11. Changing and maintaining behavior 259
  11.1. Ethical and practical considerations 259
  11.2. Changing the behavior of individuals 260
    Training new behaviors 261
    Strengthening behaviors 263
    Weakening behaviors 264
    Changing verbal contingencies with individuals 268

Generalization and maintenance of
   behavior change 270
11.3. Changing verbal communities 274
   Techniques for changing verbal communities 277

Chapter 12. Behavior analysis of particular groups
        and social issues.. 281
12.1. Politics and behavior analysis 282
12.2. Women and feminist psychology 283
   Women and power 284
   The social construction of gender 285
12.3. Children and their contingencies............................. 287
12.4. People with intellectual disabilities
      and autism 289
12.5. The aged and their contingencies 290
12.6. Organizational behavior management....................... 292
12.7. Intervention and the production
      of countercontrol 293
   Positive effects of intervention 295
   Negative effects of intervention 298
   Designing better evaluations and interventions 300

References 303

Subject index 373

Author index 380

Preface

The major aim of this book is to show that behavior analysis can cogently, and with a lot of originality, talk about and experiment with social phenomena while still keeping a natural science approach. It also aims to show that sociology, anthropology, sociolinguistics, and musicology do not have to be tacked hastily onto social psychology, but have a proper place within the social sciences where they must take over from social psychological approaches. Their phenomena do not look much like natural science (and so all sorts of meta-universes of discourse are invented), but they are ultimately, and not reductively, based in natural science.

What worries me is that a book with these aims easily swings between rushing through too much, at a speed of several hundred social phenomena explained-away-per-hour, and not saying enough to convince anyone. If one merely cites some sociology, for example, then sociologists presume that the person does not really know the area. If one spends time and goes into depth over each social phenomena, then the book either becomes too large or leaves out too much. Hence I always worry about books like this one.

For these reasons, I here apologize to all those I gloss over in this book with a mere citation, a cursory glance at their many years of hard research, or miss out altogether. I did it because of the type of book I want this to be—the type I think is needed at this point in time for both behavior analysis and social psychology. I hope the readers will follow up the fascinating details so carefully given in the original references. The real importance of all this material lies in the details, as always, and that requires following up. The many references are not there to look impressive but to use.

Writing a book such as this requires many behaviors commonly described as single-minded, dogmatic, arrogant, and unfriendly. I would like to acknowledge, thank and apologize (i.e., grovel) to all those who have come into contact with these behaviors of mine.

I especially wish to thank my three major and consistent critics who have done so much to destroy my thinking each time I thought I had got somewhere. They are Wendy Gunthorpe, James McEwan and Mary Foster. They are each worth many who merely give blanket praise or rejection. Wendy read many of the very early drafts (thanks, Gundy!), and Mary read many of the later drafts. James went over most of the arguments with me, and nicely punished me for thinking woolly thoughts.

Bits and pieces in various forms were also helped from readings and discussions with Vicki Lee, Ed Morris, Bill Temple, Mike Smithson, Rich DeGrandepre and Paul Taylor—thanks for your time and effort. And of course, the ever present anonymous reviewers: I love 'em and I hate 'em. Lastly, but not leastly, Steven and Linda Hayes, for agreeing to publish the book and for putting a lot of time into making it published.

Thanks to all of you who struggled through versions and re-versions. I hope it's worthwhile. There are many infelicities and violent abuses of English still in the book, but I alone am responsible for what remains. You all tried to warn me. My only excuse is that English is my first language and I have therefore been exposed to, and reinforced for copying, vagrant abuses of perfect English by verbal sub-communities throughout my life. The second language I am now learning is much more correct and proper because it is being verbally controlled from the start.

Finally, I want to thank all my family, friends and colleagues for support over the years of writing all this book, and sometimes even making encouraging noises. Also Bushka, *watashi no neko,* who missed out on many games while this was being written.

Bernard Guerin

Part 1

The Principles of
Behavior Analysis

Chapter 1

Introduction to Behavior Analysis

There were two goals I had in writing this book. The first goal was to write an account of behavior analysis which was up-to-date and would be interesting, and hopefully understandable, to those social scientists not familiar with the area. As a social psychologist, when I first began reading behavior analysis there was much that did not interest me because it did not seem relevant to the study of humans and their social behavior. The analyses of social behavior that were available were fine, but they passed over whole areas of social behavior–especially those of most concern to social psychologists. Although useful, many of these accounts I later found to be either very outdated or very simple analyses (Malott, 1973; McGinnies, 1970; McGinnies & Ferster, 1971; McLaughlin, 1971; Ulrich & Mountjoy, 1972). Both these problems are understandable given their time of writing, but I wanted to write the sort of book that I wish had been available from the start.

The second goal in writing this book was to develop a full analysis of social behavior, albeit preliminary, including material from sociology, sociolinguistics, musicology and anthropology. I had since found out, of course, that there were some good analyses of social behavior hidden in the behavior analysis literature, but they still needed pulling together and much more development.

This introductory chapter therefore contains two themes–an introduction and a conclusion. The introduction is to orient new readers of behavior analysis to the field; the conclusion suggests what they might get out of behavior analysis by the end of the book. I have developed the idea of verbal communities quite markedly from how it is talked about usually in behavior analysis, so those familiar with behavior analysis might want to read the concluding remarks before launching into Chapter 2 or their favourite topic.

Introductory remarks. These introductory remarks are to set the scene, especially for social scientists unfamiliar with behavior analysis, and those who think they are familiar. This is mainly to get across the message to not give in to peer pressure–that behavior analysis is not at all like you have read and heard about it. It does not reduce everything to food and sex reinforcers, nor does it throw out the window all the good things like the mind or the self or theorizing or innate behaviors or thoughts or feelings or attitudes or the brain or information or emotions or symbolic behaviors or knowledge. These are straw-person arguments which both introductory and advanced psychology books promulgate.

Please keep an open mind as you read and please keep the straw-person behaviorisms to yourself. Behavior analysts get tired of constantly fighting straw-person critiques. A few years ago I decided to give this up altogether, and to leave people alone if they did not bother to read behavior analysis and therefore believe that it throws out the window the mind or the self or theorizing...etc. This happened when I realized that such straw-person behaviorisms existed as social representations within the psychological community (see Chapter 10), and therefore would not be changed by rational argument.

If the reader is still worried that behavior analysis does do all those nasty things above, then here are three strategies to help you decide. First, keep an open mind (see, I said the word!) and read this book thoroughly. Find your favourite concepts and phenomena and see how they can be analyzed by behavior analysts, and follow up the references because I have summarized so much.

A second strategy is to read some of the rejoinders which have been given by behavior analysts to critiques. As mentioned, I get tired of thinking about them, but some writers have done an excellent job. Try the following: Todd & Morris (1992), Delprato & Midgley (1992), Lee (1988), Morris (1993), Hayes (1986), Hineline (1980, 1990, 1992).

Finally, you can consider these four thoughts of someone who has been through it. First, keep in mind that if there are effects in the world, or phenomena, then behavior analysis is not going to deny they exist. When we say we are feeling depressed or that we have an open mind, *something* is going on! What behavior analysis does differently than the rest of psychology is to look more closely at the effects themselves and what has occurred in the past when they happened. This often leads it to talk about the phenomena rather differently than other social sciences.

My second thought is that the arguments of behavior analysis, and especially the philosophies of behaviorism, form a circle. If you have learned only half the arguments then you can easily criticize the rest. Students to whom we teach this thoroughly, suddenly, one day, have an aha! experience, when the full circle of arguments joins up and they see the entire picture at once. For example, if you just understand the idea that the meaning of an event is its consequences, you can easily knock this down. But your counter-argument is almost always going to contain other assumptions with which behaviorism disagrees. Until you get the full circle of assumptions right, you cannot see how they fit together and you will not get the aha! experience. Remember, there was a reason why B. F. Skinner called his version of the philosophy, *Radical* Behaviorism. The word radical is accurate.

My third thought you could keep in mind is that behavior analysis turns out to be a bountiful ground for social scientists. Most of the mysterious qualities of human life, such as symbolic behavior, subjectivity, thought, spirit influence, mind, Zen mind, self-identity, self-awareness, linguistic meaning and grammar, conscious-ness, beliefs and attitudes, do not disappear in behavior analysis as if they never existed, but they are actually shown to be controlled by social factors (patterns of verbal community influence). They all become essential social events, and therefore provide a truly social, social science, and help argue against the individualistic interpretations of some social psychologies.

So following from the first thought I gave, these "subjective" phenomena are real enough, but they are talked about very differently by behavior analysts. They are talked about as socially derived phenomena, which is a bonus for the social sciences as I see things. As I gradually delved into behavior analysis, I was very surprised at how useful behavior analysis was for analyzing and interpreting social behavior, especially at a community and societal level—even though a common criticism is that it only works for individual animals. There are no new principles of behavior for social behavior, like a group mind or a collective representation, but the properties are so very different to individual behavior that one can understand why group minds were postulated in the first place. And these special properties of socially organized behaviors are so hidden and unobvious that one can also understand why they were all put into the body as individual minds, souls and subjectivities.

My fourth and final thought to help you through is what behavior analysis can do for you. In particular, there is a powerful history of applied behavior analysis. If your aim is to change the world then behavior analysis is right out there in front. It still needs more development in community and societal level change, however, but I have reviewed this material and made many suggestions along these lines in Chapter 11 and 12.7.

The reason I believe behavior analysis has worked so well in changing behavior is because it has paid more attention to the consequences of behavior than any other psychology. In behavior analytic terms (launching into Chapter 2 here), there are three components (not really separable, however) for the most simplest analysis of behavior: the contexts in which the behavior and its consequences occur, the behavior itself, and the previous and current consequences of the behavior in that context.

Of these components, it is the consequences which are poorly analyzed in most other psychologies, and which I believe weakens the applications made by social psychology. As I stress in this book, social psychology in particular either hides the consequences away (see 5.3), or else drags them in as a "drive for consistency", a "drive which leads us to compare ourselves with others", a "desire for positive self-esteem...[and] the need for self-definition, or structure", or as "hedonistic relevance". How is one to change behavior when one of the three essential components is analyzed in these static ways? How do you go about changing the drives, needs and desires in order to change behavior?—this is not spelled out.

It is precisely in changing behavior that behavior analysis reaps the benefits of its full analysis of behavior. The authors of the above statements do an excellent job of analyzing the situational contexts for the social behavior and the social behavior itself, but lose out by not giving enough attention to consequences (I do not want to name them here because there are so many others who do the same, and because these ones at least spell out all their assumptions). And once again, when most of the needs and desires of social psychology are analyzed they are found to refer to social factors—patterns of verbal community influence. So one of the three social bases of behavior has been glossed over as drives and desires.

Concluding remarks. In lieu of a concluding chapter (which everyone reads first anyway), I want to outline here my conclusions. I cannot hope to summarize everything in the book—there is too much. Instead, I want to give the points that I hope readers will take away with them. Those readers new to behavior analysis might want to keep re-reading this section as they read the book.

Contingencies can be usefully analyzed into the components outlined in Chapter 2. Behaviors have consequences in certain contexts which can affect their likelihood of occurring again in that context or in similar contexts. The contingencies between contexts, behaviors and consequences form the subject matter of behavior analysis (and psychology). Each component can only be defined with respect to the other components. For example, a behavior cannot be defined without the context in which it has had effective consequences in the past. In this sense, there is no such thing as just a behavior, like moving the arm. Moreover, not only gross body movements but thoughts, feelings, and talking are considered behaviors, and therefore they each have discriminative contexts and effective consequences as part of their contingencies. Behavior changes when the contingencies change.

Life, however, actually consists of multiple contingencies, which behavior analysis is starting to study more (Chapter 3). The relative strengths of the contingencies and the manner in which they come to be patterned, structured or layered determine what an animal does. For nonhuman animals, this work is starting to have an influence in the study of animal ecology.

Human contingencies are a bit more complicated but not because there are any new principles of contingent relations among stimulus contexts, behaviors, and effective consequences. Rather, the layering of multiple contingencies becomes more complex with humans. In particular for this book, humans can form groups which provide consequences to group members very loosely or indiscriminately, in the sense that there does not need to be a direct or immediate consequence for the consequence provider. This provision of loose consequences can occur because the group formation as a whole reinforces the individuals in very many ways. Without immediate, effective consequences for the provider of the loose consequences, such verbal communities are unlikely to occur with animal groups.

This way of forming groups (verbal communities) means that behaviors can become almost detached or uncoupled altogether from the nonsocial environment. This occurs if there are contingencies which consist of social contexts and social consequences, and of behaviors which have little impact on the nonsocial environment. For example, speaking has little consequence on the nonsocial environment, except to produce a small airflow, and the contexts and consequences forming the contingencies involved in speaking are social (Chapter 7). Verbal behavior, defined in this way, therefore includes language use, music, art, gestures ("non-verbal" behavior!), money use, symbolic behaviors, rituals, socially constructed knowledge, attitudes, and rumours.

Looked at in this pragmatic way, words do not refer to things, words only ever refer people to things. Words and other verbal behaviors are therefore always performative. Because of these properties which are formed through verbal communities, we are able to talk about green elephants, martians, and black holes—because the only truth of the words is the effect they have on people, not an effect "relating" to elephants or black holes.

The loose or indiscriminate reinforcements from verbal communities, which maintain such behaviors, are hardly noticeable, unlike a piece of food, a bundle of money or some water. The behaviors they maintain have therefore typically been viewed as caused or controlled by an inner self or mind, an unspecified desire, drive or need, or by spirits. Ironically, these very individualistic, internal notions turn out to be the most thoroughly and essentially social of all contingencies.

This same argument applies to thoughts, feelings, attitudes, and social knowledge. These behaviors are doubly hidden, because they are covert, unlike talking, in the sense that they cannot be seen by others, as well as having their maintenance controlled by a verbal community's system of loose reinforcement. Such "private events" are not indicative of an inner language or a private inner existence, but of generalized social maintenance. Because they are so detached from control by the nonsocial environment, unlike making a cup of coffee which is constrained by the nonsocial environment, they can probably only occur in the special verbal communities formed by humans.

A final complication with analyzing human behavior is that many behaviors function merely to maintain the verbal communities, because of their many advantages. The function of such "symbolic" behaviors therefore has little to do with what is done: the doing of the symbolic behavior or ritual is itself the function, since it acts to maintain the group as a whole. For example, the function of taking bread in the Catholic Mass should not be analyzed in terms of eating food; the function is one of maintaining the community itself.

A scheme for analyzing human behavior. As a guide to the analysis of human behavior, I will finish these introductory and concluding remarks with a scheme for approaching episodes of human behavior and analyzing them. If one person is seen to walk up to another and do something to them, for example, these are the sorts of questions you could work through to get an initial analysis of the behavior sequences.

1. What might be the consequences from the physical environment for this behavior? (Part 1 of the book). Part of behavior analysis consists of finding out what people can do with things in the environment.

2. What other contingencies might be present as alternative behaviors? (Chapter 3) Are there multiple contingencies which are having a subtle effect.

3. What are the immediate or direct effects from people in the vicinity? (Part 2 of the book) Are other people giving direct consequences, acting as discriminative stimuli, or co-acting?

4. Is there a history of a verbal community maintaining the behavior? (a group which reinforces in a loose manner; Part 3 of the book)
5. If there is a verbal community maintaining the behavior then does the behavior reinforce the maintenance of the community (a ritual or symbolic behavior, 9.3) or does the behavior have a particular reinforcing group outcome if most of the community does the behavior (a reinforcing metacontingency, Chapter 10)?
6. How might we go about changing the behavior? (Part 4 of the book; and this will depend upon the answers to 1-5 above)

To give an example of how this initial orienting analysis might go, consider the case of speeding in a car. We need to consider the following:

1. The effects from the physical environment for speeding (getting places faster, the wind, the sound of the engine, the "feel" of the road surface).
2. The immediate effects from people in the vicinity (avoiding pedestrians, ignoring strangers who shake their fist at you, using other drivers to gauge your speed).
3. The additive metacontingencies of many people driving (traffic jams, air pollution).
4. What the verbal community says and does about speeding (the law, passengers, the media presentations about speeding, generalized social punishers for speeding, family views on speeding) as well as the verbal community's advantages from the behavior (things gets done faster in a vehicular society and help the entire economy. In fact, the advantages are so many that no one would suggest outlawing cars altogether just because we cannot stop people speeding: the community's advantages are always weighed against the individual risks).
5. Whether speeding might ritually maintain any verbal sub-communities rather than providing more direct individual or community outcomes (ritual speeding to maintain adolescent male groups, or perhaps some lonely people might speed to maintain an interaction with police?).
6. To change speeding behavior we might need to change each of these different contingencies which partially control speeding (Chapter 11). Just reinforcing individuals for not speeding will not suffice if verbal communities in society strongly reinforce speeding.

These analyses are not mutually exclusive, of course, and within each of them there will be further facets to analyze. But how do you decide whether your analysis is correct or not? The answer to this is simple to give, but hard in practice.

An analysis is correct if you can show that the controlling variables actually have an effect. That is, they have to be shown by experiment or intervention, not by deduction or theorizing (Sidman, 1960; Skinner, 1950). For example, suppose we put a regular driver in a special car which was sound-proof, air-proof, and in which there was no "feel" of the road surface. If they began to speed more, but slowed down again when we brought the noise and other variables back again, then we would suspect that these three variables (all nonsocial consequences) had been controlling the speeding: that speed was reduced as the noise increased, the wind increased, etc. My supposed experiment is too simple, but particular experimental and intervention methods provide the proof of controlling variables (Sidman, 1960).

This way of conducting interventions reflects the pragmatist philosophy behind behavior analysis. The truth or meaning is the effects or consequences something has: how you talk about it does not have truth except for the effects of what you say on people. If the sound of the road is controlling speeding behavior (slowing down when the noise increases), then you must be able to show the effect by removing the variable (a sound-proof car) and returning it.

One final consideration. Behavior analysis is also a lot of fun. Being able to look for and show controlling variables is exciting enough, but being able to analyze difficult behaviors theoretically, by using the simple and layered contingencies, is even more exciting. The theoretical analyses do not amount to much until experimental or intervention studies are carried out, but they are worthwhile putting thought into. Skinner (1950) did not write that one should not theorize, as is often reported by critics, but that one should not theorize between different levels of subject matter. One of his books even had "theoretical analysis" in the title (Skinner, 1969).

Much of this book consists of theoretical analyses because the areas have not been tackled in this way before (I sometimes broach wild speculation). Where possible I have referenced experimental material from all the social sciences, and other analyses. I have tried to cover all the major areas of social science, however weakly, in order that those new to behavior analysis can see how their specialities might be tackled in a new way. I hope readers enjoy the speculation and experimental results, follow their own thoughts up with experimental research, and attack the other phenomena of social life in the spirit of behavior analysis.

Chapter 2

The Components of Behavior Analysis

2.1. Antecedent Conditions and Stimulus Contexts

One of the key phenomenon of behavior is that if a behavior is strengthened or reinforced by contingent consequences then *the context or situation in which this occurs comes to have some control over the behavior.* This is an important foundation for behavior analysis and one which has many implications. It is a key way in which antecedent stimuli, contexts or settings come to have influence over our behavior. An obvious example might be walking into a study or home office just to get something and "without thinking" suddenly finding yourself doing work which you had not "intended" doing. [The phrases in quotes highlight that the setting or context in this case has taken over control of our behavior from verbally governed behavior or thought. See 7.4. and Baum & Heath, 1992.]

The control by contextual events is not a triggering effect: a stimulus does not elicit or trigger a behavior like a billiard ball. Skinner was very particular about moving away from the Stimulus-Response formulations which had been unsuccessful in psychology, first with Watson and then with Hull and Spence (Chiesa, 1992; Iversen, 1992; Lee, 1988; Moxley, 1992). Textbooks have often confused the two since the same word "stimulus" occurs in "stimulus-response", "discriminative stimulus", and "stimulus control", but a whole new way of thinking is involved with behavior analytic stimulus control. For this reason the present book will usually refer to a context, a stimulus context, or a setting, when speaking about the "stimuli" of behavior analysis.

The stimulus context which is present when a response is strengthened or reinforced (we will explore these terms in 2.3) has a different effect from triggering a response. The stimulus context exerts its control by making the response more likely to occur in the future when that context is again present. This general property of behavior is called *stimulus control* and the context is properly called a *discriminative stimulus*.

For example, in the presence of a cat most people are far more likely to make the verbal response "cat" than the response "aardvark". In a room without a cat, the response "cat" is less likely to occur (unless there are other stimulus conditions for it). The presence of a cat does not trigger off the response "cat" in a billiard-ball mechanistic fashion, but makes the response more likely depending upon very subtle contextual conditions (see 3.2) and the history of the person (2.4).

As mentioned above, the term *stimulus context* will generally be used throughout this book rather than stimulus because I believe it is less problematic. The common way of speaking about a stimulus or many stimuli gives the impression that there must always be an object or a thing present—THE stimulus. While this is sometimes true, that a simple object present during reinforcement can control future responses, it is not always the case (cf. Kantor, 1970). Often a whole context, situation or setting comes to control the production of responses. For example, being at the doctor's surgery makes many behaviors more likely to occur, ones which might not occur in any other settings (such as compliance), but it is not just one object which controls this—the "discriminative stimulus" in this case is a very complex setting with many objects and smells. Indeed, it is often hard to verbalize exactly such a context. I believe that referring to this as a stimulus gives a misleading impression of precision (also see Deitz & Malone, 1985, for other refinements of terminology).

From what has already been said it should be clear that the way in which stimulus contexts come to control behavior is very important to behavior analysis. If a child is aggressive, you need to find out the contexts in which the aggression occurs, or the stimulus objects (possibly people) present when the aggression occurs. You will then have a good analysis of what stimulus contexts are controlling the behavior because the behavior has been strengthened in those settings in the past. Stimulus contexts are also important for behavior change. We might train an aggressive child not to fight at home, but find that they are still fighting just as much at school.

The precise study of how it is that contexts come to control behavior began with Skinner (1938), who first formulated the three-term contingency by ceasing to think of stimuli as triggers for behavior. The work has steadily grown since then and much is known about the details of stimulus or contextual control. Some of the properties of stimulus control will be given here, and their place in whole contingencies is presented later in 3.1.

Stimulus Generalization

An important property of any stimulus control is that if a stimulus context controls a response (or another whole contingency), then *any similar contexts* will also control that response to some degree (Honig & Urcuioli, 1981; Mostofsky, 1965). In the classic demonstrations, a rat's bar pressing is first strengthened (contingently reinforced) only when a red light is on. There is no strengthening with any other light colour. It is found from this that while the rat responds most strongly when the red light is on (the red light controls the behavior), and does not respond when a green or blue light is on, the rat does respond with orange and yellow lights but not as strongly as with a red light. This is called *stimulus generalization* (Skinner originally used the term *stimulus induction*, 1938).

Stimulus generalization is important for many reasons. First, it is a useful phenomenon when explaining how our more general or abstract "concepts" are formed. We can be reinforced for saying "tree" when there is a gum tree present, but we will also tend to respond likewise in the context of similar objects, such as pine trees and jacarandas. But we would not generalize to aardvarks and call them trees.

Stimulus generalization is also important when it is *not* very useful. In behavior training and therapy it is often found that people do not generalize some important contexts of stimulus control. For example, Rincover and Koegel (1975) showed that a behavior taught in a therapy situation for one boy (Cliff) would only occur in another setting if the table and chairs present during training were also present in that second setting. The stimulus control was too rigid so the behavior did not occur in other settings. Under these conditions, special procedures were needed to generalize the stimulus control beyond that which had been accidently trained.

Stimulus generalization also allows for the occurrence of new behaviors. If I respond in a context similar to one in which the behavior has previously been strengthened, then new contingencies become possible. For example, suppose a child has had patting reinforced when it was done to a cat, strengthened perhaps by the reactions of both the cat and the parents. The same behavior could then occur with a context *similar* to that of a cat—namely, a dog. This, however, is likely to produce new types of reactions from the animal (and therefore consequences for the child) which will lead to new behaviors (running away, if the dog reacts badly to patting!). So responding in similar contexts is one way that new behaviors can develop in both adults and children.

Discrimination and Perception

With the analysis of stimulus control, the realms of perception and psychophysics can be analyzed (Zuriff, 1972). We can find out what an animal can discriminate in the environment by whether that animal can respond differentially in different contexts If a red light contingently reinforces a rat's pressing of a bar, and a green light does not, then the rat would normally press the bar when the red light is on and stop pressing when the green light is on. This shows that the animal can discriminate red from green, because it responds differentially in the two different stimulus contexts. If the rat was red-green colour blind, however, then it would behave the same in both contexts. This same discrimination process occurs with humans, when we put our foot on the brake in the context of a red light and take it off for a green light, without thinking. The consequences for putting on the brake are different in the contexts of red and green lights, although they are more complicated than those for a rat, since social consequences are a part of going through red lights or not going through red lights.

A further complication for humans is that while we perform these simple discriminations all the time, we can also make verbal responses about those contingencies: "You must brake whenever there is a red light but do not put on the brake if there is a green light". It is clear, however, that we do not *have* to verbalize every time we stop at a red light. The discriminative control works without that. But in some cases the verbalization can affect a contingency, and this will be dealt with in 7.4. For the most part, though, when analyzing how people interact with the nonsocial environment, the context controls the selection of the behavior in conjunction with a previous history of reinforcement. This is what is usually referred to in psychology as responding without awareness, responding unconsciously, or responding intuitively. It must be kept in mind that this is the norm for both animals and humans; verbal behavior is just a special set of contingencies which sometimes interacts with other contingencies.

One interesting feature of perceptual analyses with discrimination as the basis is the role of the consequences. We usually do not think that perception and discrimination have anything to do with their consequences, since we just seem to look at whatever there is around us. But the implication is that if the consequences are very powerful for responding in one way, then a bias towards this will creep into even simple perceptual discriminations, although it is more obvious in studies of attention, which we will look at in the next section. Perceptual biases have traditionally been studied in psychology using signal detection models, but a behavior analysis is also appropriate (see Davison & McCarthy, 1987; McCarthy & Davison, 1981; Davison & Tustin, 1978, for excellent examples of this work). So what we can discriminate and do discriminate is a function of the previous consequences for doing so.

Attending to Stimuli

One well established finding is that attending to stimuli or contexts is a contingency. That is, the consequences and stimulus contexts of attending can determine the patterns and extent of attending. Schroeder and Holland (1968), for example, were able to control eye movements by changing the likelihood that a signal would be detected. Frazier and Bitetto (1969) found that this could be done independently at three different places requiring attention, at least for some combinations of their scheduling of consequences. Similar results can be shown for attention given to another person (Beardsley & McDowell, 1992, though see 7.3 for problems with the reinforcement used in this study).

Treating attention as a contingency means that even our complex patterns of attending to street signs, buildings, people around us, and transport, when walking down the street, can be related to our history of past consequences when attending to these things. This is an important point which is missed by most traditional and cognitive theories of attention (see Ray, 1972). Attending to this or that will depend upon the relative rates of reinforcement for attending, the amount of reinforcements involved in the past, and the inverse delays in the consequences. We often report this as our "interests," that I look at shop windows rather than the pavement because "they have more interest for me." After a few cases of finding money on the pavement, however, our interests in attention change.

Another property is that conditioned and generalized consequences (2.3) have been shown to influence attention: that is, animals will produce a response which has the consequence of letting the animal observe some other context correlated with positive consequences. These have been called "observing responses" (see

Hirota, 1972; Holland, 1958; Mueller & Dinsmoor, 1986; Wyckoff; 1952). For example, a rat will learn to press a bar for which the only contingent consequence is that it shows the rat which of the red or green lights are on. The rat can then press another bar which differentially reinforces pressing contingent on the light colour. Observing responses can be trained in many species of animals, including goldfish (Purdy & Peel, 1988).

In a similar way, Benton and Mefferd (1967) found that human subjects would pull a lever which focussed a slide projector. In this case the consequences are quite subtle and complex (Vaughan & Michael, 1982), but a probable analysis is that focussing leads to being able to respond appropriately to the pictures on the slides, which cannot be done if they are blurred, and responding appropriately to visual stimuli is almost always reinforced in some way or another as an *establishing operation*. Case, Ploog and Fantino (1990) did a similar, interesting study in which subjects played the Star Trek game on a computer. A complex (but powerful, if you have ever played the game!) social reinforcer was that of killing the Klingon invaders. Subjects could make another response, the observing response, which gave them information about the state of affairs in the Empire. It was shown that this observing response could be strengthened by the eventual reinforcement of killing Klingons.

The point of all this is that attentional responses become embedded, as it were, in very complex chains and layers of behaviors in which they act as observing responses, and are not directly or immediately reinforced at all. We do not get food pellets every time we focus our eyes or a slide projector lens; instead, focussing allows us to look at something which is a stimulus context for another contingency. We look at things, shift our eyes, and focus our eyes in order to be able to respond appropriately, even if the observing is not directly reinforced itself. In fact, most of what we do at all has a prerequisite that we look and focus clearly on something. So looking is probably the most important establishing operation of all.

Most of the time behavior analysts just assume the workings of attention without this more detailed analysis, so that if a light is placed near a rat in an experimental box, and the light changes when the consequences do, it is *assumed* that the rat will attend to this light and learn its discriminative function. But this attention is a phenomenon in itself, and more work is needed on it because, beyond the simple examples I have given, the analysis becomes harder (but even more interesting!).

Elsewhere (Guerin, 1990) I have suggested that a closer comparison to the work on perception by J. J. Gibson (1966, 1979) will point to some new ways of pursuing this line. This includes a re-thinking of the concept of a "stimulus" (cf. Gibson, 1960; Gibson & Gibson, 1955), a view of perception as an active response system rather than the passive reception of light, the consideration of classical conditioning as the operant conditioning of perceptual responses, and some speculation about how attentional and perceptual responses might be involved in equivalence classes.

Further, imagery and dreaming seem to be behaviors in which all the component attentional and perceptual responses are happening without their usual environmental context being present (Guerin, 1990). We can imagine looking at a dog when there are none around. This is possible when the direct consequences for attending are extremely powerful or when the "re-enacting" of the appropriate perceptual responses (such as moving the head and focussing) enables the organisms to then respond appropriately for other consequences (as discussed earlier for conditioned reinforcement of attention). This analysis assumes that the component responses of perception and attention are just like other behaviors and have discriminative stimuli (you only image in certain circumstances) and consequences (interesting events are made possible if you can image).

For example, a stimulus context in which "re-enacting" the perceptual responses has often been socially reinforced is that of verbal questioning. The consequences are very different following "What colour was that dog we saw yesterday?" if I can do a "re-take" of the perceptual responses I went through the previous day and give a correct answer. In principle, this is no different to being asked "How did you plant the beans yesterday?", and then "going through the motions" with my hands of what I had done but without the appropriate stimulus context of dirt and seeds. The study of imagery, then, is the study of the conditions under which I can and cannot do such re-takes of previous perceptual responses.

There is once again, however, the complication of verbal behavior with humans. If, on the previous day (when the dog was present), I had *said* to myself or someone else that the dog was black with white spots, then instead of re-enacting the perceptual responses when questioned the next day about the dog's colour, I can instead re-enact that verbal behavior. This is, in fact, probably one of the functions of verbal behavior which makes it so useful to us: it is easier to re-enact verbal behaviors than perceptual responses, probably because they become less confused with other responses over time. This means that it becomes very difficult to distinguish between people re-enacting perceptual responses and re-enacting verbal behaviors.

Whatever the responses involved, behavior analysis does not postulate a "representation" in the head to explain such events, as do most cognitive theories. The so-called "representation" is a series of perceptual or verbal behaviors, each with their own discriminative contexts and consequences, and these events do not occur just in the head. They differ from the motor behaviors usually talked about by behavior analysts, such as bar-pressing, only in that they are private events (see Chapter 8). When explaining them, cognitive theorists argue that if the perceptual behaviors are re-enacted then *a mini-replica of the original discriminative context has to exist* somewhere. Such a "replica" only "exists" in the perceptual history which has shaped the current perceptual responses, however. The same cognitive theorists would not postulate an ethereal replica of dirt and seedlings if I "went through the motions" with my hands of how I had previously planted some beans. There are still consequences and stimulus contexts when we just "go through the motions", but the are not the same ones as occurred originally.

I believe that a behavior analysis of attention and perception still has a long way to go yet (see Guerin, 1990). For those who might wish to explore this area, the following will be of help: Bickel and Etzel, 1985; Buzsaki, 1982; Case, Fantino and Wixted, 1985; Costall, 1984; Dinsmoor, 1985; Frazier and Bitetto, 1969; Goldiamond, 1962; Mackay, 1991; Malott, 1968; Mueller and Dinsmoor, 1986; Ray, 1972; Schneider and Morris, 1988; Schoenfeld and Cumming, 1963; Turvey, 1977; Turvey and Carello, 1986; Williams, 1984.

Establishing Operations and Motivative Variables

There are times when stimuli and settings affect our behavior but not in the exact way that discriminative stimuli do. For example, discriminative stimuli must have a history with reinforcement contingent upon a response only in their presence, but stimuli sometimes affect us without such a history. While in some cases this could be due to stimulus generalization, there are other cases which seem to preclude this as an explanation. These stimulus contexts have usually been called *establishing stimuli* or *setting events*, and the relevant responses *establishing operations*.

For example, we might be in the kitchen with a block of chocolate sitting in the fridge. That is, there is a contingency available in, or afforded by, the environment such that if we open the fridge then eating chocolate is possible. If we are not hungry, however, then we will usually not contact this contingency. If we are hungry, then we will likely open the fridge (if we have the pre-requisite history). This means that some antecedent condition, such as hunger or food-deprivation, is necessary before the fridge can act as a discriminative stimuli—even if other discriminative stimuli are involved as well.

Becoming hungry, then, is an establishing operation for contacting the chocolate-in-the-fridge contingency. The contingency itself and its discriminative context do not change during any of this, since my increase in hunger cannot do anything to the physical being of chocolate or fridges: being hungry for example cannot make it more likely that there is chocolate in the fridge. Rather, the reinforcing effectiveness of the chocolate is said to be changed if I am hungry. The long-term learning of the contingency is also not altered, merely a momentary change in reinforcer effectiveness.

This example involves a motivative variable, one dealing with deprivation, but there are other setting events not normally called deprivation. For example, much verbal behavior functions through establishing operations rather than through new contingencies. "I will give fifty cents for every mango you pick from the tree" will change the momentary effectiveness of mangoes as reinforcers, but the discriminative context for the contingency is still the same. Moreover, the change in mango-effectiveness in this case has nothing to do with hunger deprivation.

So establishing operations have the properties of temporarily changing whether an event can act as an effective discriminative stimulus or reinforcer, and changing the behaviors previously reinforced by that event (Michael, 1988, 1993). In the illustration above, my verbal behavior is the establishing operation and it changes the effectiveness of mangoes as reinforcers (even if I'm not hungry) and therefore increases mango picking. In this case it is an establishing operation which had to be learned at some point, whereas in the chocolate example above the food-deprivation is presumably unlearned (at least to the extent of eating when hungry).

Despite the excellent discussions on this topic, I believe that the terminology dealing with establishing operations is not yet complete. There are many controlling variables which are put together in this category merely because some observable event changes behavior and cannot otherwise be classified. Many examples involve larger units of behavior which are not well understood at present (see 3.2), as well as cases where there are very subtle consequences which are also not well understood. The terminology is certainly an advance on calling everything a discriminative stimulus, but my hunch is that the terminology will change again once these other areas are explored further. The increasing number of empirical studies on establishing operations will also help to clarify the controlling variables (Hall & Sundberg, 1987; McPherson & Osborne, 1986, 1988).

For more on establishing operations the reader could follow these leads: Chase and Hyten, 1985; Cherpas, 1993; Hall and Sundberg, 1987; Leigland, 1984; McPherson and Osborne, 1988; Michael, 1982a, 1983, 1988, 1993; Parrott, 1987; Vollmer and Iwata, 1991; Wahler and Fox, 1981).

Information, Signals and Signs

People often talk about stimulus contexts as information, signals or signs. For example, the familiar red and green lights are called "traffic signals". While this is fine for everyday talk, it is not precise enough for behavior analysts, who tend to avoid these three terms. It is not that the terms refer to events which do not exist, but rather, they lead to conceptual problems. This section discusses some of these problems.

The major problem with "information", as the term is usually used, is that it ignores the consequences involved in establishing such relations in the first place. It gives the impression that any information will be attended to, learned, and acted upon. That these behaviors also depend on the consequences in their contingencies is masked by the word and its usage. The events involved when the word information is used need to be analyzed as full contingencies with at least three components, whereas the use of the word "information" gives the impression of a Context-Response relation without any functional consequences having a role.

For example, someone might tell me that there is *information* on the class board about an exam tomorrow. Just knowing this, however, tells us little about the contexts for looking at the board, the actual responses involved in doing the exam, and especially the consequences which function to have us attend to and read the information, let alone act upon it. By talking about information divorced from consequences, as cognitive psychologists do, we only produce half the analysis of behavior. It seems to be assumed that once information is "given" the behavior will automatically follow without previous consequences. Then there is surprise when it does not (Ajzen & Fishbein, 1980). For these reasons the word information is avoided; it is imprecise and misleading and always requires further analysis.

The same comments apply to the words "signal" and "sign". While we might happily say in everyday life that the traffic lights "signalled to go", or were "a sign to drive off", this could mean any of the following: stimulus control, establishing operations, motivational (consequential) relations, or even elicited responses. Such vague terms are better avoided in scientific writing. A clearer and more detailed analysis of what is involved in traffic lights and responding in the context of traffic lights is needed. It is because we assume that people always attend to the traffic lights and drive when the lights are green that we can use the word signal. But the traffic lights might signal green without us driving off because of other contingencies, however. A shallow analysis without the consequences specified would not even consider this possibility.

2.2. Behaviors and Responses

Behavior analysis treats all our actions and conduct as behaviors, and this includes covert thinking and imaging as much as the more obvious physical body movements. There are a number of reasons why it is useful to do this. The most important of these is that it leads one to consider processes rather than objects. If we treat memory, for example, as a verb (remembering) instead of a noun (memory), different active perspectives are possible (Bartlett, 1932; Branch, 1977; Nilsson, Mantyla & Sandberg, 1987; Palmer, 1991; White, 1991).

I use the terms behavior and response interchangeably. The word response is not meant to imply an automatic response to a stimulus, however, like a reflex or triggering response. I will now discuss some major properties of behavior.

Response Classes and Operants

One of the most troublesome aspects of behavior analysis, and of psychology more generally, is that of defining behaviors. It was realized early on that it was not useful to treat each individual occurrence or instance of a response as a different response (Skinner, 1935). There seems to be something similar happening each time I repeat a response, so it is ludicrous to treat each instance individually. For example, we could treat each instance of smiling as the same response *smiling* rather than as separate and different responses.

Skinner's (1935) idea was to define a *response class* instead, where each instance would be considered a member of that class. For example, a response class might be waving your hand. Each time I wave my hand could be considered a member of that response class. The problem is still there, however, of knowing when a new class develops. Is waving my other hand a different response class, for example?

The very original way that Skinner (1935) dealt with this problem was to consider response classes as *functional units*, rather than trying to find structural or topographical (what they look like) features to define each class. That is, if the individual component responses are controlled by the same contexts and consequences, then they belong to the same response class. So if hand waving with either hand always occurs in the same circumstances, with the same controlling contexts and effective consequences, then they can be considered instances of the same response class. This way of viewing responses means that response classes have to be *demonstrated* rather than postulated. We cannot decide from our armchairs whether two instances of behavior are members of the same response class—we must show that they co-vary. This usefully puts the emphasis on experimentation.

This view also means that *behaviors cannot be defined without specifying the contingency of which they are a part.* This is an important point, since it means that the very same physical arm movement might be present in different contingencies and so the response class is different. The outcome of this is that *the basic unit of analysis is the contingency* rather than the behavior. While most views of psychology have behaviors as the basis ("Psychology is the study of behavior, emotion, and thought"), behavior analysis has the whole contingency as its unit: the response class, the functional consequences of those responses, and the contexts in which the consequences have their effect. This makes it an interactional psychology.

The definition of an *operant class* is more straightforward. An operant class is any response class which varies as a function of its consequences. Any responses which can be manipulated by changing the consequences are talked of as operants. This means that flying is normally not an operant: if I offer you $100 to wave your hands and fly, you could not easily do it. If I offered you $100 just to wave your hands, however, you could easily oblige. So waving the hands is an operant response. Notice again that operants have to be demonstrated rather than postulated or deduced.

In general, most of the so-called *voluntary behaviors* are operants, and involuntary behaviors are not. The involuntary behaviors are covered by classical conditioning or are classified as innate behaviors. So you can show by simple experiments that a cat's pawing of sand after defecating cannot be manipulated by any consequences, and is therefore likely to be an innate behavior. Similarly, you usually cannot easily stop a phobic reaction by changing consequences, and so this is likely due to previous classical conditioning. As mentioned already, most of the important everyday behaviors of humans are operants, and especially the social behaviors.

The definitions of response classes and operants we have gone through here are of great theoretical importance, by which I mean that how we talk and write about them is important and has important implications. One often finds that one way of talking is more useful than another, or that one way of talking seems useful at first but leads to all sorts of conceptual problems later.

For these reasons, behavior analysts have given a lot of time to finding the best ways to talk about response classes and operants, and only a few topics have been dealt with here. For those interested in pursuing this further, excellent discussions can be found in the following: Baer, 1976, 1982; Catania, 1973; Collier, Hirsch and Kanarek, 1977; Delprato, 1986; Galbicka, 1988; Lee, 1981a, 1983a, 1986, 1988, 1992; Midgley and Morris, 1988; Schoenfeld, 1976; Segal, 1972; Skinner, 1935, 1974; Staddon, 1967; Teitelbaum, 1977; Thompson and Lubinski, 1986; Thompson and Zeiler, 1986.

Strengthening of Response Classes

Responses are changed in a number of ways, and there are a number of ways of talking about this. The one that has been most useful to behavior analysis is to talk of the *probability of a response* (Espinosa, 1992; Johnson & Morris, 1987). That is, a response is talked about as more or less likely to occur (given an antecedent stimulus context). If a response is made more likely then we say that it has been strengthened or reinforced (like reinforced concrete). If it is made less probable then it might have been either weakened, punished or extinguished.

While there are some problems with talking this way, it has been most useful to behavior analysis, especially both in avoiding the trap of talking as if all responses are produced by a stimulus triggering a response, and in emphasizing that the response probability needs to be measured rather than hypothesized. One problem with this terminology, however, concerns the antecedent stimulus contexts. If we say that a response is highly probable but only in certain contexts, is the probability idea superfluous? Could we not say that the specific stimulus context is more or less likely and that the response will *always* occur if those specific conditions eventuate? That is, the probability might be in the environment, not "decided" by the response itself. This problem is usually avoided by talking about the components of the three term contingency as one unit, as suggested in the last section, so the response probability is a shorthand way of talking about stimulus context probability.

A second way of talking about response strength is to consider how long it takes to extinguish or stop that response when its functional consequences are stopped. Skinner (1938, 1940) originally referred to this strength as the *reflex reserve* (see also Killeen, 1988). This was the idea that each time a particular response is strengthened by its consequences, it acquires a small reserve of instances. So for example, if pressing a button was reinforced once then it might acquire 10 (fictional) points of reserve, meaning that 10 more presses could occur *without further reinforcement* until it stopped happening altogether. If it was reinforced twice, it might gain a possible 20 future presses without reinforcement, although such a linear increase is not actually found.

This version of response strength has more recently been given a better backing by the work of Nevin (1988; Nevin, Mandell & Atak, 1983; see also Mace, Hock, Lalli, West, Belfiore, Pinter & Brown, 1988). Nevin and his colleagues have defined a clearer notion which they call *behavioral momentum*, and they claim that it is a better measure of response strength than response rate (probability of response).

A third meaning which is often given to response strength is the idea of a stronger response being a more *effortful* or forceful response. This is, however, different from the above meanings, in that the force of a response is itself affected by antecedents and consequences (Eisenberger, 1989; Notterman, 1959; Notterman & Mintz, 1962). This means that the force or intensity of a response must be treated as a separate operant which has its own response strength in the earlier meaning of response probability. More forceful responses will occur under certain stimulus contexts, involve different response topographies, and have different consequences than less forceful responses.

For example, I can call your name out across the street quietly or loudly, and will get different consequences depending upon which I do, independently of what I actually call out. So producing your name in the first place turns out to be a separate operant from how loudly, or with how much effort, it is vocalized. This is given credence from studies which have set up different consequences for response strength and response force. Jackson and Wallace (1974), for example, treated a girl who could speak words (i.e., their behavioral momentum was sufficient) but was nearly inaudible. The authors trained her to speak louder.

The Natural Selection of Response Classes

A further conceptual twist to behavior analysis lies in the manner of thinking about the production of responses. Our everyday talk has us *wanting* to produce responses for consequences, or *needing* to produce responses for consequences. This is problematic since it leads us to conclude that the future can cause the present.

Instead, an *analogy* with evolutionary theory was proposed by Skinner (1981a; Glenn, Ellis & Greenspoon, 1992). In evolution, the different species produce slight genetic mutations or variations which are selected through natural selection. This means that some mutations which are adaptive, or at least harmless, will survive when those animals possessing that characteristic reproduce further members. Those which are not will die off before reproduction occurs. Another relevant point about evolution is that a large number of variations survive only in a small number of the population. For example, not everyone has red hair, but those with red hair are not necessarily dying out. These variations are important since environmental changes can select for characteristics which were previously ineffectual. Some variations might do better under the new conditions, when some environmental change has occurred, and previously dominant variations might now die off.

Skinner (1981a) proposed that the selection of responses by environmental contexts and consequences was analogous to evolutionary selection. Responses after birth consist of innate reflexes which occur under most stimulus contexts, as well as some variant responses produced through accident. But on top of this, some of these responses lead to consequences which strengthen or reinforce, meaning that the responses are more likely to be performed again under those environmental contexts. Other responses are extinguished or punished and "die off", meaning they become less likely to occur under those same environmental contexts.

A common error in reading this is to assume that Skinner was implying something about species and genetics: for instance, that reinforced responses are more likely to be passed onto new members of the species, or that some contingencies are genetically coded. It must be remembered that he was only making an analogy, that the same way of thinking about strengthening, selecting and reproducing can be used when thinking about behavior. The evolutionary method of logic transformed the biological sciences, and the same could happen in behavior analysis.

The variations which occur "naturally" in behavior can arise for a number of reasons (see Segal, 1972, for one of the few thorough papers on this, and also Epstein,

1991). For example, young children produce a wide variety of mouth sounds through reflexes. Some of these then lead to strengthening consequences from the parents, such as those resembling speech; others are extinguished because they lead to no strengthening consequences and are not *supported by the environment;* while still others will lead to punishing consequences from the parents, such as those mouth sounds resembling farts.

Segal classified five general ways of inducing operants. These were: by shaping with functional consequences, the use of deprivation, the use of reflexes, the use of innate releasers, and by emotional induction. Since each of these has many different ways of being accomplished, there is a large source of variations for our behavior. We also saw in 2.1 that stimulus generalization can lead to new responses (also Spradlin & Saunders, 1984).

Behavior variations can also be produced by *environmental changes.* When the baby mentioned above learns to hold liquid in its mouth the same "speech-like" sounds now produce brand new effects, such as gurgling and spitting, some of which might be strengthened, but most of which will be extinguished or punished by the parents. Further, there might be other more subtle consequences, such as sensory reinforcement (see 2.3), such as when the sensations in the mouth of the new gurgling reinforce the response despite the parents' punishing consequences. Or as an example of sensory punishment, some of the new sounds produced might lead to sore lips and a sore throat, and those sounds might become less probable therefore.

The production of variability in behavior also seems to be modifiable by consequences. That is, you can strengthen response variability. Pryor, Haag and O'Reilly (1969), for example, trained porpoises in a marine park to do some tricks, and later reinforced them contingent upon producing new tricks. Only behaviors which had not been produced before were reinforced. They found that a number of new responses never seen before in the porpoises appeared, although some were in the behavior repertoire of related species of porpoises. There is some controversy over strengthening the production of variability, however, and for further discussion see Barrett et al. (1987), Benjumea and Arias (1993), Machado (1989), Morris (1990), Neuringer (1993), Page and Neuringer (1985), and Schwartz (1982).

One of the main points of the natural selection analogy is to avoid talking in terms of *purpose.* This was one of Darwin's big achievements in evolutionary theory; that biologists no longer had to talk about giraffe *wanting* or *trying* to grow their necks longer *in order to* reach to high leaves. There was a plausible explanation which looked purposeful, but which was not. Animals produce many variations, the environment selects some, and these become more likely to recur. The same way of thinking applies to contexts, behaviors and consequences in the behavioral analogy. We do not have to talk about infants *wanting* to make noises *in order to* learn to speak; instead, they produce a variety of sounds some of which survive in certain contexts if the environmental (mostly social in this case) consequences support them; that is, if they have strengthening consequences.

Darwin's way of thinking also avoided having to postulate that the environment *triggered* a change in the length of a giraffe's neck; instead it *increased the probability* of long necks in the population if the giraffe's predecessors had suitable variations present in the gene pool. Applying this way of talking to behavior goes against the mechanistic S-R theories of behavior. With his evolutionary analogy, Skinner could avoid saying that the environmental context or stimulus conditions triggered a response, as Watson and Hull had done previously, thus avoiding a mechanistic and reductionist form of psychology (Chiesa, 1992; Glenn, Ellis & Greenspoon, 1992; Moxley, 1992). Instead, the environmental contexts select contingencies which are more likely to re-occur in those same contexts again. This is very different from having them triggered mechanistically in the same context.

For completeness, I wish to add one more thought. Given we cannot really subdivide the contingency unit, then we also have to pursue the evolutionary analogy to say that behaviors select contexts and consequences. If I cannot (for innate or contingency history reasons) stay afloat in water then I cannot contact a number of special contexts and consequences. I cannot see certain marine animals and I cannot blow air-bubbles in the same way I can in water. This means that we should really talk about the selection of contingencies, not behavior. But more on this in Chapter 3.

Response-induced Responses

An interesting class of responses have been called *response-response* links (Ray & Sidman, 1970). These are produced in an interesting way and have unusual properties. Although they have not had much study done on them, a few comments are added here for completeness.

The idea is that the production of some responses can act as the stimulus context for other responses (Blough, 1963). If, for example, a quick series of repeated responses lead to strengthening consequences then they can become a response class and always be performed as a group. One place they are found is in cumulative records of schedule performance. They appear as short bursts of bar pressing which act in concert (Blough, 1963).

While these response groups can be explained in the normal manner, their unusual properties arise because most consequences in the environment (except visual ones) cannot occur quickly enough, and affect the organism quickly enough, for each separate response in the burst to become separately controlled. They arise, therefore, because of speed limitations in environmental consequences. This means that it is hard to separate them out by applying consequences.

Everyday examples might include tapping all the fingers in turn when impatient, or playing a small run or sequence of notes on a piano keyboard. The latter can possibly be changed since the sounds that are a direct consequence of each response in the unit, can occur quickly enough (at the speed of sound) so that people will eventually get a new effect (consequence) by varying the repetitive series of responses. The separate notes will then have become separate operants with their own contingencies. One of the functions of teaching piano, for example, is to shape each note as a separate operant, such that any note can follow any other note just as easily.

For someone who is not properly trained on the piano, however, playing d and c when the middle finger has played e is more likely than playing f# and g#. Learning the piano requires the notes to function independently of any series of responses which happen fit together. To do this, separate consequences must be applied to each note, and luckily these consequences can sound as discriminative stimuli which travel quickly and do not have to be watched. We could arrange things so that different colours appear after each note is played, so these different consequences could also exert an influence on the individual notes in the series, but having to watch colours interferes with other aspects of piano playing and is difficult to organize when many notes are played simultaneously.

2.3. Consequences

The last of the three basic concepts of behavior analysis is that of functional consequences. The basic phenomenon is that if certain events (reinforcing events) occur *contingent* upon a response then that response class becomes more likely to occur again. If certain other events (punishing events) occur *contingent* upon a behavior then that response class becomes less likely to occur again. Lastly, many consequences or effects can be made contingent upon a response but not affect the future probability of that response class (non-functional consequences), and many effects follow a response but not in any contingent fashion. The question of consequences, then, is one of locating the functional or effective consequences and finding out how they work and how they need to be structured to be effective.

There have been a lot of problems with, and revisions of, the terms *consequences*, *reinforcements* and *strengtheners*. I could not do justice to it all in the space available here. Instead, I will discuss a few general points about the terms, and what they mean for non-behavior analysts, and then concentrate on describing many forms of them. As mentioned in a few places, there are many subtle consequences which are unknown to psychologists outside of behavior analysis but which exert a big influence on human behavior.

General Points

In the examples so far in this book I have used food as the major consequence which strengthens behavior. In modern behavior analysis, the term "reinforcer" does not always refer to quantities of food or water, nor "punishment" refer just to electric shocks. There are many subtle and unobvious events which strengthen behaviors and which are outlined below. This needs to be kept in mind since many critics believe that "reinforcer" only refers to obvious consequences like the presentation of food or water.

Some general questions need to be discussed about consequences. The first is that reinforcers should not be confused with either *rewards* or *incentives* (also see Dickinson, 1988). Both these terms are less precisely defined than the procedures of reinforcement and punishment and they mask a number of different events which need analyzing in separate components.

The word "reward" is used in everyday life when a pleasant consequence is directed towards a person for things they have done. Your boss might give you a reward for being a good worker, or parents might give their children a reward for helping to wash the dog. These usages have at least two components: they are *pleasant* events which are contingent upon completion of a *series of different behaviors*. There are two problems with this: the pleasantness aspect and the serial aspect, which I will discuss in reverse order to make life difficult for the reader.

Reinforcement is strictly the procedure of making a strengthening event contingent upon one single response class. Indeed, to be most effective, a reinforcement procedure should be made contingent as specifically as possible on only one response class. The problem with an effective reward, an event given after a series of responses, is that it will strengthen *all* the responses which took part in the action: the bad ones as well as the good ones.

If, for example, the boss gives a bonus reward for "good work in the office", and let us suppose that this bonus is actually an effective strengthener, then it will strengthen all the behaviors which were involved. These might include cheating on another office worker to do better, presenting the appearance of working hard when not really doing so, and leaving early when the boss is not there. Rewards can include many undesirable behaviors, some of which might be at cross purposes.

It is for this reason that behavior analysts try to be as specific as possible when using strengtheners and weakeners. The specific responses are identified and a specific strengthener made contingent upon that one response as far as possible. If more than one response must be involved then separate consequences should be made contingent upon those different responses. For this reason the word "reward" is usually avoided, since it suggests a procedure which is too loose and probably is not effective anyway. [Although many behaviors analysts, including Skinner, use the term casually.]

The word "incentive" involves the same problem as reward: incentives are also usually given for a series of responses, some of which might be undesirable. If the boss offers to give you a bonus at the end of the month if you can sell three more sets of encyclopaedia, then this applies to any responses which achieve the effect, which includes threatening old ladies into buying a set.

A second problem with incentives is that, although they look like a case of simple reinforcement, their *anticipatory* nature tells us that far more is involved. They are actually an example of instructional or verbal control, since the future (the incentive bonus) cannot directly cause the present behavior (selling encyclopaedia). The control and maintenance of instructions is complex and will be dealt with in 7.4. So, while the word "incentive" appears to have a simple analysis, equivalent to reinforcer, it does not and is therefore avoided by behavior analysts. Incentives exist, and are sometimes effective, but their analysis is complex and the word cannot therefore be used as a primitive term.

The other problem with both the words reward and incentive is that, as nouns, they most often are used to mean something pleasurable. Now this issue is controversial amongst behavior theorists, but the general behavior analytic position is that *pleasure is not a pre-requisite for reinforcement.* We often loosely refer to reinforcing events and consequences as pleasurable, such as food when hungry, but pleasure is seen as a separate component which is not necessary for strengthening behavior. Pleasure requires a complex analysis in itself and is not a primitive term.

The idea of pleasure came into modern psychology from Edward Thorndike with his Law of Effect. This stated that any response which was followed by "pleasure" or "satisfaction" would be made more probable; that is, have a greater response strength. Some psychologists, such as Staats (1975), still follow this conception of reinforcement.

The problems with this are many. Pleasure and satisfaction are extremely unclear terms, and it is unclear even how they could control behavior. One is less likely to attribute pleasure as a major controller of animal behavior: for example, we do not say that cats learn to open doors because doing so is pleasurable. As well, there are times when behaviors are reinforced, and we repeat them often, but we do not find them pleasurable. There are also many problem behaviors which people would *like* to be rid of but which are maintained by environmental consequences despite this. There are also many behaviors which can be shown to be maintained by environmental consequences but of which we are not aware. For example, opening doors is reinforced but it cannot really be called pleasurable or satisfying.

Further, a large part of what we mean by pleasure and satisfaction are the verbal responses which come after the event and which themselves are maintained by social consequences (see 7.1). The same is true of pain (Schoenfeld, 1981). Many people have trouble with talking in this way about pleasure and pain. The only real difference that is being urged is that pleasure and pain do not themselves directly control our behavior. The experience is real and the verbal statements about them are usually real, but these are a separate and later step from the consequences which control the behavior which brings about the pleasure or pain. Your waving and smiling might be maintained by the immediate change in the other person's demeanour when they see you; and your pleasure at seeing them is a later occurrence, though just as real. But it is considered a misleading analysis to say that the pleasure of seeing someone itself strengthened the behavior of waving to them. It is very easy to slip into talking about reinforcers as pleasurable events and punishers as painful events, but they are not synonymous.

Having dealt with the problems of rewards and incentives, the second general point about reinforcers is the *circularity* of the reinforcement concept. Like natural selection in evolutionary theory, reinforcement cannot be defined a priori but only demonstrated in action. We ask why hair is common on male humans and the answer is that it has been selected as adaptive through natural selection. If asked how we know it is adaptive we are told that since it has survived it must have been adaptive!

The basis of natural selection is circular when talking about it, but the truth of it needs to be demonstrated in practice.

Similarly we might ask how someone knows that the chocolate bar is a strengthening consequence for the child's reading of books, and be told that it is a positive reinforcer. If we ask how they know it is a positive reinforcer we are told that it strengthens the reading of books for the child.

The problem here is not as bad as it seems, since the circularity does not lead to an infinite regress. In both behavior analysis and evolutionary theory the answer is to go and look for the data rather than just talk about it. At the present moment we cannot absolutely predict what events will act as strengthening or punishing consequences—we need to try them out and demonstrate them in practice. There are no magic formulae to decide that chocolate bars will work but not fried liver (see Timberlake & Farmer-Dougan, 1991, for discussion of this).

The trick, however, is that in practice we can make pretty good guesses about what events will strengthen and weaken behavior. First, there are some obvious examples such as food for a food-deprived animal and water for a water-deprived organism. As well, electric shocks are usually effective in punishing responses for most mammals. But anything more fine grained than this need to be checked out first. Chocolate bars will not always work in every context, even with hungry children! Other practical guesses come from some recent theories which try to make a better prediction of which events or objects will strengthen contingent responses. These will be discussed later (see Premack's Principle below).

A final consideration in guessing what consequences will strengthen or weaken behavior is that to find a reinforcer (or a punisher) it is best to *know your animal*. Many animals have innate responses and innate preferences for strengthening and weakening consequences. The person who knows their animal the best will be more likely to find these out—whether this animal be human or otherwise. At present we cannot sit back in an armchair and dictate what will strengthen any animal's behavior, except for the few obvious examples mentioned above.

The third general point for talking about reinforcing and punishing consequences concerns the classification of consequences. There is a general consensus amongst behavior analysts on the technical terms to use, but the terms unfortunately have other meanings in common language and are therefore sometimes misleading. Because of this, other schemes have been proposed.

The prevailing classification is that functional consequences are called *reinforcers* if they strengthen responses (make them more likely) and *punishers* if they weaken responses (make them less likely). They are called *positive* if they add something to the situation to do this and *negative* if they remove something from the situation. This makes four possible types for a classification.

An example of a *positive reinforcer* would be food to a food-deprived organism contingent upon pressing a bar, which would probably lead to an increase in the response rate of bar pressing. By contingently adding something (the food) you strengthen the response. If, on the other hand, you turned *off* an electric shock for

10 seconds whenever the animal pressed the bar then bar pressing would most likely increase as well, and this would be classified as a *negative reinforcement* procedure because it strengthens behavior by removing something from the situation. If you *presented* the animal with an electric shock everytime it pressed the bar then bar pressing would probably stop, so this would be called a *positive punishment* procedure. Lastly, if you *took away* the animal's food contingent upon pressing the bar, this would be a *negative punishment* procedure, and the bar pressing would stop in this case also.

In my experience, the major problem people seem to have with this technical classification is with the words "positive" and "negative". A "positive" procedure would seem to mean a "nice" procedure or a "pleasant" procedure, whereas positive punishment is anything but this. Likewise, "negative" reinforcement is usually considered good (being able to switch off an electric shock). For the moment, anyway, this terminology will continue, although some have argued strongly against it (Michael, 1975). Catania (1973) has made a good suggestion that we replace the terms reinforcers and punishers with "operants" and "stoperants"!

My own preference is for the term "functional consequences" with a further specification of strengthening or weakening, leaving out whether this occurs through punishment or reinforcement procedures. Very rarely have I found it necessary to refer to whether something is added or removed from the situation, so the terms "positive" and "negative" can usually be left out. "Functional consequences" also gets shortened to just "consequences" when I use it repeatedly, but only functional or effective consequences are meant.

Another problem with terminology has been that consequences are sometimes referred to generally as reinforcements, even though weakening effects might be included. In a loose way people say: "We will have to find out what reinforcements are functional for this person", when this could mean strengthening or weakening. The only real answer to this is for people to tighten up their terminology.

There are many more angles and twists to this terminology. For other discussions consult the following excellent sources: Catania (1969, 1984), Commons, Fantino and Branch (1993), Dunham, 1977; Eisenberger (1972), Lee (1988), Michael (1975), Schoenfeld (1978), Smith (1974), and Williams (1983).

Types of consequences

Macro or Obvious Consequences. The term "macro consequences" is not a technical term but my own short-hand way of referring to those consequences which are either large or obvious. This includes common objects such as food pellets and chocolate bars, as well as events like electric shocks. Most of the work in behavior analysis, both applied and experimental, has been conducted using macro consequences. Also, as mentioned above, most critics have assumed that these are the *only* consequences with which behavior analysts deal. For these two reasons, I like to emphasize the subtle functional consequences instead, to keep everybody on their conceptual toes.

When one is analyzing perception, private events, or verbal and other social behaviors, one soon realizes that more is needed for analysis than macro consequences such as food and sex. The subtleties of verbal behavior in particular are missed if macro consequences are the only ones assumed (e.g., Chomsky, 1959). Some whole areas of study, in fact, failed because they limited contingencies to only the obvious macro consequences (see verbal conditioning, 7.3) and left out the subtleties.

I have dealt with rewards and incentives above. One other macro consequence commonly talked about in connection with humans is "feedback" (Powers, 1973; Reser & Scherl, 1988). Feedback is often treated as synonymous with reinforcement by those not well acquainted with behavior analysis, especially when it is called "knowledge of results". For example, it is often said that exam results act as feedback and can "reinforce" working hard at the next test.

Two problems exist, however, which makes "feedback" a less than useful term for behavior analysis. First, the delay between responding and feedback is often considerable—even conditioned reinforcers are not likely to be effective under such circumstances (Michael, 1980; Peterson, 1982). The effects of real reinforcers drop off very quickly with delays. Second, for feedback to be effective it depends upon a previous reinforcement history: that is, we must learn at some point in our life that knowledge of results can be reinforcing before they will work later on. They are usually treated, however, as though merely presenting feedback will make a change occur. This means that the analysis of feedback is not simply that of a reinforcer. It will depend upon intermediate verbal behaviors with their own contingencies, as well as a conditioning history of what happens when one does follow feedback. It is therefore avoided in behavior analysis, especially as a primitive term.

For behavior analysis, then, the phenomenon of feedback is real but the explanation is much more complex than it looks. It would seem to depend on conditioned reinforcers, chains of verbal behavior, and probably subtle social reinforcers and therefore have subtle conditions under which it will work. Peterson (1982) suggested that feedback is a discriminative stimulus or a conditioned reinforcer, but raised problems with these. Michael (1980) suggested that it might be a form of rule-governed behavior (7.4) but urged that more be found out first about it. In any event, feedback should not be treated as an obvious form of any consequence, since it is one of the "indirect-acting" contingencies (Malott, 1984) and will only be effective under some circumstances. More will be said about everyday examples of feedback in 12.7.

Conditioned Consequences. Conditioned consequences are a very common form of consequence (Gollub, 1977; Kelleher, 1966; Kelleher & Gollub, 1962; Wike, 1966). They were briefly discussed above in connection with contingencies of attention, and are clearly one basis for the control of establishing operations. They are consequences which, although not strengthening or weakening in themselves, can function because they are contexts for other contingencies. For this reason they are sometimes called *secondary consequences*.

Conditioned consequences are included in this section since their effect is often subtle and nonobvious (Zimmerman, 1963). Many times an analysis reveals no macro consequences and it appears that a behavior is being magically maintained without any reinforcement whatsoever. Conditioned reinforcers are often found to provide the actual environmental support for these behaviors.

Money is an example of a conditioned strengthening consequence, since in itself it is not strengthening—it consists merely of pieces of metal and paper. But because many other strengthening events and objects have been made contingent upon the context of money, it can act as a strengthening consequence in its own right. This is only so long as it still allows the further contingent consequences to occur. If it lost all power to act as a context for other consequences, it would stop being used. [More on the social aspects of money in 9.3.]

Many properties of conditioned consequences are known, although more research still needs to be done. One major problem is that they have to be periodically paired with the effective contingent consequences. If they do not occasionally lead to functional environmental consequences they will cease to work. As mentioned above, if money stopped leading to other contingencies with strengthening consequences then we would stop using it.

A classic example of conditioned consequences is the study by Findley and Brady (1965) who tried to reinforce a chimpanzee on a FR 4000 schedule. This meant that the chimp had to pull a lever *4000 times* before getting a food reinforcer! Findlay and Brady found this difficult to achieve, and the chimp showed long pauses between pulls and there were periods of hours sometimes when it did nothing at all. Findlay and Brady then started flashing the food tray light at every 400 pulls, although the chimp still did not get any food until it had completed 4000 pulls. By just doing this, however, the response rate increased dramatically and the pauses were reduced. The light was now a conditioned reinforcer and acted as an effective consequence after every 400 pulls (that is, it changed the response probability).

To an observer outside of such experiments, this can appear as a very strange situation. Everytime the light flashed the chimp would increase its response rate. To an observer it would look as if the chimp *wanted* or *needed* the light to be flashed, or that it *knew* that the light meant food. It would take a lot of careful observation to work out what was reinforcing what in this situation. This is the very condition facing behavior analysts with complex human behavior. They must observe some human behavior and decipher the events by changing the contexts and conse-quences. We might watch someone buy lottery tickets each week and conclude that they have an innate *need* for lottery tickets, since no macro consequences are ever seen (only occasionally does the person win).

One trick for recognizing conditioned consequences is to watch for the word "signal". We could have said above that the light looked like a *signal* for the chimp to keep pressing the bar. However, as mentioned in 2.1, this word has a very loose meaning and is avoided by behavior analysts. The word includes aspects of motivation, stimulus discrimination, as well as establishing operations. But when someone does use the term it is a clue that conditioned consequences are likely to be present.

Generalized Consequences. Generalized consequences are those which have been paired with more than one consequence. Money is again a good example. Money not only can produce food, it also can produce many other strengthening events and objects, as well as many other conditioned consequences. Such *generalized consequences* are subtle both for the reasons mentioned in the last section and also because they make their appearance in many different stimulus contexts. For these reasons it is hard to pinpoint the total effect money has on our behavior.

A very important group of generalized consequences are the generalized social reinforcers. These are subtle consequences which come from participating in a community which support and maintain many of our behaviors in a loose way. Perhaps the most important of these is verbal behavior. People do not actually give us chocolates and hugs everytime we speak or write a sentence, but the general effects of getting a reply and participating in conversation are conditioned, automatic (see below), and generalized consequences. They are generalized because many responses are maintained in this way, including a large part of our social behavior (see 4.2), especially verbal behavior (7.2).

So like conditioned consequences, generalized consequences can lead to the impression that some responses have no functional consequences at all. But the ever-vigilant behavior analyst is more careful about jumping to such conclusions. Given the importance of generalized consequences in complex human behavior, not enough is known about their basic properties and much more research needs to be done. It seems, for example, that generalized conditioned consequences can still have an effect even when an animal is satiated (Nevin, 1966; Wenrich, 1963). If true, this would be very important in analyzing social behaviors where no consequences are apparent.

Automatic Consequences. A curious type of consequence is the automatic consequence (Vaughan & Michael, 1982). These are cases where the very response itself *seems* to be reinforcing (cf. Herrnstein, 1977; Skinner, 1977). The best discussion is that of Vaughan and Michael (1982), who drew upon the scattered references in the works of Skinner. They divided these references up into three categories: *perceiving, producing* and *problem-solving*. Examples are given below. The reader can further consult Vaughan and Michael (1982) for examples of automatic punishment and automatic negative reinforcement. Here are some examples of each category:

a. Perceiving

> To one who is interested in dogs, simply seeing dogs is automatically reinforcing (Skinner, 1953, p. 272).
>
> We can avoid this duplication by assuming that when a visual object is automatically reinforcing, the behavior of seeing it may become so strong that is occurs in the absence of the object (Skinner, 1968, p. 125).

b. Producing

The important reinforcers are largely automatic: a sentence comes out right, it says something interesting, it fits another sentence. If these automatic reinforcers are powerful enough, the student may continue to write and improve his writing even though he receives few if any comments (Skinner, 1968, p. 160).

c. Problem-solving

Another source of automatic reinforcement is seen in "problem solving," where the speaker generates stimuli to *supplement* other behavior already in his repertoire (Skinner, 1957, p. 442).

Few pupils ever reach the stage at which automatic reinforcements follow as the natural consequences of mathematical behavior (Skinner, 1968, p. 18).

Knowing these three sources of automatic reinforcement does not help us much, since the bases for them have not been studied properly yet. More needs to be known about their relations with innate reinforcers, social reinforcers, establishing operations, conditioned reinforcers, and generalized reinforcers. They appear to be independent of deprivation levels, which make them more likely to be a type of conditioned reinforcer, although they can certainly be satiated (a dog lover seeing too many pictures of dogs). Elsewhere I have suggested that Gibson's idea of *ecological affordances* is actually one of automatic reinforcement (Guerin, 1990). This would suggest that we need to analyze the perceptual side of many of these automatic reinforcements, since they may be innate response events to environmental affordances.

Sensory Consequences. One subtle form of consequence which was mainly studied in the 1950s is sensory reinforcement. This arose from research showing that with no macro consequences, animals would press a bar which merely effected sensory changes—such as viewing pictures from projected slides (Kish, 1966). The function of this was later postulated to be that of controlling the environment by exploration, and this was often thought of as an innately reinforced response.

While the phenomenon cannot be denied, the controlling variables and the mechanisms involved have still not been satisfactorily dealt with. Some researchers believe it is innate; some believe it is avoidance of "monotony"; others believe it is a form of automatic perceptual reinforcement (or even vice versa); while still others believe that it is a response which has the function of changing the possible environmental contingencies themselves, rather than a response to any contingencies in particular (Glow, 1985).

Little has been done on this phenomenon in recent years, probably because the work was couched in terms of Hullian drive theory, which is no longer popular. It is still important, however, since it probably relates closely to a number of the other subtle consequences, such as automatic perceptual consequences, Premack's principle, avoidance conditioning, feedback, and generalized consequences. It might also turn out to be a generalized form of establishing operation or setting event. A consideration and testing of how all these fit together would clarify the whole concept of consequences, and would also clarify how so much human behavior seems to occur without macro consequences.

Natural Consequences. A further way to characterize subtle consequences has been to refer to *natural* consequences, usually contrasted with *contrived* consequences (Ferster, 1967; Kohler & Greenwood, 1986; Skinner, 1982). Natural consequences are the consequences which would support behavior or weaken behavior *in the natural environment*, although this last term is somewhat vague. It does not refer to a scene of being surrounded by trees and lakes, dressed in animal furs, hunting for your food with a spear, but refers to the consequences which maintain behaviors in our everyday lives, modern or not.

The idea has mainly arisen in applied behavior analysis where a lot of the early interventions used chocolates or lollies as the reinforcers. Although these worked quite well, it was found that such training did not always generalize to other situations, so attempts were made to utilize in training those consequences which might *ordinarily* support or prevent the behaviors. Most of our behavior in life does not normally occur because chocolates are a consequence (unfortunately!).

So natural consequences are not a new type of consequence but the utilization of common but subtle consequences. One method of doing this in applied work has been to train people to *recruit the natural consequences* (Baer & Wolf, 1970; Hrydowy, Stokes & Martin, 1984; Stokes, Fowler & Baer, 1978). This means to train people in the target behavior and also teach them to tap into, or find, naturally available sources of consequences.

Stokes and his colleagues, for example, trained children not only to do mathematics problems using praise to strengthen the behavior, but also trained the children how to put up their hands to elicit praise from their teachers (Stokes et al., 1978). Other researchers have found it necessary to train with contrived consequences because the natural consequences were too subtle or not powerful enough, but they then faded the training into natural consequences as a final phase of the program (Jones & Kazdin, 1975).

One interesting feature of this work is that while objects such as lollies were often used as contrived consequences in early applied work, the trend in finding natural consequences has been towards using social consequences. This will come up as a theme in later chapters—that social consequences are powerful and very common controllers of our behavior, but they are not as well researched as food-based consequences. Their presence and power is therefore frequently overlooked when analyzing human behavior.

Premack's Principle and Relative Deprivation. Theories of reinforcement were given a new twist in the 1960s when Premack proposed that the value of a reinforcer was relative (Premack, 1962, 1965). What is now most often called "Premack's Principle" stated that a low probability behavior can act as reinforcer for a high probability reinforcer, regardless of the actual nature of those reinforcers.

Whereas up to that time many experiments had made drinking water contingent upon running in a small wheel (for mice or rats, not for humans!), Premack (1962) showed that if deprived of wheel running and not water, then a rat would drink water if wheel running was made contingent upon this. This suggested that there was nothing special about the food or water deprivations which were nearly always used, it was the *baseline probabilities* of the behaviors which determined the relative effectiveness of their strengthening properties.

This idea changed the way of thinking about reinforcers, since in principle the reinforcing effect could be predicted from a knowledge of baseline probability of responding. This was confirmed in a series of experiments (Premack, 1962, 1965, 1971; Premack & Premack, 1963; Premack & Schaeffer, 1962; see also Bernstein & Ebbesen, 1978; Croll, 1974; Schaeffer, Bauermeister & David, 1973; Schaeffer & Nolan, 1974; Wasik, 1968). Some later experiments found it was not quite as simple as this. Eisenberger, Karpman and Trattner (1967) and Schaeffer (1965) showed that the effect actually depended upon the deprivation relative to a baseline: the principle was that a behavior below its "normal" baseline rate of responding could be used as a reinforcer for one above its normal baseline rate of responding.

This was later formalized in a few ways, as the *relative deprivation* of two responses (Timberlake & Allison, 1974), and as *equilibrium theory* (Timberlake, 1980, 1984; Timberlake & Farmer-Dougan, 1991; Hanson & Timberlake, 1983). These theories are mathematical models relating how far a response is from baseline to its relative effectiveness as a reinforcer. More recently it has been found that that the relative deprivation of one response actually affects the equilibrium point of other responses (Pierce, Epling & Boer, 1986). This now places the phenomenon as a multiple response interaction, which will be dealt with in 3.2. As will be argued there, a general theory of multiple contingencies is still needed, to show how responses and the baseline points interaction with deprivations and additions of new behaviors.

Some researchers have made use of Premack's Principle in practical applications, since it means that food deprivation and chocolate bars do not have to always be used. To strengthen a behavior you simply find a preferred activity which is less probable than the one you wish to increase and then make it contingent. For example, Homme, DeBaca, Devine, Steinhorst and Rickert (1963) found that running and screaming were more probable at baseline for children in a classroom than watching the blackboard. So to increase the latter they made a period of running and screaming contingent upon a (longer) period of watching the blackboard quietly.

For other applications see Aeschleman and Williams (1989), Bateman (1975), Hartje (1973), Konarski (1987), Konarski, Johnson, Crowell, and Whitman (1981), Mitchell and Stoffelmayr (1973), Roberts (1969), Robinson and Lewinsohn (1973), and Wasik (1970). For a criticism of some of these see Knapp (1976), and a further recent advance by Vaughan and Miller (1984), who have put forward evidence that responses are strengthened by reinforcement rather than relative deprivation.

The important point here to gain from these principles and models is that reinforcement effects are extremely subtle, and depend as much on what other responses are available as they do on the essential nature of the consequential events.

A behavior analyst needs to be aware of this when looking for reinforcing consequences in a situation. Unrelated, contingent low probability behaviors might be strengthening a behavior when no macro consequences can be found.

Self-reinforcement. One interesting feature of human behavior is the prevalence of what appears to be self-reinforcement procedures. A person will appear to arrange their own reinforcement contingencies. For example, to help finish this book I might give myself a chocolate bar for every 20 pages that I complete in one sitting. This comes across as a subtle reinforcer since there might be no overt demonstration of such a self-reinforcement: there might be no words spoken out loud nor physical movements to indicate what is controlling my behavior. It all seems to happen inside my head.

While a proper discussion of self-reinforcement will be left until Chapter 8, it should be noted that this is not an easy behavior to analyze. The evidence, in fact, suggests that self-reinforcement is maintained by generalized social reinforcement—which turn out to be even more subtle! At the least, it is *not* analogous to a rat pressing the bar 20 times before receiving a food pellet, and needs to be carefully analyzed.

Avoidance and Escape. Avoidance and escape conditioning are the effects of negative reinforcement. A response will be strengthened if it leads to the escape or avoidance of a noxious stimulus or context. Some of the properties of this are well known (Hineline, 1977; Sidman, 1966). The point of singling these out here is that they can produce some subtle effects which might be missed if an analyst is only looking for macro consequences.

In avoidance conditioning, for example, once the response has been well established, very few presentations of the noxious stimulus are needed. Suppose a rat has been trained to press a bar every 30 seconds to avoid an electric shock. What we will see from the outside, once it is properly trained, is a rat which presses the bar every 25 seconds or so and which spends the rest of its time doing other activities. It may be a long period before we see it being shocked. This means that the effects of negative reinforcers can be overlooked in analyses.

A human example might be as follows. We watch a person walking down the street and notice that everytime they reach a certain point they cross the road for no obvious reason. While we might hypothesize that there is something positively reinforcing about the other side of the road, it is just as plausible that they are avoiding something on the first side but we might not be watching that side of the road. Indeed, if we found nothing positive on the second side we would have to consider such avoidance. But the point is that we might find nothing obvious since a few trials with the avoidance can establish a very strong response.

I believe that avoidance and escape are extremely important in human social behavior (although I have little evidence for this beyond my own observations). One example is the general finding that people are very cautious about others *evaluating* what they do (Guerin, 1986; Szymanski & Harkins, 1993; Chapters 4 & 12). This seems to be a learned response to others, especially strangers: we generally feel negatively evaluated by others and do many things to avoid such a situation. This will be discussed more in 4.2 and 12.7. When more analyses of social behavior are carried out, I believe social avoidance schedules will be found to be very important.

Verbal Consequences. Another subtle consequence is referred to as verbal conditioning. This consists of phrases such as "Good!", "Well done" and "Don't do that!". These seem to act as potent consequences for humans (Holz & Azrin, 1966). They seem to be specialized conditioned generalized consequences (whew!) since they work with many of our responses but are specialized to verbal behavior. They also are intimately tied up with social consequences.

A lot of work was done in the 1950s and 1960s on conditioning verbal behavior using verbal consequences (Holz & Azrin, 1966). The issues are complex and have not really been resolved, and will be discussed in another part of this book (7.3). They should be kept in mind, however, as another source of subtle consequences which can affect our behavior without being too obvious.

Long-term and Cumulative Consequences. Another subtle strengthening effect which should also be kept in mind is that of long-term, cumulative consequences. In theory at least, a very slight strengthening effect occurring repeatedly over a long period can take control of a response if there are no other more powerful consequences. For example, Skinner has suggested that "the intraverbal 'house-home' is due to thousand of instances in which, having heard 'house' it is useful to say 'home', gaining a very slight reward" (in Vargas, 1986, p. 133, note 3). Such effects could be overlooked in an analysis if not attended carefully.

There seems to be no research on this, although the analysis is probably not as clear as it appears from the quotation given. There could be classical conditioning influences or even the formation over a long period of exposure of an equivalence class containing 'house' and 'home'. Social contingencies are also probably involved given the social nature of verbal behavior.

Social Consequences. Social consequences have already been mentioned above with regards to verbal conditioning. But there are other social effects not covered by this. Indeed, social consequences are so important to humans that Chapter 5 is devoted to the topic. It is frequently not taken into consideration, however, when analyzing human behavior. From their writings on human behavior (not usually in informal conversations, however), it appears that many behavior analysts believe that humans live in a social vacuum. Most likely, the experimental work has been heavily based on individual animals, so the social effects are not well known experimentally yet.

Social effects have some interesting properties which separate them out for study, even if all the properties can be ultimately explained in terms of the ones already mentioned. First, social consequences are dynamic, in the sense that they occur very quickly and are quickly changing. A mere glance is often sufficient to produce behavior in others, and the role of reinforcer can swap between two people very quickly.

Second, social consequences are potent and ubiquitous in humans. The fact that people will fight in wars "knowing" that they will die speaks of powerful controllers of behavior. Finally, for humans, almost everything we do is a social product, even in our own "private thoughts" (8.5 and Berger & Luckmann, 1967). It is therefore essential that they be understood.

Superstitious Consequences. Another group of subtle consequences are superstitious consequences. They are not a separate category of reinforcers but are usefully treated on their own. They refer to cases where a response has been accidently shaped by a consequence which is not contingent upon the response but which has occurred immediately in any case.

In the original work, Skinner (1948) noticed that pigeons reinforced on a random time schedule of reinforcement (noncontingent) developed particular responses which had coincidently occurred just before the random reinforcer, such as flapping their wings or turning in circles. He suggested that if the pigeons kept making this response that it was likely reinforced again on an (accidental) intermittent basis, and therefore could be maintained even longer.

This is subtle because the behavior analyst might not even notice the reinforcer, especially if it is unusual or accidental in the circumstances. As well, it could have occurred earlier in the animal's life, leaving an even more subtle history. Moreover, considering the speed and dynamics of social consequences, we would expect a lot of superstitious social responding, in which, for example, people "believe" that someone does not like them because that person coughed when they were about to speak, even though this might be accidental.

There is a lot of controversy over exactly how such superstitious effects are developed and the principles upon which they are based. The reader can consult the following for more: Davis, Hubbard and Reberg, 1973; Herrnstein, 1966; Ono, 1987; Skinner, 1948; Staddon, 1977; Staddon and Simmelhag, 1971; Timberlake and Lucas, 1985; Weisberg and Kennedy, 1969; Zeiler, 1972.

One other feature deserves a comment here. If it were not for ethical problems, superstitious consequences would be interesting in applied behavior analysis. If we wanted to maintain a useful behavior we could artificially link it to a chance reinforcing event. For example, in B-grade western movies, the cowboys frighten the Indians by supposedly turning out the sun as a consequence for non-compliance, when in fact it is a chance eclipse (as if Indians would not know about eclipses!). While unethical to carry this out, it should be kept in mind when analyzing behavior, even if it should not be used for behavior change.

Delayed, Remote and Indirect Consequences. There is a group of consequences which are often lumped together. These are *delayed*, *remote* and *indirect* consequences. Only the first has really been studied but all have appeared in analyses and will appear throughout this book. For these reasons I would like to make some clarifying remarks and suggest some points for their analysis.

Delayed consequences will be mentioned in discussing the Matching Law in 3.1 (also see Commons, Mazur, Nevin & Rachlin, 1987). If the consequences of a response are delayed then its strengthening or weakening effect is usually not as powerful. For this reason the most effective consequences are those made immediately following the response (but see Lattal & Gleeson, 1990; Wilkenfield, Nickel, Blakely & Poling, 1992).

Remote consequence is a term sometimes used which can mean one of two things. First it can just mean a delayed consequence, in that the consequence is remote in time from the response. It can also mean, however, that several events have to take place following the response before the consequence occurs, but these events are unrelated to the response itself. While these will also be delayed, more is happening which seems to involve multiple contingencies.

Indirect consequence can also mean several things. Most commonly the term refers to consequences for which there is a chain of events occurring before the consequence occurs, but these mediating events are related to, or arise from, the response itself (unlike remote consequences). This means that the immediate consequences of the response are non-functional but effects arising from these inconsequential effects are eventually functional.

While these last two terms are vague and my understanding of them probably does not agree with that of other writers , they are useful terms if treated carefully. With human behavior, and especially social behavior, many functional consequences are mediated by non-consequential events or are delayed. When I smile at someone the effects back on me are many and varied. There is not one clear consequence which stands out, and some consequences might even be mediated by other people not present at the time. So while I shall occasionally use these terms in this book as a shorthand way of referring to very complex, mediated, and delayed effects, the hope is that they can one day be either clarified or else exorcised from our scientific vocabulary. Another writer has written an excellent analysis of them, using the terms "evasive goals" and "contingencies that are not direct acting" (Malott, 1989).

Scheduling of Consequences

Analyzing contingencies is never easy, and there are many subtleties with human behavior. While details of how different contingencies can combine is left to Chapter 3, two final topics of importance need to be mentioned here.

Multiple Causation. One practical and theoretical problem in analyzing behavior is that behavior can be multiply determined. This means both that *several consequences can control a single response, and that several different responses can be controlled by a single consequence.* This issue has mainly been discussed with reference to verbal behavior, where single words can be influenced by several sources (often leading to unusual verbal slips), and where a single consequence can control several words (often leading to cliché phrases such as "pass the salt"). These have been discussed in detail by Skinner (1957). More recently, Catania and Cerutti (1986) have demonstrated how nonverbal behavior in pigeons can also be multiply determined.

The point of this is that having multiple consequences control behavior makes a clear analysis of human behavior often very difficult. One must be aware that there

might be other subtle influences occurring, even if one obvious source of consequences seems to be fully controlling a response.

Schedules of Reinforcement. Another source of subtle control in the analysis
of behavior arises with the scheduling of consequences (Ferster & Skinner, 1957;
Zeiler, 1977). Scheduling consists of varying the relations between a response and
its consequences. The best known relations are ratio relations (e.g., three responses
for every consequence–FR 3) and temporal relations (e.g., a consequence every
thirty seconds if there is at least one response–FI 30secs). Even if the same
consequence is given for every three responses and for a response after every thirty
seconds, very different patterns of behavior are observed.

By varying such relations, patterned changes can be made in responding rates.
Very subtle changes occur which cannot be understood unless the scheduling is
investigated. Extinction and collateral changes, for example, are affected by the
particular schedule in operation. A full understanding of the different schedules of
reinforcement is needed to appreciate the basics of behavior analysis, and some more
details will be given in Chapter 3. The recent work has been summarized in a number
of publications (Catania, 1966, 1984; Davey, 1981; Fantino & Logan, 1979;
Morse, 1966; Thompson & Grabowski, 1972; Zeiler, 1977, 1984) and most textbooks
on learning have an adequate summary of the very basic schedules.

Rather than repeat all the details here, I would like to mention just one under-
researched schedule of reinforcement (but see Wanchisen, Tatham & Hineline,
1992), which I believe is important in human social behavior. This is the group of
adjusting schedules, which includes progressive schedules. The adjusting schedules are
ones in which the response changes the nature of the schedule. For example, a rat
might have to press the bar three times for one pellet on the first press, five times for
the second pellet, seven times for the third, and so on. This means that the response
changes the scheduling of consequences.

The reason I believe these are important is because my informal observations
of social behavior tell me that a large part of our social behavior is based on such
schedules. I can tell a joke to someone and get a laugh from them, but if I keep on
doing this they laugh less and less. This is something about social behavior which
I believe we learn very early in our social lives. People are often called socially
unskilled precisely because they do not notice the (negatively) adjusting schedule
until the other person has left or fallen asleep!

While some work has been done on adjusting schedules, I think more is needed,
especially with human behavior (see for example, Bennett & Samson, 1987; Bhatt
& Wasserman, 1987; Mazur, 1988). How we change between different schedules
when adjusting ones are involved will be an important question for human behavior
analysis.

2.4. Contingency History

All of the points in this chapter show the importance of the *contingency history*
of the organism in determining the functioning of their behavior. For example, if

we know that an organism has had a history of avoidance by bar pressing, then we can better determine what the animal will do if punishment is used to suppress bar pressing later on. Contingency history is a useful construct since it puts the onus on the researcher to show how developmental differences in experience lead to different controlling variables later on.

The problem is, however, that it is notoriously difficult to find out the histories of organisms except when they are raised under laboratory conditions. It is also often tempting to just appeal to "conditioning history" when an analysis fails to find very much. So contingency history is both a powerful influence and a difficult one to grapple with in real cases. This usually means that it is ignored in applied cases and controlling variables are sought in other ways. Some suggestions on how this situation might be improved or studied with humans are given in Baron, Perone and Galizio (1991), Chase (1988), Donahoe and Palmer (1989), Johnson et al. (1991), LeFrancois, Chase and Joyce (1988), Shimoff (1986), Wanchisen (1990), Wanchisen, Tathem and Mooney (1989), and Weiner (1964).

Chapter 3

Combining Contingencies

We have now discussed the components of contingencies. As mentioned, behavior analysis has the contingency as its basic unit rather than behavior. Behaviors do not occur without a context and consequences, and behaviors which look the same might occur in different contingencies and therefore be different.

This chapter looks at the properties of whole contingencies and how they work together to make the larger patterns or units of our behavior. Behavior analysis has wisely taken the strategy of working from the basic principles to more complex behaviors, so not as much is known experimentally about these larger units. How to approach these is one topic of current interest (cf. Thompson & Zeiler, 1986). Traditionally, mainly chains of contingencies were analyzed, but there is much written now about first, how contingencies might be otherwise layered (my cheap word, not a technical term), and second, how it is that many contingencies work together to produce patterned streams of behavior. Because this literature is recent I will be speculating in many places. This should eventually be replaced by experimental evidence of the contingencies involved.

3.1. Layers of Contingencies

In 1986, Sidman (1986a, b; also cf. 1978 and Catania, 1980) presented the findings of stimulus control in a new way, which has excited the community of behavior analysts and led to much new research. This presentation was done to provide a basis for discussing some results he and his colleagues had been studying for some years, but it also provided a new way of thinking about the logic of contingencies. I will present the material in this fashion also, and acknowledge a debt to Sidman. His papers on this should be read carefully since they contain a lot of depth which I cannot cover.

Two-term Contingencies

The point of departure in discussing contingencies will be to consider the simplest (but fictitious) case of just a behavior and a consequence of that behavior which is strengthening (or it could be weakening). Consider a case with hand waving as the response and with a smile and a comment ("Hi there!") from another person as the consequence. We will assume that this consequence is effective in strengthening: that is, it will make hand waving more likely in the future. So we have only two components: a response and its functional consequences. [A proper analysis of such a verbal episode is actually quite complex, and involves generalized social consequences—see Chapter 7.]

In our simple example there is no stimulus context, or at least the stimulus context remains constant. With only two components or terms, the consequences are analyzed as always occurring whenever the response occurs. What we can say more formally is that *IF* this response is made *THEN* these particular consequences follow. In our example, *IF* hand waving, *THEN* smile and comment, and this does not depend upon any stimulus context. We might also generalize and say that when other responses are made these consequences do not follow. Figure 1 shows this two-term Response-Consequence contingency (R-C) in a graphic manner.

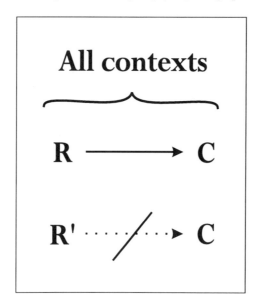

Figure 1. Two-term contingency. Probably fictitious because some context always discriminates contingent behaviors and consequences.

Despite the simplicity of the two-term contingency, in which the context (theoretically) exerts no control, it can be used to analyze a number of important properties of behavior. Most of these properties were shown originally in experimental boxes using pigeons or rats, especially in the exhaustive studies of Ferster and Skinner (1957). These authors systematically explored the possible variations in the way consequences were programmed contingent upon behaviors while the context was kept constant, and they laid down the foundations for the analysis of two-term contingencies. They were well aware that stimulus conditions would normally also control the Response-Consequence relation (Skinner, 1938), but they kept this constant through their experiments. What is being emphasized here is that changes in Response-Consequence relations or contingencies can occur without varying the stimulus context. With only two terms in our conceptual tool box we can analyze and change some important behaviors.

One way in which Response-Consequence contingencies can be manipulated and studied is by changing the manner in which the consequences follow the response. This is called the scheduling of contingencies, and was briefly mentioned in 2.3. Contingency schedules are the relations between the response and its functional consequences. In the experimental studies of behavior analysis, pigeons or hens peck a key which has the consequence of producing food, while other studies have rats pressing a bar which also has the consequence of producing food. There are at least five ways to vary the contingent relations with this simple situation.

The first contingency variation, studied by Ferster and Skinner (1957), is to change the response requirements for the production of a consequence. For example, intermittent schedules of reinforcement do not produce one reinforcer for every one response, but might produce one reinforcer contingent upon a number of responses (Ratio schedules). Alternatively, a reinforcer might be produced only when responding after a certain time period (Interval schedules). In these ways the relations between the production of the response and the production of the consequences can be varied. Important changes are found to occur in responding when this is done.

The stimulus context is not absent in such studies, however, but remains the same throughout the sessions. In fact, stimulus control is probably present anyway, since the animals only peck in the experimental boxes and not when put back into their home cages. So if nothing else, they learn to discriminate a setting in which pecking is reinforced (being put in experimental cage), and a setting in which it is not reinforced (home cage). But stimulus control cannot usefully be studied in this way.

A second way in which Response-Consequence contingencies can be varied is by changing the size or amount of the consequence. For example, if twice as much food is contingent upon a response, will the response be twice as likely to occur? A third way of varying the two-term contingency is by putting a delay between the response and the contingent consequence. This becomes the most simple analysis of memory (McCarthy & White, 1987). Over how long a period will a consequence control a response if delayed? To study more complex forms of memory requires changes in stimulus context to test the controlling relations, and to do this we need the third contingency term in our analysis (McCarthy & Davison, 1991).

A fourth way of varying the two-term Response-Consequence contingency is by increasing or decreasing the amount of deprivation the animal has had with respect to the reinforcer (Morris, in press; Skinner, 1938). For example, if food is a consequence of pressing a bar for an animal, will its response rate be doubled if it is deprived of food for twice as long?

All of the ways of studying changes in contingencies mentioned so far have had a single response with a single consequence. A final variation in the Response-

Consequence contingency is to provide an alternative response and consequence. If there are two responses available which have two different functional consequences, how does the animal divide its time between the two responses? The study of this question makes up the growing area of multiple contingencies (3.2 below).

One recent approach to all five aspects of response-consequence contingencies has been to put the different relations into a quantitative form. There is, in fact, a series of equations which predict these two-term relations in a consistent and meaningful manner. There is no such equivalent (yet) which also includes different stimulus contexts as a third term. The equation referred to is commonly called the Matching Law (Davison & McCarthy, 1988; Herrnstein, 1961) and will be discussed in 3.2. The point I wish to make here is that these relationships can be described with two-term contingencies. Even important phenomena such as self-control (how delays in consequences can affect behavior—see 8.5) or simple memory tasks can be usefully analyzed with two-term contingencies.

Three-term Contingencies

The key unit of behavior analysis has been the three-term contingency rather than the two-term (Skinner, 1938). With the addition of another level, robust analyses of some quite complex behaviors become possible. These analyses can also be used as a basis for changing behavior in applied settings.

The major difference at this level of analysis is that the stimulus context in which a two-term contingency is learned comes to have some control over the production of that two-term contingency. This is shown graphically in Figure 2. The two-term Response-Consequence (R –> C) relation only occurs in Context A1, not in Context A2. In this sense it is usually referred to as discriminative control, because the two contexts become discriminated if the consequences are effective ones, and also because the stimulus conditions are discriminative of the consequences available.

It must be remembered that such contexts can include a whole setting or situation, or just the presence of a single object or person. For example, saying certain four-lettered words might be strengthened in the presence of certain friends, while there might be aversive consequences in the presence of certain other people. So the stimulus context can be quite complex and hard to put into words, but can still be learned easily. Non-human animals can easily learn discriminations which are very hard to put into words, since verbalization is not necessary for the three-term contingencies to work.

It must be remembered, then, that we can learn to discriminate without using words, and that putting contingencies into words is *another* behavior which must be analyzed separately into its stimulus contexts and functional consequences (Chapter 7). One conceptual problem is that we, as humans, can verbally comment on the contexts. In the example above we might normally comment on the contingency by saying something like: "I can only say these four lettered words around Bill, Mary and James, not around Erica". What needs to be remembered is that the context itself

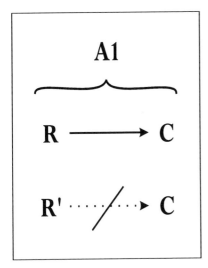 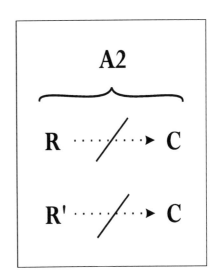

Figure 2. Three-term contingency. Response R has an effective consequence in context A1 but not A2. Context A1 is therefore discriminative of the contingency.

controls the production of responses (as well as the consequences), not the verbal behavior of commenting to oneself about the context. While verbal behavior can be shown to control behavior under some conditions (see 7.4), it is the context which controls the responses. In most cases the verbalizing of a discrimination only occurs after the discrimination has been learned.

The important point about three-term contingencies here is that they occur when the consequences are produced only in a certain context, and so *the behavior is only likely to re-occur in the same or similar contexts.* The properties of stimulus control are studied experimentally, for example, with rats pressing bars under red or green lights (with pressing only reinforced under red lights), or with pigeons pecking red or green keys (with pecking only reinforced under red keys). The basic phenomenon, first shown by Skinner (1938), is that after a while the animal will only press the bar (or peck the key) when the red light is on. In this case *the light colour is said to control the responding.*

There is one more point to make before considering the properties of this new level of analysis. This is that the context is said to select the two-term contingency rather than trigger it or cause it (2.2). What we learn in life is a repertoire of two-term contingencies which are selected by particular stimulus objects or contexts. This can be put more formally as "*IF* this Context, *THEN IF* this Response *THEN* this Consequence". Behavior analysis has a selection theory of behavior rather than a causal theory. The stimulus context and consequence are not said to cause or trigger the response, but rather the consequence selects the behavior in certain contexts. Be reminded again, as well, that the three-term contingencies do not have to be verbalized in the head before a discrimination can be made. The above is merely a formal way of stating a three-term contingency. We would be hard pressed to verbalize the contingencies of most of our behaviors.

The implication of all this is to again emphasize that *to define a behavior properly we must include both the consequences and the context in which that behavior produces the consequences.* Two-term contingencies merely hold the context constant, and do not occur in the real world. Instead, a multitude of contexts select from our repertoire of two-term contingencies. This means that the basic units of psychology must be three-term contingencies rather than behaviors or stimuli by themselves. We cannot specify any behavior without giving both the stimulus context and the consequences which have selected it. This means that all the properties discussed above for two-termed contingencies also apply to three-termed contingencies, except that the context can select (or discriminate) when those properties occur.

What, then, can the three-term contingency analyze which a two-term contingency cannot? First off, the realms of perception and psychophysics can be analyzed once the third term is added. As mentioned in 2.1, it is possible to find out what an animal can discriminate in the environment by whether that animal responds differentially in different contexts. If a red light selects for one response and a green light for another then an animal which is able to discriminate red from green will respond differentially in the two different contexts. From our example above, a rat would press the bar when the red light is on and stop pressing when the green light is on.

A second phenomenon amenable to analysis by three-term contingencies is that of conditioned consequences (2.3). This occurs when the consequences produced by one response are actually the stimulus context for another three-term contingency. If we could press a button on our desk to make available a fridge which we can then open to get chocolate, the button pushing would be strengthened as well as opening the fridge. Here we have the consequence of button pushing forming the stimulus context for another response involving the fridge door. Pushing the button has no immediate consequence which is itself strengthening of behavior (the appearance of a fridge is not reinforcing if there is no chocolate inside), but functions because it is a conditioned consequence.

To go back to our example of a rat with red and green lights, if the rat now has another bar which has the consequence of turning on the red light, the pressing of this second bar will be strengthened even though turning on a red light is not a strengthening consequence in normal circumstances. If these conditions hold, that an animal can respond in a particular way which results in a further context which can strengthen another response, then some new and important properties arise. Two of these will be discussed.

The first property is that consequences can develop beyond just those "programmed" or directly produced by the environment. If we only had two-term contingencies then only those consequences which directly follow from a response would be effective. Working for money, for example, would not be strengthened because there are no direct functional consequences from being given bits of paper. It is because money is a discriminative stimulus for many other direct consequences that any response which produces money will be strengthened indirectly. So money is a conditioned consequence and requires three-term contingencies at least for analysis.

The implication of this is that our contingencies can go beyond having food, sex and water as the only functional consequences of behavior. This also means that we can go beyond a limited range of behaviors: those that produce immediate functional consequences. Any behavior which produces money can be strengthened, no matter how wild. So the variability in our repertoires of behavior can go beyond that selected by directly interacting with the physical environment. The existence of conditioned consequences makes many new behaviors possible.

This property of conditioned consequences also makes possible behavior chains. In analyzing complex behaviors we often find sequences (rather than layers) in which the consequence of one response is the context for another and the consequence of that response is the context for another, and so on. In this way chains of behavior can be analyzed. For example, getting up from my chair is a context for leaving the room which is a context for going to the fridge, which is etc. etc. The rigid nature of chains, however, make them less relevant when analyzing human behavior. Human plans of action (relationships between contingencies) usually involve layers of stimulus control (four- and five-term contingencies) rather than fixed chains in which starting the first segment leads invariably to the last.

The second property of conditioned consequences is that generalized stimulus contexts are made possible. That is, one context can be functional for a number of different two-term contingencies. Again, money is a handy example: the stimulus context of having money can select many different two-term contingencies. Put in our more formal manner: IF money THEN new clothes; AND IF money THEN go to the movies; AND IF money THEN buy a flute. So adding a stimulus context to the two-term contingency allows for generalized stimulus control. Direct environmental contexts often only afford a limited range of two-term contingencies. How many different consequences can you produce from a blade of grass? The two-term contingencies afforded by a blade of grass are limited. Generalized stimulus contexts allow a greater variety of discriminations and responses (as Walt Whitman knew), and these can only be analyzed when we use a three-term contingency.

The role of generalized contextual control becomes even more important for humans. As we will see in Chapter 7, a large part of our verbal behavior is maintained by a generalized *social* contextual control. If left to the non-social environment, probably only a few types of verbal behavior would re-occur. Scientific reporting of the environment would not occur, since without generalized verbal control our statements about the environment would be directly controlled by the immediate consequences for reporting the environment. This would lead to biased scientific reports.

The third and final advantage of using three-term contingencies to analyze behavior is that they provide the most simple basis for analyzing *knowledge*. In these simple terms, knowledge is behaving differentially in different contexts. If I know how to make a cup of tea then this means that I can behave in a particular manner given certain objects and a context.

The same also applies to knowing that (Ryle, 1949) something is the case except that verbal behavior is now involved. If I know that Lima is the capital of Peru then this means that I can behave differentially (and hopefully correctly) in certain contexts–for example, in the context of reading: "What is the capital of Peru?" There is more to verbal behavior and knowledge, however, than can be analyzed with three-term contingencies, although Skinner did a remarkably thorough job of this in his published works (1957, 1974). For a better analysis of verbal knowledge, we need to use four-term contingencies.

Four-term Contingencies

With four-term contingency layers, the three-term contingencies now also come under stimulus control. A very simple example of this is shown in Figure 3. Sidman (1986a) refers to this as conditional discrimination, since the discriminations we have just talked about become conditional upon other stimulus conditions. It is also what we normally call contextual control. A stimulus will have an effective (functional) consequence in one context but not in another.

There is a big difference between the contexts at the level of the three-term contingency and at the level of the four-term contingency. The fourth term does not

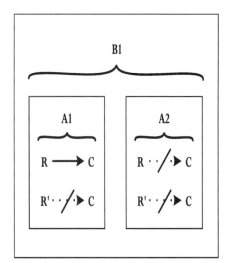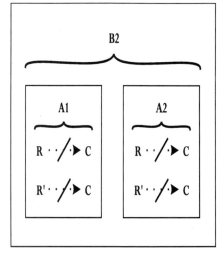

Figure 3. Four-term contingency. Context B1 is now discriminative of the entire three-term contingency in Figure 2.

determine the response-contingency relation, but determines which discriminative stimuli will control the response-consequence relations. So the fourth-term context selects from the repertoire of three-term contingencies.

The four-term contingency has some remarkable properties. Before examining the major one of these, stimulus equivalence classes, a bit more should be said about the four-term contingency.

Having four terms can help us analyze behavior in cases where the same object or the same word (as in verbal behavior) is responded to differently in different circumstances. We normally talk about this level of analysis as the significance or the meaning of objects or words. For example, the same word "mercury" can *mean* different things depending upon whether we are dealing with (have a fourth-term context of) liquids, gods, planets, personality, or music. Putting this in behavior analytic terms we can say that the same third-term context of the word "mercury" will select different two-term contingencies depending upon whether we have a fourth-term context of liquids, gods, planets, personality, or music. Merely changing the context changes all our responses and consequences in that context.

Stimulus Equivalence Classes

The most remarkable property of the four-term contingency is that of stimulus equivalence classes (Hayes & Hayes, 1992b; Sidman, 1986a, b, 1990), which have been found with interoceptive stimuli (DeGrandpre, Bickel, & Higgins, 1992), gustatory stimuli (Hayes, Tilley & Hayes, 1988) and musical stimuli (Hayes, Thompson & Hayes, 1989), in addition to the usual visual stimuli. The reasoning is that when learning most verbal behavior what is being taught are equivalences: that the word "chair" functions the same as both the sound of "chair" and the four-legged object we sit upon. Sidman took an analogy from mathematics, that to show two events are equivalent one must show three properties: identity, symmetry, and transitivity. While the use of the analogy has rightly been questioned (Saunders & Green, 1992), this is one way to begin looking at behavioral equivalences.

To follow this through let us consider a simplified example, Figure 4. Suppose we set up a conditional discrimination such that if there is Context D then under Context E a response R will have an effective consequence C. To get rid of other chains and layering effects, we say that under no other circumstances (Context E', Context D' or other responses R') will R lead to effective consequence C. Suppose we now train another conditional discrimination such that if there is Context E then under Context F the response R will again produce consequence C. Finally, given Context E and other Contexts (F') or other responses (R') there is no production of the effective consequence C. We can show all these contingency relations in set form as Figure 4.

In our example, we have now taught two discriminations, which is often represented using a common short-hand notation: that we have now taught two discrimination, D–>E and E–>F. (The problem I have with this short-hand is that we tend to forget the role of the responses and consequences in actually producing

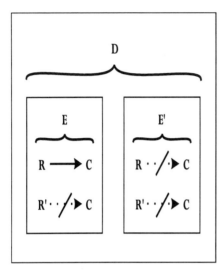 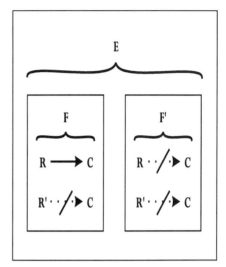

Figure 4. Example of equivalence class training and testing. Note that no direct relations between contexts D and F have been taught. If relations of Identity, Symmetry and Transitivity appear after this much training then the organism is said to have formed an equivalence class among Contexts D, E and F.

these contextual relations. It appears as if an association has been taught.) Notice that *nothing* has been taught about what happens in Context F if there is Context D, nor what happens in Context E if there is Context D and Context D'. The extremely interesting thing is that some properties which have never been taught can sometimes be found if this procedure is carried out. There are three of these properties:

1. The property of Identity is said to occur if, under Context D, an animal responds under a second Context D rather than another context which might be present (call this other Context D') when given a choice. In the short notation, D–>D is established without explicit, formal training.
2. The property of Symmetry is said to occur if in Context E the animal responds under Context D rather than any Context D'. So E–>D is also established without explicit training.
3. The final property is Transitivity, which is said to occur if under Context D the animal responds under Context F rather than any other Context F'. So D–>F is established without being trained.

If all three of these properties occur then the Contexts D, E and F are said to form a Stimulus Equivalence Class. They can each functionally substitute for one another, without the specific links between them being trained.

Before giving an example of this, a few points should be made. It seems that at the moment, equivalence classes can only be formed by humans. No convincing evidence has been shown for nonhuman animals (Hayes, 1989a) although it is still possible. Second, the phenomenon has only been shown for humans who are able to use language. Language-using intellectually disabled persons have been shown to form equivalence classes, but not language-deficient intellectually disabled persons (Devany, Hayes & Nelson, 1986), although it will be noted below that the interpretation of this is not yet certain. The final point is that these emergent relations occur immediately and spontaneously. There is no need to posit implicit cognitive processes going on which form new "connections".

To give an example of equivalence class relations, let us suppose that like most adults you have an equivalence class which consists of a verbal response "dog" and discriminated behaviors in the presence of a shape which has four legs, a wagging tail, floppy ears, etc. The power of equivalence classes can be gauged by considering what happens when I teach you that in a *Chinese context* if there is also a *dog context* then responding under a Context "gou" leads to reinforcing consequences. (Note that the actual response could be many things; pointing to or saying the word "gou" for instance.)

If I train DOG–>GOU in a *Chinese Context*, the word "gou" can immediately be substituted by normal adults for all other equivalence relations of "dog", *even though these substitutions have never been explicitly trained.* I can automatically now comment "That is a gou" when I see a dog walk past; I can comment "It's a gou's life I lead"; and I can joke that "I'm going to have a hotgou with sauce for lunch". All of these occur without the need for explicit training. This is the effect of stimulus equivalence classes on behavior.

The power of equivalence class relations can also be experienced as frustration when training language-deficient persons with intellectual handicaps or with very young children. You can reinforce saying the word "chair" in the context of objects with four legs and a place for the bottom to rest; you can also reinforce saying the word "chair" in the context of the written word CHAIR. The frustration in training comes because the CHAIR–>"chair" four-term contingency must also be explicitly trained with such people. It does not appear spontaneously and immediately as would happen with non-handicapped persons.

What has been claimed, then, is that the ability to form equivalence classes is a pre-requisite for the normal functioning of language (Sidman, 1990). Without the spontaneous and flexible formation of contextualized responses which can be substituted without teaching, language stays at a very basic level. Nonhuman animals can successfully learn even five-term contingencies (Nevin & Liebold, 1966; Santi, 1978), but the three properties of equivalence classes do not emerge from this training. This might also indicate a possible genetic basis to language use, since animals have not shown equivalence class relations. However, it might still just be that we are not training the animals properly in some way that humans can do without. So a genetic basis is not conclusive.

Others have suggested, with good evidence, that verbal behavior is a prerequisite for the formation of stimulus equivalence classes (Dugdale & Lowe, 1990; Wulfert, Dougher & Greenway, 1991), rather than the reverse. This view claims that the untrained equivalence relations appear because the organisms (again, only language-able humans)*name* the stimuli in some way and the naming relation enters unseen into the training through a long contingency history with verbal behavior. The basic phenomenon of stimulus equivalence class formation and its importance are not disputed, just the way in which it occurs (also see O'Mara, 1991). At the moment there seems to be no agreement or perfect evidence for either side of this argument although the evidence presented by Dugdale and Lowe (1990) seems hard to beat. In either case, the phenomenon itself is of vital importance.

[What is interesting to me in this dispute is that it seems to be implicit that equivalence class formation becomes possible because of language ability and, therefore, because of the formation of verbal communities and their patterns of *loose* reinforcement of behavior. This means that equivalence classes are a social phenomenon, made possible both through verbal communities reinforcing arbitrary relations between stimuli and through subjecting members to long learning sessions in order for them to become members. I believe the loose reinforcement is related to the arbitrary nature of equivalence relations.]

Equivalence classes allow for the generativity seen in the use of language, that new structures and "connections" appear spontaneously. Some have suggested that this is not possible in a behavior analytic account of language use (Chomsky, 1959), but this is true only if such views rely on a weak S-R account of verbal behavior or else they only consider a three-term contingency analysis of language use. Stimulus equivalence classes allow for spontaneous construction of word substitutions and for metaphors.

Let us consider one final property of four-term contingencies (another example of stimulus equivalence classes is given in 7.3; Silverman, Anderson, Marshall & Baer, 1986). I do this because it is important for this book that four-term contingencies and equivalence classes are well understood. As we shall see later, most of social behavior involves very subtle, shifting contextual effects, and the concatenation of many levels of contexts. Simple three-term contingencies do not take us far in analyzing social behavior (cf. Russo, 1990).

Suppose you walk into a chemistry lecture and the lecturer says, "Today I want to talk about metals". Spontaneously and immediately the words "mercury" and "iron" become more probable (presuming you have properly studied for the course) while the words "water" and "chlorine" have a lower probability of occurrence. Just the context of being in a chemistry lecture would give words such as "Aardvark" a very low probability. You are unlikely to say these words out loud, since that requires another level of context, such as occurs when questioned by the lecturer or a symbol is drawn on the board.

If, on the other hand, you walked into the lecture and the lecturer had said, "Today I want to talk about liquids" then "mercury" would again be high probability and so would "water". The relevant responses—those that have been strengthened in the past in that context—become more likely to occur. This happens spontaneously and immediately and involves a number of levels or layers of contextual control. The appearance of "mercury" requires a four-term contingency analysis because it has two meanings.

Something of the flavour of equivalence class relations can also be experienced when a person makes an oblique reference. Imagine that you are busy talking to someone about how chicken can be cooked by rubbing herb and garlic butter under the chicken skin with a spoon before it goes into the oven, and the person suddenly says to you, "That would be very useful in deep space exploration". The experience you have is that of loose verbal contextual control of responding. Equivalence classes are spontaneously formed and to put it idiomatically, "your brain goes spinning with the possibilities".

As has been said, equivalence class relations are extremely important for analyzing language use since so many relations can be formed from just a few explicitly taught relations (Hayes & Hayes, 1992). In one experiment, Wulfert and Hayes (1988) estimated that from teaching 8 conditional discriminations, about 200 others were available without training. This goes someway towards showing the importance of language use as contextual control for human behavior. To analyze these phenomena four-term contingencies are needed. There are now many applications of stimulus equivalence classes for education and people with handicaps (Green, 1991; Stromer, 1991) and more appear in each issue of the *Journal of the Experimental Analysis of Behavior*.

This concludes the discussion of how stimulus contexts can control behavior as layers of contingency relations (also see Catania and Cerutti, 1986). Five-term contingencies will not be discussed here, but Sidman (1986a) gives an interesting account. They add more complexity but have other properties. They allow that four-term contingencies (and equivalence relations, of course) can occur in some circumstances but not others. That is, equivalence relations can come under further stimulus control.

3.2. Multiple Contingencies

Up to this point we have talked about single contingencies, chains of contingencies, and layers of contingencies. In real life, however, there are always many contingencies afforded by the physical and social environments. On a Sunday afternoon, for example, there are many possible things you could do. Somehow, one or more of them occur and others do not eventuate, often the ones that have been verbalized about the most: "I must weed the garden this Sunday".

This section looks at the growing research area of how this partitioning amongst contingencies occurs. In order for behavior analysis to deal with complex human behavior, and especially social behavior, multiple contingency effects need a lot more research.

In situations of multiple responses we often talk about people having choices, as I *choose* or *decide* what to do on the lazy Sunday afternoon. The use of this terminology will be explored more fully in Chapter 8, but for now it should be said that the words "choose" and "decide" are not used much by behavior analysts. The reason for this is, again, that the words are loose and cover a number of separate events. They cannot be primitive terms since they can be broken down into more basic contingencies.

For example, when we use those two words we usually do so in contexts where some of the contingencies involve verbal behavior. If we do something "without thinking" (i.e., without verbal behavior) then we usually do not say that we decided or chose to do it. So the terms require certain conditions before we even use them, such as whether verbal behavior forms part of the multiple contingencies. To show what is really meant by choice and decision, therefore, requires specifying the social contexts under which the two terms are used and not used. This means that for the wider view of multiple contingencies they are not very useful terms.

In the recent literature, behavior analysts are now using these words, but they refer to any situation where there are multiple contingencies. If a rat has two bars to press which have different consequences, then the rat is said to choose between them. All this means is that the relative amount of bar presses or time spent pressing one bar as opposed to the other are measured, and this records the "choice". It is not implied that the rat has verbal behavior involved and thinks about its choice, and to this extent the use of the term "choice" by behavior analysts can be confusing. To say it again, the use of the terms "choice" and "decision" are confusing because we normally use them when there are multiple contingencies *and* some of them are verbal ones.

This section will consider models of what these multiple contingencies (or choices) might be. There have been a few different approaches to this question of partitioning behavior amongst multiple responses. First, given different sources of reinforcement, which maintain different responses, how is one "chosen" over another and what are the controlling variables? Second, some researchers have used Premack's Principle (2.3) and looked at what happens when responses are made contingent upon other responses in a multiple response environment. Others have looked at what happens to a group of responses when one is punished or prevented: how are the others redistributed over time? Fourth, some have looked at the effect of withdrawing a source of reinforcement: how do the responses redistribute and which of the earlier responses reappear? And finally, what happens to the entire repertoire when new responses are added?

These are very difficult questions, and equivalent questions have been posed (but also not fully answered) by most other psychological theories. For example, the same question for cognitive psychologists would be: how are plans for behavior assembled and one chosen over another to be executed (Miller, Galanter & Pribram, 1960; Schank & Abelson, 1977)? Decision theorists would ask: how are dynamic decisions made, and how are decisions made about what decisions to attempt to implement?

So the difficulty in getting answers to these questions is not the problem of behavior analysis alone. Parts of these literatures will be discussed below but no overall picture is available yet. So while selected topics only will be given below, the reader is encouraged to try and find the bigger picture.

Choices Between Contingencies

The first area pertinent to multiple contingencies is that of choosing between alternative sources of reinforcement. Until relatively recently, there was no behavioral model of choice. Skinner wisely rejected earlier attempts to develop one from choice in maze running since the number of variables left uncontrolled was great. This was one basis for his disagreements with Tolman (see Skinner, 1986b). With a different methodology, concurrent schedules of reinforcement, a behavioral model of choice became possible.

In 1961, Herrnstein proposed a new law of effect, later called the Matching Law, which left the way open for a behavioral choice model (see Findley, 1958, for an earlier start). Herrnstein (1961) proposed that if there are two sources of reinforcement, the relative number of responses will be proportional to their reinforcement values. It was a molar model of the allocation of responses (or time) to relative reinforcements. Several molecular models have been suggested as well, looking at the moment by moment details (see Commons, Herrnstein & Rachlin, 1982, for some of these debates).

In the typical modern experiment, an animal or human is provided with two responses as a "choice". Each has an independent schedule of reinforcement— usually a variable interval (VI) schedule. Such schedules provide reinforcers for responding but only after a variable amount of time. So one bar (with a rat pressing a bar) might *on average* give one reinforcer per minute whereas the other bar gives a reinforcer *on average* every two minutes. The question of choice is then one of how many responses does the animal allocate to each of the bars. [The rats cannot cheat and press both bars simultaneously!]

The original formulation suggested only that the relative allocation of behavior was proportional to the proportion of reinforcements, but a number of other controlling variables of choice are now known (Davison & McCarthy, 1988, provide an excellent review, while Rachlin, 1989, gives a less technical account. For an example of application, see Martens et al., 1990).

In the most simplified form, the matching law predicts the relative rates of responding for two behaviors (B1 and B2) as a function of the relative *rates* of reinforcement (R1 and R2), the relative *amounts* of reinforcement (A1 and A2), and the inverse relative *delays* to reinforcement (D1 and D2). It is expressed as follows:

$$\frac{B1}{B2} = \frac{R1}{R2} \quad \frac{A1}{A2} \quad \frac{D2}{D1}$$

This equation suggests (with good evidence) that the more reinforcement on average, the more that option is chosen (but there is not a linear relation); the larger the amount of reinforcer, the more that option is chosen; and the longer the delay between response and reinforcer, the less that option is chosen.

In recent research, the amount of reinforcement (A) has been standard for all experiments, hence this ratio will be ignored in the discussion. As well, weighting exponents have been left out from the above equation: to allow for individual differences and biases the three components of the equation are usually given power exponents. Finally, while the model as shown is for two choice decisions, it can be generalized to both single choice decisions and to decisions with more than two options (Herrnstein, 1970).

What this model says is that if there are two major sources of reinforcement, the relative amount of responding depends on the relative amounts of reinforcer, the rates of reinforcement, and the inverse of the delays until the reinforcer is received. If these three variables are multiplied and the proportion is, say 3:1, then the rate of responding will also be 3:1.

While this model has proved very useful in predicting the behavior of animals (Commons, Mazur, Nevin and Rachlin, 1987), and has been usefully applied to theories of animal foraging (Commons, Kacelnik and Shettleworth, 1987), applications to human choice have had some mixed results (Baum, 1975; Beardsley & McDowell, 1992; King & Logue, 1987; Pierce & Epling, 1983; Redmon & Lockwood, 1987; Schmitt, 1974). Other variables obviously play a role in human choice, and we will examine some of these when discussing human decision making in Chapter 8.

It is possible to study other controlling variables by comparing the results to those predicted by the Matching Law. For example, excellent work has been done with farm animals studying their preferences for different food types and different housing requirements (e.g., Kilgour et al., 1991; Matthews & Temple, 1979). In such research, pecking on different keys by hens might produce different types of reinforcers—wheat or barley, for example. If the keys are programmed with the same rates of reinforcement and delays to reinforcement, then the matching equation can be used to assess how much bias there is towards one or other of the food types. In this way the animals can "tell us" what types of food or housing they prefer or how aversive stimuli such as noise are to them (MacKenzie, Foster & Temple, 1993; McAdie, Foster, Temple & Matthews, 1993). This is also a great help in deciding animal welfare questions, rather than just letting people decide what animals prefer (e.g., Kilgour et al., 1984).

This is an important point beyond just an application to animal welfare. The major concern of this book is social behavior, and choices between behaving in different ways with different people do not usually have constant and identical reinforcers. While the use of constant reinforcers has been useful in developing the Matching Law, and will continue to be so in basic research, human examples need other controlling variables to be added.

Arranging Contingencies Between Multiple Responses

An early way of approaching multiple response situations was to consider the intermixing of contingency relations between different responses. The classic work on this was done by Findley (1962, 1966), who was interested in how to build up what he called multi-operant repertoires. Findley used chaining (sequential) and options (parallel) to achieve this. He showed how some complex groups of responses could be considered as a unit at another level, and these new units could be strengthened or weakened as would a simple operant. That is, a small chain of, say, three responses could be strengthened on a FR 10 schedule of reinforcement. In this way many of the multiple contingencies can be built up rather than "chosen" between. This really is an analysis of the controlling variables in planning. Findlay carried out experimental work with these ideas with rats, pigeons, monkeys and humans. These showed that some complex behaviors could indeed be analyzed in this way. Small amount of reinforcers could maintain long and complex behavior sequences.

An example of Findley's work is the male Mangabey monkey Smokey, which was trained on switches and pushbuttons to do the following: first, Response 1 required 40 presses or pushes (FR 40 schedule of reinforcement). This led (called a "tree" in Findley's terminology) to a choice situation (an "option") where the Smokey could respond with Response 2 (also FR 40) which produced food, or Response 3 (FR 40) which produced water. After food or water, the tree began again.

Having learned all of this thoroughly, the whole tree structure (40 R1s leading to either 40 R2s or 40 R3s) was placed into a FR 4 schedule of reinforcement. This meant that the monkey had to go through the tree structure four times before it could obtain any of the food or water. The results are shown in Figure 5. The cumulative responses of responding with the tree contingency show clear grouping of four, followed by a pause after reinforcement (the usual property of FR schedules). Within the tree, the monkey varied between the food and the water options, but the groupings of four are still clear. So the tree routine was built up into a larger unit of behavior with less overall reinforcement.

Before leaving this example, notice that the Matching Law would deal with the question of the relative choices between R2 and R3, as a function of various controlling variables. In this case the rates of reinforcements for R2 and R3 were the same, as were the delays (both were immediate). The major controlling variable was that of different types of reinforcers, food versus water. This was not of particular interest to Findley, but it can be seen from Figure 5 that food was chosen more frequently than water. So the study of the Matching Law forms a part of Findley's overall program of research (cf. Neef, Mace, Shea & Shade, 1992).

Bernstein and Ebbesen (1978) used a different method to look at the same question, having people live alone in a laboratory which was set up like an apartment for periods of up to 34 days. There were a limited number of activities they could perform, all of which were "self-chosen". One subject, for instance, chose the activities of artwork, candlemaking, or reading the magazines Hot Rod, National Geographic or Reader's Digest. All of the subjects could also prepare food, eat food, drink, exercise, write, and do maintenance tasks.

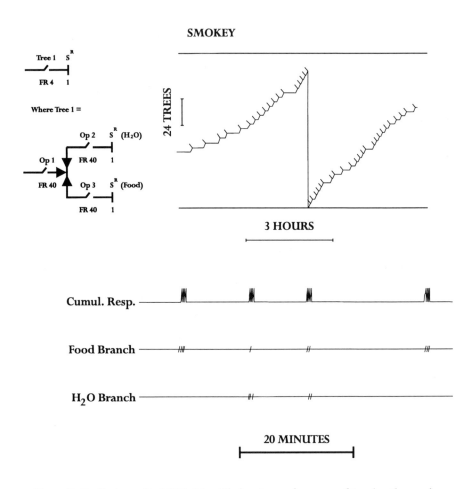

Figure 5. Findley's results (1962, Fig. 42) showing performance of Smokey the monkey. Sample record illustrating the performance after placing the tree under an FR 4 contingency. Reprinted by kind permission of The Society for the Experimental Analysis of Behavior, Inc. Copyright 1962.

These authors were interested in testing Premack's Principle (2.3), that a high probability response could act to strengthen a low probability response if it was made contingent upon completion of the latter. To do this, they first measured the baseline probabilities of all the different behaviors, and then varied the contingent relations between the responses. For example, the subject mentioned above might be required to do 70 minutes of artwork *in order to* do 45 minutes of reading.

Bernstein and Ebbesen (1978) found that the results seemed to fit Premack's Principle. The distribution of responses over time could be predicted by the contingencies between the responses. It was also found that the rate of the contingent response was never brought up to its baseline rate after it had been made contingent. In the example given above, for example, when reading was made contingent upon artwork, the amount of reading never reached its original baseline levels even though enough artwork could have been carried out to make this possible. So making one response contingent upon another led to a decrease in the baseline of the former and an increase in the latter. This can be predicted by a few different models of multiple response effects (Allison, 1976, conservation model; Mazur, 1975, value averaging model; also cf. Pierce, Epling & Boer, 1986).

A similar study also found that, when made contingent, there were increases in the low probability behaviors and decreases in the high probability behaviors (Foltin et al., 1990). An interesting finding of this study was that this change with an added contingency was exacerbated when the subjects had smoked marijuana. The drug acted as a motivator, but mainly for the instrumental (low probability) responses. Some other examples of work along these lines with humans will be mentioned in 6.7.

The experimental results in this area are partly a function of what is measured and how many activities are available. Collier et al. (1990) put rats in a environment where they could eat, drink, run on a wheel, or nest. All these were measured. The authors then increased the cost of accessing these resources by increasing an FR schedule. They found that for each resource, while the frequency of bouts of eating, drinking, wheel running and nesting decreased, the bouts themselves were longer. So by measuring both frequency of bout and bout size, different effects of changing the contingencies were recorded.

Restricting contingencies

Multiple response effects can also be studied when one or more responses are removed from the repertoire. How does a whole repertoire change if this occurs? Response restriction itself can be done in a few ways. A behavior can be punished, the stimulus context for the behavior can be removed or changed in some way, or the response could be extinguished. This latter will be dealt with separately in the following section.

Experiments on response restriction typically set up a multiple response repertoire and then either punish a response and measure the changes in the other responses, or else restrict access to a response and measure the changes in the others (e.g., Crosbie, 1990, 1991, 1993). Green and Striefel (1988), for example, let autistic children have six activities, measured the baselines on these, and then restricted access so the children could perform only three or four of the activities. The changes in rates of each activity were then measured. Lyons and Cheney (1984) used male rats for their experiment, putting them in a multi-compartment box with five activity compartments and a hallway. The compartments allowed the rats to turn off the lighting, view a female rat, turn off white noise, drink water, and eat food, while they could wait in the passageway.

Five principles have been proposed for predicting how multiple responses are redistributed when access to one response is stopped or one response is extinguished (see Green & Striefel, 1988). They are not mutually exclusive.

a. Selection substitution rule: the redistribution will be different for different individuals and must be empirically determined. Suggested by Bernstein and Ebbesen (1978) for their results.

b. Constant ratio rule: the other responses will take up the newly available time, increasing in the same proportions as their relative baselines (Luce, 1959; Rachlin & Burkhard, 1978; Rachlin, Kagel & Battalio, 1980).

c. Hierarchical rule: the most probable response remaining will take up all the newly available time while the other responses will stay at baseline levels (Dunham & Grantmyre, 1982).

d. Sequential dependence rule: responses which were sequentially dependent upon the now restricted response will also decrease in frequency (Dunham & Grantmyre, 1982).

e. Equal redistribution rule: the newly available time will be distributed equally between all the remaining responses (Lyons & Cheney, 1984).

The experimental literature at present suggests that none of these rules fits all the data, even given that the selective substitution rule does not really predict at all. Studies by Dunham and Grantmyre (1982), Lyons and Cheney (1984), and Green and Striefel (1988) have found very idiosyncratic responses redistributions. Green and Striefel also found that similarities between both the stimuli used in responses and in the topography of responses could partially predict that one would substitute if the other disappeared. This inconclusiveness means that further factors remain to be discovered.

Extinction of Responses

The approaches given above rely on removing a possible response by changing context or by changing the contingencies between responses. Another way to influence multiple responses is by the extinction (Catania, 1984) of one or more responses. This differs from the previous methods since the response is still possible for the animal but there is no longer any discriminative stimulus or consequence supporting it.

Epstein (1985a) discussed a finding, often mentioned but rarely researched, that when one response is decreased through extinction, a response previously reinforced in similar circumstances will recur. This has been called resurgence (Epstein & Skinner, 1980; cf. Kazdin, 1982). For example, if I extinguish a child's crying before going to bed, a response which previously occurred in that situation, say reading a bedtime book, might increase in frequency even though I have not directly changed its contingencies at all.

It is possible that resurgence played a role in the mixed results pointed out in the last section. The problem is that resurgence does not yet make very strong predictions about *which* of the previous responses will occur. It would be interesting to compare the two approaches. To do this you would let an animal have, say, six responses in a situation and then either place one of them under extinction or else immediately prevent that same response by removing some establishing operation for it. A comparison of the changes in the other five responses would be most interesting. Would the redistribution be different with the two procedures, and could some topographical feature of the other five responses better predict the redistribution? The experiment remains to be done.

One other well-documented finding is that if reinforcement is stopped and the behavior comes under extinction then aggression is a common outcome (Azrin, Hutchinson & Hake, 1966; Hutchinson, 1977). Todd et al. (1989), for example, found that children were two to ten times more likely than baseline to hit a punching bag when a marble-dispensing clown stopped reinforcing. This "extinction-induced aggression" seems to have been shown only in cases where there were few other alternative behaviors, however. The results in this section would suggest that it will be a function of the number of other available contingencies. It might not be indicative of an emotional reaction to extinction, but of another very salient contingency for many animals filling in the time now available. This could easily be tested.

Addition of New Responses

Little work seems to have been done on the effects of adding new responses into a repertoire, despite its importance, and despite the frequency with which behavior analysts train new behaviors. If a person had a very limited repertoire, a person with intellectual disabilities for example, then the addition of a new behavior could entail the disappearance of other behaviors since it would take up a large amount of time at first. This may not be a favourable outcome at all.

Alternatively, merely adding many new behaviors could reduce problem behaviors without any further therapy. With an aggressive child, for example, teaching them a number of new behaviors, even if totally unrelated to aggression, might reduce the aggression through a redistribution of the entire contingency repertoire. If we could predict such changes it would be of much benefit for applied behavior analysis.

Based on the predictions made earlier, we can suggest the following possible outcomes from adding new behaviors:

    a. the new redistribution will depend upon how strong the added contingencies turn out to be.

    b. if the new contingency was very strong then the previously most probable response would decrease in frequency.

    c. very low probability responses would disappear altogether.

    d. if the new responses were keystone behaviors (Evans & Meyer, 1985, meaning establishing operations) then they would allow even more new responses to occur, which would intensify the decremental effects on responses in the previous repertoire.

These points raise an interesting question about the effect of the size of a repertoire. How do overall behavior patterns compare between someone with a very large repertoire and someone with a small repertoire? The small repertoire person must experience frequent redistribution phenomena, since they are more likely to have large changes occur. This could lead to the appearance of psychological instability. A person with a large repertoire might be able to weather changes better because only small fluctuations occur in their repertoire from redistribution phenomena.

Nothing seems to have been researched along these lines as yet (but cf. Thoits, 1983). The work would probably be of great interest to applied behavior analysts. It might be especially so since both Skinner (1987) and Herbert (1981) have suggested that modern day people have smaller and smaller repertoires, because technological advances are meaning less and less actual behavior is needed for sustaining life processes.

How One Contingency can Mysteriously Affect Another

In analyzing behavior, especially complex human behavior, collateral behavior changes are often found. Nordquist (1971), for example, found that when an intervention was mounted to reduce a child's oppositional behavior towards his parents, his enuresis was also reduced even though no explicit treatment had been given.

This area of collateral changes is not well developed yet, but holds a rich potential for future behavior analysis given the areas already covered in this chapter (see Evans, Meyer, Kurkjian & Kushi, 1988, for the best summary). There are several ways I can see, from what has been reviewed above, that changes in one contingency (call the behavior A) might affect another behavior (B) without any intervention directly on B. This classification is preliminary and unsubstantiated, but it might provide a start.

a. There might be a functional relation between the two behaviors. In this case, behavior A is maintained by the same consequences as behavior B. If the intervention changes or makes more frequent the possibility of the consequences then B might become more frequent as well.

As an example, Nordquist (1971) suggested that in his reported case, both oppositional behavior and bedwetting were maintained by poor parental reinforcement procedures. When the parents were taught better procedures to reduce the oppositional behavior, the bedwetting also changed with the changed consequences. The collateral change in behavior B probably occurred because of a functional relation between the two behaviors.

b. Two behaviors might have the same or very similar contextual control or establishing operations. In this case, presenting the context for behavior A in an intervention might also lead to an increase in behavior B. For example, increasing children's drawings can be done by giving them lots of pencils and paper. This change is also a context for number of other behaviors, however, such as throwing pencils, making paper jets, writing on the wall, and doing origami.

c. Providing a schedule for one behavior might increase adjunctive behaviors. Adjunctive behaviors are not well understood, but are behaviors which increase when a schedule of reinforcement is introduced. The original finding was that putting rats onto an interval schedule for food increased their drinking even though there was no limitations on drinking at any time (Falk, 1969).

Not enough is known about adjunctive behaviors although they have been suggested as a third category of learning, alongside operant behaviors and classically conditioned behaviors (Wetherington, 1982). Suggested examples for humans include walking and pacing, smoking, eating, overall level of activity, and compulsions (e.g., Kachanoff, Leveille, McClelland & Wayner, 1973). Even though little is known for certain, this category must be considered when analyzing collateral changes. (For more on the arguments, see the following: Falk, 1977; Frederiksen & Peterson, 1974; Overskeid, 1992; Reid & Staddon, 1982; Roper, 1980; Staddon, 1977; Wetherington, 1982).

d. There might be a temporal relation such that one behavior allows a large amount of time which is likely to be filled by some other activity. This is not identical to adjunctive behavior. It means that if one behavior is changed so as to leave time available, *some* other activity must fill this and be recorded as increasing.

For example, if a behavior change means that a highly aggressive child become less so, then some other activities must fill the time previously used in aggression. This could be staring into space, watching television, being naughty, or reading books. The most interesting point is that *the new behavior might have no relationship to the other except for this temporal relation*, although Green and Striefel (1988) found that the filler activity was likely to have some topographical features in common.

As an example, when some species of animals are put together their level of fear is reduced (Guerin, 1993). This means that more time is available for other behaviors since less crying and vigilance occur. In such situations, different species do different things. If food is present then chicks together will spend the extra time eating. If rats are put together they will spend the extra time in social interaction, and eat less than when they are alone.

e. The behavior changed might be a keystone behavior for another behavior. The concept of keystone behaviors was developed by Evans and Meyer (1985). They suggested that in some cases one behavior is a pre-requisite for another By training or facilitating the keystone behavior, the other is made possible and is likely to increase in frequency.

f. The final type of collateral change to be mentioned, and the most important for this book, is that of mediation by other people. This overlaps with the other types of collateral changes, but other people are involved.

For example, if I teach you to smile then this can lead to a change in the range of consequences available from other people (cf. Buell et al., 1968). This is not quite the same as a keystone behavior effect because the first behavior is changing the contingency relations altogether. This can occur easily with other people since the social contingencies are dynamic and flexible.

These six routes to collateral changes need to be studied and tested. As an example, Haring, Roger, Lee, Breen and Gaylord-Ross (1986) found that after teaching intellectually handicapped persons how to initiate conversations, their frequency of expanding conversations (keeping the conversation going) also increased without any training. There are at least two explanations for this. First, it could be that conversational initiations are a pre-requisite behavior for expansions. This would mean that training expansions, then, would have little or no effect on initiations. Alternatively, initiations and expansions could share contexts or consequences, and form a functional response class. This would mean that training expansions *would* lead to a collateral increase in initiations of conversations. Gunthorpe and Guerin (1991) in fact found that the latter was true: training expansions did increase initiations.

I hope it can be seen that the study of multiple response interactions, including collateral response changes, promises to be very useful in the future, both for analyzing complex human behavior patterns and for providing better interventions in applied settings. They are of especial importance in studying social behavior, and I will refer to such effects through this book.

3.3. Analyzing Social Contingencies

While the whole of this book is about the social contingencies, it is worth considering briefly in this chapter social contingencies and the special properties (not principles) which put them in a class of their own. The rest of the book will then deal with the details of social contingencies in a more systematic fashion. In one sense the rest of the book can be seen as an extension of the previous section, 3.2. The most important way in which multiple behaviors can occur is if two or more people act "together" in some way to produce an effect which they could not achieve alone. So the "multiple responses" might be responses from different people which have an effect different from that produced by the individual responses alone. The production of such effects in turn has effects on the individuals involved.

What is Special About Social Behavior?

It seems to us that other people are special sorts of objects in the environment. Indeed, we do not refer to other people as "objects" or "things" at all, unless it is meant as an insult. But for an analysis of behavior we should initially treat people as just another type of object and from this find out their special properties. As we will see here, they do have properties not shared by other objects although the analysis of social behaviors is based on the same principles as for any other behaviors. People have special reinforcing properties as well as special stimulus properties.

The problem that arises is that of clearly separating social behavior from "non-social behavior", and perhaps also from verbal behavior. There has been a lot of discussion on these points within behavior analysis, and little consensus exists. Most of the obvious solutions turn out to have conceptual problems when they are fully thought through.

For example, is a behavior only learned through the mediation of other people, but which can be carried out in the absence of others, rightly called social behavior? Hake and Vukelich (1972) have used the term quasi social stimuli to refer to such problem cases. As an example of this, money does not function without other people entering into the very complex contingencies. Money is no use unless at least one person responds to it in the same way we do. Does this mean we should call all our economic behavior social? If we taught an animal to respond to money by giving us things, would this make it a social interaction?

Another position to take is that the components of any contingency, stimulus context, behavior and consequence, can be in two states: they can be such that others *have* to be involved, or they can be such that others *might* be involved. Looking at the problem this way, which of these we call *social* becomes a bit arbitrary. For example, we will see in Chapter 7 that other people have to be considered in verbal behavior contingencies, even when we talk to ourselves (cf. Wittgenstein, 1953). Aggressive behavior, on the other hand might include other people or it might not. But to say that aggressive behaviors are not to be called social behavior because they do not *have* to include other people seems a poor way of treating social behavior.

We could make another distinction and call behaviors "social" if other people *are directly* involved, but this leads to other conceptual problems, such as how to consider the exchange of money with a food machine. Other people are not involved directly in the flesh, but the contingencies would never occur without other people to set up the food machines or to teach us about money.

I wish simply to avoid all these problems here since there are no easy solutions. I will mostly refer to the social *properties* of contingencies, which will include any contingencies where another person is involved as either a stimulus context, as a determinant of consequences, or as part of the (group) behavior itself. These relations have to be demonstrated by showing that the other person is part of the contingency, rather than deduced from arguments about what is and is not social behavior. In practice, if a person is involved in any of the three terms of a contingency the behavior has sometimes been called a social behavior, and this broad usage will be followed here.

My answer to these problems is that of most importance is whether a social behavior depends or does not depend upon having a verbal community (Part 3 of the book). If definitions and conceptual distinctions have to be made, then I believe that separating social behaviors with and without a verbal community is more important than trying to separate social and nonsocial behavior. For this reason the major part of this book is divided in this way rather than as social and nonsocial behaviors.

For more on how we might define social behavior, the question I am avoiding here, the reader is referred to the following: Catania (1986), Hake (1982), Hyten and Burns (1986), Lee (1984), Parrott (1983, 1986a), Schoenfeld (1965), and Skinner (1953, 1957). Of interest might also be Bowdery (1942) and Langford (1978).

What is special about social behavior, then, is perhaps only that other people play a big role in our lives and they form special groups called verbal communities. They are in principle no different to other parts of the environment and can be a stimulus context for a contingency, part of a group behavior, or a consequence of our behavior. So if we take them as no different in the principles of behavior than a chair or a rock, then we must look for any special properties they have which differentiate them from these other parts of the environment.

Properties of Social Behavior

From the perspective developed in Chapter 2 and 3.2, we can view other people as bundles of multiple contingencies which are dynamic and interactive in a way that chairs and rocks are not, which are flexible in their behavior, which are numerous and salient in our lives, have a long contingency history, and which are mediators for many (most?) of our other contingencies. Thus they are highly intermeshed in our layers of contingencies and in the interactions between our multiple contingencies.

When we interact with someone they can react to what we say and do and in many and flexible ways. Very few things we do escape the possible mediation by other people. Despite this, my observation is that much social behavior is of little direct or immediate consequence. This, however, is not because people are not important, but because little is left to direct shaping by others. It is not very often (for most of us) that someone pushes or shoves us, gives us food contingent upon a behavior, or is regularly present to act as a discriminative stimulus Rather, much of our social behavior is mediated by verbal contexts in four- or five-term contingencies rather than through physical action. Direct physical behaviors such as touching and pushing seem to occur relatively rarely with people.

For example, often one person requires something the other has, and this forms the building block of much social behavior. We then speak of social power—the relative control of socially discriminated consequences. This will sometimes be achieved by pushing and shoving or grabbing the object, but most times the interaction will occur solely with words or gestures and be just as decisive. In both cases we are dealing with the same principles of behavior, but in the latter case the properties of generalized social consequences and verbal communities make the contingencies very different.

Skinner wrote of this division (1957, p. 2): "Behavior which is effective only through the mediation of other persons has so many distinguishing dynamic and topological properties that a special treatment is justified and, indeed, demanded." Such behaviors are called verbal behaviors (and include many behaviors called nonverbal by other psychologists): linguistic behaviors, gestures, socially shared knowledge, instructions, self-behaviors, attribution, attitudes, music, art, and dance.

The major point of this book, therefore, will be to distinguish between contingencies where people act directly as discriminative stimulus, consequence, or as co-behaver, and those where a verbal community maintains the behavior regardless of whether another person is present or not. In the former case, some other part of the environment (such as a food machine) could substitute for the person involved and the contingency could survive. In the latter case, however, other people are essential to the generalized social contingencies and the behaviors produced are therefore uniquely human, and uniquely part of social science, despite being based on the same natural science principles of behavior analysis. This is the division between verbal behaviors (which must be social) and the (social) nonverbal behaviors which still involve another person (cf., Parrott, 1986a).

The properties of these types of contingencies are so very different that they form separate divisions in this book. Chapters 4, 5 and 6 deal with other people mediating directly as stimulus context, consequence, or as co-behavers, and Chapters 7, 8, 9 and 10 deal with those social contingencies which involve generalized social consequences and verbal communities. In real life, however, these are mixed in together, and so the fourth part of the book will give some examples of how they interact to produce complex human behavior.

The whole of this book, the approach of behavior analysis, is based in the natural sciences. The foundations have been outlined in this, the first part of the book. The formation of verbal communities defines the social sciences, and the differences between social science and the other natural sciences arise from the properties of verbal comminities. The social behaviors discussed in the second part of this book fall somewhere in between. These social behaviors usually involve other people but because verbal communities are not required, other parts of the environment could substitute for the presence of people.

Part 2
Social Contingencies
Without a Verbal Community

Chapter 4

Social Discriminations

4.1. Conspecifics as Stimulus Contexts

Other people can act as discriminative stimuli and establishing operations. Technically, this means that the presence of people is correlated with changes in the behavior strengthening effects available. For example, if you are doing something by yourself, you would not expect to be laughed at or rebuked. Having someone appear and watch you perform means that there is now a discriminative context for these consequences to occur. They could also praise you for doing well, of course. Such discriminations as these are presumably learned through childhood and form part of our contingency histories.

The presence of others can be discriminative of changes in consequences which are specific to one person, or it can be discriminative of generalized changes in consequences which occur in the presence of almost any people. Verbal behavior is strengthened, for example, if someone is present who also speaks the same language.

This way of talking about people produces some interesting lines of inquiry. First, how people function as discriminative stimuli will depend on previous interactions with that person or with other similar persons. If we meet a stranger, they will act as a discriminative stimulus for only the very generalized consequences, such as verbal behavior, attention, and as a source of praise or rebuke. If they they remind us of another specific person then there will be more specific contingencies contacted: "I always think about tennis when I see Bob because he reminds me of Eric, my old tennis partner".

People we know will have more specific effects because of previous interactions with them. Meeting the Head of Department in the corridor is a discriminative stimulus for behaviors indicative of working hard, for example. Either doing these behaviors has been strengthened in the past or else not producing them has been punished in the past when the Head of Department was around.

Some researchers have concluded that a number of our social behaviors are not changed by their consequences at all, and instead are innate or "hard-wired" (e.g., Zajonc, 1980). By this they mean that the behaviors must be consequential to the species as a whole through reproduction by the individual. However, it turns out that most of these behaviors are the very ones that are maintained by generalized consequences. It is very hard to tell innate behaviors from behaviors maintained by generalized reinforcers, since you cannot ever prove that a behavior is innate, and since the generalized consequences are so diffuse and unobvious when observing human behavior. The most important of these will be described in 4.2: social compliance, verbal behavior, social facilitation, imitation, social comparison, and gesturing.

What this point has meant is that psychologists other than behavior analysts have found evidence which they interpret as supportive of innate behaviors. There are no *obvious* (macro) functional consequences so the results are talked of showing innate forms of behavior. These same results, however, can be interpreted as showing the effects of generalized social consequences. An example of this is verbal behavior: there are no obvious consequences everytime we say something which is grammatically correct, so some psychologists conclude that humans have an innate propensity to speak grammatically. Instead, the maintenance of verbal behavior is through generalized social consequences which are hard to see. Their effects lurk in our contingency histories.

Social Versus Nonsocial Discrimination

One of the early views was that there was something innate about differentiating social objects from nonsocial objects. It was said, for instance, that babies can innately distinguish peoples' faces from inanimate objects. This led to a series of experiments comparing the discrimination of social and nonsocial objects.

Following the argument above, it is suggested that there is nothing intrinsically different between social and nonsocial objects. Social objects are more dynamic, interactive, have more powerful consequences, and more generalized consequences (see 3.3). When we give these same properties to a non-social object, such as a smart computer program, people immediately and spontaneously treat them as they would a social object. This means that research should be directed to finding out how these special properties are discriminated, rather than trying to prove that they are absolutely intrinsic to social objects.

Some of the evidence in this vein came from Husted and McKenna (1966), who showed that rats could discriminate between the presence and absence of a second rat. They also found that their rats could discriminate between pairs of individual rats of the same species and the same sex. This meant that there were specific cues present to allow discrimination.

This work was extended by Danson and Creed (1970) and Millard (1979), who showed that the *rate of responding* of one animal could act as a discriminative cue for another animal, even though the discriminating rat performed with a different response. Other similar results have been found with rats and monkeys (Fushimi, 1990; Timberlake & Grant, 1975).

Hake, Donaldson and Hyten (1983) followed this work up with a replication, but in doing so found some possible non-social cues which might have been controlling the discriminations in the earlier experiments (see also Marcucella & Owens, 1975, and Volger, 1968). They found that their experimental pigeons were responding to *auditory cues* made by the stimulus pigeon. When they masked this sound the discrimination effect diminished, although a further experiment showed that another non-social auditory cue might still have been present.

The discussion of Hake, Donaldson and Hyten (1983) suggests that there are difficult problems in sorting out whether a discriminative cue comes from the social presence of another animal or some collateral effect of the other being there. From the viewpoint expressed here, however, it does not make any difference whether social objects are inherently different to non-social objects or not. If a property of social objects is that they are dynamic and have flexible behavior, then a multitude of cues must *always* be a part of recognizing social objects.

There is some interesting evidence that very young infants respond differently to animate and inanimate objects (see Gelman & Spelke, 1981). While this is to be expected, given the enormous differences between the two in sensory and other consequences, it is remarkable that it happens so young. Golinkoff and Harding (1980; cited in Gelman & Spelke, 1981) reported that 24 month old infants were surprised when a chair seemed to moved on its own but not when someone moved it. While the infants had no verbal behavior (thoughts or "understanding") about this, they could respond differentially.

In summary, there seem to be no inherent cues used innately to discriminate between social and nonsocial objects. Rather, social objects typically have different properties because they have so many changing features which can readily act as salient cues and which have a long learning history. The point, then, is to find those cues and show how they function.

Discriminative Cues

This leads us to the question of what it is about a person that can act as a discriminative stimulus. The answer: practically anything! All the features which we consider "meaningful" about a person are discriminative stimuli for differential consequences. If a person is wearing a black arm band then this means that certain responses will be strengthened (talking in a soft voice) and certain others will be punished (making crass jokes about dead bodies).

While we could talk about "social signal" or "social meaning", I believe there are two reasons why this terminology should be avoided (cf. 2.1). First, using these terms gives the impression that the significance of the "signal" lies in the object itself, or is inherent in that object. In most cases, however, any other object could have been used just as easily—such as a black headband instead of armband. In other words, the use of these terms obscures the effects of previous contingency history with those objects because it is the previous history which establishes the "meaning".

The second reason for not using the term "social signal" is that it ignores the motivational component of discriminative stimuli, and treats them as pure transfer of motivationless "information". But it is not enough to have distinguishing cues, there must be differential consequences ("shades of meaning") to those cues as well, whether these are from a past history of learning (discriminative stimuli) or from their role as establishing stimuli. Using the term discriminative cue rather than social signal reminds us that the full three-term contingency is involved and that the relation could be changed if the consequences were to be changed.

An interesting example of changing social discriminations in monkeys was published by Stammbach (1988). He taught a certain skill to *non-dominant* monkeys in a group which produced a reinforcer, so the non-dominant monkeys became the "specialists" at finding the reinforcers. The presence of these monkeys therefore now became discriminative of reinforcement. Once this was done, Stammbach found that the other monkeys would follow these trained monkeys, and the more dominant monkeys stopped chasing the specialists when in the presence of the response levers. Thus the cues involved in being dominant were clearly dependent upon the production of reinforcers, and could be changed when the reinforcers changed.

It can be seen, then, that we should not pre-judge what can and cannot be a discriminative cue, since any feature which can be seen or heard and can lead to differential consequences will do. If there are commonly used cues (such as the face) or patterns of cues (waving a limb), it is because of the way the body and environment are structured, not because the "receiver" has an innate propensity to use those cues. This means that looking for patterns in the use of social cues also has to involve looking for the changes in consequences when those cues are present.

4.2. Generalized Discriminations Provided by Other People

Because almost any feature of a person can be used as a discriminative cue if the consequences are correlated with its presence (given a particular behavior), the study of specific cues follows trivially from the principles of discrimination. Most of the research, therefore, has been on generalized discriminations, although much of it is interpreted in ways other than that given here. If there are generalized patterns of consequences then the presence of another person will be discriminative of a number of behaviors and consequences.

It is argued, then, that much of our social behavior is maintained by the cumulative effect of living in a social community, through which some very general responses are maintained. As examples, we get very similar consequences from interacting with any person who is scowling and clenching their fists; if our facial expressions look aggressive we get similar effects from most other people. In this sort of way the discriminations become generalized, at least within a social community.

Smiling is another example. When young, smiling is typically correlated with positive reinforcers and so becomes a discriminative cue when *anyone* is smiling. Later in life we discriminate the "finer shades of meaning" of smiles and treat differently the smiles of friends and of car salespersons—they typically have different consequences.

Most of this is perhaps well known and not disputed. What psychologists often need reminding of, however, is that there are consequences involved in these phenomena. The full three-term contingency is needed to analyze and change such discriminative cues. Smiles only "mean" something if there are consequences. If we changed the usual consequences then smiling could begin to "mean" (discriminate) bad events (the smile of a car salesperson?).

The remainder of this chapter will look in more detail at seven common types of generalized discriminations. It is not the purpose to review all the findings, since in most cases they have already been well reviewed. Rather, the purpose is to re-emphasize the role of consequences in these phenomena. The value of doing this is that it opens many ways of studying such phenomena if they are not assumed to be fixed or innate. Emphasizing the role of consequences in these seven research areas also means that applied work can work at changing the phenomena (if this is socially valuable) through their consequences. It must also be kept in mind that the social contingencies discussed here are only taken to be generalized in Western cultures. Other cultures might have other important social consequences which become functional with just the presence of another person. As well, various subgroups of a culture have different consequences for the same contexts and behaviors.

Social Compliance

There is a great deal of evidence that under many conditions people are generally more compliant or obedient in the presence of others. The classic studies of Asch (1956), Orne and Schreibe (1964) and Milgram (1974) supported this. Two generalized consequences are often suggested to be involved in such situations. First, all during childhood the presence of other people is probably discriminative of social approval if behavior is socially compliant; and second, discriminative of social disapproval if noncompliant. Being socially compliant or noncompliant when no one is present has no immediate effects. It is argued, then, that the extent to which these contingencies have been generalized to many people other than parents, and generalized to many different contexts and settings, will predict the extent of a person's social compliance.

While none of this will be news to social psychologists, it means that we have a focus for looking at the controlling variables of compliance and obedience. First, we should look for the contextual variables (four- or five-term contingencies) which discriminate compliance. This is the thrust of the traditional social psychological approach, to describe the settings or contexts under which we get more or less compliance. Second, we should also look for the dynamics of the consequences which maintain such compliance, as well as the consequences which prevent compliance. Many of these will come from within a subgroup rather than from the whole generalized community (Hebdige, 1979).

The role of social consequences in this area is usually found in social psychology under the label of normative influences (Deutsch & Gerard, 1955; also see Hogg & Abrams, 1988, for a good discussion of such influences). It is usually expressed as a need or a motive people have for social approval and avoidance of social disapproval. I am arguing here that we can get further if we analyze this into a generalized consequence component of our three-term contingency repertoire. Calling it a "need" does not help our analysis, and requires postulating a new "need" everytime the consequences change.

The role of the social contextual variables in this area has been referred to as the informational influences (Deutsch & Gerard, 1955; Hogg & Abrams, 1988). If the generalized social compliance in a group is very powerful and not likely to be changed by consequences more specific to the persons and the social negotiation involved, then the contextual or informational variables alone will predict behavior. This is what most of the social psychological literature has assumed. For example, if we assume that the consequences have already established generalized compliance, then knowing the "information" (discriminative context) which is present (such as "No smoking is allowed") will allow for correct predictions of behavior by social psychologists. But this is still wholly dependent upon the consequences being generalized and remaining stable. A proper analysis requires both the the normative and informational components. When more specific consequences are also present, these will also be part of the social negotiation of conformity.

The question of social psychology, therefore, of whether normative influence, informational influence, or both are present in conformity is really a red herring (cf. Hogg & Abrams, 1988). The consequences *and* the context will always play a role, as will both general and specific consequences. Given the rarefied experimental setting of the early studies of conformity, it is no wonder that generalized consequences played a major role in producing quite a lot of conformity (and obedience).

Generalized consequences will vary with group membership, as group consequences establish new discriminations and behavior (Hogg & Abrams, 1988; Watt et al., 1991) which have *reference* to a specific group rather than the whole of society. Some other social psychological studies have nicely shown how the type of group you are in changes the consequences used to influence groups (Nemeth, 1986; Nemeth & Brilmayer, 1987). Majority groups seem to use social compliance (normative consequences) to influence others, whereas minority groups use verbal behavior (discriminative stimuli) with environmental consequences. Of course, for these influence strategies to work the minority has to be in a position to have the majority attend to their verbal behavior in the first place.

Social compliance, then, is a term for the effects of general social consequences within a social community. To produce very general consequences and establishing stimuli from a group requires performing other (socially compliant) behaviors. Social compliance has both contexts in which it occurs (informational influences) and consequences (normative influences). Moreover, because generalized consequences are not at all obvious, social psychologists have been able to predict behavior by describing the setting alone.

Verbal Behavior

Verbal behavior will be dealt with at length in Chapter 7. This section is here merely for completeness: a reminder that verbal behavior is a social behavior which is maintained by generalized social consequences. Most of our verbal behavior would stop if there were no other people around. This means that the words and sentences we use are primarily social discriminative stimuli. Their presence or absence is correlated with changing consequences from other people. If I say "dog" then the consequences or subsequent patterns of behavior of another person are different than if I had said "armadillo". An important property of verbal behavior is that it allows us to produce *arbitrarily related behaviors* in other people, since the maintenance comes from other people rather than the world itself.

Verbal behaviors are some of the most important discriminative cues about a person. We spend a lot of our time and pay a lot of attention to what others say and how they say it. We can usually make finer and more accurate discriminations about consequences from what a person says than from the way they look or the way they walk, although gestures can act as autoclitics (7.2) for spoken verbal behavior.

Not all verbal behavior is thought to be maintained by generalized social consequences. Zettle and Hayes (1982) distinguish between tracking and pliance. As illustrated in Figure 6, some direct environmental events can maintain verbal behavior, as when repeating the name of something we see helps us later to do something else. Saying "I must pick the beans tonight" might be reinforced and make such verbal behavior more likely in the future. The verbal behavior is said to track our nonverbal behavior into reinforcing contingencies. When verbal behavior is made more likely by the responses of another person, however, this is referred to as pliance. These are most often generalized social consequences.

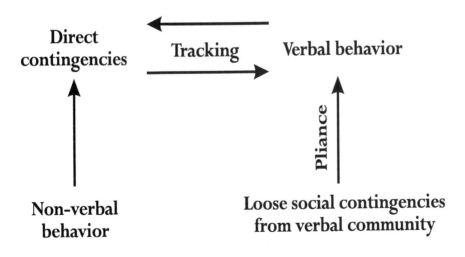

Figure 6. Verbal behavior maintained by tracking and pliance.

Social Facilitation

One of the oldest questions in social psychology is that of social facilitation: what is the effect on behavior from just the presence of another person? The original findings were that performance measures increased when in the presence of others, hence the name, social facilitation. Since then, social impairment has also been found, so current theories try to explain the conditions under which there might be either increases or decreases in performance when in the presence of another person.

There are many theories and many hundreds of social facilitation studies, which cannot be reviewed here (Guerin, 1993). Instead, we will briefly look at social facilitation from the behavior analytic perspective.

The area of social facilitation has followed the same pattern mentioned in the introductory remarks to this chapter. The theories of social facilitation have not noticed the role of generalized consequences so they needed to postulate innate or hard-wired responses to the presence of others, since similar effects occur when in the presence of many other people, even strangers. This can be better analyzed as the result of generalized consequences, however, rather than innate reactions to the presence of others.

In current theories of social facilitation there are three major phenomena. First, there are changes found when people are in the presence of others due to distraction (Sanders, 1981). The empirical problem with the distraction effects is that distraction will be found collaterally with any other changes as well, so we can never show what effects are due to distraction alone. The distraction idea is important, though, because it emphasizes how powerful people are as discriminative stimuli. If there is a person present then attention is given to them over chairs, tables, and vases of flowers. Since it is consequences which primarily determine this allocation of attention, the distraction effects show the importance of social consequences in our lives.

The second social facilitation phenomenon (Guerin, 1986) is the effect of evaluation. The research all seems to show that there is a general effect in the presence of others related to being evaluated. In behavior analytic terms, the evaluation simply means that other people are powerful sources of consequences. Throughout life, the presence of others has been discriminative of others providing consequences contingent upon our behavior, both pleasant and unpleasant. Evaluation, therefore, is this contingent relation (cf. Seta, Seta & Donaldson, 1992; Szymanski, & Harkins, 1993).

The effects of evaluation will depend upon the context, but in general they will consist of compliance, since this has produced reinforcers in the past contingent upon the presence of an evaluator. For example, evaluation can act to reduce variability in behavior (Ader & Tatum, 1963) or to increase variability (Barrett, Deitz, Gaydos & Quinn, 1987), depending upon the requirements of the context.

More specifically, for Western cultures at least, the finding seems to be that punishing consequences are generalized from evaluation settings. In common terms, people expect to receive negative evaluations from others rather than positive evaluations. This is talked about as a general evaluation apprehension effect when in the presence of others (Cottrell, 1972; Henchy & Glass, 1968). This is extremely revealing from a behavior analytic perspective. The social facilitation literature seems to show a generalized effect of compliance to avoid negative outcomes in the presence of others. If people are performing a task, such as singing a song, they will anticipate a negative evaluation from others present. The effects of this on behavior are varied (Guerin, 1986), but they say a lot about the general atmosphere in which we learn to perform in front of others in Western society.

There is more to this, however. The reference in the last paragraph to anticipation suggests that verbally mediated behavior control is playing a role here. The generalized avoidance of disapproval in the presence of others might be the result of following self-instructions rather than letting the environmental contingencies of the task itself control behavior. That is, in the presence of others, our covert verbal behaviors are likely to increase since verbal behavior in general has had strengthening consequences in the past when in the presence of others.

The chain of events in social facilitation settings might therefore be the following: that the presence of others increases verbal behavior; this results in an increase in self-instruction following which (for reasons of our societal histories) concentrates on avoidance of disapproval; and this gives rise to the reports of evaluation apprehension, which in this case would primarily be verbal behavior. As we shall see in Chapter 8, this is essentially the same view reworded as those who argue that the presence of others leads to an increase in self-awareness, which is equated here with following covert verbal self-instructions (cf. Street, 1994).

The problem with any conclusions here is that previous work has not differentiated between behaving to produce social approval and behaving to avoid disapproval, so this can only remain a working hypothesis until experimental manipulations hopefully find an answer. If true, it would suggest yet another disadvantage to verbally governed behavior, that it engenders apprehension in the presence of others.

The third social facilitation phenomenon is called the mere presence effect of another person. This can be summarized as the effects of the presence of others when there are no directly imposed consequences from that person. There is evidence that effects can be found in situations close to this (cf. Geen, 1989, 1991; Guerin, 1986, 1993; Zajonc, 1965, 1980). That is, there seem to be effects on behavior from the presence of another person even when that person does not reinforce, evaluate, communicate with, interact with, or otherwise directly influence the subject.

Some have argued that this is an innate or "hard-wired" effect (Zajonc, 1980), but in behavior analytic terms this step is not necessary. The mere presence effects are likely to be a result of being automatically reinforced through our lives for behaving more intensely in some manner or another when in front of others. While we can be mildly punished through life for hyperactivity when others are around, there are also consequences if our activity level is very low. Consider, for example, how many times in childhood you had to *look busy* when someone was present or else you got in trouble. The accumulation of such episodes would eventually lead to a higher rate of responding in the presence of others, even if they do not explicitly strengthen this with obvious consequences.

In summary, the minimal social situations studied in social facilitation research suggests three generalized contingencies involving other people. First, we have been generally reinforced for attending to other people, and this can be shown by the distraction effects (also 4.1). Second, there are generally more consequences available when others are around, and this is reflected in a general increase in behavior levels in the presence of others which gain social approval or avoid social disapproval. The increase in verbal behavior in the presence of others seems also to increase the following of self-instructions rather than environmental consequences, and this in western society seems to lead to an anticipation of punishing consequences and hence socially compliant avoidance behaviors. It will also increase any other effects of verbally-governed behavior replacing contingency-governed behavior.

Third, the presence of others is generally discriminative of strengthening consequences for more overall activity. People act more forcefully and more frequently in the mere presence of another person because of generalized cumulative consequences of the past.

Imitation

Another generalized discrimination is that of imitation. In Western society at least, it seems that a general response to the presence of others is to do what they do. Clearly this is a big part of our Western upbringing, and there must be thousands of occasions upon which doing what another person is doing has led to strengthening consequences for that behavior.

There are a few different functional groups of behaviors involved here. First, there is modeling, copying, or imitation of responses, when one person watches how another person behaves and does the same. Second, there can be a following response, where one person follows and in this way tracks (Zettle & Hayes, 1982) the same contingencies (cf. Bullock & Neuringer, 1977). Third, there is observational learning, where one person passively watches another but their behavior is found to change afterwards.

Making distinctions between these, and other subtle forms of social learning, is very difficult. This is partly because we do not have the right vocabulary to talk about the differences yet, and partly because they are hard to manipulate independently. What is clear is that they all seem to involve forms of behavior which are strengthened by generalized reinforcement. That is, through our lives doing these three forms of imitation generally has led to strengthening consequences. Like social facilitation and verbal behavior, researchers have also tried to explain imitation as innate forms of behavior because they cannot find any *obvious* sources of consequences.

In one sense, these three forms of imitation are like instruction following, in that behavior is strengthened with mediators, and the natural contingencies of doing so generally strengthen the behavior. The three different forms, modeling, following and observation learning, are slightly different ways of achieving this without relying on verbal behavior, as does self-instruction following.

Since imitation has a generalized strengthening basis, we must expect only weak control without supplementary sources of consequences. If a child imitates but does not track the natural contingencies, and there are no social sources of strengthening, then the behavior will soon cease. In most cases, then, supplementary sources of reinforcement will be needed if tracking is not strong. For example, if I watch someone eat their peas with honey on their knife, imitate them and cut my tongue, I am unlikely to continue this practice. Imitation is generally strengthened but other consequences must take over if the behaviors are to maintain, since the generalized effects will be weak. In my case this could occur through tracking the consequences (I get the honey trick to work) or through supplementary social support (someone encourages me to keep trying until I finally get it right—a sadist with a sense of humour and a straight face!).

The choices, therefore, in training for imitation, are to thoroughly strengthen any imitative behaviors to establish generalized imitation, to punish non-imitation, or to arrange so that any natural reinforcers will be quickly tracked during the imitation. The first two can have negative consequences themselves, however, as the parent soon finds when their child starts imitating the bullies at school or disreputable television characters. So either fine discriminative control of the *contexts for imitating* needs to be trained, or else careful attention given to letting imitation track the natural consequences.

There are large literatures on both imitation in animals and teaching children generalized imitation. The reader might wish to consult the following: Epstein, 1984a; Flanders, 1968; Peterson and Whitehurst, 1971; Robert, 1990; Steinman, 1970, 1977. For an interesting historical review of imitation in language acquisition, see Kymissis and Poulson (1990) and for a good critique of animal imitation studies see Howard and Keenan (1993).

Observational Learning

There are some important features of observational learning which require a discussion separate from imitation. I include in observational learning situations in which one animal observes another and its behavior changes afterwards in a way "relevant" to what was observed. A child might passively watch an adult hitting something and afterwards go and hit it as well (Bandura, 1965).

Such situations have proven a breeding ground for cognitive theories. Some psychologists believe that humans and animals must store a cognitive representation of their observations which is later utilized, and others believe that since they can see no *obvious* reinforcers for "learning" during observational learning (i.e., no food pellets or chocolates), then non-motivational processes must have occurred. In

Chapters 2 and 8 there are a number of ways suggested to analyze such cases without resorting to cognitive constructs and mental representations. Some of these were not available when the early observational learning work was done. Indeed, there was still a strong Hullian S-R influence on many of those who did keep to behavioral principles (see the papers in Parke, 1972).

An excellent behavior analysis of observational learning is given by Deguchi (1984), who reduces observational learning to three features, and then provides analyses of these features. The essence of observational learning, says Deguchi, are (1) that changes can occur after only one trial, (2) that the behavior can occur after a delay, and (3) that it works better if the animal observes the model being reinforced than if not.

I will not repeat Deguchi's analysis of these three aspects (also see the excellent papers by Baer & Deguchi, 1985, and Deguchi, Fujita & Sato, 1988). I believe that a lot more can be developed with a behavior analysis of the phenomena occurring in such situations, especially if subtle consequences are also included. As Deguchi makes clear, there are a lot of problems with the experiments so far conducted. In particular, the past history of strengthening of behavior following observation has not been controlled and generalized imitation is likely to have been learned through childhood.

There is also a case that both modeling and observational learning still have innate aspects (Deguchi, 1984; Skinner, 1966). It would certainly be of use to evolutionary reproductive survival if young animals imitated without waiting to learn imitation. Some evidence for neonatal imitation has been presented, but there may be artifacts involved (Field, Woodson, Greenberg & Cohen, 1982; Hayes & Watson, 1981; Meltzoff & Moore, 1983).

Social Comparison and Auditing

We have seen above that one animal's rate of responding can act as a discriminative stimulus for another animal (e.g., Danson & Creed, 1970). There is other work, more relevant to humans, which shows a generalized response of finding out how other people are performing. The behavior analytic groundwork for this was done by Hake and his colleagues, before Hake's untimely death (Hake & Vukelich, 1980; Hake, Vukelich & Kaplan, 1973; Vukelich & Hake, 1974, 1980). It is related to an area of traditional social psychology called social comparison theory (e.g., Festinger, 1954; Goethals & Darley, 1987; Kruglanski & Mayseless, 1987; Suls & Wills, 1991).

What has been found in the behavior analytic studies is a generalized response such that subjects will press buttons, pull levers, or otherwise respond if doing so gains access to the points scored by themselves or other subjects. Hake and his colleagues called these audit responses. There was no obvious reinforcement of audit responses in these experiments, which suggests that they were maintained by generalized consequences.

Once again, it is likely that through our lives we have been generally reinforced for finding out what others are doing, especially if we do not know how to behave, or if the situation is competitive or ambiguous (Conolley, Gerard & Kline, 1978). Clearly, we can learn quickly from watching others, rather than through trial and error on our own.. This generalized behavior will have been strengthened many times through our lives and must be closely related to generalized imitation.

There is still a lot more work to be done on this phenomenon before we really know what is going on and how it might be related to other phenomena. For instance, it seems likely that verbal behavior is usually involved with humans. If "knowledge" of results affects behavior, and especially response rate, then verbal instructional control must play a role. This means that all the limitations of instructional behavior control will be present with auditing responses. There is also considerable delay in the effects, so self-control processes must play a role to bridge the delay.

This all means that social comparison is probably much more complicated than it appears at present. What we do know is that access to a score of your own or another's performance acts as a generalized control of behavior. Social comparison might also be a verbally mediated form of observational learning, in that subjects do not observe the other's behavior but a mediational stimulus which is correlated with their behavior. Most of all we need to find out the conditions under which social comparison is more or less likely. Two conditions, competition and ambiguity, have been mentioned, but others remain to be shown. Many other conditions been spelt out by social psychologists (e.g., Suls & Wills, 1991), but they need placing into the full three terms of the contingency, rather than relying on mentalistic formulations as surrogates for the functional consequence component.

Gestures

When we come to analyze gestures there is an immediate problem with terminology. In traditional psychology, gestures are referred to as "nonverbal behavior" (though see McNeill, 1985). For behavior analysts (if the reader can remember anything of what was mentioned at the end of Chapter 3 or can prophetise Chapter 7), gestures are by definition verbal behaviors. The reason is that they are a sophisticated system of "signs" which are used as discriminative stimuli and are maintained by generalized social reinforcement. This is more obvious in the case of sign-languages, but I want here to concentrate on showing that less obvious gestures are still verbal behavior.

As an example, consider raising the eyebrows. Through a lifetime of social interaction this acts as a discriminative cue for changing schedules of social reinforcement. If someone raises their eyebrows at me during a conversation, this has, in the past, been correlated with certain changes in consequences. Since this happens with many different people (and different eyebrows) some particular effects can become generalized over different people, including strangers.

Gestures can be very fine grained and sophisticated with humans, in the sense that very minute changes can be discriminative of powerful changes in consequences. They cannot be used around corners or out of sight, however, and they are not as precise in their effects as linguistic verbal behavior. I can speak language and get someone to sing either mournfully or laughingly, but this precision of control is difficult using only gestures, especially if restricted to eyebrow movements, for example.

The biggest advantage that language has, as a social system of discriminative stimuli, is that it is not grounded in any physical reality—the words do not have to look like what they discriminate and they can be sounds or marks on paper. It is this very property which makes them so useful. Gestures are limited because there are only so many ways in which we can re-arrange our faces and postures, and even doing these often requires some training in acting school. Gestures are also probably more prone to random errors, with accidental twitches and poorly coordinated movements. As well, it is hard to imagine a standard set of gestures which could be held perfectly consistent between people, unless we all developed very well trained facial muscles. Finally, changing gestures is probably slower than changing words, and certainly more tiring (imagine giving a two-hour lecture using eyebrow movements!).

The major research questions concerning gestures have been whether they have an innate basis, and how they should be interpreted. With regards to the innateness issue, we can see that a large amount of this is probably due (yet again) to not recognizing the *generalized* strengthening effect of using gestures in social behavior. But more than this, because the gestures themselves are grounded in facial and bodily movements, it has been more tempting to look for innate bases to these movements.

Against this, is should be remembered that *any* type of movement could, in principle, act as a discriminative stimulus: even wiggling the ears! Facial gestures happen to be important because the muscles have more flexibility, and probably also because they are easily seen during interaction. Flexing the back muscle in various patterns, for example, would have less utility for this very reason. We would have to keep turning around and would then not see the person properly.

The point of this is that, because we need a flexible system of facial movements to use as discriminative stimuli with dynamic social contingencies, there might be an innate basis to the *flexibility* of the facial muscles, since this would be advantageous in evolutionary terms, but we must not infer from this that there is necessarily an innate basis to the *consequences* of those facial movements which are utilized in gestures: their meaning is not innate. That is, the muscles of the face could have evolved their flexibility because of their usefulness as discriminative stimuli (though how do you prove this?), but how exactly that flexibility is then utilized cannot be innate. While smiling is an obvious pattern to change on our faces, and therefore very good for a discriminative stimulus, it could be used for any number of consequences (the smile of a car salesperson).

What this means is that an innate basis of gestures could be shown for the wrong reasons. It might be genetically determined that we can move the sides of our mouth down in more than one way, but that this is used to "signal" impending anger or sadness would not be innate. The consequences used with particular cues are mostly arbitrary and socially determined. So humans might have an innate ability to flex the mouth muscles, which other animals might not have, but this does not show that there are specific innate consequences when these are used as discriminative contexts.

Having said this, it can still be reasonably argued that some gestures are *indirectly* related to the consequences which they discriminate. Like the use of onomatopoeia in speaking (see Chapter 7), there are probably a lot of components of functional operant classes which are present in gestures. For example, it seems likely that if you hit someone with a clenched fist for long enough and often enough, even the slowest learner would discriminate those nasty consequences merely from the raising of a clenched fist. Open palms would then be functionally correlated with not being hit. If we hit with open palms, however, then the opposite would occur. This means that any innate basis to the use of a clenched fist as a universal gesture with humans, would be because the hand is best (innately?) used as a hitting device when clenched (less air friction?), not because we have a hard-wired pattern of gesture meanings in our heads.

Some of the facial movements are more difficult to explain in this way, and they may well be nearly arbitrary. The shifts in consequences discriminated by a wink, for example, are difficult to explain in a functional way. If we follow the natural selection metaphor given in 2.2, however, it is likely that any original functional bases to gestures would have changed by now in any event. The advantages and functions for us not to live in the sea are not the same as those of our primitive ancestors who left the sea.

One needs to be very careful in sorting these problems out. If you ignore the discriminative basis of gestures, which most cognitive theorists do, then it is conceivable that the gesture could be an innate "signal" for another animal. If we take the discriminative control into account, however, it seems less plausible, though certainly possible, that there is an innate link between the gesture and the consequences which have occurred in the past following that gesture. In this sense the "link" between a gesture and its typical consequences is actually *in the environment,* not innately sitting inside our nervous system. The link is a contingency, albeit socially mediated.

Common Points

There are some common points which have appeared in each of the cases presented of generalized discriminative control in the presence of other people. First, whenever the discriminative nature of the phenomena is not recognized by other psychologists they have started assuming a referent inside the person. For example, this referent turns out to be "meaning" in the case of language use, and the "message" or "signal" in the case of gestures. A better view is that these referents are contingencies already in the environment. They are the consequences discriminated by the language use or the gesture performed.

Second, in each case, because the discrimination is widespread and without obviously noticeable consequences, the temptation has been to assume an innate or hard-wired basis. This might be an innate "Language Acquisition Device" (Chomsky) in the case of language, innate meanings to gestures, or an innate capacity to imitate. In two cases it has been suggested that there might actually be some innate basis to the behavior, but not in the usual ways suggested (imitation and gestures). In both cases, the behaviors could still be changed if the generalized contingencies were to be changed: an innate basis does mean that the behaviors cannot be changed.

The last point of commonality is that the control exerted is weak because it has only been generally reinforced. If other reinforcers were made contingent on any of the behaviors dealt with in this section, then the behaviors could be changed quite easily. With appropriate consequences we could turn a smile into a feared gesture. The problem in practice, however, is not that the generalized control is strong—it is not—but that the control is exerted by many different people in many different settings it has a powerful influence overall. So while I could punish "looking at social comparison information" in a laboratory, and totally ruin the generalized auditing contingency, as soon as the person was back in the real world the general consequences for auditing would be operational and the person would change back. The strength of the generalized discriminations, and difficulty in changing them, lies in being cumulative and widespread, rather than from having specific, highly valued reinforcers.

Chapter 5

Social Consequences

In this chapter I want to discuss the types of consequences which can be socially mediated, and the ways in which they can enter into contingencies. The first part will look at those events which involve another person and which can act to strengthen behavior or weaken behavior. The second part will look at how other people affect the scheduling of individual contingencies, whether or not the behaviors involve other people directly. The third part will show where these social consequences have been hidden in the traditional social psychological literature, since reference is rarely made to them. The following chapter will then look at the behaviors which *necessarily* involve more than one person and the remote consequences which can be contacted when such group behaviors are contacted.

Most of the literature attempting to analyze social behavior has concentrated on very direct influences which use reinforcement and punishment (Ferster, 1958; Ferster & Perrott, 1968; Sidman, 1989; Skinner, 1953), rather than how social behaviors are controlled through the use of verbal contexts and "symbolic" behaviors, which will be emphasized in this book (Chapters 7, 9, and 10). It is my contention that most of our social behavior is maintained through verbally mediated contexts rather than direct pushing, grabbing, kissing and fighting.

5.1. Properties of Social Consequences

Types of Social Consequences

Social consequences are many and varied; they are any contingent effect produced by a person which can act to strengthen or weaken someone else's behavior. We have dealt briefly with some in 2.3 and 4.1. Obviously, if any social behavior is used as a discriminative stimulus for a reinforcer or punisher then that social behavior can act as a conditioned reinforcer or punisher. If the presence of a particular person has been correlated in the past with reinforcement following a response then that person's presence can act as a reinforcer.

Of more interest, since they can be analyzed without specific case details, are the general forms of functional social consequences. First, there are all the forms of reinforcement which come under the labels of approval and affection. We have already seen in 4.2 that social facilitation research shows a general effect that people change their behavior in the presence of others to avoid disapproval. It therefore is a powerful group of social reinforcers. The approval or affection is probably not in itself reinforcing, but is correlated with other reinforcers being more likely from an approving or affectionate other person, although this might be intermittent and indirect. While this seems overly reductionist, that people are *only* affectionate because they get something out of it, the links are very complicated. Approval and affection are usually establishing operations in a long series of events, and can be equated with the loose and general reinforcements from a verbal community. In fact, if "affection" is too obviously a situation of just trying to get something specific, then we say that the affectionate person is "using" the recipient, and this is considered bad form.

For most people, contingent attention and various forms of touch also act to strengthen behavior (Hart, Reynolds, Baer, Brawley, & Harris, 1968; Zimmerman & Zimmerman, 1962). What exactly makes these and similar social events reinforcing is not quite known, although they only work in certain contexts (Morris, 1980). Some clues were found in the literatures on minimal effects of other people (4.2), and these generalized consequences presumably develop throughout socialization (Bijou & Baer, 1965; Millar, 1976). Other related cases of functional social consequences also exist, such as grooming in chimpanzee (Falk, 1958). Just being given access to the presence of other pigeons appears to be strengthening for pigeons (Peele & Ferster, 1982), while being given access to social living areas has been found to be reinforcing for baboons (Ferster, Hammer & Randolph, 1968).

Another general form of social consequences is verbally mediated control, through generalized praise and insult. If this is used then a problem arises: verbal control is usually weak unless supplemented by other consequences. It can be done though in long standing groups where generalized social compliance has been established (see Chapter 9 for some examples), or in situations such as hypnosis when special techniques are used to get tight verbal control over another person's behavior.

A fourth generalized form of social control is through aversive contact, such as pushing and hitting. It is often overlooked that forms of punishment and negative reinforcement seem to be extremely widespread in everyday social life, especially if verbal abuse is included in this (Ferster, 1958; Sidman, 1989; Skinner, 1953). Some reasons for their use were given in 2.3, but there is another reason as well. One of the major reasons for aversive techniques being so widespread is the easy availability of aversion. If you attempt to use strengthening techniques on another person then a deprivation usually needs to be established first and a number of patient, contingent trials need to be conducted (although verbal control partly gets around this). But we cannot always wait until people are hungry and thirsty before reinforcing their behavior. Further, attending to the person to observe their behavior and the need to provide positive consequences mean that much effort is required.

The clue, then, is that for social uses, aversive events are almost always easily available—a slap across the face almost always hurts although it might be even worse in some contexts. Since we usually have little control over the deprivation of others, aversive techniques are commonly employed. You do not need to build up pain deprivation first. You just have to adjust to the countercontrols (12.7) from the other person after the aversive events, and this is often handled through group membership.

If we look at these general forms of social consequences available, then, there are four major types: approval and affection, contingent attention and contact, aversive techniques, and verbally mediated consequences. The first two require some effort to employ, the third has unwanted side-effects but is easy and quick to administer and therefore common, and the fourth is a weak form of control by itself and usually needs to be supplemented.

There are many other forms of social consequence, of course, but they are not general like these four. These four tend to be used by many people and have some effect on most people. Other social consequences, such as letting you ride on my bicycle, are not generalized. They need to be studied as particular cases.

The Dynamic Scheduling of Social Contingencies

In a few places through this book social contingencies have been described as dynamic and flexible. A few different things are meant by these adjectives. First, they means that social interactions are quick. With a few changes in facial expression I can manipulate a number of contingencies. Second, dynamic also means that the contingencies frequently change. If we do the same thing to a rock five times over we usually get the same consequence. If we do the same thing *more than once* with another person, we usually get different consequences. So social contingencies often involve a type of adjusting schedule of reinforcement or punishment. If we keep repeating the same response we do not get the same consequences from another person—they "turn off". Repetition occurs quite frequently in children who have not yet learned this basic skill of social behavior (because they have not had adult contingencies applied). They just keep repeating and repeating responses: they might keep Uncle Bob doing his trick over and over again—until Uncle Bob gives off bad vibes. This is not a pure adjusting schedule, but one that gradually turns into extinction or punishment. Try telling someone the same joke over and over and see what they do.

Social contingencies are also dynamic in the sense that many are usually available, so that it appears as if we make choices between them (see 3.2). Put in everyday terms, we appear to swap between contingencies if they do not please us. If I am not enjoying talking to Paul then I can leave and go and talk with Bill instead. A fourth meaning of dynamic is that merely contacting the social contingencies can change those contingencies. While this can also occur with non-social contingencies, it is the normal effect when contacting social contingencies. So it is not just that Mary keeps changing her consequences to my behavior, but that my behavior following her consequences affects Mary's later reactions. This means that sequencing is as important as layering with social contingencies.

The final meaning of dynamic is that social contingencies are most often very subtle four- and five-term contingencies. That is, the consequences I receive depend on very subtle changes in the social contexts, whether this is a change in facial expression, a word in reply, or a pause. Each of these involve layered conditional discriminations, not simple three-term contingencies. This means that perceptual responses must be heavily used in social behavior, since there is a need to keep monitoring the swiftly changing contextual events, including hearing any words spoken.

These last two meanings of dynamic encompass a lot of what has been called interpersonal negotiation and social influence in social psychology. We negotiate interpersonal consequences by dynamically adjusting to other people and their contingencies. This means that the situation is much more complex than the simple schedules usually studied (McGinnies, 1970; McGinnies & Ferster, 1971; McLaughlin, 1971; Ulrich & Mountjoy, 1972). There are multiple responses, changing schedules of reinforcement, and complex conditional discriminations.

Verbal Control of Social Consequences

We saw earlier that there are four generalized ways in which one person can manipulate the consequences to another. The first three were approval, attention, or use of aversive stimuli (either for punishment or negative reinforcement). The fourth way to manipulate consequences was to give verbal instructions to the other person and attempt to change their behavior in this way. As has been mentioned in a number of places, this is a weak form of control unless there already is a generalized form of social compliance, or direct consequences contingent upon noncompliance. Despite this, verbal instructions are an easy and common way to change others for specific effects. They require no change in material conditions as discriminative stimuli, just the use of speech or writing. As well, they require no deprivation as an establishing operation (Nevin, 1966; Wenrich, 1963). For these reasons, attempts at verbal control are extremely common despite the weak results, and probably make up the bulk of social influence and negotiation.

An interesting study on this was done by Van Houten, Nau, MacKenzie-Keating, Sameoto and Colavecchia (1982). They tested some conditions for increasing the obedience of children to verbal reprimands. They found that reprimands worked better when the person giving the reprimand was closer to the child, and better if the child's shoulder was gripped and eye-contact made. These conditions both suggest that it is the aversive back-up to the verbal reprimands which are being manipulated. Some other conditions for increasing compliance with verbal instructions will be given in 7.4 (also Cialdini, 1987).

The key, then, for effective verbal control is to first get generalized social compliance. This is done in hypnosis, where a large part of the early procedure is aimed at getting compliance with the hypnotherapist's verbal instructions. Common rituals and ritualized social behaviors perform this same function in normal verbal communities, as we shall see in Chapter 9. These ritualized social behaviors seem irrational and purposeless, but they are ways of maintaining routine social compliance in a verbal community so as to make subsequent verbal instructions more effective.

5.2. Group Contingencies and the Allocation of Consequences

Chapter 4 outlined some of the social discriminations which are commonly made: that is, some of the more general contextual controls of social behavior. We have just discussed some of the consequences common to social events. In this section I wish to discuss ways in which other people affect the contingencies utilizing responses and consequences which are available to individual people. In the next chapter we will look at the contingencies which can only be contacted with more than one person.

When put in a group to perform a task, the contingencies are automatically changed in several ways. First, there are usually consequences for the whole group rather than the individual, which means that individuals receive only some of the consequences they might otherwise have if they had acted alone. Second, the consequences will depend to a large extent on the "structure" of the group: that is, the way in which consequences are allocated within a group. For example, if one member of a group makes a mistake but the outcome is to the group as a whole, this could reinforce that mistake for that individual (if the outcome is reinforcing). Third, the discriminative contexts for individual consequences becomes less clear in a group, since there are more interpersonal cues as discriminative contexts.

Each of these points will be taken up in turn. A further section will then address some of the special characteristics of the contingencies of large groups, where the fine discrimination of other members is very limited and interpersonal consequences therefore become more indiscriminate.

Contingencies Applied to a Whole Group

When working on a task as part of a group, contingencies can be arranged in several ways. Commonly, the group as a whole is given a remote consequence for the total production. While each person might have equal amounts of automatic strengthening merely from completing the task or their part of it, the remote consequences given afterwards to the whole group will be "diluted" according to the number of people in the group and its allocation structure.

In this situation, the schedule of reinforcement for any individual in the group will be contingent upon the other members of the group. This will affect the overall strengthening effects of the remote contingencies even if the reinforcement is divided equally. For example, if the rate of responding is doubled by one individual in a group on a fixed-ratio schedule of reinforcement, the rate of reinforcement is not doubled for that individual but for the whole group. This means that the overall rate of responding for each member will be less than that when performing alone.

An interesting experiment, similar to the above outline, was reported by Grott and Neuringer (1974). They put both individual rats and groups of three rats into experimental boxes with a lever. The overall response rates were measured.

Unfortunately, the individual rates for each individual in a group of three could not be measured, but there were some fascinating findings. First, the groups of three responding with one lever between them took longer to satiate, because there were three of them to satiate. This means that if satiation is a problem on a task, a group could be a useful way to overcome the problem. The same was also true of extinction.

When placed on a schedule of Differential Reinforcement for Low Rates of responding (DRL), the groups had higher rates of responding, even though this had the consequence of less reinforcement for all of them. While this could appear to be a case of social facilitation, facilitation of a well-learned response in the presence of others, the authors rightly point out that a competition effect is a more likely explanation. The rats in the group were competing for reinforcers with only one lever (a condition of scarce resources) and this probably controlled the higher rates of responding.

Grott and Neuringer (1974) point out how the actual schedules can be changed in the group situation.

> Under the fixed-ratio schedule, for example, one rat was often replaced at the lever by a second rat before the ratio requirement was completed, and the second rat would respond only a few times and receive reinforcement. Thus, for a given Group member, the schedule of reinforcement actually experienced was often a variable ratio. Similarly, under the fixed-interval and fixed-time conditions, the schedule of reinforcement experienced by a Group member was often variable interval and variable time, which may partially account for the shorter pauses and higher response rates emitted by Groups as compared with individuals (p. 319).

There is one other point not mentioned by these authors. This is that while the Group rats responded faster, overall they were less than the equivalent of three times the Individual rats. In Figure 3 of Grott and Neuringer (1974), for example, the individual rats responded on average about 110 times, while the Group rats initially responded on average about 210 times, rather than 330 (3 times 110). This means that overall, the rats in the groups responded less than individuals as was suggested at the beginning of the section. The problem with this conclusion is that coordination between the rats in groups may have led to the diminished relative rate of responding, since the rats could not all get at the lever equally easily.

A better test of this would be to present three levers to three rats with one common source of reinforcement. The average rate per individual would tell us more about contingencies for a whole group. Some evidence along these lines was found by Graft, Lea and Whitworth (1977), who put five rats in a box with five levers, and found that both the aggregate rate of responding and the individual rate of responding fitted the Matching Law. Unfortunately, they did not run individual rats with one lever for a comparison of individual and group reinforcement.

Fortunately, there is some clearer evidence for lower rates of responding in groups in an area of social psychology called social loafing. Social loafing refers to a decrement in performance when in a group. Members of a group are said to loaf. There is good evidence for this (Bartis, Szymanski & Harkins, 1988; Geen, 1991; Goethals & Darley, 1987; Harkins, 1987; Harkins & Szymanski, 1987, 1988; Mullen & Baumeister, 1987; Paulus, 1983; Szymanski & Harkins, 1993; Williams, Harkins & Latané, 1981).

The problem with the social loafing literature is that only a shallow analysis of consequences is made. The major condition mediating loafing, it is said, is whether or not the individuals in the group are identifiable or not. If they are, then loafing will not occur (Latané, Williams & Harkins, 1979). The other mediating variable is evaluation (Harkins & Szymanski, 1989; Chapters 4 and 12); if individuals are evaluated then loafing disappears. It should be clear by now that these are manipulations of consequences and in particular, social consequences. In a nice study by Szymanski and Harkins (1993) it was found that subjects would studiously avoid allowing the experimenter to evaluate their work, even when this led to a disadvantage to themselves. If you are made non-identifiable then the consequences change dramatically. This will be dealt with fully in 5.3.

The findings of social loafing are very robust, and show the changes in consequences arising from merely being in a group. If you are working in a group then you become less identifiable and will usually receive less reinforcement, even if your behavior does not change. Merely being in a group also means you can be evaluated (a new source of interpersonal consequences) and the consequences can again change. You increase the consequences by increasing evaluation or making the task "meaningful" (Williams & Karau, 1991).

The "Structure" of Group Contingencies

In this section we consider more complex cases of consequences apportioned to group members. This is often called the "structure" of the group, although this term is confusing in behavior analysis. In behavior analysis, *"structure" usually refers to a steady state of functioning.* Structures, whether cognitive structures, group structures or social structures, are like ossified functions: "Purely repetitive and therefore structural" (Klee, 1953, p. 23). If there is a pattern of contingencies in the environment such that the behaviors produced become patterned and repetitive, then this is labelled a structure. By forgetting the contingency basis of such structures, however, the role of consequences in producing the behaviors is usually ignored. Such analyses then mix up contexts and consequences since it seems that the behavior can be predicted from the context or structure alone. But the consequences are only hidden, not absent.

For this reason, behavior analysts try to get back the full functional bases, three-term contingencies at least, and are not content to just study structures, whether cognitive structures, language structures, or social structures (see Baer, 1982, for example). In this sense, behavior analysis gets inside the structures and finds out how they function. The consequences are always there maintaining the behavioral structures and cannot be ignored.

Many studies have varied the consequences to individuals in a group and looked for changes in group and individual performance. Quite of few of these have varied consequences under the guise of feedback, which is also a term that assumes too much about consequences (2.3) and confounds contexts and consequences (see as an example, Goltz et al., 1989). Other studies have used weaker forms of consequences, including the problematic verbal reinforcements discussed in 7.3. In fact, almost all the of the reinforcers used in traditional studies of group structure are remote and delayed, and most involve verbal mediators, so they are not necessarily reinforcers in a proper technical sense. This has meant that the results have been highly variable between studies and there are mixed findings. Any conclusions are therefore tentative and need very careful reviewing to make sense of them. Many of these experiments could be profitably replicated with better control over both the contexts and the consequences used. Examples of this work are: Goltz et al. (1989), Hall (1957), Newby and Robinson (1983), Pryer and Bass (1959), Rosenberg and Hall (1958), Shepperd (1993), Smith (1972), Stoneman and Dickinson (1989), and Zajonc (1962).

Only two relevant studies will be outlined here. In an interesting series of experiments, Glaser and Klaus (1966 and Klaus & Glaser,1970; also Egerman, 1966) varied the reinforcement structure of groups. Some groups worked in "parallel" where members did the same task and one correct task was sufficient for a group reward (which was a very remote consequence), thus making some members redundant. Other groups worked in "series" such that each member had to complete their task for the whole group to get their reward.

Glaser and Klaus found that these reinforcement "structures" could predict behavior quite accurately. The parallel arrangement interfered with individual performance as measured before joining the group, since the schedule of reinforcement changed from a continuous schedule to an intermittent variable schedule. So the individual behavior was controlled by the group schedule "structure":

> The initial drop in performance in the team setting suggests that "ease of adjustment" to a group is a function of the change in the schedule of reinforcement to which a member is introduced: this change might be especially marked if the other members of the team are performing at relatively low proficiency levels (Glaser & Klaus, 1966, p. 12).

Another experiment was reported by Burnstein and Wolff (1964, also Wolff, Burnstein & Cannon, 1964). They attempted to shape a multiple DRH-DRL schedule in individuals and groups, where the groups only received group consequences. While the individuals came under the stimulus control of the multiple schedule, only two of the five groups showed any real change after fifteen hours of training. In these two groups there was only one member responding correctly. This showed the difficulty and inefficiency of using group contingencies with multiple schedules, and also perhaps suggests that group learning of fine discriminative control will be problematic, as suggested earlier. A recent review of productivity loss in groups also comes very close to a contingency analysis (Shepperd, 1993).

Discrimination in Groups

Part of the problem with group behavior lies in discriminating the contexts for reinforcement or punishment. We have already mentioned that a lot of social discrimination consists of subtle contextual discrimination involving four- and five-term contingencies. If you are suddenly thrust into a group of strangers, the discriminations that have controlled your behavior in the past will be changed. It then takes time to contact the new possible contingencies, even though some might be very favourable (Chapter 6).

The fact that social interactions are also dynamic, in the several senses outlined at the start of this chapter, means that there are other problems. While frowning, raised eye-brows might be discriminative of impending punishment on a one-to-one basis, it has less impact if you are in a group. Indeed, there are probably more behaviors possible in a group than alone, since interacting with each member and each combination of members is possible. This means that the discrimination will be more complex and less likely to occur. This is probably one reason why less sensitive and less refined (discriminated) behavior has many times been reported for groups (Moscovici, 1985).

The effect of this is that to control groups requires different types of contingencies than to control individuals. With individuals we can influence them directly by force, or by many forms of gestures, which act as conditioned consequences or autoclitics to our verbal behavior. We also have the capacity to respond to the many effects produced by that individual and therefore shape their behavior better. You cannot control crowds, however, with subtle four- and five-term contingencies.

In a group, therefore, influence usually comes through lots of spoken verbal behavior which can affect all members of a group equally and does not dilute the consequences. An individual who normally controls through gestures (nonverbal communication) will be lost in group influence (cf. Marwell, 1963). The members of the group will not be able to attend all the discriminative cues presented, and will have to rely on any spoken verbal behavior as the key discriminative cue. This reliance on spoken verbal behavior means that group influence will be harder to accomplish than individual influence, unless the group already has strong social compliance with verbal instructions. There unfortunately appears to be no experimental studies comparing social influence tactics used on groups and individuals.

There is another possible problem with discrimination in groups. If interpersonal influences are a strengthening part of our social life, the give and take of relationships, then the argument above suggests most of us are less likely to have effects on groups. This in turn means that we are likely to form into smaller groups, that we can control better, in the long run unless there are other direct benefits from belonging to larger groups. It will be argued in the next chapter that there are remote consequences available to neither individuals nor small groups which can help glue larger groups together. But it might need time for individual members to contact the contingencies.

In summary, the previous section suggested that one inherent property of being in a group is that the consequences are usually less for any individual, or at least dramatically changed. A second property is that the visibility, and hence the use of discriminative social cues, is reduced when in groups. There is less chance to use fine discriminative stimuli in groups. Other means of control or social influence need to be implemented, especially rational, verbal behavior.

Large Groups

When we come to larger groups, we need to work out what makes a group. Is just a mass of people enough to constitute a group? One answer to this question came many years ago from Donald Campbell (1960a). He suggested several indices of larger groups which can be used to define them as social entities.

The most relevant here of Campbell's indices of aggregates is that of "common fate":

> The use of coefficients of common fate, differing from zero to unity, enables us to deal with entitativity as a matter of degree, and even in the physical world intergrades occur. Thus between the teapot and the teapot lid the inter-entity coefficients are high, though not quite as high as the intra-entity coefficients. Lower, but still high, are the inter-entity coefficients between cup and saucer. The intra-entity common fate coefficients are higher for a platoon than for a battalion, and higher for a destroyer crew than for either" (p. 191).

What seems to be suggested here is a measure of common consequences: if an aggregate of people share common consequences then they form a group. This forms a sort of social operant (this is not at technical term) in the way that Skinner (1935) defined operants. If one or more responses are controlled by the same consequence they form an operant (2.2). If two or more people share the same consequences they form a social operant. This is a dubious terminology, however, and should remain an analogy.

Large groups seems to exacerbate all the changes in contingencies so far mentioned in this chapter. In large groups the individual consequences become even less imposing for each individual, and this leads to what has been called "deindividuation" (Zimbardo, 1970). People in crowds become less personally responsible for any group outcome so crowds produce behavior (especially aggressive behaviors) which individuals would not separately. Deindividuation is probably a combined effect of the reduced means of discriminating consequences in a group and the "diluting" of consequences between people in a crowd, as will be documented in 5.3.

One recent line of argument is that deindividuation is mediated by "self-awareness" of personal standards of conduct (Carver & Scheier, 1981; Diener, 1980; Prentice-Dunn & Rogers, 1991). It is argued that normally we regulate our behavior with private self-awareness, and this keeps our behavior in check by comparing current behavior with our personal standards of behavior. In large groups and under some other conditions, however, private self-awareness is lowered and we stop regulating our behavior and therefore act against our normal standards of behavior. It is also argued that under such conditions our behavior can also get out of control. When there is less accountability to others we are said to have a lower level of public self-awareness, compare our behavior less to public standards of behavior, and therefore produce more counter-normative behaviors. Only the former is now referred to as deindividuation, however (Prentice-Dunn & Rogers, 1991).

Putting this into behavior analytic terms, the reasoning seem to be that self-regulation by covert verbal behavior (7.6) is prevented when in a large group. The problems given earlier with fine discrimination in groups might mediate such an effect. Private self-awareness would refer to verbal behavior about rules and our previous verbal behavior ("I shouldn't eat any more chocolate or I will get fat"), while public self-awareness would refer to verbal behavior about generalized social contingencies ("I shouldn't eat any more chocolate or people will laugh at my fat stomach").

The social psychologists mentioned above have found that different variables control these two "states of awareness", as we would also expect from the behavior analysis. Controlling (reducing) private self-awareness are variables of distraction, group cohesiveness (i.e., group rules usurp private rules), and socially altered thinking patterns. Public self-awareness is reduced by less accountability, group diffusion of responsibility for behavior, and anonymity. These variables will be discussed further in 5.3, but note here that they really refer to environmental changes in social consequences rather than a personal self-awareness state. In the behavior analysis sense both private and public self-awareness are social phenomena (Street, 1994).

It will be argued in 7.7 that the development of verbal self-regulation and tracking can undermine the generalized social compliance which holds so much of our social behavior in place. The reduced self-awareness idea of deindividuation is perhaps the reverse of this undermining effect. If the group is large then the maintenance of social compliance will be stronger than self-regulation, since there are greater consequences for not complying. Attempts at influencing the majority to change the social norm will therefore have little or no effect, and private self-awareness is reduced.

There are three effects, then, inherent from being in a group. In the last sections we saw that being in a group usually entails less consequences for individuals and less fine discriminative control. Added to this now is that being in a group, at least in some circumstances, leads to less verbally governed behavior.

Using Group Contingencies in Practice

There is a small literature which needs to be mentioned on using social contingencies in actual settings—mostly in classrooms. Kazdin and Geesey (1977), for example, had children working for tokens which would get them events (such as free time or a Kool Aid) or would get the whole class the same event. They found that the latter was more successful in strengthening the target behavior, attention.

Speltz, Shimamura and McReynolds (1982) tried three types of group contingencies: based on the group average, based on a particular poor student, and based on a randomly chosen student. The results seemed to show an increase with all the group contingencies, and with little difference between them. The major difference was that the identified poor students seemed to do better under the group contingency which used them as the criterion. The problem with this study is that there was no return to baseline, which would have allowed the experimenters to find out whether the contingencies were controlling the changes in behavior or something else.

For further discussion of group contingencies the reader is referred to the following: Greenwood, Hops, Delquadri and Guild, 1974; Hayes, 1976; Litow and Pumroy, 1975; Slavin, 1977; Smith and Fowler, 1984. For examples of political control, see the following: Ferster, 1958; Lamal, 1984; Segal, 1987; Sidman, 1989; Skinner, 1953, 1971.

5.3. The Hidden Consequences in Traditional Social Psychology

There is an interesting question which has been touched upon, of why traditional social psychology has not needed to conceptualize consequences explicitly in order to deal with social phenomena. How can they seem to ignore such aspects which are so crucial in behavior analysis? It will become apparent through this section that consequences *have* played a large role in social psychology, but that they have merely been hidden. We will not look here at the theoretically hidden consequences, implicit in such terms as "expectancy-value" and "hedonistic relevance", however, but just at the experimental data.

The experimental manipulations used in social psychology have disguised powerful types of consequences. In fact, social psychologists have begun to realize that a more solid functional and motivational grounding is needed (Breckler & Greenwald, 1986; Crano, 1991; Pratkanis, Breckler & Greenwald, 1989; Sorrentino & Higgins, 1986; Tetlock & Kim, 1987). This is precisely where a behavior analysis of social behavior can help.

This section (also Guerin, 1991) will show how consequences have determined the social behavior found in traditional social psychology. We will first look at ten experimental manipulations which have implicitly varied consequences. These will then be compared across ten areas of social psychology to show clearly the consequences which have been implicit. The studies selected were those with a clear experimental condition for which the behavior of the subjects had consequences and a control condition with no such consequences for subjects. As would be expected of published studies, they all found significant effects with their manipulations.

The Manipulations of Consequences

Ten areas of experimental social and organizational psychology were reviewed and any studies manipulating any forms of consequences were located. These consequences were then classified into ten types of manipulations. Although this procedure could not hope to be exhaustive, it is believed that the major forms of all the phenomena were covered. The ten types of manipulations found are outlined below with some explanation of their operation and problems. The studies which use a particular manipulation are listed in the Appendix at the end of this chapter.

It should be noted that most of the "hidden" consequences *not* reviewed here are verbally mediated ones. Social compliance can therefore be assumed as the prime generalized motivator in these cases.

1. Future interaction

The first type of manipulation is the use of future interaction to vary social consequences. In these experiments subjects are told that they will have to meet the people they are interacting with, evaluating or discussing, in future sessions. Subjects in control conditions are either told that they will not be meeting the persons again or else they are told nothing.

This manipulation has often been used to vary task involvement, without explicit discussion of why it should lead to greater involvement. The implicit assumption seems to be that the person to be met can give negative consequences to the subjects in the later session, depending upon how they behaved in the first session. If there are greater consequences then there should be greater involvement.

2. Real consequences

A second manipulation is the use of real consequences that subjects can gain or incur during interaction with others in experiments. For example, subjects in the experimental condition might gain real money or they might make suggestions which will be used by the experimenter for real purposes. The status of these with respect to behavior analysis is a bit dubious (also cf. Crano, 1991). Most are verbally mediated and not direct, despite being "real".

3. Explanations

In a third manipulation it is stressed to subjects that they must explain their behavior afterwards, or give an account, either to the experimenter or to the other participating subjects. This implicitly means that retribution, reward, evaluation, or other consequences, can be made afterwards contingent upon performance.

4. Dependency

Another manipulation of consequences makes subjects responsible for other subjects, by having the other person dependent in some way upon the subject (e.g., Berkowitz, 1972), for example. Other studies, especially ones dealing with negotiation, have varied consequences by making the subjects who negotiate the group rewards responsible for dividing up the rewards. Subjects have the others dependent on them for rewards. Most of these studies have used role-playing techniques rather than real money, however.

5. Anonymity

Some studies have manipulated anonymity in various ways, telling subjects that their results are confidential, private, or unidentifiable. If done carefully, this guarantees that there will be no interpersonal consequences since individual results are not known.

Many studies have looked at differences between behavior in public and private conditions (e.g., Carver & Scheier, 1981). A number of these confound other types of perceived consequences with privacy, however. As well, there is a large literature on deindividuation which examines the effects of anonymity in a group. Here, among other effects, consequences play a large role, as we saw earlier in this chapter. A more detailed analysis of the anonymity manipulations will be made later in this section. Problems with interpreting the results of these manipulations have been raised by Tetlock and Manstead (1985).

6. Responsibility

Consequences have also been manipulated by directly changing how responsible subjects feel for their behavior. For example, in one study on aggression in deindividuating conditions, subjects were told that the experimenter would be responsible for anything that happened (Diener et al., 1975). To what extent subjects believe such manipulations is not known but will depend on verbal compliance with the experimenter.

Other relevant research traditions are those of bystander intervention (Darley & Latané, 1968) and social loafing (Latané Williams & Harkins, 1979). One focus of these has been the diffusion of responsibility through a group. To test this, felt responsibility has been manipulated in a number of ways. We have already seen in this chapter that diffusion of responsibility in a group can be thought of as a result of having group contingencies.

7. Evaluation

Evaluation has been used as a manipulation of accountability. Subjects in this case do not have to explain their behavior, but rather, other persons evaluate their behavior. Although these others may not be able in every case to proportion consequences afterwards, there seems to be enough anxiety in being evaluated to suggest that it has important verbally mediated consequences for most subjects (Guerin, 1986; Weber & Cook, 1972). This was discussed in 4.2.

8. Status

A number of negotiation studies have used manipulations which vary how accountable the negotiators are to their constituents: what their status is with respect to the group. The negotiators may be trusted or not, may have role obligations, or may have their jobs in jeopardy. Where negotiators are trusted, for example, it has been argued that they are less accountable to their constituents so there can be less consequences. Similarly, if they are not trusted or their jobs are in jeopardy then there are greater consequences from not complying with group intentions.

9. Reversibility

A further manipulation of consequentiality concerns the reversibility of a decision or behavior. If a behavior with possible negative consequences can be reversed in the future, before negative consequences arise, this clearly means less responsibility. In line with this, some experiments have varied whether or not subjects can change their decisions or behavior after making an initial choice.

10. Control

In this last manipulation, control of the consequences is given to another person. The subject does not have control of the reinforcements in the situation except by altering their behavior to influence the controller.

These ten manipulations have been used to vary the consequentiality of subjects' behavior: they are aimed at making social consequences contingent upon interaction with others. It should be kept in mind that most of the studies were studying other effects and incidentally used these manipulations of consequences. This means that the manipulations have not always been tight ones.

A large number of studies have mixed different types of manipulations. For example, studies have manipulated accountability by having subjects face the prospect of meeting the confederate at a later date, justifying their behavior to that person, and being evaluated by that person (e.g., Tetlock, 1985). Control subjects are kept anonymous. Such studies therefore mix anonymity, evaluation, future interaction and explanations. This is not a problem for the studies themselves so long as subjects anticipate or come into contact with *some* form of consequence. The problem comes in trying to do a finer behavior analysis on the results.

Some of the manipulations entail the presence of others. These are not necessary associations but just common ones which seem to be mixed in real life. That is, they could be separated with a more stringent manipulation but are commonly lumped in together. To aid in discussing these manipulations, some of these frequent associations are now presented.

1) With manipulations of future interaction it is also usually the case that explaining previous behavior to the person is likely, that anonymity cannot be maintained, and that the person can evaluate the previous interaction.

2) Giving an explanation will also usually entail future interaction while providing the explanation, real consequences, lack of anonymity and expected evaluation of the explanation.

3) Having someone's consequences dependent upon your behavior means a change in felt responsibility and the anticipation of evaluation by that person. As well, if the dependent persons are also subjects in the experiment they will have changed consequences from lack of control over rewards.

4) Anonymity can lead to a change in felt responsibility and a change in expected evaluation.

5) Expectancy of evaluation is probably correlated with expecting real consequences (social approval from the experimenter if nothing else) and a lack of anonymity.

6) Having a change in status of trust by constituents usually entails that the constituents are dependent upon the subjects and that the felt responsibility of the subjects has changed.

7) Having consequences controlled by someone else most often has been mixed with having to justify behavior before receiving consequences, a lack of anonymity, an increase in evaluation, and some assumed status difference between the subjects and the consequences holder.

Table 1 presents the number of studies in each of ten selected research areas of social psychology which used one of the ten manipulations. It can be seen that many areas have their own preferred manipulations of consequences. For example, social loafing and deindividuation have concentrated on anonymity and responsibility in their testing; while cognitive tuning studies deal mostly with future interaction and giving explanations.

Table 1 also suggests the use of some manipulations of consequences in areas where they have not been tried before. Would the inhibiting effects of negotiating for constituents disappear if anonymity was assured? Would the effects leading to greater cooperation disappear if choices were reversible? Would allocation decisions change if subjects were asked to explain and justify their decision afterwards? Would social loafing effects disappear if the people disadvantaged by the loafing were to be met.

Not all combinations of manipulations and research areas make sense, however. This is both because some research areas only concern specific aspects of consequences and because some of the manipulations are closely related. As an example of the former, helping behavior is not usually reversible, so it makes little sense to set up an experiment to see whether people are less helpful if they know they can replay the situation and help the second time round. A time machine would be needed in real life to apply such results.

In reviewing the results of these studies it is clear that the phenomena of experimental social psychology have been produced mostly through manipulations of *generalized social contingencies,* and mostly mediated by verbal behaviors. The different manipulations of consequences have produced remarkably similar results within, and between, the different research areas. But the review also shows that the ten manipulations are not independent. Although they might be separated in laboratory experiments to find independent effects, they are usually found in combination both in real life and previous experiments. This is, I believe, important for behavior analysis. We need to know how social consequences are commonly *clustered* in real life. The regular patterns of consequences will give us the structures of social behavior. Privately, just between colleagues and myself, we call these "lumpy consequences" or "lumpy contingencies", because in the real world they

Table 1. Number of studies using a manipulation of consequences

	Conflict & cooperation	Deindiv- iduation	Allocation	Decision making	Attitudes	Attribution	Cognitve tuning	Nego- tiation	Social loafing	Helping
Future Interaction	7	4	5	4	6	12	12	4	0	2
Real consequences	11	1	0	5	4	0	0	1	1	2
Explanation	1	1	0	6	4	3	0	1	0	2
Dependency	3	2	2	4	2	1	0	6	0	10
Anonymity	13	21	2	6	2	3	0	0	11	2
Responsibility	1	12	1	4	2	0	1	0	13	4
Evaluation	2	6	0	6	3	1	15	11	3	1
Status	0	0	0	2	2	0	1	10	0	0
Reversibility	0	0	0	3	0	0	5	0	0	0
Control	1	1	1	0	0	0	13	7	0	0

usually occur lumped together and cannot be easily separated, only theoretically or in laboratory conditions.

There are many examples of such mixed manipulations. For example, a common situation in real life is having to meet someone after performing a behavior, explaining your behaviour to them, and being evaluated by that person, who then consequates according to their verbal evaluation. Organizational performance evaluations and oral dissertation defenses are two examples of this situation. For this reason many studies have knowingly included all these consequences together to get a strong, realistic manipulation.

Despite these problems with mixed manipulations, very similar results are found in most of the research areas across all the manipulations. For example, all of the aversive consequences are found to produce increased cooperation (future interaction, real losses, explanation, reduced anonymity, reduced responsibility, evaluation). As argued below, this is probably because experimental social psychology has only studied common and very general consequences. And has been said here before, by assuming the working of very generalized social consequences it looks as if the stimulus context can fully predict behavior.

Anonymity and Evaluation

Two of the manipulations have some special properties and problems, and will therefore be discussed in more detail.

Table 2 presents the different manipulations of anonymity used in the studies. Further types of anonymity manipulations can be found in the self-awareness literature. These were not reviewed because either there was no proper control condition (lack of consequences), or else because the research area was not one reviewed (see Breckler & Greenwald, 1986, for other consequence manipulations).

Anonymity has been widely used as a general manipulation of avoidance of punishing consequences. If subjects are truly anonymous, there can be no consequences to them personally, even the generalized social consequences. This would therefore be a useful experimental manipulation for behavior analysts interested in researching social behavior. The manipulations of anonymity have varied widely, however, and studies have included one form of anonymity only to have another form leave subjects totally identifiable. Many examples of this can be found in the reported studies.

The most common problem with anonymity manipulations has occurred when subjects are made anonymous to each other but the experimenter can still find out their results (Guerin, 1986, 1993). Little mention is usually made of whether the results are anonymous to the experimenter. Reis and Gruzen (1976), in fact, found that subjects used different allocation strategies depending on whether the other subjects, the experimenter or neither, knew their allocations (also Szymanski & Harkins, 1993, for an example of the power of experimenter evaluation).

Future studies should pay careful attention to each of these forms of anonymity. The important point is that *anonymity primarily manipulates avoidance of punishing*

Table 2. Manipulations of Anonymity

No names given

Arbuthnot & Andrasik (1973), Beaman et al. (1979), Diener (1976, 1979), Diener et al. (1976), Helmreich & Collins (1968), Insko et al. (1985), Johnson & Downing (1979), Kidder et al. (1977), Mouton et al. (1955-56), Mann et al. (1982), Nadler et al. (1982), Prentice-Dunn & Rogers (1980), Rogers & Ketchen (1979), Rogers & Prentice-Dunn (1981), White (1977), Zimbardo (1969)

Told confidential

Adelberg & Batson (1978), Diener (1976), Lindskold & Finch (1982), McFarland et al. (1984), Tetlock (1983a,b), Tetlock (1985b), Tetlock & Kim (1987), Worchel et al. (1975)

Told not traceable

Johnson & Downing (1979), Prentice-Dunn & Rogers (1980), Rogers (1980), Rogers & Prentice-Dunn (1981), Tetlock (1983a,b), Tetlock (1985b), Tetlock & Kim (1987)

Others will never know/ Peer awareness

Berkowitz & Daniels (1964), Bixentine et al. (1966), Bonacich (1972, 1976), Donnerstein et al. (1972), Fox & Guyer (1978), Gruder (1971), Gruder & Rosen (1971), Jerdee & Rosen (1974), Kahan (1973), Leventhal et al. (1972), Morse et al. (1976), Prentice-Dunn & Rogers (1980), Rogers & Prentice-Dunn (1981), Reis & Gruzen (1976)

Subjects kept separate or brought in separately

Jorgenson & Papciak (1981), Mann et al. (1982), Michelini (1976), Reis & Gruzen (1976), Rogers & Ketchen (1979), White (1977), Wichman (1970)

Results pooled

Brickner et al. (1986), Diener (1979), Harkins & Jackson (1985), Harkins & Petty (1982), Harkins et al. (1980), Insko et al. (1985), Jackson & Harkins (1985), Jackson & Williams (1985), Kerr & Bruun (1981), Latane et al. (1979), Mann et al. (1982), Nadler et al. (1982), Paloutzian (1975), Petty, Harkins et al. (1977), Swindell & Mann (1984), Williams et al. (1981), Weldon & Gargano (1985), White (1977), Zimbardo (1969)

Sealed envelopes

Reis & Gruzen (1976)

Results not recorded

Donnerstein & Donnerstein (1973), Prentice-Dunn & Rogers (1980, 1982), Rogers & Prentice-Dunn (1981)

Masks worn

Mathes & Guest (1976), Miller & Rowold (1979), Rogers & Ketchen (1979), Zimbardo (1969) *consequences.* Studies utilizing anonymity should carefully consider all possible sources of consequences in the experimental setting.

Table 3 presents each of the different manipulations of evaluation in the studies reviewed. As with other areas of social psychology, many of the studies have confounded evaluation in their designs (Guerin, 1986, 1993). The same problem as anonymity is found: studies have manipulated one form of evaluation and other sources of evaluation have been ignored, so subjects in control conditions may feel evaluated through another channel. All possible sources of evaluation need to be taken into account in future research.

While anonymity has been a generalized condition for avoidance of consequences, *evaluation has been a method of intensifying generalized consequences.* If reinforcements are contingent on an expected evaluation, this will intensify the effort to obtain them. Evaluation with contingent negative consequences will intensify avoidance behaviors.

There are points, then, in the manipulations of anonymity and evaluation which are obscured in theory and experimental manipulation. This brief behavior analysis of those manipulations can help show how they can be made clearer in future experiments.

The Inherent Consequences of Being in a Group

Many of the studies have compared people behaving alone with people in groups. These have shown marked differences in behavior as would be expected from Chapters 4 and 5. It has been suggested in both these chapters that there are consequences which usually arise merely from being a member of a group. Three of these have been mentioned: less consequences for individual members of a group, less effective use of discriminative cues, and a reduction in verbal self-regulation.

In terms of the manipulations discussed here, membership of a group will also usually imply the following: anticipated future interaction; real consequences (since the people are real); justifications may be required by other group members; the other group members are often dependent in some way; there is greater anonymity to others outside the group (diffusion of responsibility); there is less anonymity to those in the group; the group members will evaluate each others' behavior; and the control of group rewards will rest with all members rather than the individual.

This suggests that: *many of the properties of groups arise from the changes in consequences inherent in group membership.* This can be seen most clearly in the social loafing, deindividuation and diffusion of responsibility literatures. These have manipulated conditions which change the scheduling of consequences to group members. They reliably find that the behavior is changed.

While knowledge of the conditions specific to a situation is normally required to predict the more complex behavior of groups, the studies here show that many consequences are common to all groups. It is these generalized group consequences which have been widely used in social psychology and which make up the foundations of research on group processes. Applications to real groups, however,

Table 3. Manipulations of Evaluation

Behavior recorded
Davis et al. (1976), Donnerstein & Donnerstein (1973), Tetlock (1983a)

Give talk to peers
McAllister et al. (1978)

Future discussions
Aronson & Carlsmith (1962), Chaiken (1980), Davis et al. (1976), Gruder (1971), Gruder & Rosen (1971), Jones (1968), Klimoski & Ash (1974), Mann et al. (1982), Tetlock & Kim (1987)

Monitored by others/Salience
Benton (1975), Carnevale et al. (1981), Carnevale et al. (1979), Haccoun & Klimoski (1975), Klimoski & Ash (1974), Kogan et al. (1972), Michelini (1976), Pruitt et al. (1978,1986), Schwartz & Gottlieb (1976), Wall (1975), White (1977)

Explicit evaluation
Beckhouse et al. (1975), Breaugh & Klimoski (1977), Brown (1968), Carnevale et al. (1981), Carnevale et al. (1979), Davis et al. (1976), Haccoun & Klimoski (1975), Klimoski (1972), Klimoski & Ash (1974), Lindskold & Finch (1982), Prentice-Dunn & Rogers (1980, 1982), Pruitt et al. (1978), Rogers & Prentice-Dunn (1981), Rozelle & Baxter (1981), White (1977)

also require knowledge of the consequences specific to that group and situation, since changing the consequences will change the outcomes.

Conclusions

The experimental social psychology literature has studied a wide range of social consequences which are common to many situations. What are still needed in traditional social psychology are both methods for recognizing the specific consequences in applied settings, and methods for changing consequences. These are precisely what behavior analysis can offer. Making explicit the consequences employed by social psychology, as has been done here, holds much promise of unifying the rigours of experimental social psychology with an advanced behavioral analysis.

Traditional social psychology has been able to ignore motivation for an interesting reason first mentioned in Chapter 4: social psychology primarily deals with those social behaviors maintained by generalized social compliance, because more specific consequences do not produce the scientific generality favoured in the area. Instead, social psychologists have (quite sensibly) concentrated their efforts on very general behavior patterns which might produce general laws.

The end result of this is that most of the behaviors studied are maintained by very general social consequences. Because of this, subjects in experiments *appear* to perform the predicted behaviors without specific motivators; they seem to do it for its own sake, or because they "want to" or just "decide to". This means that *just a description of the social context has appeared to "explain" the behavior*, because the consequences were generalized, hidden, and could be relied upon in the settings chosen when averaged over a group. But if social psychologists wish to change behavior in applied settings, they must come to grips with the underlying generalized social contingencies maintaining the very behaviors they mostly study. They cannot just keep saying that usually people conform, and leave the motivational elements at such a naive level that generalized social compliance will always be present. They need to analyze the full three-term contingencies and beyond.

Chapter Appendix: Studies using
Experimental Manipulations 1 to 10

Future interaction

Adelberg & Batson, 1978; Arkes et al., 1987; Aronson & Carlsmith, 1962; Ben-Yoav & Pruitt, 1984; Berscheid et al., 1976; Brock & Fromkin, 1968; Chaiken, 1980; Cohen, 1961; Darley & Berscheid, 1967; Davis et al., 1976; Diener, 1976; Eiser & Taylor, 1972; Greenberg, 1978; Gruder, 1971; Gruder & Rosen, 1971; Harkins et al., 1977; Harkness et al., 1985; Harvey et al., 1976; Hennigan et al., 1982; Higgens et al., 1982; Hoffman et al., 1984; Holt & Watts, 1969; Jones, 1968; Kiesler & Corbin, 1965; Klimoski, 1972; Klimoski & Ash, 1974; Marlowe et al., 1966; Mazis, 1973; Michelini, 1976; Miller et al., 1978; Monson et al., 1982; Pallak & Heller, 1971; Powell, 1974; Prentice-Dunn & Rogers, 1980, 1982; Roering et al., 1975; Schlenker & Schlenker, 1975; Schoenrade et al., 1986; Shaffer & Ogden, 1986; Shaffer et al., 1987; Shapiro, 1975; Shure & Meeker, 1968; Slusher et al., 1974; Slusher et al., 1978; Taylor, 1975; Tetlock, 1983a, b; Tetlock & Kim, 1987; von Grumbkow et al., 1976; Watts & Holt, 1970; Wells et al., 1977; Worchel et al., 1975; Yamagishi & Sato, 1986; Yarkin et al., 1981; Yarkin-Levin, 1983; Zajonc, 1960.

Real consequences

Beckhouse et al., 1975; Brown, 1968; Collins & Hoyt, 1972; Evans, 1964; Gallo, 1966; Gallo et al., 1969; Gerard et al., 1964; Goethals et al., 1979; Gumpert et al., 1969; Harari & Graham, 1975; Kelly et al., 1970; Knox & Douglas, 1971; Lamm & Ochsmann, 1972; Maslach, 1974; Messe et al., 1967; Nel et al., 1969; Oskamp & Kleinke, 1970; Radlow et al., 1968; Rozelle & Baxter, 1981; Schwartz, 1970, 1974; Shaw & Thorslund, 1975; Sherman, 1970; Slovic, 1969; Swindell & Mann, 1984; Wrightsman, 1966.

Explanations

Adelberg & Batson, 1978; Arkes et al., 1987; Aronson & Carlsmith, 1962; Chaiken, 1980; Davis et al., 1976; Ford & Weldon, 1981; Gruder & Rosen,

1971; Hagafors & Brehmer, 1983; Jones, 1968; Klimoski & Ash, 1974; Mann et al., 1982; McAllister et al., 1979; Rozelle & Baxter, 1981; Schoenrade et al., 1986; Tetlock, 1983a,b, 1985b; Tetlock & Kim, 1987.

Dependency

Benton & Druckman, 1973, 1974; Ben-Yoav & Pruitt, 1984; Berkowitz & Connor, 1966; Berkowitz & Daniels, 1963, 1964; Berkowitz, Klanderman & Harris, 1964; Bershied et al., 1976; Carnevale et al., 1979; Carnevale et al., 1981; Cooper & Worchel, 1970; Cvetkovich, 1978; Daniels & Berkowitz, 1963; Geer & Jarmecky, 1973; Goranson & Berkowitz, 1966; Greenberg, 1978; Greenglass, 1969; Gruder, 1971; Lamm & Ochsmann, 1972; Nel, Heimrich & Aronson, 1969; Paloutzian, 1975; Schopler & Bateson, 1965; Schopler & Matthews, 1965; Shapiro, 1975; Slovic et al., 1969; Slusher, 1978; Slusher et al., 1978; Solomon, 1960; Vidmar, 1971; Zalenska & Kogan, 1971.

Anonymity

Adelberg & Batson, 1978; Arbuthnot & Andrasik, 1973; Beaman et al, 1979; Berkowitz & Daniels, 1964; Bixenstine et al., 1966; Bonacich, 1972, 1976; Brickner et al., 1986; Davis et al., 1976; Diener, 1976, 1979; Diener et al., 1976; Diener, Westford, Dineen & Fraser, 1973; Donnerstein & Donnerstein, 1973; Donnerstein et al., 1972; Fox & Guyer, 1978; Gruder, 1971; Gruder & Rosen, 1971; Harkins et al., 1980; Harkins & Jackson, 1985; Harkins & Petty, 1982; Helmreich & Collins, 1968; Insko et al., 1985; Jackson & Harkins, 1985; Jackson & Williams, 1985; Jerdee & Rosen, 1974; Johnson & Downing, 1979; Jorgenson & Papciak, 1981; Kahan, 1973; Kerr & Bruun, 1981; Kidder et al., 1977; Latané et al., 1979; Leventhal et al., 1972; Lindskold & Finch, 1982; Mann et al., 1982; Mathes & Guest, 1976; McFarland et al., 1984; Michelini, 1976; Miller & Rowold, 1979; Morse et al., 1976; Mouton, Blake & Olmstead, 1955/56; Nadler et al., 1982; Paloutzian, 1975; Petty, Harkins, Williams & Latané, 1977; Prentice-Dunn & Rogers, 1980, 1982; Reis & Gruzen, 1976; Rogers, 1980; Rogers & Ketchen, 1979; Rogers & Prentice-Dunn, 1981; Swindell & Mann, 1984; Tetlock, 1983a, 1983b, 1985b; Tetlock & Kim, 1987; Weldon & Gargano, 1985; White, 1977; Wichman, 1970; Williams et al., 1981; Worchel et al., 1975; Zimbardo, 1970.

Responsibility

Arbuthnot & Andrasik, 1973; Beaman et al., 1979; Brickner et al., 1986; Collins & Hoyt, 1972; Cooper, 1971; Darley & Latané, 1968; Diener, 1976; Diener et al., 1975, 1976; Diener, Westford, Diener & Beaman, 1973; Diener, Westford, Dineen & Fraser, 1973; Fleishman, 1980; Geer & Jarmecky, 1973; Harari & Graham, 1975; Harkins & Jackson, 1985; Harkins, Latané & Williams, 1980; Harkins & Petty, 1982; Hoffman et al., 1984; Ingham et al., 1974; Jackson & Harkins, 1985; Jackson & Williams,

1985; Kerr & Bruun, 1981; Latané, Williams & Harkins, 1979; Maruyama et al., 1982; Mathes & Guest, 1976; Morgan, 1978; Petty, Harkins & Williams, 1980; Petty, Harkins, Williams & Latané, 1977; Petty, Williams, Harkins & Latané, 1977; Prentice-Dunn & Rogers, 1980; Rogers & Prentice-Dunn, 1981; Schwartz, 1970, 1974; Schwartz & Gottlieb, 1976; Swindell & Mann, 1984; Wallach et al., 1964; Weldon & Gargano, 1985; Williams, Harkins & Latané, 1981; Zaccaro, 1984; Zalenska & Kogan, 1971.

Evaluation

Aronson & Carlsmith, 1962; Beckhouse et al., 1975; Benton, 1975; Breaugh & Klimoski, 1977; Brock & Fromkin, 1968; Brown, 1968; Carnevale et al., 1979; Carnevale et al., 1981; Chaiken, 1980; Cohen, 1961; Davis et al., 1976; Donnerstein & Donnerstein, 1973; Gruder, 1971; Gruder & Rosen, 1971; Haccoun & Klimoski, 1975; Harkins et al., 1977; Harvey et al., 1976; Hennigan et al., 1982; Hoffman et al., 1984; Holt & Watts, 1969; Innes, 1981; Jones, 1968; Klimoski, 1972; Klimoski & Ash, 1974; Kogan, Lamm & Trommsdorf, 1972; Leventhal, 1962; Lindskold & Finch, 1982; Mann et al., 1982; Mazis, 1973; McAllister et al., 1979; Michelini, 1976; Newston & Czerlinsky, 1974; Powell, 1974; Prentice-Dunn & Rogers, 1980, 1982; Pruitt et al., 1986; Pruitt et al., 1978; Rogers & Prentice-Dunn, 1981; Rozelle & Baxter, 1981; Schwartz & Gottlieb, 1976; Tetlock, 1983a; Tetlock & Kim, 1987; Wall, 1975a,b; Watts & Holt, 1970; White, 1977; Zajonc, 1960.

Status

Bartunek et al., 1975; Breaugh & Klimoski, 1977; Frey & Adams, 1972; Haccoun & Klimoski, 1975; Harvey et al., 1976; Hermann & Kogan, 1968; Klimoski & Ash, 1974; Kogan & Doise, 1969; Kogan et al., 1972; Lamm & Kogan, 1970; Medow & Zander, 1965; Vidmar, 1971; Wall, 1975a,b; Zander & Forward, 1968.

Reversibility

Frey, 1981; Frey, Kumpf, Irle & Gniech, 1984; Frey & Rosch, 1984; Hennigan et al., 1982; Higgens et al., 1982; Holt & Watts, 1969; Leventhal, 1962; Watts & Holt, 1970.

Control

Benton, 1972; Benton & Druckman, 1974; Ben-Yoav & Pruitt, 1984; Brock & Fromkin, 1968; Carnevale et al., 1979; Carnevale et al., 1981; Cohen, 1961; Erber & Fiske, 1984; Frey & Adams, 1972; Greenberg, 1978; Harkins et al., 1977; Harvey et al., 1976; Hennigan et al., 1982; Higgens et al., 1982; Hoffman et al., 1984; Holt & Watts, 1969; Mazis, 1973; Newston & Czerlinsky, 1974; Powell, 1974; Pruitt et al., 1978; Slusher et al., 1978; Watts & Holt, 1970; Zajonc, 1960.

Chapter 6

Social Behaviors and Social Interaction

Social behaviors have traditionally been divided into standard categories, such as cooperation and competition (e.g., Thibaut & Kelley, 1959), helping, and social skills. These categories will be followed here for convenience, but there is no reason why they must remain like this. Future analyses might find better functional ways of grouping and labelling social contingencies. For good discussions of classification of social behaviors see Buskist and Morgan, 1988; Hake and Olvera, 1978; Hake and Vukelich, 1972; Komaki, 1986b; Parrott, 1983; Patterson and Reid, 1970; Schmitt, 1981, 1984; Slavin, 1977. Some suggestions about how these categories might be eventually changed are given in this chapter.

Like Chapter 5, many studies of these phenomena have had weak manipulations of contingencies. That is, delayed "rewards" or remote consequences were often used, so the strengthening effects of these on group behavior must have had a variety of verbal and other social mediators. The results of such studies are therefore unclear, and will not be discussed here (see Schmitt, 1987, for more on these problems). In this chapter I wish only to provide some orienting instructions for making analyses of these social phenomena. There is not room for a complete review. When confronted by such phenomena I hope these comments will be useful in the search for controlling variables.

The final introductory point is that the distinction between group and individual behaviors is actually inappropriate for humans. As is stressed in this book, and more so in Chapter 8, individual human behavior is thoroughly social, because most of it is maintained by generalized social contingencies formed in verbal communities. Only when directly contacting the environment are we being non-social, for example, when digging a hole in the ground. Even in this case, however, there are many component responses which are socially maintained. For example, this would occur when digging a hole if your behavior changed when someone else was present (social facilitation), if you were imitating the way your neighbour digs holes, if someone else controlled the consequences of digging the hole, if others were helping you dig the hole, or if you were talking to others or even yourself about how you will dig and what you will do with the hole when it is finished.

The theme that runs through the material in this chapter is that most group behaviors can be analyzed in two ways. First, there are usually direct advantages to the individual from behaving in the ways described, whether cooperative, competitive, selfish, altruistic or helpful. But most of these behaviors can also occur as a way of merely maintaining the group itself, and the benefits come from this rather than from any immediate "payoffs" (9.2). This means that the obvious social advantages do not always provide a full behavior analysis–the role of carrying out the behavior to the whole group functioning needs also to be considered. This is what is sometimes described as solidarity, or team-forming behaviors. We do not attend a formal social occasion because of immediate payoffs but because doing so previously has helped "cement" a group membership which has previously led to many and varied benefits.

6.1. Advantages of Group Behavior

Human behavior is unique and seems special because verbal communities are formed which can culturally evolve special behaviors (verbal behaviors) which could not be maintained by the nonsocial environment. Such behaviors, and the ways they are developed, will be explored in Chapter 9 and 10, but the basis for all of this is that forming groups has advantages. If there were not advantages then verbal communities would fall apart, as indeed many folkways have fallen into disuse. This chapter looks at some of these group advantages, especially the more direct ones.

The major advantage of groups is that they can be used to bridge indirect, delayed and remote contingencies which an individual could not contact alone. This works in two ways. First, as will be shown in 7.6, the social maintenance of self-regulatory verbal behavior can especially facilitate contact with remote contingencies.

The second way in which groups can bridge remote contingencies is by the development of group members behaving in ways which contact contingencies not available at all to an individual. A simple example would be a group of people lifting something too heavy for any one individual to lift alone. While such effects are often thought of exclusively as cooperative behaviors, competitive behavior can also contact contingencies which an individual could not alone. The effect of competition in sport, for example, is to reach new records which are not found in individual performances.

With non-human animals we can also find examples of animals working as a group to achieve remote contingencies without verbal self-regulation. Some of this material can be found in Bertram (1978). These group strategies have either been selected over a long time or else are easily discriminated in the environment. This should be kept in mind when the role of verbal behavior in group responses is emphasized through this book. Animals can develop similar group responses over (evolutionary) time without verbal facilitation.

6.2. Cooperation

The term cooperation is commonly used for a few different types of contingency schedules which should eventually be replaced by more specialized terms. The common definitions involve something like the following: "in which every person's performance is reinforced when a group performance standard has been met" (Schmitt, 1986, p. 27); "in which the reinforcement of two or more individuals depends upon the behavior of both or all of them" (Skinner, 1953, p. 311). Other good discussions will be found in the following: Lindsley, 1966; Marwell and Schmitt, 1975; Schmitt, 1984.

Unfortunately, definitions have a way of excluding what is of interest and of being slippery. This is why I believe that further distinctions should be made of social behaviors and the terms cooperation, competition, and conflict tightened or replaced. For example, from the above definitions the distinction between the cooperating parties receiving the same or different reinforcers is unclear. If I lend a friend a hand in fixing their bicycle, is this cooperation, since the reinforcers received by the friend and myself will differ in kind and quantity?

There is one definition of cooperation which I wish to emphasize although it excludes many traditional examples of cooperation. This is to call a group behavior cooperation only if it allows contact with a contingency which could not be achieved by an individual (cf. Keller & Schoenfeld, 1950). This restricts the social episodes covered in the two earlier definitions of cooperation, but I am not arguing that this is all there is to cooperation. An example of this would be the automatic consequences to each member of a group which lifts a very large rock; contact with these reinforcers is dependent upon the other people cooperating, since the consequences could not be contacted by an individual behaving alone.

The present restricted definition excludes other examples often called cooperation, however. Consider two people who lift up a small rock together. Most definitions of cooperation would include this behavior, though the present definition does not. The reason for excluding this case from being called cooperation is that I suspect that a lot more is going on which needs to be further analyzed. The behavior is not being controlled purely by the remote contingencies of lifting, but must involve verbal instructions and ritualized social compliance to a verbal community (9.3). If we lump all these together as "cooperation" we will never properly analyze them.

So in the present definition, cooperation is controlled by remote contingencies contacted by group members and *only* by group members acting in concert. The other cases of "cooperation" (outside my definition), which do not contact individually impossible contingencies, need more analysis: that is why I would like them to be treated separately. Why for instance, are the group members carrying out a task of lifting a small rock together if they could do the task on their own? Clearly, other social contingencies must be controlling their behavior beyond the unique cooperative goal. Too many variables are contained in such examples of "cooperation"; we need to start pulling the term apart.

This now raises the question of how a group contacts the remote contingencies in the first place? It is suggested that for humans, this will primarily involve verbal influence and generalized social compliance engendered by a verbal community: "If you don't cooperate you'll be in big trouble", "If you help me it will help all of us". As mentioned earlier, animals can also contact remote group contingencies, but this must develop over a long evolutionary period (Bertram, 1978). The rapidity with which humans can shape the same behaviors shows that there is a different route.

So it is being argued that there are at least two types of "cooperative" behaviors covered by the usual definitions of cooperation and that they should be distinguished because they involve very different contingencies. What this means is that for humans, many of our cooperative social behaviors are maintained by generalized social compliance to a verbal community and not from what the group cooperation actually achieves–the immediate outcomes. Cooperative social behaviors in my sense bring about group outcomes on the environment which could not otherwise be made; that is, contact can be made with remote contingencies. This is shown in Figure 7.

For example, Wolfe, Boyd and Wolfe (1983) reinforced children for cooperating using tokens, and then faded from tokens to verbal praise. While this tells us about cooperation in the usual sense, we still do not know whether the behavior would have maintained if the praise had been faded as well. If the behavior could be maintained without praise then a cooperative contingency (in my sense) must have been contacted. If the behavior had not maintained then something else must have been controlling the cooperation. Most likely the children were being compliant towards the adults and the tokens (supposed outcomes of the cooperation) were not having a controlling influence at all. Participation in a verbal community is therefore the proper analysis of this situation rather than cooperation in my sense.

This is a point which will crop up again in later chapters: that people can act as if they are being controlled by obvious reinforcers when in fact verbal community social compliance is maintaining the behavior. People, for example, can go to a

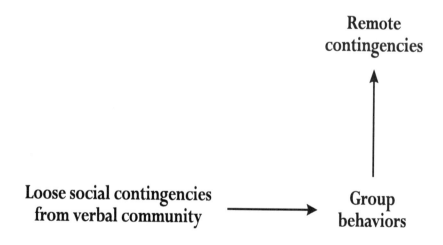

Figure 7. Verbal communities allow group behaviors to contact remote contingencies.

music performance and act as if the music is reinforcing, even to the extent of making serious faces or smiling wistfully at the (socially) appropriate times. For some of these people, however, the behaviors exhibited are maintained by generalized social contingencies and not by the music itself at all. The music might only act as a social discriminative context.

In general, the results of experiments on cooperation show that the scheduling of the consequences determine the level of cooperation, although most experiments deal with the social influence processes which promote cooperation in the present sense (a group goal) but may not sustain it (Azrin & Lindsley, 1956; Barton, 1981; Hake & Olvera, 1978; Hake & Vukelich, 1973; Hake, Vukelich & Olvera, 1975; Lindsley, 1966; Marwell & Schmitt, 1972, 1975; Olvera, & Hake, 1976; Rosenbaum, Moore, Cotton, Cook, Hieser, Shover & Gray, 1980; Schmitt, 1976; Schmitt & Marwell, 1971).

Some of these studies have also found that subjects avoid ending up with unequal amount of reinforcers (Hake, Vukelich & Olvera, 1975; Matthews, 1977), which is more difficult to achieve with three people cooperating rather than two (Marwell & Schmitt, 1972). This again seems more indicative of social compliance controlling the behavior rather than behavior controlled by remote cooperative contingencies. The problem, then, as I see it, is that previous studies of cooperation have not distinguished between the control of cooperation through social compliance with a verbal community and the effects of the cooperation for a group goal not achievable individually.

The problem I have raised resembles the (false) criticisms that radical behaviorism is reductionistic and misses out on what is truly human. I am arguing that the cooperation experiments have been too simple (not too reductionist) and have not taken the specifically human properties of verbal communities into account. The special property of our behavior is the ubiquitous social contingencies which maintain so many otherwise arbitrary behavior, such as making noises from the mouth. We have now reached a point where these cannot be ignored in analyzing human behavior. They need more careful attention in experimental work.

There is one final point to make about defining cooperation. Arguments over the definition of social behavior have centred on whether or not other people have to be involved. Is a behavior social if no one else is present? The re-orientation suggested here is towards defining any human behavior as social if it involves generalized social contingencies or verbal behavior. This is perhaps what is essentially social, not just the presence or absence of other people. The effects of such verbal communities occur even when alone.

This raises a paradox. If there are powerful generalized social consequences operating in my environment, I might perform behaviors when alone even though they are not strengthened by tracking the environment. These must be considered as social behaviors even though I am alone. To my way of thinking, the truly **social** behaviors are those which can be *maintained through other people* in a generalized way, and which control behavior whether or not someone else is present. The paradox arises since these social contingencies might be said to be most powerful when they work when someone is alone! If I can get you to do something for me when you are alone and especially when the environment does not also reinforce the behavior, not only should your behavior be considered a social behavior, but this should be considered a more effective social contingency than if I had been present and acting as a discriminative stimulus (4.1).

As mentioned earlier, the major findings reflect that it is the consequences of cooperating which determine whether or not there is cooperation between people, although only obvious, macro consequences have been manipulated in experiments. More cooperation is found when people are involved (have contingent consequences), when the people have made public statements that they will cooperate (extra social consequences applied), and when there are less people (Dawes, 1980). Verbal control of cooperation is found by showing that communication between people usually increases cooperation and that moralizing increases cooperation (Dawes, 1980; Orbell, van der Kragt, & Dawes, 1988).

6.3. Competition

The contingencies for competition appear to be more straightforward than those for cooperation: the situation is arranged such that if one person receives a consequence then the other person does not. While this sounds simple, I do not believe that it is. Excellent discussions of the behavioral literature will be found in the following: Buskist and Morgan, 1987, 1988; Schmitt, 1984, 1986.

The schedules in practice for competition are complex, adjusting, and dynamic in all senses. A reaction time competition, for example, looks like an intermittent schedule but any changes in one player's behavior which are shaped by the schedule changes the behavior of the other person and hence changes the "intermittency". It is therefore a mutual shaping which cannot be reduced to simple schedules. The best of the research recognises this (e.g., Buskist & Morgan, 1987; Schmitt, 1987). Buskist and Morgan (1988) have begun the task of distinguishing different functional types of competition by examining the contingencies operating, as I did in a small and preliminary way for cooperation in the last section. They distinguish interactive and non-interactive competition, individual and team competition, and minimal and maximal competition.

Further to this, I would also make the same argument for competition as was done for cooperation: that we must distinguish between competitive behavior which is controlled by the more direct consequences arising from the responses and competitive behavior which is controlled by verbal community contingencies. An example of the latter would be a competition in which the person's behavior is controlled by their self-statements: "I must win. I must beat this other person. I'm going to get you...whether I win the trophy or not..." With such a case it is clear that the supposed reinforcer which only one of the group will get (the trophy) is not controlling the behavior, and probably some intergroup (verbal community) conflict contingencies are operating.

In such cases as these, the behavior is at least partially controlled by verbal behavior and therefore social consequences (cf. Simmel, 1955). I would hazard to guess that more human competitions are controlled by social consequences than are controlled by the consequences of the responses made, though this will be different for non-human animals (Kanak & Davenport, 1967). Most competitions do not give enough prizes to maintain our basic requirements of life, so they must be carried out for other reasons. Experimental work on competition needs to address this, and look more carefully at such sources of control in competition. Most experimental work treats the prize or trophy as the major (or only) controlling variable and ignores verbal community effects.

Buskist, Barry, Morgan and Rossi (1984) have begun to explore experimentally these different paths to competition. They gave some of their subjects orienting instructions that the situation would be a competitive one. While subjects without these instructions still became competitive, they took longer. So in this case the verbal instructions set the occasion for competition. The subjects in Buskist et al. (1984) also reported that they enjoyed the competitive situation. This conflicts with other reports that the removal of competition can act as a reinforcer (Steigleder, Weiss, Cramer & Feinberg, 1978). Clearly there are different types of competition, and different degrees of social reinforcement for competition. In line with this interpretation, some cross-cultural differences in competition have also been reported (e.g., Carment & Hodkin, 1973).

Another variable combined in the common experimental manipulations of competition are auditing effects, which were discussed Chapter 4. The evidence presented there showed that the opportunity to audit can be used to strengthen other behaviors. Competing can also be reinforced by social comparisons (Conolley, Gerard & Kline, 1978), although the amount of auditing depends upon how close the competition is (Buskist & Morgan, 1988; Hake, Vukelich & Kaplan, 1973; Vukelich & Hake, 1974). Some interesting new experimental tests on this are presented in Buskist and Morgan (1988).

Another type of competitive situation is one in which speed determines the individual outcome rather than quality. In a test using rhesus monkeys, Washburn, Hopkins and Rumbaugh (1990) had the monkeys fire "guns" at targets and reinforced only the first monkey to hit the target. They found that the monkeys hit the target more quickly in this competitive situation, but used more shots to get that effect. That is, in this competitive situation they increased the speed but at the cost of accuracy.

As was concluded by Buskist and Morgan (1988), there are many phenomena occurring within the "simple" competitive situation. Only a few of these have been discussed here. More still lie waiting to be experimentally tested. As was suggested for cooperation, we should perhaps begin to develop alternative names for these different functional effects, rather than calling them all "competition".

6.4. Helping Behavior

There are two major questions that people have asked about helping and altruism. First, is altruism towards conspecifics innate? Second, what controls helping behavior?

Many studies have tried to deduce or experimentally show that altruism is innate (see Krebs & Miller, 1985). We saw in Chapter 4 that the question of innateness is difficult for behavior analysts because the behavior produced by generalized social contingencies closely resembles innate behaviors, and there is probably no way of showing a difference between them without completely depriving an animal of social contact from birth.

The same problem occurs with helping and altruism. Examples of human altruism might occur not from an innate basis but because of generalized social compliance with a verbal community. If generalized social compliance is the very fabric of human behavior, maintaining large portions of all our behavior, then we would expect to find helping behaviors whether or not there was any obvious, immediate payoff for the helper. It is probably impossible to show, then, that an example of altruism with a human is innate.

The control by generalized social consequences is seen in many of the statements I have heard made about helping: "I helped because it is the done thing... It was the proper thing to do". Good examples can be found in media interviews with heroes and heroines; they find it difficult to say why they were helping when there was a risk involved, "You've just got to help someone if they are in trouble, don't you?" While such statements *could* be indicative of an innate motive to help fellow humans, more likely it is part of maintaining good stead within a verbal community, and therefore getting access to the advantages of a verbal community.

With non-human animals there are many experiments purporting to show altruism (Boren, 1966; Colman, Liebold & Boren, 1969; Daniel, 1942, 1943; Massermann, Wechkin & Terris, 1964; Rice & Gainer, 1962), although problems remain (Taylor, 1975; Marcucella & Owens, 1975). The animals used, white rats and macaque monkeys, have highly flexible behaviors so it is not unlikely that there was learning taking place. On the other hand, examples of cooperative breeding in birds may show truly innate patterns of helping.

What has been shown with humans, however, is that helping behavior can readily be modified by its consequences (references can be found in Dovidio, 1984; Krebs & Miller, 1985; Latané & Darley, 1970; Piliavin, Dovidio, Gaertner & Clark, 1981; White & Gerstein, 1987). Many experiments have manipulated variables which involve changing the consequences, and they reliably find that helping behavior changes. Some of these were reviewed in 5.3. Without extrapolating to non-human animals, helping with humans seems too flexible to be purely innate. A number of these studies from traditional social psychology which incidentally manipulated consequences were listed in Tables 1 and 2 in Chapter 5.

With regards to bystander intervention (Latané & Darley, 1970), as a specific example, Cacioppo, Petty and Losch (1986) found that subjects who were helpers reported that they anticipated that other people would see them as being responsible for the recipient of help's well-being. Subjects who were onlookers also reported that they thought the helpers were responsible. So implicit (verbal community) social consequences are applied to helpers.

In a nice series of more carefully controlled experiments, Weiner (1977) explored altruistic responding when subjects had a chance to give free reinforcements to another subject ("give responding"). This was found to occur but was easily reduced by introducing some costs and constraints. As well, give responding was found to be determined by past experience with receiving reinforcement from others. This last finding suggests that a good deal of helping is maintained by social compliance in a group, perhaps including avoidance of negative evaluations from the experimenter in the laboratory case. The only other explanation is that subjects may have thought that they could get something from the other person again in the future (possible future interaction– see 5.3). This seems unlikely from the description of the experimental procedure in Weiner (1977), however.

So we are left with two routes to helping behavior in humans. First, there may be some specific consequences of helping which will strengthen or weaken helping, or at least the anticipation of an outcome will strengthen the behavior (e.g., White & Gerstein, 1987). Second, the generalized social compliance or generalized avoidance of negative evaluation leads to helping, unless there are some costs involved. Helping behaviors in this sense are part of maintaining a verbal community (9.3).

6.5. Sharing

A phenomenon related to cooperation and helping is that of sharing. The word cooperation is usually used when two parties *behave together* in some way such that both gain out of the interaction, while helping is usually used when one party *behaves towards another* without obviously gaining from it. Sharing, on the other hand, is usually used when one party *gives something to another* who is not necessarily lacking, and there is no obvious gain for the sharer. For example, if two neighbours work together to pick apples off their trees we would call that cooperation. If the neighbours had picked the apples but only one of them kept them, we would call that helping. If one neighbour had picked apples and then had given half to the other that would be called sharing rather than helping.

There is a small but fascinating behavior analytic literature on the development of sharing (Barton, 1981; Bryant & Budd, 1984; Fowler & Baer, 1981; Hake, Olvera & Bell, 1975; Hake & Schmid, 1981; Hake, Vukelich & Olvera, 1975; Kohler & Fowler, 1985; Olvera & Hake, 1976; Rogers-Warren & Baer, 1976; Rogers-Warren, Warren & Baer, 1977; Schmid & Hake, 1983; Weiner, 1977).

In one line of this research, Hake and his colleagues had subjects work on matching-to-sample problems, but only the first subject to complete a Fixed Ratio requirement could get to do the problems. The research found that subjects would alternate completing the Fixed Ratio responses so they alternately received a problem to complete (Hake, Olvera & Bell, 1975; Hake, Vukelich & Olvera, 1975; Olvera & Hake, 1976). Subjects did not give to the other but alternated their taking instead. When the Fixed Ratio requirement was increased, the sharing also increased. In other studies, attempting to train sharing in children, it has been found that modeling alone is not sufficient (Barton, 1981; Rogers-Warren & Baer, 1976; Rogers-Warren, Warren & Baer, 1977). Active rehearsal and reinforcement of the behavioral components seem to be necessary to train children to share.

The study of sharing is important because it probably forms the developmental basis for the formation of verbal communities (see Kent, 1993). Children learn through trained sharing that loosely reinforcing someone else's behavior, even when there is no immediate outcome for them, is useful in the longer term. This leads to the pattern of forming groups who reinforce most behaviors of the other person (Chapter 9), and this allows many community outcomes which are good for all the community and which would not be possible without the loose verbal community reinforcement (Chapter 10).

6.6. Social Skills and Social Interaction Patterns

What makes a person socially competent or socially skilled? In the most general terms, from what has been said in Chapters 4, 5 and 6, they must make contextual social discriminations which can be maintained in a community. This involves negotiating with other members of the community as well as maintaining the generalized social contingencies.

There have been many interventions aimed at increasing social skills. Most have targeted specific skills using specific reinforcers. The complexities of training such behaviors and maintaining them in their natural environments have been recognized by the proponents (Breen & Haring, 1991; Dattilo & Camarata, 1991; Durand & Carr, 1991; Ninness, Fuerst, Rutherford & Glenn, 1991; Serna, Schumaker, Shermen & Sheldon, 1991; Storey & Horner, 1991). For example, while shyness is often considered a product of poor social skills, it can also be used to avoid negative evaluations from other people (Snyder, Smith, Augelli & Ingram, 1985), so in that sense it is a refined social skill.

The role of the consequences contacted through social compliance to a verbal community should not be under-estimated in studying social interaction (as we saw for cooperation, competition, helping and sharing). Without taking these into account, social skills degenerate into "how to get the most from other people" because of the crude reinforcement models oftimes underlying their use. Examples of this can be seen in the early literature on "assertion training". While this was separated from aggression or rudeness, it still tended to over-estimate the importance of self-regulation as compared to the benefits of social compliance to a verbal community. As we saw in 5.2, the advantages of being socially compliant are remote and can be easily overlooked, but underlie most of our important behaviors (Chapters 9 and 10).

This mixture of contingencies available through social interaction suggests that social skills lie in handling multiple contingencies (3.2), most notably the specific contingencies afforded by the many people with whom you interact, the contingencies afforded by self-regulation, and the contingencies afforded by social compliance to a verbal community. Since we do not have a clear model of how the integration of multiple contingencies works, we cannot do the same with these sources for maintaining social interaction. This is reflected in the problems with assessing social competence (Ralph, 1990). A few suggestions will be made here, and hopefully more behavior analysts will tackle these questions.

In many ways our social behavior is like the foraging of animals for food, and the multiple contingency approaches to foraging might provide some future directions (see, for example, Bhatt & Wasserman, 1987; Commons, Kacelnik & Shettleworth, 1987; Kamil, 1983; Mellgren & Brown, 1988; Shettleworth, 1989). In the recent research on foraging it has been shown that the Matching Law and other multiple contingency approaches from behavior analysis complement the earlier foraging models. This might be able to be stretched to social situations as well.

In the foraging research (see Shettleworth, 1989, for some of its problems), animals are considered to forage from patches and "choose" between patches. One of the important points of the foraging models is that the foraging itself changes the contingencies both of that patch of food and other patches not being foraged. In the present case, we can suggest that people sample from social "patches" (other people and groups of people), and our very sampling of those patches changes the contingencies of the patches. These advanced models actually include some of the dynamics which are typical of social interaction.

There are some differences, however, which should be noted. First, we can influence the patches in ways other than depletion. We can "give" to the patches which makes them more likely to provide strengthening consequences in future foraging occasions. It is as if foraging birds were to water and fertilize the patches they deplete before leaving (and in one sense they probably do!). Of course, birds have other ways of helping the plants from which they forage; in particular, by seed dispersal. But the regulation of this has been shaped over a long period.

The other way in which social behavior differs from foraging is with the use of social contingencies. This means that some social foraging is maintained by generalized forms of social consequences, and individual encounters will have no obvious source of reinforcement. Saying "Hello!" to a total stranger in the street is an example. There does not appear to be generalized interactions between animals and their food, for example, unless we wish to stretch to a metaphor by calling innate behaviors generalized evolutionary shaping, but I will resist doing that here, however.

In summary, the question of how to study the functions and structures of social interaction is a difficult one to answer, and we need a better way of dealing with multiple contingency dynamics than we have at present. The foraging models of animal behavior might provide a means to do this.

6.7. Experimental Studies of Longer Term Social Interactions

There are a few studies which have looked at multiple contingencies over a longer time span than the usual laboratory experiments. The most impressive series has been conducted by Brady and his colleagues over a number of years (Bernstein & Brady, 1986; Bernstein & Michael, 1990; Brady, 1990, 1992; Brady, Bigelow, Emurian & Williams, 1974; Brady & Emurian, 1979; Emurian, Brady, Meyerhoff & Mougey, 1981, 1983; Emurian, Emurian, Bigelow & Brady, 1976; Emurian, Emurian, & Brady, 1978, 1982, 1985; Foltin, Fischman, Brady, Bernstein, Capriotti, Nellis & Kelly, 1990).

These authors had subjects live in a self-contained laboratory in which the contingencies of most behaviors could be measured and manipulated. They varied individual contingencies as well as social contingencies. They found that setting up contingencies which required cooperation (in the sense given in 6.2) changed the patterns of social interaction, which could be measured from the intercom system. In three-person groups some fragmentation of social interaction occurred. And when negative reinforcement was instigated (Emurian, Emurian & Brady, 1985) more aggressive verbal responses appeared (see the similar results of Cherek, Spiga, Steinberg & Kelly, 1990). When resources were made scarce (Emurian, Emurian & Brady, 1982) the group interactions included more frequent complaints and withdrawals.

There is a wealth of information from these studies which cannot all be reviewed here. They are an excellent example of how research on multiple contingencies in social behavior could be studied rigorously and in a realistic fashion. Other studies attempting to answer similar questions are Bernstein and Ebbesen, 1978; Feallock and Miller, 1976; Findley, 1962, 1966; Horcones, 1983; Winkler, 1980). As mentioned in the last section, until we begin to explore multiple contingencies further, the dynamic aspects of social interaction will be without a good foundation.

6.8. Verbal Communities, Metacontingencies, and Interlocking Social Behaviors

The three chapters making up Part 2 of this book have treated cases in which people mediate, respectively, the discriminative stimulus, the consequences, and the behaviors of contingencies. It has been impossible to exclude verbal behaviors and the effects of verbal communities from our discussion because this is a major form of human social behavior. We have seen, therefore, two types of cooperation, two types of competition, etc., one controlled by the product of the joint behaviors, the other controlled by properties of a verbal community already in place. It should be obvious that just because verbal communities can change the very nature of cooperative and competitive social behaviors they must be important. For this reason, Part 3 of this book discusses verbal communities and their effects in detail.

Before that, however, some discussion is necessary about different ways that have been put forward to describe interlocking social behaviors, the ways in which effects arise from people behaving together. Most descriptions point out that two or more people each behave and the joint product of their behaviors have effects. This has been followed in Part 2 for the most part.

Glenn has made a useful distinction between contingencies and metacontingencies (Biglan, Glasgow & Singer, 1990; Ellis, 1991; Glenn, 1985, 1986, 1988, 1989, 1991). If I have understood the distinction correctly, metacontingencies refer to the relations between social behaviors and their outcomes. For example, there are many direct effects of driving a car on an individual. But there is also a metacontingency that if everyone drives a car (because of the useful effects) then air pollution will increase and this will have a deleterious effect on all drivers. The metacontingency is between the classes of driving operants and the outcome of all those operants, irrespective of the individual outcomes also present.

A terminology problem is that the joint outcome does not control the driving operants so it is perhaps not really a contingency (therefore metacontingency) in the usual sense that the class of operants is controlled by its consequences. In Glenn's sense, then, many or all of the cooperative, helping, and competitive social behaviors discussed through Part 2 of this book were dealing with metacontingencies. There were outcomes of the interlocking actions of individuals over and above the direct effects on the individuals.

The use of language has two roles in metacontingencies. First, as Glenn (1989, 1991) points out, verbal behavior is usually required to change metacontingencies, though perhaps not always. Second, verbal behavior itself is a product of many people acting in conjunction—a cultural practice. Having a set of behaviors which affects both a listener (reader) and a speaker (writer) makes outcomes possible which would not be possible with a single individual.

What is to be described in Part 3 of this book, however, might be thought of as a special case of a metacontingency, but one which is ubiquitous and very powerful amongst humans. Verbal behaviors are a special case in which a group of people act to reinforce a wide variety of behaviors even though some of those behaviors have no reinforcement for either the individual or the group as a whole. What is beneficial in such a social system is that overall, the generalized and loose reinforcement of group members' behavior allows many useful metacontingencies to operate.

Consider the example of driving and air pollution given earlier. To overcome this problem I could punish individuals for driving too much or reinforce them for driving less, and these strategies might work through the use of verbal and other behaviors in changing a metacontingency of air pollution. Consider now that we could do the same to these same individuals to change other metacontingencies of food shortages (Glenn, 1991), infant survival, effects of smoking (Biglan, Glasgow & Singer, 1990), etc. But a more useful cultural strategy in the long run would be for a group of individuals to begin reinforcing many different behaviors rather indiscriminately or loosely in order to get the very special generalized social compliance to the group. Changing metacontingencies then becomes an easier problem to tackle, rather than having separate verbal interventions for every different problem.

To put this another way, the difference is one between a group of people behaving in a particular way which produces a specific metacontingent outcome, and a group of people acting to maintain a group by generally reinforcing most behaviors of group members and then having the compliant group work towards specific outcomes when this is useful. In the long run, of course, the latter, a verbal community, will only maintain if there are reinforcing outcomes for the individuals who form the group, but there are many examples of imbalances lasting many generations between who gives and takes from a society (the rich and the poor).

The formation of common widespread verbal communities, like the group of people who make up English speakers, have reinforcing consequences for the individuals extremely often, except when the group members are in a country which uses a non-English language. Everytime we speak we have effects which we would have trouble achieving without an English speaking verbal community.

The key feature, then, for Part 3, is that there is a community of people (even two people will do) who reinforce each other in a very loose way most of the time, not just for specific cooperative or group behaviors with positive group outcomes. This "reserve of community goodwill", as it were, is then utilized for producing group products. Thus only one certain type of metacontingency is being discussed in Part 3 of this book: Part 2 has examples of interlocking social behaviors which do not require such a verbal community.

The final point to mention here, and I do so because it alters some of the analyses in terms of metacontingencies, is that the establishment and maintenance of a verbal community is usually associated with various "ritual" behaviors. These behaviors cannot be analyzed in the terms of Part 2, because they are not maintained by their immediate social outcomes. Rather, their relevant social function is to maintain the group so that the other metacontingencies can be contacted. If analyzed by looking at the immediate effects for the individual or the group, none will be found. More will be said on this in Chapter 9, and examples have been given in this chapter for cooperation, competition, etc.

It would be ludicrous, for example, to look for the function of eating the bread in the Catholic Mass as a metacontingency involving food and the dietary intake of protein. The ritual behavior is most likely functioning in a generalized manner to maintain group compliance which is maintained because in general the group as a whole is more effective on the environment than working alone.

This difference is something like Glenn's (1985) distinction between technological and ceremonial cultural practices but I believe that she is getting at something slightly different. She acknowledges only social control through status, position, or authority (Glenn, 1986), whereas groups can develop generalized group maintenance (in my sense) without any status or specific social control (e.g., Gluckman, 1965; Middleton & Tait, 1958).

As part of this, I also disagree that ceremonial social control must be seen as restricting, rigid, and an impediment to individual operant variability. Hopefully from discussions of language use, the use of money, the construction and change in social knowledge, and music, it will be seen that forming a loosely reinforcing group is not always equivalent to getting into a rut. Indeed, I believe most of our human variable, and often arbitrary, behavior is only made possible through the formation of verbal communities which loosely reinforce many behaviors of their members without immediate outcomes.

But beyond these minor disagreement, Glenn has mapped out a very similar distinction to that which divides this book in two, and she covers some other important points which I cannot do justice to in this space. An example of this is her excellent discussions of the evolution metaphor at a cultural level (Glenn, 1991; Glenn, Ellis & Greenspoon, 1992; Glenn & Malagodi, 1991)

Part 3
Social Contingencies
with a Verbal Community

Chapter 7

Verbal Behavior and Language Use

I have already had recourse to mention verbal behavior several times in this book. It is impossible to talk about human behavior without discussing verbal behavior and verbal community control of behavior. The time has now come to deal with it in more detail, although there is still a lot we do not know about verbal behavior (Sundberg, 1991). Further details about the verbal communities themselves will be left for Chapters 9 and 10, as well as the many verbal behaviors other than linguistic verbal behavior, such as music, art, ritual, and money.

Verbal behavior is one of the major differences between human and nonhuman animals, but it is not based on new principles of analysis. While verbal behavior can control our behavior and that of others, we will see that the verbal behavior itself is controlled in the usual fashion with layers of contingencies. It is, however, a special case which has some remarkable properties (Catania, 1986; Hayes & Hayes, 1992a, b; Michael, 1984; Skinner, 1957; Winokur, 1976).

7.1. Principles of Linguistic Verbal Behavior

"Linguistic verbal behavior" is not just a fancy way to talk about language, but a whole new way of talking about *the use of language forms and other symbols to influence other people* (MacCorquodale, 1969). This is a functional view: words and sentences do not express ideas or refer to things but serve to get things done through people or have people refer to things. Verbal behavior is just another type of behavior, which has its own contingencies like any other, but one which only operates on the environment through other people. Verbal behavior has no effects on the physical environment which might lead to reinforcement: the reinforcing effects come from other people. In this way there are similarities to Austin (1962), Searle (1969) and Russell (1986/1926). The general stance towards the use of words is also unusually close to that of the Ilongots of the Philippines (Rosaldo, 1982).

The assumption is that at some point in the evolution of humans the vocal tract produced operants: that is, various sounds became capable of being affected by their consequences in the same way that bar pressing can be affected by its consequences. If I am talking about picking you up to go to a party, saying the word "car" has vastly different consequences than saying the word "bicycle". In a loose sense, verbal behavior could have developed as sign language, since all that is needed is a series of flexible behaviors which can be affected by their consequences. Or if the muscles of the ear had been developed then humans might have culturally evolved (Glenn,

1989) a "wiggly ear" language. But the fact is that there are more variations available with responses of the vocal tract and moving a pen around, and this flexibility is needed to form a useful form of language. As well, you do not need to see someone speak when listening, whereas a wiggly ear language would be no use around corners or over long distances. Telephone calls would be short with a wiggly ear language.

A consideration of the advantages of verbal behavior is important since it applies to most other social behavior involving verbal communities.

> Verbal behavior is also normally very fast, greatly exceeding the speed of nonverbal behavior with the same variety of forms and consequences. The limit appears to depend upon the mass of musculature which is set in motion. Talking is faster than gesturing, and an external medium, as in writing or typing or smoke-signalling, exacts a penalty. Speed is also encouraged by the rapid serial chaining of behavior which is possible because the speaker need not wait for the physical reaction of the listener at each stage. Extensive segments of verbal behavior are reinforced only when completed. (Skinner, 1957, p. 205).

Catania (1985) and Skinner (1986a) have some further interesting discussion about possible reasons for the evolution of verbal behavior, which will be raised at the end of Chapter 9. [Also note that the **serial** nature of linguistic verbal behavior mentioned in the quote is the basis of the single-channel hypothesis of cognitive theories. Chapter 8 has more about this.]

Verbal behavior should not be thought of as language (Lee, 1984). Language is the set of signs or symbols which is utilized in verbal behavior. These signs and symbols are behaviors which have no consequences or meaning *except in a community of people using them.* In this regard, the behavior analysis view has some similarities to that of the French linguist Saussure (1983), who also distinguished between a set of arbitrary symbols called language and the use of those symbols in a "speech community".

One can study the evolution and change in language systems, as did Saussure, and one can theoretically abstract the rules which predict grammar and other features of a language, as have psycholinguists. But it is a mistake to imply that these rules tell us anything about the use of those symbols. Instead, we must treat verbal behavior as just another (but very special) behavior and look for the contingencies which maintain it.

What one finds is that there are special properties of verbal behavior which both make it possible in the first place and which make it different to most other behaviors. First, as Saussure urged, the symbols and sounds are either arbitrary, or they might as well be. There is no meaning residing in our words beyond their social consequences (cf. Mead, 1922, 1934): they are just possible noises of the vocal tract. This has the great advantage of not tying language to environmental events (such as pointing, or wiggling the ears in a way that resembles what is being talked about) which would impede its rapid progress (see the quote from Skinner, 1957, above). On the other hand, this also means that we have to spend some considerable time learning these arbitrary symbols since they are "detached" from environmental events. It also means that they are likely to keep changing, since they have no environmental grounding.

The second feature of verbal behavior is that it is fundamentally social (Lee, 1984). Aside from a few features discussed in 7.4 and Chapter 8 (and maybe not even then), there are no consequences in the environment which strengthen verbal behavior. If we shout at rocks or brick walls we have no effect on them. Even if there is a sensory strengthening effect, perhaps talking at a "whispering wall", the actual words spoken have no differential consequences–they only have this when directed at other people. The case to consider is that of a Robinson Crusoe. After 10 years alone on an island, how much verbal behavior would still be made, and what types of verbal behavior? This experiment has not been done, since volunteers are not readily available. In the absence of data, it is suggested that only a few types of verbal behavior would remain, mostly those to do with self-control and self-regulation: the bridging of delayed environmental consequences through intermediary behaviors (see Chapter 8).

This point about verbal behavior has many implications. It means that we must always consider a listener, or possible audience, when finding out what controls particular verbal behavior. We cannot talk about individual verbal behavior performed in a social vacuum even when talking to ourselves "in our head". A child would not learn to say "Milk" if brought up alone, although they may take some time to discriminate that saying this is only strengthened when a listener is present.

There is more to this point still. All our words mean nothing (have no consequences) in the absence of a listener who is also capable of verbal behavior using the same symbols (Hayes & Hayes, 1989; Parrott, 1984; Schoneberger, 1990; Skinner, 1989). We cannot have our verbal behavior strengthened or maintained when talking to someone who also could not talk in the same language (or write if the person has a faulty vocal tract). We are only said to function as a member of a language community if we can speak the language and also act appropriately after listening to someone else speak–and we must be able to switch quickly between the two. That is, only if we can strengthen others' verbal behavior and have our verbal behavior strengthened can we be part of a verbal community. The switching between the two roles also suggests that stimulus class formation is a prerequisite for understanding, or at least for any sophisticated understanding (Hayes & Hayes, 1989).

A final implication of the social nature of verbal behavior is that derivative forms of verbal behavior, including self-instruction and even self-control, rely on social consequences. While these behaviors seem to be personal private behaviors, they need intermittent social reinforcement to be maintained (see Chapter 8 for more). It must always be kept in mind, and I keep repeating this regularly to myself, that *words do not refer to things and events: words refer people to things and events.* Verbal behavior is inherently social.

A third feature of verbal behavior is that the social reinforcement is a generalized effect. That is, there is not always a specific reinforcement for a particular word or sentence. Rather, there is automatic strengthening (just "being understood", for example) of large portions of different verbal behaviors. One type of verbal behavior does have fairly specific strengthening (mands, 7.2), but the others do not. This means that verbal behavior has to occur in a group which reinforces somewhat loosely. Such verbal communities are dealt with in Chapters 9 and 10.

While the role of *loose and generalized social consequences* seems a minor point, the implications are immense and should not be overlooked. On the negative side, it means that most verbal behavior will involve only weak control, both for the listener and for the speaker (worse still for the writer!). Instructions, for example, will almost always need to be supplemented with forms of consequences other than just generalized social reinforcement. Just saying "You should give up smoking" has little effect by itself.

On the positive side, the fact that we can produce verbal behavior with few direct consequences means that unbiased reporting of the environment is made possible. If there were always specific consequences from an audience for what I say, my verbal behavior would become heavily shaped by that audience. This, of course, applies to the development of science as much as everyday conversation. I can report that "There is a cat in the tree" since such reporting has been *generally* strengthened by others in the past. If there had to be specific consequences in order to get me to make such statements, then science would not be possible. I would either keep quiet or report only what my audience wanted me to say.

The picture that emerges is of verbal behavior being a very specialized behavior developed in groups for group benefits: the making of sounds (or marks or gestures) which is maintained by social consequences. These consequences can be specific, but most often they are generalized social consequences. This generalized strengthening makes it possible to use an arbitrary set of symbols to refer people to environmental contingencies, and also make "non-motivated" reporting of the environment possible. The production of generalized social reinforcement requires a verbal community which loosely reinforces members. These points will all be expanded in the following discussions.

7.2. Types of Verbal Behavior

Based on this functional approach to verbal behavior, a number of functional types have been investigated. The types are not based on structural features, such as nouns and verbs and prepositions, but based on their functional effects on other people. The original conceptual work was done in the 1940s by Skinner (published in 1957), but more recent changes and additions have been proposed by Catania (1980), Chase, Johnson and Sulzer-Azeroff (1985), Michael (1982b, 1985), Oah and Dickinson (1989), Smith (1983), Ulman (1985), and Vargas (1986). There is not the space here to do justice to the sophistication of this approach. The reader should consult the above sources for more detail (Oah & Dickinson, 1989, would be a good place to start). Five types of verbal behavior will be briefly outlined in this section: mands, tacts, echoics, autoclitics, and intraverbals.

A mand is a functional verbal unit which is controlled by a specific state of deprivation, and its sustaining consequence is the satisfaction of that state. If I want a drink of water I might say, "Can you get me some water?", which will usually be strengthened by having an effect: by being given some water by another person.

If you were to say a nonsense word "Grooters?", then this would not be strengthened by being given water–you would most likely be given strange looks. Conversely, if you said "Give me some water" to a brickwall, you would not get a great deal of water. So while mands are specifically motivated, the form is socially constructed within a language community, and the consequences are mediated by others but they might be nonsocial reinforcers. The important point is that they depend on a shared language and social mediation so despite the condition of individual deprivation, they are still social events.

I have already mentioned the tact in passing. This is a verbal unit which is under the control of generalized social reinforcement. A tact is usually a report on the environment which functions to refer people to the environment: "There is a cat hiding up in the tree". These are not verbalized for any specific state of deprivation (such as: "It has been weeks since I reported a cat up in a tree; I would really like to") but because similar reports have been socially reinforced in the past for many different reasons. In childhood especially, our use of words to report the state of the world is strengthened by parents and teachers in many ways. We do not have an innate need to report on the environment; tacting has been strengthened by generalized social consequences.

In a similar way, our repetition of something which has been said is often reinforced. Such verbal units are called echoics (or textuals if they involve writing). Stimulus prompts work this way ("Say perspicacious", "Perspicacious") as do fill-ins ("What is the time now in Peru?", "The time now in Peru..."). The variables which control echoics are the form of the earlier sound and a history of generalized consequences for repeating. [Note that if the fill-in was repeated because it made the following part of the sentence more understandable to the listener, then it would also be showing an autoclitic function. See below.]

Intraverbals are verbal units which are reinforced when given in response to other words. That is, they are controlled by other words and a history of those words. For example, "One, two..." might control the production of "...buckle my shoe". This is not manded, since there is no specific deprivation; it is not tacted, since it is not reporting on the environment; and it is not echoic, since the reply does not resemble what has gone before.

A large part of our knowledge about the world is made up of intraverbals, and a large part of both superficial and serious conversation is filled with intraverbals. They are controlled in the long run by generalized social reinforcement because they will be strengthened if we get them "correct", and because it is the social rather than the physical environment which corrects us. In childhood we spend a lot of time reciting words which have no direct effect except generalized approval from teachers and parents. For example, a lot of people report not actually "understanding" hymns and poems until later in life, even though they could recite them as children.

Finally, autoclitics form an important category of linguistic functions which modify the consequences of other verbal units (see Catania, 1980; Hall, 1992; Lee, 1983b; Skinner, 1957). I can mand "Get me some water" rather directly, or alternatively say "Could you please get me some water?" The first three words have no meaning in a traditional sense but they function is to modify the mand so as to make it more likely to be reinforced. This is how their use in sentences is strengthened.

Autoclitics can also be applied to tacts, as in "I believe the cat is hiding up in the tree". Again, the first two words have no meaning, but they function to modify the consequences. They will have been strengthened in the past since less social punishment will be inflicted if the cat turns out not to be hiding in the tree. Bold tacts, such as "The cat is definitely hiding up in the tree", are punished more if found to be wrong.

One other autoclitic which should be mentioned is grammar (also see Guerin, 1992b for more on this). Grammar has no meaning by itself, in the behavior analytic sense of having direct consequences. Rather, grammar makes functional consequences more likely from other parts of speech if followed. For example, if I said "Some get me water" I am not likely to be given water by anyone, but if I said the grammatically correct "Get me some water?" I am more likely to have the mand reinforced. So grammar is a particular ordering of words which we learn from a verbal community and which makes effects more likely when talking within that verbal community. In a similar way, breaking our sentences into shorter words and phrases make us more likely to be understood by a listener and hence reinforced. Saying "Thecatisdefinitelyhidingupinthetree" makes the listener less able to reinforce the behavior.

By putting together these five types of verbal units, the aim is to analyze verbal episodes. We need to know something about the context, however, and a particular word or phrase cannot be assumed to be one or other of the five types: "...we cannot tell from form alone into which class a response falls... Fire may be (1) a mand to a firing squad, (2) a tact to a conflagration, (3) an intraverbal response to the stimulus Ready, aim..., or (4) an echoic or (5) textual response to appropriate verbal stimuli." (Skinner, 1957, p. 186). This is true of all grammatical schemes, however, not just the one presented here.

There is now a large body of new research which has directly manipulated these five different verbal functions. Just two examples will be given here.

Lamarre and Holland (1985), for example, have shown that mands and tacts can act independently: learning one does not automatically ensure the other. They taught children the phrases "On the left" and "On the right" either as tacts or as mands. To train as mands they asked questions such as "Where do you want me to put the dog?" To train as tacts they asked questions such as "Where is the dog?" They found that when tested for the opposite function to that trained, the children did not respond appropriately. That is, the functions of manding and tacting were independent even though the same form, or topography, of phrases had been taught. As adults, of course, we have learned to switch between the two easily.

Another interesting study, by Lodhi and Greer (1989), looked at the hypothesis of Skinner (1957) that when talking to oneself a person acts as both listener and speaker. To do this they had children play with either anthropomorphic toys (humans-like) or nonanthropomorphic toys (puzzles, etc.). They analyzed the self-talk into the five functional types of verbal behavior we have covered above. It was found that when playing with the anthropomorphic toys the children used mands as well as tacts: that is, they were acting as both speaker and listener. With the nonanthropomorphic toys they produced few mands, and no conversations with themselves.

For other examples of this research the reader could try the following: Lee (1981b), Oah and Dickinson (1989), Stafford, Sundberg and Braam (1988), and Yamamoto and Mochizuki (1988). Much of the research is now published in a specialist journal, *The Analysis of Verbal Behavior*.

What has been briefly presented is a functional account which closely follows Skinner (1957), whose idea was to try and categorize parts of language use based upon their function: what effect do the words or phrases have upon another person? What different types of effects are there? It is very easy to find problems with such a classification, but it is difficult to find a replacement. Next time you hear someone say something, ask yourself: what was the function of that verbal episode? What might have reinforced such classes of episodes in the past? You will probably find that if you do this you will re-invent mands, tacts, autoclitics and intraverbals.

7.3. Audience Control of Verbal Behavior

Verbal Conditioning

A lot of research has been done on verbal conditioning, mostly in the 1950s and 1960s, using the Pavlovian and Hullian traditions. The idea was to show how verbal behavior was modified by changing the consequences. Typically, an experimenter would ask a subject to talk about something, and then strengthen each occurrence of a word, or type of word (such as plurals), with a reinforcer (or assumed to be) such as "Uhm", "Yes", or "Uhh hu". A good early review of this work can be found in Holz and Azrin (1966), and recent approaches in Eifert (1987). I will not attempt to evaluate all this material here, but concentrate instead on placing it into the more modern framework of this book.

One of the problems in most of this literature is that the experimental research only used a small selection of consequences, and many of those must be classed as macro consequences (Farber, 1963). While "Uhm", "Yes", and "Uhh hu" might sometimes work to select types of words, there is far more to this in real life than the use of these words. The impact of automatic strengthening cannot be over-emphasized here, as well as avoidance of silence (cf. Murray, 1971; Weiss, Lombardo, Warren & Kelley, 1971). More importantly, as mentioned above, generalized social consequences within verbal communities maintain most of our verbal behavior rather than specific verbal gestures from strangers. The subjects probably did not share many of their verbal communities with the experimenters.

From this perspective, being put in an experiment where the experimenter commented with "Uum", "Yes", and "Uhh hu" everytime you said a plural word must have seemed strange. The point is that plurals are not reinforced this way in normal verbal behavior, they are reinforced because they make other reinforcing verbal events more likely. So whether verbal conditioning works or does not work, and whether subjects have to be "aware" (be able to tell themselves) of what is going on for it to work, becomes somewhat irrelevant to how verbal behavior is usually maintained in everyday life. The traditional approach was one of having another person mediate a simple three-term contingency—as the provider of consequences (a lá Part 2 of this book)—whereas verbal behavior in our lives is part of the loose reinforcement within verbal communities.

For example, I would guess that plurals are automatically strengthened because a listener replies to our comments appropriately in the plural form, and does not refer to the singular. This automatic strengthening is subtle, and very unlike the effect of receiving "Uum", "Yes", and "Uhh hu" in reply to plural forms. The power and subtlety of this can be seen by considering the following case. Suppose you say to a listener, "There are four cats up in that tree", and they reply, "Yes, there is a cat up in the tree". The reaction you have is indicative of the subtle strengthening which did *not* occur this time as it normally would have. Just getting the appropriate response is enough to reinforce using plural forms within a verbal community, especially as a setting event or establishing operation for further conversation. Adding "Uhm", "Yes", or "Uhh hu" becomes something unusual, and which is likely to have other effects.

A second point about the verbal conditioning literature is that while tacts were almost always used in this research, the social consequences supplied by the experimenter would have functioned like disguised mands (Skinner, 1957), probably leaving subjects wondering what the experimenter was really after. As well, there was little reciprocal talk from the experimenter, making the whole exercise even more odd, since even the automatic consequences of continuing and expanding upon a conversation were missing.

In all, this is not the appropriate situation in which to research the subtle effects of consequences on verbal behavior. For these reasons, a lot of behavior analysts have ignored this large literature and tried to develop other methodologies. Whether such conditioning works will depend upon a lot of social variables which were never controlled. Someone in my immediate group might influence me by going "Mnnn" but not a stranger, unless the social context was such that the interaction was a setting event for other things.

One example of a fascinating study along these lines was that by Rosenfeld and Baer (1969). They had a subject employed to teach (without "awareness") another subject using the agreement sounds mentioned above. However, the learning subject was a "double-agent" and during the intervention phase spoke at length only when the "teacher" gave one type of sound (e.g., "Yeah"). This reinforcement from the double-agent increased the rate of the "teacher"'s response without any evidence afterwards that the "teacher" was aware of (could verbally report) that this was happening. The "teacher", though, was quite aware of the effect or phenomenon required, having been told to do this to the subject. They were not aware that it was happening to them, however!

Audience Selection of Behavior

One of the properties of verbal behavior that has been stressed is that listeners or an audience are a necessary part. It is not that we usually prepare speech in our heads which we may or may not decide to say to someone, although this can happen; rather, the audience usually selects our verbal behavior, in the selection manner discussed in 2.2. This applies as much to the content of what we say as the conversational style we use, which will be selected by our different verbal communities (Hall, 1992).

For example, if I run into my boss at work then an entire repertoire of verbal behavior is selected by the stimulus context. Things which I have meant to say to her when I saw her next suddenly "come to mind", and grammatical forms I use might be different. That is, they are selected out, even if I had not thought about them for some days. They are selected out because they are the ones which have been strengthened in the past, or which I anticipate (9.7) will be strengthened. Contrawise, things I "wanted" to tell my mother do not "come to mind" when I meet my boss at work.

Similarly, if I meet a foreigner who does not speak English, a very small repertoire is selected, a repertoire which I might not use in any other circumstances except perhaps when talking to children (cf. DePaulo & Coleman, 1986). My usual verbal behavior would not be strengthened under these circumstances, since the person could not provide any reciprocal effects which would maintain my statements.

If you think about this example of talking to foreigners, it gives the clear feeling of how important cumulative, intermittent, and generalized social reinforcement (whew!) is to the maintenance of verbal behavior. We do not usually keep talking in the absence of a responsive audience even if we do have something important to say. The verbal behavior is maintained by very generalized and subtle social reinforcement.

Further examples of audience selection can be found in the following sources, although much more needs to be done: Michael, 1984; Silverman, Anderson, Marshall and Baer, 1986; Skinner, 1957; Spradlin, 1985; Winokur, 1976. A few examples of this research will be discussed.

Some early studies found that the two social roles of listening and responding (called receptive) and speaking (called expressive) were independent (e.g., Guess, 1969; Guess & Baer, 1973; Lee, 1981b; see also Guerin & Innes, 1989). The receptive did not generalize to the expressive, as it was put, although some studies did show that the expressive could generalize to the receptive. While this was useful in the context of verbal behavior of persons with intellectual disabilities, it was a problem for normal children, since they do seem to generalize remarkably quickly.

A major breakthrough on this was with the application of stimulus equivalence classes to audience effects (Silverman, Anderson, Marshall & Baer, 1986). These authors taught children to use two repertoires which were trained by two different teachers (who were either puppets or adults). They found that the repertoires were independent, but that if one teacher taught a portion of the other repertoire then the whole of that other repertoire became available. That is, an audience could select a repertoire and also form equivalence classes with other repertoires, allowing immediate "generalization" to other forms of verbal behavior.

This shows how complex the relations between audiences and verbal repertoires can become, and also how much of the control of verbal behavior is through managing four- or five-term contingency contexts within verbal communities, rather than through simple three-term contingencies and the reinforcement of saying "Mmnnn". For example, I have a particular verbal repertoire for my work in psychology, which I am writing up at this moment. If I meet someone new at a party, I do not speak in these terms to them—the terms I am writing in now. Instead, I speak more "down to earth", or else I lose an audience. These verbal repertoires are immediately selected by the presence of that person, which acts as the highest level context in a five-term contingency. If, on the other hand, I meet someone new who happens to "speak my lingo", the entire repertoire does not have to be trained again with this new person before I can use it. Instead, the whole repertoire becomes available immediately.

Not all the audience effects are obvious. Rosenberg, Spradlin and Mabel (1961; also Spradlin, 1985) put mixed and same pairs of high- and low-verbal intellectually handicapped subjects together for conversations. They found that more verbalization were produced with same ability pairs than with mixed ability pairs. Putting two low-verbal subjects together produced as much verbal behavior as putting two high-verbal subjects together.

Other aspects of the audience involve the normal stimulus generalization functions. Someone who is similar to a regular audience is likely to select that same repertoire (Skinner, 1957; Spradlin, 1985). This can sometimes be amusing when meeting someone new who strongly "reminds you" of a close friend. You will find yourself talking to the stranger in the ways you talk to your friend, and you have to exercise some control to stop yourself. This is also why in some specific contexts we call someone by the wrong name, because the contexts selects out on the basis of our experiences with the person belonging to the wrong name.

I would like to make two more points about audiences, although there is much more work needed to be done on this topic (see Spradlin, 1985, for some suggestions). The first point is that we can act as our own audiences under some circumstances and edit our own verbal behavior (Hyten & Chase, 1991). Many of the functions of this will be discused in Chapter 8 and a relevant study by Lodhi and Greer (1989) was discussed above. Through childhood we learn to talk to ourselves as if we were another person (or multiple selves, 8.4). We can control our own verbal and nonverbal behavior therefore through our verbal behavior (7.4), although the uses of this still require a verbal community in the first instance: we do not have private languages (Wittgenstein, 1953).

The second point is that sometimes we have multiple audiences which cause a selection problem (cf. Fleming, Darley, Hilton & Kojetin, 1990). The classic case is that of adolescents trying to talk to their parents in front of a group of their peers. Again, the dynamics of this show just how important the underlying social consequences are for verbal behavior. If you are in this situation, you find yourself talking to your parents in a mixture of the two repertoires, while heavily self-editing (Hyten & Chase, 1991; Skinner, 1957). The important point is that the problem comes from having two repertoires which have many different verbal behaviors selected simultaneously. In particular, there are words and phrases spoken with the peer group which have been actively punished by the parents. The editing mostly seems to involve leaving these out.

This is also similar to Freud's examples of intrusive words and phrases, and slips of the tongue. In such cases, multiple contexts have selected different repertoires which produce a mixed output. The real task for the psychoanalyst is that of finding out what layers of context have selected which bits of the utterances, and then finding out why those contexts were functional– why they had been strengthened and who was the audience. It should be no mystery to the reader at this point that Freud found interpersonal and societal variables (permissible sexual relations) to be important in this, given the social nature of verbal behavior which has been stressed here.

7.4. Instructions and Verbally Controlled Behavior

One of the important advances in behavior analysis has been the study of conditions for verbally controlled behavior. This was introduced by Skinner in 1965 at a conference, and was later published in 1966 (and reprinted in 1969; see also Skinner, 1988). It is often called rule-governed behavior, but I prefer to use the less ambiguous term verbally controlled behavior (Vargas, 1988). I think the several meanings of "rule" confuse the former term. Instruction following is a specific case of rule-governed or verbally controlled behavior.

The idea is that human behavior can be shaped either directly by environmental contingencies or by the verbal behavior of yourself or others (Cerutti, 1989; Hayes, 1989b; Riegler & Baer, 1989). For example, I can learn not to touch hot stoves through touching a few and getting burned. In this case the environmental contingencies directly shape my responses. Alternatively, someone might say to me, "Do not touch hot stoves or you will get burned". Under certain conditions, then, I might follow their instructions and learn not to touch hot stoves. I might also, of course, test their instruction out by touching just one stove at some point.

The key point with this work is to find out those conditions under which instructions can control my behavior (for example, Bentall & Lowe, 1987; Catania, Horne & Lowe, 1989; Catania, Matthews & Shimoff, 1982; Galizio, 1979; and Riegler & Baer, 1989). Obviously we do not always follow people's verbal instructions, nor our own. The principal condition goes back to the discussion in 7.1: verbal behavior is a social behavior, so the conditions will mainly depend upon social contingencies and the verbal communities in which we live.

Behavior analysts treat instruction following as no different from any other behavior. Instructions will be followed if they have been strengthened in the past. If I have a history of people crying "Wolf!", I am less likely to follow instructions than someone who has previously followed instructions which have led to reinforcing effects. If someone I do not know well, or someone I do not trust, tells me not to touch a stove because it is hot I am likely to test this out rather than blindly obey them. If they are a member of one of my verbal communities I might trust them even if I do not know them that well because being part of that community means that we mutually reinforce in general (e.g., 10.4).

Zettle and Hayes (1982) have suggested two routes to verbal instructional shaping of behavior. These were illustrated in Figure 6 (Chapter 4). First, pliance occurs when social consequences are most important in controlling behavior. That is, when there are social consequences for which the individual might even disregard the environment. If I hold a gun towards you and instruct you to eat the red lollies because they taste the best, you would likely follow my instructions. What is controlling your behavior is the social condition of the gun, however, not the taste of the red lollies. More specifically, it is the socially mediated consequences of instructions which control the behavior.

Second, Zettle and Hayes use the term tracking for instructions which guide or track you into environmental contingencies. An example would be if I instructed you to try the red lollies and you then found that you did like them and ate them in future. My instructions have *put you onto the track of* an environmental consequence which then proceeds to maintain the future behavior rather than the social consequences of instruction following.

This division between pliance and tracking is very close to the distinction made by Glenn (following Veblen) between technological and ceremonial cultural practices (Ellis, 1991; Glenn, 1985, 1986, 1988; also 6.8). Technological contingencies work because of the direct outcomes, in the same way that tracking works (maintains the behavior or not). Ceremonial contingencies work because of the social control behind the consequences. Glenn's distinction applies to more than just instructions, however, and will be discussed further in Chapter 9.

One other property of instruction following is an insensitivity to environmental contingencies. This only occurs if pliance is the key variable affecting behavior rather than tracking. What has been found is that people who are following verbal instructions will often not tap into environment contingencies which are present. A typical experimental procedure is to give verbal instructions to some of the subjects on a reinforcement schedule, and to then change the schedule later during the sessions. Those who were instructed tend to keep responding as instructed rather than changing to the new schedule.

As Cerutti (1989) has rightly pointed out, this is not a necessary property of instruction following but depends on many other variables. If the instruction following were to turn into tracking then there would be no insensitivity to schedule changes. What is important, then, are the conditions under which pliance turns into tracking.

There is much debate at present over how to refer to, and discuss, instruction following or verbally controlled behavior. Some behavior analysts view this as a new category of behavior, special to humans, while most see it as contingency governed behavior but with special properties. Some believe that instruction following can in principle be distinguished from contingency governed behavior, while others do not (see Brownstein & Shull, 1985; Buskist & DeGrandpre, 1989; Catania, Matthews & Shimoff, 1989).

From the viewpoint developed here, it is clear that instruction following is not a new form of behavior but obeys common principles. The question should be asked, then, of why we bother to use instructions at all; they must have strengthening consequences if we continue to use them. We will first discuss the advantages and then the disadvantages of using instruction following.

Perhaps the biggest advantage of instruction following is, almost paradoxically, the fact that it can lead to insensitivity to environmental contingencies. This is extremely useful in cases of short term punishing situations which lead to longer term strengthening situations, in cases of delayed or remote consequences, and in cases of complex stimulus contexts which produce conflicting actions. In all three cases, we can usefully respond, whereas an animal might not, because we can follow instructions (backed by social consequences) rather than engage the direct environmental contingencies. We could follow self-instructions as well. For example, the environmental contingencies for spending a large amount of time writing a book need to be bridged in some way when I would rather be swimming, going to parties or playing tennis. Verbally governed behavior can regulate this, even though it is also based on contingencies. This is an important property which allows us to extend our horizons beyond animals.

A second advantage of verbally governed behavior is that they can be codified. That is, they can be put into written form. This has all sorts of benefits: it means that we can get pliance without an instructor having to be present to shape the behavior; it means that we can learn to behave in ways which we have never experienced before, and can therefore take advantage of the instructions from those who have spent a lot of time experiencing those contingencies; it means we have an easy way to pass on codified environmental contingencies; and it also means we have a chance to change the codified contingencies.

Science, in this view, is a written form of environmental contingencies (Lee, 1985), and instructions have sometimes been called Contingency-Specifying-Stimuli (Blakely & Schlinger, 1987; Schlinger & Blakely, 1987). It is as if we encapsulate environmental contingencies into writing behaviors, including equations, and these can help with our manipulations of the environment.

For example, someone in the United States might spend much of their time setting up controlled experiences (experiments) with pastry. They find that if they do A then the result is a pastry B; if they do C then they get a yummy pastry D. Through all of this they will be reinforced by the taste and the social approval of others. They will be an expert who "knows their pastries", which means that they have experienced the direct environmental contingencies and have been shaped by the environment. The important point comes when they write their final best pastry recipe down. When this is done, someone even in New Zealand can follow the recipe instructions and produce something close to the original chef's best efforts without ever experiencing all of the trial and error process at first hand, although they might fine tune the process by tracking afterwards when tasting it themselves and making slight changes.

While this is a simple scenario, it is way beyond the bounds of the behavior of animals. We can, in effect, write contingencies down so that others can easily follow instructions and contact those contingencies. This produces behavior far more easily than trying all the contingencies from scratch and continually reinventing the wheel. The power of this is often overlooked because it seems so natural to us. Books in a library contain the encapsulated contingencies experienced by many thousands of people. We do not have to reinvent the wheel every time we do something new.

Consider another example: how to behave in a bushfire. Most people have never been in a bushfire, so if they were put in one they would respond on the basis of similar past contingencies (if the fire is coming from one direction then run the other way quickly). A better way is to find someone who "knows their bushfires"; that is, someone who has experienced first hand the contingencies of bushfires (such as: if the wind blows up in a squall then X will usually happen; bushfires move more quickly uphill). If they can put these contingencies into a written instructional form then many people can benefit from this, but only if there is pliance or tracking to maintain following the instructions. This is one importance of instructions.

There are also disadvantages to following verbal instructions rather than direct environmental contingencies (also see 8.9 on how Zen Buddhism overcomes too much verbally governed behavior). First, as we have seen above, social compliance is usually needed for instruction following. This means that if there are no immediately obvious strengthening effects to following the instructions then people will ignore them. That is, if there is no quick tracking or strong pliance then people will not follow instructions. Having instructions dependent upon a verbal community also lends some bias to the instructions to which we are exposed. Just putting up signs for drivers to follow a speed limit does not work by itself.

Pliance needs supplementary forms of strengthening, many of which are problematic. We can make the social consequences of not being pliant to instructions more and more severe, but this causes other problems of countercontrol (12.7). We can also strengthen generalized instructional pliance in educational institutions, but this leads to producing sheep who blindly follow instructions (Chang, 1991).

These two problems are part of another. If we emphasize pliance too much then people will be insensitive to environmental contingencies. In some cases, perhaps not in bushfires though, it might be more wise for people to follow the environmental contingencies rather than instructions. This again means that research should try to find the conditions which change people from pliance to tracking.

This all leads to one other highly speculative problem which no one seems to have looked at. The problem is that with so much of our society based on verbally mediated behavior control, people may have become generally more insensitive to the environmental contingencies. Many people seem to live at one remove from "real life", and I suspect that a lot of the "back to nature" movement is a reaction to this. Our education thoroughly emphasizes learning of contingency specifying stimuli, simply because there is not the time available to learn everything we need to know through direct experience with the environmental contingencies. Our behavior repertoires are becoming large, but they are all filled with verbally mediated contingencies. Our repertoire learned through direct contact with environmental contingencies may be shrinking. The majority of what we know is verbal.

Moreover, I also believe that this is affecting our social relationships. Because verbal behavior is maintained by generalized social consequences, and because instructional control is verbal control (Vargas, 1988), our social relationships may be becoming dominated by verbal behavior since this is emphasized by our society. Social relationships can involve so much more than talking, but how much of our direct contact with other people is being replaced by talking, intraverbals and instructions?

7.5. Correspondence Between Saying and Doing

The Relations Between Saying and Doing

This section will look at the correspondence between saying something about your own actions, self-instructions or self-regulation, and actually carrying that action out. More will be said on this in 7.6, where we look at self-regulation, in Chapter 10, where we look at consistency between reported attitudes and actions related to those attitudes, and in Chapter 8, where we look at the question of the self and what controls the self.

From what has been said so far in this chapter, it should be clear that there is not a simple contingent relation between saying and doing. It is not that we say something and that "saying" then controls the action that it names. Nor is it so simple that saying has no relationship at all to doing. The question is this: if you say "I am going to go and wash up the dishes in the sink", how, if at all, does this verbal behavior control your actual behavior? It could be that whatever was controlling the imminent washing of dishes also led to your verbal statement; or it could be that different variables altogether led to the washing and to the verbal statement–the two might be unrelated. The fact that we often do not do what we say we will (well, myself at least), must give credence to these two possible cases.

The relations between saying and doing can get more complicated still. Suppose I observe you to wash the dishes three times without saying anything, and then on the fourth time you say "I am going to go and wash up the dishes in the sink". What do I conclude? You would probably report to me that you did the dishes *because* you said you would, but does this mean that the other three times some other variables were present which are now absent? Was the verbal behavior added the last time because more strength was needed to do the dishes? [Or was the verbal behavior making a point (a hidden mand) to me about *my* dish-washing record and had nothing to do with your actions at all?]

The behavior analytic view is that any of these cases might occur, but there is dispute over whether a verbal self-statement can directly control behavior. I think the problem is that we do not yet know enough about multiple contingencies (3.2), so we do not know how multiple control of doing and saying interact and influence each other. This is especially true between verbal and nonverbal behaviors (see Catania & Cerutti, 1986). If we could decide this then we would be able to say whether a verbal response can influence a physical action or whether other variables control them both in parallel.

Training Correspondence

There has been a lot of work done on the direct training of correspondence between saying and doing. It seems to have been first tried experimentally by Lovaas (1964), who reinforced the verbal responses of children which named food items. He found that the foods were eaten more when the verbal behavior was reinforced. The finding seems to be that correspondence between saying and doing can be reinforced.

Since this study there has been controversy over what controls what, and what is going on in this seemingly simple situation (see Baer, Detrich & Weninger, 1988; Catania, Shimoff & Matthews, 1987; Deacon & Konarski, 1987; Guevremont, Osnes & Stokes, 1986, in press; Israel, 1973, 1978; Lloyd, 1980; Matthews, Shimoff & Catania, 1987; Osnes, Guevremont & Stokes, 1987; Paniagua 1985; Paniagua & Baer, 1988; Paniagua, Pumariega & Black, 1988; Ribeiro, 1989; Riegler & Baer, 1989; Stokes, Osnes & Guevremont, 1987). I will discuss just a few of the issues involved.

First, a question which has arisen is whether the procedure of correspondence training merely reinforces the behavior and the verbal part is irrelevant (Rogers-Warren & Baer, 1976). If you reinforce when there is correspondence between saying and doing, you might just be reinforcing a correlation between behaviors and reinforcement. It has proved difficult experimentally to show that the verbal behavior is a *necessary* component.

Second, there is question of whether correspondence is just part of the larger development of self-regulation. Are the children used in these experiments regulating through self-verbalization, so the overt verbalization might be irrelevant? In fact, it is possible that the overt (adult) control of correspondence might interfere with developing self-regulation.

The last question here is that of how best to talk about correspondence. It is not enough just to refer to positive instances between saying and doing, since the instances of not saying/doing are important, as well as saying/not doing and not saying/not doing. Matthews, Shimoff and Catania (1987) call this a contingency space analysis.

The training of correspondence clearly works, although its maintenance has not yet been adequately shown (Guevremont, Osnes & Stokes, in press). As mentioned above, I think the problem here is one of multiple contingencies (3.2). The relation between saying/doing and not saying/doing needs to be related back to the analysis of a whole system of responses, since we have verbal and nonverbal responses as well as their interactions. We just do not know what is going on, and I do not believe we will until the interactions between multiple response classes are better understood. In particular, the relations between verbal behaviors and motor behaviors need more elucidation.

A recent report by Ribeiro (1989) helped broaden the issue by discussing correspondence in terms of self-tacting and self-manding. Likewise, the comprehensive review by Riegler and Baer (1989) put correspondence into the context of the development of many other verbally controlled behaviors and the bigger question of self-regulation.

As a final comment to put correspondence into another broader context, it should be noted that our society is very strict on correspondence, perhaps because it is strict on the development of self-regulation. Children get reinforced for correspondence from the time they learn to control their social environment through speaking. Even as adults, there are strong sanctions against being inconsistent in this regards. A plethora of excuses and attributions (10.1) are needed to help us with correspondence failures beyond our control (verbal or nonverbal control). If I told you "I'll meet you at the pictures at 7pm" and did not show up, there would be strong sanctions unless I could show it was more than mere non-correspondence between my saying and doing.

This all depends upon our verbal community because some cultures do not strengthen correspondence between saying and doing in the way our culture does. Harris (1984, 1987) reports that in north-east Arnhem Land, correspondence is not strict. If the Arnhem Lander promises to meet you the next morning to go fishing and does not turn up, it is not to be taken as rude (non-correspondence). For the Arnhem Lander:

... there need be no direct connection between what he does and what he promises to do. Also from his point of view, it seems very strange behavior to carry out a commitment to a pleasure, if what looked like a pleasure yesterday has turned into a chore today. (Harris, 1987, p. 2)

For six Fridays in ten weeks, Dja___, a man of about fifty, went to considerable trouble to find me and arrange to go and look at his country on the following Saturday. Not once did he turn up, and on following Fridays he showed no embarrassment about having missed the previous arrangement, and no slackening of enthusiasm. The entire initiative had come from him. When I questioned him, the answer was, "I was tired, my boy" with a friendly laugh. "We'll try next week". (Harris, 1984, p. 128)

7.6. Verbal Behavior and Self-regulation

While self behaviors will be dealt with in Chapter 8, some discussion is necessary at this point. Self-regulation does not occur only through verbal behaviors, but such forms are some of the most important in adult humans. We can, for example, regulate our future behavior by tying a string around our finger, but even this is made easier by verbal behavior. Skinner (1953) gives many examples of nonverbal self-regulation.

At the same time, it should be remembered that verbal behavior occurs through special properties of nonverbal behavior, and is not fundamentally different from other behaviors—it does not exist in a nether world of mental representations or cognitions. The main properties are that it can occur without overt signs, and that it can be maintained by generalized social reinforcement rather than specific deprivation. This in turn allows other special properties detailed earlier: it can occur without others being present, for example.

The special feature relating to self-regulation is that verbal behavior seems to help bridge remote contingencies. If we need to remember to put the rubbish out at night we can repeat verbal statements, overtly or covertly, and by keeping this behavior strong we are more likely to "remember". As mentioned, there are other ways of doing this without verbal behavior, especially through utilizing other people to bridge the remote contingencies (see Chapter 6). We can also arrange stimulus conditions to make the behavior more likely; for instance, by putting your bedtime pajamas next to the rubbish bin. But once again it is the special properties of verbal behavior which make this medium the most effective: verbal behavior is fast, it is not directly tied to environmental controls, it has a generalized strengthening from a community of speakers, the behaviors used can be arbitrary and not controlled by other variables, and it does not have to rely on an immediate state of deprivation. All of these features make it a good sort of behavior to utilize for self-regulation.

The relationship between verbal behavior, self-regulation and remote contingencies is shown in Figure 8. Generalized social consequences make verbal behavior possible. Verbal behavior can also be maintained if tracking occurs. Once established, verbal behavior can be used as a means of self-regulating, and this self-

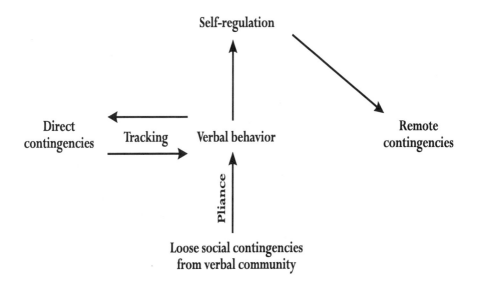

*Figure 8. Pliance and tracking maintain verbal behavior, which can be used by
individuals to contact remote contingencies.*

regulation is useful because it facilitates remote contingencies which could not
otherwise be contacted. Nonhuman animals can contact some of these remote
contingencies (such as building dams) only through long evolutionary changes via
reproductive strategies. We can learn to do many of them in the first ten years of
our lives.

It needs to be kept in mind that the idea of self-regulation is somewhat different
to that of other psychologists, although these other versions could be translated into
behavior analytic terms (Luria, 1961, for example; see Paniagua & Baer, 1988). As
we will see in Chapter 8, most of the psychological notions of self assume an "inner"
determination, and leave the source of this determination up in the air. Behavior
analysts, however, do not take this determination for granted, and look for its control
as well, mainly in a verbal community and a past reinforcement history. Figure 8
shows some of the pathways and variables which determine the inner-determina-
tion.

7.7. Social Compliance and Self-regulation

We have seen through Chapters 4, 5, 6, and 7 that there are complex relations
between self-regulation and social compliance. It is time to bring all these strands
together. The major point so far is that generalized social compliance from taking
part in a verbal community maintains both verbal behavior and a large part of our
social behavior. Verbal behavior, in turn, makes possible and maintains self-
regulation, and one effect of this is to allow contact with remote contingencies and

remote reinforcing effects (Figure 6). We have also seen in Chapter 5 that many of our group behaviors can also facilitate contact with remote contingencies. In particular, the use of social compliance and verbal behavior in groups can greatly facilitate coordination between members of a group and thus improve cooperative group behaviors (see Figure 7 and Emurian, Emurian, & Brady, 1978).

These complex relations between self-regulation and social operants are shown in Figure 9 but without detailing the effects they might have. Given that the use of either self-regulation or social compliance can contact remote contingencies, there can be conflicts between the two.

The first interaction is that group solutions to remote contingencies can be disadvantageous to self-regulation, and can inhibit the development and maintenance of self-regulation. If one has group support for maintaining all the necessary remote contingencies then self-regulation might be unlikely to develop. So there are costs in having groups working together on tasks which could be performed by individuals. For example, if children are raised to always join together on tasks in the interest of harmonious family relations (ritual behaviors to maintain a very useful verbal community), even simple tasks, then this will not be conducive to the development of the children's own self-regulation which might be necessary later in life. Such children will not have the chance to make contact by themselves with remote contingencies and track them for future use. A dark side to dependency occurs here.

On the other side of the coin, the development of self-regulation can undermine the maintenance of generalized social compliance. If most of the remote contingencies in life can be contacted without group cooperation, by using self-regulation, then generalized social compliance will be weakened since the cooperative maintenance of social operants will be redundant. This is shown in Figure 9.

This problem is the one which is most obvious in western countries, because of the emphasis on self-regulation. Once children can begin to achieve remote effects without their family and peers, it is no longer reinforcing to achieve the effects in such a cooperative manner. In some other countries, and some areas of western countries, in which there is a heavy emphasis on generalized social compliance, self-regulation is discouraged as dangerous, since it undermines the social control.

A side-effect of this occurs with helping behaviors. If, as suggested in 6.4, a large part of helping is maintained only by generalized social compliance, then we can expect less helping behavior motivated in this fashion when there is an increase in self-regulation. The self-regulator who is no longer reinforced by the remote contingencies gained through verbal communities will have no "compunction" to help others unless there is a more specific reinforcing effect. People will then need to be explicitly taught about the generalised consequences of helping if they are going to ever contact them. People become more determined by immediate outcomes not mediated by a verbal community (see 9.1), so they will be less likely to help "for the good of the community" (cf. Kitty Genovese: Latané & Darley, 1970).

A second effect can also be predicted for verbal behavior. As people learn to regulate their own verbal behavior, they will be reinforced less for complying with the "traditions" of the verbal community. They will not lose many remote consequences by changing words and sounds for their own specific consequences even though they become less well understood by the larger verbal community. This means that subculture languages will become more prevalent in conditions where self-regulation replaces social compliance as the means of contacting remote contingencies (Hebdige, 1979).

As we will see in Chapter 9, in traditional societies the elders usually had rituals to maintain compliance with the verbal community, so the group could continue to contact the remote contingencies only obtainable through social compliance. With the development of better self-regulation, as the young were educated in missionary and government schools, most remote contingencies could be contacted without the elders and the ritually maintained group support (see Achebe, 1988, for a realistic account of this). While increased self-regulation seems a good idea to us,

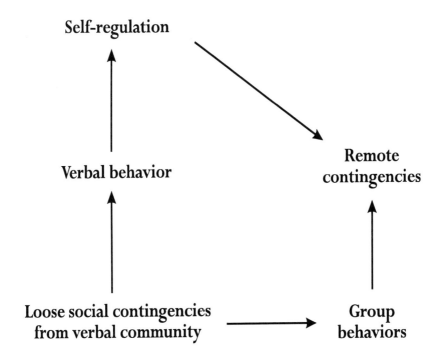

Figure 9. Conflict between self-regulation and social compliance when both can contact remote contingencies. Either group behavior weakens for self-regulating individuals or the group attempts to control self-regulation.

it has meant that some other important regulatory functions (remote contingencies) of social compliance have been lost.

The development of self-regulation is also encouraged by the verbal community use of money. Younger people in western countries can earn as much, if not more, money than their elders and so gain all the objects and effects necessary to run their lives without any help from a group. Money therefore encourages independence from groups (Simmel, 1978/1900, p. 342) and promotes impersonal relations between people (Simmel, 1978/1900, p. 297). 9.3 has more on this.

There is a tradeoff, then, between self-regulation and social compliance. To the extent that they are maintained by the same remote consequences they will undermine each other. To groups controlled by social compliance, self-regulation will seem either not worthwhile or else a threat. To groups who function individually through self-regulation, social compliance will seem a waste of time with no benefit and a threat to self.

The difficulty with these effects is that both the loss of self-regulation and the loss of social compliance will only be felt gradually and over a long period, since it is the remote consequences which are no longer contacted. What is in most danger of being lost are those behaviors for which social compliance is always necessary for maintenance. Helping and verbal behavior have been suggested as two of these. Helping, for example, is really only tenable through generalized social compliance, since so few episodes of helping have remote reinforcers which could reinforce self-regulation apart from group maintenance. Altruistic type helping will not occur with weak or absent verbal communities.

7.8. Other Linguistic Verbal Behaviors

Many other aspects of verbal behavior been pursued by behavior analysts, both experimentally and conceptually (see Hayes & Chase, 1991; Hayes & Hayes, 1992b). Some other topics, including sociolinguistics and verbal behaviors other than linguistic, will be dealt with in the next chapters. The interested reader is recommended the following as a selection of other topics about linguistic verbal behaviors: maladaptive verbal behavior (Alford, 1986; Burns, Heiby & Tharp, 1983; Glenn, 1983; Layng & Andronis, 1984); descriptive analyses of verbal interactions (Bijou, Umbreit, Ghezzi & Chao, 1986; Parrott, 1985, 1986b); language use with autistic children (Secan, Egel & Tilley, 1989; Yamamoto & Mochizuki, 1988); logic and reasoning (Terrell & Johnston, 1989); grammar (Catania, 1972; Schoenfeld, 1969; Zuriff, 1976), and spelling (Lee & Pegler, 1982; Lee & Sanderson, 1987), and content analysis (Lee et al., 1989).

Chapter 8

Social Cognition and Behavior Analysis

8.1 Cognitive Psychology and Behavior Analysis

Background to Cognition

In the 1950s there was a radical change in the dominant psychology. Hullian behaviorism had been predominant in psychology for many years, and it had several strong claims which were imposed. First, the original idea of some behaviorisms had been to eschew talking about events which could not be seen. At the time, this seemed a useful advance on the very loose form of introspection that was taking place. Following from the last chapter, just getting people to talk about what they see and feel tells us more about their verbal community than it does about how people function. In fact, introspection is probably a good way of finding out about verbal community practices (e.g., Herzlich, 1973), as long as one does not believe that people are verbalizing the true causes of their behavior.

The second claim of Hullian behaviorism was a strong Stimulus-Response basis, which was also a great advance from its predecessors. It led to a very mechanistic view of the world, however (Morris, 1993, in press), and each link in a Stimulus-Response chain had to be observable and measurable. The idea was sensible for the time because Sherrington had published his basic axioms of neural stimulus-response reflexes and Pavlov had shown how reflexes could be extended to non-reflex behaviors. Thus it seemed reasonable at the time that a complex version of this extension from reflexes to new behaviors could build up complex human behavior (cf. Iversen, 1992).

This scheme held good for a number of years, but in the 1950s, more and more intervening variables which were not observable became part of the Hull-Spence system (Hull, 1943; Spence, 1956). Most psychologists became impatient to use hypothetical models of such unobservable events, especially when this strategy had proved so useful in physics and chemistry, and since so much interesting human behavior seemed private. So was born the "Cognitive Revolution" (Miller, Galanter & Pribram, 1960). [As we have seen, the behavior is not actually "private" but social in origin: the contingencies are not obvious therefore they seems private.]

The arguments ushering in the study of cognition were varied: there was no single strand of thought. In part, the new study of cognition was merely formalizing the use of hypothetical, unobservable, intervening variables, and Spence himself saw that this was not really different from the Hullian systems (Spence, 1960). Miller, Galanter and Pribram (1960), for example, hypothesized a TOTE unit, which could be conceptually placed as a building block for the unseen mental processes. An organism had goals which were occasionally tested (T) against the current state of the organism and the organism then operated (O) in some fashion to meet the goal, this was tested (T) again and the operation stopped or exited (E) if the goal was met (cf. Carver & Scheier, 1981).

A second part to the cognitive revolution was the introduction of information theory ideas. Stimuli were reconceptualized as "having" information which organisms picked up, processed and remembered. The basic phenomenon was that our worlds do not correspond to the real world. This was also the building block to the introduction of "representations" ("images" in the original, Miller, Galanter & Pribram, 1960). The information picked up from the world (re-processed) was stored as a representation of the world, and it no longer matched the real world. The representations must therefore be stored as memories or images, retrieved when required, and further re-processed when necessary. Cognitive psychology therefore required elaboration upon the organization of such storage and retrieval.

Third, artificial intelligence and cybernetics had got to the point where there were plausible mechanisms which could act **as if** goal seeking but which were programmed instead with plans for action. The computer analogy also emphasized an orderly process of taking in information (like typing at a keyboard) which is transformed and taken into a processing environment (the CPU), further transformed based on the organization of previous storages of transformed information, and finally further storage (RAM) or output (screen activity). By transforming keystrokes into some other form (digital signals) which could be serially stored and changed, the computer revolution had been extremely successful, especially when the serial changes had been speeded up to present day standards. This was therefore a sensible analogy, but only an analogy, to use for the extremely complex and difficult arena of human behavior.

Finally, Miller, Galanter and Pribram (1960) emphasized "plans" in the structuring of behavior. They argued correctly that behavior is poorly dealt with by only trying to specify the immediately preceding behavior or stimulus in order to explain it. They provided examples of the role of planning:

Mrs. Jones *has* a recurrent Plan for keeping her house running that she *revises* and *executes* daily. She also *has* a nonrecurrent Plan to visit her sister in Baltimore. And she is *collaborating* in a shared Plan to get her neighbor elected sheriff. With all of these Plans (and more) *running* at one time, her problem is to *perform* those acts that simultaneously advance the greatest number of them. Thus, Mrs. Jones may *decide* to drive to town, *get* her hair done before she leaves to see her sister, pick up the election posters at the print shop, and buy the week's groceries. One trip to town serves to advance three Plans at once. (Miller, Galanter & Pribram, 1960, p. 95, italics mine)

This emphasizes the active nature put onto the information processor; Mrs Jones does a lot of having and deciding and revising. Whereas previous attempts along these lines before Hull had fallen into the trap of pre-supposing a little homunculus in the head who could do all the deciding and revising, the computer and cybernetic analogies made a self-regulating system without an homunculus more plausible.

Modern cognitive psychology usually works within a group of broad areas, which each have their own phenomena they deal with. This is important to remember, because the phenomena studied must be dealt with by whatever system of psychology is current. Behavior analysis must be able to explain and experiment with the cognitive phenomena if it intends changing the cognitive metaphors. Gone are the days of early behaviorism when you could just claim that such phenomena did not exist or that the details were not important. Increasingly, though, behavior analysts are attempting to work with the phenomena which cognitive psychologists have been working on (White, McCarthy & Fantino, 1989), but without using the cognitive metaphors outlined above.

The broad areas of cognitive psychology are attention, perception, working memory (processing/ short term memory/ thinking), long term memory, and psycholinguistics. The broad picture of cognition is that organisms attend to stimuli and events, and the changes are put into another form which preserves information contained in the stimuli. The form of the information is digital in the computer, but is left unspecified (Anderson, 1978) for humans. The attention processes can be determined by the stimulus or be guided by past experience (schema-driven). The point at which it becomes guided is unclear, some arguing that stimuli are coded early on in attention and others that a relatively "raw" source of information is only coded later.

The working memory or main processing proceeds to handle the information which has been attended and coded. The goals of this processing are not clear, but this probably reflects the variety of uses humans have for what they see. Some people might see an apple and eat, some might see and apple and throw it, whereas still others might want to give it to a doctor. The "workings" of the working memory have been specific to the area being studied. Cognitive psychologists have mostly looked at accuracy and speed of recognition, labelling with names, and the effects of different ways of processing on later recall. When dealing with, for example, reading words and making up rhymes, it is assumed that the stimuli will be recognized and this part of the cognitive process is not studied.

The major impetus to all this work has been to show the effects of previous storage on current usage. If I talk to you about nurses and doctors and then present you with some words and nonsense words, you will be quicker to recognize that "hospital" is a word than "cat". The previous experience has had an effect on the way in which current stimuli are processed—in this case, semantically related words are recognized quicker. Or in another case, Ostrom, Lingle, Pryor and Geva (1980) had subjects predict whether a person would suit a particular occupation on the basis of traits describing them. It was later found that subjects recalled more of the traits which were relevant to the occupation. Another experiment also suggested that the occupation name changed the encoding process to facilitate later recall of those items. Thus processing and organization of memory is based on the task goals or verbal labels.

There has also been a lot of research on processing representations of stimuli which are not present. This comes in the areas of recall speed and accuracy, imagery, and solving problems with remembered stimuli. For example, if I ask you to say whatever words come to mind, why are the words usually thematically related? Can you imagine what a giraffe would look like turned on its head?—what angle would its neck form with respect to an upright tree? Each of these problems asks you to process stimuli without the stimuli being present. Because we can do such tasks, they are taken as evidence that we have representations of giraffe in our heads which we can process in the absence of the real thing.

Behavior Analysis and the Cognitive Phenomena

With such a large literature on cognition it is a daunting task for behavior analysts to try and approach the area. It is no wonder that many have decided to ignore or reject the approach and work independently on the same phenomena. The entire range of phenomena cannot be dealt with here, but I wish to suggest a few guiding principles which might help both behavior analysts and cognitive psychologists to see the others' way of talking about what people do (Schlinger, 1992; Skinner, 1985).

My first guiding principle is to try and separate those cognitive phenomena which are based on verbal behavior and those which are not. This is a great source of confusion within cognitive psychology of which cognitive psychologists do not seem aware. As we saw in Chapter 7, the contingency bases of verbal and nonverbal behavior are very different, and so we should not lump them together and assume the processes are the same. For example, the study outlined above by Ostrom et al. (1980) was based on learning verbal labels and involved a history of verbal community practices, whereas the effects of recognizing objects around us might not. Coming up with *labels* for objects around us (tacting) is certainly a verbal behavior though. Indeed, my observation is that much of the cognitive literature is built around verbal phenomena to do with how we build up a repertoire of names, how we apply the names to new objects, and how tacting can help us remember, attend, and search (verbally governed behavior). Behavior analysis can already suggest from this much that social sources of control will be involved in such verbal behaviors. We will look further at verbal/nonverbal difference when considering unconscious and automatic processing below.

The second guiding principle is that for behavior analysts, there is a different way of talking about the effects of past experience on current behavior. Rather than talk about taking in information and storing it for later use, behavior analysts work on a model that the organism is changed when it remembers. *There is not a constant processing environment which processes changing and changeable information, but the organism just behaves and this experience changes the organism. The change is the remembering.* This might seem a minor translation of metaphors but the implications for talking about psychology are immense .

Consider an analogy of a spherical ball of putty or plasticine. Suppose we hit it (mildly) with a hammer. It will retain an indent of the head of the hammer. In the sense of behavior analysis the plasticine has remembered the hammer-hit because the organism was changed: it is not the same spherical ball that it was. Suppose we now have a new spherical ball of plasticine plus the old bent one. We strike them both with a knife. The two balls are different in shape and will therefore behave differently. First, the original plasticine ball might have a deeper cut from the knife because of its past history with the hammer. Second, the behavior of the two balls might be different (perhaps only marginally in this example). For example, the original ball of plasticine might hold more liquid if it some poured into the hammer marks and cuts. They might also roll with a different movement if released on an incline—or perhaps the original ball of plasticine might not roll at all.

The point of this is that experience is said to have an effect by changing the organism, not by the organism storing information about the experience and retrieving it later while maintaining an unchanging processing environment. The latter could be used for a computer simulation of hitting plasticine, as a metaphor, but it is not what happens with real organisms. It might be said that this is fine for an inanimate, passive object like a ball of plasticine, but what about moving organisms? The answer is that it is even more important in such cases, because the number and amount of changes will be increased and the possibilities of interacting changes will also be increased.

To put this into a behaviorally better computer model, as we input information into the computer the keyboard must be changed to reflect the experience of inputting and the keyboard would therefore behave differently the next time we input data. To repeat, *there is no unchanging processing environment in organisms.* The changes in the "processing environment" **are** the remembering. (also see Branch, 1977; Palmer, 1991; Schlinger, 1992).

One implication of this change of metaphor is that responding becomes an inseparable part of learning, because it is part of the contingencies. This applies not just the observable motor responses but also the events occurring inside the eyes and brain. When organisms learn they are changed for the future; it is not just that some representation gets changed while the processing structure remains constant. This emphasis on overt and covert responding and how it is changed by experience is also reflected in the paucity of data and reasoning about responses within the cognitive psychology literature. The history and experience of the organism becomes mapped into a store of representations and so the motor responses emitted are taken to be a trivial later function of these. For the behavior analyst, however, the history of the organism is the very stuff of remembering, attention and "memory organization".

What all this means is that when talking about schema, concepts and memories, cognitive psychologists are nominalizing the changes which have occurred to the organism from a previous history of interacting with the environment. We clearly do not have a brain and spinal cord full of plasticine, but the events taking place within these parts of the body are many and varied. The changes from any particular event of the organism and the environment are also probably distributed through different parts of the nervous system and not localized in a memory storage area of the brain.

Skinner used another analogy to help demystify these notions. He likened the effects of experience on the history of the organism to a car battery (he probably took it from Bentley, 1941, p. 16). When charging a battery we do not put electricity into the battery in the sense of passing electrons through an unchanging environment (the anodes and cathodes) to a storage area for stacking-up electrons. Rather, what we do is to change the battery itself so that it behaves differently the next time we use it. The battery which has been charged has a new history, is a different battery, and behaves differently when used.

Having said all of this, it must be said further that behavior analysts are no better off in knowing what exactly this "changing the organism" means physiologically than cognitive psychologists are about the basis of the mental representations. The advantages though are ones of logical consistency with natural science, keeping an event-based model instead of a thing-based model, allowing a reasonable distributed processing basis, and still allowing all the cognitive phenomena to be dealt with.

Using the first two guiding principles, mental representations are dealt with in a few ways by behavior analysts. First, the term representation is sometimes used as a substitute for behavior—the organism is just behaving in some fashion, usually covertly. Having an image is behaving covertly in some way, and there will be contingencies for which this occurs. Second, representations sometime mean that the organism has been changed. If I have a representation stored of something I have learned, this only means that I have been changed by those original events and I will behave differently because of this.

A third guiding principle to help digest both behavior analysis and cognitive psychology concerns the time-frame for the events being talked about. Cognitive psychology has the organism on a temporal scheme of taking in information, processing it, and responding or storing the information. The processing might also be a bit quicker if there is a history of responding.

For the behavior analyst this temporal scheme is mistaken. The "processing" was done when the organism was changed by the previous events, and it does not have to be dragged out as a representation when it confronted by new events. This is why responding can be so quick, because immediately after a change has occurred the organism will respond in the new way, it does not take further retrieval and processing time to carry this out. To go back to our analogy, when put on an incline for the first time, the plasticine ex-spherical ball does not have to start processing the old information about the hammer-hit and the knife-slash, reconstruct this as a representation of the dents in it, decide how to roll, and then proceed to do it. As soon as it has interacted with the hammer and knife it will behave differently if put on an incline. Likewise the battery does not have to wait to give out electricity after being charged; it is ready to be used immediately.

Let us now consider all the guiding principles so far discussed, and use them to "translate" a modern quote from cognitive psychology into a form amenable to behavior analysis while still preserving the essential phenomena being talked about. Consider the following:

> Concepts are stored in the brain in the form of "dormant" records. When these records are reactivated, they can re-create the varied sensations and actions associated with a particular entity or a category of entities. A coffee cup, for example, can evoke visual and tactile representations of its shape, color, texture and warmth, along with the smell and taste of the coffee or the path that the hand and the arm take to bring the cup from the table to the lips. All these representations are re-created in separate brain regions, but their reconstruction occurs fairly simultaneously. (Damasio & Damasio, 1992, p. 70).

First, the "dormant" records are really changes in the organism. This is like calling the hammer marks in our plasticine a dormant record; fine for a metaphor but it mis-represents how things are. Second, the example is partly talking about responding to the word "cup" and the verbal responses to do with coffee, and partly the "perceiving" of (nonverbal, real) coffee cups. One can respond to coffee cups without noticing all the events mentioned in the quote (color, texture, warmth), so the question arises of what contingencies must be present if we *do* re-create all these sensations and arm movements. It is likely that extra social/verbal contingencies are involved when we re-create sensations as described in the quote because we normally handle coffee cups without all this occurring. Finally, the covert behaviors occasioned by the coffee cup might well be distributed throughout the brain: there is no reason why they should not be. In fact, the idea of having all the coffee cup behaviors together somewhere in the brain is rather strange.

We have now seen how the major metaphors are dealt with in behavior analysis. I wish to discuss, before moving on to particular areas of social cognitive psychology, some of the commonly used terms and how we might better talk about them. Some major terms have already been dealt with. "Attending", "imaging" and "information", for example, were also covered in 2.1.

Another common idea is that of single channel processing. The idea is that we can only process one event at a time, or that there are limits on processing. We cannot look at a large scene and take it all in immediately, for instance. This usage is ambiguous, though, for behavior analysts. First, there can be multiple sources of control, as we saw in 3.2. I can do several things at the same time, especially if some are covert. So single channel processing might refer to one of two other ideas. First, it could mean that usually only a single response can be carried out at one time. I cannot tap in a 7/8 rhythm with one finger and 3/4 in another. This however, is an artifact of learning history: I have known people who had learned to do just this with a lot of practice, although cognitive psychologists might claim that the two have now formed a single unit which can be processed simultaneously.

The second idea that single channel processing might mean is that verbal behavior is being talked about and only one stream of verbal behavior can occur at once, whether covert or overt. This is important because it tells us something about verbal behavior even though it changes the original idea about the single channel hypothesis. Verbal behavior can be utilized for many behaviors, and is especially useful to specify multiple contingencies and to extend control over time. It is easier to remember "dog" over a time period than it is to remember all the features of a dog and how to respond appropriately. The cost is that responding later on the basis of "dog" is imprecise.

This point means that a lot of cognitive experiments are really about using verbal behavior to substitute for other behaviors. Prototypes are probably a reference to verbal behaviors reinforced by my verbal community when put together; my idea or concept of a dog is based around "dog" and the related perceptual and verbal behaviors. If words or verbal rules are controlling behavior then all the same effects as occur for prototypes, schema and concepts are found (generalization, etc.). So the equivalent of single channel processing is verbally governed behavior.

There are many other areas of cognitive psychology which arise because verbal behavior has different contingencies than nonverbal behavior. Several areas of research, for example, detail how there are two ways or modes (Hayes & Broadbent, 1988) of learning to do tasks. Task performance can be controlled by verbal behavior, in which case they are said to be carried out with "conscious representation", "knowing that", "explicit knowledge", "verbalizable knowledge", "articulation", "mindfulness", "explicit mode", "conscious cognition", or "conscious abstraction" (Berry & Broadbent, 1988; Broadbent, FitzGerald & Broadbent, 1986; Dulany, 1991; Greenwald, 1992; Perruchet, Gallego & Savy, 1990; Reber, Kassin, Lewis & Cantor, 1980; Sanderson, 1989; Street, 1987, 1988). If they are controlled in nonverbal contingencies (Part 1 of this book) then they are said to be carried out with "nonconscious acquisition of information", "unconscious abstraction", "unconscious cognition", "mindlessness" "knowing how", "implicit mode", "implicit knowledge", "unconscious acquisition" (Berry & Broadbent, 1988; Broadbent, FitzGerald & Broadbent, 1986; Cohen & Squire, 1980; Greenwald, 1992; Lewicki, 1986; Lewicki, Hill, & Czyzewska, 1992; Perruchet, Gallego & Savy, 1990; Reber, Kassin, Lewis & Cantor, 1980).

These distinctions were covered in 7.4 when discussing verbally governed behavior. In each case tasks can be controlled by verbally specified contingencies but only if the person has a history of social reinforcement which includes such verbal behavior. I can teach you an algorithm to follow when solving problems, but there still needs to be social contingencies to follow my instructions or quick tracking of the consequences of problem solving which maintain algorithm following.

The examples are difficult, however, because I can act as if I am following a verbal rule if the environment has the rule structured into it, as it were. For example, I can catch Frisbees from having learned and practiced to catch them. I could also catch it (perhaps!) by verbally working out the trajectory and speed and verbally knowing the place to stand in order to catch it. Part of the work discussed in 7.4 was aimed at developing experimental methods to tell these two "modes" apart.

The work of cognitive science is most impressive in developing models which mathematically specify the contingencies involved in human tasks. This does not mean, however, that humans must know (verbally) those rules of the environment in order to do them, just as a dog does not need to know the computer algorithms on a spaceship which track a trajectory in order to catch a Frisbee moving in the same trajectory. Such verbal rules are required for computer programming, but a different process of shaping takes place with humans (Palmer & Donahoe, 1992).

The place of verbal behavior is interesting in this regard. As shown in 7.4, we can learn a behavior through shaping (controlled by the environment) or through following verbal rules (controlled by social contingencies). But the learning of verbal behavior itself is not learned through following rules. For example, we learn to behave in accordance with the rules of grammar long before we can verbally specify those rules and explicitly follow them. Most people I know can correctly use plural forms of verbs but cannot tell me what rule they are following. [Hint: many cats run but one cat runs.]

This mixed heritage of verbal behavior comes through, surprisingly enough, in the modern idea of an unconscious (Bowie, 1979; Greenwald, 1992; Lacan, 1977; Moscovici, 1993). The unconscious has been used sometimes to refer to behavior which we cannot verbally specify: for example, I can play a series of notes on the piano without "consciously" (verbally) thinking about each of them. More importantly, the unconscious has been used to refer to our verbal behavior about the world, the social construction of knowledge. In this regard, then, Lacan (1977) writes that *the unconscious is the structure of language.* That is, our most important unconscious behaviors are the verbal behaviors which we use to specify the contingencies of the world but which are not themselves verbally specifiable to us. This is also probably the meaning of a current cognitive psychology term, the "cognitive unconscious" (Greenwald, 1992).

Of importance from this is that most of the writers on this topic acknowledge the social basis of this sort of unconscious (Lacan, 1977; Moscovici, 1993). Moscovici, for example, writes that after considering the emphasis on conscious processes and cognitive orientations:

And yet I knew that, in the life of societies, as was observed by Mauss and Lévi-Strauss, relationships, beliefs, or institutions are seldom created deliberately and reflexively. That is to say, shared motivations and significations, just as the representations rooted in a language or culture, because they are the work of a collectivity, cannot be entirely conscious. (Moscovici, 1993, p. 40)

What this means, and what it means for behavior analysis, is that our behaviors are shaped by either the physical or social environment. Behaviors shaped by the physical environment are called "unconscious" but are often not discussed by psychologists or psychoanalysts as part of the unconscious. Verbal behaviors which control behavior (7.4) are considered to be the "conscious" behaviors but as Lacan points out, we do not consciously produce or control them. That is, (unconscious?) social contingencies shape the verbally governed behaviors which are considered conscious. Finally, the most important unconscious behaviors are those which have been shaped by social contingencies rather than the physical environment, and so some psychologists and psychoanalysts talk about the unconscious as being social in origin.

Chunking (Simon, 1979) is another example of a covert behavior which can be both verbally and nonverbally controlled. Chunking can occur first when a single utterance of verbal behavior controls a lot of nonverbal behavior. For example, if I say "Please make me a sandwich", and the social contingencies are strong and there is a past contingency history, then a lot behavior might follow from this simple sentence. You do not have to remember (respond appropriately to) the entire sequence explicitly, verbally, or consciously, but just the words "make a sandwich" (see Skinner, 1957, Chapter 9).

On the other hand, chunking sometimes refers to nonverbal scheduling of multiple behaviors (Findley, 1962). An example was given in Chapter 3 of work by Findley with a monkey called Smokey, who could carry out large "chunks" of behavior with little reinforcement because careful trees and options were built into the scheduling. Similarly, I can look at a very complex chess board pattern and say "The Pillsbury attack" and later reproduce the pattern of pieces fairly reliably. This occurs only because of the history of social reinforcement of the organism.

Another verbal phenomena in cognitive psychology is that of anchoring and adjustment. Tversky & Kahneman (1974) suggested that in situations of uncertainty (no verbal rules learned or no prior history) there is a cognitive strategy of anchoring your judgment at some point and adjusting from there based on stimulus discrimination. For example, if asked to guess quickly the answer to 20 X 30 X 40 X 50 X 60 X 70, people give lower estimates than for 70 X 60 X 50 X 40 X 30 X 20. The phenomenon seems to be one of anchoring on a higher initial value in the second case and making smaller adjustments.

Many of these cases of anchoring and adjustment seem to involve an initial verbal behavior (the anchor), followed by some inaccurate verbal or nonverbal adjustment of the value (Block & Harper, 1991; Cervone & Peake, 1986; Davis, Hoch & Ragsdale, 1986; Einhorn & Hogarth, 1985; Kahneman, 1982; Northcraft & Neale, 1987; Plous, 1989; Switzer & Sniezek, 1991). They are found in situations of uncertainty, which means by definition that there is weak control from the physical stimuli involved. In the case given above, for example, the long multiplication stimuli do not control our behavior (unless you have really learned your long multiplication tables very thoroughly). The utilization of verbal behavior to perform such tasks and come up with a rough, heuristic answer has presumably been reinforced for most of us because we rarely get verbal feedback to say that we are wrong.

8.2. Some Private Events

Behaviorism has a very special way of dealing with hidden events occurring within the skin (Bentley, 1941; Day, 1976; Hayes & Brownstein, 1987; Moore, 1980, 1984; Skinner, 1974; Zuriff, 1979). Unlike some of the early behaviorisms, and methodological behaviorism, such private events as they are called are considered real and ever present. Feelings and thinking are not denied, merely talked about differently. The first point to make is a distinction between verbal behaviors and non-verbal events occurring privately in the body (unobservable to anyone else). What happens during pain and how you talk about pain to either yourself or someone else are two different events. Both are real but have different sources of control: they are reinforced in different ways and under different stimulus conditions.

We saw in Chapter 2 that "seeing" can mean different things. Consider driving through the countryside for a number of miles. When you reach your destination someone asks you whether you drove through the town of Huntly. In one sense of "seeing" you did not see Huntly, because you cannot actually remember anything about driving through the town, although you know you must have because there is no alternative route and you planned to come that way. But in another sense of "seeing" you must have seen the road, the traffic lights, the cars in front, etc., as you went through Huntly otherwise you would have had a very nasty car accident. So you both saw Huntly and did not see Huntly.

What is going on here, of course, is that the first sense of "seeing" means that you did not verbally comment to yourself or someone else as you went through Huntly so you cannot remember verbal reports of seeing Huntly. But the contingencies of driving through Huntly were contacted (automatic processing, in cognitive psychology terms) but without verbal comment (without awareness).

This form of reasoning will hopefully be familiar at this stage of the book. The trick with private events is that the same form of reasoning is applied to events going on within the body with no difference just because of their unobservability. When I cut myself there are various behaviors which form the contingencies: that is, I behave differently, and have learned to behave differently, when I am cut. Under some conditions, very special ones such as an emergency or hypnosis, I might not even behave differently when cut. At the same time as this is going on, I might or might not comment to myself about the cut and my different behavior. The verbal behavior also forms part of what we call pain but has different controlling variables, in particular, there are social variables for whether or not I comment to myself or out loud when I am "in pain", and the terms I use are learned from a verbal community.

So the trick to thinking about private events is to treat them as if the event was taking place outside the body but no one else could see it. The same principles as for all other behavior then apply equally.

Anticipation

While anticipation is used frequently in everyday accounts of behavior, it is by no means a simple event. In fact, I will argue there are at least two different meanings of anticipation, although both can be reduced to behavior analytic terms.

The first meaning of "anticipation" is the one that Skinner most frequently used as a translation. This is that anticipating something is behaving in ways that have been strengthened in the past. So on a VI 30secs schedule of reinforcement we might comment that it looks as if the rat is pressing because it is anticipating the reinforcement after about 30 seconds. As Skinner and others have rightly pointed out, the future cannot *cause* the present so a future event cannot determine the rat's bar pressing. This is equivalent to saying that giraffe evolved long necks *in order to* get food at the tops of trees. Instead, the rats are behaving in ways that were reinforced (shaped or selected) in the past.

While this is a correct and proper answer in most cases, there are human situations in which I think we mean more than just this by the word anticipation. These are cases where I *predict verbally* what will happen and call this an anticipation. I anticipate that if I do X then Y will occur and that if Y occurs then Z will certainly follow. These cases are still controlled by the present and the past rather than the future, but it is verbal behavior which is involved. The anticipations do not control behavior in any sense but are merely pseudo-tacts about the future.

I think that most cases of anticipation fall into this pattern. The only other type is where the anticipation is a self-instruction which is then followed prior to the time of the prediction, such as: "I anticipate that I will do X when I get home". In these cases the verbal behavior might control behavior (if suitably strengthened), but the pseudo-tact about the future itself does not control behavior, it is actually controlled by whatever source made the person make such a remark in the first place.

So in both senses of "anticipation" the controlling variables are past or present contingencies, and no new principles of behavior need be invoked.

Intention

Intention has been covered in many places in this book. To summarize briefly, Skinner used the Darwinian way of thinking to overcome the problems of having intention (2.2). Organisms behave (overtly and covertly) and these behaviors are sometimes selected by the environment (reinforced) and become more probable in the future.

Intention therefore has two meanings. One meaning is that organisms look as if they intend to do things because the behavior has been reinforced in the past. So a cat might paw and open the door of a cupboard seemingly **in order to** get at the food therein. Past reinforcement, however, explains this without recourse to intention. The other meaning of intention is that we produce verbal behavior which specifies what we are going to do: "I intend going to the shops now". This, however, depends on other contingencies which maintain the verbal behavior rather than the action of going to the shop, and might or might not correspond to what I then do (7.5; Lloyd, 1980). The two sets of contingencies are separate and there is no necessary connection.

8.3. Thinking

In many ways we have already dealt with thinking in this book. For behavior analysts, thinking is behavior like any other, although some of it cannot be observed in bodily movements. In this sense, we have covered thinking in discussion of stimulus contexts (especially 2.1), response classes (2.2), consequences (2.3), multiple contingencies (3.2), and most of all with verbal behavior and its ramifications (especially 7.4, and the present chapter). These discussions covered many of the ordinary uses of the word "thinking" (see Skinner, 1974). Thinking often just means behaving with respect to someone or some thing, but it can also entail verbal behavior with the speaker as the audience; "talking to oneself" about events. Insofar as thinking is used for solving problems, it is an example of verbally controlled behavior (7.4): "I thought about it before I acted".

What is going on, then, is something not very well understood yet. There are multiple contingencies occurring, including ones purely within the person. Out of this, physically observable behavior occurs in patterns. To this situation we often comment that we are thinking about things, even if there is no verbal behavior occurring. In this sense Skinner (1974) writes of thinking as "behaving weakly".

Thinking, then, is just seen as an extension of other behaviors which appear out of multiple contingencies, in contrast to cognitive models which make them independent processes having dubious relations with other behaviors (the automatic processes). What cognitive psychologists mean by thinking in this sense is probably the distinction we have made between direct contingencies and verbally governed behaviors. Their models do give the impression, however, that most human behavior could not occur without us thinking about it first. We have discussed in 7.4 the basis for this; that verbally controlled behavior arises from direct contingencies in the long run anyway.

The use of verbally controlled behavior is particularly important in logic and reasoning (Skinner 1957; Terrel & Johnston, 1989), but a distinction has to be made between behavior which is patterned and behavior which is controlled by a verbal rule (cf. rule-characterized and rule-governed, in Terrel and Johnston, 1989). Animals can forage in patterns which are analyzed into a few simple decision rules (see Commons, Kacelnik & Shettleworth, 1987) but this does not mean that they *followed* these rules: that the rules controlled their behavior.

As pointed out by many behavior analysts (see Skinner 1957; Terrel & Johnston, 1989), we can act in accordance with grammatical rules or probabilistic analyses of chess moves, but this does not mean these rules are functional, especially as verbalized rules. We act according to rules because we are tracking environmental consistencies or because they are strengthened by a verbal community (although these usually track the environment if they survive for long enough). That is, the probabilities of chess moves are in the environment rather than rules in our verbal behavior, and it is this way that we come to act in patterned ways.

Of course, we can have our behavior verbally governed, as when we study a book of chess moves very closely and use this (make them functional) while playing chess. But this is merely a behavioral extension of reading the book as we are playing, which is usually not allowed and would take too long to be useful. We make the responses of reading the book so strong that we can behave in that way without the book in front of us. Under these circumstances it is as if we can read the book in our heads while the chess game is going on: "She has put her bishop in front of the pawn. When that happens the book said I would be in danger of a blocking move..."

So the proper study of "thinking processes" is in the role of verbal behavior in governing other behaviors, such as making deductions, chess and decision making. I believe the cognitive psychologists have been misled by not distinguishing either between behavior governed by direct contingencies and verbally controlled behavior, or between pliance and tracking within the latter. The area is important, and their models can help behavior analysts get started in this area (cf. Johnson-Laird, 1983), but these distinctions need to be thrashed out properly beforehand.

8.4. Self-events

It is usually the case that discussions of self-events come early in books (exceptions are Keller & Schoenfeld, 1950; Skinner, 1953). Once the basics of the self-events are outlined, social behavior is then covered. This follows the traditional social psychological view that social behavior is built from individual self behavior. With the behavior analytic view presented in this book, however, self-events are seen as secondary to social events. Or rather, self-events are specialized social events.

The view is that self-processes are derivatives of generalized social contingencies such as verbal behavior and gesturing and are learned through a verbal community. They are not a personal, inner secret store of veridical experiences. This view, or something close to it, is shared by others outside of behavior analysis (Bem, 1965; Berger & Luckmann, 1967; Michel Foucault, 1988; Jacques Lacan, see Bowie, 1979; Mead, 1924/1925, 1934, see Miyamoto & Dornbusch, 1956; Sampson, 1985; and Wittgenstein, 1953, see also Day, 1969).

While this point of view seems strange to Western culture, it is worth pursuing. At first it seems as if all the precious aspects of self are being adulterated, but this is not the case. The phenomena are merely being talked about differently.

What is the "Self"?

The main problem of the self for psychology is that it is not self-explanatory and has many meanings (Pratkanis & Greenwald, 1985). Saying that so-and-so did something because of self-processes gets us nowhere. We still have to explain these self-processes. The notion of the self has had such a big impact on the West since its development (Foucault, 1985) that it has often been taken as a "given" and not analyzed further.

On the present view the "self" is something like this: it is the behavior of verbalizing to yourself about yourself. We begin in life by talking to others about our behavior, and about our overt behaviors in particular (Bem, 1965). We then begin to do this in the absence of an audience. So all the physiological events involved in producing verbal behavior can be carried out without the final response of speaking. Once we can "talk" about ourselves to ourselves, we can become quite sophisticated in doing this and conduct many responses without overt movements.

The key point though is that self-processes depend on verbal behaviors, which in turn depend upon generalized social reinforcement or tracking for maintenance. This means that the self is a social product and in most instances requires social consequences for maintenance. There are times when social support is not required, and these are comparable to tracking. If covert verbalizations about your own responses lead you directly to strengthening environmental consequences, then it might be sustained independently of the social support.

For example, consider the behavior of covertly planning (forming self-instructions of) future behavior. It can be noticed that people usually "need" to tell others all about their plans in order for them to actually carry them out. This indicates that they require social consequences. Other people do not need to this because their history of self-instruction following has led to (or self-tracked?) other forms of strengthening consequences. Indeed, just having self-instructions correctly followed might strengthen such responses.

An implication of this view of the self is that the whole notion of a self is like a developing verbal story throughout your life, a social and verbal construction, rather than a continuing readout of privileged data (cf. Day, 1977; Gergen & Gergen, 1988; Nisbett & Wilson, 1977). Since most of the self-talk about yourself will be built from contingencies and events that are also observable to others, and which are reinforced by others, it is possible on this view that someone else might be in a better position to assess you than yourself. This view is contrary to most psychological views of the self, for which the person themself is always better able to judge their "real self" than anybody else. This view also means that there is no true or "real" self. Indeed, multiple selves are implicated by the behavior analysis view because the self-talk about ourselves will change with different audiences and contexts (cf. Cushman, 1990; Markus & Nurius, 1986; Thoits, 1983).

A person will usually be a better judge of the physiological events occurring within their body, although overt measurements can be made of most parts of our bodies with medical equipment. The only other private, privileged data of the self are the past covert verbalizations which were never overtly expressed to others. This is in fact what many people think of as their true secret self: the *never expressed verbalizations about themselves.* The problem with this for people's idea of their self is that these past unexpressed verbalizations do not necessarily deal with real contingencies in either the social or physical environments. In fact, they seem to me to correspond to what Lacan (1977) calls the Imaginary. To be "Real" they need to have environmental consequences, even if these are generalized social consequences. This sets them apart from socially maintained fictions, such as Father Christmas for children, which contact some sort of social consequences.

A final implication of this view of the self to be mentioned here is that the ultimate control of self-processes lies in the social and physical environment (cf., Mageo, 1989; Sampson, 1985). Even if we talk to ourselves about ourselves and keep this totally secret, there will some environmental control on this. It might be a tracking effect which has taken the control away from generalized social contingencies, or it might be a social avoidance response if previous self-reports have been socially punished when verbalized. This is saying that the most private and unspoken self-thoughts are only unspoken because of punishing past social contingencies for saying them aloud.

The self-processes give great advantages to humans over the other animals. They allow us to accomplish delayed and mildly-punished behaviors which we would not otherwise do. We need only think about the role of self-management in human conduct to see the influence it has on our lives. As behavior analysts we need to be careful in analyzing the control of such behaviors since common sense notions fail us here.

Other psychologists still adhere to common sense views of the self, although recent views are coming closer to that of behavior analysts (Baldwin & Holmes, 1987; Cushman, 1990; Markus & Nurius, 1986; Sampson, 1985, 1989). The major directions this is taking is to argue for a social basis to the self, though without giving good reasons for a socially constructed basis to the self, and for the self as a multiple set of responses. In this sense the self can be a multiple set of behavior repertoires, but mostly verbal behaviors (Markus & Nurius, 1986; Thoits, 1983).

Self-Reporting of Behavior

We must first distinguish self-reporting of covert events within the skin from reporting past and present behaviors which could potentially be reported by another person just as well. All covert events are potentially reportable if we had the medical equipment, but usually they can only be reported by the person having the events. For example, normally only a person in pain can report this, but medical equipment could report to others that someone is having pain events. Such equipment will not be reporting exactly the same thing, but the pain events can be reported.

So what happens when we report pain, then? First, some events inside the skin are discriminable—they can become discriminative stimuli. Pain is an example of this. Other events inside the skin are not discriminable. Changes in electrical activity in the brain are an example of this. We are not normally able to discriminate "alpha" from "theta" activity, although it is claimed that this can be done through intensive training and although recording devices can measure this. So it is possible to measure covert events which we ourselves cannot discriminate, and it is possible to learn to discriminate covert events which we normally do not discriminate.

Animals can also discriminate internal events. In a nice study, Lubinski and Thompson (1987) taught one pigeon to peck a key which another pigeon had been taught to respond to by reporting on its drug state (it either had saline, cocaine or pentobarbital). Correct reports mutually reinforced both animals. It was found that the reporting also generalized to other drugs which the animals had not taken before, but which had related effects.

There is more though that occurs when we report a covert event like pain. What happens is that a verbal behavior is discriminative of pain events. In no sense do we behave the pain—it is just an event inside the skin—nor do we create pain in someone else when we report it. All that happens is that we speak and this is not the pain but another discriminated behavior. Furthermore, the source of the words is not the pain—pain does not give us our vocabulary. Our vocabulary comes from other people not from the pain. What this means is that we can only report pain if the verbal community has given us words to use (Skinner, 1957; Wittgenstein, 1957). And the accuracy of those words will be a function of how closely the verbal community has shaped the verbal behavior.

For example, if we have a headache then we usually get away with saying just that much. A doctor might continue questioning further, and ask what sort of pain and where does it feel like it is coming from. It is instructive that the different sorts of pain are described using analogies from elsewhere in our vocabulary—sharp pains, dull pains—this shows that we use a public vocabulary to describe our pains to others and have the appropriate effect on them.

The discriminative stimuli controlling self-reports become clearer at this point. First, the accuracy of self-reports depends upon how well the discrimination is made in the first-place. As we have seen above, for covert events this varies depending upon the event. For past and present overt behaviors this also varies. For instance, you can probably report quite well how many fingers you have but not very well what you ate for breakfast three mornings ago. Reporting on the variables which affect your behavior also varies in accuracy (this is called meta-cognition if about verbal behavior). If you are hungry then you will say that food is a potent reinforcer at that time. If you are asked to add 12 and 4 together (to get 16) you probably cannot report on the major variables affecting this behavior—especially since so much of the control is in your past reinforcement history.

An interesting case comes when verbal behavior is controlling your behavior, because you can probably report your behavior quite accurately in this case also (Hayes, 1986). In fact, people can be so accurate that they believe that the self-report itself is controlling their behavior. This is the essence of "planning". If we are planning to go shopping there are many verbal behaviors controlling different parts of this action. If we are asked what we are doing, these verbal behaviors can be accurately reported, although the variables controlling the verbal planning behaviors themselves cannot be reported. For example, if asked what I was doing I could reply, "I was thinking about whether to get cabbage or cauliflower at the supermarket when I get there". If I am now asked what made me think about cabbages and cauliflower, or decide between them, the answer is a very dubious self-report.

So far we have discussed the discriminative stimuli for self-reports. The behaviors themselves depend upon our verbal training and, as mentioned in connection with pain, this in turn depends upon our verbal community and learning of the language. If you ask me how I am and I reply "Grouse!", this might not have the appropriate effect on you if you were not brought up in the same verbal community. [I believe the term "grouse" comes from various British verbal communities, circa 1950/1960.]

The third component of self-report contingencies, the consequences of self-reports, are more difficult to get a fix on. Self-reports are not like reading off a secret inner source of privileged information, but are motivated (are maintained by consequences). If they are maintained by generalized social consequences then they can be accurate reports on what you have discriminated about your present and past behaviors (we could call them self-tacts perhaps). If, on the other hand, there are specific social contingencies or audience characteristics (7.3), then self-reports will become biased towards these. This should make us wary about what we attribute to self-reports. Since they are verbalizations of socially strengthened responses they can be mands, tacts or intraverbals. We need to know which before accepting them as accurate reports of our own behavior (cf. Hayes, 1986; Nisbett & Wilson, 1977; White, 1988).

As an example, different verbal communities have different ways of reporting their health and illness (cf. Herzlich, 1973), and using other terms in your self-reports of illness will be socially punished unless you are a medical doctor. Therefore, some control for self-reports comes from the social consequences. Different communities and groups provide different consequences for using the terms "headache" and "migraine". The use of these two terms are probably only distinguished by the consequences from the verbal community. Some communities I have known never "have" migraines whereas other groups have them all the time. It is the community consequences for the terms which determine the self-reporting.

The consequences of self-reporting can be more subtle than this. If people learn to report about themselves to themselves (also called meta-cognition) then this can be a very useful behavior, and can act as a setting event for improved remembering over time, improved problem solving, and other accomplishments. "Now let's see, I put the red one on top of the blue one first, and then took away the green one". So self-reporting to yourself can track contingencies and rely less and less on social contingencies, although this might only occur in the first place if the social consequences are very generalized.

There are a few lines of research which have developed recently around self-reports. Bernstein and his colleagues have looked at the accuracy with which people can report on the relative rates of reinforcement which are controlling their behavior (Bernstein, 1986; Bernstein & Ebbesen, 1978; Bernstein & Michael, 1990). We discussed a study by Bernstein and Ebbesen (1978) in Chapter 3, in which people lived in an environment for a few weeks with the contingencies between their activities controlled. This study also found that people had reasonably accurate self-reports on the reinforcers controlling their behavior; or in everyday terms: what was of value to them. Bernstein and Michael (1990) went further and arranged contingent relations between activities which were based on either the actual observed time distribution of activities or the self-reports of time distribution. The former predicted the resultant time re-distribution better than did the self-reports. Thus while the two were similar in reporting, the observation was more accurate and more predictive of behavior *after* the contingencies were changed.

Bernstein and Michael (1990) make a very good point in their discussion, that despite the various sources of control with verbal self-reports, we often cannot measure the actual or real values so we must depend upon self-reports anyway. The rest of psychology has been doing this for many years already, but the importance of the behavior analysis point of view is that the conditions under which self-reports are accurate or not can be studied, because the controlling factors of the self-reports are taken into account. They are not assumed to be accurate "direct read-outs" of privileged information, but depend upon the stimulus contexts and social consequences.

This means that we can either train people for better self-reports (similar to correspondence training, 7.5) or learn more about the conditions for normal accurate self-reports. The latter has been the goal of research by Critchfield and Perone (1990, 1993; Critchfield, 1993). In a series of studies, these authors have had subjects carry out tasks with a time limit and an accuracy requirement (they must get a correct recognition within a certain period) and the have them report on whether they got the points for their answer. The results seem to show a bias towards reporting that they successfully got the points.

This was also found using a signal detection approach (Critchfield, 1993). The response bias towards reporting success dropped when subjects were doing worse but still showed a positive bias. Also of interest was that as the recognition task became harder with more sample stimuli the self-report sensitivity dropped, and when the number of comparison stimuli increased self-report sensitivity increased. Thus the response bias and sensitivity to report correctly on one's behavior were differently affected by the nature of the task. Like all work in this area, the social consequences (from the experimenter) have not been varied so subjects can "get away with" positively biased self-reports. Manipulating generalized social consequences, however, is very tricky in practice.

There has also been interest shown by some behavior analysts in protocol analysis—the analysis of what people say out loud while they are doing a task

(Ericsson & Simon, 1984; Hayes, 1986). Wulfert, Dougher and Greenway (1991) did an interesting study in which subjects learned stimulus equivalence classes of geometrical shapes (see 3.1). While they were doing this they were asked to report out loud what they were thinking. Analysis of these protocols showed that the subjects who thought about relations between the stimulus items, such as "Circle goes with the open triangle" (p. 492), were the ones who successfully formed equivalence classes. Subjects who did not form equivalence classes were mainly those who spoke about the two stimuli as a compound, such as "Together they look like a house" (p. 492). A second study then had an intervention which made subjects attend to either the relational or compound aspects and this predicted who formed equivalence classes. So this study successfully used protocol analysis to find something others had not before about stimulus equivalence classes.

Self-reinforcement

There has been a lot of controversy over self-reinforcement. This has mostly been over whether there are "inner" processes controlling the phenomenon or whether there is environmental control. Some cognitivists have thought that behavior analysts deny that self-reinforcement exists, but the questions has always been one of where the control comes from, not whether it exists (Catania, 1975). As outlined above, the control of self-processes comes from environmental consequences, usually social consequences. This is the point being made, not that self-processes do not exist.

Consider, for example, someone who lets themself have one chocolate bar for every two pages of an assignment they get done (not a very subtle contingency!). Are they "reinforcing" themself in the same way that someone else might reinforce them? It looks just like a rat pressing a bar: two presses (pages) and they get one food pellet (chocolate bar). The only difference is that *they* provide the chocolates, not the equipment or the experimenter.

Despite looking like a simple reinforcement procedure, there is a lot more going on. We need to consider the control over starting the whole procedure (the rat gets forced into the cage), the control over completing two pages (the rat is controlled by the equipment), and the control over actually receiving the food (which the equipment delivers). This means that there are many different responses by the person conducting the "self-reinforcement", and the (possibly) separate sources of control for these need to be found.

Most behavior analysts who have considered such cases, or experimented with them, have concluded that environmental contingencies control all these other responses which make up self-reinforcement (e.g., Baer, 1984; Goldiamond, 1976; Gross & Wojnilower, 1984; Nelson, Hayes, Spong, Jarrett & McKnight, 1983; Roberts, Nelson & Olson, 1987). For this reason "self-reinforcement" is considered a misnomer.

Let us look at possible sources of control. First, the person in our example is wanting to write an essay for some consequence: to gain social approval or perhaps to avoid failing a university subject. This must be a powerful source of control over all the responses involved in the self-reinforcement procedure. If not, the whole procedure is likely to fail. Second, in making self-instructions about how to proceed with the procedure, generalized social control is involved. This is shown by people reporting their procedure to others. If no one knows about the procedure and its expected outcomes (chocolate bars), then the procedure might not work at all. Hayes, Rosenfarb, Wulfert, Munt, Korn and Zettle (1985), in fact, found that a common self-reinforcement procedure did not work if it was kept totally anonymous. Only when the experimenter would know the results did it work. This strongly implicates generalized social consequences as a source of control (also see Hayes, Munt, Korn, Wulfert, Rosenfarb & Zettle, 1986; Rosenfarb & Hayes, 1984).

A third possible source of control is the effect of previous tracking. If such self-reinforcement procedures have led to reinforcing consequences in the past then this source of control might maintain the current self-reinforcement. In our example, the control might not be from any future effects of good essay marks, nor from others approving a successful outcome, but because previous uses of the techniques have worked successfully. In these cases it could perhaps be kept anonymous and still be carried through to the end, unlike the results of Hayes et al. (1985).

The importance of generalized social consequences in making self-reinforcement procedures work is underscored by comments from people who have used them, to the effect that such techniques work only if the clients are already motivated. That is, if there is already a source of control to maintain the whole procedure, whatever this might be, then the procedure itself has a good chance of succeeding (Gintner & Poret, 1988). In summary, the self-reinforcement are really social and not self-motivated.

This point has important implications for designing self-reinforcement procedures. In the past, the reinforcement part has been assumed to be controlled by the "self" and the real sources of control have been ignored. We need to design such procedures around these other sources of control, rather than ignore them, or else any changes brought about by self-reinforcement techniques will not maintain afterwards. Most obviously, the social controls on self-reinforcement need to be specifically and explicitly programmed into self-reinforcement techniques.

Self-control

Self-control is closely related to self-reinforcement in many cases, but the examples considered here are those in which a person must control behavior in order to achieve larger delayed consequences rather than smaller immediate consequences (Epstein, 1984b). There is a large literature on this topic, which is still growing, and not just by behavior analysts (see Brigham, 1980; Commons, Mazur, Nevin & Rachlin, 1987; Darcheville, Riviére & Weardon, 1992; Flora & Pavlik, 1992; King & Logue, 1987; Mahoney & Thorensen, 1974; Mischel & Patterson, 1976; Rachlin, 1974). As we have already seen in Chapter 6 and 7.7, group behavior allows another way of controlling behavior for remote contingencies when there is no self-control.

Like self-reinforcement, the control over behavior is not simple. While animals can be trained to choose larger delayed reinforcers over smaller immediate reinforcers, special techniques are usually needed (Grosch & Neuringer, 1981; Haaren, van Hest & van de Poll, 1988; Mazur & Logue, 1978; Rachlin & Green, 1972; Schweitzer & Sulzer-Azaroff, 1988). Most animals, if left with just the environmental contingencies, do not develop control for delayed reinforcement. The contingencies need to be carefully adjusted (Grosch & Neuringer, 1981; Mazur & Logue, 1978).

Likewise with humans, there is probably a large influence in human self-control from self-instruction following (7.4). We use verbal behavior to control the delaying behavior. This means that generalized social contingencies will usually play a role in self-control, since they control self-instructions unless a tracking effect occurs. Indeed, Nelson, Hayes, Spong, Jarrett and McKnight (1983) suggested that self-reinforcement procedures might only be functional if they act as cues to delayed reinforcement and self-control. Even with animals, a precurrent "commitment" response can help self-control (Rachlin, 1974).

Self-reference and Self-attribution

There has already been some mention of self-reference and self-attribution. The point was that in reporting about one's self, there is only a small source of responses which are not accessible to another person. Most of the verbalizations refer back to observable behavior (Bem, 1965). The small amount which is really private consists mainly of intraverbals about previous behavior which have not been spoken. Even these are controlled in the long run by social contingencies, as was argued above. The only other components are reports of physiological changes in the body, to which most other people have no access. The point of this is to argue against the common idea that self-reference has some privileged status as a source. In this sense we are like strangers in our bodies, although once you get used to the idea it no longer seems paradoxical.

One of the problems is that there is a long intellectual history in the West of using metaphors of depth when talking about people. People have "hidden depths" about them, we must look for the "deep unconscious", and anyone else is considered "shallow". Some philosophers and psychologists have tried to work against this metaphor (e.g., Bentley, 1941; Deleuze & Guattari, 1981), but it is persistent. Self-references to *deep* aspects of the self usually mean a reference to controlling variables which are generalized and social (and therefore nonobvious) or ones due to a nonobvious past reinforcement history.

Further, as Bem (1965) has argued, attributions about the self derive from the same sources as attributions about other people, and the attributions will be learned through a verbal community. As was mentioned above for self-reports of health and illness, explaining health and illness also depend upon what is learned through specific verbal communities. This will be covered in detail when discussing verbal communities (9.1), social attributions (9.1), and social constructions of knowledge (10.2)

8.5. Affect and Emotion

Cognitive psychology, and particularly social cognitive psychology, has recently seen much research into affect and emotion. As argued elsewhere (Guerin, 1992b), affect seems to be another name for nonverbal contingencies. Psychologists have been showing that we can respond differentially towards objects without verbalizing about them (Zajonc, 1980), and this loose sense of evaluative responding is called affect. It serves the same function as the term "unconscious" did for another verbal community of psychologists. We desire, evaluate, or judge affectively objects and events without thinking about them. This simply means that we have learned to respond differentially towards them without verbalizing (cognitive or conscious processing).

Emotion, on the other hand, has a long background in psychology and seems to cover many phenomena. First, there are physiological reactions which occur in certain circumstances. One way of stating such circumstances is that they involve contingency transitions (this idea appears to have originally come from Michael Davison, and was handed down to me, probably embellished, by Mary Foster). That is, when contingencies are changing and the overall change is to richer sources of reinforcement then the emotional response is one of happiness or similar. If the change is back to normal leaner sources of reinforcement or a change to less than usual reinforcement schedules then depression, unhappiness, etc. result.

The evidence seems to be that the physiological events which occur in emotional states are not specific to the emotion, which means that the label and hence the verbal experience of *particular* emotions must be learned through a verbal community (Buck, 1988). What this means is that emotion, and even the experience of emotion in so far as this includes covert verbal behaviors, is socially constructed (cf. Fisher & Chon, 1989; Kemper, 1987). Whether something is called happiness or elation will be determined by the definitions (in use) provided by a verbal community, and the stimulus control coming from the contingency transition event itself. That is, elation will only be the emotion in certain circumstances of happiness, and which circumstances these are depends jointly on the verbal community and what it calls elation (some religious groups say they experience elation over almost every trivial event in life), and on the stimulus event itself (if you found $1 on the footpath you might be happy but not elated, and the circumstances partly dictate this).

8.6. Intrinsic Motivation

Another area to impinge on self-processes and cognition is that of "intrinsic motivation", although this has several meanings (Rotter, 1990). Intrinsic motivation is a term for motivation which has no obvious external control: "...behavior is intrinsically motivated when there are no apparent external rewards... Intrinsically motivated behaviors are ones that are involved with the human need for being competent and self-determining" (Deci, 1975; also Deci & Ryan, 1980). Apart from the vagueness of these negative definitions we can see that subtle social consequences are (yet again) not taken into account, and so appeals are made to "human needs" for motivated behavior. This is clearly not sufficient from a behavior analytic point of view.

The area arose from a finding that when "external rewards" were given for behaviors which were "intrinsically motivated", the intrinsic motivation decreased. This was used as evidence that behavior modifiers could ruin an already existing intrinsic motivation if macro consequences were applied. There are all sorts of problems with this literature, and only some will be mentioned. While the phenomenon is not to be denied, the conclusions certainly can be (see Bernstein, 1990; Dickinson, 1989; Feingold & Mahoney, 1975; Flora, 1990; Mawhinney, 1979; Mawhinney, Dickinson, & Taylor, 1989; Scott, 1975; Scott, Farh & Podsakoff, 1988).

First, the whole range of subtle consequences have been ignored and a very simple version of reinforcement theory used as a straw-person theory. This is apparent when intrinsic motivation is seen to rest on a need for being competent and self-determining. These terms are not further analyzed.

Second, most often in experiments the subject's whole behavior has been "rewarded" rather than single responses. As mentioned in 2.3, this has the effect of strengthening all responses even those which conflict with the performance goal. Even when contingencies are brought in, they are "rewards" contingent upon a whole performance, not a single response (Ryan, Mims & Koestner, 1983). Thus interference from multiple contingencies must underlie the decrease in intrinsic motivation. Since the individual responses have not been clearly delineated for reinforcement procedures, it is indicative that the term "reward" is used. A poorly administered strengthener will certainly undermine both subtle and macro strengtheners already maintaining a response. There is no problem for behavior analysts in this. Their concern is to better analyze what controls the "intrinsic motivators".

For example, the most common intrinsically motivated tasks used in experiments are a puzzle game and a hidden figures task. There would almost certainly be social consequences contingent upon completion and noncompletion of such tasks, from when we learned to play games in social settings through our development. To ignore this leads to the superficial analyses of saying that there are intrinsic needs for playing games.

For a better analysis one can ask a simple question: why should humans worry about their competence? Presumably the answer is because it has been reinforced by tracking environmental consequences or it has been strengthened by reporting competence to others people for generalized social reinforcement. Similar arguments apply to "self-determination". It is also noteworthy that both seem to refer to verbal behavior about competence and self-determination, rather than the direct control of these.

8.7. Creativity

Creativity was always a problem for stimulus-response theories of behavior since new behaviors were hard to explain except as the result of a changing environment. The key to this comes with the natural selection model of behavior (2.2), a view similar to that of Campbell (1960b). For a variety of reasons, new behaviors are produced; some of these are strengthened and survive, others extinguish (Epstein, 1991).

The question of creativity then becomes one of finding the conditions under which new behaviors are produced, and some of these conditions were covered in 2.2 (also Segal, 1972). First, there can be changes in the environment which change the behavior. Second, there is response generalization, which might lead to behaving in an old way in a new environment, which subsequently shapes the old behavior into something new. Third, the production of new behaviors or variations on previous behaviors can be strengthened itself (Machado, 1989; Page & Neuringer, 1985; Pryor, Haag & O'Reilly, 1969; Schwartz, 1982). This is also shown by many behavior modification programmes which aim to increase variability of behavior (Goetz & Baer, 1973; Sloane, Endo & Della-Piana, 1980; Winston & Baker, 1985).

Fourth, increased variability can probably result from verbally governed behavior, although this has not been experimentally tested properly yet (though see Meichenbaum, 1975). It certainly appears as if we can create new behaviors by "thinking about it". This may be a result of re-arranging stimulus control, however, as when you turn a half-drawn picture upside-down in order to "see it differently" and produce something creative. Such verbally governed behaviors are emphasized in creative writing and creative drawing classes. Future research on creativity needs to look at the manipulation of stimulus classes using the technology of higher-term contingencies and stimulus equivalence classes.

Finally, "creative" behavior can be produced by new arrangements of older behaviors, although the control of the recombination may reside in one of the above four methods. Epstein (1985b, 1987, 1991) has shown this with pigeons, that new behaviors can emerge from previously unconnected behaviors. In one study he taught pigeons three separate behaviors and then gave them a problem which required all three together to make an "insightful" or creative solution—which they did. In another interesting experiment, Nakajima and Sato (1993) showed that whether a pigeon removes an obstacle or not which prevented solving a problem depended upon the pigeons' previous history with removing the obstacle. Thus again, the solution might be new and original but solving the problem is built from previous behaviors.

8.8. Decision Making and Choice

From the behavior analytic point of view, there are several confusions in the traditional approach to decision making. First, there is a confusion between behavior maintained through environmental contingencies directly and behavior maintained through verbal mediation. Second, there is a confusion in positing a chooser or decision maker as an internal actor. Decision behavior sometimes resembles this when verbal behavior mediates the "choice", but in most cases any internal verbal commentary comes afterwards or concurrently and is socially based in any case.

The third confusion arises from the first two: that the decisions are not treated in a wider framework of all possible behaviors. That is, the question of decision making is the question of relative strengths of multiple contingencies, including the contingencies maintaining verbal control of behavior. In this sense, decision making is one way to approach multiple contingencies (see 3.2). Moreover, if verbal behaviors do mediate some human decision making, they are merely one more element in the integration of multiple contingencies; they are not a new special type of process.

To the extent that decision making merely means that an animal behaves one way rather than another, the work on direct contingencies covers this. Decision making is often taken this broadly in the traditional literature, but saying that an animal *chose* to press a bar rather than drink from a water spout merely avoids an analysis of control, and just describes the event instead. We will ignore this wider sense of the term decision making. It has, in effect, been covered in all the first part of this book. Instead, we will concentrate on two senses of decision making: cases where there are a few alternative contingencies with similar "values", and cases where verbal behaviors are involved in multiple contingencies.

Traditional decision making theory has concentrated on eliciting the subjective probability of choice options and the reported utility of those options from the decision makers, and predicting choice from these (e.g., von Winterfeldt & Edwards, 1986). This work has developed mostly static decision models designed to predict one-off decisions. Discussion of decision making over time and dynamic decision making has been minimal within this approach, but there are some useful advances (see Bjorkman, 1984; Edwards, 1962; Kleiter, 1970; Rapoport, 1975).

Traditional decision making research has also concentrated on developing cognitive models, which has meant that the link between a (cognitive) decision and the actual behavior has been weak, in the same way as we saw in 7.5. As well, a number of anomalies have appeared to confront axiomatic decision theory (Machina, 1987), and overcoming these has required further assumptions (Kahneman & Tversky, 1979, 1984). These developments should interest behavior analysts, since it is argued here that the traditional models are really models of multiple contingency effects. One problem is the interpretation of delay (D) when dealing with humans. Another is the effect of following rules or instructions when choosing, which animals do not do. A further problem concerns how one-off decisions might be made, if there is no relative proportion over time. These problems will be discussed in turn below.

A Behavioral Model of Choice

An extension to the behavioral model of choice (3.2) has dealt with the interpretation of delay with humans. Rachlin et al. (1986) proposed that probability could be thought of as delay: small probabilities correspond to long delays and high probabilities correspond to short delays. It was shown that by making this assumption, the results of Kahneman and Tversky's Prospect Theory (1979, 1984) could be accounted for in a behavioral model of choice, as well as other anomalies of axiomatic decision theory. Some experimental evidence for this has been presented using human subjects (Rachlin, Logue, Gibbon & Frankel,.1986; Rachlin, Castrogiovanni & Cross, 1987), although other data go against this (Silberberg, Murray, Christensen & Asano, 1988).

Using this "behavioral" equation given in 3.2, Rachlin et al. (1986) make some translations of traditional decision models into behavioral terms. The utility of a choice option in traditional decision models equates with the amount of reinforcer (A). The probability of choice events equates with the rate of reinforcement (R). The delay to reinforcement does not appear in cognitive decision making models, but, as we have seen, it can also be interpreted as a form of probability. With these equivalences, the major tenets of Kahneman and Tversky's Prospect Theory (1979) can be handled by a simple behavioral model. So the expanded model of behavioral decision making, which equates probability with delay in the Matching Law, can incorporate traditional decision models. As well, it has several other advantages over traditional formulations of decision making (see Rachlin et al., 1986). For the purposes of this book, there are two advantages of particular note.

First, it provides an improved method of tackling decision making over time and dynamic decision making. Rather than dealing with one-off probabilities, or even a series of one-off probabilities (Friedman, Carterette & Anderson, 1968), it uses the more continuous and flexible rates of reinforcement. Very similar changes to traditional decision making theory have been called for by others in the cognitive tradition (Lopes, 1981).

The second advantage of the expanded behavioral model is that with some modifications it can differentiate between a verbally specified probability and an experienced probability (or delay). That is, it differentiates between rule-governed presentations of probabilities and the experience of outcomes over time. Some suggestions will be made as to how to incorporate these in below.

Verbal Behavior and Decision Making

While the Matching Law captures nicely the effects of direct environmental contingencies, I believe it has problems when verbal behavior is involved (Rachlin's, 1989, comments on verbal behavior notwithstanding; see also Silberberg, Murray, Christensen & Asano, 1988). The are several ways that verbal behavior complicates decision making. We will cover only some of these. More developments along these lines should develop in the next few years as the work on verbal behavior increases (Hayes, 1989b).

[Those within the traditional decision making literature have also found problems which I believe arise from missing the distinction between direct and verbal control of behavior. Some examples are: Broadbent, FitzGerald and

Broadbent (1986); Cohen, Chesnick and Haran (1972); Gilovich (1983); Keren and Wagenaar (1987); Lopes (1981); Montgomerey and Adelbratt (1982); Svenson and Edland (1987); Tversky and Kahneman (1973), although these cannot all be expounded here.]

The first effect of verbally governed behavior on behavioral decision making is to precipitate two conditions for which there will be poor decision making over time. The first route to poor decision making results from an adherence to verbal rules of probability in the face of experienced violations of the expected outcomes (cf. Einhorn, 1980). Similar violations have been found when human subjects follow instructions for responding to simple reinforcement schedules rather than experience with the actual schedules themselves (Hayes, Brownstein, Haas & Greenway, 1986; Shimoff, Matthews & Catania, 1986), as we saw in 7.4. An example of this for decision making would be gamblers following self-instructed dictums, such as "I have to win sometime", and not being "aware" that they are repeatedly losing and getting no payoff at all. These dictums will have been strengthened by social contingencies or tracking by previous verbal rule-following.

The distinction we are following allows development of a model of intuitive decision making, which decision theorists are beginning to tackle (Hammond, Hamm, Grassia & Pearson, 1987). For the behavior analyst, intuitive decision making refers to behaving in accordance with the multiple environmental contingencies acting at that time (3.2). Nonintuitive means that decision behavior has become verbally governed in some way and verbal rules are controlling the decision behavior through pliance or tracking.

A second route to poor decision making occurs when someone has been reinforced in the past for following limited experience of outcomes rather than reliable verbal instructions about the outcomes. For example, despite repeated (verbal) warnings from experts that certain areas such as flood plains face natural risks, people still build on such areas without taking risk insurance (Fischhoff, Lichtenstein, Slovic, Derby & Keeney, 1981). In these cases, limited experience with outcomes leads to ignoring the instructions derived from careful risk assessments. There is no tracking of punishing outcomes and the pliance from the warnings does not control behavior.

We can see from these examples the role played by the "experts". Some experts have learned from repeated exposure to, or experience of, the contingencies of the decision alternatives. They may be able to advise verbally what should be done but not give (verbal) reasons for their own choice. The most useful expert is one who can verbalize clearly **and** accurately the contingencies experienced and provide reasons. Other experts deal purely with verbal reports and verbal (perhaps mathematical) models of environmental contingencies. If their sources are accurate there is no reason why they should not make accurate original verbal statements about environmental consequences, although laypeople distrust this type of expert who has no hands-on experience. I once knew a person who built excellent and useful mathematical models of fish populations but had no hands-on experience with actual fish in the sea. His verbal rules (mathematical models) were still well used by the authorities.

A second effect of verbally governed behavior on decision making is a reliance in decision making on easily "available" or "representative" stimuli (Tversky & Kahneman, 1973). It is suggested that this results also from following verbal behavior rather than experienced outcomes (but see Nevin, 1991) which leads to over-reacting to local variations in rates of reinforcement. This will be especially apparent when people are directed to discover rules of probability. A similar effect has been found when people are using an anchor-and-adjust strategy in judgment, as posited by several cognitive models (for example, Lopes, 1985).

A third effect of verbally governed behavior concerns delays in choice reinforcement. It is suggested that as well as equating probability with delay, as Rachlin et al. (1986) have done, verbally instructed or specified probabilities should be treated in Matching Law terms (3.2) as having a shorter delay (D) than experienced outcomes, even when scheduled probabilities of reinforcement are equal to the instructed probabilities.

That is, when instructed with a probability and its outcome, the *total probability which controls the choice behavior* will still be higher than that experienced during the scheduling of the same stated probability. This occurs because the short delay between verbal instructions and outcome, when probabilities and outcomes are both presented, effectively means that a higher total probability is controlling the behavior. In terms of the model given in 3.2, if one or both of R1 and R2 are verbally instructed rather than experienced, then D1 and D2 are effectively reduced.

What this means is that decisions for which you have previously *experienced* the actual contingencies and the rates (probabilities) of the consequences should be more conservative (less risky) than those where you are *told* the probabilities which you have not experienced but which have strong pliance. This is because we must take into account the delay involved in experiencing some environmental contingencies (usually long if done properly) and in being told a probability (usually short).

As an example, consider being given a coin which might or might not be biased. You could spend time trying out the coin in repeated throws, or you could be told that heads comes up three times as often as tails. While the rate of reinforcement remains the same for any choice behavior, in predicting the behavior you must take the delay in finding out into account as well. The short delay when told a probability predicts that choices will be more risky or impulsive. *Being told rather than experiencing should lead to more risky or impulsive choices.*

The behavioral decision making model is yet to make much impact in applied work although it holds much potential (see McDowell, 1982; Myerson & Hale, 1984). It has been successfully applied, however, in the study of foraging in birds and other animals. I believe, however, that it will have problems in human work because of there are always multiple responses with humans. So response allocation in humans will involve many responses, and choosing one will affect all the others, as we saw in 3.2. There is still the challenge, however, that there are ways to overcome these difficulties which I think will follow from developments in multiple response work. The solutions lie in the future.

8.9. Zen and the Art of Contingency-Governed Behavior

Before leaving social cognition, I wish to make some interesting parallels between the verbally-governed/contingency-governed distinction and the art of Zen. We have seen that the distinction reappears continuously when discussing human behavior, and is equivalent to that between automatic and controlled processing in cognitive psychology, and conscious and unconscious elsewhere in psychology. We have also seen in various places in this book how both advantages and problems are created for humans by having two sources of control. Verbally governed behavior is an advantage, for example, if "self-control" via socially reinforced verbal behavior can control our behavior rather than immediate environmental consequences. We would probably do little but eat chocolate all day otherwise.

The problems with verbally governed behavior are cases where people might fail to act because they are telling themselves what to do rather than responding to the contingencies present in the environment. Social training makes us all not do things which might be good for us, or makes us ruminate excessively if we have done the things we are not supposed to. A number of psychological therapies are aimed at sorting out sensible verbal control from stifling verbal control (Haley, 1973; Hayes, 1987; Poppen, 1989).

Zen can be seen as an approach to the same problem. The state of nirvana for Zen Buddhists would appear to be one of almost complete contingency-governed behavior. When people try and attain nirvana, bliss or pure happiness, they typically think and talk about it to themselves or to others, or try to verbally direct themselves into nirvana. This, says Zen, is not the Way:

The way that can be spoken of
is not the constant way
(Lao Tzu, 1963, p. 75)

The practice of Zen, then, seems strange because it consists of attempts to stop verbal contingencies from cluttering (controlling) our other contingencies. The emphasis is upon acting and learning through consequences, rather than thinking about acting and its consequences. While this might seem to include unethical behaviors, and we could visualize Zen monks going wild at parties, such behavior is usually absent, it is pointed out, because it happens through thinking. If we try and formulate verbally some ethical principles to guide behavior, already we have strayed into verbally governed behavior. Nor does Zen mean an escape from sense experience: "This is why 'the sage makes provision for the stomach and not for the eye', which is to say that he judges by the concrete content of the experience, and not by its conformity with purely theoretical standards" (Watts, 1957, p. 47).

The idea is to trust the environmental contingencies over approximate verbal specifications of those contingencies. "We 'know' how to move our hands, how to make a decision, or how to breathe, even though we can hardly begin to explain in words how we do it. We know how to do it because we just do it!" (Watts, 1957, p. 33). This clearly makes the distinction we have seen between doing and talking about doing.

Zen teachers employ the method of presenting little vignettes with paradoxical meanings in an attempt to show people a way out of words (e.g., Reps, 1957). The conversations in these vignettes usually continue until the student does something which is directly controlled by nonverbal contingencies rather than words-especially words about seeking the truth.

> Shuzan held out his short staff and said: 'If you call this a short staff, you oppose its reality. If you do not call it a short staff, you ignore the fact. Now what do you wish to call this? (Reps, 1957, p.127).

Or consider the sarcasm and cynicism applied to rule-governed behavior in the following story (p. 104), with the Master talking sarcastically to himself:

> Zuigan called out to himself every day: 'Master.'
> Then he answered himself: 'Yes, sir.'
> And after that he added: 'Become sober.'
> Again he answered: 'Yes, sir'
> 'And after that,' he continued, 'do not be deceived by others.'
> 'Yes, sir; yes, sir,' he answered.

This also presents with cynicism the criticism we saw in 8.5 of self-reinforcement being controlled by a self.

So Zen does not mean to become 'intentionally' spontaneous or deviant, but to trust your behavior, the result of which is behavior similar to others but done for reasons other than verbal control, and stronger because of the environmental control not reliant upon verbal mediation. Animals, the Zen poets sometimes remind us, do quite nicely without words:

> Coming, going, the waterfowl
> Leaves not a trace,
> Nor does it need a guide.
> (Dogen, in Stryk & Ikemoto, 1977, p. 63)

As found in behavior analytic laboratories over the world, pigeons, rats and hens can learn complicated behaviors through interacting with contingencies which are very difficult to specify. People, rather than animals, have problems from words and dreaming. Even when sick, people will talk and verbally dream rather than act:

Sick on a journey—
over parched fields
dreams wander on.
(Basho, 1985, p. 81).

Finally, we can also apply the Zen teachings to the methodology of behavior analysis, which rejects approaches based purely on verbally specifying what psychology is about, what the data should look like, and other armchair theorizing (Skinner, 1950). Instead, the point has been to find out by interacting with the environment, which in the case of behavior is from interacting with living organisms such as pigeons, rats and people and finding out what they do under varied conditions and contingencies. Armchair verbalizing might correctly specify the environment but it is only as accurate as the tacts it works from, and these tacts can only be accurate if they come from methodically interacting with the social and physical environments.

A Zen student told Ummon: 'Brilliancy of Buddha illuminates the whole universe'.
Before he finished the phrase Ummon asked: 'You are reciting another's poem, are you not?'
'Yes', answered the student.
'You are sidetracked', said Ummon.
(Reps, 1957, p.123).

Or to take an excample from our own field, by an otherwise great psychologist:

A great psychologist wrote, "Self, as a conscious experience, is any complex of mental processes that means some temporary phase of this combination; and a self-consciousness is a consciousness in which the self, as a conscious experience, is focal." (Titchener, 1915, p. 544)
Long after he finished the sentence, Skinner (1950) asked: 'You are only reciting words and not interacting with the world, are you not?'
'Yes', answered the great psychologist.
'You are sidetracked', said Skinner.

Chapter 9

Verbal Communities

In the last two chapters we have looked at the basic properties of verbal behavior and how they apply to individuals, even though the properties are ultimately social and rely upon a community of other people. The key point has been that *using verbal behavior we can change the environment without interacting with it: we cause other people to interact instead.* Words do not refer to things, they refer people to things: verbal behaviors have an effect in the world through other people. More importantly, verbal behavior can only be organized (only culturally evolve) if a group of people loosely reinforce many behaviors which might have no immediate functional consequences for them. That is, verbal behaviors depend upon a verbal community.

Once these points are grasped, a large part of our lives can be seen as functioning through other people rather than through interacting with the environment. I do not go and chop down trees and make paper when I want to write a letter. Instead, I go to the local newsagents who sell me some paper if I give them some money. And I do not get money by forging metal and making it–I get money by doing behaviors which have no relationship whatsoever to the money itself nor with how I spend the money later.

The first major point therefore is that a (very) large part of our lives is based on indirect effects which arise from the properties of verbal behavior–made possible by extensive generalized, social contingencies. From this, three additional points arise which form the basis of the social sciences, and which will form the basis of the next two chapters. The second major point is that all of this system of verbal behavior depends on having a community, however small, which "goes along" with it; third, that when analyzing such behaviors a useful shortcut is not to ask "What are the specific reinforcers and under what conditions are they contingent?", but "Who is the functional audience"; and fourth, that many of our social behaviors function to maintain the verbal community rather than to get the community to have effects on the environment, and analyses can be misleading if this is not taken into account.

The importance of these four points cannot be overestimated. As mentioned, they form the basis of the social sciences and a large part of this chapter will document how anthropology, sociology, sociolinguistics, musicology, and social psychology have dealt with them. They are so special that it has many times been claimed that the social sciences cannot be reduced to a natural science because there is a discontinuity in subject matter when dealing with people (e.g., Gergen, 1985; Winch, 1958). The behavior analytic approach has its cake and also eats it: the principles of human verbal/social behavior are firmly established in the natural sciences (Parts 1 and 2 of this book), but the special properties of verbal behavior make a separate study of the social sciences necessary (cf. Baldwin & Baldwin, 1978). The verbal communities which have culturally evolved for humans have very different properties (but not principles) from any groups of nonhuman animals.

It is impossible to completely review anthropology, sociology, musicology, and social psychology in this book (I'm already too old), so I will discuss the major thoughts of each with a few examples. One last point to mention about this approach is that when these avenues are pursued the result looks less and less like traditional behavior analysis. This is because traditional behavior analysis has usually analyzed very direct three-term contingencies between contexts, behaviors and consequences, even when talking about social behavior. When considering social behaviors in a verbal community, however, the effects are very indirect and new ways of thinking and acting must be introduced. The result looks much less like an experimental chamber situation than behavior analysis usually does but there is no reason why verbal communities cannot also be researched experimentally.

9.1. Conceptions of Verbal Communities

Social Science Conceptions of Community

There are many ideas about communities which have been proposed in the social sciences, and most of them have at least some validity, even if the terms used are not behavioral ones. Most of these ideas have moved away from defining communities in terms of physical distance and proximity. Most social scientists wisely saw that we might live near someone and yet not form any sort of community with them. On the other hand, living near people often creates some sort of community or social reinforcement structure (Festinger, Schachter & Back, 1950) and so there are complex links between the two uses of the term "community" (Gusfield, 1975).

One of the earliest views on community was that of Tönnies (1957/1887) who argued that there were two kinds of communities, which he called (and they usually retain their German) Gemeinschaft and Gesellschaft. The first was a more traditional form of community with an authority based on that tradition. This involved close family and community identification with common, interlinking bonds. The basis was said to be a "natural will", but we also read that this natural will was based on family and the soil: presumably meaning that the community generalized reinforcement structures were based on common reciprocation (see Chapter 6) within a tight group and based around food (soil) production.

Gesellschaft, on the other hand, was based on a "rational will"; based around authority as law and rationality rather than around more direct reciprocation between community members. The major feature, however, was that reciprocation between members of the Gesellschaft was for a particular end or function. Tönnies also argued that there was little or no identification with the community (at large), although there must still be smaller communities which supported role-specific behaviors within the larger community. The rise of Gesellschaft was clearly related to the rise of urban industrial capitalism.

This is a very brief outline of Tönnies, and his two types of social groups were not meant to be found in such pure forms. There are two major points which we can draw from his distinction, however. First, the nature of social relations changes with the introduction of written and other verbally-governed social behavior. But I believe that it is untrue that the Gemeinschaft and Gesellschaft distinction is primarily one between contingency- and verbally-governed social behaviors. My reading suggests that the prime distinction Tönnies made was between groups based around loose and generalized social reinforcers and those based around more direct reinforcers for which other people are a necessary part.

In a Gemeinschaft the social reinforcers are highly interconnected. There is also the feature that many social acts are ends in themselves: that is, they function to maintain the group and have no other purpose, or no other purpose more directly involving the nonsocial environment. The key feature of Gesellschaft, on the other hand, is the directness of the social contingencies, which exist only for some other ends. This key feature of Gesellschaft probably means that verbally-governed behavior is more prevalent but only as a side-effect. If there is social interaction with other people for some end, then verbal control would be expected to play a large role. Contractual relationships would be prevalent. To summarize in terms of Figure 9 (Chapter 7), Gesellschaft social structures are predicated on verbal self-regulation for specific remote contingencies and Gemeinschaft based on contacting remote contingencies through community behavior. It was the tension between the two that Tönnies described.

Durkheim (1933/1893) pursued many avenues of sociological thought and derived implications from these for both society and individuals. Community was cast into mechanical and organic forms. Mechanical solidarity was the older form (based in Durkheim mostly around a tribal image) where everyone was similar. People did the same kinds of things and opinions were common to a group. The common opinions were called "collective representations", very similar to the notion of "social representations" which will be discussed later.

The later "organic" style of community derived from the rational division of labour into social roles. The solidarity of a community had to be based around interdependence, and therefore it followed that if you were not dependent upon someone there was no need to form a community with them. Self-sufficiency was no longer possible, however, because a computer specialist does not have time to grow food and make clothes, so a system of weak ties (Granovetter, 1973, 1982) developed which provided remote contingencies through payment rather than access through a community to whom payment would appear rude.

The division of roles had many other implications which Durkheim derived (cf. Turner, 1990). For example, lifestyles no longer had to be homogenous, indeed it was difficult to maintain a common, community lifestyle with such varying roles in society (what do a computer specialist, a shop owner and a janitor have to share?).

Similarly, opinions and values were divided concurrently with the division of roles in society, especially since there was no longer a need to maintain collective representations if there were only weak ties between people. So whereas in past societies the close neighbourhoods could serve for most remote functions, different primary groups now took over different functions for members with the increase in role differentiation (Litwak & Szelenyi, 1969).

Durkheim had perhaps a more positive view of modern society than others, and saw the modern organic solidarity as a necessary feature which had positive as well as negative effects. He claimed that while organic solidarity was beneficial to maintaining a complex society which was good for most people, some people could become completely isolated from their usual communities. To this end he researched the mediation of societal forms in causing suicide (1951/1897). In this way suicide can be seen as a verbal/social phenomenon (also Hayes, 1992).

Societies based on mechanical and organic solidarity are almost synonymous with Gemeinschaft and Gesellschaft but there are differences. Durkheim perhaps can be seen as having answered a question about Tönnies' two types: what are the specific ends which people in Gesellschaft societies start using social relationships to obtain? For Durkheim, the analysis of the rise of using social relationships for specific ends rests in the division of labour into specifically reinforced pursuits. Once I am being reinforced primarily for doing a specific task, my social relationships become bound up in this and my way of life changes. I no longer need generalized verbal communities to gain my ends (Figure 9).

Once again, this is a fairly glib outline of an important figure in social science. Durkheim drew out many other pertinent points for analyzing communities (and their lacks). For instance, he also analyzed the role of rituals in maintaining early forms of community (Durkheim, 1915/1912), and made the point we shall raise in the next chapter: that much of our behavior (that called ritual in particular) functions to maintain a community rather than any more direct effects and might therefore appear to be without a function at all.

Weber (1948) studied the transformation of society towards increasing rationalization. The rational approach for Weber was one based on the ends of efficiency and maximum monetary return, and clearly involves the explicit use of verbal behavior and self-regulation to control other behavior. He traced, for example, how religion turned from a community involvement for its basis to "book religion" where verbal dogma were authorized. He also traced the rationalization of law, and even the rationalization of music from spontaneous and sound-shaped behavior (my term, not his) to the standardized western art music which followed social rules rather than shaping by sounds. As Weber pointed out (along with others), there was a strong role played in this transformation by the development of the western (verbal) system of notation (Weber, 1958). That is, the development of putting music into a standardized rule-governed notation changed the music itself.

The four-fold division of actions used by Weber can be seen to contain the Gemeinschaft and Gesellschaft distinction. Weber argued that three other bases of social action besides the rational one (zweckrational) were pursuing an absolute ethical, religious or aesthetic value (wertrational), emotional actions (affektuell), and traditional actions (traditional). All three would appear to be socially maintained in a behavior analytic sense, thus this group of properties combined match quite closely the Gemeinschaft. In particular, the pursuit of an absolute goal (wertrational) is one way of maintaining a Gemeinschaft community, through rituals and taboos related to the absolute value.

These common properties of generalized group reinforcement to maintain a community were also emphasized by Cooley (1909). Primary groups, as he called them, interacted face-to-face, had an unspecified character (i.e., generalized social reinforcers), were relatively permanent, usually involved a small number of people, and had a high level of intimacy between the people. All these properties again point to generalized and loose social reinforcement between a tight-knit group who directly interact with one another. Similar properties are to be found in the "folk society" of Redfield (1947).

As Durkheim had pointed out, Gemeinschaft groups become harder to maintain with a high level of division of labour and when individuals can follow rational, self-regulated (rule-governed) means to get ends without the group helping. This theme was further developed by Simmel (1950) who saw money as a key mediator of these changes in community functioning, which he described as a "web of group-affiliations" (Simmel, 1955). Money, as a common generalized social reinforcer, allowed peoples' behavior to become removed from the system of a verbal community, and so the community's group goals (emphasized in Chapter 6 and 7.7) became less important.

Like Tönnies, Durkheim and Weber, Simmel (1978/1900) traced out the implications of this for our behavioral and societal lifestyles. An emphasis upon money as the mediator of community reciprocation leads to an emphasis on intellect and verbally-governed behavior over physical skills (p. 434 ff), on time-scheduling, on beliefs in causality, on individuality and impersonal relations between people (p. 297 ff), and on a rational attitude towards other people rather than an emotional (community) one. In fact, Simmel's major book on money (Simmel, 1978/1900) can be read by behavior analysts as a case study on the implementation of a system of generalized reinforcers on verbal community relations. More will be said about money later in this chapter.

Once again, there is more to this writer than the parts I have superficially outlined. Simmel wrote convincingly on the weak ties in society (Simmel, 1955), on forms of competition (Simmel, 1955), on secrecy and knowledge as social constructions (Erickson, 1981; Simmel, 1950), and the effects of modern life on thinking (Simmel, 1950, and 10.9). The works on secrecy are interesting because they show how smaller communities can form and maintain within a larger industrial society. This is perhaps the beginnings of the sociology of modernity, which we will treat later: how to maintain a small, but viable (reinforcing), verbal community in the overall systems of generalized communities within which we live.

The major ideas which we can take from these classical writers are that even communities in the original sense are not maintained by a simple system of reward interdependence, but rather, have a very complex system of sharing and hidden negotiation. Primary groups reinforce a wide range of behaviors of their members even if specific individual ends might not be met by these groups. But the evolved group goals which loosely reinforce all members maintain the group as a whole. On top of this group functioning are the more recent trends towards social relationships based on contractual (rule-governed) obligations and specific goals of the individual (Baldwin & Baldwin, 1978). Other people participate in such goals but the work they actually do is unrelated to the outputs. For example, a typist in a company types not to produce the pages of type written material, but to draw a wage which is is used in ways that are totally unrelated to typing. Finally, the contractual social relationships seem to lead to an increase in verbally-governed behavior, and in less emphasis on face-to-face reinforcement. Verbally-governed behavior is obviously present in Gemeinschaft groups as well, but as a form of behavior which can get people to do specific behaviors, an increase should be apparent in Gesellschaft groups where people are used for specific ends.

Sociolinguistic Speech Communities

While psycholinguists have typically followed Chomsky's lead and treated language use as an internally generated phenomenon, sociolinguists have been sensitive to the social nature of verbal communities for many years—at least since Saussure (1983/1916) spoke in his seminars about "speech communities" and "linguistic communities" (Culler, 1976). Groups of people form speech communities which change the language they utilize either as a result of some environmental or accidental change, or else through language's functional use as a ritual device which helps maintain the group (Guerin, 1992a).

As an example of the latter, a member of a verbal community might initially use a new word with their ingroup for a variety of reason. They might accidently mispronounce a word, they might have made a joke about the word, it might be "deliberately" coined or mispronounced to differentiate their group from another group. However the word is introduced, if it is reinforced by effective use or by explicit ritual approval by the ingroup then the word might maintain a usage even though members of other groups in the same society (the larger verbal community) do not behave appropriately to the word. A new "buzzword" or phrase can therefore be introduced because it acts to keep the group solidified, and this has been reinforced when using ritual "buzzwords" in the past. Sociolinguists therefore find that under conditions of strong ingroup/outgroup conflict or competition, the verbal behavior within groups changes rapidly. In common terms, there is a proliferation of buzzwords.

To measure such changes, one aim of sociolinguistics, therefore, has been to map out the different speech communities and resultant social networks on the basis of the linguistic terms and accents that they use (Coates & Cameron, 1988; Eckert

& McConnell-Ginet, 1992; Labov, 1972, 1990; Milroy, 1987a, b; Romaine, 1982; Trudgill, 1984). This does not tell us about the content of verbal behavior which a verbal community reinforces and maintains, but it does tell us about the pronunciations (autoclitics) reinforced by a verbal community and how these pronunciations change with changing social relations between groups. This obviously provides an important, but not exhaustive, way of showing the existence of a verbal community. As such, the techniques and findings should therefore be of interest in the study of verbal behavior.

All the different sociolinguistic methods cannot be reviewed here, but the basic steps in the methodology are to gain access to communities, to analyze the phonological and syntactical variation in the speech styles of a sample of the communities (as representative as possible in the field), and to find out further details about social networks, marriage and friendship patterns—who speaks to whom and who learns to speak from whom (e.g., Milroy, 1987a, b). These measures are then usually related to community and sociological variables (e.g., Labov, 1990). Many of the social network measures are self-reports, but sociolinguists emphasize that observations should back up the self-reports (Milroy, 1987a).

On a more detailed level than this, studies in the social psychology of language and in anthropology have looked at "psychological" variables and conditions which affect language use in groups, particularly the role of group membership (Coupland, 1984; Coupland, Giles & Wiemann, 1991; Frazer & Cameron, 1989; Gallois, Callan & Johnstone, 1984; Giles & Johnson, 1981, 1987; Hamilton, 1988a; Henley, 1989; Kramarae, 1990; Ng, 1990a, b). While this work has usually been worded in cognitive terms, with little explicit reference to a verbal community's reinforcement of "appropriate" linguistic variations in verbal content and pronunciation, such behavior analytic variables are clearly involved.

For example, we read: "...when an outgroup language is the societal norm, ethnolinguistic differentiation can invoke considerable social sanctions as a consequence. Moreover, in some situations, little cognitive effort may be involved in maintaining one's own dialect or language within the private and 'safe' confines of the home" (Giles & Johnson, 1987, p. 69). We can have little quarrel with such an approach if the second sentence is re-worded as: "One's own dialect or language can be maintained within the confines of the home because this situation is private and 'safe', which means that it has been reinforced in the past or at least not punished as it is in public".

With such slight re-wordings, the details of such studies tell us much about autoclitic functioning under social control. Saying a word with a particular pronunciation makes it more likely to be reinforced in some social contexts (ingroup) but not in others (outgroup). The linguistic ingroups and outgroups are the verbal sub-communities maintaining the linguistic variables being studied, and many of the variables clearly reflect the strength of generalized social reinforcement within a verbal community.

One measure of the strength of generalized social reinforcement within a verbal community has recently been called "ethnolinguistic vitality" (e.g., Giles & Johnson, 1987). Leaving aside the cognitive jargon used, ethnolinguistic vitality seems to be measuring how many facets of the group members' verbal and nonverbal behavior are also reinforced by the verbal community—in effect: how loose is the community reinforcement of member behavior? Typical questions on a self-report measure ask how highly a minority language is valued, how much the groups intermarry, how well-represented the linguistic groups are represented in business, and how strong and active they consider the linguistic group to be (Bourhis, Giles & Rosenthal, 1981; Pittam, Gallois & Willemyns, 1991). Even if we accept the use of self-reports, these sorts of sociolinguistic methods do not reveal individual change in verbal behavior, only general patterns and general changes in verbal behavior across verbal communities. While this has not been the traditional approach of behavior analysts to verbal behavior, it is a valid part of studying verbal communities.

When looking at the verbal functioning of individuals, there are other findings from the social psychology of language which are more directly relevant and useful for behavior analysts. One relevant finding is that within conversations there seems to be a common behavior (an autoclitic function) of accommodating speech to that of the speaker on many dimensions. For example, someone listening to a speaker who has a strong Japanese accent might start using more of the Japanese vowel phonemes, even when talking in English, or might start clipping their phonemes. Clearly, changing your speech to match that of a speaker has been reinforced in the past, and the accommodation studies can inform us of some of the social variables and stimulus conditions which control this.

Many discriminative conditions for speech accommodation have been proposed and measured by social psychologists of language (Coupland, 1984; Giles, Coupland & Coupland, 1991; Street & Giles, 1982), although the reinforcing or punishing conditions are not usually dealt with explicitly. As has been argued elsewhere in this book, while a study of the functional consequences of speaking is necessary for a complete analysis of verbal behavior, because verbal behaviors are typically reinforced in either a generalized manner or by altering other verbal functions (Schlinger, 1993), the specific consequence variables are easily overlooked and the behavior can appear to occur without any reinforcement (Guerin, 1992b).

As an example of speech accommodation research, Coupland (1984) studied an assistant (Sue) in a travel-agency in Cardiff, recorded her speech to customers, and found that she accommodated her speech to their accents. The methodology of recording verbal behavior (autoclitic accents in this case) over time of a single subject with an intervention applied at different times (different customers) is not unlike the methodology of behavior analysis (Sidman, 1960). While averages were also reported, whole transcripts, sentence-by-sentence, from the conversations were used by Coupland to show very specific control of Sue's speech by that of the customers. This methodology comes very close to being a behavior analytic study of verbal behavior.

The importance of control by consequence was also partly appreciated in this research, albeit not in behavioral terms. Coupland (1984, p. 63) wrote:

It has been speculated that the rewards to Sue of this speech accommodation are that she gains her interlocutors' approval and/or makes her communication more efficient. Arguably, travel-agency assistants not only 'desire a gratifying interaction' (Giles & Powesland, 1975, p. 158) but are employed partly to ensure that this comes about.

This type of research, and the transcripts given, provide very good examples of autoclitic functioning during conversation.

Like sociolinguistics, the social psychology of language most commonly studies pronunciation variations, and therefore tells us little about the content (substantive mands and tacts) of verbal behavior maintained by a verbal community. Two people might be in groups which maintain identical pronunciations but one group reinforces statements about God and one group punishes such statements. So these types of studies do not exhaust the verbal behaviors maintained in communities. Other theories in social psychology, however, have explored the wider verbal behaviors which can be maintained, and these tend now to be dealt with as social identity theories or as social representations (see Guerin, 1992c for the latter).

Self-categorization and Social Identity Theories

Social identity theories examine how people come to report an identity with their social groups and how this social identity leads to group phenomena such as conformity, group cohesiveness and intergroup discrimination (Abrams & Hogg, 1990; Hogg, 1992; Hogg & Abrams, 1988; Tajfel, 1974; Tajfel & Turner, 1979; Turner, Hogg, Oakes, Reicher & Wetherall, 1987; Turner & Oakes, 1989). Of particular note is that, like the concept of a verbal community, such theories do not define just any behaviors involving two or more people as a social identity group. If I happen to be assigned to work with three other people this does not guarantee that I will develop a social identity with that group. The groups being talked about said to be "real" groups rather than "nonsense" groups (Fraser & Foster, 1984), and they are probably identical to reference and membership groups (Charters & Newcomb, 1966; Killian, 1952; Merton, 1957; Newcomb, 1966). Most importantly, they are not just haphazard groups but groups which have the properties of a verbal community (Guerin, 1992c; Skinner, 1957).

For the behavior analyst, then, social identity means being reinforced by a verbal community. If I "have an identity" with a church group it is because they shape many (but perhaps not all) of my behaviors, and they reinforce them loosely—without very much discrimination in the short-term if behavior is within certain bounds. My "social identity" therefore consists of my verbalizations (often covert) about the verbal communities which reinforce me, with some of these "self" verbalizations having been constructed by those verbal communities in the first place (8.4 and

Guerin, 1992c). We have already seen above that the languages and sub-languages we use are said to form a part of our social identity (Giles & Johnson, 1987), but at the same time there are other verbal communities which maintain other behaviors which form part of our social identity.

This way of viewing social identity theories makes them important to behavior analysis because they spell out some conditions under which we report belonging to a verbal community or not. The conditions for developing a system of reinforcement characteristic of verbal communities are the same conditions which social identity theorists argue differentiate social identity groups from people who happen to be in the same place at the same time. For example, even if the group I am in fails at a major goal, and there is no supposed "group reinforcement", I still consider myself as belonging to that group because of the generalized reinforcers which have been given intermittently in the past (cf. Turner, Hogg, Turner & Smith, 1984). So like the verbal communities of behavior analysis, specific, immediate and repeated reinforcement are not necessary conditions for social identity. Rather, they are groups with generalized, intermittent systems of loose mutual reinforcement which have usually been developed over time. In colloquial terms, verbal communities are said to be "forgiving" in the short term; in anthropological terms these have been called generalized reciprocity relationships (Sahlins, 1965).

One large part of the social identity research has been to look at how "cognitive" categorization based on social identity with groups leads to various social psychological phenomena. That is, the research has looked at how "cognitively" labelling a group as an ingroup leads to a variety of effects (Turner & Oakes, 1989). For behavior analysts this means studying the ways in which verbalizing or naming an ingroup/outgroup affects future verbal behavior and any verbally governed behavior. Some research has found that even arbitrary labels can affect behavior in groups (e.g., Tajfel, Billig, Bundy & Flament, 1971; Tajfel & Wilkes, 1963). If there are two arbitrarily labelled groups A and B, and I am assigned to be a member of group A, then my future verbal behavior (or any verbally governed nonverbal behavior) is found to be partially controlled by those labels because this has been reinforced in the past.

Such an approach is important for informing behavior analysts about the effects of verbally governed behavior on other socially maintained behaviors. Naming of a group affects (controls) social identity (verbalizing about the group and behavior) which affects future group behaviors which are primarily verbal or verbally governed. This research is slightly different in emphasis to social identity theories. It is sometimes called "self-categorization theory" (e.g., Turner & Oakes, 1989—an interesting case in itself of naming groups to differentiate them) although both terms probably refer to the same phenomena in the long run. Self-categorization theory is more concerned with how people come to name aspects about themselves and the groups they belong to, and the effects that arise by using those names and the names of other groups.

Like sociolinguistics, then, social identity theories (including self-categorization theory) can provide us with information about the behavior of people when their behavior is controlled by the generalized reciprocity systems of verbal communities, and especially about how verbal behaviors interact with other social behaviors (also Price, 1989).

Social identity theories, on the other hand, can learn much from behavior analysis about the "motivational" bases (the effective consequences) of verbal behavior and how to best talk about them. At the moment, the systems of verbal community reinforcement are talked about by social identity theorists in the following ways: as a "drive which leads us to compare ourselves with others" (Abrams & Hogg, 1990, p. 3); as the "desire for positive self-esteem...[and] the need for self-definition, or structure" (Abrams & Hogg, 1990, p. 6); "Individuals strive to achieve or to maintain positive social identity" (Tajfel & Turner, 1979, p. 40); and as a weak criticism of a straw-person form of reinforcement or "rewards" (e.g., Turner & Oakes, 1989, p. 235). It is not that these needs and desires are particularly wrong, it is just that they are a very shallow analysis of behavior: why should people want positive self-esteem or want self-definition? Social identity theorists can learn from Skinner (1950) and behavior analysis about better ways to word such "need" and "drive" statements.

More detailed summaries of the theories and experimental findings of the literature in this area are available in the following: Hogg, 1992; Hogg and Abrams, 1988; Turner and Giles, 1981; Turner, Hogg, Oakes, Reicher and Wetherall, 1987; Turner and Oakes, 1989.

"Community" in Community Psychology

There has been some debate in community psychology over what is meant by "community" (Chavis & NewBrough, 1986), but a large part of this has followed sociological discussions closely, as detailed earlier. The main impetus has been around the two notions of a "psychological sense of community" and the "empowerment" of communities (Fawcett, 1991; Fawcett et al., in press; McMillan & Chavis, 1986; Rappaport, 1987; Sarason, 1974; Seidman, 1988; Smith, Fawcett & Balcazar, 1991).

In my terms, the psychological sense of community has been carefully differentiated by community psychologist from people just living close together precisely because there must be generalized reinforcing of community members before there can be that elusive "psychological sense of community". Community psychologists often speak out against the community interventions as usually practiced by behavior analysts (Society for the Experimental Analysis of Behavior, 1987b), which target specific reinforcers to individuals. Rather, community psychologists continually urge that something more be done to empower communities and this would appear to be the establishment of verbal communities which provide generalized reinforcers to members. It is not that direct individual reinforcement to change communities is wrong, but that verbal community intervention is also needed.

The community psychology aim to empower (or develop) communities to do this more effectively comes from research showing better mental and physical adjustment with a better sense of community. From what has been said so far from sociology, sociolinguistics, and social identity theory, this is not surprising: so much of our behavior is mediated verbally and nonverbally by the layers of communities to which we reciprocate (belong). More will be said about this in Chapter 10.

One input that has been made from community psychology is in the measurement of community, which is interesting despite its reliance upon self-reports of community "feeling". Glynn (1981) developed a questionnaire for measuring "psychological sense of community" (PSC) where "psy chological sense" primarily meant self-reports of both behavior and verbal community-reinforced statements about communities and neighbourhood. The latter is usefully measured by asking respondents to rate the items for their "ideal" community. Some of the items were "Most of my friends in this community are here to stay", "In an ideal community there would be community leaders whom you could trust", and "People can depend on each other in this community" (Glynn, 1981).

Glynn (1981) found that this scale differentiated between people living in three different communities, which were expected on other grounds to have more or less sense of community (see Table 1 in Glynn, 1981). An interesting finding was that the strongest predictor of psychological sense of community was the number of years the respondent expected to live in the community. While the direction of causality is doubtful here, people report that the future interactions they expect to have determine how close they "feel" to the community. [But alternatively, if people do not "feel" part of the community then they might expect not to be in the community as long.]

Glynn (1986) followed this work up by comparing the results of the PSC to the sense of neighbourhood. Respondents were asked whether, if someone asked them "What is your community?", they would reply with family, friends, work, neighbourhood, town or city, group or club, church, or other. The major finding was that neighbourhood was mentioned quite frequently, despite the sociological suggestions that neighbourhoods are no longer important to people (also found by Campbell, 1990). What this highlights, however, is the lack of clarity about what the respondents might mean by community and that there can be multiple communities in which people participate. As we have seen, in the broadest sense we might answer to the question "What is your community?" with "Speakers of the my language" and with good reason (Milroy, 1987a). The problem is one of people not having terms for the sorts of communities being studied.

A better approach is to measure specific functional aspects of a well-defined type of community (e.g., the sociolinguistic communities outlined above). Good examples of this comes from community psychology itself–the measurement of social networks which provide social support (see Chapter 10), the functional definition of settings which support community activities (Barker & Associates, 1978; Perkins, Burns, Perry & Nielsen, 1988), and communities in the workplace

(Klein & D'Aunno, 1986). And in this regard, behavior analysts are lagging behind in defining and studying functional communities.

One last point to make is that we often do not notice how much gets done for us in our environment through verbal communities rather than through any direct action of our own—even direct social behavior. It is only when we lose our verbal communities that the difference is most noticed: so many small things we could previously rely on happening, with perhaps only a small setting event from us, no longer occur. In the extreme this leads to culture shock, trauma, and disorientation (Furnham & Bochner, 1986; Nicassio, 1985). In extreme cases, such as total war, reciprocity even in small interactions cannot be relied upon, and these small events show the ubiquitous reach of the verbal communities in which we participate:

> People walked abruptly out of one another's lives. A friend who'd waved goodbye on a Kawasaki Station platform died the same night in a fire-bomb attack; a kindly factory hand who'd given the girls a share when the workers had a special ration of frozen mandarins received his draft papers and wasn't at his bench one morning. As each day began, the exchange of greetings was full of the joy of having met again, while eyes meeting in farewell each evening held the sorrow of knowing that this might be the last time. (Gō, 1985, p. 90)

As we will see in Chapter 10, this can be overcome with social support through social networks, which is a way of saying that they are verbal communities which can still be relied upon. For instance, number of friends or acquaintances in a new place predicts better adjustment (Nicassio, 1983).

The "Stranger" in Sociology

One other fertile area for the study of verbal communities has been in the sociological study of strangers and "deviants" (Simmel, 1950). While this literature might look from the outside to be of interest only to psychologists directly involved with the so-called deviants of society, it does in fact contain much that is relevant to verbal communities.

Rather than investigate how communities tie themselves together and socialize their members, the study of strangers looks at how people face an already intact community when they are an outsider (Harman, 1988). This might be a "bag lady" living in a modern city, an anthropologist meeting a new tribal group for the first time, or a school child on the first day in a new school. Where there is no normal function for the person in society, they can in fact live their entire life as a marginal member of society.

Harman (1988) summarizes most of this literature well, and shows how the variables involved in maintaining verbal communities play a role when strangers confront groups and negotiate access. These include linguistic membership and fluency, the social role to be played by the stranger, previous social ties to group members, and resource scarcity within the group.

9.2. Social Behavior as Discriminative Context and Consequence

There is a distinction which needs to be made when analyzing behaviors in the context of a verbal community. When the effects of a behavior are not found in the environment, and a verbal community looks suspiciously like the culprit maintaining the behavior, it is tempting to look immediately for effects which directly benefit the community. For example, not eating pork might have a community payoff of reducing disease vectors or "...because pig farming was a threat to the integrity of the basic cultural and natural ecosystems of the Middle East" (Harris, 1974, p. 35). Whatever the explanation, there is a tendency when behaviors are found which seem *irrational with respect to their environmental effects,* to look for a direct community payoff (e.g., Barrett, 1984; Kottak, 1980; Harris, 1974, 1979; Ross, 1980, for some of the most sensible examples).

As long as such explanations do not invoke a "group mind" which "tries" to gain a benefit for its community, such analyses can be insightful and useful (Biglan, Glasgow & Singer, 1990; Glenn, 1988, 1989; Lloyd, 1985; Malagodi & Jackson, 1989; Malott, 1988; Vargas, 1985). However, such views have been strongly criticized in social anthropology for missing something out (Barrett, 1984; Friedman, 1974; Keesing, 1981). Some of these criticisms we can ignore, because behavior analysis would not make the mistakes impuned: that there is a group mind, that there are no payoffs for individuals but only for the group, and that mediating behaviors do not exist.

There is one point though which has cropped up repeatedly in this book. This relates to behaviors often called "symbolic" or "ritual" by the critics (Barrett, 1984; Friedman, 1974; Keesing, 1981). It is argued that many behaviors are done not for any individual or group reinforcing effects, but because they are symbolic or ritual. In behavior analytic terms, what they are getting at with these term is that the consequences of such behaviors are not the reinforcing consequences, but rather, the behaviors are discriminative stimuli for more generalized community contingencies. In particular, most of the behaviors referred to have a consequences of maintaining the group itself.

As an example, consider the behavior of a group who drink in a particular pub, occasionally calling on one of their members to gulp a pint of beer admidst laughing and cheering. The beer itself might act as a reinforcer but there is clearly more involved here. The group approach might be to look for a "group outcome" or metacontingency which would benefit the group in the long-run, such as the increased health and vigour of group members as opposed to groups who do not encourage drinking beer (perhaps unlikely!). What is being argued here is that the beer gulping behavior might be irrelevant or arbitrary, and that the major function of the behavior is to reinforce the maintenance of the group itself: the cheers and laughter would reinforce belonging to that group and the "beneficial group outcome" is in merely belonging to that group and keeping it together rather than in drinking beer or doing some other ritual behavior.

> ...anthropology has known since Durkheim's time that rituals establish or enhance solidarity among those joining in their performance...Yet we have much to learn about just *how* ritual creates this solidarity. (Rappaport, 1984, p. 347, italics in original).

The point here is not to deny the existence of metacontingencies or group outcomes, but to caution against finding a direct function in all cases, especially ritual behaviors. Such behaviors include the many ritual behaviors we have, including all the "polite" behaviors and greeting rituals, the use of language itself, taboos, symbols, money, and the many verbally-governed behaviors. For example, it is sometimes said in behavior analysis that the reinforcement for saying "Hello!" to someone you meet is the effect it has on them: they reply to you; they might tip their hat. But as well as any reinforcing effects thus gained, saying "Hello!" reinforces the community of polite speakers as well: it is a discriminative stimulus for a large range of generalized community reinforcers the likes of which I have obtained from smiling people in the past. Such symbolic functions should not be ignored in analyses of human social behavior. The same point will occur when discussing notions of rationality.

9.3. Behaviors Maintaining a Community

One of the guiding principles of this book is that most human behaviors do not have immediate, obvious consequences. Instead, many nonobvious consequences were outlines in Chapter 2. This is especially apparent in the maintenance of verbal communities. The reason for this is that with a verbal community not only can the effect your behavior has on another person be reinforcing, but as we saw immediately above, it can also be a discriminative stimulus for a whole range of other community reinforcers (Guerin, 1992a).

This difference has confused many social scientists since obvious reinforcers cannot often be found for social behavior. In particular, ritualistic behaviors will often be discriminative stimuli for all the many reinforcers available from having a verbal community or social identity in the first place. That is, carrying out a ritual functions to maintain the group rather than being reinforcing in itself. From this, many social scientists have concluded that ritual behaviors are unmotivated, because there are no obvious reinforcers.

This means that when analyzing behaviors in a verbal community, the effects of the behaviors might have immediate reinforcement but might also function to keep the verbal community together as well. If I act polite towards a group of people and politely shake hands with them, this is likely to have immediate effects on their behaviors and also to include me in the group for future occasions of loosely discriminated reinforcement. Some of these types of social behaviors are analyzed in this section.

Languages and Paralanguages

We have already seen how sociolinguistic groups form verbal communities. It is likely that speaking a language also acts to reinforce the members and therefore maintain the community. This is perhaps not obvious until one lives in a foreign country where one speaks the minority language. Merely being able to speak to any member of your linguistic community is reinforcing, not because of anything mysterious about language but because you cease to have easy and accurate effects on other people as soon as you stop speaking the same language. In order to cause someone to get you food, someone who does not speak your language, you have to make all sorts of hand-signals, and even then you cannot accurately specify the particular food you want. Languages maintain a verbal community because you are able to get so many very precise effects if you speak the language correctly.

So there is a circle of effects which occurs: language is only possible with a group; the group over time evolves and changes what effects occur when a word of phrase is said; and talking in that language has those effects but also has the added effect of making it more likely that the verbal community will continue to talk together that way in the future. So verbal communities maintain a language or subculture (Fine & Kleinman, 1979; Hebdige, 1979) and the language or subculture at the same time reinforces belonging to the group (social identity).

I have briefly dealt with gestures and paralanguages in 4.2–the so-called "nonverbal" behaviors. Having covered verbal communities we can now see how gestures fit into the wider community rather than being specific effects which might be innate. A wink has no effect except on other people who are part of a verbal community for which particular ways of behaving following winks have been reinforced or punished, as the case might be.

The functional study of gestures, prosody, and paralinguistics is the study, then, of autoclitics and the verbal communities which support them (Patterson, 1990; Street, 1990). A small change in gesture, emphasis or accent can be a discriminative stimulus in that verbal community for a very different effect, and therefore for a very different social control. The function might also be one of helping the verbal behavior be understood easier, in the same way that grammar facilitates ease of responding (Guerin, 1992b). Both are social events, but the latter facilitates other consequences and does not have social consequences specific to its production.

The verbal community basis of gestures also is traced by Geertz (1973) in his discussion of Ryle's (1971) idea of "thick description". Based on Ryle, Geertz compared one boy contracting his eyelids because of an involuntary twitch, another shutting his eyelids as a conspiratorial wink, and another who is parodying the first boy's twitch. All the eyelid movements appear the the same but they are obviously very different. It is the supposed interpretation (the thick description) of the latter two events that Geertz believes makes cultural analysis different from analyses in the physical sciences.

As we have seen when approaching this same type of argument elsewhere in this book (2.3 and 10.3 for example), the difference or the meaning of the twitches lies in the sources of consequences. The twitch might have no functional consequences if it is involuntary, although it might have Pavlovian setting events. The other two eyelid movements are maintained by social consequences but of different types. So no new social science or cultural foundations are required; the natural science approach can explain the difference between these behaviors. The foundations for each type of wink are still very different and cannot be treated as the same because their consequences are very different.

Totems, Taboos and Rituals

The same pattern just mentioned in connection with Geertz, that two behaviors can look the same but be analyzed very differently because of two different sources of consequences, will continue through this section as well. For each of the topics covered here, totem, taboos and rituals, some social scientists have contended that they have a basis in material functions such as food and sex, while others have contended that they have a symbolic or cultural foundation. In each case some of the latter social scientists also contend that the one cannot be reduced to the latter. However, behavior analysis does this by showing a very different foundation to symbolic or cultural behaviors—a foundation in verbal communities—while maintaining at the same time that verbal communities are ultimately built upon principles of natural science—principles outlined in the first part of this book.

It is interesting to compare this to the phenomena in Chapter 4. When no obvious reinforcers were found for imitation, gestures, social facilitation and observational learning, an innate basis was usually proposed by someone or another. In the present section, when no obvious reinforcers are found for community-involved social behaviors, a separate social science discipline—textual, hermeneutic, interpretive or postmodern—has almost always been suggested by psychologists, sociologists or anthropologists. Once again we can actually deal with these phenomena as having special properties belonging to verbal communities (when groups become mutually reinforcing in a loosely discriminating way) but at the same time have these special properties based in pure natural science with no new principles of behavior needed for analysis.

Totems. Totems are often thought of as separate from religion, although many important writers have argued against this (e.g., Durkheim, 1915/1912). With totems we can see a simple type of group maintenance. A group inherits or proclaims a totem, and behaviors associated with that totem must be carried out in the future. Failure to do so is usually socially punished. What the group then do with this socially maintained authority will vary between any two groups. Some will use the group cohesion to legitimize interests of particular people in the group: others will use it to advantage all the group in the long run.

This social system behind totems can be seen in the close connection between the social aspects of the group and the totem, a closer connection than any metaphysical beliefs which might accompany the totemic behaviors (Durkheim, 1915/1912). Indeed, "the sentiments produced by the dominance of society over the individual become attached to the totem as the most distinctive symbol of the group" (Giddens, 1978, p. 91).

The social contingencies which maintain the totems, and which in turn maintain the group cohesion, have usually evolved some typical features. First, explicit, overt behaviors are reinforced rather than just the verbal recitation of the name of the totem. Explicit behaviors allow explicit social consequences to be made contingent upon completion of the behaviors. Second, the totems are usually arbitrary common events or objects, although the supernatural aspects verbally reported might lead one to suspect that mysterious objects would be preferable. The reason that mysterious objects are not preferable, however, is that common events or objects allow more frequent contact with totems and therefore more common group reinforcement or avoidance of punishment. A group with ritual behaviors based around a once-in-ten years appearing totem would find little to maintain generalized reinforcement between-times. The use of classes of objects rather than a single object also increase the frequency of contact, especially if this becomes shaped into language forms in use (Lévi-Strauss, 1963a, 1966; Lévy-Bruhl, 1966).

Taboos. Taboos are often thought to have two separate functions. The first is equivalent to what has been talked about so far: that they serve to maintain and localize social compliance which is then useful for other group activities, and in the long run probably advantageous (also Lambek, 1992). The second is to do with certain events such as danger, blood, handling corpses, menstruation, childbirth, and killing and gutting animals. For example:

> And we find expressed in the same term, those of taboo, two quite separate social functions: (1) the classification and identification of transgressions (which is associated with, though it can be studied apart from, processes of social learning), and (2) the institutional localization of danger, both by the specification of the dangerous and by the protection of society from endangered, and hence dangerous, persons. (Steiner, 1956, p. 147)

This second function seems more to do with classical conditioning of avoidance, the minor phobias to do with unpleasant and dangerous events. Similar occurrences can be found with vertigo, snake phobias, aversions to eating liver, and general dirty objects (Douglas, 1966). Most of us would show similar "symptoms" if we had to handle a corpse!

It is important to note that in the anthropological literature, social compliance is still utilized for group cohesion in handling such messy events, so the two functions of taboo cannot be totally separated, as Steiner (1956) also emphasized.

So long as people have minor phobias, whatever their source, this can be used as a way of maintaining social compliance for other ends.

This suggests that phobias and avoidance are like a free form of motivation which can be used for group maintenance purposes. This property was mentioned in 2.3. Once an avoidance or negative reinforcement contingency is set up, it needs little input to keep it going. Merely having nothing happen reinforces the behavior. Given the problem we have encountered of how groups are to maintain social compliance and cohesion when their benefits are often remote and not obvious, it is no wonder this form of maintenance has been widely utilized.

The same can be said, in fact, for superstitious consequences (2.3). They require little maintenance in themselves once they have been made, unlike positive reinforcement and punishment, so they too can be utilized for group purposes. And indeed the anthropological literature gives some examples of this. The point being made, however, emphasizes with anthropology that "natives" do not work for superstitions because they do not have "higher thinking" like we do, but because the superstitious behavior can be seen to be a way of allowing remote contingencies to benefit the group—not by keeping people ignorant but by maintaining the group verbal behaviors and instruction following. So the people are acting quite rational with respect to the subtle verbal community contingencies. It was the early anthropologists and psychologists who missed the subtleties of what was going on when studying "superstitious" maintenance of religions and taboos.

Similar events can be seen in our societies. Standing up and singing a national anthem does not change any direct environmental contingencies of much note, but rather, it maintains the verbal community and a whole way of life which has many benefits. And this "whole way of life" is one solution to gaining remote consequences for the whole community. It is not the only way, nor perhaps even the best way, but it cannot be sustained by the remote consequences alone.

Rituals. We have seen in the last section that a large part of the social rituals and social relations involve the allocation of consequences or accountability (Douglas, 1980; Gluckman, 1972). It is precisely because verbal mediators do not require direct contact with environmental contingencies that all sorts of "irrational" beliefs can mediate the allocation of consequences. As long as there is generalized social compliance maintained by some means or another, the social control thus exercised will work just as well as if there were "rational", direct environmental consequences acting.

What is happening in rituals, then? It again seems to be the exercise of social control: that is, the social contexts and social consequences are maintaining the ritual rather than any consequences of the acts that are actually performed. The verbal comments on these acts by participants might invoke consequences from a God or from another source, but these probably do not tact the functional consequences. As Bloch (1989a, p. 29) rightly points out, formal ritual languages make social cohesion even more likely by reducing the number of options of reply available and therefore precluding dissension.

So both taboos and rituals will develop for both individuals and groups when there is either a clash between consequences (3.2) or a need to bridge a remote contingency. On a group level, taboos and rituals will also develop when there are clashes between the consequences for the group and for the individuals. What taboos and rituals seem to do is to provide a measure of social control to mediate some important changes of consequences which occur during our lives. It should not be thought, however, that rituals are therefore static or unchanging. As Harrison (1992) points out, the existence of rituals can be seen as the property of the groups or leaders of the groups, and struggles occur to control the rituals. New leaders will make small, distinctive changes to reinforce their version of the verbal community. And depending upon the background social changes, the rituals might not even work properly (Geertz, 1973, p. 146).

Consider the following three examples. If Marvin Harris (1979) is correct about the ecological and dietary basis for not eating certain food types then this will be an extremely remote contingency, showing an effect only over many generations. This alone could not sustain the prohibitions, so ritualized forms of social control are needed. Hence we have a large variety of rituals and taboos evolved (selected) to enforce the verbal prohibition and therefore bridge the delay.

Or consider secondly the changes in contingency contexts and consequences when a member of a family marries someone from another family and leaves to live with this other family. Many large and many subtle changes take place during such an event and clashes between multiple individual contingencies and between group and individual contingencies occur. In line with this, many rituals and taboos have culturally evolved for such events, which function to provide a delay in the changes so as they can be dynamically shaped and the long term consequences can become apparent (tracking). Third, what about the long-term consequences of behaving as a member of a nation, when events like paying taxes puts one off? To maintain the nationhood, various rituals such as saluting a flag or standing up during a national anthem have culturally evolved.

The role of rituals in sustaining compliance with verbal rules produces an interesting conclusion: that the breakdown in traditional rituals, taboos and religious observances has occurred through both the development of self-regulation and through the weakening of family consequences. On the first point, the development of verbal self-regulation means that the remote contingencies can be contacted without needing group guidance through ritual and social control (Figure 9 in Chapter 7). Good decisions can be made without consulting your elders or praying in a church.

On the second point, our most important contingencies, such as those to do with food, marriage and careers, no longer involve family or social leaders as was the case in other times (once again I am referring to western societies here). Anyone who can earn money can gather food without relying on their family members, so the long term consequences of breaking family related taboos no longer apply. Indeed, most of us would not even consider asking our elders for advice on most life events. We make our own decisions.

In considering life in tribal centers, however, this is not the case, and the major contingencies are mediated by family and tribal elders. This allows them to develop a strong source of social compliance which can then function to maintain other the verbal parts of the rituals and taboos. And these can further support remote contingencies which are strengthening in the long run for the group and could not be gained individually. The whole tight social system, then, operates to enhance social compliance which allows the group to contact beneficial remote contingencies, which they cannot obtain through their own self control or other means of bridging delay.

Food and Eating Rituals. With the importance of food and nutrition to all people, and its common power to act as a strengthener of behavior, it is no wonder that it plays a central role in most cultures. And given the importance, therefore, of food in regulating the social powers in a group of people (who controls the food?), it is no wonder that food also comes to play a major role in the symbolic behaviors of all people if the verbal behavior controls the regulation of food.

The study of food and its ramifications has been done in a number of different ways. Some have concentrated on the religious, taboo or symbolic aspects of food: how certain foods are not allowed to be eaten, how certain rituals (behaviors) have to be carried out before eating the food, and how food can only be prepared in certain ways (Douglas, 1966; Steiner, 1956). In the present terms these deal with the exercise of social control through verbal control of behaviors connected with eating.

Others have described the ecological aspects of food: how much food can be produced given the affordances of the environment; how much food does a person need, how do different groups maintain a nutritional balance; and how does ecological balance determine population size, various customs related to food, and migration (Feil, 1987; Harris, 1979; Lee & DeVore, 1968; Rappaport, 1984; Schwimmer, 1973).

Still others have focussed specifically on the exchange of food and its relation to social organization: how ecologically rare food items can be gained; how intergroup consequences can be shaped through the exchange of food items; how food items themselves can become discriminative stimuli rather than consequences and therefore come to act as symbols mediating social control (offerings of food); and the ritual (social control) function of sharing food between people (Blau, 1964; Evans-Pritchard, 1940; Kent, 1993; Krige & Krige, 1939; Mauss, 1966; Sahlins, 1972; Schwimmer, 1973).

All of these facets show how much more complex food is in a behavior analysis than the mistaken idea that its function is always as a primary reinforcer in the three-term contingency. It is this role of social consequences and the discriminative social contexts of verbal behavior which gives behavior analysis an advantage over other forms of psychology for interpreting anthropological materials. These two roles of food have been recognized in anthropology but not psychology: "...while in 1929,

Radcliffe-Brown believed that interest was conferred upon animals and plants because they were 'eatable', in 1951 he saw clearly that the real reason for this interest lay in the fact that they are, if I may use the word, 'thinkable' " (Lévi-Strauss, 1963b, p. 2). The behavior analyst does not see these as exclusive roles, though, as Lévi-Strauss implies.

Politics, the Family and Social Relationship Rituals. With regards to the social organization and social relations in different cultures, one can see a wide range of maintaining consequences. At one end of this, some relations are shaped by direct contingencies, which might involve fighting, kissing, pushing and the exchange of goods with balanced or negative reciprocity (Sahlins, 1965). At the other extreme, some relations are maintained very ritualistically, which means that they are primarily rule-governed or verbal community controlled (generalized reciprocity, Sahlins, 1965). Most cultures are, of course, a mixture of these, and it is their unravelling which will involve an anthropological behavioral analysis.

This also suggests that social groups can have two types of rulers or heads. Crudely put, these are the rulers by direct contingencies and the rulers by indirect or verbal contingencies. As can be extrapolated from all that has been said in Chapter 7, the problem for the rulers by direct contingencies is that control must be taken over the motivators: the food, sexual relations, and means of production. The problem for the rulers by verbal contingencies is that of getting social compliance to the verbal statements made since verbal behavior is only as strong as the social compliance.

Direct control was probably the original control before verbal behavior appeared. Its operation required direct social reinforcement and punishment. Such forms of social behavior can be seen in the interactions of young children who push and pull to get their way. The rise of verbal control can be seen in the rise of religious control. An interesting task would be to analyze how social compliance was maintained in order for the religious pronouncements to work in the first place. The Inquisition springs to mind!

With the early combinations of verbal and direct control of social groups we see the beginnings of the modern state. How powerful it must have been to have the compliance to social verbal rules maintained by direct contingencies. If this was done then almost any arbitrary verbal statements could be imposed on large groups of people. Thus we can begin to analyze the functioning of witchdoctors, the mediaeval Roman Catholic church, and religious dictatorships, by asking how social compliance to their verbal behaviors was maintained. Witchdoctors seem to use verbal behavior itself (like car salespersons) or else superstitious reinforcement; the others used state superstructures (means of production; control of primary motivators) to reinforce social compliance to their verbal rules.

As we have seen in studying groups in this chapter, the primary groups are those that have the most important consequences. In most small social groups this is the family unit, as well as the heads of whatever form of government might be in power. The consequences are likely to be verbally mediated in such forms and therefore do not appear as simple punishments or response costs. Anthropologists have found the same, that a large part of social rituals and social relations involve the allocation of consequences (Gluckman, 1972), or the method of "tracing accountability" (Douglas, 1980, p. 12). And part of the wisdom of the group elders is in knowing the contexts for the different social consequences (Evans-Pritchard, 1976).

Since the family is in large part the controller of consequences, or the controller of the contexts of consequences, the relations between family members will become a major focus in small groups (Evans-Pritchard, 1951). Such small groups have tight regulations on who can marry whom, and who can do what towards whom. Family trees are known in great detail (Fox, 1967), probably maintained because of their mediating role in current consequences. Old family events and rituals can determine the allocation of consequences even in a contemporary situation (Tanizaki, 1957).

At the risk of oversimplifying, consider the following about remembering and kinship relations: "Lines of relationships, so complex to the outsider to unravel, would be crystal clear and easy to recall to the person who stands to gain a cow or an ox from correctly computing them" (Douglas, 1980, p. 75). The cows and oxen do not act as primary reinforcers here in a simple minded version of reinforcement, but are part of complex community contingencies.

Another point discovered by anthropologists is that in tribal societies the larger family is as important as the nuclear family. While a husband and wife (or wives!) might live in the same compound, they live with many relatives and have contact with many others besides the spouse. So the consequences are not tightly tied to one spouse as they tend to be in western society. This change in group contingencies leads to a change in group behavior. Some examples have been presented in novel form of the changes in social contingencies when a man marries more than one wife (e.g., Achebe, 1988; Bâ, 1981).

Money and Commodity Exchange

One view of money in society is that money is an evil influence which destroys relationships and wreaks havoc on the moral order of a community. While this view is implicit (and less extreme) in some sociology and anthropology, we must beware treating it as fixed (Bloch, 1989b). From both behavior analysis and anthropology (Bloch & Parry, 1989), money can be seen as a secondary reinforcer which only exists by virtue of there being a community in the first place. Durkheim also wrote, in a similar way, that there must be prior non-contractual elements in all contracts. Simmel (1978/1900, p. 345) also wrote that: "under specific historical conditions, money simultaneously exerts both a disintegrating and a unifying effect". So money assumes the existence of a prior verbal community, and the non-contractual elements are the loose mutual reinforcing of a verbal community.

In analyzing the effects of money we must therefore look for variables related to the social community and the commodities of exchange rather than to money itself. Socially destructive effects of money, for example, might be more likely to arise from divisions of labour than from money, although the division of labour encourages the use of monetary systems (Durkheim, 1933/1893; Simmel, 1978/ 1900). Further, there is evidence that monetary systems were alive and well long before western capitalism took over, and the effects of many of these monetary systems was extremely positive to the social communities involved (for examples, see Dalton, 1965; Einzig, 1949; Parry & Bloch, 1989; Sahlins, 1972). Simple causal views relating money and barter also seem to be misplaced (Humphrey, 1985), as do simple notions of gifts and reciprocity (Mauss, 1966; Parry, 1986).

Hart (1986) has written about the two ways of looking at money (the "two sides of the coin" as he puts it). Money is a social institution which exists only because a community goes along with it, but it is also something which can be exchanged for goods or services. As Hart writes, "It is thus both a token of authority and a commodity with a price" (1986, p. 637). His concern was that the two sides of money had been confused by anthropologists, sociologists and economists, some insisting on the commodity value of money, others on the social aspects of money.

From a behavior analytic perspective, the same problems emerge. Money can be looked at as a symbolic exchange: that is, a secondary reinforcer made possible only because a verbal community "goes along with it". On the other hand, under normal circumstances we can assume the working of the monetary systems in a community and think of money as something which gets people something else. We find this latter sense when behavior analysts analyze money simply as a reinforcer, with statements like "The subjects were reinforced with 10¢ for every point they received". Statements such as this are only true *given the existence of the social monetary system*. A full analysis of money must include the verbal community which makes it possible.

Note that this is similar to points made earlier (7.3) that the words "Good" and "Umm" can only act as reinforcers *given the existence of a verbal community*. Similarly, using a light as a secondary reinforcer in an experimental chamber will only work given the contingency set up by an experimenter. Any effects found in an experimental chamber presuppose this (social?) relationship arranged by the experimenter because such a contingency between lights and food is not found in nature.

The pertinent question, then, is the following: under what circumstances can we assume the existence of verbal and monetary communities? Hart (1986) also poses this question when he suggests that different states of social relations can lead to different monetary methods of getting the same ends (1986, p. 648) While this is clearly an empirical question, a few suggestions can be made.

First, when dealing with large, long-term, or well-defined communities, we can assume the working of such social systems. In the same way that we do not bother to check on the social system of banking and the state of the government debt everytime we make a simple bank transaction, so also we do want to analyze the entire verbal community everytime we try to analyze why someone said something. Interesting cases occur with large societies when they begin breaking down. At the beginning of a large civil war, for example, currencies fluctuate and the country's currency will often become worthless or abnormally inflated, not because the gold reserves have changed, but because the social system of community reciprocation has broken down. Stock markets are sensitive to such social changes (see also 10.4).

Second, when dealing with small, isolated communities, such as have been researched by anthropologists, the relations between commodity and social (or symbolic) aspects of money cannot just be assumed. To give a crude example, if dealing with a pacific island community who use shells as a type of currency, we cannot assume to go into the island with a large number of shells collected elsewhere and be considered rich. The community would not accept our money, a case where the commodity and social aspects of money interact. We can assume, however, to go into most large banks around the world with gold bullion, good plastic cards, or lots of paper notes of a decent currency and have our transaction accepted.

Many good examples of how the two aspects of money interact in some circumstances are to be found in the anthropological literature, see Parry and Bloch (1989) for a good starting point. Indeed, one of the points of their book is to argue that commodity and symbolic, social aspects cannot be easily separated (Bloch & Parry, 1989; Dalton, 1965).

An example is discussed by Hart (1986) to clarify the ethnography of Malinowski (1922). The islanders in question had two forms of commodity exchange between different communities with a division of labour (fishing and agricultural communities were separate). One form of commodity exchange (*wasi*) was highly ceremonial, in which community leaders made speeches and presented large quantities of goods as a gift. Naturally this gift was later reciprocated by the receiving community with other products. At the same time, exchange went on between individuals of the two communities (*vava*), with the types of negotiation and haggling not present in the ceremonial *wasi*.

What Hart shows is that the two types are adaptive for different conditions. If there is a *general feeling of goodwill* (i.e., a verbal community) between the two communities then haggling exchanges can be made by individuals with a safety of consequences and expectations of making a good deal. If there is conflict present then the communities as a whole will barter and this will be backed by ceremonials and other ritualized behaviors. So the smaller, individual exchanges will only work if there is a stable social system already working. In times of war, for example, bartering between nations becomes the perogative of the state, and individual companies cannot barter internationally without consulting the government. Thus, as Hart (1986) nicely points out, individualism is not an outcome of social unrest but an outcome of social rest. Similarly, in times of government stability, I can carry out individual transactions quite happily just between me and an electronic bank terminal. In times of government economic instability I am more likely to band together with a cooperative to make transactions.

The other avenue of thought which has been followed in economic sociology and economic anthropology is the effects on social relations from implementing monetary relations. We have seen some of these above when discussing Simmel: money can lead to impersonal relationships, new types of social groups, an emphasis on intellect and rationality, and an increase in secrecy (Simmel, 1978/1900). Simmel (1950, p. 335), for example, claims three bases by which money can lead to secrecy. First, money is "compressible" by which Simmel meant that a lot of money can be put into one cheque or one credit card. Second, monetary transactions are abstract and with few intrinsic qualities to make them obvious. And third, money can have effects at remote times and remote places, which makes the initiator of consequences unknown. Properties such as these give communities based heavily upon money certain features which appear inevitable, but which derive from the generalized and arbitrary nature of the money objects. Monetary societies are therefore excellent case studies in the implementation of token economies.

Verbally Controlled Behavior: Bureaucracy, Law and Rationality

We have seen in Chapters 7 to 9 that verbally controlled behavior is extremely important in analyzing human behavior. Humans do not only engage in contingencies in which the physical environment shape the form of the behavior by providing contexts and consequences, but they also can have behavior shaped and maintained by social consequences for following a contingency which is verbally specified. Put simply, I can avoid touching stoves because I touch a few and the consequences shape my future behavior, or because someone in a verbal community shapes me by social consequences to follow their rules and then specifies either: "Do not touch that stove" or "If you touch that stove you will be burned". Both of these latter have implicit social consequences involved, as well as specified environmental consequences in the latter case.

Verbally controlled behaviors are commonplace in our everyday lives. There are also three forms of verbally controlled behavior which act to maintain verbal communities. These are bureaucracies, law systems, and rational systems of behavior. I will only touch briefly on each to give some of the flavour.

Bureaucracies. I have already mentioned above the work of Max Weber, who was one of the first modern social scientists to discuss bureaucracy. He related social systems and the increasing rationality-driven western society to the development of bureaucracies and the "typical" bureaucrat. That is, rule-governed behavior has proved so useful, despite its "evils", that it has paid off for groups that have been thus driven. In turn, the bureaucracies provide an evolutionary niche for certain ways of organizing work and hence the lives of the bureaucrats.

For example, if a group of people are to benefit from running their group with a rational routine which follows various useful rules of conduct, then people must be available to make those rules happen. This comes about because the consequences of following or not following rules are from other people rather than the rule-following tracking, and so the bureaucrats must be kept in check for social motivation. The most common way of checking these social consequences is to have them watched over a regular period of work, so the existence of a working day routine (9.00am to 5.00pm) follows from the rule-following properties. This in turn means that the bureaucrats' own private lives have to be organized around five working day and free weekends. This is turn affects the way in which interpersonal relations can function for the bureaucrats because families must accommodate. The development of a society based on following rules therefore ramifies all the way down to the private life functioning and organization of bureaucrats.

The following is what Weber saw as the basic bureaucrat produced by the organization necessary to have a functioning bureaucracy:

1. They are personally free and subject to authority only with respect to their impersonal official obligations.
2. They are organized in a clearly defined hierarchy of offices.
3. Each office has a clearly defined sphere of competence in the legal sense.
4. The office is filled by a free contractual relationship. Thus, in principle, there is free selection.
5. Candidates are selected on the basis of technical qualification...They are appointed, not elected.
6. They are remunerated by fixed salaries in money...
7. The office is treated as the sole, or at least the primary, occupation of the incumbent.
8. It constitutes a career. There is a system of 'promotion' according to seniority or to achievement, or both. Promotion is dependent upon the judgement of superiors.
9. The official works entirely separately from ownership of the means of administration and without appropriation of his position.
10. He is subject to strict and systematic discipline and control in the conduct of the office.

(Weber, 1947, p. 333)

We can see in this that the evolution of rule-following by societies has led to a way of doing things that was due to the contingencies, and not just due to someone's whim: "The management of the office follows general rules, which are more or less stable, more or less exhaustive, and which can be learned. Knowledge of these rules represents a special technical learning which the officials possess" (Weber, 1948, p. 198).

The social consequences necessary for rule-governed behavior to maintain can be found in points 1, 2, 6, 8, 9 and 10. A structure of promotion and remuneration is required because following the rules themselves does not reinforce the rule following in these cases (there is no tracking). That all means that scrutiny is required so forms of evaluation (8) and accountability are therefore required as further ramifications. Other checks are then needed for countercontrols (also see 12.7).

As we saw in 9.1, many sociologists, including Weber, Durkheim and Simmel, have remarked on the further ramification of the development of bureaucracy that people become "disenchanted" or alienated from their work and their lives. This arises because the (social) consequences maintaining their (rule-governed) behavior are not the consequences which arise from their work. It is not just, loosely following

Marx, that in our modern lifestyles we are no longer close to the contingencies of the physical environment, but more, that even the verbal consequences of our work do not maintain our coming to work and following rules–the remote salaries and promotions do instead.

Thus the development of rule-following societies sometimes leads to better standards of living because the rules work well, but they also have ramifications down to the very way we live. People end up living lifestyles to fit society's rule-following because only in that way can a good standard of living be maintained for all.

Laws. The other major form of societal rule-following is the development of legal systems. In this case the societal purpose is not rule-following to get better production and standard of living (whatever the disenchantment of individuals) but the overall protection of members of the group and the regulation of morality. Once again, for the general advantage of all individuals in the community, the problems of some individuals are ignored. That is, following legal rules might be better for us all (at least on paper), but mistakes happens and the blind, bureaucratic legal systems can sometimes damage individuals in a verbal community.

The functioning of legal systems can of course be found in pre-literate societies, but simple rules seem to be used in any case (Moore, 1978; Roberts, 1979). There will usually be an oral tradition remembered by the elders, although, being an oral tradition, consequences can determine what is "remembered" in any particular case. As for bureaucracy, the advent of writing changed many of the contingencies for following rules (Goody, 1986, 1987). Laws could be applied with less variation and with less local coloring due to immediate social consequences. The written laws can be learned more easily, cross-checked, and be open to anyone's scrutiny.

The anthropology of law shows a nice continuity between our systems of laws and tribal laws (Moore, 1978; Roberts, 1979). In each case the system is based on the group of most consequence to people, the small tribe or the larger society. A compromise or negotiation is sought between what people in that group can do and what hurts or affects individual others too much for the good of the whole group. While this can be negotiated interpersonally, either by direct action or by verbal negotiation, at some point written forms are used to set down the law, and this changes the nature of the disputations and negotiations.

Like the disenchantment we saw in bureaucracies, the implementation of written laws means that the whole process of disputing the law becomes detached from the moral event which started the dispute in the first place, and rests instead on the words of the law. Once again, the consequences involved in the dispute (X stole my car) are not the consequences which mediate the process of the law: lawyers' fees and payments for impartial judges. So the verbal community's running of moral disputes takes them out of the context of consequences with which the disputes started. I therefore suggest that the alienation or disenchantment of working on a job for a salary is identical to the frustration and lack of satisfaction people have with the law process. Again, the overall benefit to the community for strict rule-following has ramifications for individuals engaged in the process.

Rationality. Rationality has been touched upon a few times in this book. One of the problems is the multiple definitions it evokes. Let us consider some of these:

1. Being rational as following the course of action with the best outcome. If there is a choice between ten and twenty dollars, only someone irrational would choose the ten dollars. If I am hungry and there is food in one jar and no food in the other the rational thing would be to pick up the one with the food.
2. Rational as following the best verbal instructions available. If you told me that a stove is hot and yet I still touch it, then I would be acting irrationally.
3. Rational as not being swayed by mere opinion and custom. If the evidence shows that garlic does not cure warts then it is irrational to suppose it does or to continue to put garlic on warts just because your parents told you it does work.
4. Rational as acting with a (verbal) knowledge of the reasons or causes of why you are doing the action. If I tried baking bread with ground rice just to see what happens then I am acting irrationally. If I know (verbal) that yeast makes cakes rise by giving off gas then I am acting rational if I try putting yeast to make bread rise.

From a behavior analytic point of view we can see some problems immediately. Most of these points depend upon having verbal knowledge of some events before or after acting. From Chapter 7 it is clear that all verbal behavior is maintained (at least initially) in social contingencies, therefore what is rational or not will depend upon the verbal community. Further, this point also means that there is always *an alternative source of consequences to consider* when making judgments about rationality: what were the alternative social consequences maintaining the rationality or the irrationality?

Thus I hope it can be seen that *irrationality is a case of strong alternative social consequences in most instances* (dementia aside, but perhaps even then). For this reason anthropologists and sociologists have been very careful and very wise to analyze the social context of so-called irrational behaviors (Beattie, 1970; Durkheim, 1951/1897; Evans-Pritchard, 1976; Winch, 1958). They also make the point that there are no irrational behaviors, just ones that are culturally different to ours. While this view can quickly slip into a full blown cultural relativism, the behavior analytic way of stopping this is to point out that it is the social consequences which still determine what any culture will produce as rational or irrational behaviors.

Thus if African villagers say they believe that whether a chicken dies or not from poison tells them the guilt in a legal dispute, they are acting rational with respect to the verbal community's contingencies. The conflict with scientific views on chickens and poisons does not really come into question because there are all sorts of loopholes for retrials with another chicken and the like (Evans-Pritchard, 1976).

Consider perhaps the most pure case of irrationality, if a hungry pigeon in a cage with two keys to peck, one a VI 300 secs and the other a CRF, were to peck only the VI schedule key. If this actually happened we would immediately look for problems with the training (a superstitious avoidance of the CRF key) or some other source of reinforcement. Similarly, if we find "irrational" human behavior we should be looking for other sources of control, and given most of the questions about reason and rationality (e.g., Descartes; see Gellner, 1992) are about following what is specified by verbal behaviors, we should look for alternative social sources of control in the first instance.

This position means that the real question of rationality is whether to do what the verbal community specifies, be this a community of scientists or villagers. Whether we act in accordance with the latest rules of science will depend upon the outcomes for following those rules and the community's benefit if everyone roughly does what science says (usually it pays off for some people). Clearly, in western societies, there is a great emphasis through childhood on the benefits to everyone for following the rules "discovered" by science. The reason, in turn, for this is because this helps establish a scientific community that is not reinforced for specific findings which people will follow, but for "knowledge" which is true for everyone.

In summary, there is a cycle here that science works best to track the physical environment and put this into words if there is nonspecific reinforcement for doing science applied to a scientific community (Rorty, 1987). Nonspecific reinforcement for science is in turn best arranged if society as a whole reinforces all of the work of scientists rather than only what turn out to be useful. This in turn is best accomplished by having everyone usually follow any rule produced by science, and believe it to be the best and most recent finding of "knowledge". So while science can make mistakes, someone who goes against scientific findings is not just going against that isolated finding, but against the whole community enterprise for setting up a useful, unbiased and productive scientific community. This is why science has many times become a political issue (e.g., Gellner, 1992): because the community as a whole maintains the scientific community from bias. So such people get labelled as "irrational" even if science happened to be wrong.

The point of making consequences the source of rationality, rather than whether or not something is "rational", also helps solve the criticisms against rationality while retaining a sense of reality. Gellner (1992), for example, provides a useful "Checklist of Reason-bashing" (p. 132). If reason and rationality consist of finding verbal reasons for doing something before acting, for example (Gellner, p. 132, item 2), then there is no certain rationality because the verbal behaviors are determined by many contingencies, especially social contingencies.

So accepting that there is no certain or universal rationality does not entail that there is no certain or universal reality, only that there is no certain verbal specification of reality. That is, we and all the other animals find our way around this world or perish, but we cannot put all of those contingencies which we contact into a verbal form which will always be perfectly followed or which would always work out perfectly if they were followed. The world is there and real, perfectly naked in its contingencies, but our verbal specifications of those contingencies are imperfect and following them depends upon many things, not least the community support for an unbiased science.

9.4. The Evolution of Verbal Communities

Historical

For many centuries in philosophy, and later in anthropology and psychology, there has been speculation over the origins of language. While the thoughts expressed can only be speculative, they are interesting and useful in that they make us assess the foundations for language use more carefully.

I have already discussed in Chapter 7 some of the points essential for verbal behavior. There must be a behavior which has flexible and arbitrary variations. For example, there are enough muscular variations on pointing and moving the hands that a sign language can be used to get other people who also "know" the sign language to do appropriate events. Without further muscular development of the ear, however, it is doubtful that very many variations could be made using that part of the body. While many different parts of the body could possibly be used for a total language, this makes attending very difficult and parts of "sentence" would be lost without giving full attention to the person "speaking".

As Skinner (1957, 1986) points out, the vocal musculature was an important development, because vocal sounds can function in the dark, around corners, over long distances, when busy doing something else, with little effort, and very quickly so there can be more immediate reinforcement (Holland, 1992). We can have effects on other people even when they are not watching us and when we are busy with some other activity, simply by asking them to do whatever it is.

The other important pre-condition for language use is a verbal community. If other people do not respond appropriately to what is said then the whole point of a language is missed. Moreover, just saying something does not make it happen: there needs to be functional consequences to behaving appropriately to the words and sentences, and there also needs to be functional consequences to learning behavior appropriately in the first place.

Further, it is not enough for language to assume that another person knows the language and that if I am powerful enough they will behave appropriately to my words and sentences. Instead, for easy and proper functioning of language we need a verbal community. That is, verbal behavior is going to work best in a community which reinforces the members for many and arbitrary behaviors in a loosely discriminative way. Once people in a group are socially compliant in general, because the group reinforces many behaviors, behaving appropriately to arbitrary vocal sounds can be made to work more easily. *This all means that it is the evolution of verbal communities rather than the evolution of language per se that is important.* A language of sorts would work with noises and strong social consequences even without a verbal community, but flexible and reciprocal language use requires a mutually and loosely reinforcing group (Hayes & Hayes, 1989: 6.5).

Once a verbal community was first in place, people could be made to do things that were not supported by the physical environment. Thus the evolution of arbitrary signs and symbols is closely tied to developments in social structures (Noble

& Davidson, 1991), in particular, the special features of a verbal community. Once the basic verbal community and language use were in place then verbally specified contingencies could begin to work as effectively as the contingencies themselves (Catania, 1985), and as we noted in Chapter 7, the advantages of this for a verbal community, as well as for individuals, becomes enormous. For example, behaviors can be "tried out first" as it were, with verbally governed behavior (cf. Kendon, 1991), and contingencies with long delays to reinforcement can be bridged with the mediation by a verbal community.

The Life of Communities over Time

As well as speculating on how verbal communities might have formed in the first place, we can also look for patterns in how real groups form, how they spend their time, and how they eventually come to an end. We have seen earlier that Tönnies and Durkheim mapped out such scenarios for Western society as a whole. It was thought that originally (Gemeinschaft and mechanical solidarity) the verbal community of Western society was homogeneous and close, with a system of generalized reinforcers. Durkheim, in particular, argued that the introduction of division of labour led to contractual relationships and verbally governed systems of reinforcers with little other reinforcers involved. This led to individualisms of many sorts, such that individual sources of reinforcers outweighed (in a matching law sense) what a community could produce. So for Durkheim, it was the division of labour which brought about these changes.

Looking at smaller groups which form a tight verbal community, several researchers have proposed stages through which groups move (e.g., Gersick, 1988; Tuckman, 1965; Worchel, Coutant-Sassic & Grossman, 1992). Most of the research, however, has used groups with a limited life-span, so it is not surprising that the time constraint itself heavily determines the pattern of the group life. Gersick (1988), for example, found in her eight naturally-occurring teams that about halfway through their existence they moved from group goals to considering their own goals individual more.

It is common with time limited groups, then, that the first period is spent with a lot of social interaction (forming the verbal community commitments, roles and reciprocity) and very loose social reinforcement, the middle period carrying out the tasks of the group (contacting the remote consequences that the individuals could not get on their own), and the final period with individuals considering their own position more than that of the group's (Gersick, 1988; Tuckman, 1965).

Many natural groups have no time constraints, such as flower societies, cat clubs, and sewing groups. In these cases the re-shuffling of the community reinforcers seems to occur with the particular events controlling the outcomes. So an imminent Cat Show might lead to members of the cat club interacting more and re-establishing the loose group contingencies which gave the initial start to the verbal community; the commencement of another sewing club might lead to the original sewing club to falter, with another source of generalized reinforcement becoming available for some of its members.

After studying many real groups, Worchel, Coutant-Sassic and Grossman (1992) suggested that groups come into existence from discontent and precipitating events. People might not be getting a fair deal from the government or smaller verbal communities and so the reinforcement available from another verbal community becomes a powerful influence. The evidence also suggests that at this stage of forming a group, the members report being homogeneous; while forming a verbal community they stress the similarities they have and perhaps exacerbate the differences to other groups (c.f., Tajfel & Turner, 1981).

While the group is working on its mission, the original sources of control which arranged the verbal community will lose their influence, probably in many different ways. If the group is working on a project, then the actual work has to be organized, which means that different members get different tasks and therefore somewhat different outcomes. The results coming back to the group as a whole have to be divided, and this can often be inequitable. Also, the organization of the project requires some people to tell others what to do, and this also introduces new, unintended consequences differentially to individual members. All of these effects can be seen as products of the division of labour, but on a smaller scale than that envisaged by Durkheim. These effects all lead to new sources of control on the individual (punishing or reinforcing) which compete against the original loose group reinforcers maintaining the verbal community, and these new sources of control are the ones that can eventually lead to the group's disintegration. At this point in a group's life the members report that their group is heterogeneous compared to other groups.

While Worchel, Coutant-Sassic and Grossman (1992) do not talk in the terms I have above, their account is clearly plausible in behavior analytic terms. While not precise, and it cannot be—given the generalized sources of control involved with verbal communities, it provides an interesting account which could be followed up empirically.

Chapter 10

Behaviors Maintained by a Verbal Community

A question asked about verbal communities towards the end of Chapter 3 was: why bother to maintain these generally reinforcing groups? We saw in Part 2 that much useful social behavior can occur without such verbal communities. We also saw in Chapter 9 that modern societies are characterized by more interactions without the "village" type of close community (Gemeinschaft), so either most of our behavior now occurs without a verbal community or else the types of verbal communities have changed. It is the latter that will become most apparent in this chapter. So why are there still verbal communities, albeit of a different type? What functions do they serve?

In the last chapter we looked at some of the group behaviors which maintain a verbal community: ritual behaviors, laws, language systems, and money. It was pointed out that some of these (the latter two in particular) are useful behaviors in their own right. That is, while the everyday use of speech and writing can function to maintain a verbal community of speakers and writers, in the short term their use also gets things done for us. So they reinforce the individual at the same time as they reinforce the maintenance of the verbal community. Each of these behaviors should therefore be included in this chapter, as behaviors which are maintained by a verbal community. However, as I do not wish to discuss each of those behaviors again, we will take Chapter 9 as read.

In the present chapter, then, I wish to discuss other behaviors which appear to be in part maintained by a verbal community but which have not been covered in the last chapter. For example, if a person brought up without western music were to listen to Mozart, or indeed if a person from a western country brought up on Tchaikovsky were to listen to some Gubaidulina, they would not show the "appropriate" behaviors. This suggests that a verbal community is maintaining at least part of our musical behavior repertoire.

There is clearly no firm cutoff point between the different sources of control; behaviors can have effects from the environment, effects from another person without a verbal community, and verbal community maintained effects, all at once. Taking the example given above, while making sounds can be maintained for many reasons due to the sounds themselves, it is likely that making particular "Mozart sounds" or "Gubaidulina sounds" is prepared for us by a verbal community. The scheme of questions given in Chapter 1 is appropriate here, although we will only look at verbal behaviors in this chapter.

10.1. Attributions and Social Attributions

Attributions are the reasons or causes we give for events that occur: why did the driver not stop at the red light; why did Mary and James not get married and live in Seattle; why am I afraid of heights? All these require that I arrive at some verbal behavior which specifies the causes of events, and of particular interest are those which give the causes of our own behavior or the behavior of other people.

Attribution theory began with some very particular observations and phenomena (Heider, 1958): that people explain their own behavior differently than the behavior of others (Jones & Nisbett, 1972); that people often attribute responsibility to victims of accidents (Walster, 1966); and that people are usually satisfied with one salient explanation as a cause (Jones & Davis, 1965). As these particular questions were pursued, attributions came to encompass almost anything which was thought about anything. If I said that "That vase is blue" then I would be attributing blueness to the vase and an attribution was being made.

So from three particular phenomena the theoretical control was lost for some years. [For this reason only some topics will be mentioned here.] The area also developed into cognitive models of attribution, which fitted with cognitive models of thinking around at the time (see Chapter 8). And finally, the area became inconclusive when the debate between motivational and cognitive (or informational) variables in attribution was found to be vacuous and unanswerable (Tetlock & Levi, 1982; Tetlock & Manstead, 1985). Were attributions made because of the information people had or were they made to serve a function?

From these developments there are perhaps two strands of theory and research (Kelley & Michela, 1980): first, attribution theory, how people provide reasons and causes for events; and second, attributional theory, how attributing a reason or cause can affect future behavior (see Svartdal, 1988). An example of the first might be if I give the reason for my poor exam mark as being that the exam was hard and I hardly studied for it. An example of the second might be that were I were to attribute my poor exam mark to not liking the subject material of the exam then I might be less motivated to study the next time around, whereas if I attributed my poor exam mark to illness, I might be more motivated to study the next time around.

Before discussing these two findings, one behavior analytic version of attribution theory should be mentioned: Bem's (1965) self-perception theory. Following Skinner (1957), Bem suggested that a behavioral approach to the difference between attributions about ourselves and about others would be that we learn to tact our own behavior in the same way that we learn to tact other people's behavior, and that any differences therefore result from differential reinforcement from a verbal community (see Chapter 8 and below for more). Therefore, if I have a different explanation of why I go to church and why my nextdoor neighbor goes to church it could be because the verbal community reinforces talking in those terms, because I have very different sources of tacting in both cases, or because I have learned such reasons from other people or the mass media.

In each case of the attribution sources just given, note that the verbal community is involved. This point will become important, that because we are dealing with verbal behavior in attributions, the verbal community influences what is said and when it is said.   Thus both cognition (what is said—social consequences) and motivation (when it is said—social discrimination) are involved in any attribution. As has been emphasized in Chapter 8 and elsewhere, the cognitive part looks unmotivated because the social basis of thought is ignored.

Looking first at the reasons given for events, attribution theory, these will come from tacts about the sources of control of our behavior (and the behavior of others), from the many intraverbals we have learned to say when talking about our behavior, from the verbal community and what we learned through childhood and schooling, and from what the verbal community currently reinforces. For example, there are standard, public reasons which can be given for why I might have failed an exam. Since the verbal community can only reinforce correspondence that it can check on, I can usually get reinforced for replying to the question "Why did you fail the exam?" with any of the excuses publicly available. Replying "Because of my goldfish" is not a current verbal community reason and so I would be punished unless more verbal detail was forthcoming. Also, replying "Because my family all died", when this can easily be shown to be false, would also be punished.

This means that the emphasis on employing salient reasons and causes in attributions is really a reflection that the verbal community only reinforces some explanations, and these explanations in turn probably reflect how much the verbal community can check on the correspondence. Following also from this, the use of private events as reasons ("I failed because I had a headache that day") is also very useful because these cannot easily be checked by a verbal community (Street, 1994; Zettle & Hayes, 1989).

The second question, of attributional theory, really concerns verbally-governed behavior. If I verbally report that the reason I failed was because I am not **smart** enough to learn Japanese, how does this affect my behavior when I next study Japanese? That is, how does my verbally reported lack-of-smartness control my future behavior. The question of verbally governed behavior was dealt with in 7.4, along with data to show some conditions under which verbal behavior could govern reinforcement schedule performance with humans. This replaces (for a behavior analyst) any attributional accounts of the same phenomena (e.g., Kleinke, 1982). Once again, the verbal community enters into the control of behavior because of the pliance control of verbally-governed behavior: we learn most of our rules from other people, and this differs between cultures (Miller, 1984).

The conclusion of all this is that attributions mean talking about how we tact events and behavior, or make intraverbals about them, and about how these verbal behaviors can control future behavior. It has been emphasized that this cannot be separated from a verbal community which maintains certain explanations and punishes others, nor from a verbal community which provides most of our explanations in the first place.

Having presented a brief behavior analytic view of attribution processes, it should not be surprising that the social psychological literature has also begun to recognize the essential social bases of attributions (e.g., Hewstone, 1989). This has occurred in four ways (cf. Hewstone & Jaspars, 1984).

First, it was found that the actor/observer effects depend on group membership (Jones & Nisbett, 1972). The common finding had been that people typically explained their own behavior in terms of environmental variables but the behavior of others in terms of dispositional variables. But this finding was found to depend upon the groups to which the person, and the person having their behavior explained, belonged (e.g., Duncan, 1976; Hewstone & Ward, 1985). So the entire attribution process was changed depending upon the verbal community to which the attributer and attributee belonged. Interestingly, Ichheiser (1949) had long ago suggested that this attribution error was due to the way we are brought up in western society, not to a personal error of judgment (also cf. Hineline, 1992 and Miller, 1984).

The second source of socialness in attribution was that most of the attributions were made in a social context. In behavior analytic terms, the major consequences for giving this or that attribution are social ones. Third, the research on attributions increasingly looked at explanations for social phenomena. People seemed to spend more time explaining social events than events in the physical environment. [I consider this to be the same as the reported focus of social representations on explaining the unfamiliar, see 10.2.]

Finally, the attribution research began to emphasize that attributions were common or shared across members of groups, or verbal communities. There was no fictitious individual who rationally considered all the events in the world and individually developed the reasons and causes for those events. Rather, people learned from their verbal communities what sorts of events were suitable or not as explanations, with the result that researchers usually found a small range of socially determined attributions (e.g., Hewstone, Jaspars & Lalljee, 1982; Howard, 1984; Pandey, Sinha, Prakash & Tripathi, 1982). So, for example, it is not that people all individually examine the accidents or uncontrollable events they have experienced and all happen to conclude that victims are partly responsible for their accidents, but rather, we all learn that this is an acceptable explanation (reinforced, not punished) in our western society verbal communities (Howard, 1984; Walster, 1966).

The attribution research, then, is left acknowledging the essential role of verbal communities in making attributions. This has led to an increase in research on how verbal communities can construct and maintain whole knowledges which might not have any factual basis. And while the attribution research was being conducted primarily in the Unite States, researchers in Europe and Britain were looking more closely at socially constructed knowledges maintained by a community.

10.2. The Social Construction of Knowledge

The notion of socially constructed knowledge is really a topic of verbal behavior. Many areas of social science, including psychology, talk and write about people having socially constructed realities, or about the social construction of various phenomena. Little has been mentioned of these trends in the behavior analytic literature, although I believe that behavior analysis presents an excellent basis for investigating such phenomena (see Guerin, 1992c for more details; also Sá, no date).

Claims about social constructions are made by a number of social science writers, the following a merely few examples (Atkinson, 1990; Austin-Broos, 1987; Berger & Luckmann, 1967; Bruner, 1991; Dake, 1992; Duveen & Lloyd, 1990; Echabe & Rovira, 1989; Farr & Moscovici, 1984; Fisher & Chon, 1989; Fraser & Gaskell, 1990; Galli & Nigro, 1987; Gamson, Croteau, Hoynes & Sasson, 1992; Gergen, 1985, 1988; Katz, 1979; Lacan, 1977; Leont'ev, 1981; Mead, 1934, also see Roberts, 1977; Miller, Potts, Fung, Hoogstra & Mintz, 1990; Saussure, 1983, also Guerin 1991b; von Cranach, Doise & Mugny, 1992; Vygotsky, 1978, see Wertsch, 1985; Willer, 1971).

These authors argue that there is a separate reality which exist only for humans, and that this reality is created by other people. We cannot individually change that reality since it is already in place from the time we are born. But through our interactions with others we partake of this cultural realm and a large part of our "knowledge" comes from these social origins.

The analysis I have made suggests that the term social construction is only justified in cases for which the behaviors are verbal or verbally governed and are almost uniquely maintained by the loose social consequences of a verbal community (Guerin, 1992c). Such behaviors have all the properties claimed by their proponents: they are particular to (maintained by) a social group; the do not rely on obvious motivations (macro consequences); they are arbitrary; they do not have to correspond to physical reality in order to maintain; they are the underpinnings of culture; and they differentiate us from other animals.

So it is not that all reality is socially constructed. The parts that are commonly called intuitive, unconscious, automatic, affective, unregulated, unaware, or spontaneous, will be controlled by direct environmental contingencies. It is the special properties of the generalized, loosely discriminative social consequences provided by verbal communities which make possible the human behaviors which seem independent of the environmental contingencies. These are the basis to social constructions.

So it turns out that behavior analysis provides an excellent foundation for discussing social constructions: it clearly differentiates between socially constructed and other behaviors, and it provides a natural science foundation to such constructions rather than leave the foundation up in the air, in a parallel universe, or worse—in a post-modern quagmire of socially-maintained specialist words. This prevents a problem that everything humans do now seems to get prefaced by "The social construction of...". Using "social representations" or "widespread beliefs", on the other hand (Allansdottir , Jovchelovitch & Stathopoulou, 1993; Farr & Moscovici, 1984; Fraser & Gaskell, 1990; Guerin, 1992c; von Cranach, Doise & Mugny, 1992), restricts us usefully to the specific properties of verbal communities and how they shape and maintain knowledges. This seems to be a more useful delineation than simply prefacing everything with "The social construction of..." whenever there is any involvement of other people at all. If that is the only criterion then almost everything we do could be prefaced thus (3.3).

A behavior analysis of social constructions also provides many new ideas as well. For example, following what was said in section 7.4, the conditions for turning pliance into tracking will be those conditions for breaking society's control over a socially constructed phenomenon. It also suggests a number of ways in which verbal community representations might be changed which nicely compliment the methods researched at present (11.3, and Sotirakopoulou & Breakwell, 1992).

10.3. Attitudes and Attitude Change

The term "attitudes" has a variety of meanings, only some of which we can deal with here, since the literature is so vast (Guerin, 1994). The major idea is that attitudes are a generalized affective response to stimuli and contexts. For example, "I like going to the beach." In this sense of attitudes, particularly when dealing with the behavior itself rather than the statement, we are dealing with generalized multiple responses (3.2): we "like" events and contexts according to their relative strengthening effects.

The term "belief" is used to refer to verbal knowledge we might have about something: "I believe that fish live in the ocean", "I believe for every drop of rain that falls, a flower grows". The beliefs do not necessarily have to be liked or disliked. This is what separates them from attitudes.

Both the dual nature of attitudes and the role of beliefs in attitudes have caused a lot of discussion, with three major foci. First, there is argument about attitude-behavior consistency, in which the observed behavior does not match the verbally reported liking or disliking. Second, Bem (1965) has suggested that our reports of attitudes and liking are derived from self-observation of what we do, so reported attitudes are verbal behavior about our self-observed attitudes. Third, there is the question of the relationship between beliefs (primarily intraverbals and tacts) and attitudes. I might believe that smoking is a health hazard and yet smoke; and moreover I might also believe that smoking is a health hazard and yet report that I like smoking. Clearly beliefs do not control attitudes or reported attitudes.

Attitudes and Verbal Behavior

The present outline will consider the case of attitudes as verbal behavior (also see Guerin, 1994). In this sense attitudes are a commentary on one's behavior to oneself or to others. They are not comments on hidden internal beliefs or latent processes of behavior, but are a phenomenon to be studied. They do not reveal a secret source of knowledge but comment on overt and covert behavior.

This idea of attitudes is not new, nor is it confined to behavior analysis (Bem, 1965; Fraley, 1984). What behavior analysis can offer, however, is a better analysis of the sources of control in attitudes. For example, a statement referring to "my attitude towards fluoridation" is a verbal behavior which has varied sources of control. There may or may not be any control coming from the environment relevant to fluoridation: the control might be all social.

It can be seen that behavior analysis produces a functional analysis of attitudes. While functional analyses are not new in attitude research, behavior analysis adds a lot that is new (cf. Herek, 1986 1987; Katz, 1960; Pratkanis, Breckler & Greenwald, 1989; Smith, Bruner & White, 1956; Snyder & DeBono, 1987). For example, from the verbal basis of reported attitudes it will be clear that social consequences and contexts from verbal communities must play a role in producing such reports. This provides a sound basis for research on the social context of attitudinal reports (Eiser & van der Pligt, 1984).

Attitudes and Tacting. Tacting is assumed in traditional social psychology to be the major function of attitudes: to report a generalized verbal comment on previous or possible self-behaviors; just reporting on the environment seems to be maintained by generalized social consequences from a verbal community. This was the basis of the tacting function, and the analysis could extend to reporting self-behaviors. So from "I rescued a cat from up a tree the other day" we could generalize to "I really like cats." While this last attitudinal statement looks like a tact, it is a complex reporting of self-behavior.

Another functional basis for providing an attitude statement is as a reply to a question. If asked "What do you think of the situation in the Middle East?" we ordinarily are required to respond. Refusals are generally punished through childhood. Try refusing to answer sometime when someone asks you a simple question and observe the social consequences you elicit. Rather than list every belief we can (intraverbals) about the situation in the Middle East, a common reply which does not bore our listener is to say "I don't like the look of the situation in the Middle East".

A further possibility is that reporting attitudes has functioned as a ritual social event rather than anything that crucially depends on the attitudes reported. This means that reporting attitudes could function merely to provide social conversation, to avoid silence, or to maintain a verbal community (Murray, 1971; Skinner, 1957). While conversations often initially tact certain key topics such as the weather, reporting opinions might be reinforced by escape or avoidance of silence. Thus exchanging opinions, even if ignored, can help maintain a verbal community.

Another possible source of tacting attitudes is involved with self-regulation of behavior through verbal behavior (see 7.5). If people have the accurate reporting of their own behavior strengthened, they might provide less biased self-observations. This is one goal of most therapies: to get a client to observe accurately their own behavior and be able to report it. Like other forms of self-control this is might be

238   Chapter 10

self-reinforcing or tracking. Some tacting of attitudes might be maintained in this way.

A final way that "tacting" of attitudes might be maintained is through generalized manding. As will be discussed in the next section, reported attitudes can be disguised requests or mands. If this disguise is frequently strengthened then reporting attitudes will sustain or create a generalized compliance in another person. So these verbal behaviors are halfway between manding and tacting. They appears to be tacting but there is a long term mand which achieves generalized compliance.

Since attitudinal tacts have a clear source of motivation unrelated to the tact content itself (what is verbally specified), pure attitudinal tacts are unlikely to ever occur. Almost always the attitude reported will in some way fit the consequences which have elicited the report. Because, as has been argued, this will include social consequences, the community in which an attitude is reported will be a function of the verbal and nonverbal behavior of that community. That is, social context will in most cases bias reported attitudes (cf. Eiser & van der Pligt, 1984; Silver, Abramson, & Anderson, 1986).

So this approach also affirms another point: that the study of attitudes and attitude change belongs to a social psychology. Traditional social psychology has often treated attitudes as purely individual reports of a private nature. The area has also moved to cognitive foundations and the social nature of attitudes has been lost to a large extent (cf. Crocker, Fiske & Taylor, 1984; Sherman, 1987). The behavior analytic approach shows more clearly why attitudes are a social phenomenon: through the verbal behavior used in attitude statements, through the "self" processes occurring (see Chapter 8), through the mutual shaping indicated by the use of mands and autoclitics, and through the social maintenance of attitude tacting (cf. Erickson, 1982; Kiecolt, 1988; Verplank, 1955).

Attitudes, Manding and Autoclitics. Some comments have already been made about the manding function of attitude statements. Making attitude statements can result in specific positive or negative consequences, they can be shaped, and they can be used to shape others. If your boss remarks that she does not like people who drink coffee while they work, it is not just an innocent tact of her private attitude. It will very likely shape the way you behave, and it may or may not have been "intended" to shape your behavior. In any event, it will function as if she had manded: "I do not want you to drink coffee while you work".

This means that there is a dynamic quality to attitude statements beyond pure tacting. This is also reflected in the use of autoclitics. Qualifications will be made to attitude statements to modify the consequences. For example, "It seems to me that...", "I had always believed that...", "I think that I like...", "I rather like...", and "I tend not to go in for...".

If there are negative consequences for attitude statements, they can be avoided in various ways. For example, instead of remarking "I like cats" you can say "I quite like cats". Any negative consequences can later be easily averted with this second statement. Another strategy is to provide verbal discriminative contexts after a negative verbal reply. If "I like dogs" receives a reply, "But they always bark which is annoying", then you can qualify your attitude thus: "Oh yeah, I mean that I only like dogs that don't bark".

Many examples of autoclitics can be found in the social psychological areas of impression management and self-presentation (Baumeister, 1982; Tedeschi, 1981). These areas do not distinguish, however, between overt behaviors to modify consequences (shaping) and verbal behavior which modifies consequences (autoclitics).

Attitudes and Intraverbals. An interesting point follows from what was said earlier, that reporting attitudes could be strengthened by the escape from conversational silence and its consequences, such as the way that discussing the weather is often negatively reinforced. This implies that attitudes can also be treated as intraverbals, if the presentation of an already formed statement will function just as well as one under the control of the immediate physical or social environment. Listen to a conversation about the weather and judge how much is controlled by the environment (tacting the weather) and how much consists of previously learned functional units of verbal behavior. That is, many attitude statements are controlled by previous verbal behaviors. These effects are most often seen in casual conversations where the fact that you are talking at all is more important (has more consequences) than what is actually said. Whole conversations can be totally disconnected from the actual environment, the control coming from previous verbal behavior.

This also has plausibility since, as we have seen, attitudes are generalized statements. The environment cannot control the production of a statement such as, "I like all cats", since no one has interacted with all the cats in the universe. Therefore, attitudes are intimately tied up with verbal behavior and hence with generalized social control.

It is at this point that research start talking about beliefs. I can have beliefs about nuclear energy which have no positive or negative evaluation: "The likelihood of a nuclear accident is quite large over a ten year period". I can also have attitudes about nuclear energy: "I do not like the use of nuclear energy". I can also claim that the attitude is somehow based upon the belief: "Because the risk of nuclear accidents is high, I do not like the use of nuclear energy".

What has been argued elsewhere (Guerin, 1994) is that whether a statement is presented in the form of a belief or an attitude is itself an autoclitic and depends upon the verbal community. In some social contexts, statements are reinforced more if presented as attitudes and sometimes more if presented as beliefs. Just like the socially-determined grey area mentioned earlier between attitudes presented as tacts and as intraverbals, so too attitudes and beliefs vary depending upon the audience. If I present a statement as a belief is it a more persuasive statement, but it can also be refuted more easily than if presented as an attitude. Compare: "Nuclear power is dangerous" and "I do not like nuclear power".

Attitude and Behavior Consistency. One of the questions which has perplexed attitude researchers is the relationship between attitude and behavior (Ajzen & Madden, 1986; Fazio & Zanna, 1981; Fishbein & Ajzen, 1975; Lloyd, 1980, 1994). People are not always consistent between their attitudes and their behavior. They can report that they "like" cats but be seen to mistreat cats and keep them away from their home.

From all that has been said in this chapter, it should be clear that there is no automatic link between attitudes and behavior (Fraley, 1984; Lloyd, 1980). Traditional social psychological models assume that attitudes report an inner source which must be close to veridical, so they therefore have problems with attitude-behavior inconsistencies (cf. Fishbein & Ajzen, 1975). They then divide attitude change, for example, into changes made to the veridical belief structure and other "peripheral" changes (Petty & Cacioppo, 1986).

For the behavior analyst, on the other hand, the problem is that there are so many ways in which inconsistencies between attitudes and behavior can arise (see also 7.5). Any of the different sources of control given earlier in this section could lead to inconsistencies. For example, if a verbal community strengthened liking of dogs rather than cats this would strengthen the verbal behavior of reporting liking for dogs. If there were other conflicting contingencies, however, which strengthened positive behaviors towards cats, an attitude-behavior inconsistency would occur.

To put this succinctly, the "truth" of attitudes is not whether they correspond to behavior but what effect they have on the person who hears them spoken. Given the less than perfect control of our behavior by verbal reports, the behavior analyst is more likely to wonder how so much consistency can possibly happen. The correspondence literature (7.5) suggests that there are strong contingencies operating from childhood onwards to make us consistent in our attitudes and behaviors (cf. Riegler & Baer, 1989).

The same contingencies towards consistency probably apply to consistencies between all our behaviors, and the verbal/nonverbal is only one case. There are mild forms of punishment for someone who does one thing one day and the opposite the next day. As Walt Whitman (1855/1986, line 1314) pointed out, consistency is not a logical necessity of life:

Do I contradict myself?
Very well then....I contradict myself;
I am large....I contain multitudes.

What this means is that with our large repertoires of behavior we should expect inconsistencies. This is especially so with verbal behavior which, as we have seen in Chapter 7, has a contingent relationship with reporting real events. To put it succinctly, the physical environment to a large degree will select consistency between sequential behaviors acting on the environment, but because verbal behavior only contingently tacts the environment, the consistency between verbal behavior and nonverbal behavior will be weaker. As has been found in the social psychology literature, shaping by experience with contingencies and shaping by a verbal community lead to different types of attitude-behavior consistencies (Fazio & Zanna, 1981).

Attitude Change

There has been a lot written about attitude change, but little from behavior analysts. With the multiple sources of control it is important to establish what exactly is changed in attitude change. First, our behavior might be changed through changing the contingencies and the observation might be that we have changed our attitudes. For example, if I was to give my cat away and buy three dogs, people might report that I had changed my attitudes towards dogs, and possibly also towards cats.

Second, the contingencies of intraverbals or the relationships between intraverbals (Terrell & Johnston, 1989) might be changed such that your "beliefs" change and different attitudes are reported afterwards. For example, I could strengthen some intraverbals concerning the advantages of having dogs rather than cats as pets. Alternatively, the verbal behavior of the persuader could act as a establishing operation (Michael, 1982a). For example, "Did you know that your rich uncle who will die soon dislikes cats intensely?"

Third, attitude change can also mean a change in expressed attitudes, whether or not behavior or beliefs are consistent with the attitude. In this case, a change of contingencies changes the reported attitudes but this might be logically inconsistent (Terrell & Johnston, 1989) with other intraverbals and might bear no resemblance to actual behavior. A common case of this revolves around the basic property of verbal behavior stressed in this book: that it is ultimately based on generalized social contingencies and social compliance with a verbal community. An example would be if you were taken to a dog-lovers meeting and asked to stand up and comment on the relative joys of owning cats and dogs. In this case the reported attitudes will be directly affected by the social community, and no doubt your talk would be full of autoclitics and impression management behaviors.

It is all these varying sources of control which social psychologists have not taken into account when dealing with attitude change (except perhaps Fishbein & Ajzen, 1975). By assuming a tight relationship between attitudes and behavior, and by ignoring the role of social consequences, they have missed some important sources of control. Of special importance are the verbally governed versus contingency governed distinction, and the social basis of attitudes through generalized social consequences.

The distinction between attitudes which are primarily verbal reports and attitudes controlled mostly by environmental contingencies (reporting what you observe yourself to do), means that to change attitudes we either need to change the environment in some way or else we need to change only attitudes which have little control exercised from the environment. In this sense it is easier to change someone's attitudes towards fluoridation than to change their liking for cats or dogs because there is little environmental impact on most people from fluoridation—it is mostly intraverbal behavior. The consequences of fluoridation are learned through reading rather than direct environmental contingencies.

One of the best models of attitude change includes some of the behavior analytic distinctions, but like the attitude-behavior consistency literature, it ignores the full role of consequences. This is the Elaboration Likelihood Model (ELM, Petty & Cacioppo, 1986) which suggests two routes to attitude change: one through changing beliefs following thoughtful assessment, the other through peripheral cues. The former concerns intraverbals primarily; the second concerns verbal community influences.

In the ELM there are several postulates which mask the role of consequences. One stage of the model assesses whether or not the person (being persuaded) is "motivated" to process thoughts about the issue. It is here that consequences will be found which maintain or change attitudes, but consequences cannot adequately be dealt with only as a first step in a process model.

Other than generalized social consequences, the posited "motivators" in the ELM rely on needs and vague desires as surrogates for verbal community consequences. There is said to be a "need for cognition", a sense of personal responsibility, personal relevance, motivational affect, motivation to agree with experts, etc. It is not that the phenomena behind these words are wrong or do not exist, but rather, the behavior analytic position must go further than this in looking for motivators to change attitudes. Consequences have dynamic properties and cannot be dealt with as a semi-permanent, reified "need" or "desire".

These problems with relegating functional consequences to a minor and stable role are most apparent in the small literature on maintenance of attitude change (Cook & Flay 1978; Guerin & Innes, 1990). One can assume that "People are motivated to hold correct attitudes" (Petty & Cacioppo, 1986, p. 5), but to know whether attitudes will maintain we need to know more about the dynamics of the implied motivators. One could arrange contingencies such that a person has a high "need for cognition" and so thinks about attitudes frequently, but also such that they do not maintain such attitudes. Implicit in most of the attitude change models is the view that a changed attitude will continue without further motivation as a stable state. This problem also arises from not dealing adequately with the social consequences maintaining attitudes and beliefs.

From a behavior analytic perspective, if the attitude change is primarily controlled through intraverbal contingencies (beliefs), and if there are contingencies present to maintain consistency, then an attitude change attempt might succeed in maintaining over time. Second, if the attitude change is primarily controlled by social contingencies for reporting attitudes (peripheral cues in the ELM) then the maintenance will depend upon the strength of the verbal community's consequences and the social contexts in which the attitudes are embedded (cf. Smith, Bruner & White, 1956). Finally, if the attitudes are primarily self-descriptions of behavior, as described earlier, then the maintenance will primarily depend on the strength of the particular environmental contingencies to maintain the behaviors described.

It can be seen that by analyzing all three-terms of the contingencies, the maintenance of attitudes becomes more complex but easier to predict and change. We do not have to find out when the "need for cognition" will play a role, but instead look for contingencies which reinforce intraverbal behaviors. There is some weak evidence, in fact, that the effects of an attempt to change attitudes, by changing intraverbals about those attitudes, maintained only when the contingencies for maintaining production of the intraverbals were also maintained (Guerin & Innes, 1990).

Attempts to change attitudes through social contingencies, on the other hand, will have to change the larger verbal community in order to maintain any attitude changes. The weaker effects in maintaining peripheral attitude change (Petty & Cacioppo, 1986) probably arise from not making permanent changes in the social communities. If the right social contingencies are arranged then long term attitude change through peripheral means will be possible. The problem is, of course, that it is hard to arrange people's social contexts. Classic studies in changing social contexts and measuring attitude change and maintenance suggest that it is successful (e.g., Newcomb, 1943). Most usually a social control for attitude change is implemented successfully, but the person returns then to their usual verbal communities and the attitude change disappears (11.3 also discusses these problems).

The Theory of Reasoned Action

One of the most successful theories of attitudes, beliefs and behavior is the Theory of Reasoned Action (Ajzen & Fishbein, 1977, 1980; Fishbein & Ajzen, 1975; Sheppard, Hartwick & Warshaw, 1988). There are some interesting similarities between this theory and a behavior analytic perspective, which I will briefly comment upon. First, the model restricts itself to situations in which the person has control over the events taking place and the behavior is "voluntary" (though see Ajzen, 1985; Madden, Ellen & Ajzen, 1992). So to begin with, the domain is set out as that of human operant behavior.

Second, the theory only predicts consistency among beliefs, attitudes, intentions to behave, and behavior in specific instances. That is, "I like cats" would not predict whether or not I am going to buy a cat this weekend, but "I would very much like to buy a cat soon" and "I intend buying a cat this weekend" would be better predictors. What this means is that specific contingencies are being specified rather than generalized statements, which this whole section has stressed are problematic for attitude-behavior consistency on a behavior analytic analysis.

Third, the TRA model assumes (with evidence) that the best predictor of behavior is the verbal intention to perform the behavior. That is, except for measuring my actual behavior of cat-buying-on-the-weekend, the best predictor is whether or not I report that my specific intention is to buy a cat on the weekend. While this might seem either a trivial or a false extension, if we are dealing with situations over which we have "control", then these are likely to be situations involving verbally governed behavior. So the best predictor is therefore the report of what verbal behavior will govern my future behavior, although this will be by no means foolproof (Ajzen & Fishbein, 1980). So we can for the most part equate behavioral intentions with verbally governed behavior.

There are two predictors, in turn, of behavioral intention. One is the sum of the various beliefs I might have about whether the behavior in question will lead to the expected outcomes, each multiplied by the evaluation of that outcomes. For example, one belief might be that if I get a cat then it will probably (5/7 on a belief strength scale) catch the mice I have seen around my home. My evaluation might be that this would be a very good thing (6/7). I might also believe (not very strongly though) that getting a cat would lead to more noise at night (1/7) and my evaluation is that this would be bad if it occurred (5/7). So mathematically, my attitude towards the behavior is (30/49) + (5/49). Obviously, the first belief has more influence over my intention to perform the cat-buying behavior than the second belief.

What do all these equations mean then? Well firstly, the beliefs and evaluations are a measure of the different contingencies involved in getting a cat (belief strength) and their anticipated (8.2) reinforcement or punishment strength (evaluation). As Bernstein (1986; Bernstein & Michael, 1990) found, people can give reasonably good estimates of such values, especially if there is specificity and only "voluntary" behaviors. The second part of the equation business is that adding together all the different beliefs and evaluations is like putting together all the multiple contingencies which are involved in the particular behavior. As mentioned in 3.2, we have no way at present of combining multiple contingencies to make predictions, except in the most simple cases. The Theory of Reasoned Action is a quick method of doing this by relying on verbal reports, and the multiplicative result is not unlike a multiple contingency Matching Law for verbally governed behavior (Chapter 3).

The other predictor of behavioral intention is the "subjective norm". As has been pointed out many times in this book, the word "subjective" in psychology usually means "social", because the generalized social contingencies and their history are not obvious and are therefore assumed to reside inside the person. In the present case, the subjective norm is the pressure to act one way or another by people who are important or salient to the belief. That is, this predictor measures the verbal community contingencies.

There are two predictors, in turn, of the subjective norm which are again multiplied and all added together. These are whether each of a few salient or important people believe you should or should not do the behavior, and your motivation to comply with those persons. To follow our example, my spouse might think it a good idea to get a cat (6/7) and I always (?) comply with her (7/7). On the other hand, my mother might think that I should not get a cat at the moment (1/7) but I rarely comply with her (3/7) in any case. So in this way the verbal communities relevant to the behavior are brought into the equation and a weak verbal measure taken of their influence.

I hope it can be seen that the Theory of Reasoned Action brings together the major variables also dealt with by behavior analysis: verbally governed behavior, verbal tacts about contingencies and reports of their value, combining the multiple contingencies involved to get an overall prediction, and the verbal community contingencies. The major doubt is perhaps the over-reliance of verbal behavior reports, but restricting its application to voluntary behaviors and only for specific behaviors makes it quite useful in situations where observed behavior is hard to measure (also Bernstein, 1986; Bernstein & Michael, 1990).

10.4. Impersonal Trust

A number of behaviors maintained by very general verbal communities have been discussed as "impersonal trust". This refers to a very general trust we usually have in social institutions and groups. For example, if we have our fortnightly pay placed directly into a bank account then we are, in a very loose way, trusting that we can get the money out again. We are also trusting that the money will be worth something (exchangeable). The implicit trust, therefore, points us towards large, societal communities in which we regularly participate.

Zucker (1986) has made a very interesting analysis of some cases in which these types of trust have broken down. For example, in times of depression people will often not trust the banks or even the value of government currency, and will buy gold or land instead. Zucker isolated three ways of increasing the impersonal trust: through personal reputation or direct past experience which leads to trust; trust based on past experience with similar others or similar institutions; and trust based on rational certification and professionalism.

As an example of the different productions of trust, in the past people might have been more likely to put money into stocks of shares of a company which was owned by a relative or member of a similar racial or cultural group. We might be more likely these days to trust our investments to someone with professional qualifications and perhaps a good reputation. The different modes of extracting trust from the social system shows the different types of verbal communities which are present. Shapiro (1987) further makes an analysis of the safeguards which impersonal trust engender and the costs and problems with trying to simultaneously trust a verbal community and trust the guardians of the trustees.

As one further example of this research, Lewis and Weigert (1985a, b) have made a suggestion, which mirrors the approach of behavior analysis to trust as verbal community loose reinforcement, in the context of the differences between social atomism and holism. Social atomism holds that groups are reducible to individuals while social holism holds that group properties are not reducible to individual behavior. Lewis and Weigert suggest that both views are correct and that it is impersonal trust which gives a group "holistic" properties. Changes to the group trust will likewise affect the individual social behavior.

This view of Lewis and Weigert agrees with the analysis made in this book that social behavior can be divided into social behavior relying upon a verbal community and social behavior which does not. The latter becomes the former when a system of generalized or loose reinforcement occurs in the group (i.e., loose behaviors of trust). Although we will not repeat it here, Lewis and Weigert (1985a) trace these ideas through sociology from Durkheim and Simmel to the present day (Barber, 1983; Luhmann, 1979).

10.5. Social Support, Weak Ties and Network Theories

We saw in the last chapter, did we not, that community psychologists, anthropologists and sociologists have each looked at the networks of social relations (Cohen, 1969; Killworth, Bernard & McCarty, 1984; Marsden & Lin, 1982; Mitchell, 1969). The primary problem was that of defining the functional relation between the recipients: when was there a community, a neighbourhood, or a friendship? From the current perspective we would expect many different functional relations in social networks, and verbal communities in the present definition would involve generalized or loose reinforcement between members of the community. Indeed, there is some evidence that functional relations between different forms of groups have differentiated. The results of Litwak and Szelenyi (1969) suggested, for example, that in modern western societies neighbours help with immediate emergencies, kin and family help with goals involving long term commitment, and friends help to provide variety of interests and exploration.

What we should learn from this as behavior analysts is that the behaviors maintained by different types of verbal communities might be generalized over a limited range of behaviors. That is, neighbours might function as a verbal community in dealing with emergencies and immediate problems in the area, and they might have their own linguistic terms, socially constructed knowledges, attitudes and beliefs, rituals, etc. Kin and family have been found to figure in discussions of important matters (Marsden, 1987), for instance, as well as helping (Amato, 1990). Networks even change during different phases of a relationship (Milardo, 1982).

The variation of function in different groups means that research results will be vague unless the function of the group or network being studied is made clear and measured (e.g., Marsden, 1987, 1990). Thus even the "weak ties" have been found to sustain verbal communities with functions that are very important but only used in some circumstances (Granovetter, 1973, 1982). One factor which has been identified in social relationships is the reciprocity, but the generality of the exchange also needs to be investigated (Sahlins, 1965; van Tilburg, van Sonderen & Ormel, 1991).

Family are perhaps the only remnant in modern western societies of verbal communities which reinforce (with loose reinforcers) a very large range of behaviors. Families support kin in many different endeavours whereas other communities, such as work groups, have a restricted range of loosely reinforced behaviors.

The most researched functional communities are those which provide (or do not provide) support for a person during times of physical or mental stress. Even within this topic, different functional support behaviors are defined (Barrera & Ainlay, 1983). In general, the results show better adjustment, health and psychological well-being with more social support, but this depends upon the type of support and the timing of the support (Beckman, 1981; Berkman, 1985; Brownell & Shumaker, 1984; Cobb, 1976; Cohen, Mermelstein, Kamarck & Hoberman, 1985; Cohen & Wills, 1985; Gottlieb, 1981; Jacobson, 1986; Mermelstein, Cohen, Lichtenstein, Baer & Kamarck, 1986).

As would also be expected from a behavior analysis, there are costs as well as benefits from maintaining such communities and their functions, as has been found from a number of studies and from a number of different theoretical perspectives (e.g., Riley & Eckenrode, 1986; Rook, 1984, 1987), but again this depends upon the type of support provided (Rook, 1987).

10.6. Social Remembering

Another group outcome, or metacontingency (Glenn, 1991), which can be maintained by a verbal community is social remembering. We saw in Chapter 8 that remembering is usually thought of as an individual behavior, whether an individual can remember to do or say something. This notion in turn pivots upon whether an individual can recreate the stimulus conditions under which a behavior was previously emitted. As an individual, if I am asked to remember the capital of Peru, I might try and recreate the discriminative contexts of emitting the correct behavior.

Once remembering is viewed as stimulus control techniques and as highly verbal, then we can begin to accept that one function of verbal communities is that they can remember for us. That is, if we are part of a verbal community, the community can provide us with the stimulus conditions (verbal or nonverbal) for remembering correctly. Part of this group benefit is rather obvious: that through verbal community-maintained written instructions I can better remember. This amounts simply to a wordy way of saying that I can look something up in a book or ask someone! Because the existence of writing depends upon a verbal community this can be considered a benefit of belonging to a verbal community.

Others have looked at other, less obvious forms of social remembering (Center for Human Information Processing, 1987; Clark & Stephenson, 1989; Clark, Stephenson & Rutter, 1986; Connerton, 1989; Elkine, 1927; Fentress & Wickham, 1992; Halbwachs, 1980/1950; Hartwick, Sheppard & Davis, 1982; Stephenson, Clark & Wade, 1986; Wegner, 1987).

One method of social remembering is for the verbal community's power of compliance to be used to have members repeat and rehearse oral histories of the group, and the useful knowledge that goes with this. While western youths typically need to be coaxed into such things, the benefit to a group is usually better appreciated (verbally) by older members of the community. So oral histories can be seen as social remembering (Bauman, 1986; Goody, 1987; Henige, 1982; Tonkin, 1991) maintained by general social compliance.

A second form of social remembering comes from group members providing discriminative stimuli for remembering, a type of snow-balling effect (Wegner, 1987). In an interesting series of experiments, Stephenson and colleagues gave subjects recordings of a simulated police interrogation and a few minutes afterwards asked them to remember as much as they could alone, in dyads, or in groups of four. It was found firstly that larger groups remembered more correctly, but not in proportion to their numbers (although with most memory data there is a ceiling on how much can be remembered). More interestingly, from a verbal behavior point of view, individuals made more metastatements when recalling than did the groups (Clark & Stephenson, 1989; Clark, Stephenson & Wade, 1986). Metastatements are comments made about the material to be remembered rather than repeating the material. This result suggests that the individuals were making more (meta)statements which could be discriminative stimuli for remembering than did people in the groups. Thus the group replaced, to some extent, the use of precurrent verbal operants for remembering–the metastatements (Parsons, Taylor, & Joyce,1981).

10.7. Music and Writing

When we come to behavioral analyses of the Arts, we find little available except a small amount on writing. There were also a few comments made in 9.3 about the effects of writing laws on behavior. Because of this paucity, I will briefly mention some behavior analyses of writing and then elaborate (i.e., wildly extrapolate) about music.

Writing. Skinner provided analyses of writing both fiction and nonfiction (Skinner, 1934, 1939, 1957, 1968, 1972, 1981b). One other paper outlined some self-control techniques used by authors (Wallace, 1977), and one other on helping elderly people to write letters which were more reinforcing to the recipients (Goldstein & Baer, 1976).

The main analyses of writing center on the strengtheners involved. Since neither the acclaim for a piece of writing nor good sales figures occur for some time after the writing has been finished, supplementary sources of reinforcement or self-control techniques are needed to maintain writing. Writers have found various techniques to solve this problem (Wallace, 1977). As we saw in 8.5, "self-reinforcement" is not a simple procedure and involves other people, and for this reason many of the techniques of writers also involve the help of friends to maintain their writing.

Another way to view this is to compare the strengthening of letter writing over the years. In some (usually wealthy) families many years ago, letters would be sent across town by messengers, and a return letter might appear within a matter of hours. This must have sustained writing more than the current postal systems where a return letter can take forever.

The messenger letter system has probably been replaced by the telephone, for which an immediate answer strengthens the behavior. The side-effect of this is that while the immediacy of telephones make their use almost automatically strengthened, it turns out to be punishing when there is no answer on the telephone. At least letters were sure to get where they were going by messenger. An engaged signal on the telephone is not conducive to making lots of calls.

Music. With regards to music, very little has been written (cf. Skinner, 1980), so most of the following is my speculation. I hope it prompts an experimental program in music behavior. I will only touch on a few points.

What makes a person play music? This is by no means a simple question, since there appears to be no obvious gain. To pursue this, let us consider three audiences for music, assuming (as I do) that music has primarily social functions (cf. Guerin, 1991c; Weber, 1958).

The first audience is the musicians themselves. There might be some automatic strengthening from completing passages and whole pieces of music. Just completing a large piece of music, especially for the first time, seems to be strengthening, it is certainly pleasing. As well, playing "interesting" passages or inventing new passages might strengthen the behavior. It must be kept in mind that this should not be construed as an expression of the self. This strengthening might be from sensory aspects, from generalized social consequences, or from observational learning ("I've seen others get social approval when completing this piece of music").

Second, there is often an audience of other musicians playing at the same time. They will probably select a different series of responses than the "self-audience" or an audience of non-musicians. Social consequences could results from more "fancy" playing in front of other musicians, as well as from imitation and adaptation of passages that the others play. Further, the effects made when a group of musicians are playing together is especially strong. For learning musicians (remarkably like children with verbal behavior), the combined loudness brought about by playing in groups seems to be reinforcing. For the more mature musician, the combined harmonies and contrapuntal effects are especially "worthwhile", and presumably strengthening of music playing.

Against this is the finding that with many in the group the individual strengthening is reduced (Chapter 5). An interesting case of this was once told to this author by the wife of a professional musician in an orchestra. I do not know if this is a common procedure, but this orchestra kept moving the violin desks around except for the 1st violin desk. This was done because the violin players at the back, if they stayed there, would begin to play slower and softer. Social loafing at its best.

A third audience is the "real" audience, the ones who are there only to listen to the music. They provide some strengthening for the musicians through fees and applause. This is most likely verbally mediated, however, since the applause only comes at the end of a performance, and might not otherwise sustain an entire performance. This analysis in fact suggests that the fees and applause only strengthen the attendance of the musicians: that is, they only reinforce the musicians showing up. The applause is too remote from the dynamics of the performance to strengthen the quality of the performance, unless it is verbally mediated by the musicians ("I played really well, and I seem to be getting more applause than ever before"). But verbally mediated forms of control are weak and supplementary strengthening will be required (from the first two types of audiences presumably).

I believe that this weak control has the effect of making musicians not very responsive to audiences during performances, unless they can see the gestures of the audience (which might be reinforcing). This effect probably helps create the image of stone-faced musicians who have little stage presence. Further, it is the performers who are playing only for the money and glory, and not for other more serious reasons, who stay entirely responsive to an audience (they are said to "woo" the audience).

A final consideration is the reinforcing effect of the music itself. It is here that things get murky. It is not at all certain what makes a passage of music either pleasurable or reinforcing "in itself". The progression of Western music has seen the creation and violation of musical "rules", where the rules are not verbally expressed but are environmental contingencies. They are like systems of sounds, in the sense of which I wrote about language as a system of symbols in Chapter 7.

So there is no "meaning" to any sound; like language, the meaning is not inherent but is the difference or effect anything makes to the whole system–the consequences. This goes against common sense, since most people believe that it is the sounds they "like", not the discrimination from other sounds and the consequences. However, it is plausible to me when I listen to the full range of "mere sounds" which people have found pleasing, from the Scottish bagpipes to the Gamelan music of Indonesia to contemporary Western classical music (e.g., May, 1980). To me, this shows the socially defined nature of musical tastes. It is not the sounds themselves but their relations to the social system of sounds approved through a verbal community's history.

The sweetest sounds often seem to be those that only just violate a "rule", which again suggests strong social control, and verbally governed control in particular. In Western music this went out of control in the later music of Wagner and Strauss, where the addition of chromatics, which gave the special flavour to Mozart, was stretched to blandness. Nothing more could be done within that system of sounds, and Schoenberg invented a new system of sounds. Schoenberg's system of sounds was almost certainly a case of instruction following, however, and not reinforcement from the musical contingencies themselves, because many people find such serial music "unsatisfying"; for them the rule following has not tracked "natural" contingencies (although I also suggest there are few nonsocial contingencies in music; like language it is a constructed system, but effects such as octaves might provide reinforcement from the physical environment).

There also seems to be a curious reinforcing effect of repetition in music. Favourite pieces are repeated almost compulsively. I am not sure what is happening here, although I guess that it is related to the development of musical themes. Is it the repetition of "rule breaking" passages which form a new musical stimulus equivalence class within the whole sound system? Is the rule breaking and further development a form of escape from punishment? A lot of interesting work could be done on this, which would probably also lead to a better understanding of the subtle consequences in areas other than music as well.

A related concern is the existence of records, cassettes and compact discs. These allow an exact repetition each time they are heard, and this (informally to me) leads to a profound increase in the compulsive listening quality mentioned above. I suspect it has something to do with the way that perceptual response systems (Guerin, 1990) are formed and maintained, but this is really wild speculation. Research on this would also help clarify non-musical repetition effects (Rabbit & Banerji, 1989).

As far as composing music goes, the comments are similar to those mentioned above with respect to writing. The composition itself must be strengthening enough to keep the listeners' attention, although most classical music requires attention to have supplementary motivation, usually social or self-instructed (which amounts to the same). Some music does not consider the audience's attention as its major priority. The riots accompanying the first performance of Stravinsky's Rite of Spring suggests that not only was he ahead of his time, but that the music did not strengthen the audience's attention. That is, the audience could not find any strengthening effects in the music. Later audiences did.

10.8. Rumours

Once there is a community of people who share knowledge which also might be socially constructed, and who share weak ties with members of other communities, the scene is set for the spreading of rumours and gossip (Allport & Postman, 1947; Back, Festinger, Hymovitch, Kelley, Schachter & Thibaut, 1950; Epstein, 1969; Firth, 1956; Peterson & Gist, 1951; Prasad, 1950; Rosnow, 1980, 1991; Rosnow, Esposito & Gibney, 1987; Sinha, 1952; Walker & Blaine, 1991).

The two questions of interest are: why do people talk about rumours, and what are the conditions for spreading rumours? In both cases the answer seems to be that rumours are involved when there are changing social contingencies. When there is general anxiety in a verbal community, that is, when there are uncertain or changing social contingencies, then rumours seem to be most prevalent (Rosnow, 1980). When there is no certain answer to the rumour and the stakes are high, rumours also spread faster. Moreover, anxiety-provoking "dread" rumours are more prevalent than "wish" rumours (Walker & Blaine, 1991).

Rumours, then, are a function of socially constructed knowledge and important changes in verbal community contingencies. This makes them like a generalized social comparison or auditing which spreads through an entire verbal community. They also require a verbal community or social network which is intermeshed with other verbal communities, in a similar way to that in which public opinion is formed and spread through communities (Katz & Lazarsfeld, 1955). They have positive as well as negative functions, and help to maintain a verbal community as much as they are a negative side-effect of its existence (Firth, 1956).

10.9. Modernity, Mass Media and Computer Communication

Modernity. It was mentioned above that families are perhaps the only remnant in modern western societies of verbal communities which reinforce (with loose reinforcers) a large range of behaviors. A number of writers have commented on other changes in social life we are currently undergoing (Cushman, 1990; Giddens, 1990, 1991; Sampson, 1989; Skinner, 1987). Most of the themes put forward by these different authors are similar. Giddens (1990) perhaps summarizes these themes best as the pace of changes, the scope of changes, and the nature of modern institutions. He suggests that there are discontinuities with the past: that modern social institutions and institutional arrangements are different in kind to those of the past.

In particular, Giddens singles out the three strands for attention. First, that the nature of space and time have changed in modern society in a radical way. What he means by this, for behavior analysis, is that a great many of our behaviors are not discriminated by specific times and places anymore. I can find a generic supermarket in most places in the world open most times of the day and can do my generic shopping for generic items which are likely to be in stock in very similar packaging (all this is meant for the western world of course!). This behavior is not contextualized to a particular time and place. Further, while we still must go to Athens to view the Parthenon (or the bits in the British Museum), we can also view pictures of it, watch televised documentaries on it, and read about its background and details, probably better at home than in Athens, for those privileged to live in western countries.

Giddens' point then (and he is not the first to make this point) is that the discriminative stimuli for many of our modern behaviors have become generalized in time and space. From this follows his second point: that social relations have become "disembedded" because of these generalized context for behaviors. Money in particular has disembedded social relations from interactions, as we saw in 9.3. I can make monetary exchanges with someone in another country without interacting socially at all. The other aspect of disembedded social relations is that technology has become independent of the persons using it (Murdock, 1993). Doctors around the world will employ almost identical treatments for most common diseases, and building construction is based on standard procedures around the world. The epitome of this is to attempt standard forms of therapy which can be "plugged in", as it were, like modules.

It must not be thought that time/space generalization and disembedded social relations are all bad. Clearly there are benefits as well as costs of these changes to society. Giddens (1990, 1991) and others try to detail the costs and benefits of such changes. Giddens (1991), for example, showed how ideas of self and identity have changed from the changes in societal functioning. This topic was briefly dealt with in the last chapter. Likewise, Hart (1986, p. 642) has commented on how plastic money, easy credit and other generalized (disembedded) means of getting people to do things has affected our ideas of personal identity (also cf. Sampson, 1989).

All of these changes lead to a disembedding of experience from our worlds (Giddens, 1991; Moscovici, 1987; Skinner, 1990; Thompson, 1990). Getting anything done becomes heavily reliant upon verbal behavior to get other people to do things, which means both that other people become more of a means than an end, and also that we end up trusting anonymous others for much of what we do. If we wanted to travel over a bridge in a strange city we rely upon using money earned in some irrelevant manner to pay impersonally a taxi driver to take us over the bridge. At the same time there is impersonal trust in the taxi driver and the bridge builders (that the bridge does not fall down). Giddens (1991) claims that such increases in impersonal trust has led to people in modern society having a type of anxiety about all the loose ends they must take for granted. It is not that we now have more anxiety than previous eras, but that the type of anxiety is different. Television has been suggested as both a source and a remedy for this anxiety (cf. Silverstone, 1993).

The third feature which Giddens summarizes is "institutional reflexivity", that knowledge about society is itself now used to regulate society. That is, knowledge about people is used to organize social institutions even though much of this knowledge is socially constructed. Put another way, with a bit of extrapolation, much of our social behavior is now verbally governed or guided by rules which are taken from what is known or constructed about society (Skinner, 1987). Examples of this would be learning what you want to wear by reading magazines which tell you what people *should* want to wear this season, and this information is itself taken from what is known about society, or more likely is socially constructed by those in positions of power. So unlike previous ages of human history, society is reflexive and can quickly change depending upon what it finds out or makes up about itself.

Mass Media. A common element in all the suggested changes of modernity is the presence of a mass media system. While little has been said from behavior analysis about the mass media and its effects, a few suggestions are probably in order. This will only include a few points of direct relevance to behavior analysis, and only to do with television viewing. There are many other important features of the mass media which need to be understood at a behavioral level (Behr & Iyengar, 1985; Cook, Kendzierski & Thomas, 1983; Doob & Macdonald, 1979; Gamson, Croteau, Hoynes & Sasson, 1992; Hansen, 1991; Keating & Latané, 1976; Livingstone, 1990; Moscovici, 1990; Murdock, 1993; Oskamp. 1988; Roberts & Maccoby, 1985; Robinson & Levy, 1986; Silverstone, 1993; Thompson, 1990; Tyler & Cook, 1984; Wegner, Wenzlaff, Kerker & Beattie, 1981; Wober, 1990).

First, television is the focus for a large amount of peoples' time. This means that there are powerful consequences at work with television viewing, but more difficult is the problem of establishing what they might be. Sensory reinforcement is one possibility (see 2.3) although that in itself requires further elucidation. Generalized avoidance of other settings might be another possibility. Alternatively, social reinforcement for television viewing is a likelihood. This might occur in two ways. First, talking about what is seen on television could be reinforced socially, or at least avoidance of punishment for not viewing television. [As someone who has foregone television for many years, it has been obvious to me that a great part of modern conversation is based around television viewing. Not being able to talk about television programmes is clearly punishable.]

The second way in which television viewing might be socially reinforced is in determining the symbols or totems around which rituals and symbolic behaviors are based. Television also acts to construct or provide the context for how to behave in order to be socially acceptable. In this way the comment has been made that television can set the agenda for symbolic social behaviors (Gamson, Croteau, Hoynes & Sasson, 1992; Hansen, 1991). As a highly verbal medium (Thompson, 1990), television is perfect to assume such a role.

The dependence of TV culture on verbal behavior and verbal communities means that all the social construction phenomena outlined earlier in this chapter will be found for TV. For example, rumours, disembedding, and tight subculture verbal communities (fan clubs), not only exist for TV, but are extremely powerful (e.g., Jenkins, 1992).

A second feature of television is that it requires minimal physical behavior on the part of the viewer to keep it going, and therefore qualifies for Skinner's (1987) loose term of a "pleaser". The audience does not have to react or have an effect in any way to keep the action going. Indeed the television is notoriously unresponsive to comments made in the living-room about commercials or B-grade movies. As such, the television teaches an unresponsiveness of its own, that things can keep going without any social responding. This is unlike interacting with real people, however, as some responding is needed.

Further to this, television can be watched alone and behaviors can therefore develop outside of normal social communities. Most people, however, seem to prefer to watch with others, thus emphasizing the likely social reinforcement implicit in television watching. As mentioned above, what is perhaps more worrying is that the television can symbolically define the types of audiences with whom we watch, or go to the movies with, and can therefore organize our social relations or verbal communities.

All of these points add up to emphasize the points discussed above from Giddens (1991), that our social life has become disembedded from social interactions with important others, has become global and generalized, and our primary social institutions have become reflexive. Mass media clearly play a role in producing these effects, and we can see this even at the level of individual behavior.

Computer Communication. One other way in which technology is changing how people affect each other is in the use of computer communications–the use of EMail and networking. When we interact with someone over a computer network rather than face-to-face, many contingencies are changed. First, the interaction is purely verbal, there are no more direct effects possible over communication links (until virtual realities stop being virtual!). Second, any effects of, say, manding which are made over computer networks will have little direct effect on the mander because nothing can be seen of the results and results are delayed. Also, effects of gestures will be lost altogether, so autoclitic functioning must be made explicitly in written form when using EMail messages.

The effects of such changes might not be all bad. For example, people might be more likely to tell the truth over an EMail link because there will not be an immediate punishing effect back on them. This might give time to countercontrol a punishing effect which is returning over the EMail. Similarly, some statements might be easier to make if the recipient cannot see the facial expressions or other gestures of the sender. In either case, the nature of the social interaction certainly must change with EMail communication.

The most extensive series of studies are by Kiesler and colleagues (Huff, Sproull & Kiesler, 1989; Kiesler, Siegel & McGuire, 1984; Kiesler & Sproull, 1992; McGuire, Kiesler & Siegel, 1987; Siegel, Dubrovsky, Kiesler & McGuire, 1986; Sproull & Kiesler, 1986, 1991a, b) who researched how computer-mediated communications affect social behaviour. They have done this both through looking at already existing electronic mail channels (Sproull & Kiesler, 1986) and through laboratory experiments (Siegel, Dubrovsky, Kiesler & McGuire, 1986).

Their results show that when electronically networked groups make decisions, the participation rates are more equal, they come up with more ideas for action, and speak more frankly with more self-expression. While the greater democracy is useful in getting ideas, it also has the disadvantage of taking longer and making it less likely that anything will be done (less successful manding). Some evidence also shows that less arguments were pursued in electronic discussions (McGuire, Kiesler & Siegel, 1987), and that people can try and dominate the network by making it impossible for others to interrupt. Like Spears, Lea and Lee (1990), there was some evidence for more uninhibited behaviours during electronic discussions (Siegel, Dubrovsky, Kiesler & McGuire, 1986), which can be both a positive effect, if people say things they would not normally say, or negative, if people start making anti-social comments or inappropriate jokes. Finally, the effects of status also decrease during electronic networking, since the cues for status are not so obvious when the other people cannot be seen.

Many of these results are from laboratory settings where the participants have little experience with electronic mail, but others show the effects on managerial styles and performance (Huff, Sproull & Kiesler, 1989; Kiesler & Sproull, 1992; Sproull & Kiesler, 1991b). With increased experience it is likely that rules or standards for discussion would emerge so the decision time would decrease, but that the many benefits, such as equal participation, would also decrease. Further research should provide answers. In behaviour analytic terms it is argued that the social consequences change dramatically when communication is not face-to-face, and so the EMail communication link could be a good way of researching the effects of social consequences.

Part 4
Applying Behavior Analysis

Chapter 11

Changing and Maintaining Behavior

11.1. Ethical and Practical Considerations

Before talking about changing behavior something needs to be said about the issues involved in doing this. First, in one sense we are always changing other peoples' behavior when we interact with them at all. All interaction is a dynamic mixture of presenting verbal contingencies or using nonverbal contingencies–even to get another person to start or stop interacting! Therefore, we need to be clear about what we mean by the ethics of changing behavior: the ethical issue is perhaps really one of whether you "should" attempt to change the behavior of someone who is unwilling to participate. But this is still not clear. If I want a friend to buy my old records and I therefore try to persuade them, is this ethical? Are car salespersons unethical?

There are two types of "control" which are confused when talking in this area. In the behavior analytic sense we are always controlling the behavior of other people and cannot stop doing this. My writing is controlling your behavior to some extent, even if this is only to put you to sleep.

The real ethical sense of "control", on the other hand, is whether or not a community is going to restrict someone's behavior repertoire to protect other members of the community. Because of the loose control by a verbal community, people can get away with hurting others and depriving others. Practical ethics consists of a community "deciding" (culturally evolving, Glenn, 1989) a point at which the person doing the hurting should be stopped in order to protect the whole society and not threaten the system of loose contingencies. The cutoff is not really arbitrary but it does vary depending upon the goals and outcomes achieved in different societies. Different groups will have different ethics not because it is all arbitrary, but because the groups differ in what they can achieve for members who participate within the rules (cf. Marin, 1993). There is nothing in behavior analysis, then, which can dictate to any community where its cutoff point should be. The control talked about in behavior analysis is of a different sort.

While not trying to be too pedantic, I hope it can be seen how complex the issues are. What is most important is to not attempt behavior changes unless you are sure they conform to at least the requirements of your local Psychological Society or the American Psychology Association, that you have professional standing to carry out such a change, and the person is willing to participate and their protection has been safeguarded.

On the more practical side, it should be made clear that changing people's behavior is not as easy as it appears in books. It should not be thought that people are resistant to change attempts, but rather, that there are always other contingencies operating which are stronger than those used to make changes (cf. Haley, 1973). In real life the contingencies acting upon a person are many and varied; they are both verbal and nonverbal.

In this regard one cannot go in to solve a behavior problem equipped only with a knowledge of the principles of behavior analysis. One also needs to know a lot about the contingencies acting on the people being dealt with and their environment. For example, one cannot sit down with an intellectually handicapped person and explain to them new ways of behaving–they may simply not understand (behave appropriately to the words). It is no use setting up a fancy stimulus discrimination for an elderly person if their attention patterns no longer allow them to make those sorts of discriminations.

I call this procedure "know you animal". If you know the innate and contingency history of whatever or whoever you are training, then you can make more efficient change programs. Often several steps of a procedure can be cut out if you know something about the animal with which you are dealing. In particular, almost all attempts to change peoples' behavior utilizes an assumed participation in several overlapping verbal communities. For these reasons, Chapter 12 will consider some special groups of people and look at the special contingencies under which they commonly operate. In each of these cases, to really carry out behavior changes one must discover the normal contingencies operating and the contingencies for each person as an individual.

Ethical behavior change is not just a function of the change procedures used. Another important concern is whether or not the outcome of the change is useful to the person being changed. For this reason there has been a lot of discussion within applied behavior analysis about the social validity of any change (Baer, Wolf & Risley, 1987; Fawcett, 1991; Schwartz & Baer, 1991; Stolz, 1981; Wolf, 1978). This means that before a behavior intervention has been carried out, a check needs to be made on whether the people involved report the change as useful or not, and afterwards, whether it actually worked or not and was seen as useful. It is hard to justify making a change if it is of no use.

11.2. Changing the Behavior of Individuals

The behavior change literature and practice is less advanced than the experimental literature. The foundations are based on some of the older experimental work. The areas of multiple response effects, stimulus equivalence classes, and verbal control of behavior are likely to have a big impact on applied techniques in the future, but they have not yet infiltrated.

The approach is the same as for the experimental analysis of behavior: define the relevant behaviors, find the contexts in which they occur, and find the consequences which strengthen and maintain those behaviors in those contexts. Applied behavior analysis goes one step further than this and arranges to change the contexts or, more usually, change the consequences.

Only a quick overview is possible here. Those interested can read some good textbooks on this (Cooper, Heron & Heward, 1987; Sulzer-Azaroff & Mayer, 1977). Keeping up with the *Journal of Applied Behavior Analysis* is also a necessity. The Society for the Experimental Analysis of Behavior (1987a, b) has reprinted a large number of these articles in four volumes.

Training New Behaviors

Shaping is the name given to a procedure of teaching a new behavior. You start by defining the target behavior wanted, and go on to define other behaviors which are successively closer to the target behavior. The idea is to start with a behavior that even vaguely resembles the target behavior, and strengthen this with reinforcement. You then wait until a variation in that behavior appears which is closer to the target behavior and strengthen that second one. A key point is to stop strengthening earlier approximations once you have moved onto a behavior closer to the target. This is also called the method of successive approximations.

For example, if you wished to teach intellectually disabled children to wave (cf. Stokes, Baer & Jackson, 1974), you might start with any movement of the hand above the elbow and reinforce that. You might next reinforce only those movements which are lateral; you would then stop reinforcing just any movement of the hand above the elbow. Your next step might be to reinforce this new behavior only when a person appears and greets the client. This is training for a specific stimulus context: we usually wave only when greeting someone who appears. You would then stop reinforcing waves which did not occur in such contexts.

Shaping is a useful and powerful technique if used properly. The key points are to plan ahead what you are after, to stop reinforcing earlier approximations once you have moved on, and to use the organism's already existing behaviors where possible. It takes patience and forethought.

A second way of training new behaviors is through modeling or imitation. Something has already been said about imitation and observational learning in Chapter 4. Modeling in training can be of many kinds, and might involve role-playing a situation which includes the target behavior; it might be exact copying of a behavior from a model; or it might mean watching a video and imitating what happens there. A key point that was made in Chapter 4 was that modeling and imitation are useful only if they are taught first. That is, the person has to cooperate and be capable of generalized imitation for these procedures to work. Unless the model's behavior actually controls the client's behavior, imitation will not work. So you have to get to a position such that your behavior can control generalized imitation in the client.

A warning should be repeated here. It may not always be desirable to teach generalized imitation. It should be made context specific: occurring only in the training environment. Otherwise the person might imitate dangerous or aggressive behaviors from others (or from the television).

A third way of training new behaviors is through verbal instructions or prompting (e.g., Anjoh & Yamamoto, 1991). This simply refers to telling someone what to do rather than showing them what to do. And in that lies the problem. As we saw throughout Chapter 7, the verbal control of behavior relies on generalized social compliance through social consequences and is therefore weak. This needs to be stressed. If you walk up to someone and say "Please walk three paces forward" they probably will not do it, at least straight away. So in the same way that modeling needs a generalized imitation skill, verbal control needs generalized social compliance first. If you have this then verbal instructions can quickly do what might take a long time with shaping, and it can supplement modeling and make it far more efficient.

There is one other catch to the use of verbal control in training behavior, however. This is, that if verbal control is used to teach a behavior, then it will be the generalized social consequences which immediately maintain the behavior (Chapter 7). If I use verbal control to teach you to wave "Put your hand up like this and move it back and forth when you greet someone" then the response is only responding initially to the generalized social consequences which give control to the verbal behavior. If you wish the behavior to maintain then alternative sources of consequences need to be made contingent on the response.

Usually, the automatic consequences of a behavior take over or track quickly; for example, the greetings in response to the new waving behavior will likely sustain the new behavior and the verbal prompts can be quickly dropped. But this needs to be checked out carefully and provision made for it if necessary. Too many times someone is taught a behavior through verbal means (lectures, for example) and the behavior itself never tracks any consequences available. So verbal training needs to be supplemented by rehearsal—but only rehearsal which allows good contact with the natural contingencies, not mere verbal rehearsal.

The generalized compliance with verbal instructions probably explains a lot of the procedures of hypnosis. Many of the early sessions of hypnosis consist in building up a generalized compliance to the hypnotherapist's instructions (Erickson, 1980). As we learn more about verbal control of behavior (see Chapter 7 for some clues) we should learn better techniques for such procedures. Getting people to follow their own verbal instructions better might help, for example (see 7.5 for some clues).

A fourth way of training new behaviors is to use physical guidance. This also needs cooperation from the client but not generalized compliance to model or follow instructions. Here you use a minimum pressure to physically guide the person in the behavior. So to train hand waving you might lightly hold the the person's wrist and lift their hand up and move it as a wave.

The problem with physical guidance is that the touch of the guidance can act as a powerful discriminative stimulus for the response. That is, the person might not do the behavior if the guidance is not there (see for example, Rincover & Koegel, 1975, the case of Joey). To overcome this, the physical guidance should use the minimum pressure needed and should be faded as soon as possible. This means to reduce gradually the pressure until only a light touch is needed, and then let the person respond without any touch at all. The control can also be transferred to verbal or modeling techniques.

One method that is becoming common is to use graduated prompts. With this, the person is first trained using verbal prompts and instructions. If this does not work then modeling is carried out. If this fails then physical guidance is used. So there is a graduated series of methods which are used in turn if the previous one fails to control the behavior.

These, then, are the major ways of training a new behavior. See also resurgence in 3.2. Some recommended examples are the following: Horner and Keilitz (1975); Reid and Hurlbut (1977); Wacker and Berg (1983).

Strengthening Behaviors

A lot of time has already been spent in Section 2.3 on the types of consequences which can strengthen behavior, and some of the problems with them. We have seen that natural positive reinforcers are used wherever possible for many good reasons. If this is not possible then the behavior is trained with contrived reinforcers and these should be faded into natural ones as a last phase of the intervention (see Jones & Kazdin, 1975, for a good example of this). We also saw in 2.3 that for best results, the reinforcement needs to be contingent, immediate, not satiating, appropriate to the individual, varied, stronger than competing consequences, and faded to intermittent, natural reinforcement.

Some people view the use of positive reinforcement as a form of bribery. To me it seems that the forms of bribery are only those that use contrived reinforcement. Cases utilizing natural reinforcements are common and are not perceived as bribery.

A second form of increasing the rate of responding is not widely used. This is negative reinforcement. It is seen as unethical, except in drastic circumstances perhaps, to increase behaviors through escape and avoidance. A noxious situation usually needs to be created so the person will increase the escape or avoidance behavior. This technique itself should be avoided unless the circumstances are life-threatening. Despite this, parents, teachers and governments frequently use this method "You are not leaving the table until you have eaten all your spinach!" "Do X and We won't put you in prison" (see Sidman, 1989).

There is one other way of strengthening behavior, although it is technically the same as positive reinforcement. This is the use of positive rehearsal. Getting someone to repeat a behavior usually seems to make it more probable in the future. This has not yet been clearly analyzed by behavior analysts, and still needs some work done on it. Some suggestions will be given.

It may be that what occurs during effective positive rehearsal is that the natural consequences begin to take over from the contrived consequences, the generalized imitation consequences, and the generalized verbal consequences. It might also be that the stimulus context has a better chance of taking over control of the behavior when rehearsals are carried out. A third possibility is that verbal self-regulation gets a chance to control behavior during rehearsal, although it is not clear then why the effect should occur for nonhuman animals as well. Other than these suggestions, there are no clearly demonstrated reasons why merely repeating a behavior should strengthen it.

Weakening Behaviors

There are a number of general techniques which can be used to reduce the rate of responding. We must be cautious in using these, however, for ethical and practical reasons. First, they do not by themselves train any behaviors to replace those reduced, and so the newly available time might not be used constructively. Second, it was suggested in 3.2 that any increase in the number of responses in the repertoire (providing they are reasonable behaviors) is probably a good thing in the long run. Reducing the number of responses may lead to long term problems if overdone.

The major reason for being cautious with reducing behaviors, however, is an ethical one: that most of the techniques rely on aversive conditions. These are generally avoided unless absolutely necessary, as for instance with children repeatedly hurting themselves. Usually the change can be accomplished with extinction and the reinforcement of incompatible behaviors, which will be considered below. In any event, the techniques should be used only with the permission of the clients, or their guardians if they cannot make such decisions themselves.

The first way of reducing behaviors is through extinction procedures. This simply means withholding the reinforcement for the behavior in question. It is a very easy technique to use, is very powerful if done properly, and has only a few problematic side-effects. The major problem with extinction is that if it is done inconsistently, usually withholding the reinforcement but occasionally lapsing, then it turns into an intermittent schedule of reinforcement. Intermittent schedules are very hard to extinguish, so the lapses make it very difficult in the long run. A practical problem with extinction is that consistency is often hard to accomplish in the real world, especially if more than one person is involved in the behavior change.

A second problem is that extinction almost always initially produces an increase in the rate of responding. When the reinforcement is first withheld, humans and animals both increase their rate of responding. If the extinction is continued then it soon drops off. This produces problems because one is tempted to stop extinction during this immediate increase, or at least lapse occasionally with the results mentioned earlier.

A third problem is one that is not often mentioned. Extinction with humans often consists of withholding attention from a person, since, as has been stressed throughout this book, a large portion of human behavior is maintained by social consequences. There are some problems with this, I believe, although I have no strong evidence for them. The problem seems to be that withholding attention also leads to an extinction of verbal community membership, which might generalize beyond the specific case being dealt with and lead to a general withdrawal from community.

The problem, then, is that in the long run, mutual shaping and extinction by presenting and withholding attention may be undesirable. If parents withhold attention from their children for compliance this could lead to a behavior repertoire dominated by (maintained by) parental approval. Freud would have called this an over-active superego! That is, most of the child's behavior would need intermittent reinforcement from the parents to be maintained at all whereas one goal for raising children is to get them self-regulating.

A second way of reducing a behavior is through Differential Reinforcement for Low Rates of Responding, or DRL. The idea here is to strengthen lower and lower rates of responding, until the behavior is stopped or else has reached a minimum acceptable criterion. It is less aversive than some of the other techniques and is tolerant, in the sense that it does not require an immediate cessation of behavior.

One problem with it, however, is that it takes some time to accomplish. Having to gradually reduce the rate of responding can be a lengthy procedure, and if the behavior is an unpleasant one for the person or other people around them then it would be wiser not to use it. A second problem is that it focuses the attention (and verbal behavior) of the client on the undesirable behavior. If the rate of this behavior is being measured and reinforcement is contingent upon it, then the client will naturally focus upon the behavior.

For these reasons, a better technique is the Differential Reinforcement for Other Behaviors, or DRO. It is also sometimes called Omission Training or OT. This reinforces for any behavior other than the one to be reduced. While it is similar to DRL it focuses attention onto other behaviors rather than the problematic one. The problem with DRO, however, is that some of the other behaviors might be just as bad as the one to be reduced. While this is usually taken care of by training new behaviors and reinforcing only a selection of other behaviors, problems can still arise.

A better way, then, to ensure that all these problems are taken care of is to use Differential Reinforcement for Incompatible Behavior or DRI. Here a behavior is strengthened which cannot be done simultaneously with the one to be reduced. For example, if a child is always getting out of their seat in a class, and this is considered undesirable, then the source of reinforcement for getting out of the seat could be removed (extinction) and the behavior of sitting in the seat reinforced as well, since this is incompatible with getting up. This gets over the problem of reinforcing worse behaviors and also the problem of focussing attention on the undesirable behavior. It is a very useful technique to use in conjunction with other techniques for reducing behavior. It is constructive and does not focus attention onto the problem itself.

With a bit of imagination an incompatible behavior can be found for most problem behaviors.

The remaining techniques to be discussed are all effective if used properly, but they rely on having aversive conditions and so should be avoided. This means that they should not be used without a careful consideration of the ethics involved, and the rights of the client. As mentioned, they should be discussed with the clients or their guardians beforehand, and be approved by a local Ethics Board. Despite this, it is interesting that they are all techniques that are commonly used by educators, government, police and the armed forces, although they are not always used very effectively even then (Sidman, 1989).

Response Cost refers to removing a portion of reinforcement contingent upon doing the behavior to be reduced. The most common form of this is the system of fines. If you speed in your car (and get caught) then a portion of money or your free time is taken away. This is widely used by police, governments, parents and education systems.

If done properly response costing can be quick and effective, but to do it properly is usually difficult. It needs to be consistent and immediate, and contingent on the behavior. Speeding fines, for example, have none of these properties. You can speed for years and not get caught, and there is a lot of verbal mediation involved in the costing procedure, which makes it neither immediate nor properly contingent. The other problem with response costing, and all the remaining techniques is that if the person can escape from the total situation then this escape will be negatively strengthened. Escape might be carried out through cheating or lying, or physically withdrawing.

An interesting but controversial technique for reducing a response is timeout. The means that the person is removed from the sources of reinforcement contingent upon the response. So, for example, if a child is being noisy and disturbing a class, they might be removed to a bare room elsewhere for a few minutes each time they are noisy. Apart from the problems to be mentioned, this can be a quick and effective way of reducing behaviors if done properly. It is also quite easy under most circumstances.

Having said that, there are serious problems with timeout. First, it is illegal in some states and countries, since it is considered a punishment (which it technically is). Other educational systems have banned it although it is not officially illegal. One of its other problems is that if the other room or setting is not actually bare, then there could be other sources of reinforcement present which will strengthen the response which gets them removed from the original setting. The same can happen if the setting with the problem response is aversive, stressful or just plain boring. Even removal to a neutral environment can then strengthen the problem response! As well, the technique itself can negatively reinforce escape and avoidance behaviors. In the case given above, if the child is repeatedly removed from the classroom and this is made aversive to them, they might stop turning up for school altogether, thereby avoiding the timeout and the classroom.

In practise, one of the problems encountered is that behavior change agents have used timeout as an escape of their own. If the child is sent out then the teacher does not have to deal with the problem any longer. More than this, the longer the child is out the stronger this is. So timeout ends up being a long sojourn into a bare environment rather than a very short period away from the reinforcers. Timeout is most effective if short, but longer periods can unfortunately strengthen its use by the change agent.

One of the reasons that timeout is best done for short periods is that it is not a constructive method by itself. It does not train useful behaviors to replace the undesirable ones. For this reason, the person is better having a short timeout followed by re-introduction to the original setting combined with DRI or DRO. This also reduces the chance of escape and avoidance.

There is a related problem in classroom settings. Children are present in classroom to learn, and sending them out has the side-effect of removing them from learning as well. They not only do not learn replacement behaviors, but they do not learn the educational material either. Foxx and Shapiro (1978) developed an interesting variation on timeout to overcome this problem, using timeout ribbons. The school children were given ribbons to put in their hair, and every once in a while those children with ribbons were given praise and some edibles. In this case, the undesired responses led to contingent removal of the ribbon for a short period. So the children were effectively removed from the sources of reinforcement without having to be removed from the classroom itself.

Another way of reducing responses is overcorrection (MacKenzie-Keating & McDonald, 1990). This is again an aversive technique, but it attempts to make the aversive part constructive. The idea is that contingent upon the response, the person is made to correct the situation to how it was before the response, and then to overcorrect as well. This is combined with positive practise of the correct behavior. For example, Foxx and Azrin (1973) dealt with children who were mouthing objects. They made overcorrection contingent upon mouthing an object. The overcorrection in this case consisted of having them clean their teeth and wash their mouth out with mouthwash. So the correction was relevant to the undesired behavior, and was constructively aversive.

The major problem with overcorrection is the same as for response cost and timeout. You need to have sufficient control over the person that they cannot escape or avoid the overcorrection procedure itself. If they can, then the whole procedure will be strengthening escape or avoidance. Overall, overcorrection seems to be an efficient and useful technique where it can be applied. Its constructive approach says much for it.

The final technique to be discussed is punishment. Here an aversive stimuli is made contingent upon the response. To be effective a number of conditions need to be met (Azrin & Holz, 1966). The punishment needs to be immediate, it needs to be as intense as possible, it needs to be consistent, and escape and avoidance have to be prevented. Needless to say, these conditions are rarely met for many ethical and practical reasons, so punishment is rarely effective when used by parents, teachers, and governments.

There are also many side-effects of the use of punishment, even when carried out effectively. For example, a complete reduction in all behaviors is often found. The problem behavior is reduced as well as most other behavior, and this probably reflects that punishment will punish participation in a verbal community as well as the behavior intended to be punished. Problems also occur when verbal statements are used instead of direct aversive stimuli. These occur because of the weak control of verbal instructions (see Chapter 7).

Despite these problems, punishment is extremely (most behavior analysts would say depressingly) common in everyday life. It is used by spouses, friends and enemies, parents, educational systems, governments, armies, and police services (Sidman, 1989). And it is not effectively used. One reason for its widespread use is that in the short term it often strengthens the punishing behavior itself for the punisher. If a parent slaps a child contingent upon a response, the child usually stops quickly, and negatively strengthens the parent's slapping behavior. The problems and side-effects mentioned above only show up in the long term, so the immediate impact seems effective, at least for the parents. Worse than this, most alternatives to punishment, such as positive reinforcement have much more delayed effects and require a lot of forethought and effort.

Most behavior analysts do not use punishment at all. Indeed, Skinner has remarked how he is proud of the alternatives that behavior analysts have devised to replace punishment (Griffin, Paisey, Stark & Emerson, 1988). However, he, and many other behavior analysts believe it is useful and more humane in certain circumstances. In particular, situations with self-abusive children who will injure or kill themselves if not treated quickly seem to justify the use of carefully controlled punishment, but the cases need to be carefully thought out.

Such a case might be one described by Sajwaj, Libet and Agras (1974) in which lemon juice was squirted into a 6-month old infant's mouth contingent upon her bringing up her food. She was rapidly losing weight from vomiting and would likely have starved to death, since she did not keep any food down. The punishment was effective very quickly and she rapidly gained weight. While aversive, lemon juice in the mouth seems a reasonable compromise to save a life.

This completes the discussion of techniques for reducing behaviors. It must be kept in mind that these are not simple techniques nor ones to be used lightly. They all have some ethical problems which need to be thought out and discussed before starting. As well, they should not be ever used in isolation, but should be combined with more constructive approaches such as positive reinforcement, which strengthen new behaviors.

Changing Verbal Contingencies with Individuals

Throughout this book the role of generalized social contingencies from verbal communities has been emphasized. Much of our behavior occurs because of a learned general compliance to other people in our verbal communities. This keeps us talking and writing in the language of a verbal community, it keeps us within certain codes and practices of a community's ethical norms, and it keeps social interaction between people as a function of certain variables. These behaviors do not occur in a motivational vacuum but have generalized consequences to maintain them.

This leads to the question of how we should go about changing behaviors of individuals which are maintained by verbal communities; whether we should change such behaviors; and whether it is even possible to change them. For example, if a person started speaking exclusively French in an English speaking community, how would or should we deal with this? Should we treat it as an aberrant behavior and try and weaken it while reinforcing any attempts to speak English?

Such questions as these have been a dilemma for psychotherapy: how culture dependent are the various forms of psychotherapy? Should we treat someone from another culture if the "target" behavior is "normal" in their society? I hope it can be seen that the social constructionist basis to verbal behavior which is implicit in behavior analysis allows some new directions to these questions. For example, the enormous role of verbal behavior in traditional psychotherapy shows the reliance on generalized social contingencies. A major feature of these psychotherapies is that they spend a lot of time trying to control the client's behavior through talking to them, or having the client talk (Hayes & Wilson, 1993).

Even in modern "cognitive therapies" the behaviors are dealt with verbally. For example, many therapies have the client imagine events. For a toad phobic they might be asked to imagine walking into a room full of toads. All of the covert responses which occur are being controlled by the therapist's verbal behavior, and hence, by generalized social contingencies. Other forms of therapy such as Rational Emotive Therapy are even more based on verbally controlled behavior (Poppen, 1989; Hayes, Kohlenberg & Melancon, 1989; Zettle & Hayes, 1980, 1982).

While the effects of generalized social contingencies need to be treated somehow, we should be clear what such approaches are up against. The problem for the therapist is that the maintenance of the presenting problems arises from the generalized impact of a whole community. The therapist can try and remove the client from that community, as has sometimes been done (Erickson, 1980; Haley, 1973). Alternatively, the therapist can build discriminations about the community: of when and where the client might not socially comply.

Whatever the change required, the means of accomplishing it might necessarily have to be verbal behavior, since this is our best means of getting at generalized social contingencies. This is what is commonly meant as making the client see things from a new perspective, or "cognitive" reframing. Simply training new behaviors when the problem behavior is one which is supported by generalized social contingencies will probably not maintain and generalize, unless the impact of the community is weakened. This latter step might have unwanted side-effects, however. The final alternative is to change the verbal community itself, and this is dealt with later in this chapter.

Generalization and Maintenance of Behavior Change

With some powers of social compliance through authority or status, I do not believe it is too difficult to get people to immediately change their behavior. The number of brands of psychotherapy claiming success testifies to this. As well, this is a large part of what hypnosis is about; it builds social compliance to the point that the hypnotherapist's verbal behavior controls the client's behavior. All of these forms of behavior change depend on gaining instructional control through generalized social compliance.

Applied behavior analysis and behavior therapy go beyond merely talking about things and trains new behaviors and changes old ones. But even here, social compliance and instructional control are usually needed. Just to get someone to come into an office needs some control. Getting them to carry out self-management tasks, or to attend to some presented stimuli, requires some social compliance.

The real question for therapies, then, is not how to get an immediate change in behavior. Given some social compliance this can be quite easy. Rather, the real questions are how to get the behavior to occur outside of the therapy setting and how to keep it occurring after the therapy or training has officially finished. If the new behaviors only occur in the therapy setting and it do not maintain afterwards, any "successful" therapy can be considered useless. We therefore turn to the questions of generalization and maintenance of behavior changes.

Generalization. Stimulus control means that a stimulus context which is consistently present when strengthening of behavior occurs will come to control that behavior. Stimulus generalization means that stimulus contexts similar to the original can also control the behavior to some extent. The practical problems of stimulus control are twofold. First, undesired behaviors might generalize too much. So, for example, we learn a new four-letter word from a friend and the proceed to use it in all contexts, which produces negative social consequences. In such a case the stimulus control needs to be tightened. The specific contexts in which the word can be used need to be better discriminated.

The second problem of stimulus control, and the one that will be dealt with in detail, is the lack of generalization of a desired behavior to contexts other than ones in which it was explicitly learned. So, for example, an intellectually handicapped child is taught how to initiate conversations through training in a therapy setting. It is then found that they do not use this skill outside of that setting.

Lack of generalization has been a major problem in all psychotherapies and behavior therapy. Most often the generality of the changes is not reported. But there are many reports of behavior changes which have not generalized beyond the therapy setting (see Rincover & Koegel, 1975, for some fascinating examples). To overcome this, several techniques for increasing generalization have been outlined. As well, if any occurrences of spontaneous generalization occur during training, these should be immediately reinforced. Finally, any contingencies present in the settings for generalization which might actually block or prevent generalization should be removed or changed.

The major paper in this area is that of Stokes and Baer (1977). They presented nine methods of increasing generalization. At least one of these was not a proper method, however. The usual procedure at that time was called "Train and Hope" by Stokes and Baer. People trained a new behavior and proceeded to hope that it would work. They aimed to make a better technology than this. Stokes and Osnes (1989, and also 1988) have expanded this categorisation and provided new examples of the techniques. They have twelve types of generalization training divided into three major categories. Only a brief outline will be given here. Interested readers should read the papers mentioned as well as Edelstein (1989) and the papers in a book edited by Horner, Dunlap and Koegel (1988).

The first category of generalization techniques has been called Exploit Current Functional Contingencies (Stokes & Osnes, 1989). This means to use the contingencies (contexts, responses and consequences) which will be in the environments where the behaviors changed are to be used in the future. So one should use natural consequences (2.3) for the types of responses "normally" used. It also means training how to recruit natural consequences rather than hoping they will appear in the real world (for example, Stokes, Fowler & Baer, 1978).

The second category of techniques is called Train Diversely. This simply means that the contexts, responses, and consequences should be varied, at least after the behavior change has been effected. So the behavior should be rehearsed in different stimulus contexts and the response should be slightly varied. As well, multiple trainers can be brought in so the person rehearses with different strangers (see, for example, Stokes, Baer & Jackson, 1974). All these methods help ensure that the behavior will generalize outside of the therapy setting and with people other than the therapist.

Another technique is to make consequences less discriminable by using intermittent reinforcement, delayed reinforcement, and unpredictable reinforcement. Once again, these can be used after the training is complete, since regular contingent reinforcement is usually needed in training. In fact, noncontingent reinforcement has been used to help generalization, but only after training is complete.

The final category of generalization is called Incorporate Functional Mediators. This refers to techniques in which someone or something mediates between the training of a behavior and the carrying out of that behavior in other settings and at other times. That is, there are discriminative stimuli which can be present on other occasions to assist in generalization. This includes the use of verbal mediators as well as tying a string around your finger.

Maintenance. With the problem of maintaining behavior change we are on shaky ground. There has been no clear categorisation of the methods like generalization (though see Owen, 1981, and Sulzer-Azeroff, 1990). In fact, there is little conceptual work done at all. Further, the methods overlap to some extent with the methods for increasing generalization. This is understandable, though, since most behaviors which generalize to a number of settings will be more likely to persist, and behaviors which maintain will usually need to be carried out in multiple settings.

The problem with maintenance is the same as for generalization. A lot of reports of behavior changes do not say whether the behavior continued much beyond the time of training. Training is next to useless if it does not continue after the explicit training sessions stop. Luckily, most published report of behavior therapy now give results of follow-up measures.

Four topics about maintenance will be discussed. The first is the use of natural contingencies. This is probably the best way to promote maintenance of behavior change. If the contexts, responses and consequences match those in the environments in which they will be used then this will help maintenance. Like generalization, this means that intermittent or even noncontingent consequences may need to be used (Nation & Woods, 1980). Automatic consequences also will help (see 2.3). These are what maintain much of our behavior in the real world.

One useful method which should be used for all behavior change interventions is to go and observe similar people to the client in similar settings doing the target behavior. An attempt can then be made to establish what maintains the behavior in these people, and the results used to promote maintenance following behavior change. For example, following the case given in the last section: what exactly does maintain the way we initiate conversation in everyday life? Under what normal conditions do we initiate conversations and when do we keep doing this? If we can find this out then similar consequences should be used to train conversation.

Given the large amount of human behavior which is maintained by social consequences in social contexts, these need to play a large role in training for maintenance. Unfortunately, involving spouses, peers and parents in training is only now becoming a widespread practice. These are the people who will provide the sustaining consequences and contexts in the person's life, so they should be incorporated in training.

A second technique for promoting maintenance is to utilize self-events. If a person can be trained in self control as part of the behavior change then they will be better able to withstand delays and absences of reinforcers in their normal environment. They can give self-instructions, monitor their own behavior and provide self-management of means and ends. The problem with this which was discussed in 8.4 is that self-events are also under the control of social contexts and social consequences. This means that they cannot be self-sustaining forever but need to have other intermittent social reinforcers. This, however, can be explicitly arranged if it is acknowledged. A person who is self-observing and providing their own "reinforcers" can be taught to recruit intermittent comments and praise from others. This will help sustain the verbal behavior involved in controlling these events.

The third topic about maintenance concerns lifestyle changes. It has already been noted that most behaviors can be changed in the short term in a therapy setting, and that the problem is to make this maintain after the therapy is finished. Unfortunately, some of the changes made require major changes of lifestyle if they are to be maintained at all outside of the therapy setting. For example, you could teach an intellectually handicapped person how to clean houses so that they could make a living doing cleaning jobs. But the practical problem is that to maintain this, they need to get a job and this will have many effects on the rest of their life, especially in their allocation of time between behaviors.

In the foregoing case, most of the problems were practical rather than ethical. But consider a case of teaching a woman how to defend her rights as a person and not be told what to do by her husband. The maintenance of this will require drastic changes in her life—perhaps even divorce from her husband if they will always fight in future. While it is hard not to teach someone such a worthwhile behavior, the ethical problems are tremendous. Presumably some form of marital therapy with built-in the maintenance required by changing the husband's behavior as well (see Jacobson, 1989, for some ideas on how to proceed in other cases).

Similar problems occur when teaching healthy behaviors such as jogging, or how to quit smoking or reduce weight. The practical problem is to change the person's lifestyle so as to find the time required for these activities. The ethical problem concerns things like the person having to stop seeing friends who provide food or encourage smoking, or whether to involve a spouse in the program to promote maintenance. I am hopeful that when we know more about the ways in which multiple responses interact across whole repertoires of behavior (3.2), we will be able to spell out better procedures for large scale behavior changes, and hopefully find ways to reduce the ethical problems tied up in such changes.

These problems relate to the final area of discussion: that of maintaining changes in more physiological oriented behaviors. By this is meant changes in smoking habits, substance abuse, obesity, and other health related areas. The maintenance of changes in these areas has a poor record, something like only 30% maintenance after six months (see for example, Brownell, Marlatt, Lichtenstein, & Wilson, 1986; Marlatt & Gordon, 1985; Owen, 1981; Perri, McAllister, Gange, Jordan, McAdoo & Nezu, 1988). In fact, it is talked about as relapse prevention rather than maintenance of change.

These cases are tricky for a number of reasons. First, as we have seen, they do require more of a lifestyle change if maintenance is to be successful (for instance, Manning, Osland & Osland, 1989). Second, the natural positive consequences of not smoking or not being fat are delayed and indirect. This means they are hard to utilize in training. Third, and less certain, there is something physiological about these types of changes which means they probably involve a lot more than operants. Classical conditioning and even innate behaviors are involved, so pure operant changes will not be as effective.

11.3. Changing Verbal Communities

The strategies used for changing human behavior depend upon the type of functional consequences operative for a given behavior. Most interventions in behavior analysis, even community interventions (Society for the Experimental Analysis of Behavior, 1987b), only consider direct effects from the physical environment and from people acting as extensions of the physical environment. We will briefly consider these, although 11.2 has covered this ground in much more depth, before looking at verbal communities.

Shaping and Maintenance from the Physical Environment. The principles of shaping and maintaining behavior by changing the way the environment functions are well known and studied (11.2). Nonhuman animal studies re-arrange the scheduling of reinforcers and reliably change the behavior of the organism. The second best (but not always possible) way to get someone to stop eating chocolate is to remove all the chocolate from their environment.

Direct Shaping from Other Persons. While both applied behavior analysis and behavior modification make use of changes in physical environment to change behavior, the situation is usually not quite as simple as animal studies. This is because most human interventions have a person mediating the change in environmental contingencies. The change agents will usually mediate the discriminative stimuli while trying not to become discriminative stimuli themselves (remove any pictures of chocolate in the house), mediate the behavior itself with prompting and modeling, or mediate the consequences and scheduling of consequences (Cooper, Heron & Heward, 1987).

In practice, change agents usually find it quicker and easier to accomplish these contingency mediations if they reinforce the client's behavior as a verbal community might, which is, after all, the value of having verbal communities (see the section above on changing verbal contingencies with individuals). But the basic changing of the physical environment and the direct effects from people who act as extensions of the environment are all basic methods and techniques of applied behavior analysis.

Many examples of interventions where the change agents work without necessarily being part of a verbal community can be found in work with children, persons with intellectual disabilities, and the autistic. In theory at least, change agents who reinforce immediately for target behaviors could be replaced by machines or other reinforcement dispensers in the physical environment. In practice, however, some generalized reinforcement or "rapport" is developed, even if only to maintain attention.

Other examples of behavior change agents acting mostly as three-term contingency mediators are the large-scale community interventions, as most often practiced in applied behavior analysis (Society for the Experimental Analysis of Behavior, 1987b) and elsewhere (Perkins, Burns, Perry & Nielson, 1988). This approach is to change the community-wide sources of reinforcers, and in this sense, the change agents act as an extension of the physical environment. Once again, writing this is not meant to slight such interventions, since other techniques are not yet widely used. The problem is that a great deal of cost and energy is required to tackle most social problems in this way. Those that are amenable have been successful, but many problems are not amenable to such interventions. Political (i.e., large-scale verbal community) interventions are required in many cases of social change.

Changing Additive Metacontingencies. When many people act together and have joint effects the intervention decision is between having change agents directly reinforce individual behavior on a large scale, to use verbal communities to change the individual behaviors, or to do both if possible (cf., Jeffery, 1989). To change the problem of air pollution from cars, for example, one could try an intervention with many individuals of reinforcing less driving, or more efficient driving. This would have to be carried out on a large scale or else wait for the "small wins" to accumulate (Weick, 1984).

The other possible method of intervention would be to use verbal communities to change the additive metacontingency. In the case of additive metacontingencies, however, the individuals are not necessarily part of a verbal community which means that such an intervention would not work unless a verbal community was explicitly arranged or trained ("We would like all you drivers listening to this radio station to work together to slow down. If you are listening to this then slow down, and wave and grin to the driver next to you if they also slow down"). If the overall benefits of such a specifically arranged verbal community were not high then this strategy is unlikely to maintain for long (also see Rothschild, 1979).

Changing with Verbal Communities. The very advantage of verbal communities which make them possible is that the social compliance gained can be used for remote benefits not otherwise achievable by individuals acting alone or in additive metacontingencies. Changing behavior through verbal communities is not easy, however, because members can leave if reinforcement becomes too intermittent, because the community might not gain from the intervention, and because there are competing contingencies (Ellis, 1990; Rothschild, 1979). Influence through changing a community can be very powerful when it does work, and there is research available on how best to change whole communities (Katz & Lazarsfeld, 1955; Marin, 1993; Moscovici, Mugny & Van Avermaet, 1985; Mugny & Pérez, 1991; Rogers, 1983).

Changing behavior with a verbal community usually involves having the verbal community restrict its generalized contingencies (usually rule-governed) and enforce this by the power of its overall benefits of membership. To change driving patterns to reduce speeding, for example, a change agent might attempt to have families restrict their generalized reinforcement of the driver's behaviors only if the driver does not speed. Passengers would be asked, through the mass media for example, to reinforce slower driving by the driver (and try not to resort to negative reinforcement by "nagging"). This sort of approach using verbal communities can be seen world-wide in interventions to reduce drink driving through verbal communities of peers.

Token economies have sometimes been used as an effective method of changing the behavior of larger groups of people (e.g., Allyon & Azrin, 1968; Milan, 1987; Winkler, 1980). Token systems, however, form communities which are unlike the normal verbal communities because, while many different behaviors might lead to receiving tokens, the tokens are not usually exchangeable for reinforcers other than tangible ones. Tokens are not usually exchangeable for "verbal replies", in the way that being an English speaker is automatically reinforced by having people reply to what you say. For the specific cases token economies have been used for, this does not make any difference, but they should not be seen as a model for intervening in any type of verbal community. The key property of loose reinforcement amongst verbal community members is missing in most token economies.

Changing with Ritual Behaviors. Ritual behaviors, defined in 9.2, can be both a problem for change and also a method for change. In some adolescent groups, for example, smoking might have a ritualistic function and this will lead to problems if it is treated solely as a simple social behavior. That is, those in a group who smoke are more likely to have many other behaviors reinforced by different members of the group. Since this ritual behavior maintains the group as a whole and there are multiple social functions that follow from this, just requesting a member of the group to give up smoking is unlikely to succeed, and providing particular replacement reinforcers might not substitute for the multiple social advantages of smoking.

Alternative change strategies for ritual behaviors are to break up the verbal community, to provide an alternative verbal community which does not have smoking as a ritual behavior, or to attempt to substitute a new ritual behavior for smoking. The first of these is both difficult and probably unethical in most cases. Changing ritual behaviors by changing communities can be effective if it is possible. Felner, Ginter and Primavera (1982) provide an example in which new verbal communities were pre-arranged for students moving to a high school, in order to help with their transition. Useful behaviors such as attendance and completing school work were arranged as defining features of these verbal communities, which were formed by stabilizing the transitory peer groups which usually develop across different classes.

While changing ritual behaviors might seem difficult, the often arbitrary nature of ritual behaviors should make them easily substitutable. Evidence for this can be found in the swiftness with which new fads and fashions occur in everyday life, as groups redefine who will be reinforced by the group depending upon whether they keep up with the fashions. As well, hypnosis begins by going through a number of sometimes arbitrary rituals which act to allow the hypnotherapist to have effective control of the client's behaviors through generalized verbal control (Erickson, Rossi & Rossi, 1976). Establishing rapport in many types of interventions amounts to the same pattern: there is the development of "trust" and mutual reinforcement through reinforcing many arbitrary behaviors, and demonstrations that few behaviors will be punished. The compliance gained is then used to develop verbal or nonverbal control of the client's behavior. This is as true for the "talking" therapies as for the behavior modifier trying to get a client to carry out their behavioral homework.

Techniques for Changing Verbal Communities

Many different approaches to social and community change have been taken (Fawcett, Mathews & Fletcher, 1980; Fawcett, White, Balcazar, Suarez-Balcazar, Mathews, Paine, Seekins & Smith, in press; Katz, 1974; Kelly, Snowden & Munoz, 1977). I will write about only a few here, and then only briefly. When changing behavior on a community level it seems to be important to use a variety of techniques rather than try for the one best approach (Sheth & Frazier, 1982; Winett, King & Altman, 1989).

Where. There are a variety of settings which are useful for community change (Glanz, Lewis, & Rimer, 1990; Iverson, Fielding, Crow & Christenson, 1985; Winett, King & Altman, 1989). Some settings follow from the nature of the problem to be changed. Treating change with an education approach makes adult and child education settings useful places (Glanz, Lewis, & Rimer, 1990; Green,1984; Perry, Telch, Killen, Burke & Maccoby, 1983). For medical problems, the local doctor can be utilized as a key member of a relevant verbal community (Schofield, Redman & Sanson-Fisher, 1991). For more traditional medical changes, traditional communities might be used (Schneider, Cavanaugh, Kasture, Rothenberg, Averbach, Robinson, & Wallace, 1990).

More recently, the workplace has been seen as a useful setting for social and community change. There are many verbal communities of the type discussed in Chapters 9 and 10 in the workplace (e.g., Klein & D'Aunno, 1986). Successful interventions have been carried out on a variety of issues (Borland, Chapman, Owen & Hill, 1990; Fielding, 1984; Glasgow & Terborg, 1988).

How. A few methods of community change will be briefly outlined. Many of these also involve individual change techniques which have been discussed earlier in this chapter (Fawcett et al., in press; Winett, King & Altman, 1989). Very little can be said here about each, and the particular issues involved in their use, but references should provide an opening to find out more.

One very effective method of changing community behavior is to *change the law or public policy* directly (Fawcett, Bernstein, Czyzewski, Greene, Hannah, Iwata, Jason, Mathews, Morris, Otis-Wilborn, Seekins, & Winett, 1988; Milio, 1986). This is the community equivalent to changing behavior by changing the environment. It was mentioned earlier that the second best way to stop someone eating chocolate was to remove all the chocolate from their home environment. The best way is to outlaw any chocolate getting into the country!

The rationale for public policy is that the community as a larger whole imposes rule-governed behaviors which have fines, taxes, and incentives of excises attached to them as consequences. For example, prohibiting the advertising of cigarettes and the setting of speed limits are community dictated rules with sanctions attached, brought in for the general good of most community members. Such policy changes are usually very effective if they can be brought in, but making the policy changes can be long and hard, and will often not be brought in merely because they cannot be policed adequately. So there are still fundamental limitations imposed by the physical and social environments on what can and cannot be made law. In most cases the rights of individual community members, or a prohibitive cost, override a feasible method of saving a few lives (or cavities from eating chocolate). In other cases, very imaginative and simple interventions can help change policy decisions (Seekins & Fawcett, 1987).

Borland, Chapman, Owen and Hill (1990) present a nice example in which government bans on smoking in enclosed places led to the banning of smoking in workplaces. The effect of the ban was not just less smoking at work but a general reduction in smoking, especially for the heavy smokers.

Another approach to community change is to follow the *innovation* or implementation at a societal level, following the course as it becomes diffused through groups in society. In this way, principles for successful innovation have been suggested (Burt, 1987; Fawcett, Mathews & Fletcher, 1980; Orlandi, Landers, Weston & Haley, 1990; Rogers, 1983; Stolz, 1981). Rogers (1983) presents an excellent summary of the principles found from the introduction of technical innovations (inventions, new drugs). This includes the way in which many strategies for change were implemented and the populations they were used upon.

All the innovation studies find that social contacts and communities are important for successful innovation but often in very subtle ways (Burt, 1987; Katz & Lazarsfeld, 1955; Rogers, 1983). Burt (1987), for example, re-analyzed some medical innovation data from a classic study of the introduction of a new drug. It was shown that the adoption of the new drug by doctors was not simply from having conversations with colleagues (a cohesive verbal community), but from what was seen as the proper action for someone in their social position with regard to colleagues (called structural equivalence). That is, the innovation did not proceed from immediate talks within the verbal community but followed how the verbal community had already evolved the roles within the community.

Many of the principles from innovation studies can be re-modeled into behavior analysis, hopefully with some new ideas coming from the translation. For example, Orlandi et al. (1990) list as one feature of successful innovations that they are flexible: "Innovations that can be unbundled and used as separate components will be applicable in a wider variety of user settings" (1990, p. 290). This means that if the change technique can be used for more than what intended, and can be used in more settings than intended, then it will maintain better and be adopted by more people gradually. For behavior change, this means that behaviors which can be part of many behavior repertoires and which can generalize (cf. 11.2 above) easily will be the better ones to implement.

Many of the community changes *utilize the mass media* for implementing change, with different degrees of success (Elliott, 1989; Flay 1987; Flora, Maibach & Maccoby, 1989; Redman, Spencer & Sanson-Fisher, 1990; Wallack, 1990). The principle involved here would seem to reflect how closely the behavior is involved in contingencies with the physical environment or with other people mediating. If the behaviors are maintained mostly by the support of a verbal community, that is, socially constructed knowledges (10.3), then mass media presentations are likely to be effective. If the major sources of functional consequences come from outside the mass media then it might not be as effective–unless a mix of strategies is applied at the same time (Redman, Spencer & Sanson-Fisher, 1990; Sheth & Frazier, 1982).

This suggestion is indirectly supported by evidence that different aspects of behavior are affected by mass media campaigns. Booth, Bauman, Oldenburg, Owen and Magnus (1992), for example, found that a mass media campaign to increase exercise only changed some people from no walking to moderate walking. This can be interpreted as showing that the contingencies for regular or vigorous exercise rely on many other functional consequences than those provided by a verbal community. If exercise were completely socially constructed we might expect a better response. So the strategy must be to try and influence those socially constructed aspects of exercise, or just intentions to exercise (Ajzen & Fishbein, 1980), in order to get some change. Similarly, people in different stages of exercise, such as precontemplation, contemplation, preparation, or action, might be differentially affected by mass media campaigns (Booth, Macaskill, Owen, Oldenburg, Marcus & Bauman, in press; DiClemente, Prochaska, Fairhurst, Velicer, Velasquez & Rossi, 1991; Donovan & Owen, 1993). Again, it can be suggested that the nature of mass media as purely verbal suggests that the degree of influence will be proportional to the degree to which a verbal community supports the knowledge or behavior. We are more likely to be convinced from mass media about nuclear power plants, with which most of us have no nonverbal contact whatsoever, than about eating less chocolate.

This problem is also reflected in a study by Tyler and Cook (1984). They presented a number of types of mass media information materials to people and measured the change produced in verbal attitudes and intentions. They found that the mass media materials changed what people thought society in general was like or should be like, but they did not affect the person's own views. For example, reading about the dangers of speeding would lead people to change their views on how risky speeding is for people in general, but not for themselves.

More recently, *social marketing* principles have been used to change communities (Donovan & Owen, 1993; Hastings & Haywood, 1991; Kotler & Roberto, 1989; Novelli, 1990; Sheth & Frazier, 1982). This approach applies principles propounded by marketing analysts but adapted to sell social issues to people. To a large extent this includes the approaches we have already outlined, but they are put into a new perspective.

Of particular focus in social marketing are determining who the market is, setting out what is being exchanged for what in the "soft sell", the customer value, and market research techniques to get an initial feel for the marketing constraints before starting a campaign. It has already been pointed out that in transferring techniques from a competitive, economic marketplace to a setting of monopoly (in many cases) and nonprofit, there are limitations (Rothschild, 1979). But these limitations can at least be recognized and overcome.

A final technique is to utilize verbal communities directly, in their role as *social support* for behavior, to change the community behavior. This includes self-help groups, social support groups, community support groups, and advocacy groups (Fawcett, White, Balcazar, Suarez-Balcazar, Mathews, Paine, Seekins & Smith, in press; Felner, Ginter & Primavera, 1982; Felton & Shinn, 1992; Minkler, 1990; Paine, Suarez-Balcazar, Fawcett & Borck-Jameson, 1992; Schofield, Redman & Sanson-Fisher, 1991). In some cases change has been implemented through action research—even by creating social networks which did not exist in the first place (Engelstad & Gustavsen, 1993; Levin, 1993).

The role of verbal communities in behavior change is also found in the minority influence area. Doms and Van Avermaet (1985) found that both minorities and majorities worked through the support they were given, rather than through other principles based on relative processing of information. That is, the basis of influence and persuasion is social, even in what to think about a social issue (also Abrams, Wetherall, Cochrane, Hogg & Turner, 1990).

On a larger scale, the influence of verbal communities can be seen in the slow changes brought about by changes in a community's language. One way of improving respect for women has been to change the way they are talked about, and change the way in which "Man" substitutes for all people. A gradual process of changing the use of such androcentric phrases can act as a successful long-term intervention to change many facets about the treatment of women in our society (Cooper, 1984; Eckert & McConnell-Ginet, 1992; Hamilton, 1988b; Henley, 1989; Ng, 1990a).

Chapter 12

Behavior Analysis of Particular Groups and Social Issues

In this final chapter I wish to present some of the characteristics of certain groups of people and certain social issues into which behavior analysts have had some input or could have some input. This cannot be a complete review of these areas, but a starting point for thinking about these groups and issues in behavior analytic terms. For this reason I will not review the thousands of empirical studies but show the major features of their contingencies.

For those interested in the behavior analyses and intervention with other groups and issues, some references are briefly provided here. The *Journal of Applied Behavior Analysis* and *The Behavior Analyst* are always good places to start; try the ten-yearly index of JABA. As well, there are now four volumes of JABA reprints which are remarkably inexpensive: on community interventions, on developmental disabilities, on education, and on applied measurement and experimental design. The back pages of JABA give details (for example, Society for the Experimental Analysis of Behavior, 1987a, b). For other applications of behavior analysis here are a few references, in no particular order.

For *environmental protection* and *energy conservation* see Cone and Hayes (1980), DeGrandpre and Buskist (1991), Dwyer, Leeming, Cobern, Porter and Jackson (1993), and Geller, Winett and Everett (1982). For applications to improving *zoo and animal training technology* for both the animals and the visitors, see Markowitz (1978, 1979) and Pryor (1984).

For applications to *delinquency*, start with Wolf, Braukmann and Ramp (1987) and Morris and Braukmann (1987). For *education*, try Alberto and Troutman (1986) as well as recent issues of the *Journal of Applied Behavior Analysis*. The use of parents and peers in training is discussed in the following: Forehand (1977), McClannahan, Krantz and McGee (1982), O'Dell (1974), Smith and Fowler (1984), Van Hasselt, Sisson and Aach (1987).

For *economic* behavior see Lea, Tarpy and Webley (1987). For *behavioral pharmacology* see Thompson, Pickens and Meisch (1970), Poling (1986), Carlton (1983), and Barrett and Sanger (1991). For *safety* see the special issue of the *Journal of Applied Behavior Analysis*.(1988, *21*, Number 3).

For applications to *social work* see Thyer (1983, 1987). For a number of issues of *political, social or moral importance* see Ellis (1987), Glenn (1985, 1986), Lamal

(1984, 1991), Lamal and Greenspoon (1992), Malagodi (1986), Malagodi and Jackson (1989), Murphy (1986), Parrott and Hake (1983), Segal (1987), Thyer and Himle (1986); as well as issues of *Behavior Analysis and Social Action*, which is now called *Behavior and Social Issues*.

For interesting *therapeutic* and *clinical* applications see: Dougher (1993), Edwards (1991), Hayes (1987), Hayes and Wilson (1993), Jacobson (1989), Kohlenberg, Hayes and Tsai (1993), Nordquist (1971), Voeltz and Evans (1982), Wahler (1975), Zettle and Hayes (1980).

12.1. Politics and Behavior Analysis

There are a few points which behavior analysis can make about politics, in the broad sense of that term rather than about particular governments or Congresses (see Lamal, 1984; Lamal and Greenspoon, 1992). One first point is that politics is, or should be, about nonverbal doing, but that it gets caught in verbal doing because of the nature of modern society. That is, politics is really about getting things done in our social and physical world—organizing people and spaces so that re-organizing is not constantly needed. This means collecting and sharing resources for different layers of verbal communities and trying to find a workable mix between the layers in order to share life's experiences and resources.

While politics should be about getting things done or changed, most of this involves getting other people to do things. That is, politics must, in our present society at least, involve the organization and re-organization of verbal communities. This means that rhetoric and persuasion become a major part of politics, and the game of politics then forms its own verbal community which develops its own rituals and language. Thus it often seems that politicians and other on-the-ground people working in politics talk too much and get too little accomplished. But the problem they face is not one of simply providing reinforcers and punishers to change behavior; rather, they have to change social knowledge which both sustains verbal communities and creates verbal communities.

Behind this aspect of politics there are still the basic questions of resources and their community distribution, and in the long run, politicians, if they are to be successful, must face the "dirt" behind the talk—what resources people are actually after for their verbal community. Utopias do not exist, only utopians. This is also why economics is also a large part of what politicians do. Politics is not just about making a convincing or stirring speech to "sway the hearts and minds of men" [sic], but rather, of getting your figures correct on what the background economics is of the issue under consideration. That is, resource allocations now work via the verbal behaviors of economics.

The consideration, then, is that politics must play two inter-related roles. First, the goods and resources must be moved around people in the community since there is very specific division of labour. To do this requires verbal behavior (and hence politicians try to be part of many verbal communities) because we must get other people (or organizations) to do this. Different governments play different roles in this part of the politics game. Some have tried to take complete verbal control of the organization and distribution of goods, while others have tried to merely arbitrate (in general, verbally) any problems in the distribution which will only otherwise be solved by direct pushing around of people rather than by verbal behavior.

The second role of politics is one of welding many verbal communities into working cooperatively so a united distribution system can work. This role requires the full command of symbolic mediation and rhetoric to juggle the verbal communities, as well as backing by actual resources. The United Nations is perhaps the highest level verbal community established to get other verbal communities to work cooperatively for common outcomes, excepting for science fiction examples (e.g., Le Guin, 1969). Feudal systems provide examples of small communities which brought a variety of different groups together for work towards a common goal (perhaps not equally in all their best interests, however).

The theme of this whole book, then, can also be seen in politics: that social behavior is an interplay between having resources and sharing resources in a community which might have an overall benefit to at least some of the members. Forming tighter communities which loosely reinforce can benefit all the members in the longrun in many different ways. In all of this, verbal behaviors can create the communities, maintain the communities, and can be used to reinforce the communities.

12.2. Women and Feminist Psychology

Over the last twenty years, there have developed several psychologies for women, by women (Crawford & Marecek, 1989; Hare-Mustin & Marecek, 1988; Riger, 1992; Wittig, 1985). There have been at least two major goals: first, to empower women so that resources might be more equally shared through all verbal communities rather than based on historical precedent (e.g., Lather, 1988); and second, to change the ways in which "women" and "gender" have been talked about and represented by the whole verbal community, and to sort out the multiple ramifications of such a change. These two goals are naturally inter-related.

Behavior analysis can make some interesting approaches to a feminist psychology, most of which can be drawn out from discussion elsewhere in this book (contra Unger, 1988, who seems to generalize Hullian behaviorism to "behaviorism"). Specifically, the following are some of the ideas and goals shared by behavior analysts and feminist psychologists: the control of talking and thought in behavior analysis is said to rely on social power; behavior analysis makes a strong critique of traditional psychology (cf. Squire, 1990); the behavior analytic notion of control is a non-blaming one; non-traditional methodologies are available, especially ones for dealing with individual cases rather than averages; behavior analysis is, or should be, reflexive in its science, with scientists examining themselves as example of what they preach; a clear separation between control of behavior from the environment and from control from social contingencies, with an emphasis (in this book) on just how much control of human behavior comes from social sources and historical power bases; and, partly from the last point, an inordinate faith based on research and philosophy that most things can change with training and intervention, and that we do not have to be stuck with innateness and historical precedence forever.

All of these goals and outcomes of behavior analysis are shared by at least some feminist psychologies, which means that they might find it useful to explore the assumptions of (modern) behavior analysis from a feminist perspective. A few of these themes will be mentioned below and an analysis started.

Women and Power

For behavior analysis, power is where the control lies, in either who arranges the consequences, who arranges the stimulus conditions which select behaviors, or who determines which behaviors can be shaped. In theory, and according to many men, women also hold the power to go against any of their conditions if they are really unhappy. However, from the view of multiple contingencies (3.2), this depends upon what alternative contingencies have been trained and are available. Theoretically, behavior analysis claims that the pigeon or rat controls the experimenter just as the experimenter controls the pigeon, but given the balance of power (who is able to arrange what), the experimenter has greater power in reality. Consistent behavior analysts must therefore analyze social behavior by looking at the relative availabilities of contingencies, or social roles of power.

Traditionally, then, women have been verbally and nonverbally represented in media and life as discriminative of only a few, limited roles. While men have also been restricted to some roles and not allowed others, the variability has always been greater for men. On a basic level, women have been in roles which allow only drudge behaviors (Momsen & Kinnaird, 1993), and through Africa, for example, a significant part of the economy relies on women's unpaid work. Domination, in this sense, means being restricted to a limited behavior repertoire through historical power over arranging contingencies.

Moreover, it has been stressed through this book how traditional psychology and common thought both usually translate social contingencies into "subjective" (if specific social contingencies, Chapter 8) or "innate" (if generalized social contingencies, Chapter 5) causes of behavior. In the same way of misguided thinking there is a long history of supposing that women must either *want* their restricted roles (subjectivity) or *be made for* their particular roles (innateness). If there is no obvious physiological basis to wrongly back the latter up then the role is usually linked in some obscure way to reproductive differences in anatomy. Reading arguments about why women should be restricted to this or that behavior, one continually comes across these three vacuous arguments tailored for the particular behavior.

In analyzing the control over behavior, however, it seems obvious that the control for such specific roles cannot come from the physical environment–there is nothing in the physical contingencies of doing housework, for example, that controls women but not men. Further, behavior analysts luckily do not have the fallback position of the rest of psychology–that it is a "subjective" cause and that women actually have some hidden need to do housework. Clearly, the control is from social contingencies, but very subtle ones that are not always easy to recognize. I hope that these can be spelled out following the analyses of social behavior in this book.

In a similar way, most behaviors enacted by humans do not rely on physical differences in anatomy, but are heavily controlled by social contingencies. For many years women were not allowed (i.e., a social contingency) to continue far into an education. This also produced explanations that women did not want to be educated and were happy not to be educated, and also that women could not be educated, there was something about their genetic make-up that stopped them from going on (again, often obscurely linked to reproductive difference in anatomy). We must make analyses based on the current verbal community's patterns of reinforcement practices rather than using a three-term contingency with nonsocial control.

The Social Construction of Gender

Behavior analysis is probably unique in psychology for the ways in which social control over thought and other covert behaviors can be talked about, and this is also essential to a feminist psychology (Chapter 8; Bordo, 1987; Condor, 1986; Crawford & Gentry, 1989; Marshall & Wetherall, 1989; Mednick, 1989; Young-Eisendrath, 1988).

We have already seen in this book that how people talk about themselves can govern what they will do (Chapter 7), and that how people talk about themselves is heavily learned from a verbal community rather than purely through experience—even how we talk about our self-identities (Chapters 9 and 10; Bargad & Hyde, 1991; Downing & Roush, 1985; Giddens, 1991; Hamilton, 1988b; Kramarae, 1990; Skevington & Baker, 1989). Therefore, the range of behaviors engaged in, the variability in behavior repertoire, the range of settings and consequences exposed to, and the amount of verbally governed behavior are all a function of the social constructions of, and reinforcement by, the verbal community (Breakwell, 1990; Frazer & Cameron, 1989; Mascia-Lees, Sharpe, & Cohen, 1989). And in the case of women, we are not talking about the prejudices of a small insignificant verbal sub-community: the verbal community at the level of all the language users of English has reinforced certain statements about women and punished others (Breakwell, 1990; Coates & Cameron, 1988; Deaux & Lewis, 1984; Eagly & Mladinic, 1989; Hamilton, 1988a, b; Hansen & O'Leary, 1985; Smith & Walker, 1992; Spence & Sawin, 1985; Tuchman, Daniels & Benét, 1978; Wetherall, 1986).

The key point of this for women is that the efficacy of verbal behaviors to survive in a verbal community ultimately relies upon the social consequences which they effect. This has meant that the ultimate social power has not been, in general, in the control of women. With few sources of control coming from the physical environment, the control over defining who women are and what they are capable of, has been left wide open to abuse. As examples, the physical environment puts constraints on having a population think that women have six arms, because of the enormous social control that would be necessary to get a population to say this. But as mentioned earlier, because there are relatively few of these constraints when talking about gender it has been possible to have populations believe ideas such as these four: that women like housework, women cannot be educated properly, women are romantic at heart, or that women are inherently kinder and more nurturing than men (e.g., Piliavin & Unger, 1985).

The key point for behavior analysis, then, is not to show that these four ideas are wrong for all women, which would fall into the same trap again, but to show how they can be changed. By changing the verbal community reinforcement practices these ideas should disappear unless there is another source of control somewhere. However, because this entails changing verbal communities and the ways they talk and think, the change is liable to be slow and indirect (Chapter 11).

Another important way in which the social construction of knowledge affects behavior towards women is in science: the ways in which scientists talk about women has affected the ways in which they are studied (Acker, Barry & Esseveld, 1983; Haack, 1992; Lather, 1988; Longino, 1988; Milton, 1979; Riger, 1992; Skevington & Baker, 1989). Part of the feminist critique of psychology is to have input into not just how women are studied, but how women are thought about and talked about when deriving methodologies for study.

It has been suggested in many different ways that a feminist psychology would or should use different methodologies than traditional psychology (Gergen, 1988; Jacklin, 1987; Kitzinger, 1986; Riger, 1992; Wittig, 1985). While behavior analysis embraces many methods not used in traditional psychology, there are some reservations about the methods which have been suggested. In particular, many of the methods suggested in feminist critiques of methodology require an acceptance that verbal behavior fully controls non verbal behavior. The critique has been that trying to measure "objectively" is either wrong or else is not sufficient, and that the "subjective" reports of women should also be sought (cf. Acker, Barry & Esseveld, 1983; Bhavnani, 1993).

As argued elsewhere (Chapter 7, 9.3 on rationality, and Guerin, 1992b), it is not that there is not a reality out there, but that *verbal statements about reality cannot be true in any absolute sense.* I cannot walk through walls no matter what I think or say about my walking through walls, and this is real, but I can make the *statement* "I can walk through walls" true in a pragmatic sense if I have an appropriate effect on other people (if they nod, for example). Thus the "subjective" measures fail for the same reason as "objective" measures of reality. The trick is to get both and look at their different sources of control.

This means again that when dealing with behavior and power (consequences) there are things which can be done and which are real (no amount of wishful thinking is going to change them), but when talking about putting things or events into words, almost anything goes with the right amount of social pressure and power. For a feminist methodology, then, the first point is that just asking people about the controlling variables of their behavior will not always help, unless no other methods are possible. Verbal reports are valid measures of verbal community reinforcement patterns (often called "subjective reality"), but not veridical reports on the world (see 8.4 and Guerin, 1992b).

The second point for feminist methodology, however, is more encouraging: that with respect to the verbal community and its influence, talking to people, hermeneutics, and Q-sort methodologies (Kitzinger, 1986), are probably just the right way to go about it. As I have put it elsewhere (Guerin, 1992b), behavior analysis is probably more hermenteutical than traditional hermeneutics over this point. Verbal behavior should not taken seriously as reporting absolute causes of behavior or as an infallible guide to why behavior occurs, but verbal behavior should be taken very seriously as showing what behavior a verbal community reinforces or punishes. This study of verbal-verbal relations is not well developed in behavior analysis, unfortunately, and some of the proposed feminist methodologies would be extremely useful to adopt.

So the argument is that there is a reality we learn through interacting with the environment but that there is no true reality or objectivity in what we *say* about the world we learn. If we need to know the controlling variables of behavior then talking to people is only sometimes useful (see 8.4). But if the object is to find out about what words and social constructions are used about women or other groups to control or change them, and how to intervene and change this, then the feminist verbal methodologies mentioned above are just the right ones, and laboratory experiments would be inappropriate.

12.3. Children and Their Contingencies

The analysis of children is in a funny position, in that so much has been done and yet there has been little pulling together of the generalities (cf. Baer's excellent comments in Morris, Hursh, Winston, Gelfand, Hartmann, Reese & Baer, 1982; also Bijou, 1993; Gewirtz & Peláez-Nogueras, 1992; Schlinger, 1992). After an early statement of the general principles (Bijou & Baer, 1961), the work went into empirical studies of modifying the behavior of children. While the advances made in modifying socially important behaviors of children are impressive, I wish to give a general framework here rather than just review a whole lot of studies.

One of the major questions of traditional developmental psychology is that of how much influence the environment has on development and how much is "preprogrammed". It seems clear by now that this question is not a fruitful one to ask. Learning itself is obviously preprogrammed in some sense: I cannot learn to do things which other animals can learn, and there were things I could not learn to do when I was young which I can learn now (though there could be many reasons for this).

This mixing of "learned" and "innate" is well known to behavior analysts (Skinner, 1966, 1977). The problem, however, is that we can manipulate experimentally the environment but not the "innateness", so it has seemed wise to try modifying any behaviors until it proves hopeless. In this way, many behaviors which had been assumed to be preprogrammed into developmental sequences have been modified using techniques outlined in the last chapter (see, as one example, Piagetian conservation in Parsonson & Naughton, 1988).

As behavior analysts, even if a developmental sequence is found which seems to occur only as a developmental stage, there are other questions to ask before accepting it as an innate process. First, is there a change in the environmental contingencies which occurs consistently at a particular age? That is, are the "innateness" and the developmental stages *in the environment* rather than in the organism?

The second question that can be asked is whether there has been an accumulation of setting events, keystone behaviors or establishing operations which have changed the probability of some event, which may have been present all along, such that it now becomes functional. These setting events could be environmental or part of the multiple response repertoire. For example, being taken to school and allowed to stay there for the entire day allows many new contingencies to be contacted. It can appear, though, that a new innate stage is developed because certain behaviors start appearing which were not there before. Or again, having the use of autoclitics shaped into one's repertoire is a setting event for many other contingencies.

Unfortunately, there is a common serious misconception that behavior analysis is wedded to a naive environmentalism and allows for no innate influences in development (see Morris et al., 1982; Reese, 1982 for discussion, and Gould & Marler, 1987, for a typical example of misconception). While this is not true, the working assumption of trying to modify any behavior rather than assuming it functions innately seems to pay off. We have no empirical demonstrations of innateness, only failures to modify, which means that a guiding assumption of innateness arises only in *talking about* behavior, not in testing it. The behavior analytic commitment is not to environmentalism per se, but to empirical determination rather than purely conceptual determination, although the two look similar to the outsider.

What are the contingency features of children, then? First, we must consider that when born an infant has mainly innate behavior patterns which might or might not be modifiable (Bijou & Baer, 1978; Millar, 1976). As development continues, the major contingencies come either from the parents or through the parents. This includes learning the environmental contingencies, such as not to touch a hot stove. Children also do not have verbally governed behavior to utilize.

A further important point to be kept in mind that children have a very limited repertoire of responses, and I believe that there are important consequences to this (3.2). As new behaviors are learned, the changes in total allocation of behavior can theoretically fluctuate more than in an adult with a large repertoire. If the child has only one source of reinforcement contacted in a particular context and then learns a new contingency, this would form the equivalent of an unstable system in system theory terms. Thus swinging "moods" and childish whims could be thought of in terms of an unstable system due to the small initial repertoire. However, until more is found out empirically about multiple response repertoires, we should treat such statements as working ideas.

Some of these main features of the contingencies of childhood suggest some of Freud's "instinctive" developmental stages of childhood. The lack of verbally governed behavior suggests a lack of ego at this age, and the parental mediation of contingencies suggests the development of the superego. With a small behavior repertoire and a limited range of contingencies, a few contingencies will direct the child's behavior and this is like Freud's conception of the id, except that he located it in the person rather than in the environment (Hineline, 1992).

The special tasks for childhood, then, are to develop a large range of behaviors, with more contextual control than most other animals, and to develop self-regulation through a verbal community. In this way, many of the properties of childhood behavior can be viewed as the side-effects of having few contextual constraints on behavior. For example, I believe it is common experience that children often remember things which parents cannot. This might occur because of their fewer contextual contingencies. With many contextual discriminations learned, responding with responses irrelevant to a situation would be more difficult. This again is a question of multiple response allocation, which hopefully will be better understood someday (cf. Wahler & Dumas, 1989).

12.4. People with Intellectual Disabilities and Autism

A vast amount of behavior analysis has been applied to people with intellectual and and physical disabilities. Bijou (1966) stated the general approach for behavior analysis: the intellectually disabled person does not contact environmental contingencies as easily or as quickly as others. At an early age most children will respond differentially to consequences of their actions; the intellectually disabled, almost by definition, do not.

The source of this disability could be at any stage of the contingency. There might be problems in learning attentional contingencies which are setting events for learning other contingencies; there might be problems in the effectiveness of automatic or conditioned reinforcers—they might not be effective in strengthening behavior in these persons; there might be problems actually performing the responses which would contact the relevant consequences—the covert responses in particular; or finally, there might be learned aversive contingencies which interfere with learning new contingencies (see Wolf, Risley & Mees, 1964, for example).

While there is a lot of research done on modifying the behavior of the intellectually disabled, less is done on more general features such as finding the locus or loci of the disability. One recent finding is the absence of stimulus equivalence class formation in the intellectually disabled (Devany, Hayes & Nelson, 1986), although even this could be due to a number of other things. Given that the emphasis outside of behavior analysis is on cognitive deficits of the intellectually disabled (for example, Weiss, Weisz & Bromfield, 1986), this new area of research is promising. It will help provide a foundation to such statements as the following:

"...the mentally retarded are at risk because of cognitive limitations leading to a lack of understanding about how to behave in various social settings" (Andrasik & Matson, 1985). Clearly what is being discussed is the ability to use three-, four- and five-term contingencies, which also shows in problems with under and over generalizing. The next few years should see applicable research coming from more basic behavior analytic studies on equivalence classes.

While the majority of autistic children also have intellectual disabilities, they have some characteristics which set them apart (Schreibman, 1988). Foremost of these are the frequency of self-stimulatory behavior, lack of social responsiveness, and severe attentional problems (Lovaas & Smith, 1989). These have all been modified by consequences to different degrees in many hundreds of behavioral studies. Unlike intellectual disability, two recent authors have tried to some formulate general principles of autism from a behavioral analytic perspective (Lovaas & Smith, 1989; Schreibman, 1988). One advantage of behavior analysis is that behaviors are broken down into component behaviors. Since it is thought that autism is not a single definable problem, this strategy has helped.

The guiding model of Lovaas and Smith (1989) has four propositions. First, the behaviors exhibited by autistic children are maintained by their consequences, and can be changed accordingly. Second, there are several developmental delays in autism rather than one central deficit, as has often been suggested. Third, if put into a suitable context, autistic children can learn and have their behaviors modified. Fourth, autistic children have a mismatch between their responses and the normal environment which needs the environment to be modified.

All of these tenets amount to a more complicated view than that proposed by others, but there is evidence for the tenets. For example, Carr and Durand (1985) suggest at least three possible functions of self-injurous and aggressive behaviors: escape from an aversive context, such as stress or punishment; as reinforced by attention and other positive reinforcers; and as self-stimulatory, which is automatically reinforcement gone to extremes (Lovaas, Newson & Hickman, 1987).

Given the mixed nature of autistic "symptoms", we might expect some multiple contingency effects to emerge, but one of the problems in treatment is that response covariations and generalizations seem hard to forge with autistic children. The evidence all shows an emphasis on being overly selective, focussing on only a few dimensions. Correcting overselectivity seems to lead to a number of treatment gains, suggesting it is a keystone behavior for some of these children (Schreibman, 1988). With proper training autistic children have been taught to tact private events and to mand (Haneda & Yamamoto, 1991; Yamamoto, & Mochizuki, 1988).

12.5. The Aged and their Contingencies

While the behavior analysis of old age had an early start with Lindsley (1964), only bits and pieces have been done until more recently (see Burgio & Burgio, 1986; Hussian, 1984; Patterson & Jackson, 1980; Rosenthal & Carstensen, 1988; Skinner, 1983; Skinner & Vaughan, 1983; Williamson, 1986; Wisocki, 1984).

There are several features of the behavior of old people which suggest a contingency basis: their contingencies change markedly during this period; reinforcement schedules which were effective when young no longer sustain the same rates of behavior; and stimulus control seems less effective, both in needing more easily discriminated stimuli and in the use of four- and five-term contingencies.

One key feature of old age is that the contingencies change. Old friends leave or die, there is no longer a job with regular setting events taking place, children grow up and leave, you can no longer travel as much, and you may have to move into a smaller house or a nursing home. If no new contingencies are contacted then a form of depression can be the result (Skinner, 1983; for a similar analysis see 3.2 and 8.5). This means that a key point for the elderly is to find replacement contingencies as the ones which maintained adult life change.

To exacerbate the problem of changing contingencies, the strength of reinforcers also seems to weaken with old age (Skinner, 1983; Wisocki, 1984). Foods no longer have as strong a taste, the eyes become less sensitive, hearing becomes weaker, and genital tissues have become less sensitive.

All of these problems have ramifications beyond the immediate sensory loss. Wisocki (1984, Table 1) has an excellent description of some of these, while Skinner (1983; and Skinner & Vaughan, 1983) has many remedies for getting around the problematic ramifications. For example, less sensitive taste can lead to poor nutritional diet, loss of weight, and poor dental hygiene. The latter can further lead to dentures and the like which can change speech patterns and enunciation, and lead to changes in social contingencies (communication problems).

These problems mean that old people often have a low rate of responding–any type of responding. Even responding itself can be painful, and can lead to a further avoidance of responding. This is part of the basis for why in nursing homes for the elderly there is often little behavior in evidence. It is not that the old folk are prevented from behaving, but that the many ramifications make it unlikely unless new contingencies are instigated. So one of the major problems of behavioral gerontology is getting the old people to do something. Many other problems disappear if this is managed.

The third feature of old age was that stimulus control weakens. This means that confusion appears, since complex contingencies no longer function. If stimuli are made sufficiently salient (see Hussian, 1984, for examples) then some behavior can be recovered, but many of the higher term contingencies are still lost (Skinner, 1983). For example, recognition can be improved with better manipulation of stimuli so they act as prompts, either through self-management (Skinner, 1983) or behavior modification. Recall, on the other hand, needs self-prompting, so unless there is the history of intellectual self-management from adulthood, it is less likely to improve.

Other problems of old age seem to be common ones across any age range, except that the changes are related to the above three points. For example, incontinence is a major problem for the elderly but techniques applicable to children do not work effectively because of the ramifications given above (Schnelle, Traughber, Morgan,

Embry, Binion & Coleman, 1983). For interventions such as these, one cannot rely on teaching self-management or verbal self-regulation given the three problems which occur. Rather, much of it still needs to be carried out by modifying the environment to fit the elderly rather than trying to modify the elderly (Lindsley, 1964; Skinner & Vaughan, 1983).

12.6. Organizational Behavior Management

One of the most recent areas of applying behavior analysis, but also one of the fastest growing, is that of organizational behavior management. Here, the principles of behavior analysis are applied to organizations and the behavior of people in such environments. Despite its recent origins, there are already a few books and summary articles available (Andrasik, Heimberg & McNamara, 1981; Brethower, 1972; Frederiksen, 1982; Komaki, 1986a; O'Brien, Dickinson & Rosnow, 1982). There is also a journal devoted to the area: *Journal of Organizational Behavior Management*.

Before giving some examples of this work, a few cautions are in order. First, a lot of the published work uses only very loose behavior principles and cannot be considered behavior analysis. These include interventions which use "rewards" or "incentives" in a most non-behavior analytic way, or which do not do a proper analysis before starting and therefore, for example, assume that money will always strengthen behavior and other strengtheners are either weak or not present. Some examples of these are given by Dickinson and Poling (1994), Poling and Foster (1993), and Mawhinney (1975).

The second caution is that the interventions used are still primitive by behavior analytic standards, not through any weakness of the researchers (on the contrary!), but because of the newness of the area and the massive constraints imposed on any research in organizations. Most interventions involve only two-term contingencies, or else very simple "feedback" as a contextual discrimination. The application of complex discriminations, multiple contingencies and contingencies of social behavior has not really begun yet but should be far-reaching (see Eubanks & Lloyd, 1992; Komaki, Collins & Penn, 1982; Komaki, Desselles & Bowman, 1989, and Thompson & Luthans, 1983, for some starting points).

It is probably a reflection of previous poor management techniques, in fact, that simply providing feedback and some positive reinforcement (although usually in the weaker forms of rewards and incentives) to people in organizations has led to sometimes substantial increases in productivity. In many cases it is just the contingency relation which has been missing from reinforcers used: the usual problem with rewards and incentives (2.3).

Crowell, Anderson, Abel and Sergio (1988) used some simple techniques to improve customer relations with bank tellers. It was found, first, that merely clarifying the types of behavior categories led to a 12% increase in desired behaviors. Adding feedback and praise had a slower effect. It must be pointed out, from what has been said in 2.3, that clarifying the behavior categories must have involved many types of subtle strengtheners of these behaviors, and led to "anticipated" evaluation and accountability. Section 12.7 says more about these.

In a study of another facet of organizational behavior, Sulzer-Azaroff and de Santamaria (1980) used a package of feedback and praise with safety performance in an industrial organization. The frequencies of hazards dropped by an average of 60% over all the groups studied.

Other areas which have been put forward in behavior analytic terms are organizational culture (Eubanks & Lloyd, 1992), goal-setting (Fellner & Sulzer-Azaroff, 1984), absenteeism (Reid, Schuh-Wear & Brannon, 1978), theft reduction (Carter, Holmstrom, Simpanen & Melin, 1988), power (Thompson & Luthans, 1983), supervision (Komaki, 1986b; Komaki, Desselles & Bowman, 1989), and leadership (Mawhinney & Ford, 1977; Rao & Mawhinney, 1991).

12.7. Intervention and the Production of Countercontrol

If one ignores the social context in which people are immersed, then an obvious solution to many social problems would be to increase the scrutiny and accountability of people. Indeed, Government actions in most western countries has led to increased accountability in all walks of life, especially where economics is of concern. As well, behavioral interventions usually increase the scrutiny and consequences of people's behavior. These have been mentioned throughout this book (especially Chapter 11 and 4.2) with occasional reminders that people can behave dynamically and produce countercontrol (Skinner, 1953) to any intervention.

This section looks at some examples of everyday control and countercontrol as well as some laboratory work which supports the findings. Side-effects of evaluation and attempts to change human behavior are emphasized but the categories outlined can be applied to any forms of control which leads to countercontrol. Because there seems to be no overall review of the very common and broad social control by evaluation and accountability, I will give more details in this section than the others.

In recent years evaluation and accountability have become prominent. Government departments, private organizations, social welfare institutions, schools, universities, and research establishments, have all been under pressure to improve their efficiency, evaluate their performance, reduce unnecessary expenditure, and be accountable for their results. It is clear, however, from both experimental research and organizational anecdotes, that increasing accountability and evaluation does not always lead to increases in efficiency and productivity. In some cases, in fact, more evaluation can lead to reduced efficiency and production. A more common report is that there is an immediate change for the better, but that after a short time efficiency and productivity drop back to previous levels.

The types of evaluation and accountability are varied, and include individual performance appraisals, program evaluation, financial auditing, and organizational accountability. As we saw in 12.6, behavior analysts have also begun to work in organizations to increase productivity. In fact, any form of behavioral intervention can produce countercontrol because we can never control the settings and social environment sufficiently—nor would we want to. The production of countercontrol therefore is not a case of the subjects being wrong or doing the wrong thing, but of there being other contingencies present which were not taken into account—or not taken seriously. As Skinner put it, even when there is countercontrol produced, the organism is always right.

Apart from behavior analysis, accountability and evaluation have been discussed in many areas from many points of view (Baker, 1980; Blatz, 1972; Chippendale & Wilkes, 1977; Coyle, 1987; Deterline, 1971; Eikenberry, 1985; Elling, 1983; England, 1982; Goldring, 1987; Jaques, 1956; Kaufman, 1971; Kaufmann, Majone & Ostrom, 1986; Krapfl, 1975; Krauthammer, 1987; Munro, 1985; Newman & Turem, 1974; Romzek & Dubnick, 1987; Semin & Manstead, 1983; Sheldrake & Linke, 1979; Smith & Carroll, 1982; Smith & Weller, 1978; Tetlock, 1985; Thynne & Goldring, 1981; Ward, 1985; Wirth, 1986; Wise, 1985).

From definitions given in the above references, accountability and evaluation typically rely on one or more of the following:

1) Having to justify or present an account of conduct
2) Having to justify the economic aspects of conduct
3) Having to defend conduct from criticism
4) Having conduct rated, scaled or evaluated
5) Having conduct compared with standards
6) Facing consequences if conduct does not meet standards
7) Being responsible even when justification is impossible
8) Being legally responsible for conduct

All of these depend on a verbal matching of observed behavior to some verbally governed criterion. This process can be divided into three stages of evaluation: a scrutiny process, matching to standards of comparison, and consequences contingent upon the evaluation outcome. Further, these same three processes can be shown to occur in the three major types of evaluation: performance appraisal, program evaluation, and organizational accountability, as well as the behavior change methods given in Chapter 11. They each observe or measure performance or behavior; they compare the observations and measurements with a standard or expected value; and they all have explicit or implicit consequences from the results of the comparison.

The difference between the definitions of evaluation and accountability seems to be that the term "evaluation" is used when the scrutiny aspect is highlighted, while "accountability" is used when the consequences are highlighted. Standards of comparison are important to both. Evaluation and accountability can be seen as parts of a general and common intervention process involving verbally-governed scrutiny, comparison with standards, and increasing consequences.

Positive Effects of Intervention

Increased Effort. Evaluation, in most circumstances, clearly leads to increased effort and performance. It has been shown experimentally to lead to better decision making (Chaiken, 1980; Hagafors & Brehmer, 1983; McAllister, Mitchell & Beach, 1979). More processing is conducted, more time is taken to decide, more analytic decision strategies are used, and a more thorough search process is made. This increase in effort has also been shown to lead to less bias in decision making and judgment and to fairer decisions (Tetlock, 1985).

Increased effort is probably the major reason for evaluating in organizations. It is thought that if performance is not evaluated the effort will not be expended by employees. The problem, of course, is to channel the increased effort into efficient performance while balancing any negative side-effects. For example, the longer time spent in decision making when accountable could be a drawback if quick decisions are required (Ford & Weldon, 1981). This needs to be anticipated and weighed carefully before imposing evaluations, especially where consequences are contingent.

In behavior analytic terms, the extra "effort" comes partly from tying the outcomes more directly to the behaviors and the stimulus conditions, and partly from better reinforcement of the verbal/social rules which are to be followed.

Feedback. The other positive feature about evaluation is that it can provide new information and feedback to all levels of an organization, not just those requiring the evaluation. While supervisors often do not want to know about their subordinates' behavior (Kaufman, 1973), the evaluation can make this information more easily available to them. In behavior analytic terms, the feedback here refers to providing verbal rules which can be used to control performance—but only if the social consequences are present (2.3).

There are three ways in which evaluation might improve feedback. First the increased scrutiny during evaluation can provide new and more frequent feedback and hence improve the control by verbal rules. Many performance appraisals and program evaluations give feedback to personnel about their level of work which they would not otherwise receive, since new or more frequent measures are taken. With only an annual performance appraisal, personnel can work for a whole year not knowing how they are performing (Yerbury, 1981, p. 214).

A second way in which evaluation can improve feedback is with the comparison process: new standards of comparison used in evaluation can help people view their work in a new light. The comparison rules used are frequently inherited from earlier phases of organizational development, and may have even evolved by chance. So making new comparisons by evaluating can again support verbal rules in controlling performance. Until recently, for example, the evaluation of academic teaching and research was largely haphazard.

A third improvement in feedback can come from the consequences. Explicitly tying the evaluation outcomes to consequences sharpens up the control by verbal rules. Often personnel do not know how their behavior is tied to their social consequences, if indeed it is. There are negative side-effects of tying consequences to specific comparisons, however, which will be discussed below.

Negative Effects of Intervention

Apprehension. One common feature of evaluation is that people are generally apprehensive about being evaluated and prefer not to be evaluated (4.2; Cottrell, 1972; Guerin, 1986; Rosenberg, 1969; Sanchez & Clark, 1981; Szymanski & Harkins, 1993). From the relevant literatures on this topic, it is unclear whether the apprehension arises from being scrutinized, from being compared to verbal rules, from the consequences, or from some mixture of these. Consequences probably play a large role in generating evaluation apprehension. It would seem that most people have received only negative consequences when explicitly evaluated in the past (4.2), and evaluation is therefore commonly regarded a negative process. Care should be taken with this, therefore, when conducting an evaluation; reassurance is usually needed about the consequences of the evaluation.

There is no reason, however, why evaluation has to result in only negative consequences. It should be possible to design evaluation systems and interventions which have primarily positive consequences. Rather than being apprehensive, people might even look forward to these evaluations, or even request them (Ashford & Cummings, 1983). This is probably a long term goal for evaluation professionals, and new methods will need to be tested, since most people will continue to associate evaluation with negative consequences.

Distraction and Disruption. The process of evaluative scrutiny must always be disruptive. The evaluation apprehension mentioned above can itself be disruptive under some circumstances (Baron, Moore & Sanders, 1978). As well, merely having to provide details to an evaluator about performance measures and practices can disrupt performance. One less obvious source of disruption comes from the increased effort associated with evaluation. Under some circumstances, increased effort on complex tasks leads to worse performance (Cottrell, 1972). Tasks need to be well-learned if increased effort is to have its benefits.

Avoiding disruption from evaluation will depend heavily on the exact implementation used in any evaluation. This again needs to be anticipated and reduced as much possible, as early as possible. If it continues then normal behavior will not be measured during the baseline period, and the personnel made even more apprehensive.

Superficiality. With an increase in evaluation there is often an increase in superficial compliance with the standards of comparison (like behavioral autoclitics). If the consequences are not closely tied to the measures used in evaluation then any behaviors or outputs which *resemble* the measures will be adequate. People will give the superficial impression of behaving according to the evaluation comparison when in fact they are not. This can be noticed in both a lack of real commitment and the transitory nature of any changes which occur.

Some of these problems have been discussed in the literature on self-presentation strategies (Giacalone & Rosenfeld, 1986; Jones & Pittman, 1982). Self-presentation is one important form of superficial compliance. It is used both to avoid negative consequences and to contact positive consequences. Two commonly avoided negative consequences are effort and negative evaluations. Any behavior which leads to avoidance of these will increase in frequency, even if they are only superficial. Once this is learned, the (covert verbal) anticipation of evaluation will be sufficient to elicit them.

Another form of superficial avoidance which can occur if the standards of comparison are known is that of finding loopholes. Looking for excuses and scapegoats to remove blame and avoid responsibility for a poor evaluation is a common bureaucratic form of avoidance (Mansfield, 1982). On an individual level, Balsam and Bondy (1983) have described an interesting pattern which they call the "lawyer's syndrome": clients on behavior therapy contracts look for loopholes in the contracts which they themselves have written.

Ridgway (1956) provides many examples from the early organizational literature of superficial compliance for avoidance. He was comparing the problems of evaluating with a single criterion, with multiple criteria, and with composite criteria. It is clear from his work that just varying the number or type of standard of comparison is not sufficient to remove superficiality. Changes to the consequences are needed to overcome the problems.

A serious problem which arises from these avoidance strategies is that further evaluation is needed to keep check on the avoidance behaviors. This can escalate until frequent checks are needed which were irrelevant to the original evaluation purpose. This commonly occurs in performance appraisals and bureaucratic accountability. Extra checks are needed to make sure superficial compliance is not present. If it can be reduced by careful evaluation planning then an escalation of costs can be prevented.

Having discussed superficiality resulting from avoidance of negative consequences, we now turn to superficiality engendered from positive consequences: positive controls can also reinforce inappropriate behaviors. A common example in evaluation is attention to the evaluator, which is strengthened since it usually leads to better outcomes. [This is learned all through childhood in my experience.] Inordinate attention is often given to finding out about the evaluators, the comparisons they will use, and how they might be influenced. Superficiality can equally appear if these lead to positive consequences. Cheating and undesirable competition, for example, can be strengthened by positive controls, and eventually lead to gross negative side-effects.

Related to this is the effect that positively strengthening some behaviors has on other behaviors. For example, if there is a job promotion contingent upon a particular behavior then a promotion might be demanded for other behaviors as well. Employees might refuse to perform other behaviors if positive consequences are not also forthcoming. In practice, this leads to the need for tight job specifications: the full range of behaviors for the job have to be spelt out exactly. Once this is done, it is harder to get employees to carry out any non-specified tasks. What seemed a reasonable solution to one problem creates another. Job restructuring in Australia, New Zealand and elsewhere is at present trying to sort out historically fashioned job requirements to make them more flexible.

Even more directly, an increase in evaluated behaviors due to possible (therefore verbal) positive consequences can lead to a decrease in other behaviors. There might be less time spent on behaviors which are not evaluated and have no contingent positive consequences, even if the employee has no objections to carrying them out. These might include useful but unevaluated tasks. The multiple behavior approach of 3.2 needs to be explored to research this.

Research and anecdotes provide many examples of superficial behaviors arising from both negative and positive contingent consequences. Caplan (1968) found that evaluated social workers had an inflated number of case reports which were near successes: a "near success pile-up". Clearly, reporting near successes resulted in the same consequences as reporting complete case successes, and better consequences than reporting case failures. Hence, the near success pile-up.

A number of studies have shown that when negotiators are being evaluated by their constituents, they show more self-presentation behaviors and have worse negotiation outcomes (Ben-Yoav & Pruitt, 1984; Carnevale, Pruitt & Britton, 1979; Klimoski, 1972; Klimoski & Ash, 1974). The impression of looking tough, for the sake of the constituents, is incompatible with flexible negotiation, and the evaluation process itself seems to elicit such impression management.

Other studies have shown that low consequences and specific standards of comparison lead to less thorough performance. If the measures are known to those being evaluated then they only have to produce the minimum acceptable performance. Tetlock (1983) and McFarland, Ross and Conway (1984) both found superficial processing of arguments when the attitudes (presumably the comparison) of the persuader (also the evaluator) were known.

That changes in evaluated behavior can be transitory is shown by a report of Bassett and Blanchard (1977). Scrutiny of prison officers in a prison token economy program led to a decrease in their taking away tokens as punishment, which was the aim. When the Director left for a few months, however, the use of token punishment increased and many new categories of punishment were created. The use of punishment dropped again when the Director returned.

Reduced Flexibility and Creativity. A common report in the literature is that evaluation and accountability reduce flexibility and creativity. While this is by no means a necessary side-effect of evaluation, it does seem to be prevalent with the evaluation methods used at present, because variability can be reinforced (Page & Neuringer, 1985; also 8.7)

Amabile (1983) and Bartis, Szymanski and Harkins (1988) have shown experimentally that creativity is reduced by evaluation. Bartis et al. (1988) also showed that this effect changes with different standards of comparison. When their subjects believed that the number of creative ideas was being measured, they produced more ideas when evaluated. When they thought the creativity of the ideas was being measured the numbers went down and the creativity increased–but only when there was no evaluation.

The consequences of evaluations are likely to mediate such reductions in creativity, which means that new conditions must be found under which the consequences are conducive to creativity. Clearly, the absence of negative consequences has this effect (Bartis et al., 1988, No Evaluation Condition), but whether evaluations which have either positive consequences contingent on creativity or have no consequences can further increase creativity, remains to be tested.

The negotiation studies mentioned earlier also show how flexibility can be reduced with increased evaluation. The evaluation by constituents led to less flexible negotiation and worse outcomes. The notion of reduced flexibility and independence occurring with increased accountability has also been aired with respect to interventions within bureaucracies (Arrow, 1974; Blau, 1955; Mansfield, 1982; Mosher, 1982, p. 72).

Increase in Caution. Accountability and evaluation have been shown experimentally to lead to greater caution and this has also been mentioned with regards to bureaucracies (Staats, 1982, p. 32). This seems to be a function of the avoidance of consequences. Caution might be most noticeable when the consequences are either negative or unknown (Tetlock, 1983).

Anderson (1981) found that the foreign policy decisions during the Cuban Missile Crisis were determined both from having to justify the decisions to Congress and from the necessity of having precedents for any action. The policy decisions were more cautious if justification was needed or if there were no precedents for the decisions. Similar processes probably occur in organizational decision making of many types (Janis, 1972).

Reduced Task Interest. There is evidence that if a behavior is already motivated then adding external consequences can lead to an overall loss of motivation (Lepper & Greene, 1978). So the effect of having an evaluation which leads to consequences may not only be a superficial, transitory increase in the appropriate behaviors, but an undermining of the original task interest as well. When the evaluation is finished, the motivation for the behaviors may fall to below the original levels. The exact conditions for this are not yet known (Dickinson, 1988), and some contrary results have been found (Feingold & Mahoney, 1975). More needs to be known about this aspect, both experimentally and applied (see 8.6).

Lack of Guidance. An indirect side-effect of aversive consequences is that punishment does not specify the correct behavior and so is not educational or corrective. The behavior is suppressed but not explicitly replaced with the correct behavior. Employees might have a good idea of what not to do but little idea of more efficient behaviors to use instead. Training in new behaviors is essential if this approach is taken in evaluations (11.2).

Designing Better Evaluations and Interventions

Many recommendations have been made above to help administrators, behavior change agents, and program managers design evaluation and intervention systems when experimental control is difficult (i.e., the real world). There is little one can do to improve a one-off evaluation or intervention conducted in isolation, since there is not time to reduce evaluation apprehension, provide feedback, and tradeoff specific comparisons and specific consequences with their resultant superficial behaviors. A lot can be done, however, to improve the long term evaluation of whole systems if one designs such evaluations around the points made in the previous sections, being sensitive to their interactions and tradeoffs. The major points relevant to this goal are now summarized in terms of the consequences, the comparisons, and the scrutiny of performance.

Consequences. The points that have been made with respect to consequences all suggest that more needs to be done to generate positive rather than negative consequences for evaluations (cf. Sidman, 1989). Positive consequences have only a few possible side-effects (superficiality, for example) and many good points (less reduction in flexibility, for example). While a whole lifetime of negative experiences with evaluation cannot be easily overcome, much can be done interpersonally by the professional evaluator within a particular evaluation setting to initiate reversal.

Peters and Waterman (1982) have discussed similar points and shown that positive systems can work, although organizations need to develop a tolerance for errors. If employees are to be more flexible, more creative, less cautious, and less superficial, they need to be free of possible aversive consequences incurred from evaluations. At the least there could be a two tiered system such that those who regularly perform to a specified standard can be on a "positive only track", while those who repeatedly fail enter a "negative track", complete with negative consequences.

Instigation of positive evaluation systems requires patience as well as tolerance for errors. Punishment is a natural reaction for most people because it is reinforcing to the punisher. The negative side-effects are mostly long term ones and not associated with the use of punishment. It is therefore hard to stop the use of punishment or threats of punishments.

If positive control systems are to work, skill training must be widespread so that employees can take advantage of the positive consequences. They must have the skills first. So positive consequence systems which use evaluations with positive consequences require that consequences are closely tied to behavior, while avoiding the side-effects of this mentioned above (superficiality, for example).

Verbal Rules and Standards of Comparison. One overall conclusion from the effects and side-effects of evaluation detailed above is that clearer specification of standards of comparison are needed. There will still be problems when the criteria are necessarily vague and therefore hard to measure: such as with evaluating creativity, or friendliness to other workers. One possible solution to avoid this problem would be to set up special contexts or settings so employees can discriminate periods of vague criteria from periods of clear criteria. Creating a clear discriminative context of loose criteria for consequences is one feature of brainstorming settings. Similar practices could be more widely used in evaluations.

With regards to locating the comparison to be used, naturally occurring performance standards should be utilized, with greater reliance placed on finding out employee self-evaluation criteria and informal peer evaluation criteria. Employees often have the best idea of what constitutes a good performance because they contact the contingencies. At the worse, poor natural criteria can be corrected if they happen to be found while consulting with employees.

Finally, while multiple criteria have some drawbacks, they seem clearly preferable to the use of single criteria (Ridgway, 1956). Evaluation measures should be long term rather than continuous where possible, since this avoids a number of the negative side-effects mentioned above. It should also be kept in mind that the criteria will usually need a shaping procedure to get them working. It is idealistic to develop new comparison criteria and expect employees to be immediately sensitive to them. They need to be trained or explained. Some interesting methods for mutual shaping of organizational behaviors has been discussed by Majone (1986).

Scrutiny Processes. One major limitation with the increasing use of current evaluation procedures is that they are disruptive. As has been recommended above, building them into the organizational control provides a less disruptive alternative. If disruption and evaluation apprehension can be reduced, then continuous evaluation, with its advantages, becomes possible. Disruption and evaluation apprehension seem to be the two factors preventing the use of continuous evaluation. Continuous evaluation is a more realistic possibility also if negative consequences can be reduced. Employees can appreciate greater feedback about how they are doing and how they are rewarded if apprehension over negative evaluations is reduced.

Another possibility often mentioned is to use "evaluationless" feedback systems. If employees are working towards positive consequences rather than avoidance, they might better utilize feedback which has no contingent consequences. This will help them shape up before the public evaluation (with its real consequences) is due. It is when negative consequences are expected that feedback from scrutiny is avoided.

Like comparisons and consequences, utilization of naturally occurring scrutiny processes is recommended. For example, we do not know how much peers assess and influence each others' work, nor do we know the extent of self-evaluations which normally occur. These could be more widely tapped as naturally occurring scrutiny processes. In this way, a self-evaluating organization is not a far-fetched idea (Spann, 1979, p. 503; Wildavsky, 1972).

Naturally occurring communication channels have been shown to be underutilized (Kaufman, 1973). New channels could be developed to allow evaluation information to be passed on without having a formal scrutiny at all. While this is likely to have unwanted side-effects with negatively controlled evaluation systems, the use of positive controls might lead to an increase in information volunteering, if employees know there will be no negative consequences from reporting failures, errors or mishaps. It works in some organizations already (Peters & Waterman, 1982), and could lead to a greater use of evaluationless feedback techniques.

References

Abrams, D., & Hogg, M. A. (Eds.). (1990). *Social identity theory: Constructive and critical advances.* New York: Springer-Verlag.

Abrams, D., Wetherall, M., Cochrane, S., Hogg, M. A., & Turner, J. C. (1990). Knowing what to think by knowing who you are: Self-categorization and the nature of norm formation, conformity and group polarization. *British Journal of Social Psychology, 29,* 97-119.

Achebe, C. (1988). *The African trilogy.* London: Pan Books.

Acker, J., Barry, K., & Esseveld, J. (1983). Objectivity and truth: Problems in doing feminist research. *Women's Studies International Forum, 6,* 423-435.

Adelberg, S., & Batson, C. D. (1978). Accountability and helping: When needs exceed resources. *Journal of Personality and Social Psychology, 36,* 343-350.

Ader, R., & Tatum, R. (1963). Free-operant avoidance conditioning in individual and paired human subjects. *Journal of the Experimental Analysis of Behavior, 6,* 357-359.

Aeschleman, S. R., & Williams, M. L. (1989). A test of the response deprivation hypothesis in a multiple-response context. *American Journal on Mental Retardation, 93,* 345-353.

Ajzen, I. (1985). From intentions to actions: A theory of planned behavior. In J. Kuhl & J. Backmann (Eds.), *Action control: From cognition to behavior* (pp. 11-39). New York: Springer-Verlag.

Ajzen, I., & Fishbein, M. (1977). Attitude-behavior relations: A theoretical analysis and review of empirical research. *Psychological Bulletin, 84,* 888-918.

Ajzen, I., & Fishbein, M. (1980). *Understanding attitudes and predicting social behavior.* Englewood Cliffs, NJ: Prentice-Hall.

Ajzen, I., & Madden, T. J. (1986). Prediction of goal-directed behavior: Attitudes, intentions, and perceived behavioral control. *Journal of Experimental Social Psychology, 22,* 453-474.

Alberto, P. A., & Troutman, A. C. (1986). *Applied behavior analysis for teachers.* Columbus, Ohio: Merrill.

Alford, B. A. (1986). Behavioral treatment of schizophrenic delusions: A single-case experimental analysis. *Behavior Therapy, 17,* 637-644.

Allansdottir, A., Jovchelovitch, S., & Stathopoulou, A. (1993). Social representations: The versatility of a concept. *Papers on Social Representations, 2,* 3-10.

Allison, J. (1976). Contrast, induction, facilitation, suppression, and conservation. *Journal of the Experimental Analysis of Behavior, 25,* 185-198.

Allport, G. W., & Postman, L. (1947). *The psychology of rumor.* New York: Holt, Rinehart & Winston.

Allyon, T., & Azrin, N. (1968). *The token economy.* New York: Appleton-Century-Crofts.

Amabile, T. M. (1983). *The social psychology of creativity.* New York: Springer Verlag.

Amato, P. R. (1990). Personality and social network involvement as predictors of helping behavior in everyday life. *Social Psychological Quarterly, 53,* 31-43.

Anderson, J. R. (1978). Arguments concerning representations for mental imagery. *Psychological Review, 85,* 249-277.

Anderson, P. A. (1981). Justifications and precedents as constraints in foreign policy decision-making. *American Journal of Political Science, 25,* 738-761.

Andrasik, F., & Matson, J. L. (1985). Social skills training for the mentally retarded. In L. L'Abate & M. A. Milan (Eds.), *Handbook of social skills training and research* (pp. 418-454). New York: Wiley.

Andrasik, F., Heimberg, J. S., & McNamara, J. R. (1981). Behavior modification of work and work-related problems. In M. Hersen, R. M. Eisler & P. M. Miller (Eds.), *Progress in behavior modification* (Vol. 11, pp. 117-161). New York: Academic Press.

Anjoh, Y., & Yamamoto, J. (1991). [Improving throwing skills in baseball by high school students: An analysis of the effects of behavioral coaching.] *Japanese Journal of Behavior Analysis, 6,* 3-22. With English summary.

Arbuthnot, J., & Andrasik, F. (1973). Situational influences on moral judgment. *Proceedings of the 81st Annual Convention of the American Psychological Association, 8,* 217-218.

Arkes, H. R., Christensen, C., Lai, C., & Blumer, C. (1987). Two methods of reducing overconfidence. *Organizational Behavior and Human Decision Processes, 39,* 133-144.

Aronson, E., & Carlsmith, J. M. (1962). Performance expectancy as a determinant of actual performance. *Journal of Abnormal and Social Psychology, 65,* 178-182.

Arrow, K. J. (1974). *The limits of organization.* New York: Norton.

Asch, S. E. (1956). Studies of independence and submission to group pressure: A minority of one against a unanimous majority. *Psychological Monographs, 70,* 416-688.

Ashford, S. J., & Cummings, L. L. (1983). Feedback as an individual resource: Personal strategies for creating information. *Organizational Behavior and Human Performance, 32,* 370-398.

Atkinson, P. (Ed.). (1990). *The ethnographic imagination: Textual constructions of reality.* London: Routledge.

Austin, J. (1962). *How to do things with words.* Oxford: Oxford University Press.

Austin-Broos, D. J. (Ed.). (1987). *Creating culture: Profiles in the study of culture.* Sydney: Allen & Unwin.

Azrin, N. H., & Holz, W. C. (1966). Punishment. In W. K. Honig (Ed.), *Operant behavior: Areas of research and application* (pp. 380-447). Englewood Cliffs, NJ: Prentice Hall.

Azrin, N. H., & Lindsley, O. R. (1956). The reinforcement of cooperation between children. *Journal of Abnormal and Social Psychology, 52,* 100-102.

Azrin, N. H., Hutchinson, R. R., & Hake, D. F. (1966). Extinction-induced aggression. *Journal of the Experimental Analysis of Behavior, 9,* 191-204.

Bâ, M. (1981). *So long a letter.* Harare, Zimbabwe: Zimbabwe Publishing House.

Back, K., Festinger, L., Hymovitch, B., Kelley, H., Schachter, S., & Thibaut, J. (1950). The methodology of studying rumor transmission. *Human Relations, 3,* 307-312.

Baer, D. M. (1976). The organism as host. *Human Development, 19,* 87-98.

Baer, D. M. (1982). The imposition of structure on behavior and the demolition of behavioral structures. In D. J. Bernstein (Ed.), *Response structure and organization: Nebraska Symposium on Motivation 1981* (Vol. 29, pp. 217-254). Lincoln, Nebraska: University of Nebraska Press.

Baer, D. M. (1984). Does research on self-control need more control? *Analysis and Intervention in Developmental Disabilities, 4,* 211-218.

Baer, D. M., & Deguchi, H. (1985). Generalized imitation from a radical-behavioral viewpoint. In S. Reiss & R. R. Bootzin (Eds.), *Theoretical issues in behavior therapy* (pp. 179-217). New York: Academic Press.

Baer, D. M., & Wolf, M. M. (1970). The entry into natural communities of reinforcement. In R. Ulrich, T. Stachnik & J. Mabry (Eds.), *Control of human behavior. Volume 2, From cure to prevention.* (pp. 319-324). Glenview, IL: Scott Foresman.

Baer, D. M., Wolf, M. M., & Risley, T.R. (1987). Some still-current dimensions of applied behavior analysis. *Journal of Applied Behavior Analysis, 20,* 313-327.

Baer, R. A., Detrich, R., & Weninger, J. M. (1988). On the functional role of the verbalization in correspondence training procedures. *Journal of Applied Behavior Analysis, 21,* 345-356.

Baker, W. A. (1980). Accountability, responsiveness and public sector productivity. *Canadian Public Administration, 23,* 542-557.

Baldwin, J. D., & Baldwin, J. I (1978). Behaviorism on verstehen and erklären. *American Sociological Review, 43,* 335-347.

Baldwin, M. W., & Holmes, J. G. (1987). Salient private audiences and awareness of the self. *Journal of Personality and Social Psychology, 52,* 1087-1098.

Balsam, P. D., & Bondy, A. S. (1983). The negative side effects of reward. *Journal of Applied Behavior Analysis, 16,* 283-296.

Bandura, A. (1965). Influence of a model's reinforcement contingencies on the acquisition of imitative responses. *Journal of Personality and Social Psychology, 1,* 589-595.

Barber, B. (1983). *The logic and limits of trust.* New Brunswick, NJ: Rutgers University Press.

Bargad, A., & Hyde, J. S. (1991). Women's studies: A study of feminist identity development in women. *Psychology of Women Quarterly, 15,* 181-201.

Barker, R. G., & Associates. (1978). *Habitats, environments, and human behavior.* San Fransisco: Jossey-Bass.

Baron, A., Perone, M., & Galizio, M. (1991). Analyzing the reinforcement process at the human level: Can application and behavioristic interpretation replace laboratory research? *The Behavior Analyst, 14,* 95-105.

Baron, R. S., Moore, D., & Sanders, G. S. (1978). Distraction as a source of drive in social facilitation research. *Journal of Personality and Social Psychology, 36,* 816-824.

Barrera, M., & Ainlay, S. L. (1983). The structure of social support: A conceptual and empirical analysis. *Journal of Community Psychology, 11,* 133-143.

Barrett, D. H., Deitz, S. M., Gaydos, G. R., & Quinn, P. C. (1987). The effects of programmed contingencies and social conditions on response stereotypy with human subjects. *The Psychological Record, 37,* 489-505.

Barrett, J. E., & Sanger, D. J. (Eds.). (1991). Special issue on behavioral pharmacology. *Journal of the Experimental Analysis of Behavior, 56* (2).

Barrett, R. A. (1984). *Culture and conduct: An excursion in anthropology.* Belmont, CA: Wadsworth.

Bartis, S., Szymanski, K., & Harkins, S. G. (1988). Evaluation and performance: A two-edged knife. *Personality and Social Psychology Bulletin, 14,* 242-251.

Bartlett, F. C. (1932). *Remembering.* Cambridge: Cambridge University Press.

Barton, E. J. (1981). Developing sharing: An analysis of modeling and other behavioral techniques. *Behavior Modification, 5,* 386-398.

Bartunek, J. M., Benton, A. A., & Keys, C. B. (1975). Third party intervention and the bargaining behavior of group representatives. *Journal of Conflict Resolution, 19,* 532-557.

Basho. (1985). *On love and barley: Haiku of Basho.* Harmondsworth, Middlesex: Penguin.

Bassett, J. E., & Blanchard, E. B. (1977). The effect of the absence of close supervision on the use of response cost in a prison token economy. *Journal of Applied Behavior Analysis, 10,* 375-379.

Bateman, S. (1975). Application of Premack's generalization on reinforcement to modify occupational behavior in two severely retarded individuals. *American Journal of Mental Deficiency, 79,* 604-610.

Baum, W. M. (1975). Time allocation in human vigilance. *Journal of the Experimental Analysis of Behavior, 23,* 45-53.

Baum, W. M., & Heath, J. L. (1992). Behavioral explanations and intentional explanations in psychology. *American Psychologist, 47,* 1312-1317.

Bauman, R. (1986). *Story, performance, and event: Contextual studies of oral narrative.* Cambridge: Cambridge University Press.

Baumeister, R. F. (1982). A self-presentational view of social phenomena. *Psychological Bulletin, 91,* 3-26.

Beaman, A. L., Klentz, B., Diener, E., & Svanum, S. (1979). Self-awareness and transgression in children: Two field studies. *Journal of Personality and Social Psychology, 37,* 1835-1846.

Beardsley, S. D., & McDowell, J. J. (1992). Application of Herrnstein's hyperbola to time allocation of naturalistic human behavior maintained by naturalistic social reinforcement. *Journal of the Experimental Analysis of Behavior, 57,* 177-185.

Beattie, J. H. M. (1970). On understanding ritual. In B. R. Wilson (Ed.), *Rationality* (pp. 240-268). Oxford: Basil Blackwell.

Beckhouse, L., Tanur, J., Weiler, J., & Weinstein, E. (1975). ...and some men have leadership thrust upon them. *Journal of Personality and Social Psychology, 31,* 557-566.

Beckman, L. J. (1981). Effects of social interaction and children's relative inputs on older women's psychological well-being. *Journal of Personality and Social Psychology, 41,* 1075-1086.

Behr, R. L., & Iyengar, S. (1985). Television news, real-world cues, and changes in the public agenda. *Public Opinion Quarterly, 49,* 38-57.

Bem, D. J. (1965). An experimental analysis of self-persuasion. *Journal of Experimental Social Psychology, 1,* 199-218.

Benjumea, S., & Arias, M. F. (1993). Pigeons' novel behavior governed by multiple controlling stimuli. *The Psychological Record, 43,* 455-470.

Bennett, R. H., & Samson, H. H. (1987). Human performance under progressive ratio contingencies. *The Psychological Record, 37,* 213-218.

Bentall, R. P., & Lowe, C. F. (1987). The role of verbal behavior in human learning: III. Instructional effects in children. *Journal of the Experimental Analysis of Behavior, 47,* 177-190.

Bentley, A. F. (1941). The human skin: Philosophy's last line of defense. *Philosophy of Science, 8,* 1-19.

Benton, A. A. (1972). Accountability and negotiations between group representatives. *Proceedings, 80th Annual Convention, American Psychological Association, 7,* 227-228.

Benton, A. A. (1975). Bargaining visibility and the attitudes and negotiation behavior of male and female group representatives. *Journal of Personality, 43,* 661-677.

Benton, A. A., & Druckman, D. (1973). Salient solutions and the bargaining behavior of representatives and non-representatives. *International Journal of Group Tension, 3,* 28-39.

Benton, A. A., & Druckman, D. (1974). Constituent's bargaining orientation and intergroup negotiations. *Journal of Applied Social Psychology, 4,* 141-150.

Benton, R. G., & Mefferd, R. B. (1967). Projector slide changing and focusing as operant reinforcers. *Journal of the Experimental Analysis of Behavior, 10,* 479-484.

Ben-Yoav, O., & Pruitt, D. G. (1984). Accountability to constituents: A two edged sword. *Organizational Behavior and Human Performance, 34,* 283-295.

Berger, P. L., & Luckmann, T. (1967). *The social construction of reality.* Harmondsworth, Middlesex: Penguin.

Berkman, L. F. (1985). The relationship of social networks and social support to morbidity and mortality. In S. Cohen & S. L. Syme (Eds.), *Social support and health* (pp. 241-262). New York: Academic Press.

Berkowitz, L. (1972). Social norms, feelings, and other factors affecting helping and altruism. In L. Berkowitz (Ed.), *Advances in experimental social psychology*, (Vol. 6, pp. 63-108). New York: Academic Press.

Berkowitz, L., & Connor, W. H. (1966). Success, failure, and social responsibility. *Journal of Personality and Social Psychology, 4*, 664-669.

Berkowitz, L., & Daniels, L. R. (1963). Responsibility and dependency. *Journal of Abnormal and Social Psychology, 66*, 429-436.

Berkowitz, L., & Daniels, L. R. (1964). Affecting the salience of the social responsibility norm: Effects of past help on the response to dependency relationships. *Journal of Abnormal and Social Psychology, 68*, 275-281.

Berkowitz, L., Klanderman, S., & Harris, R. (1964). Effects of experimenter awareness and sex of subject and experimenter on reactions to dependency relationships. *Sociometry, 27*, 327-337.

Bernstein, D. J. (1990). Of carrots and sticks: A review of Deci and Ryan's *Intrinsic motivation and self-determination in human behavior. Journal of the Experimental Analysis of Behavior, 54*, 323-332.

Bernstein, D. J. (1986). Correspondence between verbal and observed estimates of reinforcement value. In P. N. Chase and L. J. Parrott (Eds.), *Psychological aspects of language* (pp. 187-205). Springfield, IL: Charles C. Thomas.

Bernstein, D. J., & Brady, J. V. (1986). The utility of continuous programmed environments in the experimental analysis of behavior. In H. W. Reese and L. J. Parrott (Eds.), *Behavior science: Philosophical, methodological, and empirical advances* (pp. 229-245). Hillsdale, NJ: Erlbaum.

Bernstein, D. J., & Ebbesen, E. E. (1978). Reinforcement and substitution in humans: A multiple-response analysis. *Journal of the Experimental Analysis of Behavior, 30*, 243-253.

Bernstein, D. J., & Michael, R. L. (1990). The utility of verbal and behavioral assessments of value. *Journal of the Experimental Analysis of Behavior, 54*, 173-184.

Berry, D. C., & Broadbent, D. E. (1988). Interactive tasks and the implicit-explicit distinction. *British Journal of Psychology, 79*, 251-272.

Berscheid, E., Graziano, W., Monson, T., & Dermer, M. (1976). Outcome dependency: Attention, attribution and attraction. *Journal of Personality and Social Psychology, 34*, 978-989.

Bertram, B. C. R. (1978). Living in groups: Predators and prey. In J. R. Krebs & N. B. Davies (Eds.), *Behavioural ecology: An evolutionary approach* (pp. 64-96). Oxford: Blackwell Scientific Publications.

Bhatt, R. S., & Wasserman, E. A. (1987). Choice behavior of pigeons on progressive and multiple schedules: A test of optimal foraging theory. *Journal of Experimental Psychology: Animal Behavior Processes, 13*, 40-51.

Bhavnani, K-K. (1993). Tracing the contours: Feminist research and feminist objectivity. *Women's Studies International Forum, 16*, 95-104.

Bickel, W. K., & Etzel, B. C. (1985). The quantal nature of controlling stimulus-response relations as measured in tests of stimulus generalization. *Journal of the Experimental Analysis of Behavior, 44*, 245-270.

Biglan, A., Glasgow, R. E., & Singer, G. (1990). The need for a science of larger social units: A contextual approach. *Behavior Therapy, 21*, 195-215.

Bijou S. W. (1966). A functional analysis of retarded development. In N. R. Ellis (Ed.), *International review of research in mental retardation* (pp. 1-19). New York: Academic Press.

Bijou, S. W. (1993). *Behavior analysis of child development* (3rd ed.). Reno, NV: Context Press.

Bijou, S. W., & Baer, D. M. (1961). *Child development: I. A systematic and empirical theory.* New York: Appleton-Century-Crofts.

Bijou, S. W., & Baer, D. M. (1965). *Child development II. Universal stage of infancy.* New York: Appleton-Century-Crofts.

Bijou, S. W., & Baer, D. M. (1978). *Behavior analysis of child development.* Englewood Cliffs, NJ: Prentice-Hall.

Bijou, S. W., Umbreit, J., Ghezzi, P. M., & Chao, C-C. (1986). Manual of instructions for identifying and analysing referential interactions. *The Psychological Record, 36,* 491-518.

Bixenstine, V. E., Levitt, C. A., & Wilson, K. V. (1966). Collaboration among six persons in a Prisoner's Dilemma game. *Journal of Conflict Resolution, 10,* 488-496.

Bjorkman, M. (1984). Decision making, risk taking and psychological time: Review of empirical findings and psychological theory. *Scandinavian Journal of Psychology, 25,* 31-49.

Blakely, E., & Schlinger, H. (1987). Rules: Function-altering contingency-specifying stimuli. *The Behavior Analyst, 10,* 183-187.

Blatz, C. V. (1972). Accountability and answerability. *Journal of the Theory of Social Behaviour, 2,* 101-120.

Blau, P. (1964). *Exchange and power in social life.* New York: Wiley.

Blau, P. M. (1955). *The dynamics of bureaucracy.* Chicago: University of Chicago Press.

Bloch, M. (1989a). *Ritual, history and power: Selected papers in anthropology.* London: The Athlone Press.

Bloch, M. (1989b). The symbolism of money in Imerina. In J. Parry & M. Bloch (Eds.), *Money and the morality of exchange* (p. 165-190). Cambridge: Cambridge University Press.

Bloch, M., & Parry, J. (1989). Introduction: Money and the morality of exchange. In J. Parry & M. Bloch (Eds.), *Money and the morality of exchange* (p. 1-32). Cambridge: Cambridge University Press.

Block, R. A., & Harper, D. R. (1991). Overconfidence in estimation: Testing the anchoring-and-adjustment hypothesis. *Organizational Behavior and Human Decision Processes, 49,* 188-207.

Blough, D. S. (1963). Interresponse time as a function of continuous variables: A new method and some data. *Journal of the Experimental Analysis of Behavior, 6,* 237-246.

Bonacich, P. (1972). Norms and cohesion as adaptive responses to potential conflict: An experimental study. *Sociometry, 35,* 357-375.

Bonacich, P. (1976). Secrecy and solidarity. *Sociometry, 39,* 200-208.

Booth, M., Bauman, A., Oldenburg, B., Owen, N., & Magnus, P. (1992). Effects of a national mass-media campaign on physical activity participation. *Health Promotion International, 7,* 241-247.

Booth, M., Macaskill, P., Owen, N., Oldenburg, B., Marcus, B. H., & Bauman, A. (in press). The descriptive epidemiology of stages of change in physical activity. *Health Education Quarterly.*

Bordo, S. (1987). The Cartesian masculinization of thought. In S. Harding & J. F. O'Barr (Eds.), *Sex and scientific inquiry* (pp. 247-264). Chicago: University of Chicago Press.

Boren, J. J. (1966). An experimental social relation between two monkeys. *Journal of the Experimental Analysis of Behavior, 9,* 691-700.

Borland, R., Chapman, S., Owen, N., & Hill, D. (1990). Effects of workplace smoking bans on cigarette consumption. *American Journal of Public Health, 80,* 178-180.

Bourhis, R. Y., Giles, H., & Rosenthal, D. (1981). Notes on the construction of a 'subjective vitality questionnaire' for ethnolinguistic groups. *Journal of Multilingual and Multicultural Development, 2,* 145-155.

Bowdery, B. K. (1942). Usages of the term 'social'. *Philosophy of Science, 9,* 356-361.

Bowie, M. (1979). Jacques Lacan. In J. Sturrock (Ed.), *Structuralism and since: From Lévi-Strauss to Derrida* (pp. 116-153). New York: Oxford University Press.

Brady, J. V. (1990). Toward applied behavior analysis of life aloft. *Behavioral Science, 35,* 11-23.

Brady, J. V. (1992). *Continuously programmed environments and the experimental analysis of human behavior.* Cambridge, MA: Cambridge Center for Behavioral Studies.

Brady, J. V., Bigelow, G., Emurian, H. & Williams, D. M. (1974). Design of a programmed environment for the experimental analysis of behavior. In D. H. Carson (Ed.), *Man-environment interactions: Evaluations and applications. 7: Social ecology* (pp. 187-208). Milwaukee: Environmental Design Research Association.

Brady, J. V., & Emurian, H. H. (1979). Behavior analysis of motivational and emotional interactions in a programmed environment. In H. E. Howe (Ed.), *Nebraska Symposium on Motivation, 1978* (Vol. 26, pp. 81-122). Lincoln, Nebraska: University of Nebraska Press.

Branch, M. N. (1977). On the role of "memory" in the analysis of behavior. *Journal of the Experimental Analysis of Behavior, 28,* 171-179.

Breakwell, G. M. (1990). Social beliefs about gender differences. In C. Fraser & G. Gaskell (Eds.), *The social psychology of widespread beliefs* (pp. 210-225). Oxford: Clarendon Press.

Breaugh, J. A., & Klimoski, R. J. (1977). The choice of a group spokesman in bargaining: Member or outsider? *Organizational Behavior and Human Performance, 19,* 325-336.

Breckler, S. J., & Greenwald, A. G. (1986). Motivational facets of the self. In R. M. Sorrentino & E. T. Higgins (Eds.), *Handbook of motivation and cognition: Foundations of social behavior,* (pp. 145-164). New York: Guilford Press.

Breen, C. G., & Haring, T. G. (1991). Effects of contextual competence on social initiations. *Journal of Applied Behavior Analysis, 24,* 337-347.

Brethower, D. M. (1972). *Behavioral analysis in business and industry: A total performance system.* Kalamazoo, MI: Behaviordelia.

Brickner, M. A., Harkins, S. G., & Ostrom, T. M. (1986). Effects of personal involvement: Thought-provoking implications for social loafing. *Journal of Personality and Social Psychology, 51,* 763-769.

Brigham, T. A. (1980). Self-control: Or why doesn't anyone actually read Skinner (1953). *The Behavior Analyst, 3,* 25-33.

Broadbent, D. E., FitzGerald, P., & Broadbent, M. H. P. (1986). Implicit and explicit knowledge in the control of complex systems. *British Journal of Psychology, 77,* 33-50.

Brock, T. C., & Fromkin, H. L. (1968). Cognitive tuning set and behavioral receptivity to discrepant information. *Journal of Personality, 36,* 108-125.

Brown, B. R. (1968). The effects of need to maintain face on interpersonal bargaining. *Journal of Experimental Social Psychology, 4,* 107-122.

Brownell, A., & Shumaker, S. A. (1984). Social support: An introduction to a complex phenomenon. *Journal of Social Issues, 40,* 1-9.

Brownell, K. D., Marlatt, G. A., Lichtenstein, E., & Wilson, G. T. (1986). Understanding and preventing relapse. *American Psychologist, 41,* 765-782.

Brownstein, A. J., & Shull, R. L. (1985). A rule for the use of the term, "Rule-governed behavior". *The Behavior Analyst, 8,* 265-267.

Bruner, J. (1991). The narrative construction of reality. *Critical Inquiry, 18,* 1-21.

Bryant, L. E., & Budd, K. S. (1984). Teaching behaviorally handicapped preschool children to share. *Journal of Applied Behavior Analysis, 17,* 45-56.

Buck, R. (1988). *Human motivation and emotion.* New York: Wiley.

Buell, J., Stoddard, P., Harris, F. R., & Baer, D. M. (1968). Collateral social development accompanying reinforcement of outdoor play in a preschool child. *Journal of Applied Behavior Analysis, 1,* 167-173.

Bullock, D., & Neuringer, A. (1977). Social learning by following: An analysis. *Journal of the Experimental Analysis of Behavior, 25,* 127-135.

Burgio, L. D., & Burgio, K. L. (1986). Behavioral gerontology: Application of behavioral methods to the problems of older adults. *Journal of Applied Behavior Analysis, 19,* 321-328.

Burns, C. E. S., Heiby, E. M., & Tharp, R. G. (1983). A verbal behavior analysis of auditory hallucinations. *The Behavior Analyst, 6,* 133-143.

Burnstein, D. D., & Wolff, P. C. (1964). Shaping of three-man teams on a multiple DRL-DRH schedule using collective reinforcement. *Journal of the Experimental Analysis of Behavior, 7,* 191-197.

Burt, R. S. (1987). Social contagion and innovation: Cohesion versus structural equivalence. *American Journal of Sociology, 92,* 1287-1335.

Buskist, W. F., Barry, A., Morgan, D., & Rossi, M. (1984). Competitive fixed interval performance in humans: Role of "orienting" instructions. *The Psychological Record, 34,* 241-257.

Buskist, W. F., & DeGrandpre, R. J. (1989). The myth of rule-governed behavior. *Experimental Analysis of Human Behavior Bulletin, 7,* 4-6.

Buskist, W. F., & Morgan, D. (1987). Competitive fixed-interval performance in humans. *Journal of the Experimental Analysis of Behavior, 47,* 145-158.

Buskist, W. F., & Morgan, D. (1988). Method and theory in the study of human competition. In G. Davey & C. Cullen (Eds.), *Human operant conditioning and behavior modification* (pp. 167-195). New York: John Wiley.

Buzsaki, G. (1982). The "where is it?" reflex: Autoshaping the orienting response. *Journal of the Experimental Analysis of Behavior, 37,* 461-484.

Cacioppo, J. T., Petty, R. E., & Losch, M. E. (1986). Attributions of responsibility for helping and doing harm: Evidence for confusion of responsibility. *Journal of Personality and Social Psychology, 50,* 100-105.

Campbell, D. T. (1960a). Common fate, similarity and other indices of the status of aggregates of persons as social entities. In D. Willner (Ed.), *Decisions, values and groups* (Vol. 1, pp. 185-201). Oxford: Pergamon Press.

Campbell, D. T. (1960b). Blind variation and selective retention in creative thought as in other knowledge processes. *Psychological Review, 67,* 380-400.

Campbell, K. E. (1990). Networks past: A 1939 Bloomington neighborhood. *Social Forces, 69,* 139-155.

Caplan, N. (1968). Treatment intervention and reciprocal interaction effects. *Journal of Social Issues, 24,* 63-88.

Carlton, P. L. (1983). *A primer of behavioral pharmacology: Concepts and principles in the behavior analysis of drug action.* New York: Freeman.

Carment, D. W., & Hodkin, B. (1973). Coaction and competition in India and Canada. *Journal of Cross-Cultural Psychology, 4,* 459-469.

Carnevale, P. J. D., Pruitt, D. G., & Britton, S. D. (1979). Looking tough: The negotiator under constituent surveillance. *Personality and Social Psychology Bulletin, 5,* 118-121.

Carnevale, P. J. D., Pruitt, D. G., & Seilheimer, S. D. (1981). Looking and competing: Accountability and visual access in integrative bargaining. *Journal of Personality and Social Psychology, 40,* 111-120.

Carr, E. G., & Durand, V. M. (1985). The social-communicative basis of severe behavior problems in children. In S. Reiss & R. R. Bootzin (Eds.), *Theoretical issues in behavior therapy* (pp. 219-254). New York: Academic Press.

Carter, N., Holmstrom, A., Simpanen, M., & Melin, L. (1988). Theft reduction in a grocery store through product identification and graphing of losses for employees. *Journal of Applied Behavior Analysis, 21,* 385-389.

Carver, C. S., & Scheier, M. F. (1981). *Attention and self-regulation: A control-theory approach to human behavior.* New York: Springer-Verlag.

Case, D. A., Fantino, E., & Wixted, J. (1985). Human observing: Maintained by negative information stimuli only if correlated with improvement in response efficiency. *Journal of the Experimental Analysis of Behavior, 43,* 289-300.

Case, D. A., Ploog, B. O., & Fantino, E. (1990). Observing behavior in a computer game. *Journal of the Experimental Analysis of Behavior, 54,* 185-199.

Catania, A. C. (1966). Concurrent operants. In W. K. Honig (Ed.), *Operant behavior: Areas of research and application* (pp. 213-270). Englewood Cliffs, NJ: Prentice Hall.

Catania, A. C. (1969). On the vocabulary and the grammar of behavior. *Journal of the Experimental Analysis of Behavior, 38,* 845-846.

Catania, A. C. (1972). Chomsky's formal analysis of natural languages: A behavioral translation. *Behaviorism, 1,* 1-15.

Catania, A. C. (1973). The concept of the operant in the analysis of behavior. *Behaviorism, 1,* 103-116.

Catania, A. C. (1975). The myth of self-reinforcement. *Behaviorism, 3,* 192-199.

Catania, A. C.(1980). Autoclitic processes and the structure of behavior. *Behaviorism, 8,* 175-186.

Catania, A. C. (1984). *Learning* (2nd Ed.). Englewood Cliffs, NJ: Prentice Hall.

Catania, A. C. (1985). Rule-governed behavior and the origins of language. In C. F. Lowe, M. Richelle, D. E. Blackman, & C. M. Bradshaw (Eds.), *Behavior analysis and contemporary psychology* (pp.135-156). Hillsdale, NJ: Erlbaum.

Catania, A. C. (1986). On the difference between verbal and nonverbal behavior. *The Analysis of Verbal Behavior, 4,* 2-9.

Catania, A. C. & Cerutti, D. T. (1986). Some nonverbal properties of verbal behavior. In In T. Thompson and M. D. Zeiler (Eds.), *Analysis and integration of behavior units* (pp. 185-211). Hillsdale, NJ: Erlbaum.

Catania, A. C., Horne, P., & Lowe, C. F. (1989). Transfer of function across members of an equivalence class. *The Analysis of Verbal Behavior, 7,* 99-110.

Catania, A. C., Matthews, B. A., & Shimoff, E. (1982). Instructed versus shaped human verbal behavior: Interactions with nonverbal responding. *Journal of the Experimental Analysis of Behavior, 38,* 233-248.

Catania, A. C., Matthews, B. A., & Shimoff, E. (1989). Mything the point about rule-governed behavior: A reply to Buskist and DeGrandpre. *Experimental Analysis of Human Behavior Bulletin, 7,* 22-23.

Catania, A. C., Shimoff, E., & Matthews, B. A. (1987). Correspondence between definitions and procedures: A reply to Stokes, Osnes, and Guevremont. *Journal of Applied Behavior Analysis, 20,* 401-404.

Center for Human Information Processing. (1987). Collective memory and remembering. [Special issue]. *The Quarterly Newsletter of the Laboratory of Comparative Human Cognition, 9* (1).

Cerutti, D. T. (1989). Discrimination theory of rule-governed behavior. *Journal of the Experimental Analysis of Behavior, 51,* 259-276.

Cervone, D., & Peake, P. K. (1986). Anchoring, efficacy, and action: The influence of judgmental heuristics on self-efficacy judgments and behavior. *Journal of Personality and Social Psychology, 50,* 492-501.

Chaiken, S. (1980). Heuristic versus systematic information processing and the use of source versus message cues in persuasion. *Journal of Personality and Social Psychology, 39,* 752-766.

Chaiken, S. (1980). Heuristic versus systematic information processing and the use of source versus message cues in persuasion. *Journal of Personality and Social Psychology, 39,* 752-766.

Chang, J. (1991). *Wild swans: Three daughters of China.* London: HarperCollins.

Charters, W. W., & Newcomb, T. M. (1966). Some attitudinal effects of experimentally increased salience of a membership group. In E. E. Maccoby, T. M. Newcomb & E. L. Hartley (Eds.), *Readings in social psychology* (pp. 276-281). London: Methuen.

Chase, P. N. (1988). A problem of history: Assessing and controlling the learning history of sophisticated subjects. *Experimental Analysis of Human Behavior Bulletin, 6,* 3-8.

Chase, P. N., & Hyten, C. (1985). A historical and pedagogic note on establishing operations. *The Behavior Analyst, 8,* 121-122.

Chase, P. N., Johnson, K. R., & Sulzer-Azeroff, B. (1985). Verbal relations within instruction: Are there subclasses of the intraverbal? *Journal of the Experimental Analysis of Behavior, 43,* 301-313.

Chavis, D. M., & NewBrough, J. R. (1986). The meaning of "Community" in community psychology. *Journal of Community Psychology, 14,* 335-340.

Cherek, D. R., Spiga, R., Steinberg, J. L., & Kelly, T. H. (1990). Human aggressive responses maintained by avoidance or escape from point loss. *Journal of the Experimental Analysis of Behavior, 53,* 293-303.

Cherpas, C. (1993). Do establishing operations alter reinforcement effectiveness? *The Behavior Analyst, 16,* 347-349.

Chiesa, M. (1992). Radical behaviorism and scientific frameworks: From mechanistic to relational accounts. *American Psychologist, 47,* 1287-1299.

Chippendale, P. R., & Wilkes, P. V. (1977). *Accountability in education.* St. Lucia: University of Queensland Press.

Chomsky, N. (1959). Review of Skinner's *Verbal behavior. Language, 35,* 26-58.

Cialdini, R. B. (1987). Compliance principles of compliance professionals: Psychologists of necessity. In M. P. Zanna, J. M. Olson & C. P. Herman (Eds.), *Social influence: The Ontario symposium, Volume 5* (pp. 165-184). Hillsdale, NJ: Erlbaum.

Clark, N. K., & Stephenson, G. M. (1989). Group remembering. In P. B. Paulus (Ed.), *Psychology of group influence* (2nd Ed., pp. 357-391). Hillsdale, New Jersey: Erlbaum.

Clark, N. K., Stephenson, G. M., & Rutter, D. R. (1986). Memory for a complex social discourse: The analysis and prediction of individual and group recall. *Journal of Memory and Language, 25,* 295-313.

Coates, J., & Cameron, D. (1988). *Women in their speech communities: New perspectives on language and sex.* New York: Longman.

Cobb, S. (19876). Social support as a moderator of life stress. *Psychosomatic Medicine, 38,* 300-314.

Cohen, A. R. (1961). Cognitive tuning as a factor affecting impression formation. *Journal of Personality, 29,* 235-245.

Cohen, J., Chesnick, E. I., & Haran, D. (1972). A confirmation of the inertial-psi effect in sequential choice and decision. *British Journal of Psychology, 63,* 41-46.

Cohen, N. J., & Squire, L. R. (1980). Preserved learning and retention of pattern-analyzing skill in amnesia: Dissociation of knowing how and knowing that. *Science, 210,* 207-210.

Cohen, S., & Wills, T. A. (1985). Stress, social support, and the buffering hypothesis. *Psychological Bulletin, 98,* 310-357.

Cohen, S., Mermelstein, R., Kamarck, T., & Hoberman, H. M. (1985). Measuring the functional components of social support. In I. G. Sarason & B. R. Sarason (Eds.), *Social support: Theory, research, and applications* (pp. 73-94). Boston: Martinus Nijhoff.

Cohen, Y. A. (1969). Social boundary systems. *Current Anthropology, 10,* 103-126.

Collier, G., Hirsch, E., & Kanarek, R. (1977). The operant revisited. In W. K. Honig and J. E. R. Staddon (Eds.), *Handbook of operant behavior* (pp. 28-52). Englewood Cliffs, NJ: Prentice Hall.

Collier, G. H., Johnson, D. F., CyBulski, K. A., & McHale, C. A. (1990). Activity patterns in rats (*Rattus norvegicus)* as a function of the cost of access to four resources. *Journal of Comparative Psychology, 104,* 53-65.

Collins, B. E., & Hoyt, M. F. (1972). Personal responsibility-for-consequences: An integration and extension of the "forced compliance" literature. *Journal of Experimental Social Psychology, 8,* 558-593.

Colman, A. D., Liebold, K. E., & Boren, J. J. (1969). A method for studying altruism in monkeys. *The Psychological Record, 19,* 401-405.

Commons, M. L., Fantino, E., & Branch, M. N. (Eds.). (1993). The nature of reinforcement [Special issue]. *Journal of the Experimental Analysis of Behavior, 60* (1).

Commons, M. L., Herrnstein, R. J., & Rachlin, H. (Eds.). (1982). *Quantitative analyses of behavior. Volume 2. Matching and maximizing accounts.* Hillsdale, NJ: Erlbaum.

Commons, M. L., Kacelnik, A., & Shettleworth, S. J. (Eds.). (1987). *Quantitative analyses of behavior. Volume 6. Foraging.* Hillsdale, NJ: Erlbaum.

Commons, M. L., Mazur, J. E., Nevin, J. A., & Rachlin, H. (Eds.). (1987). *Quantitative analyses of behavior. Volume 5. The effects of delay and intervening events on reinforcement value.* Hillsdale, NJ: Erlbaum.

Condor, S. (1986). Sex role beliefs and "traditional" women: Feminist and intergroup perspectives. In S. Wilkinson (Ed.), *Feminist social psychology: Developing theory and practice* (pp. 97-118). Milton Keynes, England: Open University Press.

Cone, J. D., & Hayes, S. C. (1980). *Environmental problems: Behavioral solutions.* Monterey, CA: Brooks/Cole.

Connerton, P. (1989). *How societies remember.* New York: Cambridge University Press.

Conolley, E. S., Gerard, H. B., & Kline, T. (1978). Competitive behavior: A manifestation of motivation for ability comparison. *Journal of Experimental Social Psychology, 14,* 123-131.

Cook, T. D., & Flay, B. (1978). The temporal persistence of experimentally induced attitude change: An evaluative review. In L. Berkowitz (Ed.), *Advances in experimental social psychology* (Vol. 11, pp. 1-57). New York: Academic Press.

Cook, T. D., Kendzierski, D. A., & Thomas, S. V. (1983). The implicit assumptions of television research: An analysis of the 1982 NIMH Report on *Television and behavior. Public Opinion Quarterly, 47*, 161-201.

Cooley, C H. (1909). *Social organization.* New York: Charles Scribner's Sons.

Cooper, J. (1971). Personal responsibility and dissonance: The role of foreseen consequences. *Journal of Personality and Social Psychology, 18*, 354-363.

Cooper, J., & Worchel, S. (1970). Role of undesired consequences in arousing cognitive dissonance. *Journal of Personality and Social Psychology, 16*, 199-206.

Cooper, J. O., Heron, T. E., & Heward, W. L. (1987). *Applied behavior analysis.* Columbus, Ohio: Merrill.

Cooper, R. L. (1984). The avoidance of androcentric generics. *International Journal of the Sociology of Language, 50*, 5-20.

Costall, A. P. (1984). Are theories of perception necessary? *Journal of the Experimental Analysis of Behavior, 41*, 109-115.

Cottrell, N. B. (1972). Social facilitation. In C. G. McClintock (Ed.), *Experimental social psychology* (pp. 185-236). New York: Holt, Rinehart & Winston.

Coupland, N. (1984). Accommodation at work: Some phonological data and their implications. *International Journal of the Sociology of Language, 46*, 49-70.

Coupland, N., Giles, H., & Wiemann, J. M. (Eds.). (1991). *"Miscommunication" and problematic talk.* London: Sage.

Coyle, C. (1987). Public administration and the theory of accountability. *Administration, 35*, 107-116.

Crano, W. D. (1991). Pitfalls associated with the use of financial incentives (and other complex manipulations) in human social research. *Basic and Applied Social Psychology, 12*, 369-390.

Crawford, M., & Gentry, M. (Eds.). (1989). *Gender and thought: Psychological perspectives.* New York: Springer-Verlag.

Crawford, M., & Marecek, J. (1989). Feminist theory, feminist psychology: A bibliography of epistemology, critical analysis, and applications. *Psychology of Women Quarterly, 13*, 477-491.

Critchfield, T. S. (1993). Signal-detection properties of verbal self-reports. *Journal of the Experimental Analysis of Behavior, 60*, 495-514.

Critchfield, T. S., & Perone, M. (1990). Verbal self-reports of delayed matching to sample by humans. *Journal of the Experimental Analysis of Behavior, 53*, 321-344.

Critchfield, T. S., & Perone, M. (in press). Verbal self-reports about matching-to-sample: Effects of the number of elements in a compound sample stimulus. *Journal of the Experimental Analysis of Behavior, 59*, 193-214.

Crocker, J., Fiske, S. T., & Taylor, S. E. (1984). Schematic bases of belief change. In R. J. Eiser (Ed.), *Attitudinal judgment* (pp. 197-226). New York: Springer-Verlag.

Croll, W. L. (1974). Some limitations on the Premack principle. *Bulletin of the Psychonomic Society, 3*, 375-376.

Crosbie, J. (1990). The effects of punishment on unpunished behaviour. *Behaviour Change, 7*, 25-34.

Crosbie, J. (1991). The effects of punishment on unpunished reinforced free-operant responses. *Australian Journal of Psychology, 43*, 1-5.

Crosbie, J. (1993). The effects of response cost and response restriction on a multiple-response repertoire with humans. *Journal of the Experimental Analysis of Behavior, 59*, 173-192.

Crowell, C. R., Anderson, D. C., Abel, D. M., & Sergio, J. P (1988). Task clarification, performance feedback, and social praise: Procedures for improving the customer service of bank tellers. *Journal of Applied Behavior Analysis, 21,* 65-71.

Culler, J. (1976). *Saussure.* Glasgow: Fontana.

Cushman, P. (1990). Why the self is empty: Toward a historically situated psychology. *American Psychologist, 45,* 599-611.

Cvetkovich, G. (1978). Cognitive accommodation, language and social responsibility. *Social Psychology, 41,* 149-155.

Dake, K. (1992). Myths of nature: Culture and the social construction of risk. *Journal of Social Issues, 48* (4), 21-37.

Dalton, G. (1965). Primitive money. *American Anthropologist, 67,* 44-62.

Damasio, A. R., & Damasio, H. (1992, September). Brain and language. *Scientific American 267,* 63-71.

Daniel, W. J. (1942). Cooperative problem solving in rats. *Journal of Comparative Psychology, 34,* 361-369.

Daniel, W. J. (1943). Higher order cooperative problem solving in rats. *Journal of Comparative and Physiological Psychology, 35,* 297-305.

Daniels, L. R., & Berkowitz, L. (1963). Liking and response to dependency relationships. *Human Relations, 16,* 141-148.

Danson, C., & Creed, T. (1970). Rate of response as a visual stimulus. *Journal of the Experimental Analysis of Behavior, 13,* 233-242.

Darcheville, J. C., Riviére, V., & Weardon, J. H. (1992). Fixed-interval performance and self-control in children. *Journal of the Experimental Analysis of Behavior, 57,* 187-199.

Darley, J. M., & Berscheid, E. (1967). Increased liking as a result of the anticipation of personal contact. *Human Relations, 20,* 29-40.

Darley, J. M., & Latané, B. (1968). Bystander intervention in emergencies. *Journal of Personality and Social Psychology, 8,* 377-383.

Dattilo, J., & Camarata, S. (1991). Facilitating conversation through self-initiated augmentative communication treatment. *Journal of Applied Behavior Analysis, 24,* 369-378.

Davey, G. (1981). *Animal learning and conditioning.* London: Macmillan.

Davis, H. L., Hoch, S. J., & Ragsdale, E. K. E. (1986). An anchoring and adjustment model of spousal predictions. *Journal of Consumer Research, 13,* 25-37.

Davis, H., Hubbard, J., & Reberg, D. (1973). A methodological critique of research on "superstitious" behavior. *Bulletin of the Psychonomic Society, 1,* 447-449.

Davis, J. H., Stasser, G., Spitzer, C. E., & Holt, R. W. (1976). Changes in group members' decisions preferences during discussion: An illustration with mock juries. *Journal of Personality and Social Psychology, 34,* 1177-1187.

Davison, M., & McCarthy, D. C. (1987). The interaction of stimulus and reinforcer control in complex temporal discrimination. *Journal of the Experimental Analysis of Behavior, 48,* 97-116.

Davison, M., & McCarthy, D. C. (1988). *The matching law: A research review.* Hillsdale, NJ: Erlbaum.

Davison, M., & Tustin, R. D. (1978). The relation between the generalized matching law and signal-detection theory. *Journal of the Experimental Analysis of Behavior, 29,* 331-336.

Dawes, R. M. (1980). Social dilemmas. *Annual Review of Psychology, 31,* 169-193.

Day, W. F. (1969). On certain similarities between the *Philosophical Investigations* of Ludwig Wittgenstein and the operationism of B. F. Skinner. *Journal of the Experimental Analysis of Behavior, 12,* 489-506.

Day, W. F. (1977). On the behavioral analysis of self-deception and self-development. In T. Mischel (Ed.), *The self: Psychological and philosophical issues* (pp. 224-249). Oxford: Basil Blackwell.

Day, W. F. (1976). Analyzing verbal behavior under the control of private events. *Behaviorism, 4,* 195-200.

Deacon, J. R., & Konarski, E. A. (1987). Correspondence training: An example of rule-governed behavior? *Journal of Applied Behavior Analysis, 20,* 391-400.

Deaux, K., & Lewis, L. L. (1984). Structure of gender stereotypes: Interrelationships among components and gender label. *Journal of Personality and Social Psychology, 46,* 991-1004.

Deci, E. L. (1975). Notes on the theory and metatheory of intrinsic motivation. *Organizational Behavior and Human Performance, 15,* 130-145.

Deci, E. L., & Ryan, R. M. (1980). The empirical exploration of intrinsic motivational processes. In L. Berkowitz (Ed.), *Advances in experimental social psychology* (Vol. 13, pp. 39-80). New York: Academic Press.

DeGrandpre, R. J., Bickel, W. K., & Higgins, S. T. (1992). Emergent equivalence relations between interoceptive (drug) and exteroceptive (visual) stimuli. *Journal of the Experimental Analysis of Behavior, 58,* 9-18.

DeGrandpre, R. J., & Buskist, W. (1991). Culture, contingencies, and conservation. *The Psychological Record, 41,* 507-522.

Deguchi, H. (1984). Observational learning from a radical-behavioristic viewpoint. *The Behavior Analyst, 7,* 83-95.

Deguchi, H., Fujita, T., & Sato, M. (1988). Reinforcement control of observational learning in young children: A behavioral analysis of modeling. *Journal of Experimental Child Psychology, 46,* 362-371.

Deitz, S. M., & Malone, L. W. (1985). Stimulus control terminology. *The Behavior Analyst, 8,* 259-264.

Deleuze, G., & Guattari, F. (1981). Rhizome. *I & C, 8,* 49-71.

Delprato, D. J. (1986). Response patterns. In H. W. Reese and L. J. Parrott (Eds.), *Behavior science: Philosophical, methodological, and empirical advances* (pp.61-113). Hillsdale, NJ: Erlbaum.

Delprato, D. J., & Midgley, B. D. (1992). Some fundamentals of B. F. Skinner's behaviorism. *American Psychologist, 47,* 1507-1520.

DePaulo, B. M., & Coleman, L. M. (1986). Talking to children, foreigners, and retarded adults. *Journal of Personality and Social Psychology, 51,* 945-959.

Deterline, W. A. (1971). Applied accountability. *Educational Technology, 11,* 15-20.

Deutsch, M., & Gerard, H. B. (1955). A study of normative and informational influences upon individual judgment. *Journal of Abnormal and Social Psychology, 51,* 629-636.

Devany, J. M., Hayes, S. C., & Nelson, R. O. (1986). Equivalence class formation in language-able and language-disabled children. *Journal of the Experimental Analysis of Behavior, 46,* 243-257.

Dickinson, A. M. (1988). The detrimental effects of extrinsic reinforcement on "intrinsic motivation". *The Behavior Analyst, 12,* 1-15.

Dickinson, A. M., & Poling, A. D. (1994). Schedules of monetary reinforcement in organizational behavior management: Latham and Huber (1992) revisited. Journal of Organizational Behavior Management, 14.

DiClemente, C. C., Prochaska, J. O., Fairhurst, S. K., Velicer, W. F., Velasquez, M. M., & Rossi, J. S. (1991). The process of smoking cessation: An analysis of precontemplation,

contemplation, and preparation stages of change. *Journal of Consulting and Clinical Psychology, 59,* 295-304.

Diener, E. (1976). Effects of prior destructive behavior, anonymity, and group presence on deindividuation and aggression. *Journal of Personality and Social Psychology, 33,* 497-507.

Diener, E. (1979). Deindividuation, self-awareness, and disinhibition. *Journal of Personality and Social Psychology, 37,* 1160-1171.

Diener, E. (1980). Deindividuation: The absence of self-awareness and self-regulation in group members. In P. B. Paulus (Ed.), *Psychology of group influence* (pp.209-242). Hillsdale, NJ: Erlbaum.

Diener, E., Dineen, J., Endresen, K., Beaman, A. L., & Fraser, S. C. (1975). Effects of altered responsibility, cognitive set, and modeling on physical aggression and deindividuation. *Journal of Personality and Social Psychology, 31,* 328-337.

Diener, E., Fraser, S. C., Beaman, A. L., & Kelem, R. T. (1976). Effects of deindividuation variables on stealing among Hallowe'en trick-or-treaters. *Journal of Personality and Social Psychology, 33,* 178-183.

Diener, E., Westford, K. L., Diener, C., & Beaman, A. L. (1973). Deindividuating effects of group presence and arousal on stealing by Hallowe'en trick-or-treaters. *Proceedings of the 81st Annual Convention of the American Psychological Association, 8,* 219-220.

Diener, E., Westford, K.L., Dineen, J., & Fraser, S.C. (1973). Beat the pacifist: The deindividuating effects of anonymity and group presence. *Proceedings of the 81st Annual Convention of the American Psychological Association, 8,* 221-222.

Dinsmoor, J. A. (1985). The role of observing and attention in establishing stimulus control. *Journal of the Experimental Analysis of Behavior, 43,* 365-381.

Doms, M., & Van Avermaet, E. (1985). Social support and minority influence: The innovation effect reconsidered. In S. Moscovici, G. Mugny, & E. Van Avermaet (Eds.), *Perspectives on minority influence* (pp. 53-74). New York: Cambridge University Press.

Donahoe, J. W., & Palmer, D. C. (1989). The interpretation of complex human behavior: Some reactions to *Parallel Distributed Processing,* edited by J. L. McClelland, D. E. Rumelhart, and the PDP Research Group. *Journal of the Experimental Analysis of Behavior, 51,* 399-416.

Donnerstein, E. & Donnerstein, M. (1973). Variables in interracial aggression: Potential ingroup censure. *Journal of Personality and Social Psychology, 27,* 143-150.

Donnerstein, E., Donnerstein, M., Simon, S., & Ditrichs, R. (1972). Variables in interracial aggression: Anonymity, expected retaliation, and a riot. *Journal of Personality and Social Psychology, 22,* 236-245.

Donovan, R. J., & Owen, N. (1993). Social marketing and mass intervention. In R. K. Dishman (Ed.), *Exercise adherence: Its impact on public health* (2nd Ed.). Champaign, IL: Human Kinetics.

Doob, A. N., & Macdonald, G. E. (1979). Television viewing and fear of victimization: Is the relationship causal? *Journal of Personality and Social Psychology, 37,* 170-179.

Dougher, M. J. (1993). Introduction to Special Section on clinical behavior analysis. *The Behavior Analyst, 16,* 269-270.

Douglas, M. (1966). *Purity and danger.* New York: Praeger.

Douglas, M. (1980). *Evans-Pritchard.* London: Fontana.

Dovidio, J. F. (1984). Helping behavior and altruism: An empirical and conceptual overview. In L. Berkowitz (Ed.), *Advances in experimental social psychology,* (Vol. 17, pp. 361-427). New York: Academic Press.

Downing, N. E., & Roush, K. L. (1985). From passive acceptance to active commitment: A model of feminist identity development for women. *The Counseling Psychologist, 13,* 695-709.

Dugdale, N., & Lowe, C. F. (1990). Naming and stimulus equivalence. In D. E. Blackman & H. Lejeune (Eds.), *Behaviour analysis in theory and practice* (pp. 115-138). Hillsdale, NJ: Erlbaum.

Dulany, D. E. (1991). Conscious representation and thought systems. In R. S. Wyer & T. K. Srull (Eds.), *Advances in social cognition* (Vol. 4, pp. 97-120). Hillsdale, NJ: Erlbaum.

Duncan, B. L. (1976). Differential social perception and attribution of intergroup violence: Testing the lower limits of stereotyping of blacks. *Journal of Personality and Social Psychology, 34,* 590-598.

Dunham, P. J. (1977). The nature of reinforcing stimuli. In W. K. Honig and J. E. R. Staddon (Eds.), *Handbook of operant behavior* (pp.98-124). Englewood Cliffs, NJ: Prentice Hall.

Dunham, P. J., & Grantmyre, J. (1982). Changes in a multiple-response repertoire during response-contingent punishment and response restriction. *Journal of the Experimental Analysis of Behavior, 37,* 123-133.

Durand, V. M., & Carr, E. G. (1991). Functional communication training to reduce challenging behavior: Maintenance and application to new settings. *Journal of Applied Behavior Analysis, 24,* 251-264.

Durkheim, E. (1915/1912). *The elementary forms of religious life: A study in religious sociology.* New York: Macmillan.

Durkheim, E. (1933/1893). *The division of labour in society.* New York: Macmillan.

Durkheim, E. (1951/1897). *Suicide: A study in sociology.* Glencoe: Free Press.

Duveen, G., & Lloyd, B. (1990). *Social representations and the development of knowledge.* Cambridge: Cambridge University Press.

Dwyer, W. O., Leeming, F. C., Cobern, M. K., Porter, B. E., & Jackson, J. M. (1993). Critical review of behavioral interventions to preserve the environment: Research since 1980. *Environment and Behavior, 25,* 275-321.

Eagly, A., & Mladinic, A. (1989). Gender stereotypes and attitudes towards women and men. *Personality and Social Psychology Bulletin, 15,* 543-558.

Echabe, A. E., & Rovira, D. P. (1989). Social representations and memory: The case of AIDS. *European Journal of Social Psychology, 19,* 543-551.

Eckert, P., & McConnell-Ginet, S. (1992). Think practically and look locally: Language and gender as community-based practice. *Annual Review of Anthropology, 21,* 461-490.

Edelstein, B. A. (1989). Generalization: Terminological, methodological and conceptual issues. *Behavior Therapy, 20,* 311-324.

Edwards, K. A. (1991). Behavioral analysis of clinical practice in the United States. In P. A. Lamal (Ed.), *Behavioral analysis of societies and cultural practices* (pp. 165-179). New York: Hemisphere Publishing.

Edwards, W. (1962). Dynamic decision theory and probabilistic information processing. *Human Factors, 4,* 59-73.

Egerman, K. (1966). Effects of team arrangement on team performance: A learning theoretic analysis. *Journal of Personality and Social Psychology, 3,* 541-550.

Eifert, G. H. (1987). Language conditioning: Clinical issues and applications in behavior therapy. In H. J. Eysenck and I. Martin (Eds.), *Theoretical foundations of behavior therapy* (pp. 167-193). New York: Plenum Press.

Eikenberry, K. O. (1985). Government tort litigation and the balance of power. *Public Administration Review, 45,* 742-745.

Einhorn, H. J. (1980). Learning from experience and suboptimal rules in decision making. In T. Wallsten (Ed.), *Cognitive processes in choice and decision making* (pp. 1-20). Hillsdale, NJ: Erlbaum.

Einhorn, H. J., & Hogarth, R. M. (1985). Ambiguity and uncertainty in probabilistic inference. *Psychological Review, 92,* 433-461.

Einzig, P. (1949). *Primitive money in its ethnological, historical and economic aspects.* London: Eyre and Spottiswoode.

Eisenberger, R. (1972). Explanation of rewards that do not reduce tissue needs. *Psychological Bulletin, 77,* 319-339.

Eisenberger, R. (1989). Can response force be shaped by reinforcement? *Perceptual and Motor Skills, 68,* 725-726.

Eisenberger, R., Karpman, M., & Trattner, J. (1967). What is the necessary and sufficient condition for reinforcement in the contingency situation? *Journal of Experimental Psychology, 74,* 342-350.

Eiser, J. R., Taylor, S. J. (1972). Favouritism as a function of assumed similarity and anticipated interaction. *European Journal of Social Psychology, 2,* 453-454.

Eiser, J. R., & van der Pligt, J. (1984). Attitudes in a social context. In H. Tajfel (Ed.), *The social dimension: European developments in social psychology* (Vol. 2, pp. 363-378). Cambridge: Cambridge University Press.

Elkine, D. (1927). De l'influence du groupe sur les fonctions de la mémoire. *Journal de Psychologie Normal et Pathologique, 24,* 827-830.

Elling, R. C. (1985). Bureaucratic accountability: Problems and paradoxes; panaceas and (occasionally) palliatives. *Public Administration Review, 45,* 82-89.

Elliott, B. (1989). *Effective road safety campaigns: A practical handbook* (Report CR80). Adelaide, South Australia: South Australian Department of Transport.

Ellis, J. (1987). Feminist forum. *Behavior Analysis and Social Action, 6,* 28.

Ellis, J. (1991). Contingencies and metacontingencies in correctional settings. In P. A. Lamal (Ed.), *Behavioral analysis of societies and cultural practices* (pp. 210-217). New York: Hemisphere Publishing.

Emurian, H. H., Brady, J. V., Meyerhoff, J. L., & Mougey, E. H. (1981). Behavioral and biological interactions with confined microsocieties in a programmed environment. In J. Grey & L. A. Hamden (Eds.), *Space manufacturing* (Vol. 4, pp. 407-421). New York: American Institute of Aeronautics and Astronautics.

Emurian, H. H., Brady, J. V., Meyerhoff, J. L., & Mougey, E. H. (1983). Small groups in programmed environments. *Pavlovian Journal of Biological Sciences, 18,* 199-210.

Emurian, H. H., Emurian, C. S., Bigelow, G. E., & Brady, J. V. (1976). The effects of a cooperative contingency on behavior in a continuous three-person environment. *Journal of the Experimental Analysis of Behavior, 25,* 293-302.

Emurian, H. H., Emurian, C. S., & Brady, J. V. (1978). Effects of a pairing contingency on behavior in a three-person programmed environment. *Journal of the Experimental Analysis of Behavior, 29,* 319-329.

Emurian, H. H., Emurian, C. S., & Brady, J. V. (1982). Appetitive and aversive reinforcement schedule effects on behavior: A systematic replication. *Basic and Applied Social Psychology, 3,* 39-52.

Emurian, H. H., Emurian, C. S., & Brady, J. V. (1985). Positive and negative reinforcement effects on behavior in a three-person microsociety. *Journal of the Experimental Analysis of Behavior, 44,* 157-174.

Engelstad, P. H., & Gustavsen, B. (1993). Swedish network development for implementing national work reform strategy. *Human Relations, 46,* 219-231.

England, G. (1982). Efficiency audit and public sector enterprise: Problems and options. *Policy Studies, 2,* 142-151.

Epstein, A. L. (1969). Gossip, norms and social network. In J. C. Mitchell (Ed.), *Social networks in urban situations: Analyses of personal relationships in Central African towns.* Manchester: Manchester University Press.

Epstein, R. (1984a). Spontaneous and deferred imitation in the pigeon. *Behavioural Processes, 9,* 347-354.

Epstein, R. (1984b). An effect of immediate reinforcement and delayed punishment, with possible implications for self-control. *Journal of Behavior Therapy and Experimental Psychiatry, 15,* 291-298.

Epstein, R. (1985a). Extinction-induced resurgence: Preliminary investigations and possible applications. *The Psychological Record, 35,* 143-153.

Epstein, R. (1985b). The spontaneous interconnection of three repertoires. *The Psychological Record, 35,* 131-141.

Epstein, R. (1987). The spontaneous interconnection of four repertoires of behavior in a pigeon (*Columbia livia*). *Journal of Comparative Psychology, 101,* 197-201.

Epstein, R. (1991). Skinner, creativity, and the problem of spontaneous behavior. *Psychological Science, 2,* 362-370.

Epstein, R., & Skinner, B. F. (1980). Resurgence of responding after the cessation of response-independent reinforcement. *Proceedings of the National Academy of Sciences, 77,* 6251-6253.

Erber, R., & Fiske, S. T. (1984). Outcome dependency and attention to inconsistent information. *Journal of Personality and Social Psychology, 47,* 709-726.

Erickson, B. H. (1981). Secret societies and social structure. *Social Forces, 60,* 188-210.

Erickson, B. H. (1982). Networks, ideologies, and belief systems. In P. V. Marsden & N. Lin (Eds.), *Social structure and network analysis* (pp. 159-172). London: Sage.

Erickson, M. H. (1980). *Innovative hypnotherapy.* New York: Irvington Publishers.

Erickson, M. H., Rossi, E. L., & Rossi, S. I. (1976). *Hypnotic realities: The induction of clinical hypnosis and forms of indirect suggestion.* New York: Irvington.

Ericsson, K. A., & Simon, H. A. (1984). *Protocol analysis: Verbal reports as data.* Cambridge, MA: MIT Press.

Espinosa, J. M. (1992). Probability and radical behaviorism. *The Behavior Analyst, 15,* 51-60.

Eubanks, J. L., & Lloyd, K. E. (1992). Relating behavior analysis to the organizational culture concept and perspective. *Journal of Organizational Behavior Management, 12,* 27-44.

Evans, G. (1964). Effect of unilateral promise and value of rewards upon cooperation and trust. *Journal of Abnormal and Social Psychology, 69,* 587-590.

Evans, I. M., & Meyer, L. M. (1985). *An educative approach to behavior problems.* London: Paul H. Brookes.

Evans, I. M., Meyer, L. M., Kurkjian, J. A., & Kushi, G. S. (1988). An evaluation of behavioral interrelationships in child behavior therapy. In J. C. Witt, S. N. Elliott, & F. M. Gresham (Eds.), *Handbook of behavior therapy in education* (pp. 189-215). New York: Plenum Press.

Evans-Pritchard, E. E. (1940). *The Nuer.* Oxford: Oxford University Press.

Evans-Pritchard, E. E. (1951). *Kinship and marriage among the Nuer.* Oxford: Oxford University Press.

Evans-Pritchard, E. E. (1976). *Witchcraft, oracles, and magic among the Azande.* Oxford: Clarendon Press.

Falk, J. L. (1958). The grooming behavior of the chimpanzee as a reinforcer. *Journal of the Experimental Analysis of Behavior, 1,* 83-85.

Falk, J. L. (1969). Conditions producing psychogenic polydipsia in animals. *Annals of the New York Academy of Science, 157,* 569-593.

Falk, J. L (1977). The origin and functions of adjunctive behavior. *Animal Learning and Behavior, 5,* 325-335.

Fantino, E., & Logan, C. A. (1979). *The experimental analysis of behavior: A biological perspective.* San Francisco: W.H. Freeman.

Farr, R. M., & Moscovici, S. (Eds.). (1984). *Social representations.* Cambridge: Cambridge University Press.

Farber, I. E. (1963). The things people say to themselves. *American Psychologist, 18,* 185-197.

Fawcett, S. B. (1991). Some values guiding community research. *Journal of Applied Behavior Analysis, 24,* 621-636.

Fawcett, S. B., Bernstein, G. S., Czyzewski, M. J., Greene, B. F., Hannah, G. T., Iwata, B. A., Jason, L. A., Mathews, R. M., Morris, E. K., Otis-Wilborn, A., Seekins, T., & Winett, R. A. (1988). Behavior analysis and public policy. *The Behavior Analyst, 11,* 11-25.

Fawcett, S. B., Mathews, R. M., & Fletcher, R. K. (1980). Some promising dimensions for behavioral community technology. *Journal of Applied Behavior Analysis, 13,* 505-518.

Fawcett, S. B., White, G. W., Balcazar, F. E., Suarez-Balcazar, Y., Mathews, R. M., Paine, A. L., Seekins, T., & Smith, J. F. (in press). A contextual-behavioral model of empowerment: Case studies with people with physical disabilities. *American Journal of Community Psychology.*

Fazio, R. H., & Zanna, M. P. (1981). Direct experience and attitude-behavior consistency. In L. Berkowitz (Ed.), *Advances in experimental social psychology* (Vol. 14, pp. 161-202). New York: Academic Press.

Feallock, R., & Miller, L. K. (1976). The design and evaluation of a worksharing system for experimental group living. *Journal of Applied Behavior Analysis, 9,* 277-288.

Feil, D. K. (1987). *The evolution of Highland Papua New Guinea societies.* Cambridge: Cambridge University Press.

Feingold, B. D., & Mahoney, M. J. (1975). Reinforcement effects on intrinsic interest: Undermining the overjustification effect. *Behavior Therapy, 6,* 367-377.

Fellner, D. J., & Sulzer-Azeroff, B. (1984). A behavioral analysis of goal setting. *Journal of Organizational Behavior Management, 6,* 33-51.

Felner, R. D., Ginter, M., & Primavera, J. (1982). Primary prevention during school transitions: Social support and environmental structure. *American Journal of Community Psychology, 10,* 277-290.

Felton, B. J., & Shinn, M. (1992). Social integration and social support: Moving "Social support" beyond the individual level. *Journal of Community Psychology, 20,* 103-115.

Fentress, J., & Wickham, C. (1992). *Social memory.* Oxford: Basil Blackwell.

Ferster, C. B. (1958). Reinforcement and punishment in the control of human behavior by social agencies. *Psychiatric Research Reports,* December, 101-118.

Ferster, C. B. (1967). Arbitrary and natural reinforcement. *The Psychological Record, 17,* 341-347.

Ferster, C. B., & Perrott, M. C. (1968). *Behavior principles.* New York: Appleton-Century-Crofts.

Ferster, C. B., & Skinner, B. F. (1957). *Schedules of reinforcement.* New York: Appleton-Century-Crofts.

Ferster, C.B., Hammer, C., & Randolph, J. (1968). An experimental space combining individual and social performances. *Journal of the Experimental Analysis of Behavior, 11,* 209-220.

Festinger, L. (1954). A theory of social comparison processes. *Human Relations, 7,* 117-140.

Festinger, L., Schachter, S., & Back, K. (1950). *Social pressures in informal groups: A study of human factors in housing.* New York: Harper.

Field, T. M., Woodson, R., Greenberg, R., & Cohen, D. (1982). Discrimination and imitation of facial expressions by neonates. *Science, 218,* 179-181.

Fielding, J. E. (1984). Health promotion and disease prevention at the worksite. *Annual Review of Public Health, 5,* 237-265.

Findley, J. D. (1958). Preference and switching under concurrent scheduling. *Journal of the Experimental Analysis of Behavior, 1,* 123-144.

Findley, J. D. (1962). An experimental outline for building and exploring multi-operant behavior repertoires. *Journal of the Experimental Analysis of Behavior, 5,* 113-166.

Findley, J. D. (1966). Programmed environments for the experimental analysis of behavior. In W. K. Honig (Ed.), *Operant behavior: Areas of research and application* (pp.827-848). Englewood Cliffs, NJ: Prentice Hall.

Findley, J. D., & Brady, J. V. (1965). Facilitation of large ratio performance by use of conditioned reinforcement. *Journal of the Experimental Analysis of Behavior, 8,* 125-129.

Fine, G. A., & Kleinman, S. (1979). Rethinking subculture: An interactionalist analysis. *American Journal of Sociology, 85,* 1-20.

Firth, R. (1956). Rumor in a primitive society. *Journal of Abnormal and Social Psychology, 53,* 122-132.

Fischhoff, B., Lichtenstein, S., Slovic, P., Derby, S. L., & Keeney, R. L. (1981). *Acceptable risk.* Cambridge: Cambridge University Press.

Fishbein, M. & Ajzen, I. (1975). *Belief, attitude, intention, and behavior: An introduction to theory and research.* Reading, MA: Addison-Wesley.

Fisher, G. A., & Chon, K-K. (1989). Durkheim and the social construction of emotions. *Social Psychology Quarterly, 52,* 1-9.

Flanders, J. P. (1968). A review of research on imitative behavior. *Psychological Bulletin, 69,* 316-337.

Flay, B. R. (1987). Mass media and smoking cessation: A critical review. *American Journal of Public Health, 77,* 153-160.

Fleishman, J. A. (1980). Collective action as helping behavior: Effects of responsibility diffusion on contributions to a public good. *Journal of Personality and Social Psychology, 38,* 629-637.

Fleming, J. H., Darley, J. M., Hilton, J. L., & Kojetin, B. A. (1990). Multiple audience problem: A strategic communication perspective on social perception. *Journal of Personality and Social Psychology, 58,* 593-609.

Flora, J. A., Maibach, E. W., & Maccoby, N. (1989). The role of media across four levels of health promotion intervention. *Annual Review of Public Health, 10,* 181-201.

Flora, S. R. (1990). Undermining intrinsic interest from the standpoint of a behaviorist. *The Psychological Record, 40,* 323-346.

Flora, S. R., & Pavlik, W. B. (1992). Human self-control and the density of reinforcement. *Journal of the Experimental Analysis of Behavior, 57,* 201-208.

Foltin, R. W., Fischman, M. W., Brady, J. V., Bernstein, D. J., Capriotti, R. M., Nellis, M. J., & Kelly, T. H. (1990). Motivational effects of smoked marijuana: Behavioral contingencies and low-probability activities. *Journal of the Experimental Analysis of Behavior, 53,* 5-19.

Ford, J. K. & Weldon, E. (1981). Forewarning and accountability: Effects on memory-based interpersonal judgments. *Personality and Social Psychology Bulletin, 7,* 264-268.

Forehand, R. (1977). Child compliance to parental requests: Behavior analysis. In M. Hersen, R. M. Eisler & P. M. Miller (Eds.), *Progress in behavior modification* (Vol. 5, pp. 111-147). New York: Academic Press.

Foucault, M. (1985). *The uses of pleasure.* Harmondsworth, Middlesex: Penguin.

Foucault, M. (1988). Technologies of the self. In L.H. Martin, H.Gutman, & P.H.Hutton (Eds.), *Technologies of the self* (pp.16-49). London: Tavistock Publications.

Fowler, S. A., & Baer, D. M. (1981). "Do I have to be good all day?" The timing of delayed reinforcement as a factor in generalization. *Journal of Applied Behavior Analysis, 14,* 13-24.

Fox, J., & Guyer, M. (1978). "Public" choice and cooperation in n-person Prisoner's Dilemma. *Journal of Conflict Resolution, 22,* 469-481.

Fox, R. (1967) *Kinship and marriage.* Harmondsworth: Penguin.

Foxx, R. M., & Azrin, N. H. (1973). The elimination of autistic self-stimulatory behavior by overcorrection. *Journal of Applied Behavior Analysis, 6,* 1-14.

Foxx, R. M., & Shapiro, S. T. (1978). The timeout ribbon: A nonseclusionary timeout procedure. *Journal of Applied Behavior Analysis, 11,* 125-136.

Fraley, L. E. (1984). Belief, its inconsistency, and the implications for the teaching faculty. *The Behavior Analyst, 7,* 17-28.

Fraser, C., & Foster, D. (1984). Social groups, nonsense groups and group polarization. In H. Tajfel (Ed.), *The social dimension: European developments in social psychology* (Vol. 2, pp. 473-497). Cambridge: Cambridge University Press.

Fraser, C., & Gaskell, G. (Eds.). (1990). *The social psychological study of widespread beliefs.* Oxford: Oxford Science Publications.

Frazer, E., & Cameron, D. (1989). Knowing what to say: The construction of gender in linguistic practice. In R. Grillo (Ed.), *Social anthropology and the politics of language* (pp. 25-40). London: Routledge.

Frazier, T. W., & Bitetto, V. E. (1969). Control of human vigilance by concurrent schedules. *Journal of the Experimental Analysis of Behavior, 12,* 591-600.

Frederiksen, L. W. (Ed.). (1982). *Handbook of organizational behavior management.* New York: Wiley.

Frederiksen, L. W. & Peterson, G. L. (1974). Schedule-induced aggression in nursery school children. *The Psychological Record, 24,* 343-351.

Frey, D. (1981). Reversible and irreversible decisions: Preference for consonant information as a function of attractiveness of decision alternatives. *Personality and Social Psychology Bulletin, 7,* 621-626.

Frey, D., Kumpf, M., Irle, M., & Gniech, G. (1984). Re-evaluation of decision alternatives dependent upon the reversibility of the decision and the passage of time. *European Journal of Social Psychology, 14,* 447-450.

Frey, D., & Rosch, M. (1984). Information seeking after decisions: The roles of novelty of information and decision reversibility. *Personality and Social Psychology Bulletin, 10,* 91-98.

Frey, R. L., & Adams, J. S. (1972). The negotiator's dilemma: Simultaneous in-group and out-group conflict. *Journal of Experimental Social Psychology, 8,* 331-346.

Friedman, J. (1974). Marxism, structuralism and vulgar materialism. *Man* (N.S), *9,* 444-469.

Friedman, M. P., Carterette, E. C., & Anderson, N. H. (1968). Long-term probability learning with a random schedule of reinforcement. *Journal of Experimental Psychology, 78*, 442-455.

Furnham, A., & Bochner, S. (1986). *Culture shock: Psychological reactions to unfamiliar environments.* London: Methuen.

Fushimi, T. (1990). A functional analysis of another individual's behavior as discriminative stimulus for a monkey. *Journal of the Experimental Analysis of Behavior, 53*, 285-291.

Galbicka, G. (1988). Differentiating *The behavior of organisms. Journal of the Experimental Analysis of Behavior, 50*, 343-354.

Galizio, M. (1979). Contingency-shaped and rule-governed behavior: Instructional control of human loss avoidance. *Journal of the Experimental Analysis of Behavior, 31*, 53-70.

Galli, I., & Nigro, G. (1987). The social representation of radioactivity among Italian children. *Social Science Information, 25*, 535-549.

Gallo, P. S. (1966). Effects of increased incentive upon the use of threat in bargaining. *Journal of Personality and Social Psychology, 4*, 14-20.

Gallo, P. S., Funk, S. G., & Levine, J. R. (1969). Reward size, method of presentation, and number of alternatives in a prisoner's dilemma game. *Journal of Personality and Social Psychology, 13*, 239-244.

Gallois, C., Callan, V. J., & Johnstone, M. (1984). Personality judgements of Australian Aborigine and white speakers: Ethnicity, sex, and context. *Journal of Language and Social Psychology, 3*, 39-57.

Gamson, W. A., Croteau, D., Hoynes, W., & Sasson, T. (1992). Media images and the social construction of reality. *Annual Review of Sociology, 18*, 373-393.

Geen, R. G. (1989). Alternative conceptions of social facilitation. In P.B. Paulus (Ed.), *Psychology of group influence* (2nd ed., pp. 15-51). Hillsdale, New Jersey: Erlbaum.

Geen, R. G. (1991). Social motivation. *Annual Review of Psychology, 42*, 377-399.

Geer, J. H., & Jarmecky, L. (1973). The effect of being responsible for reducing another's pain on subjects' response and arousal. *Journal of Personality and Social Psychology, 26*, 232-237.

Geertz, C. (1973). *The interpretation of cultures.* New York: Basic Books.

Geller, E. S., Winett, R. A., & Everett, P. B. (1982). *Preserving the environment: New strategies for behavior change.* New York: Pergamon.

Gelman, R., & Spelke, E. (1981). The development of thoughts about animate and inanimate objects: Implications for research on social cognition. In J.H. Flavell & L. Ross (Eds.), *Social cognitive development: Frontiers and possible futures* (pp. 43-66). Cambridge: Cambridge University Press.

Gellner, E. (1992). *Reason and culture: The historic role of rationality and rationalism.* Oxford: Basil Blackwell.

Gerard, H. B., Blevans, S. A., & Malcolm, T. (1964). Self-evaluation and the evaluation of choice alternatives. *Journal of Personality, 32*, 395-410.

Gergen, K. J. (1985). The social constructionist movement in modern psychology. *American Psychologist, 40*, 266-275.

Gergen, K. J. (1988). If persons are texts. In S. B. Messer, L. A. Sass, & R. L. Woolfolk (Eds.), *Hermeneutics and psychological theory* (pp. 28-51). New Brunswick, NJ: Rutgers University Press.

Gergen, K. J., & Gergen, M. M. (1988). Narrative and the self as relationship. In L. Berkowitz (Ed.), *Advances in experimental social psychology* (Vol. 21, pp. 17-56). San Diego, CA: Academic Press.

Gergen, M. M. (Ed.). (1988). *Feminist thought and the structure of knowledge.* New York: New York University Press.

Gersick, C. J. G. (1988). Time and transition in work teams: Toward a new model of group development. *Academy of Management Journal, 31,* 9-41.

Gewirtz, J. L., & Peláez-Nogueras, M. (1992). B. F. Skinner's legacy to human infant behavior and development. *American Psychologist, 47,* 1411-1422.

Giacalone, R. A., & Rosenfeld, P. (1986). Self-presentation and self-promotion in an organizational setting. *Journal of Social Psychology, 126,* 321-326.

Gibson, J. J. (1960). The concept of the stimulus in psychology. *American Psychologist, 15,* 694-703.

Gibson, J. J. (1966). *The senses considered as perceptual systems.* Boston: Houghton Mifflin.

Gibson, J. J. (1979). *An ecological approach to visual perception.* Boston: Houghton Mifflin.

Gibson, J. J., & Gibson, E. J. (1955). Perceptual learning: Differentiation or enrichment? *Psychological Review, 62,* 32-41.

Giddens, A. (1978). *Durkheim.* Glasgow: Fontana.

Giddens, A. (1990). *The consequences of modernity.* Cambridge: Polity Press.

Giddens, A. (1991). *Modernity and self-identity.* Cambridge: Polity Press.

Giles, H., Coupland, J., & Coupland, N. (Eds.). (1991). *Contexts of accommodation: Developments in applied sociolinguistics.* Cambridge: Cambridge University Press.

Giles, H., & Johnson, P. (1981). The role of language in ethnic group relations. In J. C. Turner & H. Giles (Eds.), *Intergroup behavior* (pp.199-243). Oxford: Basil Blackwell.

Giles, H., & Johnson, P. (1987). Ethnolinguistic identity theory: A social psychological approach to language maintenance. *International Journal of the Sociology of Language, 68,* 68-99.

Gilovich, T. (1983). Biased evaluation and persistence in gambling. *Journal of Personality and Social Psychology, 44,* 1110-1126.

Gintner, G. G., & Poret, M. K. (1988). Factors associated with maintenance and relapse following self-management training. *The Journal of Psychology, 122,* 79-87.

Glanz, K., Lewis, F. M., & Rimer, B. K. (Eds.). (1990). *Health behavior and health education: Theory, research and practice.* San Francisco: Jossey-Bass.

Glaser, R., & Klaus, D. J. (1966). A reinforcement analysis of group performance. *Psychological Monographs, 80* (13, Whole No. 621).

Glasgow, R. E., & Terborg, J. R. (1988). Occupational health promotion programs to reduce cardiovascular risk. *Journal of Consulting and Clinical Psychology, 56,* 365-373,

Glenn, S. S. (1983). Maladaptive functional relations in client verbal behavior. *The Behavior Analyst, 6,* 47-56.

Glenn, S. S. (1985). Some reciprocal roles between behavior analysis and institutional economics in post-Darwinian science. *The Behavior Analyst, 8,* 15-27.

Glenn, S. S. (1986). Metacontingencies in Walden Two. *Behavior Analysis and Social Action, 5,* 2-8.

Glenn, S. S. (1988). Contingencies and metacontingencies: Towards a synthesis of behavior analysis and cultural materialism. *The Behavior Analyst, 11,* 161-180.

Glenn, S. S. (1989). Verbal behavior and cultural practices. *Behavior Analysis and Social Action, 7,* 10-15.

Glenn, S. S. (1991). Contingencies and metacontingencies: Relations among behavioral, cultural, and biological evolution. In P. A. Lamal (Ed.), *Behavioral analysis of societies and cultural practices* (pp. 39-73). New York: Hemisphere Publishing.

Glenn, S. S., Ellis, J., & Greenspoon, J. (1992). On the revolutionary nature of the operant as a unit of behavioral selection. *American Psychologist, 47,* 1329-1336.

Glenn, S. S., & Malagodi, E. F. (1991). Process and content in behavioral and cultural phenomena. *Behavior and Social Issues, 1,* 1-14.

Glow, P. H. (1985). Response contingent schedule-control: Control over the environment motivates bar pressing. *Australian Journal of Psychology, 37,* 233-255.

Gluckman, M. (1956). *Custom and conflict in Africa.* Oxford: Basil Blackwell.

Gluckman, M. (1965). *Politics, law and ritual in tribal society.* Oxford: Basil Blackwell.

Gluckman, M. (Ed.). (1972). *The allocation of responsibility.* Manchester: Manchester University Press.

Glynn, T. J. (1981). Psychological sense of community: Measurement and application. *Human Relations, 34,* 789-818.

Glynn, T. J. (1986). Neighborhood and sense of community. *Journal of Community Psychology, 14,* 341-352.

Gō, S. (1985). *Requiem.* London: The Women's Press.

Goethals, G. R., & Darley, J. M. (1987). Social comparison theory: Self-evaluation and group life. In B. Mullen & G. R. Goethals (Eds.), *Theories of group behavior.* New York: Springer-Verlag.

Goethals, G. R., Cooper, J., & Naficy, A. (1979). Role of foreseen, foreseeable, and unforeseeable behavioural consequences in the arousal of cognitive dissonance. *Journal of Personality and Social Psychology, 37,* 1179-1185.

Goetz, E. L., & Baer, D. M. (1973). Social control of form diversity and the emergence of new forms in children's blockbuilding. *Journal of Applied Behavior Analysis, 6,* 209-217.

Goldiamond, I. (1962). Perception. In A. J. Bachrach (Ed.), *Experimental foundations of clinical psychology* (pp. 280-340). New York: Basic Books.

Goldiamond, I. (1976). Self-reinforcement. *Journal of Applied Behavior Analysis, 9,* 509-514.

Goldring, J. (1987). The accountability of judges. *The Australian Quarterly, 47,* 145-161.

Goldstein, R. S., & Baer, D. M. (1976). R.S.V.P.: A procedure to increase the personal mail and number of correspondents for nursing home residents. *Behavior Therapy, 7,* 348-354.

Gollub, L. (1977). Conditioned reinforcement: Schedule effects. In W. K. Honig and J. E. R. Staddon (Eds.), *Handbook of operant behavior* (pp. 288-312). Englewood Cliffs, NJ: Prentice Hall.

Goltz, S. M., Citera, M., Jensen, M., Favero, J., & Komaki, J. L. (1989). Individual feedback: Does it enhance effects of group feedback? *Journal of Organizational Behavior Management, 10,* 77-92.

Goody, J. (1986). *The logic of writing and the organization of society.* Cambridge: Cambridge University Press.

Goody, J. (1987). *The interface between the written and the oral.* Cambridge: Cambridge University Press.

Goranson, R. E., & Berkowitz, L. (1966). Reciprocity and responsibility reactions to prior help. *Journal of Personality and Social Psychology, 3,* 227-232.

Gottlieb, B. H. (Ed.). (1981). *Social networks and social support.* London: Sage.

Gould, J. L., & Marler, P. Learning by instinct. *Scientific American, 256,* January, 62-73.

Graft, D. A., Lea, S. E., & Whitworth, T. L. (1977). The matching law in and within groups of rats. *Journal of the Experimental Analysis of Behavior, 25,* 183-194.

Granovetter, M. (1973). The strength of weak ties. *American Journal of Sociology, 78,* 1360-1380.

Granovetter, M. (1982). The strength of weak ties: A network theory revisited. In P. V. Marsden & N. Lin (Eds.), *Social structure and network analysis* (pp. 105-130). London: Sage.

Green, G. (1991). Everyday stimulus equivalences for the brain-injured. In W. Ishaq (Ed.), *Human behavior in today's world* (pp.123-132). New York: Praeger.

Green, G., & Striefel, S. (1988). Response restriction and substitution with autistic children. *Journal of the Experimental Analysis of Behavior,50,* 21-32.

Green, L. W. (1984). Health education models. In J. D. Matarazzo, S. M. Weiss, J. A. Herd, N. A. Miller & S. M. Weiss (Eds.), *Behavioral health: A handbook of health enhancement and disease prevention* (pp. 181-198). New York: Wiley.

Greenberg, J. (1978). Effects of reward value and retaliative power on allocation decisions: Justice, generosity, or greed? *Journal of Personality and Social Psychology, 36,* 367-379.

Greenglass, E. R. (1969). Effects of prior help and hindrance on willingness to help another: Reciprocity or social responsibility? *Journal of Personality and Social Psychology, 11,* 224-231.

Greenspoon, J. (1991). Behavioral analysis in higher education. In P. A. Lamal (Ed.), *Behavioral analysis of societies and cultural practices* (pp. 141-164). New York: Hemisphere Publishing.

Greenwald, A. G. (1992). New look 3: Unconscious cognition reclaimed. *American Psychologist, 47,* 766-779.

Greenwood, C. R., Hops, H., Delquadri, J., & Guild, J. (1974). Group contingencies for group consequences in classroom management: A further analysis. *Journal of Applied Behavior Analysis, 7,* 413-425.

Griffin, J. C., Paisey, T. J., Stark, M. T., & Emerson, J. H. (1988). B. F. Skinner's position on aversive treatment. *American Journal for Mental Retardation, 93,* 104-105.

Grosch, J., & Neuringer, A. (1981). Self-control in pigeons under the Mischel paradigm. *Journal of the Experimental Analysis of Behavior,35,* 3-21.

Gross, A. M., & Wojnilower, D. A. (1984). Self-directed behavior change in children: Is it self-directed? *Behavior Therapy, 15,* 501-514.

Grott, R., & Neuringer, A. (1974). Group behavior of rats under schedules of reinforcement. *Journal of the Experimental Analysis of Behavior, 22,* 311-321.

Gruder, C. L. (1971). Relationships with opponent and partner in mixed-motive bargaining. *Journal of Conflict Resolution, 15,* 403-415.

Gruder, C. L., & Rosen, N. A. (1971). Effects of intergroup relations on intergroup bargaining. *International Journal of Group Tensions, 1,* 301-317.

Guerin, B. (1986). Mere presence effects in humans: A review. *Journal of Experimental Social Psychology, 22,* 38-77.

Guerin, B. (1990). Gibson, Skinner and perceptual responses. *Behavior and Philosophy, 18,* 43-54.

Guerin, B. (1991a). Anticipating the consequences of social behavior. *Current Psychology: Research and Reviews, 10,* 131-162.

Guerin, B. (1991b). *Saussure and the analysis of verbal behavior.* Unpublished paper, University of Waikato.

Guerin, B. (1991c). *Some contingencies of music.* Unpublished paper, University of Waikato.

Guerin, B. (1992a). Social behavior as discriminative stimulus and consequence in social anthropology. *The Behavior Analyst, 15,* 31-41.

Guerin, B. (1992b). Behavior analysis and social psychology. *Journal of the Experimental Analysis of Behavior, 58,* 589-604.

Guerin, B. (1992c). Behavior analysis and the social construction of knowledge. *American Psychologist, 47,* 1423-1432.

Guerin, B. (1993). *Social facilitation*. Cambridge: Cambridge University Press.

Guerin, B. (1994). Attitudes and beliefs as verbal behavior. *The Behavior Analyst, 17*.

Guerin, B., & Innes, J. M. (1989). Cognitive tuning sets: Anticipating the consequences of communication. *Current Psychology: Research & Reviews, 8*, 234-249.

Guerin, B., & Innes, J. M. (1990). Varieties of attitude change: Cognitive responding and maintenance of cognitive responding. *Australian Journal of Psychology, 18, 42*, 139-155.

Guess, D. (1969). A functional analysis of receptive language and productive speech: Acquisition of the plural morpheme. *Journal of Applied Behavior Analysis, 2*, 55-64.

Guess, D., & Baer, D. M. (1973). An analysis of individual differences in generalization between receptive and productive language in retarded children. *Journal of Applied Behavior Analysis, 6*, 311-329.

Guevremont, D. C., Osnes, P. G., & Stokes, T. F. (1986). Programming maintenance after correspondence training interventions with children. *Journal of Applied Behavior Analysis, 19*, 215-219.

Guevremont, D. C., Osnes, P. G., & Stokes, T. F. (In press). Generalization and maintenance of verbal control using correspondence training. *Behavior Modification*.

Gumpert, P., Deutsch, M., & Epstein, Y. (1969). Effect of incentive magnitude on cooperation in the prisoner's dilemma game. *Journal of Personality and Social Psychology, 11*, 66-69.

Gunthorpe, W., & Guerin, B. (1991). *The use of multiple trainers in promoting generalization*. Unpublished paper, University of Newcastle, Australia.

Gusfield, J. R. (1975). *Community: A critical response*. Oxford: Basil Blackwell.

Haack, S. (1992). Science 'From a feminist perspective'. *Philosophy, 67*, 5-18.

Haaren, F. van, Hest, A. van, & Poll, N. E. van de. (1988). Self-control in male and female rats. *Journal of the Experimental Analysis of Behavior,49*, 201-211.

Haccoun, R. R., & Klimoski, R. J. (1975). Negotiator status and accountability source: A study of negotiator behavior. *Organizational Behavior and Human Performance, 14*, 342-359.

Hagafors, R., & Brehmer, B. (1983). Does having to justify one's judgments change the nature of the judgment process? *Organizational Behavior and Human Performance, 31*, 223-232.

Hake, D. F. (1982). The basic-applied continuum and the possible evolution of human operant social and verbal behavior. *The Behavior Analyst, 5*, 21-28.

Hake, D. F., Donaldson, T., & Hyten, C. (1983). Analysis of stimulus control by social behavioral stimuli. *Journal of the Experimental Analysis of Behavior, 39*, 7-23.

Hake, D. F., & Olvera, D. (1978). Cooperation, competition, and related social phenomena. In A. C. Catania & T. A. Brigham (Eds.), *Handbook of applied behavior analysis: Social and instructional processes* (pp. 208-245). New York: Irvington Publishers.

Hake, D. F., Olvera, D., & Bell, J. C. (1975). Switching from competition to sharing or cooperation at large response requirements: Competition requires more responding. *Journal of the Experimental Analysis of Behavior, 24*, 343-354.

Hake, D. F., & Schmid, T. L. (1981). Acquisition and maintenance of trusting behavior. *Journal of the Experimental Analysis of Behavior, 35*, 109-124.

Hake, D. F., & Vukelich, R. (1972). A classification and review of cooperation procedures. *Journal of the Experimental Analysis of Behavior, 18*, 333-343.

Hake, D. F., & Vukelich, R. (1973). Analysis of the control exerted by a complex cooperation procedure. *Journal of the Experimental Analysis of Behavior, 19*, 3-16.

Hake, D. F., & Vukelich, R. (1980). Rate of auditing self and coactor performance scores as a supplementary monitor of reinforcer effectiveness. *Behavior Modification, 4*, 265-280.

Hake, D. F., Vukelich, R. & Kaplan, S. J. (1973). Audit responses: Responses maintained by access to existing self or coactor scores during non-social, parallel work, and cooperation procedures. *Journal of the Experimental Analysis of Behavior, 19*, 409-423.

Hake, D. F., Vukelich, R., & Olvera, D. (1975). The measurement of sharing and cooperation as equity effects and some relationships between them. *Journal of the Experimental Analysis of Behavior, 23*, 63-79.

Halbwachs, M. (1980/1950). *The collective memory.* New York: Harper Row.

Haley, J. (1973). *Uncommon therapy: The psychiatric techniques of Milton H. Erickson, M.D.* London: Norton.

Hall, G. A. (1992). Aspects of conversational style-linguistic versus behavioral analysis. *The Analysis of Verbal Behavior, 10*, 81-86.

Hall, G., & Sundberg, M. L. (1987). Teaching mands by manipulating conditioned establishing operations. *The Analysis of Verbal Behavior, 5*, 41-53.

Hall, R. L. (1957). Group performance under feedback that confounds responses of group members. *Sociometry, 20*, 297-305.

Hamilton, M. C. (1988a). Masculine generic terms and misperception of AIDS risk. *Journal of Applied Social Psychology, 18*, 1222-1240.

Hamilton, M. C. (1988b). Using masculine generics: Does generic *He* increase male bias in the user's imagery? *Sex Roles, 19*, 785-799.

Hammond, K. R., Hamm, R. M., Grassia, J., & Pearson, T. (1987). Direct comparison of the efficacy of intuitive and analytical cognition in expert judgment. *IEEE Transactions on Systems, Man, and Cybernetics, SMC-17*, 753-770.

Haneda, F., & Yamamoto, J. (1991). [Tacts on private events by autistic children: Acquisition and generalization.] *Japanese Journal of Behavior Analysis, 6*, 23-40. With English summary.

Hansen, A. (1991). The media and the social construction of the environment. *Media, Culture and Society, 13*, 443-458.

Hansen, R. D., & O'Leary, V. E. (1985). Sex-determined attributions. In V. E. O'Leary, R. K. Unger & B. S. Wallston (Eds.), *Women, gender, and social psychology* (pp. 67-99). Hillsdale, NJ: Erlbaum.

Hanson, S. J., & Timberlake, W. (1983). Regulation during challenge: A general model of learned performance under schedule constraint. *Psychological Review, 90*, 261-282.

Harari, O., & Graham, W. K. (1975). Tasks and task consequences as factors in individual and group brainstorming. *Journal of Social Psychology, 95*, 61-65.

Hare-Mustin, R. T., & Marecek, J. (1988). The meaning of difference: Gender theory, postmodernism, and psychology. *American Psychologist, 43*, 455-464.

Haring, T. G., Roger, B., Lee, M., Breen, C., & Gaylord-Ross, R. (1986). Teaching social language to moderately handicapped students. *Journal of Applied Behavior Analysis, 19*, 159-171.

Harkins, S. G. (1987). Social loafing and social facilitation. *Journal of Experimental Social Psychology, 23*, 1-18.

Harkins, S. G., Harvey, J. H., Keithly, L., & Rich, M. (1977). Cognitive tuning, encoding, and the attribution of causality. *Memory and Cognition, 5*, 561-565.

Harkins, S. G., & Jackson, J. M. (1985). The role of evaluation in eliminating social loafing. *Personality and Social Psychology Bulletin, 11*, 457-465.

Harkins, S. G., Latané, B., & Williams, K. (1980). Social loafing: Allocating effort or taking it easy? *Journal of Experimental Social Psychology, 16*, 457-465.

Harkins, S. G., & Petty, R. E. (1982). Effects of task difficulty and task uniqueness on social loafing. *Journal of Personality and Social Psychology, 43,* 1214-1229.

Harkins, S. G., & Szymanski, K. (1987). Social loafing and social facilitation: New wine in old bottles. In C. Hendrick (Ed.), *Group processes and intergroup relations* (pp. 167-188). London: Sage.

Harkins, S. G., & Szymanski, K. (1988). Social loafing and self-evaluation with an objective standard. *Journal of Experimental Social Psychology, 24,* 354-365.

Harkins, S. G., & Szymanski, K. (1989). Social loafing and group evaluation. *Journal of Personality and Social Psychology, 56,* 934-941.

Harkness, A. R., DeBono, K. G., & Borgida, E. (1985). Personal involvement and strategies for making contingency judgments: A stake in the dating game makes a difference. *Journal of Personality and Social Psychology, 49,* 22-32.

Harman, L. D. (1988). *The modern stranger: On language and membership.* New York: Mouton de Gruyter.

Harris, M. (1979). *Cultural materialism.* New York: Random House.

Harris, S. (1984). *Culture and learning: Tradition and education in north-east Arnhem Land.* Canberra: Australian Institute of Aboriginal Studies.

Harris, S. (1987). Yolngu rules of interpersonal communication. In W. H. Edwards (Ed.), *Traditional Aboriginal society.* Melbourne: Macmillan.

Harrison, S. (1992). Ritual as intellectual property. *Man* (N.S.), *27,* 225-244.

Hart, B. M., Reynolds, N. J., Baer, D. M., Brawley, E. R., & Harris, F. R. (1968). Effect of contingent and non-contingent social reinforcement on the cooperative play of a preschool child. *Journal of Applied Behavior Analysis, 1,* 73-76.

Hart, K. (1986). Heads or tails? Two sides of the coin. *Man* (N.S.), *21,* 637-656.

Hartje, J. C. (1973). Premackian reinforcement of classroom behavior through topic sequencing. *Journal of Psychology, 84,* 61-74.

Hartwick, J., Sheppard, B. H., & Davis, J.H. (1982). Group remembering: Research and implications. In R. A. Guzzo (Ed.), *Improving group decision making in organizations* (pp. 41-72). New York: Academic Press.

Harvey, J. H., Harkins, S. G., & Kagehiro, D. K. (1976). Cognitive tuning and the attribution of causality. *Journal of Personality and Social Psychology, 34,* 708-715.

Hastings, G., & Haywood, A. (1991). Social marketing and communication in health promotion. *Health Promotion International, 6,* 135-145.

Hayes, L. A. (1976). The use of group contingencies for behavioral control: A review. *Psychological Bulletin, 83,* 628-648.

Hayes, L. A., & Watson, J. S. (1983). Neonatal imitation: Fact or artifact? *Developmental Psychology, 17,* 655-660.

Hayes, L. J., & Chase, P. N. (Eds.). (1991). *Dialogues on verbal behavior.* Reno, Nevada: Context Press.

Hayes, L. J., Thompson, S., & Hayes, S. C. (1989). Stimulus equivalence and rule following. *Journal of the Experimental Analysis of Behavior, 52,* 275-291.

Hayes, L. J., Tilley, K. J., & Hayes, S. C. (1988). Extending equivalence class membership to gustatory stimuli. *The Psychological Record, 38,* 473-482.

Hayes, N. A., & Broadbent, D. E. (1988). Two modes of learning for interactive tasks. *Cognition, 28,* 80-108.

Hayes, S. C. (1986). The case of the silent dog—Verbal reports and the analysis of rules. *Journal of the Experimental Analysis of Behavior, 45,* 351-363.

Hayes, S. C. (1987). A contextual approach to therapeutic change. In N. Jacobson (Ed.), *Cognitive and behavioral therapies in clinical practice* (pp. 327-387). New York: Guilford Press.

Hayes, S.C. (1989a). Nonhumans have not yet shown stimulus equivalence. *Journal of the Experimental Analysis of Behavior, 51,* 385-392.

Hayes, S. C. (Ed.). (1989b). *Rule-governed behavior: Cognition, contingencies, and instructional control.* New York: Plenum Press.

Hayes, S. C. (1992). Verbal relations, time and suicide. In S. C. Hayes & L. J. Hayes (Eds.), *Understanding verbal relations* (pp. 109-118). Reno, Nevada: Context Press.

Hayes, S. C., & Brownstein, A. J. (1987). Mentalism, private events, and scientific explanation: A defense of B. F. Skinner's view. In S. Modgil & C. Modgil (Eds.), *B. F. Skinner: Consensus and controversy* (pp. 207-218). New York: Falmer Press.

Hayes, S. C., Brownstein, A. J., Haas, J. R., & Greenway, D. E. (1986). Instructions, multiple schedules, and extinction: Distinguishing rule-governed from schedule-controlled behavior. *Journal of the Experimental Analysis of Behavior, 46,* 137-147.

Hayes, S. C., & Hayes, L. J. (1989). The verbal action of the listener as a basis for rule-governance. In S. C. Hayes (Ed.), *Rule-governed behavior: Cognition, contingencies, and instructional control* (pp. 153-190). New York: Plenum Press.

Hayes, S. C., & Hayes, L. J. (1992a). Verbal relations and the evolution of behavior analysis. *American Psychologist, 47,* 1383-1395.

Hayes, S. C., & Hayes, L. J. (Eds.). (1992b). *Understanding verbal relations.* Reno, Nevada: Context Press.

Hayes, S. C., Kohlenberg, B. S., & Melancon, S. M. (1989). Avoiding and altering rule-control as a strategy of clinical intervention. In S. C. Hayes (Ed.), *Rule-governed behavior: Cognition, contingencies, and instructional control* (pp. 359-385). New York: Plenum Press.

Hayes, S. C., Munt, E. D., Korn, Z., Wulfert, E., Rosenfarb, I., & Zettle, R. D. (1986). The effect of feedback and self-reinforcement instructions on studying performance. *The Psychological Record, 36,* 27-37.

Hayes, S. C., Rosenfarb, I., Wulfert, E., Munt, E. D., Korn, Z., & Zettle, R. D. (1985). Self-reinforcement effects: An artifact of social standard setting? *Journal of Applied Behavior Analysis, 18,* 201-214.

Hayes, S. C., & Wilson, K. G. (1993). Some applied implications of a contemporary behavior-analytic account of verbal events. *The Behavior Analyst, 16,* 283-301.

Hebdige, D. (1979). *Subculture: The meaning of style.* London: Methuen.

Heider, F. (1958). *The psychology of interpersonal relations.* New York: Wiley.

Helmreich, R., & Collins, B. E. (1968). Studies in forced compliance: Commitment and magnitude of inducement to comply as determinants of opinion change. *Journal of Personality and Social Psychology, 10,* 75-81.

Henchy, T., & Glass, D. C. (1968). Evaluation apprehension and the social facilitation of dominant and subordinate responses. *Journal of Personality and Social Psychology, 10,* 446-454.

Henige, D. (1982). *Oral historiography.* London: Longman.

Henley, N. M. (1989). Molehill or mountain? What we know and don't know about sex bias in language. In M. Crawford & M. Gentry (Eds.), *Gender and thought: Psychological perspectives* (pp. 59-78). New York: Springer-Verlag.

Hennigan, K. M., Cook, T. D., & Gruder, C. L. (1982). Cognitive tuning set, source credibility and the temporal persistence of attitude change. *Journal of Personality and Social Psychology, 42,* 412-425.

Herbert, F. (1981). *God emperor of Dune.* London: Victor Gollancz.

Herek, G. M. (1986). The instrumentality of attitudes: Towards a neofunctional theory. *Journal of Social Issues, 42,* 99-114.

Herek, G. M. (1987). Can functions be measured? A new perspective on the functional approach to attitudes. *Social Psychological Quarterly, 50,* 285-303.

Hermann, M., & Kogan, N. (1968). Negotiation in leader and delegate groups. *Journal of Conflict Resolution, 12,* 332-344.

Herrnstein, R. J. (1961). Relative and absolute strength of response as a function of frequency of reinforcement. *Journal of the Experimental Analysis of Behavior, 4,* 267-272.

Herrnstein, R. J. (1966). Superstition: A corollary of the principles of operant conditioning. In W. K. Honig (Ed.), *Operant behavior: Areas of research and application* (pp.33-51). Englewood Cliffs, NJ: Prentice Hall.

Herrnstein, R. J. (1970). On the law of effect. *Journal of the Experimental Analysis of Behavior, 13,* 243-266.

Herrnstein, R. J. (1977). The evolution of behaviorism. *American Psychologist, 32,* 593-603.

Herzlich, C. (1973). *Health and illness: A social psychological analysis.* New York: Academic Press.

Hewstone, M. (1989). *Causal attribution: From cognitive processes to collective beliefs.* Oxford: Basil Blackwell.

Hewstone, M., & Jaspars, J. M. F. (1984). Social dimensions of attribution. In H. Tajfel (Ed.), *The social dimension: European developments in social psychology* (pp. 379-404). Cambridge: Cambridge University Press.

Hewstone, M., Jaspars, J. M. F. & Lalljee, M. (1982). Social representations, social attribution and social identity: The intergroup images of 'public' and comprehensive' schoolboys. *European Journal of Social Psychology, 12,* 241-269.

Hewstone, M., & Ward, C. (1985). Ethnocentrism and causal attribution in Southeast Asia. *Journal of Personality and Social Psychology, 48,* 614-623.

Higgins, E. T., McCann, C. D., & Fondacaro, R. (1982). The "Communication Game": Goal-directed encoding and cognitive consequences. *Social Cognition, 1,* 21-37.

Hineline, P. N. (1977). Negative reinforcement and avoidance. In W. K. Honig and J. E. R. Staddon (Eds.), *Handbook of operant behavior* (pp. 354-414). Englewood Cliffs, NJ: Prentice Hall.

Hineline, P. N. (1980). The language of behavior analysis: Its community, its function, and its limitations. *Behaviorism, 8,* 67-86.

Hineline, P. N. (1990). The origins of environment-based psychological theory. *Journal of the Experimental Analysis of Behavior, 53,* 305-320.

Hineline, P. N. (1992). A self-interpretive behavior analysis. *American Psychologist, 47,* 1274-1286.

Hirota, T. T. (1972). The Wyckoff observing response–A reappraisal. *Journal of the Experimental Analysis of Behavior, 18,* 263-276.

Hoffman, C., Mischel, W., & Baer, J. S. (1984). Language and person cognition: Effects of communicative set on trait attribution. *Journal of Personality and Social Psychology, 46,* 1029-1043.

Hogg, M. A. (1992). *The social psychology of group cohesiveness: From attraction to social identity.* New York: Harvester Wheatsheaf.

Hogg, M. A., & Abrams, D. (1988). *Social identifications: A social psychology of intergroup relations and social processes.* London: Routledge.

Holland, J. G. (1958). Human vigilance. *Science, 128,* 61-67.

Holland, J. G. (1992). Language and the continuity of the species. In S. C. Hayes & L. J. Hayes (Eds.), *Understanding verbal relations* (pp. 197-209). Reno, Nevada: Context Press.

Holt, L. E., & Watts, W. A. (1969). Salience of logical relationships among beliefs as a factor in persuasion. *Journal of Personality and Social Psychology, 11,* 193-203.

Holz, W. C., & Azrin, N. H. (1966). Conditioning human verbal behavior. In W. K. Honig (Ed.), *Operant behavior: Areas of research and application* (pp. 790-826). Englewood Cliffs, NJ: Prentice Hall.

Homme, L. E., DeBaca, P. C., Devine, J. V., Steinhorst, R., & Rickert, E. J. (1963). Use of the Premack principle in controlling the behavior of nursery school children. *Journal of the Experimental Analysis of Behavior, 6,* 544.

Honig, W. K., & Urcuioli, P. J. (1981). The legacy of Guttman & Kalish (1956): Twenty-five years of research on stimulus generalization. *Journal of the Experimental Analysis of Behavior, 36,* 405-445.

Horcones. (1983). Natural reinforcement in a Walden Two community. *Revista Mexicana de Analisis de la Conducta, 9,* 141-143.

Horner, R. D., & Keilitz, I. (1975). Training mentally retarded adolescents to brush their teeth. *Journal of Applied Behavior Analysis, 8,* 301-309.

Horner, R. H., Dunlap, G., and Koegel, R. L. (Eds.). (1988). *Generalization and maintenance: Life-style changes in applied settings.* Baltimore, MD: Paul Brookes.

Howard, J. A. (1984). Societal influences on attribution: Blaming some victims more than others. *Journal of Personality and Social Psychology, 47,* 494-505.

Howard, M. L., & Keenan, M. (1993). Outline for a functional analysis of imitation in animals. *The Psychological Record, 43,* 185-204.

Hrydowy, E. R., Stokes, T. F. & Martin, G. L. (1984). Training elementary students to prompt teacher praise. *Education and Treatment of Children, 7,* 99-108.

Huff, C., Sproull, L., & Kiesler, S. (1989). Computer communication and organizational commitment: Tracing the relationship in a city government. *Journal of Applied Social Psychology, 19,* 1371-1391.

Hull, C. L. (1943). *Principles of behavior: An introduction to behavior theory.* New York: Appleton-Century-Crofts.

Humphrey, C. (1985). Barter and economic disintegration. *Man* (N.S.), 20, 48-72.

Hussian, R. A. (1984). Behavioral geriatrics. In M. Hersen, R. M. Eisler, & P. M. Miller (Eds.), *Progress in behavior modification* (Vol. 16, pp. 159-183). New York: Academic Press.

Husted, J. R., & McKenna, F. S. (1966). The use of rats as discriminative stimuli. *Journal of the Experimental Analysis of Behavior, 9,* 677-679.

Hutchinson, R. R. (1977). By-products of aversive control. In W. K. Honig and J. E. R. Staddon (Eds.), *Handbook of operant behavior* (pp. 415-431). Englewood Cliffs, NJ: Prentice Hall.

Hyten, C., & Burns, R. (1986). Social relations and social behavior. In H. W. Reese and L. J. Parrott (Eds.), *Behavior science: Philosophical, methodological, and empirical advances* (pp. 163-183). Hillsdale, NJ: Erlbaum.

Hyten, C., & Chase, P. N. (1991). An analysis of self-editing: Method and preliminary findings. In L. J. Hayes & P. N. Chase (Eds.), *Dialogues on verbal behavior.* (pp. 67-81) Reno, Nevada: Context Press.

Ichheiser, G. (1949). Misunderstandings in human relations: A study of false social perception. *American Journal of Sociology, 55,* 1-70.

Ingham, A. G., Levinger, G., Graves, J., & Peckham, V. (1974). The Ringelmann effect: Studies of group size and group performance. *Journal of Experimental Social Psychology, 10,* 371-382.

Innes, J. M. (1981). Polarization of response as a function of cognitive tuning set and individual differences. *Social Behavior and Personality, 9,* 213-218.

Insko, C. A., Smith, R. H., Alicke, M. D., Wade, J., & Taylor, S. (1985). Conformity and group size: The concern with being right and the concern with being liked. *Personality and Social Psychology Bulletin, 11,* 41-50.

Israel, A. C. (1973). Developing correspondence between verbal and nonverbal behavior: Switching sequences. *Psychological Reports, 32,* 1111-1117.

Israel, A. C. (1978). Some thoughts on correspondence between saying and doing. *Journal of Applied Behavior Analysis, 11,* 271-276.

Iversen, I. H. (1992). Skinner's early research: From reflexology to operant conditioning. *American Psychologist, 47,* 1318-1328.

Iverson, D. C., Fielding, J. E., Crow, R. S., & Christenson, G. M. (1985). The promotion of physical activity in the United States population: The status of programs in medical, worksite, community and school settings. *Public Health Reports, 100,* 212-224.

Jacklin, C. N. (1987). Feminist research and psychology. In C. Farnham (Ed.), *The impact of feminist research in the academy* (pp. 95-107). Bloomington: Indiana University Press.

Jackson, D. A., & Wallace, R. F. (1974). The modification and generalization of voice loudness in a fifteen-year-old retarded girl. *Journal of Applied Behavior Analysis, 7,* 461-471.

Jackson, J. M., & Harkins, S. G. (1985). Equity in effort: An explanation of the social loafing effect. *Journal of Personality and Social Psychology, 49,* 1199-1206.

Jackson, J. M., & Williams, K. D. (1985). Social loafing on difficult tasks: Working collectively can improve performance. *Journal of Personality and Social Psychology, 49,* 937-942.

Jacobson, D. E. (1986). Types and timing of social support. *Journal of Health and Social Behavior, 27,* 250-264.

Jacobson, N. S. (1989). The maintenance of treatment gains following social learning-based therapy. *Behavior Therapy, 20,* 325-336.

Janis, I. L. (1972). *Victims of groupthink.* Boston: Houghton Mifflin.

Jaques, E. (1956). *Measurement of responsibility.* London: Heineman.

Jeffery, R. W. (1989). Risk behaviors and health: Contrasting individual and population perspectives. *American Psychologist, 44,* 1194-1202.

Jenkins, H. (1992). *Textual poachers: Television fans & participatory culture.* New York: Routledge.

Jerdee, T. H., & Rosen, B. (1974). Effects of opportunity to communicate and visibility of individual decisions on behavior in the common interest. *Journal of Applied Psychology, 59,* 712-716.

Johnson, L. M., & Morris, E. K. (1987). When speaking of probability in behavior analysis. *Behaviorism, 15,* 107-129.

Johnson, L. M., Bickel, W. K., Higgins, S. T., & Morris, E. K. (1991). The effects of schedule history and the opportunity for adjunctive responding on behavior during a fixed-interval schedule of reinforcement. *Journal of the Experimental Analysis of Behavior, 55,* 313-322.

Johnson, R. D., & Downing, L. L. (1979). Deindividuation and valence of cues: Effects on prosocial and antisocial behavior. *Journal of Personality and Social Psychology, 37,* 1532-1538.

Johnson-Laird, P. N. (1983). *Mental models.* Cambridge: Cambridge University Press.

Jones, E. E., & Davis, K. E. (1965). From acts to dispositions: The attribution process in person perception. In L. Berkowitz (Ed.), *Advances in experimental social psychology* (Vol. 2, pp. 219-266). New York: Academic Press.

Jones, E. E., & Nisbett, R. E. (1972). The actor and the observer: Divergent perceptions of the causes of behavior. In E. E. Jones, D. E. Kanouse, H. H. Kelley, R. E. Nisbett, S. Valins, & B. Weiner (Eds.), *Attribution: Perceiving the causes of behavior* (pp. 79-94). Morristown, NJ: General Learning Press.

Jones, E. E., & Pittman, T. S. (1982). Toward a general theory of strategic self-presentation. In J.Suls (Ed.), *Psychological perspectives on the self* (Vol. 1, pp. 231-262). Hillsdale, NJ: Erlbaum.

Jones, R. T., & Kazdin, A. E. (1975). Programming response maintenance after withdrawing token reinforcement. *Behavior Therapy, 6,* 153-164.

Jones, S. C. (1968). Expectation, performance, and the anticipation of self-revealing events. *Journal of Social Psychology, 74,* 189-197.

Jorgenson, D. O., & Papciak, A. S. (1981). The effects of communication, resource feedback, and identifiability on behavior in a simulated commons. *Journal of Experimental Social Psychology, 17,* 373-385.

Kachanoff, R., Leveille, R., McClelland, J. P., & Wayner, M. J. (1973). Schedule induced behavior in humans. *Physiology and Behavior, 11,* 395-398.

Kahan, J. P. (1973). Noninteraction in an anonymous three-person prisoner's dilemma game. *Behavioral Science, 18,* 124-127.

Kahneman, D. (1992). Reference points, anchors, norms, and mixed feelings. *Organizational Behavior and Human Decision Processes, 51,* 296-312.

Kahneman, D., & Tversky, A. (1979). Prospect theory: An analysis of decision under risk. *Econometrica, 47,* 263-291.

Kahneman, D., & Tversky, A. (1984). Choices, values, and frames. *American Psychologist, 39,* 341-350.

Kamil, A. C. (1983). Optimal foraging theory and the psychology of learning. *American Zoologist, 23,* 291-302.

Kanak, N. J., & Davenport, D. G. (1967). Between-subject competition: A rat race. *Psychonomic Science, 7,* 87-88.

Kantor, J. R. (1970). An analysis of the experimental analysis of behavior (TEAB). *Journal of the Experimental Analysis of Behavior, 13,* 101-108.

Katz, D. (1960). The functional approach to the study of attitudes. *Public Opinion Quarterly, 24,* 163-204.

Katz, D. (1974). Factors affecting social change: A social-psychological interpretation. *Journal of Social Issues, 30* (3), 159-180.

Katz, E., & Lazarsfeld, P. F. (1955). *Personal influence: The part played by people in the flow of mass communication.* New York: The Free Press.

Katz, J. (1979). Concerted ignorance: The social construction of cover-up. *Urban Life, 8,* 295-316.

Kaufman, H. (1973). *Administrative feedback: Monitoring subordinates' behavior.* Washington, DC: Brookings Institute.

Kaufman, R. A. (1971). Accountability, a system approach and a quantitative improvement of education—an attempted integration. *Educational Technology, 11,* 21-26.

Kaufmann, F. X., Majone, G., & Ostrom, V. (1986). *Guidance, control, and evaluation in the public sector.* Berlin: De Gruyter.

Kazdin, A. E. (1982). Symptom substitution, generalization, and response covariation: Implications for psychotherapy outcome. *Psychological Bulletin, 91*, 349-365.

Kazdin, A. E., & Geesey, S. (1977). Simultaneous-treatment design comparisons of the effects of earning reinforcers for one's peers versus for oneself. *Behavior Therapy, 8*, 682-693.

Keating, J. P., & Latané, B. (1976). Politicians on TV: The image is the message. *Journal of Social Issues, 32*, 116-132.

Keesing, R. M. (1981). *Cultural anthropology: A contemporary perspective* (2nd ed.). New York: Holt, Rinehart and Winston.

Kelleher, R. T. (1966). Chaining and conditioned reinforcement. In W. K. Honig (Ed.), *Operant behavior: Areas of research and application* (pp. 160-212). Englewood Cliffs, NJ: Prentice Hall.

Kelleher, R. T., & Gollub, L. R. (1962). A review of conditioned reinforcement. *Journal of the Experimental Analysis of Behavior, 5*, 543-597.

Keller, F. S., & Schoenfeld, W. N. (1950). *Principles of psychology: A systematic text in the science of behavior*. New York: Appleton-Century-Crofts.

Kelley, H. H., & Michela, J. L. (1980). Attribution theory and research. *Annual Review of Psychology, 31*, 457-503.

Kelley, H. H., Shure, G. H., Deutsch, M., Faucheux, C., Lanzetta, J. T., Moscovici, S., Nuttin, J. M., Rabbie, J. M., & Thibaut, J. W. (1970). A comparative experimental study of negotiation behavior. *Journal of Personality and Social Psychology, 16*, 411-438.

Kelly, J. G., Snowden, L. R., & Munoz, R. F. (1977). Social and community interventions. *Annual Review of Psychology, 28*, 323-361.

Kemper, T. D. (1987). How many emotions are there? Weeding the social and the autonomic components. *American Journal of Sociology, 93*, 263-289.

Kendon, A. (1991). Some considerations for a theory of language origins. *Man* (N.S.), *26*, 199-221.

Kent, S. (1993). Sharing in an egalitarian Kalahari community. *Man* (N.S.), *28*, 479-514.

Keren, G., & Wagenaar, W. A. (1987). Violation of utility theory in unique and repeated gambles. *Journal of Experimental Psychology: Learning, Memory, and Cognition, 13*, 387-391.

Kerr, N. L., & Bruun, S. E. (1981). Ringelmann revisited: Alternative explanations for the social loafing effect. *Personality and Social Psychology Bulletin, 7*, 224-231.

Kidder, L. H., Bellettirie, G., & Cohn, E. S. (1977). Secret ambitions and public performances: The effects of anonymity on reward allocations made by men and women. *Journal of Experimental Social Psychology, 13*, 70-80.

Kiecolt, K. J. (1988). Recent developments in attitudes and social structure. *Annual Review of Sociology, 14*, 381-403.

Kiesler, C. A., & Corbin, L. H. (1965). Commitment, attraction, and conformity. *Journal of Personality and Social Psychology, 2*, 890-895.

Kiesler, S., Siegel, J., & McGuire, T. W. (1984). Social psychological aspects of computer-mediated communication. *American Psychologist, 39*, 1123-1134.

Kiesler, S., & Sproull, L. (1992). Group decision making and communication technology. *Organizational Behavior and Human Decision Processes, 52*, 96-123.

Kilgour, R., Foster, T. M., Temple, W., Matthews, L. R., & Bremner, K. J. (1991). Operant technology applied to solving farm animal problems. An assessment. *Applied Animal Behaviour Science, 30*, 141-166.

Kilgour, R., Matthews, L. R., Temple, W., & Foster, T. M. (1984). Using operant test results for decisions on cattle welfare. In W. F. Hall (Ed.), *The behavior and welfare of farm animals:*

Proceedings of Conference on the Human-Animal Bond (pp. 205-217). Minneapolis, MN: Humane Information Services.

Killeen, P. R. (1988). The reflex reserve. *Journal of the Experimental Analysis of Behavior, 50,* 319-331.

Killian, L. M. (1952). The significance of multiple-group membership in disaster. *American Journal of Sociology, 57,* 309-314.

Killworth, P. D., Bernard, H. R., & McCarty, C. (1984). Measuring patterns of acquaintance-ship. *Current Anthropology, 25,* 381-397.

King, G. R., & Logue, A. W. (1987). Choice in a self-control paradigm with human subjects: Effects of changeover delay duration. *Learning and Motivation, 18,* 421-438.

Kish, G. B. (1966). Studies of sensory reinforcement. In W. K. Honig (Ed.), *Operant behavior: Areas of research and application* (pp. 109-159). Englewood Cliffs, NJ: Prentice Hall.

Kitzinger, C. (1986). Introducing and developing Q as a feminist methodology: A study of accounts of lesbianism. In S. Wilkinson (Ed.), *Feminist social psychology* (pp. 151-172). Milton Keynes, England: Open University Press.

Klaus, D. J., & Glaser, R. (1970). Reinforcement determinants of team proficiency. *Organizational Behavior and Human Performance, 5,* 33-67.

Klee, P. (1953). *Pedagogical sketchbook.* London: Faber & Faber.

Klein, K. J., & D'Aunno, T. A. (1986). Psychological sense of community in the workplace. *Journal of Community Psychology, 14,* 365-377.

Kleinke, C. L. (1982). Operant behavior under a falsely perceived response-reinforcement contingency: An attributional analysis. *Personality and Social Psychology Bulletin, 8,* 239-241.

Kleiter, G. D. (1970). Trend-control in a dynamic decision-making task. *Acta Psychologica, 34,* 387-397.

Klimoski, R. J. (1972). The effects of intragroup forces on intergroup conflict resolution. *Organizational Behavior and Human Performance, 8,* 363-383.

Klimoski, R. J., & Ash, R. A. (1974). Accountability and negotiation behaviour. *Organizational Behavior and Human Performance, 12,* 409-425.

Knapp, T. J. (1976). The Premack principle in human experimental and applied settings. *Behavior Research and Therapy, 14,* 133-147.

Knox, R. E., & Douglas, R. L. (1971). Trivial incentives, marginal comprehension, and dubious generalizations from prisoner's dilemma studies. *Journal of Personality and Social Psychology, 20,* 160-165.

Kogan, N., & Doise, W. (1969). Effects of anticipated delegate status on level of risk taking in small decision-making groups. *Acta Psychologica, 29,* 228-243.

Kogan, N., Lamm, H., & Trommsdorff, G. (1972). Negotiation constraints in the risk-taking domain. *Journal of Personality and Social Psychology, 23,* 143-156.

Kohlenberg, R. J., Hayes, S. C., & Tsai, M. (1993). Radical behavior therapy: Two contemporary examples. *Clinical Psychology Review, 13,* 579-592.

Kohler, F. W., & Fowler, S. A. (1985). Training prosocial behaviors to young children: An analysis of reciprocity with untrained peers. *Journal of Applied Behavior Analysis, 18,* 187-200.

Kohler, F. W., & Greenwood, C. R. (1986). Towards a technology of generalization: The identification of natural contingencies of reinforcement. *The Behavior Analyst, 9,* 19-26.

Komaki, J. L. (1986a). Applied behavior analysis and organizational behavior: Reciprocal influence of the two fields. *Research in Organizational Behavior, 8,* 297-334.

Komaki, J. L. (1986b). Toward effective supervision: An operant analysis and comparison of managers at work. *Journal of Applied Psychology, 71,* 270-279.

Komaki, J. L., Collins, R. L., & Penn, P. (1982). The role of performance antecedents and consequences in work motivation. *Journal of Applied Psychology, 67,* 334-340.

Komaki, J. L., Desselles, M. L., & Bowman, E. D. (1989). Definitely not a breeze: Extending an operant model of effective supervision to teams. *Journal of Applied Psychology, 74,* 522-529.

Konarski, E. A. (1987). Effects of response deprivation on the instrumental performance of mentally retarded persons. *American Journal of Mental Deficiency, 91,* 537-542.

Konarski, E. A., Johnson, M. R., Crowell, C. R., & Whitman, T. L. (1981). An alternative approach to reinforcement for applied researchers: Response deprivation. *Behavior Therapy, 12,* 653-666.

Kotler, P., & Roberto, E. L. (1989). *Social marketing: Strategies for changing public behavior.* New York: The Free Press.

Kottak, C. P. (1980). The material conditions of variation in Betsileo ceremonial life. In E. B. Ross (Ed.), *Beyond the myths of culture: Essays in cultural materialism.* New York: Academic Press.

Kramarae, C. (1990). Changing the complexion of gender in language research. In H. Giles & W. P. Robinson (Eds.), *Handbook of language and social psychology* (pp. 345-361). New York: John Wiley.

Krapfl, J. E. (1975). Accountability for behavioral engineers. In W. Scott Woods (Ed.), *Issues in evaluating behavior modification* (pp. 219-236). Illinois: Research Press.

Krauthammer, C. (1987). Responsibility should bear consequences. *The Guardian,* August 16, 17.

Krebs, D. L., & Miller, D. T. (1985). Altruism and aggression. In G. Lindzey & E. Aronson (Eds.), *Handbook of social psychology* (Vol. 2, pp. 1-71). New York: Random House.

Krige, E. G., & Krige, J. D. (1939). The significance of cattle exchange in Lovedu social structure. *Africa, 12.*

Kruglanski, A. W., & Mayseless, O. (1987). Motivational effects in the social comparison of opinions. *Journal of Personality and Social Psychology, 53,* 834-842.

Kymissis, E., & Poulson, C. L. (1990). The history of imitation in learning theory: The language acquisition process. *Journal of the Experimental Analysis of Behavior, 54,* 113-127.

Labov, W. (1972). *Sociolinguistic patterns.* Oxford: Basil Blackwell.

Labov, W. (1990). The intersection of sex and social class in the course of linguistic change. *Language Variation and Change, 2,* 205-254.

Lacan, J. (1977). *Écrits: A selection.* London: Tavistock.

Lamal, P. A. (1984). Contingency management in the People's Republic of China. *The Behavior Analyst, 7,* 121-130.

Lamal, P. A. (Ed.). (1991). *Behavioral analysis of societies and cultural practices.* New York: Hemisphere Publishing.

Lamal, P. A., & Greenspoon, J. (1992). Congressional metacontingencies. *Behavior and Social Issues, 2,* 71-81.

Lamarre, J., & Holland, J. G. (1985). The functional independence of mands and tacts. *Journal of the Experimental Analysis of Behavior, 43,* 5-19.

Lambek, M. (1992). Taboo as cultural practice among Malagasy speakers. *Man* (N.S.), *27,* 245-266.

Lamm, H., & Kogan, N. (1970). Risk taking in the context of intergroup negotiation. *Journal of Experimental Social Psychology, 6,* 351-363.

Lamm, H., & Ochsmann, R. (1972). Factors limiting the generality of the risky-shift phenomenon. *European Journal of Social Psychology, 2,* 455-458.

Langford, G. (1978). Persons as necessarily social. *Journal of the Theory of Social Behaviour, 8,* 263-283.

Lao Tzu. (1963). *Tao te ching.* Harmondsworth, Middlesex: Penguin.

Latané, B., & Darley, J. M. (1970). *The unresponsive bystander: Why doesn't he help?* New York: Appleton-Century-Crofts.

Latané, B., Williams, K., & Harkins, S. (1979). Many hands make light the work: The causes and consequences of social loafing. *Journal of Personality and Social Psychology, 37,* 823-832.

Lather, P. (1988). Feminist perspectives on empowering research methodologies. *Women's Studies International Forum, 11,* 569-581.

Lattal, K. A., & Gleeson, S. (1990). Response acquisition with delayed reinforcement. *Journal of Experimental Psychology: Animal Behavior Processes, 16,* 27-39.

Layng, T. V. J., & Andronis, P. T. (1984). Towards a functional analysis of delusional speech and hallucinatory behavior. *The Behavior Analyst, 7,* 139-156.

Le Guin, U. K. (1969). *The left hand of darkness.* New York: Ace Books.

Lea, S. E. G., Tarpy, R. M., & Webley, P. (1987). *The individual in the economy.* Cambridge: Cambridge University Press.

Lee, R. B., & DeVore, I. (1968). *Man the hunter.* Chicago: Aldine.

Lee, V. L. (1981a). The operant as a class of responses. *Scandinavian Journal of Psychology, 22,* 215-221.

Lee, V. L. (1981b). Prepositional phrases spoken and heard. *Journal of the Experimental Analysis of Behavior, 35,* 227-242.

Lee, V. L. (1983a). Behavior as a constituent of conduct. *Behaviorism, 11,* 199-224.

Lee, V. L. (1983b). A note on the composition of verbal response forms. *The Analysis of Verbal Behavior, 2,* 3-4.

Lee, V. L. (1984). Some notes on the subject matter of Skinner's *Verbal Behavior. Behaviorism, 12,* 29-40.

Lee, V. L. (1985). Scientific knowledge as rules that guide behavior. *The Psychological Record, 35,* 183-192.

Lee, V. L. (1986) Act psychologies and the psychological nouns. *The Psychological Record, 36,* 167-179.

Lee, V. L. (1988). *Beyond behaviorism.* Hillsdale, NJ: Erlbaum.

Lee, V. L. (1992). Transdermal interpretation of the subject matter of behavior analysis. *American Psychologist, 47,* 1337-1343.

Lee, V. L., Barnett, K., Crisp, S., Young, L., Bron, M., Vatmanidis, P. C., & Atkinson, L. Low interrater agreement on the semantic base of textual material. *The Analysis of Verbal Behavior, 7,* 91-97.

Lee, V. L., & Pegler, A. M. (1982). Effects on spelling of training children to read. *Journal of the Experimental Analysis of Behavior, 37,* 311-322.

Lee, V. L., & Sanderson, G. M. (1987). Some contingencies of spelling. *The Analysis of Verbal Behavior, 5,* 1-13.

LeFrancois, J. R., Chase, P. N., & Joyce, J. H. (1988). The effects of a variety of instructions on human fixed-interval performance. *Journal of the Experimental Analysis of Behavior, 49,* 383-393.

Leigland, S. (1984). On "setting events" and related concepts. *The Behavior Analyst, 7,* 41-45.

Leont'ev, A. N. (1981). Sign and activity. In J. V. Wertsch (Ed.), *The concept of activity in Soviet psychology* (241-255). New York: M.E.Sharpe, Inc.

Lepper, M. R., & Greene, S. (Eds.). (1978). *The hidden costs of reward*. Hillsdale, NJ: Erlbaum.

Leventhal, G. S., Michaels, J. W., & Sanford, C. (1972). Inequity and interpersonal conflict: Reward allocation and secrecy about reward as methods of preventing conflict. *Journal of Personality and Social Psychology, 23*, 88-102.

Leventhal, H. (1962). The effects of set and discrepancy on impression formation. *Journal of Personality, 30*, 1-15.

Lévi-Strauss, C. (1963a). *Totemism*. Boston: Beacon Press.

Lévi-Strauss, C. (1963b). The bear and the barber. *Journal of the Royal Anthropological Institute, 43*, 1-11.

Lévi-Strauss, C. (1966). *The savage mind*. London: Weidenfeld & Nicolson.

Levin, M. (1993). Creating networks for rural economic development in Norway. *Human Relations, 46*, 193-218.

Lévy-Bruhl, L. (1966). *The "soul" of the primitive*. Chicago: Henry Regnery.

Lewicki, P. (1986). Processing information about covariations that cannot be articulated. *Journal of Experimental Psychology: Learning, Memory and Cognition, 12*, 135-146.

Lewicki, P., Hill, T., & Czyzewska, M. (1992). Nonconscious acquisition of information. *American Psychologist, 47*, 796-801.

Lewis, J. D., & Weigert, A. (1985a). Social atomism, holism, and trust. *The sociological Quarterly, 26*, 455-471.

Lewis, J. D., & Weigert, A. (1985b). Trust as a social reality. *Social Forces, 63*, 967-985.

Lindskold, S., & Finch, M. L. (1982). Anonymity and the resolution of conflicting pressures from the experimenter and from peers. *Journal of Psychology, 112*, 79-86.

Lindsley, O. R. (1964). Geriatric behavioral prosthetics. In R. Kastenbaum (Ed.), *New thoughts in old age* (pp. 41-61). New York: Springer-Verlag

Lindsley, O. R. (1966). Experimental analysis of cooperation and competition. In T. Verhave (Ed.), *The experimental analysis of behavior* (pp. 470-501). New York: Appleton-Century-Crofts.

Litow, L., & Pumroy, D. K. (1975). A brief review of classroom group-oriented contingencies. *Journal of Applied Behavior Analysis, 8*, 341-347.

Litwak, E., & Szelenyi, I. (1969). Primary group structures and their function: Kin, neighbors, and friends. *American Sociological Review, 34*, 465-481.

Livingstone, S. M. (1990). *Making sense of television: The psychology of audience interpretation*. New York: Pergamon Press.

Lloyd, K. E. (1980). Do as I say, not as I do. *New Zealand Psychologist, 9*, 1-8. [See Lloyd, 1994 for a reprint of this paper.]

Lloyd, K. E. (1994). Addenda. *The Behavior Analyst, 17*.

Lloyd, K. E. (1985). Behavioral anthropology: A review of Marvin Harris' *Cultural Materialism. Journal of the Experimental Analysis of Behavior, 43*, 279-287.

Lodhi, S., & Greer, R. D. (1989). The speaker as listener. *Journal of the Experimental Analysis of Behavior, 51*, 353-360.

Longino, H. E. (1988). Science, objectivity, and feminist values. *Feminist Studies, 14*, 561-574.

Lopes, L. L. (1981). Decision making in the short run. *Journal of Experimental Psychology: Human Learning and Memory, 7*, 377-385.

Lopes, L. L. (1985). Averaging rules and adjustment processes in Bayesian inference. *Bulletin of the Psychonomic Society, 23*, 509-512.

Lovaas, I., Newsom, C., & Hickman, C. (1987). Self-stimulatory behavior and perceptual reinforcement. *Journal of Applied Behavior Analysis, 20,* 45-68.

Lovaas, O. I. (1964). Control of food intake in children by reinforcement of relevant verbal behavior. *Journal of Abnormal and Social Psychology, 68,* 672-678.

Lovaas, O. I., & Smith, T. (1989). A comprehensive behavioral theory of autistic children: Paradigm for research and treatment. *Journal of Behavior Therapy and Experimental Psychiatry, 20,* 17-29.

Lubinski, D., & Thompson, T. (1987). An animal model of the interpersonal communication of interoceptive (private) states. *Journal of the Experimental Analysis of Behavior, 48,* 1-15.

Luce, R. D. (1959). *Individual choice behavior: A theoretical analysis.* New York: Wiley.

Luhmann, N. (1979). *Trust and power.* New York: Wiley.

Luria, A. R. (1961). *The role of speech in the regulation of normal and abnormal behavior.* New York: Pergamon Press.

Lyons, C. A., & Cheney, C. D. (1984). Time reallocation in a multiresponse environment. *Journal of the Experimental Analysis of Behavior, 41,* 279-289.

MacCorquodale, K. (1969). B. F. Skinner's *Verbal Behavior:* A retrospective appreciation. *Journal of the Experimental Analysis of Behavior, 12,* 831-841.

Mace, F. C., Hock, M. L., Lalli, J.S, West, B. J., Belfiore, P., Pinter, E., & Brown, D. K. (1988). Behavioral momentum in the treatment of noncompliance. *Journal of Applied Behavior Analysis, 21,* 123-142.

Machado, A. (1989). Operant conditioning of behavioral variability using a percentile reinforcement schedule. *Journal of the Experimental Analysis of Behavior, 52,* 155-166.

Machina, M. J. (1987). Decision-making in the presence of risk. *Science, 236,* 537-543.

Mackay, H. A. (1991). Conditional stimulus control. In I. H. Iversen & K. A. Lattal (Eds.), *Experimental analysis of behavior, part 1* (pp. 301-350). Amsterdam: Elsevier.

MacKenzie, J. G., Foster, T. M., & Temple, W. (1993). Sound avoidance by hens. *Behavioural Processes, 30,* 143-156.

MacKenzie-Keating, S. E., & McDonald, L. (1990). Overcorrection: Reviewed, revisited and revised. *The Behavior Analyst, 13,* 39-48.

Madden, T. J., Ellen, P. S., & Ajzen, I. (1992). A comparison of the theory of planned action and the theory of reasoned action. *Personality and Social Psychology Bulletin, 18,* 3-9.

Mageo, J. M. (1989). Aga, amio and loto: Perspectives on the structure of the self in Samoa. *Oceania, 59,* 181-199.

Mahoney, M. J., & Thorensen, C. E. (1974). *Self-control: Power to the people.* Monterey, CA: Brooks/Cole.

Majone, G, (1986). Mutual adjustment by debate and persuasion. In F. X. Kaufmann, G. Majone & V. Ostrom (Eds.), *Guidance, control, and evaluation in the public sector* (pp. 445-458). Berlin: De Gruyter.

Malagodi, E. F. (1986). On radicalizing behaviorism: A call for cultural analysis. *The Behavior Analyst, 9,* 1-17.

Malagodi, E. F., & Jackson, K. (1989). Behavior analysts and cultural analysis: Troubles and issues. *The Behavior Analyst, 12,* 17-33.

Malinowski, B. (1922). *Argonauts of the Western Pacific.* New York: Dutton.

Malott, R. W. (1968). Perception revisited. *Perceptual and Motor Skills, 28,* 683-693.

Malott, R. W. (1973). *Humanistic behaviorism and social psychology.* Kalamazoo, MI: Behaviordelia, Inc.

Malott, R. W. (1984). Rule-governed behavior, self-management, and the developmentally disabled: A theoretical analysis. *Analysis and Intervention in Developmental Disabilities, 4,* 199-209.

Malott, R. W. (1988). Rule-governed behavior and behavioral anthropology. *The Behavior Analyst, 11,* 181-204.

Malott, R. W. (1989). The achievement of evasive goals: Control by rules describing contingencies that are not direct acting. In S. C. Hayes (Ed.), *Rule-governed behavior: Cognition, contingencies, and instructional control* (pp. 269-322). New York: Plenum Press.

Mann, L., Newton, J. W., & Innes, J. M. (1982). A test between deindividuation and emergent norm theories of crowd aggression. *Journal of Personality and Social Psychology, 42,* 260-272.

Manning, M. R., Osland, J. S., & Osland, A. (1989). Work-related consequences of smoking cessation. *Academy of Management Journal, 32,* 606-621.

Mansfield, H. C. (1982). Accountability and congressional oversight. In B. L. R. Smith & J. D. Carroll (Eds.), *Improving the accountability and performance of government* (pp. 61-68). Washington, DC: Brookings Institute.

Marcucella, H., & Owens, K. (1975). Cooperative problem solving by albino rats: A re-evaluation. *Psychological Reports, 37,* 591-598.

Marin, G. (1993). Defining culturally appropriate community interventions: Hispanics as a case study. *Journal of Community Psychology, 21,* 149-161.

Markowitz, H. (1978). Engineering environments for behavioral opportunities in the zoo. *The Behavior Analyst, 1,* 34-47.

Markowitz, H. (1979). Environmental enrichment and behavioral engineering for captive primates. In J. Erwin, T. L. Maple, & G. Mitchell (Eds.), *Captivity and behavior* (pp. 217-238). New York: Van Nostrand Reinhold.

Markus, H., & Nurius, P. (1986). Possible selves. *American Psychologist, 41,* 954-969.

Marlatt, G. A., & Gordon, J. R. (Eds.). (1985). *Relapse prevention: Maintenance strategies in addictive behavior change.* New York: Guilford Press.

Marlowe, D., Gergen, K. J., & Doob, A. N. (1966). Opponent's personality, expectation of social interaction, and interpersonal bargaining. *Journal of Personality and Social Psychology, 3,* 206-213.

Marsden, P. V. (1987). Core discussion networks of Americans. *American Sociological Review, 52,* 122-131.

Marsden, P. V. (1990). Network data and measurement. *Annual Review of Sociology, 16,* 435-463.

Marsden, P. V., & Lin, N. (Eds.). (1982). *Social structure and network analysis.* London: Sage.

Marshall, H., & Wetherall, M. (1989). Talking about career and gender identities: A discourse analysis perspective. In S. Skevington & D. Baker (Eds.), *The social identity of women* (pp. 106-129). London: Sage.

Martens, B. K., Halperin, S., Rummel, J. E., & Kilpatrick, D. (1990). Matching theory applied to contingent teacher attention. *Behavioral Assessment, 12,* 139-155.

Maruyama, G., Fraser, S. C., & Miller, N. (1982). Personal responsibility and altruism in children. *Journal of Personality and Social Psychology, 42,* 658-664.

Marwell, G. (1963). Visibility in small groups. *The Journal of Social Psychology, 61,* 311-325.

Marwell, G., & Schmitt, D. (1972). Cooperation in a three-person prisoner's dilemma. *Journal of Personality and Social Psychology, 21,* 376-382.

Marwell, G., & Schmitt, D. (1975). *Cooperation: An experimental analysis.* New York: Academic Press.

Mascia-Lees, F. E., Sharpe, P., & Cohen, C. B. (1989). The postmodernist turn in anthropology: Cautions from a feminist perspective. *Signs: Journal of Women in Culture and Society, 15,* 7-33.

Maslach, C. (1974). Social and personal bases of individuation. *Journal of Personality and Social Psychology, 29,* 411-425.

Massermann, J. H., Wechkin, S., & Terris, W. (1964). "Altruistic" behavior in rhesus monkeys. *American Journal of Psychiatry, 121,* 584-585.

Mathes, E. W., & Guest, T. A. (1976). Anonymity and group antisocial behavior. *Journal of Social Psychology, 100,* 257-262.

Matthews, B. A. (1977). Magnitudes of score differences produced within sessions in a cooperative exchange procedure. *Journal of the Experimental Analysis of Behavior, 27,* 331-340.

Matthews, B. A., Shimoff, E., & Catania, A. C. (1987). Saying and doing: A contingency-space analysis. *Journal of Applied Behavior Analysis, 20,* 69-74.

Matthews, L. R., & Temple, W. (1979). Concurrent schedule assessment of food preference in cows. *Journal of the Experimental Analysis of Behavior, 32,* 245-254.

Mauss, M. (1966). *The gift.* London: Routledge & Kegan Paul.

Mawhinney, T. C., Dickinson, A. M., & Taylor, L. A. (1989). The use of concurrent schedules to evaluate the effects of extrinsic rewards on "intrinsic motivation." *Journal of Organizational Behavior Management, 10,* 109-129.

Mawhinney, T. C. (1975). Operant terms and concepts in the description of individual work behavior: Some problems of interpretation, application, and evaluation. *Journal of Applied Psychology, 60,* 704-712.

Mawhinney, T. C. (1979). Intrinsic X extrinsic work motivation: Perspectives from behaviorism. *Organizational Behavior and Human Performance, 24,* 411-440.

Mawhinney, T. C., & Ford, J. D. (1977). The path goal theory of leader effectiveness: An operant interpretation. *Academy of Management Review, 2,* 398-411.

May, E. (1980). *Musics of many cultures.* Berkeley: University of California Press.

Mazis, M. B. (1973). Cognitive tuning and receptivity to novel information. *Journal of Experimental Social Psychology, 9,* 307-319.

Mazur, J. E. (1975). The matching law and quantifications related to Premack's principle. *Journal of Experimental Psychology: Animal Behavior Processes, 1,* 374-386.

Mazur, J. E. (1988). Estimation of indifference points with an adjusting-delay procedure. *Journal of the Experimental Analysis of Behavior, 49,* 37-47.

Mazur, J. E., & Logue, A. (1978). Choice in a "self-control" paradigm: Effects of a fading procedure. *Journal of the Experimental Analysis of Behavior, 30,* 11-17.

McAdie, T. M., Foster, T. M., Temple, W., & Matthews, L. R. (1993). A method for measuring the aversiveness of sounds to domestic hens. *Applied Animal Behaviour Science, 37,* 223-238.

McAllister, D. W., Mitchell, T. R., & Beach, L. R. (1979). The contingency model for the selection of decisional strategies: An empirical test of the effects of significance, accountability and reversibility. *Organizational Behavior and Human Performance, 24,* 228-244.

McCarthy, D. C., & Davison, M. (1981). Towards a behavioral theory of bias in signal detection. *Perception and Psychophysics, 29,* 371-382.

McCarthy, D. C., & Davison, M. (1991). The interaction between stimulus and reinforcer control on remembering. *Journal of the Experimental Analysis of Behavior, 56,* 51-66.

McCarthy, D. C., & White, K. G. (1987). Behavioral models of delayed detection and their application to the study of memory. In M. L. Commons, J. E. Mazur, J. A. Nevin, & H. Rachlin (Eds.), *Quantitative analyses of behavior: Vol. 5. The effect of delay and of intervening events on reinforcement value* (pp. 29-54). Hillsdale, NJ: Erlbaum.

McClannahan, L. E., Krantz, P. J., & McGee, G. G. (1982). Parents as therapists for autistic children: A model for effective parent training. *Analysis and Intervention in Developmental Disabilities, 2,* 223-252.

McDowell, J. J. (1982). The importance of Herrnstein's mathematical statement of the Law of Effect for behavior therapy. *American Psychologist, 37,* 771-779.

McFarland, C., Ross, M., & Conway, M. (1984). Self-persuasion and self-presentation as mediators of anticipatory attitude change. *Journal of Personality and Social Psychology, 46,* 529-540.

McGinnies, E. (1970). *Social behavior: A functional analysis.* Boston: Houghton Mifflin.

McGinnies, E., & Ferster, C. B. (Eds.). (1971). *The reinforcement of social behavior.* Boston: Houghton Mifflin.

McGuire, T. W., Kiesler, S., & Siegel, J. (1987). Group and computer-mediated discussion effects in risk decision making. *Journal of Personality and Social Psychology, 52,* 917-930.

McLaughlin, B. (1971). *Learning and social behavior.* New York: The Free Press.

McMillan, D. W., & Chavis, D. M. (1986). Sense of community: A definition and theory. *Journal of Community Psychology, 14,* 6-23.

McNeill, D. (1985). So you think gestures are nonverbal? *Psychological Review, 92,* 350-371.

McPherson, A., & Osborne, J. G. (1986). The emergence of establishing operations. *The Psychological Record, 36,* 375-386.

McPherson, A., & Osborne, J. G. (1988). Control of behavior by an establishing stimulus. *Journal of the Experimental Analysis of Behavior, 49,* 213-227.

Mead, G. H. (1922). A behavioristic account of the significant symbol. *Journal of Philosophy, 19,* 157-163.

Mead, G. H. (1924/1925). The genesis of the self and social control. *International Journal of Ethics, 35,* 251-277.

Mead, G. H. (1934). *Mind, self, and society from the standpoint of a social behaviorist.* Chicago: University of Chicago Press.

Mednick, M. T. (1989). On the politics of psychological constructs: Stop the bandwagon, I want to get off. *American Psychologist, 44,* 1118-1123.

Medow, H., & Zander, A. (1965). Aspirations for the group chosen by central and peripheral members. *Journal of Personality and Social Psychology, 1,* 224-228.

Meichenbaum, D. H. (1975). Enhancing creativity by modifying what subjects say to themselves. *American Educational Research Journal, 12,* 129-145.

Mellgren, R. L., & Brown, S. W. (1988). Discrimination learning in a foraging situation. *Journal of the Experimental Analysis of Behavior, 50,* 493-503.

Meltzoff, A. N., & Moore, M. K. (1983). New-born infants imitate adult facial gestures. *Child Development, 54,* 702-709.

Mermelstein, R., Cohen, S., Lichtenstein, E., Baer, J. S., & Kamarck, T. (1986). Social support and smoking cessation and maintenance. *Journal of Consulting and Clinical Psychology, 54,* 447-453.

Merton, R. K. (1957). *Social theory and social structure.* New York: The Free Press.

Messe, L. A., Bolt, M., & Sawyer, J. (1967). Nonstructural determinants of cooperation and conflict in the replicated prisoner's dilemma game. *Psychonomic Science, 25,* 238-240.

Michael, J. (1975). Positive and negative reinforcement, a distinction that is no longer necessary: Or a better way to talk about bad things. *Behaviorism, 3*, 33-44.

Michael, J. (1980). Flight from behavior analysis. *The Behavior Analyst, 3*, 1-21.

Michael, J. (1982a). Distinguishing between discriminative and motivational functions of stimuli. *Journal of the Experimental Analysis of Behavior, 37*, 149-155.

Michael, J. (1982b). Skinner's elementary verbal relations: Some new categories. *The Analysis of Verbal Behavior, 1*, 1-3

Michael, J. (1983). Evocative and repertoire altering effects of an environmental event. *The Analysis of Verbal Behavior, 2*, 19-21.

Michael, J. (1984). Verbal behavior. *Journal of the Experimental Analysis of Behavior, 42*, 363-376.

Michael, J. (1985). Two kinds of verbal behavior plus a possible third. *The Analysis of Verbal Behavior, 3*, 2-5.

Michael, J. (1988). Establishing operations and the mand. *The Analysis of Verbal Behavior, 6*, 3-9.

Michael, J. (1993). Establishing operations. *The Behavior Analyst, 16*, 191-206.

Michelini, R. L. (1976). Effects of prior interaction, contact, strategy, and expectation of meeting on game behavior and sentiment. *Journal of Conflict Resolution, 15*, 97-103.

Middleton, J., & Tait, D. (1958). *Tribes without rulers: Studies in African segmentary systems.* London: Routledge & Kegan Paul.

Midgley, B. D., & Morris, E. K. (1988). The integrated field: An alternative to the behavior-analytic conceptualization of behavior units. *The Psychological Record, 38*, 483-500.

Milan, M. A. (1987). Token economy programs in closed institutions. In E. K. Morris & C. J. Braukman (Eds.), *Behavioral approaches to crime and delinquency* (pp. 195-222). New York: Plenum.

Milardo, R. M. (1982). Friendship networks in developing relationships: Converging and diverging social environments. *Social Psychology Quarterly, 45*, 162-172.

Milgram, S. (1974). *Obedience to authority: An experimental view.* New York: Harper & Row.

Milio, N. (1986). *Promoting health through public policy.* Ottawa: Canadian Public Health Association.

Millar, W. S. (1976). Operant acquisition of social behaviors in infancy: Basic problems and constraints. In H. W. Reese (Ed.), *Advances in child development and behavior* (Vol. 11, pp. 107-140). New York: Academic Press.

Millard, W. J. (1979). Stimulus properties of conspecific behavior. *Journal of the Experimental Analysis of Behavior, 32*, 283-296.

Miller, D. T., Norman, S. A., & Wright, E. (1978). Distortion in person perception as a consequence of the need for effective control. *Journal of Personality and Social Psychology, 36*, 598-607.

Miller, F. G., & Rowold, K. L. (1979). Hallowe'en masks and deindividuation. *Psychological Reports, 44*, 422.

Miller, G. A., Galanter, E., & Pribram, K. H. (1960). *Plans and the structure of behavior.* New York: Holt, Rinehart and Winston.

Miller, J. G. (1984). Culture and the development of everyday social explanation. *Journal of Personality and Social Psychology, 46*, 961-978.

Miller, P. J., Potts, R., Fung, H., Hoogstra, L., & Mintz, J. (1990). Narrative practices and the social construction of self in childhood. *American Ethnologist, 17*, 292-311.

Milroy, L. (1987a). *Language and social networks.* Oxford: Basil Blackwell.

Milroy, L. (1987b). *Observing & analysing natural language.* Oxford: Basil Blackwell.

Milton, K. (1979). Male bias in anthropology. *Man* (N.S.), *14*, 40-54.

Minkler, M. (1990). Improving health through community organization. In K. Glanz, F. M. Lewis, & B. K. Rimer (Eds.), *Health behavior and health education: Theory, research and practice* (pp. 257-287). San Francisco: Jossey-Bass.

Mischel, W., & Patterson, C. J. (1976). Substantive and structural elements of effective plans for self-control. *Journal of Personality and Social Psychology, 34*, 942-950.

Mitchell, J. C. (Ed.). (1969). *Social networks in urban situations: Analyses of personal relationships in Central African towns.* Manchester: Manchester University Press.

Mitchell, W. S., & Stoffelmayr, B. E. (1973). Application of the Premack principle to the behavioral control of extremely inactive schizophrenics. *Journal of Applied Behavior Analysis, 6*, 419-423.

Miyamoto, S. F., & Dornbusch, S. M. (1956). A test of interactionist hypotheses of self-conception. *The American Journal of Sociology, 61*, 399-403.

Momsen, J. H., & Kinnaird, V. (Eds.). (1993). *Different places, different voices: Gender and development in Africa, Asia and Latin America.* London: Routledge.

Monson, T. C., Keel, R., Stephens, D., & Genung, V. (1982). Trait attributions: Relative validity, covariation with behavior, and prospect of future interaction. *Journal of Personality and Social Psychology, 42*, 1014-1024.

Montgomery, H., & Adelbratt, T. (1982). Gambling decisions and information about expected value. *Organizational Behavior and Human Performance, 29*, 39-57.

Moore, J. (1980). On behaviorism and private events. *The Psychological Record, 30*, 459-475.

Moore, J. (1984).On privacy, causes, and contingencies. *The Behavior Analyst, 7*, 3-16.

Moore, S. F. (1978). *Law as process: An anthropological approach.* London: Routledge & Kegan Paul.

Morgan, C. J. (1978). Bystander intervention: Experimental test of a formal model. *Journal of Personality and Social Psychology, 36*, 43-55.

Morris, C. J. (1990). The effects of satiation on the operant control of response variability. *The Psychological Record, 40*, 105-112.

Morris, E. K. (1980). The differential effectiveness of social reinforcement with children in laboratory and natural settings: A conditioned reinforcement analysis. *The Psychological Record, 30*, 9-16.

Morris, E. K. (1993). Behavior analysis and mechanism: One is not the other. *The Behavior Analyst, 16*, 25-43.

Morris, E. K. (in press). *The behavior of organisms*: A context theory of meaning. In J. T. Todd & E. K. Morris (Eds.), *Modern perspectives on classical and contemporary behaviorism.* Westport, CT: Greenwood Press.

Morris, E. K., & Braukmann, C. J. (1987). *Behavioral approaches to crime and delinquency: A handbook of application, research, and concepts.* New York: Plenum.

Morris, E. K., Hursh, D. E., Winston, A. S., Gelfand, D. M., Hartmann, D. P., Reese, H. W., & Baer, D. M. (1982). Behavior analysis and developmental psychology. *Human Development, 25*, 340-364.

Morse, S. J., Gruzen, J., & Reis, H. T. (1976). The nature of equity-restoration: Some approval-seeking considerations. *Journal of Experimental Social Psychology, 12*, 1-8.

Morse, W. H. (1966). Intermittent reinforcement. In W. K. Honig (Ed.), *Operant behavior: Areas of research and application* (pp. 52-108). Englewood Cliffs, NJ: Prentice Hall.

Moscovici, S. (1985b). *The age of the crowd: A historical treatise on mass psychology.* Cambridge: Cambridge University Press.

Moscovici, S. (1990). The generalized self and mass society. In H.T. Himmelweit & G. Gaskell (Eds.), *Societal psychology* (pp. 66-91). London: Sage.

Moscovici, S. (1993). The return of the unconscious. *Social Research, 60* (1), 39-93.

Moscovici, S., Mugny, G., & Van Avermaet, E. (Eds.). (1985). *Perspectives on minority influence.* New York: Cambridge University Press.

Mosher, F. C. (1982). Comment. In B. L. R. Smith & J. D. Carroll (Eds.), *Improving the accountability and performance of government* (pp. 71-74). Washington, DC: Brookings Institute.

Mostofsky, D. I. (Ed.). (1965). *Stimulus generalization.* Stanford: Stanford University Press.

Mouton, J. S., Blake, R. R., & Olmstead, J. S. (1955-56). The relations between frequency of yielding and the disclosure of personal identity. *Journal of Personality, 24,* 338-347.

Moxley, R. A. (1992). From mechanistic to functional behaviorism. *American Psychologist, 47,* 1300-1311.

Mueller, K. L., & Dinsmoor, J. A. (1986). The effect of negative stimulus presentations on observing-response rate. *Journal of the Experimental Analysis of Behavior, 46,* 281-291.

Mugny, G., & Pérez, J. A. (1991). *The social psychology of minority influence.* New York: Cambridge University Press.

Mullen, B., & Baumeister, R. F. (1987). Group effects on self-attention and performance: Social loafing, social facilitation, and social impairment. In C. Hendrick (Ed.), *Group processes and intergroup relations* (pp. 189-206). London: Sage.

Munro, C. (1985). The accountability of police. *Criminal Law Review* (London), 581-588.

Murdock, G. (1993). Communications and the constitution of modernity. *Media, Culture and Society, 15,* 521-539.

Murphy, C. M. (1986). Contingencies to prevent catastrophe: Behavioral psychology and the anti-nuclear arms movement. *Behavior Analysis and Social Action, 5,* 30-35.

Murray, D. C. (1971). Talk, silence, and anxiety. *Psychological Bulletin, 75,* 244-260.

Myerson, J., & Hale, S. (1984). Practical implications of the matching law. *Journal of Applied Behavior Analysis, 17,* 367-380.

Nadler, A., Goldberg, M., & Jaffe, Y. (1982). Effects on self-differentiation and anonymity in group on deindividuation. *Journal of Personality and Social Psychology, 42,* 1127-1136.

Nakajima, S., & Sato, M. (1993). Removal of an obstacle: Problem-solving behavior in pigeons. *Journal of the Experimental Analysis of Behavior, 59,* 131-145.

Nation, J. R., & Woods, D. J. (1980). Persistence: The role of partial reinforcement in psychotherapy. *Journal of Experimental Psychology: General, 109,* 175-207.

Neef, N. A., Mace, F. C., Shea, M. C., & Shade, D. (1992). Effects of reinforcer rate and reinforcer quality on time allocation: Extensions of matching theory to educational settings. *Journal of Applied Behavior Analysis, 25,* 691-699.

Nel, E., Helmreich, R., & Aronson, E. (1969). Opinion change in the advocate as a function of the persuasibility of his audience: A clarification of the meaning of dissonance. *Journal of Personality and Social Psychology, 12,* 117-124.

Nelson, R. O., Hayes, S. C., Spong, R. T., Jarrett, R. B., & McKnight, D. L. (1983). Self-reinforcement: Appealing misnomer or effective mechanism. *Behavior Research and Therapy, 21,* 557-566.

Nemeth, C. (1986). Differential contributions of majority and minority influence. *Psychological Review, 93,* 23-32.

Nemeth, C., & Brilmayer, A. G. (1987). Negotiation versus influence. *European Journal of Social Psychology, 17,* 45-56.

Neuringer, A. (1993). Reinforced variation and selection. *Animal Learning & Behavior, 21,* 83-91.

Nevin, J. A. (1991). Signal-detection analysis of illusions and heuristics. In M. L. Commons, J. A. Nevin & M. C. Davison (Eds.), *Signal detection mechanisms, models, and applications* (pp. 257-274) Hillsdale, NJ: Erlbaum.

Nevin, J. A. (1966). Generalized conditioned reinforcement in satiated rats. *Psychonomic Science, 5,* 191-192.

Nevin, J. A. (1988). Behavioral momentum and the partial reinforcement effect. *Psychological Bulletin, 103,* 44-56.

Nevin, J. A., & Liebold, K. (1966). Stimulus control of matching and oddity in the pigeon. *Psychonomic Science, 5,* 351-352.

Nevin, J. A., Mandell, C., & Atak, J. R. (1983). The analysis of behavioral momentum. *Journal of the Experimental Analysis of Behavior, 39,* 49-59.

Newby, T. J., & Robinson, P. W. (1983). Effects of grouped and individual feedback and reinforcement on retail employee performances. *Journal of Organizational Behavior Management, 5,* 51-68.

Newcomb, T. M. (1943). *Personality and social change.* New York: Dryden.

Newcomb, T. M. (1966). Attitude development as a function of reference groups: The Bennington study. In E. E. Maccoby, T. M. Newcomb & E. L. Hartley (Eds.), *Readings in social psychology* (pp. 265-275). London: Methuen.

Newman, E., & Turem, J. (1974). The crisis of accountability. *Social Work, 19,* 5-16.

Newston, D., & Czerlinsky, T. (1974). Adjustment of attitude communications for contrasts by extreme audiences. *Journal of Personality and Social Psychology, 30,* 829-837.

Ng, S. H. (1990a). Androcentric coding of *Man* and *His* in memory by language users. *Journal of Experimental Social Psychology, 26,* 455-464.

Ng, S. H. (1990b). Language and control. In H. Giles & W. P. Robinson (Eds.), *Handbook of language and social psychology* (pp. 271-285). New York: John Wiley.

Nicassio, P. M. (1983). Psychological correlates of alienation: Study of a sample of Indochinese refugees. *Journal of Cross-Cultural Psychology, 14,* 337-351.

Nicassio, P. M. (1985). The psychosocial adjustment of the Southeast Asian refugee: An overview of empirical findings and theoretical models. *Journal of Cross-Cultural Psychology, 16,* 153-173.

Nilsson, L-G., Mantyla, T., & Sandberg, K. (1987). A functionalist approach to memory: Theory and data. *Scandinavian Journal of Psychology, 28,* 173-188.

Ninness, H. A. C., Fuerst, J., Rutherford, R. D., & Glenn, S. S. (1991). Effects of self-management training and reinforcement on the transfer of improved conduct in the absence of a supervisor. *Journal of Applied Behavior Analysis, 24,* 499-508.

Nisbett, R. E., & Wilson, T. D. (1977). Telling more than we can know: Verbal reports on mental processes. *Psychological Review, 84,* 231-259.

Noble, W., & Davidson, I. (1991). The evolutionary emergence of modern human behaviour: Language and its archaeology. *Man* (N.S.), *26,* 223-253.

Nordquist, V. M. (1971). The modification of a child's enuresis: Some response-response relationships. *Journal of Applied Behavior Analysis, 4,* 241-247.

Northcraft, G. B., & Neale, M. A. (1987). Experts, amateurs, and real estate: An anchoring-and-adjustment perspective on property pricing decisions. *Organizational Behavior and Human Decision Processes, 39,* 84-97.

Notterman, J. M. & Mintz, D. E. (1962). Exteroceptive cueing of response force. *Science, 135,* 1070-1071.

Notterman, J. M. (1959). Force emission during bar pressing. *Journal of Experimental Psychology, 58,* 341-347.

Novelli, W. D. (1990). Applying social marketing to health promotion and disease prevention. K. Glanz, F. M. Lewis, & B. K. Rimer (Eds.), *Health behavior and health education: Theory, research and practice* (pp. 342-369). San Francisco: Jossey-Bass.

O'Brien, R. M., Dickinson, A. M., & Rosnow, M. P. (Eds.). (1982). *Industrial behavior modification.* New York: Pergamon.

O'Dell, S. (1974). Training parents in behavior modification: A review. *Psychological Bulletin, 81,* 418-433.

O'Mara, H. (1991). Quantitative and methodological aspects of stimulus equivalence. *Journal of the Experimental Analysis of Behavior, 55,* 125-132.

Oah, S., & Dickinson, A. M. (1989). A review of empirical studies of verbal behavior. *The Analysis of Verbal Behavior, 7,* 53-68.

Olvera, D., & Hake, D. F. (1976). Producing a change from competition to sharing: Effects of large and adjusting response requirements. *Journal of the Experimental Analysis of Behavior, 26,* 321-333.

Ono, K. (1987). Superstitious behavior in humans. *Journal of the Experimental Analysis of Behavior, 47,* 261-271.

Orbell, J. M., van der Kragt, A. J. C., & Dawes, R. M. (1988). Explaining discussion-induced cooperation. *Journal of Personality and Social Psychology, 54,* 811-819.

Orlandi, M. A., Landers, C., Weston, R., & Haley, N. (1990). Diffusion of health promotion innovations. K. Glanz, F. M. Lewis, & B. K. Rimer (Eds.), *Health behavior and health education: Theory, research and practice* (pp. 288-313). San Francisco: Jossey-Bass.

Orne, M. T., & Schreibe, K. E. (1964). The contribution of nondeprivation factors in the production of sensory deprivation effects: The psychology of the panic button. *Journal of Abnormal and Social Psychology, 68,* 3-12.

Oskamp, S. (Ed.). (1988). *Television as a social issue: Applied social psychology annual, Vol. 8.* London: Sage.

Oskamp, S., & Kleinke, C. (1970). Amount of reward as a variable in the prisoner's dilemma game. *Journal of Personality and Social Psychology, 16,* 133-140.

Osnes, P. G., Guevremont, D. C., & Stokes, T. F. (1987). Increasing a child's prosocial behaviors: Positive and negative consequences in correspondence training. *Journal of Behavior Therapy and Experimental Psychiatry, 18,* 71-76.

Ostrom, T. M., Lingle, J. H., Pryor, J., & Geva, N. (1980). Cognitive organization of person impressions. In R. Hastie, T. M. Ostrom, D. L. Hamilton, R. S. Wyer, E. Ebbesen, & D Carlston (Eds.), *Person-memory: The cognitive basis of social perception* (pp. 55-88). Hillsdale, NJ: Erlbaum.

Overskeid, G. (1992). Is any human behavior schedule-induced? *The Psychological Record, 42,* 323-340.

Owen, N. (1981). Facilitating maintenance of behavior change. In E. Boberg (Ed.), *Maintenance of fluency* (pp. 31-70). New York: Elsevier.

Page, S., & Neuringer, A. (1985). Variability is an operant. *Journal of Experimental Psychology: Animal Behavior Processes, 11,* 429-452.

Paine, A. L., Suarez-Balcazar, Y., Fawcett, S. B., & Borck-Jameson, L. (1992). Supportive transactions: Their measurement and enhancement in two mutual-aid groups. *Journal of Community Psychology, 20,* 163-180.

Pallak, M. S., & Heller, J. F. (1971). Interactive effects of commitment to future interaction and threat of attitudinal freedom. *Journal of Personality and Social Psychology, 17,* 325-331.

Palmer, D. C. (1991). A behavioral interpretation of memory. In L. J. Hayes, & P. N. Chase (Eds.), *Dialogues on verbal behavior* (pp. 259-285). Reno, Nevada: Context Press.

Palmer, D. C., & Donahoe, J. W. (1992). Essentialism and selectionism in cognitive science and behavior analysis. *American Psychologist, 47,* 1344-1358.

Paloutzian, R. F. (1975). Effects of deindividuation, removal of responsibility, and coaction on impulsive and cyclical aggression. *Journal of Psychology, 90,* 163-169.

Pandey, J., Sinha, Y., Prakash, A., & Tripathi, R. C. (1982). Right-Left political ideologies and attribution of the causes of poverty. *European Journal of Social Psychology, 12,* 327-331.

Paniagua, F. A. (1985). Development of self-care skills and helping behaviors in adolescents in a group home through correspondence training. *Journal of Behavior Therapy and Experimental Psychiatry, 16,* 237-244.

Paniagua, F. A., & Baer, D. M. (1988). Luria's regulatory concept and its misplacement in verbal-nonverbal correspondence training. *Psychological Reports, 62,* 371-378.

Paniagua, F. A., Pumariega, A. J., & Black, S. A. (1988). Clinical effects of correspondence training in the management of hyperactive children. *Behavioral Residential Treatment, 3,* 19-40.

Parke, R. D. (Ed.). (1972). *Recent trends in social learning theory.* New York: Academic Press.

Parrott, L. J. (1983). Defining social behavior: An exercise in scientific system building. *The Psychological Record, 33,* 533-550.

Parrott, L. J. (1984). Listening and understanding. *The Behavior Analyst, 7,* 29-39.

Parrott, L. J. (1985). Toward a descriptive analysis of verbal interaction. *Experimental Analysis of Human Behavior Bulletin, 3,* 12-15.

Parrott, L. J. (1986a). On the differences between verbal and social behavior. In P. N. Chase and L. J. Parrott (Eds.), *Psychological aspects of language* (pp. 91-117). Springfield, IL: Charles C. Thomas.

Parrott, L. J. (1986b). Practices of description and the definition of verbal behavior. *Experimental Analysis of Human Behavior Bulletin, 4,* 6-8.

Parrott, L. J. (1987). On the distinction between setting events and stimuli. *Experimental Analysis of Human Behavior Bulletin, 5,* 6-11.

Parrott, L. J., & Hake, D. F. (1983). Toward a science of history. *The Behavior Analyst, 6,* 121-132

Parry, J. (1986). *The Gift,* the Indian gift and the "Indian gift". *Man* (N.S.), *21,* 453-473.

Parry, J. & Bloch, M. (Eds.). (1989). *Money and the morality of exchange.* Cambridge: Cambridge University Press.

Parsons, J. A.., Taylor, D. C., & Joyce, T. M. (1981). Precurrent self-prompting operants in children: "Remembering". *Journal of the Experimental Analysis of Behavior, 36,* 253-266.

Parsonson, B. S., & Naughton, K. A. (1988). Training generalized conservation in 5-year-old children. *Journal of Experimental Child Psychology, 46,* 372-390.

Patterson, G. R., & Reid, J. B. (1970). Reciprocity and coercion: Two facets of social systems. In C. Neuringer & J. L. Michael (Eds.) *Behavior modification in clinical psychology* (pp. 133-177). New York: Appleton-Century-Crofts.

Patterson, M. L. (1990). Functions of non-verbal behavior in social interaction. In H. Giles & W. P. Robinson (Eds.), *Handbook of language and social psychology* (pp. 101-120). New York: John Wiley.

Patterson, R. L., & Jackson, G. M. (1980). Behavior modification with the elderly. In M. Hersen, R. M. Eisler, & P. M. Miller (Eds.), *Progress in behavior modification* (Vol. 9, pp. 205-239). New York: Academic Press.

Paulus, P. B. (1983). Group influences on individual task performance. In P. B. Paulus (Ed.), *Basic group processes* (pp. 97-120). New York: Springer-Verlag

Peele, D. B., & Ferster, C. B. (1982). Autoshaped key pecking maintained by access to a social space. *Journal of the Experimental Analysis of Behavior, 38,* 181-189.

Perkins, D. V., Burns, T. F., Perry, J. C., & Nielson, K. P. (1988). Behavior setting theory and community psychology: An analysis and critique. *Journal of Community Psychology, 14,* 355-372.

Perri, M. G., McAllister, D. A., Gange, J. J., Jordan, R. C., McAdoo, W. G., & Nezu, A. M. (1988). Effects of four maintenance programs on the long-term management of obesity. *Journal of Consulting and Clinical Psychology, 56,* 529-534.

Perruchet, P., Gallego, J., & Savy, I. (1990). A critical reappraisal of the evidence for unconscious abstraction of deterministic rules in complex experimental situations. *Cognitive Psychology, 22,* 493-516.

Perry, C. L., Telch, M. J., Killen, J., Burke, A., & Maccoby, N. (1983). High school smoking prevention: The relative efficacy of varied treatments and instructors. *Adolescence, 18,* 561-566.

Peters, T. J., & Waterman, R. H. (1982). *In search of excellence.* New York: Harper & Row.

Peterson, N. (1982). Feedback is not a new principle of behavior. *The Behavior Analyst, 5,* 101-102.

Peterson, R. F., & Whitehurst, G. J. (1971). A variable influencing the performance of generalized imitative behaviors. *Journal of Applied Behavior Analysis, 4,* 1-9.

Peterson, W. A., & Gist, N. P. (1951). Rumor and public opinion. *American Journal of Sociology, 57,* 159-167.

Petty, R. E., & Cacioppo, J. T. (1986). *Communication and persuasion: Central and peripheral routes to attitude change.* New York: Springer-Verlag

Petty, R. E., Harkins, S. G., & Williams, K. D. (1980). The effects of group diffusion of cognitive effort on attitudes: An information-processing view. *Journal of Personality and Social Psychology, 38,* 81-92.

Petty, R. E., Harkins, S. G., Williams, K. D., & Latané, B. (1977). The effects of group size on cognitive effort and evaluation. *Personality and Social Psychology Bulletin, 3,* 579-582.

Petty, R. E., Williams, K. D., Harkins, S. G., & Latané, B. (1977). Social inhibition of helping yourself: Bystander response to a cheeseburger. *Personality and Social Psychology Bulletin, 3,* 575-578.

Pierce, W. D., & Epling, W. F. (1983). Choice, matching, and human behavior: A review of the literature. *The Behavior Analyst, 6,* 57-76.

Pierce, W. D., Epling, W. F., & Boer, D. P. (1986). Deprivation and satiation: The interrelations between food and wheel running. *Journal of the Experimental Analysis of Behavior, 46,* 199-210.

Piliavin, J. A., Dovidio, J. F., Gaertner, S. L., & Clark, R. D. (1981). *Emergency intervention.* New York: Academic Press.

Piliavin, J. A., & Unger, R. K. (1985). The helpful but helpless female: Myth or reality. In V. E. O'Leary, R. K. Unger & B. S. Wallston (Eds.), *Women, gender, and social psychology* (pp. 149-189). Hillsdale, NJ: Erlbaum.

Pittam, J., Gallois, C., & Willemyns, M. (1991). Perceived change in ethnolinguistic vitality by dominant and minority subgroups. *Journal of Multilingual and Multicultural Development, 12,* 449-457.

Plous, S. (1989). Thinking the unthinkable: The effects of anchoring on likelihood estimates of nuclear war. *Journal of Applied Social Psychology, 19,* 67-91.

Poling, A. (1986). *A primer of human behavioral pharmacology.* New York: Plenum Press.

Poling, A., & Foster, M. (1993). The Matching Law and organizational behavior management revisited. *Journal of Organizational Behavioral Management, 14,* 83-97.

Poppen, R. L. (1989). Some clinical implications of rule-governed behavior. In S. C. Hayes (Ed.), *Rule-governed behavior: Cognition, contingencies, and instructional control* (pp. 325-357). New York: Plenum Press.

Powell, F. A. (1974). Cognitive tuning and differentiation of arguments in communication. *Human Communication Research, 1,* 53-61.

Powers, W. T. (1973). Feedback: Beyond behaviorism. *Science, 179,* 351-356.

Prasad, J. (1950). A comparative study of rumours and reports in earthquakes. *British Journal of Psychology, 41,* 129-144.

Pratkanis, A. R., Breckler, S. J., & Greenwald, A. G. (Eds.). (1989). *Attitude structure and function.* Hillsdale, NJ: Erlbaum.

Pratkanis, A. R., & Greenwald, A. G. (1985). How shall the self be conceived? *Journal for the Theory of Social Behaviour, 15,* 311-329.

Premack, D. (1962). Reversibility of the reinforcement relation. *Science, 136,* 255-257.

Premack, D. (1965). Reinforcement theory. In D. Levine (Ed.), *Nebraska symposium on motivation* (Vol. 13, pp.123-180). Lincoln: University of Nebraska Press.

Premack, D. (1971). Catching up with common sense or two sides of a generalization: Reinforcement and punishment. In R. Glaser (Ed.), *The nature of reinforcement* (pp.121-150). New York: Academic Press.

Premack, D., & Premack, A. (1963). Increased eating in rats deprived of running. *Journal of the Experimental Analysis of Behavior, 6,* 209-212.

Premack, D., & Schaeffer, R. W. (1962). Distributional properties of operant-level locomotion in the rat. *Journal of the Experimental Analysis of Behavior, 5,* 89-95.

Prentice-Dunn, S., & Rogers, R. W. (1980). Effects of deindividuating situational cues and aggressive models on subjective deindividuation and aggression. *Journal of Personality and Social Psychology, 39,* 104-113.

Prentice-Dunn, S., & Rogers, R. W. (1982). Effects of public and private self-awareness on deindividuation and aggression. *Journal of Personality and Social Psychology, 43,* 503-513.

Prentice-Dunn, S., & Rogers, R. W. (1989). Deindividuation and the self-regulation of behavior. In P. B. Paulus (Ed.), *Psychology of group influence* (2nd ed., pp. 87-109). Hillsdale, New Jersey: Erlbaum.

Price, V. (1989). Social identification and public opinion: Effects of communicating group conflict. *Public Opinion Quarterly, 53,* 197-224.

Pruitt, D. G., Carnevale, P. J. D., Forcey, B., & Slyck, M. V. (1986). Gender effects in negotiation: Constituent surveillance and contentious behavior. *Journal of Experimental Social Psychology, 22,* 264-275.

Pruitt, D. G., Kimmel, M. J., Britton, S., Carnevale, P. J. D., Magenau, J. M., Peragallo, J., & Engram, P. (1978). The effect of accountability and surveillance on integrative bargaining. In H. Sauermann (Ed.), *Beitrage zur experimentellen wirtschaftsforschung* (Vol. 7, pp. 310-343). Tobingen: Mohr.

Pryer, M. W., & Bass, B. M. (1959). Some effects of feedback on behavior in groups. *Sociometry, 22,* 56-63.

Pryor, K. (1984). *Don't shoot the dog! The new art of teaching and training.* New York: Bantam Books.

Pryor, K. W., Haag, R., & O'Reilly, J. (1969). The creative porpoise: Training for novel behavior. *Journal of the Experimental Analysis of Behavior, 12,* 653-661.

Purdy, J. E., & Peel, J. L. (1988). Observing response in goldfish (*Carassius auratus*). *Journal of Comparative Psychology, 102*, 160-168.

Rabbit, P., & Banerji, N. (1989). How does very prolonged practice improve decision speed? *Journal of Experimental Psychology: General, 118*, 338-345.

Rachlin, H. (1974). Self-control. *Behaviorism, 2*, 94-107.

Rachlin, H. (1989). *Judgment, decision, and choice: A cognitive/behavioral synthesis.* New York: Freeman.

Rachlin, H., & Burkhard, B. (1978). The temporal triangle: Response substitution in instrumental conditioning. *Psychological Review, 85*, 22-47.

Rachlin, H., Castrogiovanni, A., & Cross, D. (1987). Probability and delay in commitment. *Journal of the Experimental Analysis of Behavior, 48*, 347-353.

Rachlin, H., & Green, L. (1972). Commitment, choice, and self-control. *Journal of the Experimental Analysis of Behavior, 17*, 15-22.

Rachlin, H., Kagel, J. H., & Battalio, R. C. (1980). Substitutability in time allocation. *Psychological Review, 87*, 355-374.

Rachlin, H., Logue, A. W., Gibbon, J., & Frankel, M. (1986). Cognition and behavior in studies of choice. *Psychological Review, 93*, 33-45.

Radlow, R., Weidner, M. F., & Hurst, P. M. (1968). The effect of incentive magnitude and "motivational orientation" upon choice behaviour in a two-person nonzero-sum game. *Journal of Social Psychology, 74*, 199-208.

Ralph, A. (1990). Discriminant validity of a measurement system for assessing social competence. *Behaviour Change, 7*, 76-83.

Rao, R. K., & Mawhinney, T. C. (1991). Superior-subordinate dyads: Dependence of leader effectiveness on mutual reinforcement contingencies. *Journal of the Experimental Analysis of Behavior, 56*, 105-118.

Rapoport, A. (1975). Research paradigms for studying dynamic decision behavior. In D. Wendt & C. Vlek (Eds.), *Utility, probability, and human decision making* (pp. 349-369). Dordrecht: Reidel.

Rappaport, J. (1987). Terms of empowerment/exemplars of prevention: Towards a theory for community psychology. *American Journal of Community Psychology, 15*, 121-148.

Rappaport, R. A. (1984). *Pigs for the ancestors.* London: Yale University Press.

Ray, B. A. (1972). Strategy in studies of attention: A commentary on D. I. Mostofsky's *Attention: Contemporary theory and analysis. Journal of the Experimental Analysis of Behavior, 17*, 293-297.

Ray, B. A., & Sidman, M. (1970). Reinforcement schedules and stimulus control. In W. N. Schoenfeld (Ed.), *The theory of reinforcement schedules* (pp. 187-214). New York: Appleton-Century-Crofts.

Reber, A. S., Kassin, S. M., Lewis, S., & Cantor, G. (1980). On the relationship between implicit and explicit modes in the learning of a complex rule structure. *Journal of Experimental Psychology: Human Learning and Memory, 6*, 492-502.

Redfield, R. (1947). The folk society. *American Journal of Sociology, 52*, 293-306.

Redman, S., Spencer, E. A., & Sanson-Fisher, R. W. (1990). The role of mass media in changing health-related behaviour: A critical appraisal of two models. *Health Promotion International, 5*, 85-105.

Redmon, W. K., & Lockwood, K. (1987). The matching law and organizational behavior. *Journal of Organizational Behavior Management, 8*, 57-72.

Reese, H. W. (1982). Behavior analysis and life-span developmental psychology. *Developmental Review, 2*, 150-161.

Reid, A. K., & Staddon, J. E. R. (1982). Schedule-induced drinking: Elicitation, anticipation, or behavioral interaction? *Journal of the Experimental Analysis of Behavior, 28,* 1-18.

Reid, D. H., & Hurlbut, B. (1977). Teaching nonvocal communication skills to multihandicapped retarded adults. *Journal of Applied Behavior Analysis, 10,* 591-603.

Reid, D. H., Schuh-Wear, C. L., & Brannon, M. E. (1978). Use of a group contingency to decrease staff absenteeism in a state institution. *Behavior Modification, 2,* 251-266.

Reis, H. T., & Gruzen, J. (1976). On mediating equity, equality, and self-interest: The role of self-presentation in social exchange. *Journal of Experimental Social Psychology, 12,* 487-503.

Reps, P. (1957). *Zen flesh, Zen bones.* Harmondsworth, Middlesex: Penguin.

Reser, J. P., & Scherl, L. M. (1988). Clear and unambiguous feedback: A transactional and motivational analysis of environmental challenge and self encounter. *Journal of Environmental Psychology, 8,* 269-286.

Ribeiro, A de F. (1989). Correspondence in children's self-report: Tacting and manding aspects. *Journal of the Experimental Analysis of Behavior, 51,* 361-367.

Rice, G. E., & Gainer, P. (1962). "Altruism" in the albino rat. *Journal of Comparative and Physiological Psychology, 55,* 123-125.

Ridgway, V. F. (1956). Dysfunctional consequences of performance measures. *Administrative Science Quarterly, 1,* 240-247.

Riegler, H. C., & Baer, D. M. (1989). A developmental analysis of rule-following. In H. W. Reese (Ed.), *Advances in child development and behavior* (Vol. 21, pp. 191-219). New York: Academic Press.

Riger, S. (1992). Epistemological debates, feminist voices: Science, social values, and the study of women. *American Psychologist, 47,* 730-740.

Riley, D., & Eckenrode, J. (1986). Social ties: Subgroup differences in costs and benefits. *Journal of Personality and Social Psychology, 51,* 770-778.

Rincover, A., & Koegel, R. L. (1975). Setting generality and stimulus control in autistic children. *Journal of Applied Behavior Analysis, 8,* 235-246.

Robert, M. (1990). Observational learning in fish, birds, and mammals: A classified bibliography spanning over 100 years of research. *The Psychological Record, 40,* 289-311.

Roberts, A. E. (1969). Development of self-control using Premack's differential rate hypothesis: A case study. *Behavior Research and Therapy, 7,* 341-344.

Roberts, B. (1977). George Herbert Mead: The theory and practice of his social philosophy. *I & C, 2,* 81-106.

Roberts, D. F., & Maccoby, N. (1985). Effects of mass communication. In G. Lindzey & E. Aronson (Eds.), *Handbook of social psychology* (Vol. 2, pp. 539-598). New York: Random House.

Roberts, R. N., Nelson, R. O., & Olson, T. W. (1987). Self-instructions: An analysis of the differential effects of instructions and reinforcement. *Journal of Applied Behavior Analysis, 20,* 235-242.

Roberts, S. (1979). *Order and dispute: An introduction to legal anthropology.* Harmondsworth, Middlesex: Penguin.

Robinson, J. C., & Lewinsohn, P. M. (1973). Experimental analysis of a technique based on the Premack principle changing verbal behavior of depressed individuals. *Psychological Reports, 32,* 199-210.

Robinson, J. P., & Levy, M. R. (1986). Interpersonal communication and news comprehension. *Public Opinion Quarterly, 50,* 160-175.

Roering, K. J., Slusher, E. A., & Schooler, R. D. (1975). Commitment to future interaction in marketing transactions. *Journal of Applied Psychology, 60,* 386-388.

Rogers, E. M. (1983). *Diffusion of innovations* (3rd Ed.). New York: The Free Press.

Rogers, R. W. (1980). Expressions of aggression: Aggression-inhibiting effects of anonymity to authority and threatened retaliation. *Personality and Social Psychology Bulletin, 6,* 315-320.

Rogers, R. W., & Ketchen, C. M. (1979). Effects of anonymity and arousal on aggression. *Journal of Psychology, 102,* 13-19.

Rogers, R. W., & Prentice-Dunn, S. (1981). Deindividuation and anger-mediated interracial aggression: Unmasking regressive racism. *Journal of Personality and Social Psychology, 41,* 63-73.

Rogers-Warren, A., & Baer, D. M. (1976). Correspondence between saying and doing: Teaching children to share and praise. *Journal of Applied Behavior Analysis, 9,* 335-354.

Rogers-Warren, A., Warren, S. F. & Baer, D. M. (1977). A component analysis: Modeling self-reporting, and reinforcement of self-reporting in the development of sharing. *Behavior Modification, 1,* 307-321.

Romaine, S. (1982). *Sociolinguistic variation in speech communities.* London: Edward Arnold.

Romzek, B. S., & Dubnick, M. J. (1987). Accountability in the public sector: Lessons from the Challenger tragedy. *Public Administration Review, 45,* 227-238.

Rook, K. S. (1984). The negative side of social interaction: Impact on psychological well-being. *Journal of Personality and Social Psychology, 46,* 1097-1108.

Rook, K. S. (1987). Reciprocity of social exchange and social satisfaction among older women. *Journal of Personality and Social Psychology, 52,* 145-154.

Roper, T. J. (1980). Behavior of rats during self-initiated pauses in feeding and drinking, and during periodic response-independent delivery of food and water. *Quarterly Journal of Experimental Psychology, 32,* 459-472.

Rorty, R. (1987). Science as solidarity. In J. S. Nelson, A. Megill, & D. N. McCloskey (Eds.), *The rhetoric of the human sciences* (pp. 38-52). Madison, Wisconsin: The University of Wisconsin Press.

Rosaldo, M. Z. (1982). The things we do with words: Ilongot speech acts and speech act theory in philosophy. *Language and Society, 11,* 203-237.

Rosenbaum, M. E., Moore. D. L., Cotton, J. L., Cook, M. S., Hieser, R. A., Shovar, M. N., & Gray, M. J. (1980). Group productivity and process: Pure and mixed reward structures and task interdependence. *Journal of Personality and Social Psychology, 39,* 626-642.

Rosenberg, M. J. (1969). The conditions and consequences of evaluation apprehension. In R. Rosenthal & R. L. Rosnow (Eds.), *Artifact in behavioral science* (pp. 279-349). New York: Academic Press.

Rosenberg, S., & Hall, R. L. (1958). The effects of different social feedback conditions upon performance in dyadic teams. *Journal of Abnormal and Social Psychology, 57,* 271-277.

Rosenberg, S., Spradlin, J. E., & Mabel, S. (1961). Interaction among retarded children as a function of their relative language skills. *Journal of Abnormal and Social Psychology, 63,* 402-410

Rosenfarb, I., & Hayes, S. C. (1984). Social standard setting: The Achilles heel of informational accounts of therapeutic change. *Behavior Therapy, 15,* 515-528.

Rosenfeld, H. M., & Baer, D. M. (1969). Unnoticed verbal conditioning of an aware experimenter by a more aware subject: The double-agent effect. *Psychological Review, 76,* 425-432.

Rosenthal, T. L., & Carstensen, L. L. (Eds.). (1988). Mini-series on aging: Clinical needs and research opportunities. *Behavior Therapy, 19,* 257-384.

Rosnow, R. L. (1980). Psychology of rumor reconsidered. *Psychological Bulletin, 87,* 578-591.

Rosnow, R. L. (1991). Inside rumor: A personal journal. *American Psychologist, 46,* 484-496.

Rosnow, R. L., Esposito, J. L., & Gibney, L. (1987). Factors influencing rumor spreading: Replication and extension. *Language and Communication, 7,* 1-14.

Ross, E. B. (Ed.). (1980). *Beyond the myths of culture: Essays in cultural materialism.* New York: Academic Press.

Rothschild, M. L. (1979, Spring). Marketing communications in nonbusiness situations or why it's so hard to sell brotherhood like soap. *Journal of Marketing, 43,* 11-20.

Rotter, J. B. (1990). Internal versus external control of reinforcement. *American Psychologist, 45,* 489-493.

Rozelle, R. M., & Baxter, J. C. (1981). Influence of role pressure on the perceiver: Judgments of videotaped interviews varying judge accountability and responsibility. *Journal of Applied Psychology, 66,* 437-441.

Russell, B. (1986/1926). The meaning of meaning. *Journal of the Experimental Analysis of Behavior, 45,* 109-113.

Russo, D. C. (1990). A requiem for the passing of the three-term contingency. *Behavior Therapy, 21,* 153-165.

Ryan, R. M., Mims, V., & Koestner, R. (1983). Relation of reward contingency and interpersonal context to intrinsic motivation: A review and test using cognitive evaluation theory. *Journal of Personality and Social Psychology, 45,* 736-750.

Ryle, G. (1949). *The concept of mind.* London: Hutchinson.

Ryle, G. (1971). *Collected papers. Volume 2.* London: Hutchinson.

Sá, C. P. de. (no date). *On the relationship between social representations, social-cultural practices and behavior.* Unpublished paper, UERJ, Rio de Janeiro.

Sahlins, M. D. (1965). On the sociology of primitive exchange. In M. Banton (Ed.), *The relevance of models for social anthropology* (pp. 139-236). London: Tavistock.

Sahlins, M. (1972). *Stone age economics.* London: Tavistock.

Sajwaj, T., Libet, J., & Agras, S. (1974). Lemon-juice therapy: The control of life-threatening rumination in a six-month old infant. *Journal of Applied Behavior Analysis, 7,* 557-563.

Sampson, E. E. (1985). The decentralization of identity: Toward a revised concept of personal and social order. *American Psychologist, 40,* 1203-1211.

Sampson, E. E. (1989). The challenge of social change for psychology: Globilization and psychology's theory of the person. *American Psychologist, 44,* 914-921.

Sanchez, H., & Clark, N. T. (1981). Test of Weiss and Miller's social facilitation hypothesis: Are audiences aversive? *Perceptual and Motor Skills, 53,* 767-772.

Sanders, G. S. (1981). Driven by distraction: An integrative review of social facilitation theory and research. *Journal of Experimental Social Psychology, 17,* 227-251.

Sanderson, P. M. (1989). Verbalizable knowledge and skilled task performance: Association, dissociation, and mental models. *Journal of Experimental Psychology: Learning, Memory, and Cognition, 15,* 729-747.

Santi, A. (1978). The role of physical identity of the sample and the correct comparison stimulus in matching-to-sample paradigms. *Journal of the Experimental Analysis of Behavior, 29,* 511-516.

Sarason, S. B. (1974). *The psychological sense of community: Prospects for a community psychology.* San Fransisco: Jossey-Bass.

Saunders, R. R., & Green, G. (1992). The nonequivalence of behavioral and mathematical equivalence. *Journal of the Experimental Analysis of Behavior, 57,* 227-241

Saussure, F. de. (1983/1916). *Course in general linguistics.* London: Duckworth.

Schaeffer, R. W. (1965). The reinforcement relation as a function of instrumental response baserate. *Journal of Experimental Psychology, 69*, 419-425.

Schaeffer, R. W., & Nolan, R. J. (1974). Verbal learning and reinforcement: A reexamination of the Premack Hypothesis. *Bulletin of the Psychonomic Society, 2*, 431-433.

Schaeffer, R. W., Bauermeister, J. J., & David, J. H. (1973). A test of Premack's "indifference principle". *Bulletin of the Psychonomic Society, 1*, 399-401.

Schank, R. C., & Abelson, R. P. (1977). *Scripts, plans, goals, and understanding.* Hillsdale, NJ: Erlbaum.

Schlenker, B. R., & Schlenker, P. A. (1975). Reactions following counterattitudinal behavior which produces positive consequences. *Journal of Personality and Social Psychology, 31*, 962-971.

Schlinger, H. D. (1992). Theory in behavior analysis: An application to child development. *American Psychologist, 47*, 1396-1410.

Schlinger, H. D. (1993). Separating discriminative and function-altering effects of verbal stimuli. *The Behavior Analyst, 16*, 9-23.

Schlinger, H. D., & Blakely, E. (1987). Function-altering effects of contingency-specifying-stimuli. *The Behavior Analyst, 10*, 41-45.

Schmid, T. L., & Hake, D. F. (1983). Fast acquisition of cooperation and trust: A two-stage view of trusting behavior. *Journal of the Experimental Analysis of Behavior, 40*, 179-192.

Schmitt, D. R. (1974). Effects of reinforcement rate and reinforcer magnitude on choice behavior of humans. *Journal of the Experimental Analysis of Behavior, 21*, 409-419.

Schmitt, D. R. (1976). Some conditions affecting the choice to cooperate or compete. *Journal of the Experimental Analysis of Behavior, 25*, 165-178.

Schmitt, D. R. (1981). Performance under cooperation or competition. *American Behavioral Scientist, 24*, 649-679.

Schmitt, D. R. (1984). Interpersonal relations: Cooperation and competition. *Journal of the Experimental Analysis of Behavior, 42*, 377-383.

Schmitt, D. R. (1986). Competition: Some behavioral issues. *The Behavior Analyst, 9*, 27-34.

Schmitt, D. R. (1987). Interpersonal contingencies: Performance differences and cost-effectiveness. *Journal of the Experimental Analysis of Behavior, 48*, 221-234.

Schmitt, D. R., & Marwell, G. (1971). Taking and the disruption of cooperation. *Journal of the Experimental Analysis of Behavior, 15*, 405-412.

Schneider, R. H., Cavanaugh, K. L., Kasture, H. S., Rothenberg, S., Averbach, R., Robinson, D., & Wallace, R. K. (1990). Health promotion with a traditional system of natural health care: *Maharishi Ayur-Veda. Journal of Social Behavior and Personality, 5*, 1-27.

Schneider, S. M., & Morris, E. K. (1988). Comments on quanta in the analysis of stimulus control. *The Psychological Record, 38*, 501-514.

Schnelle, J. F., Traughber, B., Morgan, D. B., Embry, J. E., Binion, A. F., & Coleman, A. (1983). Management of geriatric incontinence in nursing homes. *Journal of Applied Behavior Analysis, 16*, 235-241.

Schoenfeld, W. N. (1965). Learning theory and social psychology. In O. Klineberg & R. Christie (Eds.), *Perspectives in social psychology* (117-135). New York: Holt, Rinehart and Winston.

Schoenfeld, W. N. (1969). J. R. Kantor's *Objective psychology of grammar* and *Psychology and logic*: A retrospective appreciation. *Journal of the Experimental Analysis of Behavior, 4*, 329-347.

Schoenfeld, W. N. (1976). The "response" in behavior theory. *Pavlovian Journal of Biological Science, 11*, 129-149.

Schoenfeld, W. N. (1978). "Reinforcement" in behavior theory. *Pavlovian Journal of Biological Science, 13,* 135-144.

Schoenfeld, W. N. (1981). Pain: A verbal response. *Neuroscience and Biobehavioral Reviews, 5,* 385-389.

Schoenfeld, W. N., & Cumming, W. W. (1963). Behavior and perception. In S. Koch (Ed.), *Psychology: A study of a science* (Vol. 5, pp. 213-252). New York: McGraw-Hill.

Schoenrade, P. A., Batson, C. D., Brandt, J. R., & Loud, R. E. (1986). Attachment, accountability, and motivation to benefit another not in distress. *Journal of Personality and Social Psychology, 51,* 557-563.

Schofield, M. J., Redman, S., & Sanson-Fisher, R. W. (1991). A community approach to smoking prevention: A review. *Behaviour Change, 8,* 17-25.

Schoneberger, T. (1990). Understanding and the listener. *The Analysis of Verbal Behavior, 8,* 141-150.

Schopler, J., & Bateson, N. (1965). The power of dependence. *Journal of Personality and Social Psychology, 2,* 247-254.

Schopler, J., & Matthews, M. W. (1965). The influence of the perceived causal locus of partner's dependence on the use of interpersonal power. *Journal of Personality and Social Psychology, 2,* 609-612.

Schreibman, L. (1988). *Autism.* Beverly Hills, CA: Sage.

Schroeder, S. R., & Holland, J. G. (1968). Operant control of eye movements. *Journal of Applied Behavior Analysis, 1,* 161-166.

Schwartz, B. (1982). Failure to produce response variability with reinforcement. *Journal of the Experimental Analysis of Behavior, 37,* 171-181.

Schwartz, I. S., & Baer, D. M. (1991). Social-validity assessments: Is current practice state of the art? *Journal of Applied Behavior Analysis, 24,* 189-204.

Schwartz, S. H. (1970). Elicitation of moral obligation and self-sacrificing behavior: An experimental study of volunteering to be a bone marrow donor. *Journal of Personality and Social Psychology, 15,* 283-293.

Schwartz, S. H. (1974). Awareness of interpersonal consequences, responsibility denial, and volunteering. *Journal of Personality and Social Psychology, 30,* 57-63.

Schwartz, S. H., & Gottlieb, A. (1976). Bystander reactions to a violent theft: Crime in Jerusalem. *Journal of Personality and Social Psychology, 34,* 1188-1199.

Schweitzer, J. B., & Sulzer-Azaroff, B. (1988). Self-control: Teaching tolerance for delay in impulsive children. *Journal of the Experimental Analysis of Behavior, 50,* 173-186.

Schwimmer, E. (1973). *Exchange in the social structure of the Orokaiva.* London: C. Hurst.

Scott, W. E. (1975). The effects of extrinsic rewards on "intrinsic motivation". *Organizational Behavior and Human Performance, 15,* 117-129.

Scott, W. E., Farh, J-L., & Podsakoff, P. M. (1988). The effects of "intrinsic" and "extrinsic" reinforcement contingencies on task behavior. *Organizational Behavior and Human Decision Processes, 41,* 405-425.

Searle, J. (1969). *Speech Acts.* Cambridge: Cambridge University Press.

Secan, K. E., Egel, A. L., & Tilley, C. S. (1989). Acquisition, generalization, and maintenance of question-answering skills in autistic children. *Journal of Applied Behavior Analysis, 22,* 181-196.

Seekins, T., & Fawcett, S. B. (1987). Effects of a poverty-clients' agenda on resource allocations by community decision makers. *American Journal of Community Psychology, 15,* 305-320.

Segal, E. F. (1972). Induction and the provenance of operants. In R. M. Gilbert and J. R. Millenson (Eds.), *Reinforcement: Behavioral analyses* (pp. 1-34). New York: Academic Press.

Segal, E. F. (1987). Walden Two: The morality of anarchy. *The Behavior Analyst, 10,* 147-160.

Seidman, E. (1988). Back to the future, community psychology: Unfolding a theory of social intervention. *American Journal of Community Psychology, 16,* 3-24.

Semin, G. R., & Manstead, A. S. R. (1983). *The accountability of conduct: A social psychological analysis.* New York: Academic Press.

Serna, L. A., Schumaker, J. B., Sherman, S. A., & Sheldon, S. B. (1991). In-home generalization of social interactions in families of adolescents with behavior problems. *Journal of Applied Behavior Analysis, 24,* 733-746.

Seta, J. J., Seta, C. E., & Donaldson, S. (1992). The implications of a resource-investment analysis of goal value for performance in audience and solitary settings. *Basic and Applied Social Psychology, 13,* 145-164.

Shaffer, D. R., & Ogden, J. K. (1986). On sex differences in self-disclosure during the acquaintance process: The role of anticipated future interaction. *Journal of Personality and Social Psychology, 51,* 92-101.

Shaffer, D. R., Ogden, J. K., & Wu, C. (1987). Effects of self-monitoring and prospect of future interaction on self-disclosure reciprocity during the acquaintance process. *Journal of Personality, 55,* 75-96.

Shapiro, E. G. (1975). Effects of expectations of future interaction on reward allocations in dyads: Equity or equality? *Journal of Personality and Social Psychology, 31,* 873-880.

Shapiro, S. P. (1987). The social control of impersonal trust. *American Journal of Sociology, 93,* 623-658.

Shaw, J. I., & Thorslund, C. (1975). Varying pattern of reward cooperation: The effects in a Prisoner's Dilemma game. *Journal of Conflict Resolution, 19,* 108-122.

Sheldrake, P., & Linke, R. (1979). *Accountability in higher education.* Sydney: George Allen & Unwin.

Sheppard, B. H., Hartwick, J., & Warshaw, P. R. (1988). The theory of reasoned action: A meta-analysis of past research with recommendations for modifications and future research. *Journal of Consumer Research, 15,* 325-343.

Shepperd, J. A. (1993). Productivity loss in performance groups: A motivational analysis. *Psychological Bulletin, 113,* 67-81.

Sherman, S. (1970). Attitudinal effects of unforeseen consequences. *Journal of Personality and Social Psychology, 16,* 510-520.

Sherman, S. J. (1987). Cognitive processes in the formation, change and expression of attitudes. In M. P. Zanna, J. M. Olson & C. P. Herman (Eds.), *Social influence: The Ontario symposium, Volume 5* (pp. 75-106). Hillsdale, NJ: Erlbaum.

Sheth, J. N., & Frazier, G. L. (1982, Winter). A model of strategy mix choice for planned social change. *Journal of Marketing, 46,* 15-26.

Shettleworth, S. J. (1989). Animals foraging in the lab: Problems and promises. *Journal of Experimental Psychology: Animal Behavior Processes, 15,* 81-87.

Shimoff, E. (1986). Post-session verbal reports and the experimental analysis of behavior. *The Analysis of Verbal Behavior, 4,* 19-22.

Shimoff, E., Matthews, B. A., & Catania, A. C. (1986). Human operant performance: Sensitivity and pseudosensitivity to contingencies. *Journal of the Experimental Analysis of Behavior, 46,* 149-157.

Shure, G., & Meeker, R. J. (1968). Empirical demonstration of normative behavior in the prisoner's Dilemma game. *Proceedings of the Seventy-Sixth Annual Convention, American Psychological Society.*

Sidman, M. (1966). Avoidance behavior. In W. K. Honig (Ed.), *Operant behavior: Areas of research and application* (pp. 448-498). Englewood Cliffs, NJ: Prentice Hall.

Sidman, M. (1978). Remarks. *Behaviorism, 6,* 265-268.

Sidman, M. (1986a). Functional analyses of emergent verbal classes. In T. Thompson & M. D. Zeiler (Eds.), *Analysis and integration of behavioral units* (pp. 213-245). Hillsdale, NJ: Erlbaum.

Sidman, M. (1986b). The measurement of behavior development. In N. A. Krasnegor, D. B. Gray & T. Thompson (Eds.),*Developmental behavioral pharmacology*(pp.43-52). Hillsdale, NJ: Erlbaum.

Sidman, M. (1989). *Coercion and its fallout.* Boston, MA: Authors Cooperative.

Sidman, M. (1990). Equivalence relations: Where do they come from? In D. E. Blackman & H. Lejeune (Eds.), *Behaviour analysis in theory and practice* (pp. 93-114). Hillsdale, NJ: Erlbaum.

Siegel, J., Dubrovsky, V., Kiesler, S., & McGuire, T. W. (1986). Group processes in computer-mediated communication. *Organizational Behavior and Human Decision Processes, 37,* 157-187.

Silberberg, A., Murray, P., Christensen, J., & Asano, T. (1988). Choice in the repeated-gambles experiment. *Journal of the Experimental Analysis of Behavior, 50,* 187-195.

Silver, B. D., Abramson, P. R., & Anderson, B. A. (1986). The presence of others and overreporting of voting in American National Elections. *Public Opinion Quarterly, 50,* 228-239.

Silverman, K., Anderson, S. R., Marshall, A. M., & Baer, D. M. (1986). Establishing and generalizing audience control of new language repertoires. *Analysis and Intervention in Developmental Disabilities, 6,* 21-40.

Silverstone, R. (1993). Television, ontological security and the transitional object. *Media, Culture and Society, 15,* 573-598.

Simmel, G. (1950). *The sociology of Georg Simmel.* New York: The Free Press.

Simmel, G. (1955). *Conflict* and *The web of group-affiliations.* New York: The Free Press.

Simmel, G. (1978/1900). *The philosophy of money.* London: Routledge& Kegan Paul.

Sinha, D. (1952). Behaviour in a catastrophic situation: A psychological study of reports and rumours. *British Journal of Psychology, 43,* 200-209.

Skevington, S., & Baker, D. (Eds.). (1989). *The social identity of women.* London: Sage.

Skinner, B. F. (1934, January). Has Gertrude Stein a secret? *Atlantic Monthly, 153,* 50-57.

Skinner, B. F. (1935). The generic nature of the concepts of stimulus and response. *Journal of General Psychology, 12,* 40-65.

Skinner, B. F. (1938). *The behavior of organisms.* New York: Appleton-Century-Crofts.

Skinner, B. F. (1939). The alliteration in Shakespeare's sonnets: A study in literary behavior. *The Psychological Record, 3,* 186-192.

Skinner, B. F. (1940). The nature of the operant reserve. *American Psychologist, 37,* 423.

Skinner, B. F. (1948). "Superstition" in the pigeon.*Journal of Experimental Psychology,* 38, 168-172.

Skinner, B. F. (1950). Are theories of learning necessary? *Psychological Review, 57,* 193-216.

Skinner, B. F. (1953). *Science and human behavior.* New York: The Free Press.

Skinner, B. F. (1957). *Verbal behavior.* Englewood Cliffs: Prentice Hall.

Skinner, B. F. (1966). The phylogeny and ontogeny of behavior. *Science, 153,* 1205-1213.

Skinner, B. F. (1968). *The technology of teaching*. New York: Appleton-Century-Crofts.

Skinner, B. F. (1969). *Contingencies of reinforcement: A theoretical analysis*. Englewood Cliffs: Prentice Hall.

Skinner, B. F. (1971). *Beyond freedom and dignity*. New York: Knopf.

Skinner, B. F. (1972). On "having" a poem. *Saturday Review*, July 15th.

Skinner, B. F. (1974). *About behaviorism*. New York: Alfred Knopf.

Skinner, B. F. (1977). Herrnstein and the evolution of behaviorism. *American Psychologist, 32*, 1006-1012.

Skinner, B. F. (1980). *Notebooks*. Englewood Cliffs, NJ: Prentice-Hall.

Skinner, B. F. (1981a). Selection by consequences. *Science, 213*, 501-504.

Skinner, B. F. (1981b). How to discover what you have to say—A talk to students. *The Behavior Analyst, 4*, 1-8.

Skinner, B. F. (1982). Contrived reinforcement. *The Behavior Analyst, 5*, 3-8.

Skinner, B. F. (1983). Intellectual self-management in old age. *American Psychologist, 38*, 239-244.

Skinner, B. F. (1985). Cognitive science and behaviourism. *British Journal of Psychology, 76*, 290-301.

Skinner, B. F. (1986a). The evolution of verbal behavior. *Journal of the Experimental Analysis of Behavior, 45*, 115-122.

Skinner, B. F. (1986b). Some thoughts about the future. *Journal of the Experimental Analysis of Behavior, 45*, 229-235.

Skinner, B. F. (1987). What is wrong with daily life in the western world? *American Psychologist, 41*, 568-574.

Skinner, B. F. (1988). A fable. *The Analysis of Verbal Behavior, 6*, 1-2.

Skinner, B. F. (1989). The behavior of the listener. In S. C. Hayes (Ed.), *Rule-governed behavior: Cognition, contingencies, and instructional control* (pp. 85-96). New York: Plenum Press.

Skinner, B. F., & Vaughan, M. (1983). *Enjoy old age*. New York: Norton.

Slavin, R. E. (1977). Classroom reward structure: An analytical and practical review. *Review of Educational Research, 47*, 633-650.

Sloane, H. N., Endo, G. T., & Della-Piana, G. (1980). Creative behavior. *The Behavior Analyst, 3*, 11-21.

Slovic, P. (1969). Differential effects of real versus hypothetical payoffs on choices among gambles. *Journal of Experimental Psychology, 80*, 434-437.

Slovic, P., Weinstein, M. S., & Lichtenstein, S. (1969). Sex differences in the risks a person selects for himself and the risks he selects for someone else. *Oregon Research Bulletin, 7*, n. 10.

Slusher, E. A. (1978). Counterpart strategy, prior relations, and constituent pressure in a bargaining simulation. *Behavioral Science, 23*, 470-477.

Slusher, E. A., Rose, G. L., & Roering, K. J. (1974). The effects of commitment to future interaction in single plays of three games. *Behavioral Science, 19*, 119-132.

Slusher, E. A., Rose, G. L., & Roering, K. J. (1978). Commitment to future interaction and relative power under conditions of interdependence. *Journal of Conflict Resolution, 22*, 282-298.

Smith, B. L. R., & Carroll, J. D. (Eds.). (1982). *Improving the accountability and performance of government*. Washington, DC: Brookings Institute.

Smith, J. F., Fawcett, S. B., & Balcazar, F. E. (1991). Behaviour analysis of social-action constructs: The case of empowerment. *Behaviour Change, 8*, 4-9.

Smith, K. (1974). The continuum of reinforcement and attenuation. *Behaviorism, 2*, 124-145.

Smith, K. H. (1972). Changes in group structure through individual and group feedback. *Journal of Personality and Social Psychology, 24,* 425-428.

Smith, L. K. C., & Fowler, S. A. (1984). Positive peer pressure: The effects of peer monitoring on children's disruptive behavior. *Journal of Applied Behavior Analysis, 17,* 213-227.

Smith, M., & Walker, I. (1992). The structure of attitudes to a single object: Adapting Critical Referents Theory to measure attitudes to 'woman'. *British Journal of Social Psychology, 31,* 201-214.

Smith, M. B., Bruner, J. S., & White, R. W. (1956). *Opinions and personality.* New York: Wiley.

Smith, R. F. I., & Weller, P. (1978). *Public service inquiries in Australia.* St. Lucia: University of Queensland Press.

Smith, T. L. (1983). Vargas on the autoclitic. *The Analysis of Verbal Behavior, 2,* 11-12.

Snyder, C. R., Smith, T. W., Augelli, R. W., & Ingram, R. E. (1985). On the self-serving function of social anxiety: Shyness as a self-handicapping strategy. *Journal of Personality and Social Psychology, 48,* 970-980.

Snyder, M., & DeBono, K. G. (1987). A functional approach to attitudes and persuasion. In M. P. Zanna, J. M. Olson & C. P. Herman (Eds.), *Social influence: The Ontario symposium, Volume 5* (pp. 107-125). Hillsdale, NJ: Erlbaum.

Society for the Experimental Analysis of Behavior (1987a). *Behavior analysis in developmental disabilities.* Lawrence, Kansas: Department of Human Development, University of Kansas.

Society for the Experimental Analysis of Behavior (1987b). *Behavior analysis in the community.* Lawrence, Kansas: Department of Human Development, University of Kansas.

Solomon, L. (1960). The influence of some types of power relationships and game strategies upon the development of interpersonal trust. *Journal of Abnormal and Social Psychology, 61,* 223-230.

Sorrentino, R. M., & Higgins, E. T. (Eds.). (1986). *Handbook of motivation and cognition: Foundations of social behavior.* New York: Guilford Press.

Sotirakopoulou, K. P., & Breakwell, G. M. (1992). The use of different methodological approaches in the study of social representations. *Papers on Social Representations, 1,* 29-38.

Spann, R. D. (1979). *Government administration in Australia.* Sydney: George Allen & Unwin.

Spears, R., Lea, M., & Lee, S. (1990). De-individuation and group polarization in computer-mediated communication. *British Journal of Social Psychology, 29,* 121-134.

Speltz, M. L., Shimamura, J. W., & McReynolds, W. T. (1982). Procedural variations in group contingencies: Effects on children's academic and social behaviors. *Journal of Applied Behavior Analysis, 15,* 533-544

Spence, J. T., & Sawin, L. L. (1985). Images of masculinity and femininity: A reconceptualization. In V. E. O'Leary, R. K. Unger & B. S. Wallston (Eds.), *Women, gender, and social psychology* (pp. 35-66). Hillsdale, NJ: Erlbaum.

Spence, K. W. (1956). *Behavior theory and conditioning.* New Haven: Yale University Press.

Spence, K. W. (1960). Cognitive versus stimulus response theories of learning. In K. W. Spence (Ed.), *Behavior theory and learning: Selected papers* (pp. 245-265). Englewood Cliffs, NJ: Prentice-Hall.

Spradlin, J. E. (1985). Studying the effects of the audience on verbal behavior. *The Analysis of Verbal Behavior, 3,* 6-10.

Spradlin, J. E., & Saunders, R. R. (1984). Behaving appropriately in new situations: A stimulus class analysis. *American Journal of Mental Deficiency, 88,* 574-579.

Sproull, L., & Kiesler, S. (1986). Reducing social context cues: Electronic mail in organizational communication. *Management Science, 32*, 1492-1512.

Sproull, L., & Kiesler, S. (1991a, September). Computer, networks and work. *Scientific American, 265*, 84-91.

Sproull, L., & Kiesler, S. (1991b). *Connections: New ways of working in the networked organization*. Cambridge, MA: MIT Press.

Squire, C. (1990). Feminism as antipsychology: Learning and teaching in feminist psychology. In E. Burman (Ed.), *Feminists and psychological practice* (pp. 76-88). London: Sage.

Staats, A. W. (1975). *Social behaviorism*. Chicago: Dorsey Press.

Staats, E. B. (1982). Governmental performance in perspective: Achievements and challenges. In B. L. R. Smith & J. D. Carroll (Eds.), *Improving the accountability and performance of government* (pp. 19-34). Washington, DC: Brookings Institute.

Staddon, J. E. R. (1967). Asymptotic behavior: The concept of the operant. *Psychological Review, 74*, 377-391.

Staddon, J. E. R. (1977). Schedule-induced behavior. In W. K. Honig and J. E. R. Staddon (Eds.), *Handbook of operant behavior* (pp. 125-152). Englewood Cliffs, NJ: Prentice Hall.

Staddon, J. E. R., & Simmelhag, V. L. (1971). The "superstition" experiment: A reexamination of its implications for the principles of adaptive behavior. *Psychological Review, 78*, 3-43.

Stafford, M. W., Sundberg, M. L., & Braam, S. J. (1988). A preliminary investigation of the consequences that define the mand and the tact. *The Analysis of Verbal Behavior, 6*, 61-71.

Stammbach, E. (1988). Group responses to specially skilled individuals in a *Macaca fascicularis* group. *Behavior, 107*, 241-266.

Steigleder, M. K., Weiss, R. F., Cramer, R. E., & Feinberg, R. A. (1978). Motivating and reinforcing functions of competitive behavior. *Journal of Personality and Social Psychology, 36*, 1291-1301.

Steiner, F. (1956). *Taboo*. Harmondsworth: Penguin.

Steinman, W. M. (1970). The social control of generalized imitation. *Journal of Applied Behavior Analysis, 3*, 159-167.

Steinman, W. M. (1977). Generalized imitation and the setting event concept. In B. C. Etzel, J. M. LeBlanc, & D. M. Baer (Eds.), *New developments in behavioral research: Theory, method and application* (pp. 103-109). Hillsdale, NJ: Erlbaum.

Stephenson, G. M., Clark, N. K., & Wade, G. S. (1986). Meetings make evidence? An experimental study of collaborative and individual recall of a simulated police interrogation. *Journal of Personality and Social Psychology, 50*, 1113-1122.

Stokes, T. F., & Baer, D. M. (1977). An implicit technology of generalization. *Journal of Applied Behavior Analysis, 10*, 349-367.

Stokes, T. F., Baer, D. M., & Jackson, R. L. (1974). Programming the generalization of a greeting response in four retarded children. *Journal of Applied Behavior Analysis, 7*, 599-610.

Stokes, T. F., Fowler, S. A., & Baer, D. M. (1978). Training preschool children to recruit natural communities of reinforcement. *Journal of Applied Behavior Analysis, 11*, 285-303.

Stokes, T. F., & Osnes, P. G. (1988). The developing applied technology of generalization and maintenance. In R. H. Horner, G. Dunlap, and R. L. Koegel (Eds.), *Generalization and maintenance: Life-style changes in applied settings* (pp. 5-19). Baltimore, MD: Paul Brookes.

Stokes, T. F., & Osnes, P. G. (1989). An operant pursuit of generalization. *Behavior Therapy, 20*, 337-355.

Stokes, T. F., Osnes, P. G., & Guevremont, D. C. (1987). Saying and doing: A commentary on a contingency-space analysis. *Journal of Applied Behavior Analysis, 20,* 161-164.

Stolz, S. B. (1981). Adoption of innovations from applied behavioral research: "Does anybody care?" *Journal of Applied Behavior Analysis, 14,* 491-506.

Stoneman, K. G., & Dickinson, A. M. (1989). Individual performances as a function of group contingencies and group size. *Journal of Organizational Behavior Management, 10,* 131-150.

Storey, K., & Horner, R. H. (1991). Social interactions in three supported employment options: A comparative analysis. *Journal of Applied Behavior Analysis, 24,* 349-360.

Street, R. L. (1990). The communicative functions of paralanguage and prosody. In H. Giles & W. P. Robinson (Eds.), *Handbook of language and social psychology* (pp. 121-140). New York: John Wiley.

Street, R. L., & Giles, H. (1982). Speech accommodation theory: A social cognitive approach to language and speech behavior. In M. E. Roloff & C. R. Berger (Eds.), *Social cognition and communication* (pp. 193-226). London:Sage.

Street, W. R. (1987). *A behavior analysis of social psychology and the social psychology of behavior analysis.* Presented to the annual meeting of the Association for Behavior Analysis, Nashville, Tennessee, May 27th.

Street, W. R. (1994). "Mindfulness" and "self-focused attention": A behavioral reconstruction. *The Behavior Analyst, 17.*

Stromer, R. (1991). Stimulus equivalence: Implications for teaching. In W. Ishaq (Ed.), *Human behavior in today's world* (pp.109-122). New York: Praeger.

Stryk, L., & Ikemoto, T. (Eds.). (1977). *The Penguin book of Zen poetry.* Harmondsworth, Middlesex: Penguin.

Suls, J. & Wills, T. A. (Eds.). (1991). *Social comparison: Contemporary theory and research.* Hillsdale, NJ: Erlbaum.

Sulzer-Azeroff, B. (1990). Strategies for maintaining change over time. *Behaviour Change, 7,* 3-15.

Sulzer-Azeroff, B., & Mayer G. R. (1977). *Applying behavior-analysis procedures with children and youth.* New York: Holt, Rinehart & Winston.

Sulzer-Azeroff, B., & Santamaria, M. C. de. (1980). Industrial safety hazard reduction through performance feedback. *Journal of Applied Behavior Analysis, 13,* 287-295.

Sundberg, M. L. (1991). 301 research topics from Skinner's book *Verbal Behavior. The Analysis of Verbal Behavior, 9,* 81-96.

Svartdal, F. (1988). The covert behavior of attributing: A review of Bernard Weiner's *An attributional theory of motivation and emotion. Behaviorism, 16,* 167-173.

Svenson, O., & Edland, A. (1987). Change of preferences under time pressure: Choices and judgements. *Scandinavian Journal of Psychology, 28,* 322-330.

Swindell, A., & Mann, L. (1984). *Social loafing and social effort in preparing for a decision making task.* Paper read at the 13th Annual Meeting of Australian Social Psychologists, Adelaide.

Switzer, F. S., & Sniezek, J. A. (1991). Judgment processes in motivation: Anchoring and adjustment effects on judgment and behavior. *Organizational Behavior and Human Decision Processes, 49,* 208-229.

Szymanski, K., & Harkins, S. G. (1993). The effect of experimenter evaluation on self-evaluation within the social loafing paradigm. *Journal of Experimental Social Psychology, 29,* 268-286.

Tajfel, H. (1974). Social identity and intergroup behaviour. *Social Science Information, 13* (2), 65-93.

Tajfel, H., Billig, M., Bundy, R. P., & Flament, C. (1971). Social categorization and intergroup behaviour. *European Journal of Social Psychology, 1,* 149-177.

Tajfel, H., & Turner, J. (1979). An integrative theory of intergroup conflict. In S. Worchel & W. G. Austin (Eds.), *Psychology of intergroup relations* (pp. 33-47). Chicago: Nelson.

Tajfel, H., & Wilkes, A. L. (1963). Classification and quantitative judgement. *British Journal of Psychology, 54,* 101-114.

Tanizaki, J. (1957). *The Makioka sisters.* New York: Alfred A. Knopf.

Taylor, C. J. (1975). Study of altruism in rats in an appetitive situation. *Psychological Reports, 36,* 571-574.

Taylor, S. E. (1975). On inferring one's attitudes from one's behavior: Some delimiting conditions. *Journal of Personality and Social Psychology, 31,* 126-131.

Tedeschi, J. T. (Ed.). (1981). *Impression management theory and social psychological research.* New York: Academic Press.

Teitelbaum, P. (1977). Levels of integration of the operant. In W. K. Honig and J. E. R. Staddon (Eds.), *Handbook of operant behavior* (pp. 7-27). Englewood Cliffs, NJ: Prentice Hall.

Terrell, D. J., & Johnston, J. M. (1989). Logic, reasoning, and verbal behavior. *The Behavior Analyst, 12,* 35-44.

Tetlock, P. E. (1983a). Accountability and complexity of thought. *Journal of Personality and Social Psychology, 45,* 74-83.

Tetlock, P. E. (1983b). Accountability and the perseverance of first impressions. *Social Psychology Quarterly, 46,* 285-292.

Tetlock, P. E. (1985a). Accountability: The neglected social context of judgment and choice. *Research in Organizational Behavior, 7,* 297-332.

Tetlock, P. E. (1985b). Accountability: A social check on the fundamental attribution error. *Social Psychology Quarterly, 48,* 227-236.

Tetlock, P. E., & Kim, J. I. (1987). Accountability and judgment processes in a personality prediction task. *Journal of Personality and Social Psychology, 52,* 700-709.

Tetlock, P. E., & Levi, A. (1982). Attribution bias: On the inconclusiveness of the cognition-motivation debate. *Journal of Experimental Social Psychology, 18,* 68-88.

Tetlock, P. E., & Manstead, A. S. R. (1985). Impression management versus intrapsychic explanations in social psychology: A useful dichotomy? *Psychological Review, 92,* 59-77.

Thibaut, J. W., & Kelley, H. H. (1959). *The social psychology of groups.* New York: John Wiley.

Thoits, P. A. (1983). Multiple identities and psychological well-being: A reformulation and test of the social isolation hypothesis. *American Sociological Review, 48,* 174-187.

Thompson, J. B. (1990). *Ideology and modern culture.* Oxford: Polity Press.

Thompson, K. R., & Luthans, F. (1983). A behavioral interpretation of power. In R. W. Allen & L. W. Porter (Eds.), *Organizational influence processes* (pp. 72-86). Glenview, IL: Scott Foreman.

Thompson, T., & Grabowski, J. G. (1972). *Reinforcement schedules and multioperant analysis.* New York: Appleton-Century-Crofts.

Thompson, T., & Lubinski, D. (1986). Units of analysis and kinetic structure of behavioral repertoires. *Journal of the Experimental Analysis of Behavior, 46,* 219-242.

Thompson. T., Pickens, R., & Meisch, R. A. (Eds.). (1970). *Readings in behavioral pharmacology.* New York: Appleton-Century-Crofts.

Thompson, T. & Zeiler, M. D. (Eds.). (1986). *Analysis and integration of behavioral units.* Hillsdale, NJ: Erlbaum

Thyer, B. A. (1983). Behavior modification and social work practice. In M. Hersen, P. Miller & R. Eisler, R. (Eds.), *Progress in behavior modification* (Vol 15, pp. 172-226). New York: Academic Press.

Thyer, B. A. (1987). Can behavior analysis rescue social work? *Journal of Applied Behavior Analysis, 20,* 207-211.

Thyer, B. A., & Himle, J. (1986). Applied behavior analysis in social and community action: A bibliography. *Behavior Analysis and Social Action, 5,* 14-16.

Thynne, I., & Goldring, J. (1981). Government "responsibility" and responsible government. *Politics, 16,* 197-207.

Titchener, E. B. (1915). *A text-book of psychology.* New York: The Macmillan Company.

Timberlake, W. (1980). A molar equilibrium theory of learned performance. In G. H. Bower (Ed.), *The psychology of learning and motivation* (Vol. 14, pp. 1-58). New York: Academic Press.

Timberlake, W. (1984). Behavior regulation and learned performance: Some misapprehensions and disagreements. *Journal of the Experimental Analysis of Behavior, 41,* 355-375.

Timberlake, W., & Allison, J. (1974). Response deprivation: An empirical approach to instrumental performance. *Psychological Review, 81,* 146-164.

Timberlake, W., & Farmer-Dougan, V. A. (1991). Reinforcement in applied settings: Figuring out ahead of time what will work. *Psychological Bulletin, 110,* 379-391.

Timberlake, W., & Grant, D. L. (1975). Auto-shaping in rats to the presentation of another rat predicting food. *Science, 190,* 690-692.

Timberlake, W., & Lucas, G. A. (1985). The basis of superstitious behavior: Chance contingency, stimulus substitution, or appetitive behavior? *Journal of the Experimental Analysis of Behavior, 44,* 279-299.

Todd, J. T., & Morris, E. K. (1992). Case histories in the great power of study misrepresentation. *American Psychologist, 47,* 1441-1453.

Todd, J. T., Morris, E. K., & Fenza, K. M. (1989). Temporal organization of extinction-induced responding in preschool children. *The Psychological Record, 39,* 117-130.

Tonkin, E. (1991). *Narrating our pasts: The social construction of oral history.* Cambridge: Cambridge University Press.

Tönnies, F. (1957/1887). *Community and society.* East Lansing, MI: Michigan State University Press.

Trudgill, P. (Ed.). (1984). *Applied sociolinguistics.* New York: Academic Press.

Tuchman, G., Daniels, A. K., & Benét, J. (Eds.). (1978). *Hearth and home: Images of women in the mass media.* New York: Oxford University Press.

Tuckman, B. (1965). Developmental sequence in small groups. *Psychological Bulletin, 63,* 384-399.

Turner, J. C., & Giles, H. (1981). *Intergroup behavior.* Oxford: Basil Blackwell.

Turner, J. C., Hogg, M. A., Oakes, P. J., Reicher, S. D., & Wetherall, M. (1987). *Rediscovering the social group: A self-categorization theory.* Oxford: Basil Blackwell.

Turner, J. C., Hogg, M. A., Turner, P. J., & Smith, P. M. (1984). Failure and defeat as determinants of group cohesiveness. *British Journal of Social Psychology, 23,* 97-111.

Turner, J. C., & Oakes, P. J. (1989). Self-categorization theory and social influence. In P. B. Paulus (Ed.), *Psychology of group influence* (2nd ed., pp. 233-275). Hillsdale, New Jersey: Erlbaum.

Turner, J. H. (1990). Emile Durkheim's theory of social organization. *Social Forces, 68,* 1089-1103.

Turvey, M. T. (1977). Preliminaries to a theory of action with reference to vision. In R. Shaw and J. D. Bransford (Eds.), *Perceiving, acting, and knowing* (pp. 211-265). Hillsdale, NJ: Erlbaum.

Turvey, M. T., & Carello, C. (1986). The ecological approach to perceiving-acting: A pictorial essay. *Acta Psychologica, 63,* 133-155.

Tversky, A., & Kahneman, D. (1973). Availability: A heuristic for judging frequency and probability. *Cognitive Psychology, 5,* 207-232.

Tversky, A., & Kahneman, D. (1974). Judgment under uncertainty: Heuristics and biases. *Science, 185,* 1124-1131.

Tyler, T. R., & Cook, F. L. (1984). The mass media and judgments of risk: Distinguishing the impact on personal and societal level judgements. *Journal of Personality and Social Psychology, 47,* 693-708.

Ulman, J. D. (1985). The promotive: A verbal operant related to production. *The Analysis of Verbal Behavior, 3,* 18-20.

Ulrich, R., & Mountjoy, P. (Eds.). (1972). *The experimental analysis of social behavior.* New York: Appleton-Century-Crofts.

Unger, R. K. (1988). Psychological, feminist, and personal epistemology: Transcending contradiction. In M. M. Gergen (Ed.), *Feminist thought and the structure of knowledge* (pp. 124-141). New York: New York University Press.

Van Hasselt, V. B., Sisson, L. A., & Aach, S. R. (1987). Parent training to increase compliance in a young multihandicapped child. *Journal of Behavior Therapy and Experimental Psychiatry, 18,* 275-283.

Van Houten, R., Nau, P. A., MacKenzie-Keating, S. E., Sameoto, D., & Colavecchia, B. (1982). An analysis of some variables influencing the effectiveness of reprimands. *Journal of Applied Behavior Analysis, 15,* 65-83.

van Tilburg, T., van Sonderen, E., & Ormel, J. (1991). The measurement of reciprocity in ego-centered networks of personal relationships: A comparison of various indices. *Social Psychological Quarterly, 54,* 54-66.

Vargas, E. A. (1985). Cultural contingencies: A review of Marvin Harris' *Cannibals and kings. Journal of the Experimental Analysis of Behavior, 43,* 419-428.

Vargas, E. A. (1986). Intraverbal behavior. In P. N. Chase and L. J. Parrott (Eds.), *Psychological aspects of language* (pp. 128-151). Springfield, IL: Charles C. Thomas.

Vargas, E. A. (1988). Verbally-governed and event-governed behavior. *The Analysis of Verbal Behavior, 6,* 11-22.

Vaughan, M. E., & Michael, J. L. (1982). Automatic reinforcement: An important but ignored concept. *Behaviorism, 10,* 217-227.

Vaughan, W., & Miller, H. L. (1984). Optimization versus response-strength accounts of behavior. *Journal of the Experimental Analysis of Behavior, 42,* 337-348.

Vidmar, N. (1971). Effects of representational roles and mediators on negotiation effectiveness. *Journal of Personality and Social Psychology, 17,* 48-58.

Verplank, W. S. (1955). The control of the content of conversation: Reinforcement of statements of opinion. *Journal of Abnormal and Social Psychology, 51,* 668-676.

Voeltz, L. M., & Evans, I. M. (1982). The assessment of behavioral interrelationships in child behavior therapy. *Behavioral Assessment, 4,* 131-165.

Volger, R. E. (1968). Possibility of artifact in studies of cooperation. *Psychological Reports, 23,* 9-10.

Vollmer, T. R., & Iwata, B. A. (1991). Establishing operations and reinforcement effects. *Journal of Applied Behavior Analysis, 24,* 279-291.

von Cranach, M., Doise, W., & Mugny, G. (Eds.). (1992). *Social representations and the social bases of knowledge.* Bern: Hogrefe & Huber.

von Grumbkow, J., Deen, E., Steensma, H., & Wilke, H. (1976). The effect of future interaction on the distribution of rewards. *European Journal of Social Psychology, 6,* 119-123.

von Winterfeldt, D., & Edwards, W. (1986). *Decision analysis and behavioral research.* Cambridge: Cambridge University Press.

Vukelich, R., & Hake, D. F. (1974). Effects of the difference between self and coactor scores upon the audit responses that allow access to these scores. *Journal of the Experimental Analysis of Behavior, 22,* 61-71.

Vukelich, R., & Hake, D. F. (1980). Basic research in a natural setting: Auditing or social comparison behavior as a function of class rank. *The Psychological Record, 30,* 17-24.

Vygotsky, L. S. (1978). *Mind in society: The development of higher psychological functions.* Cambridge, MA: Harvard University Press.

Wacker, D. P., & Berg, W. K. (1983). Effects of picture prompts on the acquisition of complex vocational tasks by mentally retarded adolescents. *Journal of Applied Behavior Analysis, 16,* 417-433.

Wahler, R. G. (1975). Some structural aspects of deviant child behavior. *Journal of Applied Behavior Analysis, 8,* 27-42.

Wahler, R. G., & Dumas, J. E. (1989). Attentional problems in dysfunctional mother-child interactions: An interbehavioral model. *Psychological Bulletin, 105,* 116-130.

Wahler, R. G., & Fox, J. J. (1981). Setting events in applied behavior analysis: Toward a conceptual and methodological expansion. *Journal of Applied Behavior Analysis, 14,* 327-338.

Walker, C. J., & Blaine, B. (1991). The virulence of dread rumors: A field experiment. *Language and Communication, 11,* 291-297.

Wall, J. A. (1975a). The effects of constituent trust and representative bargaining visibility on intergroup bargaining. *Organizational Behavior and Human Performance, 14,* 244-256.

Wall, J. A. (1975b). Effects of constituent trust and representative bargaining orientation on intergroup bargaining. *Journal of Personality and Social Psychology, 31,* 1004-1012.

Wallace, I. (1977). Self-control techniques of famous novelists. *Journal of Applied Behavior Analysis, 10,* 515-525.

Wallach, M. A., Kogan, N., & Bem, D. J. (1964). Diffusion of responsibility and level of risk taking in groups. *Journal of Abnormal and Social Psychology, 68,* 263-274.

Wallack, L. (1990). Media advocacy: Promoting health through mass communication. K. Glanz, F. M. Lewis, & B. K. Rimer (Eds.), *Health behavior and health education: Theory, research and practice* (pp. 370-386). San Francisco: Jossey-Bass.

Walster, E. (1966). Assignment of responsibility for an accident. *Journal of Personality and Social Psychology, 3,* 73-79.

Wanchisen, B. A. (1990). Forgetting the lessons of history. *The Behavior Analyst, 13,* 31-37.

Wanchisen, B. A., Tatham, T. A., & Hineline, P. N. (1992). Human choice in "counterintuitive" situations: Fixed- versus progressive-ratio schedules. *Journal of the Experimental Analysis of Behavior, 58,* 67-85.

Wanchisen, B. A., Tatham, T. A., & Mooney, S. E. (1989). Variable-ratio conditioning history produces high- and low-rate fixed-interval performance in rats. *Journal of the Experimental Analysis of Behavior, 52,* 167-179.

Ward, J. M. (1985). Accountability and responsibility: The university challenges of the 1980's. *Australian Journal of Public Administration, 44,* 73-85.

Washburn, D. A., Hopkins, W. D., & Rumbaugh, D. M. (1990). Effects of competition on video-task performance in monkeys (*Macaca mulatta*). *Journal of Comparative Psychology, 104*, 115-121.

Wasik, B. H. (1968). A postcontingency test of the effectiveness of reinforcement. *Psychonomic Science, 13*, 87-88.

Wasik, B. H. (1970). The application of Premack's generalization on reinforcement to the management of classroom behavior. *Journal of Experimental Child Psychology, 10*, 33-43.

Watt, A., Keenan, M., Barnes, D., & Cairns, E. (1991). Social categorization and stimulus equivalence. *The Psychological Record, 41*, 33-50.

Watts, A. W. (1957). *The way of Zen*. Harmondsworth, Middlesex: Penguin.

Watts, W. A., & Holt, L. E. (1970). Logical relationships among beliefs and timing as factors in persuasion. *Journal of Personality and Social Psychology, 16*, 571-582.

Weber, M. (1947). *The theory of social and economic organization*. Oxford: Oxford University Press.

Weber, M. (1948). *From Max Weber: Essays in sociology*. London: Routledge & Kegan Paul.

Weber, M. (1958). *The rational and social foundations of music*. Carbondale, Illinois: Southern Illinois University Press.

Weber, S. J., & Cook, T. D. (1972). Subject effects in laboratory research: An examination of subject roles, demand characteristics, and valid inference. *Psychological Bulletin, 77*, 273-295.

Wegner, D. M. (1987). Transactive memory: A contemporary analysis of the group mind. In B. Mullen & G. R. Goethals (Eds.), *Theories of group behavior* (pp. 185-208). New York: Springer-Verlag.

Wegner, D. M., Wenzlaff, R., Kerker, R. M., & Beattie, A. E. (1981). Incrimination through innuendo: Can media questions become public answers? *Journal of Personality and Social Psychology, 40*, 822-832.

Weick, K. E. (1984). Small wins: Redefining the scale of social problems. *American Psychologist, 39*, 40-49.

Weiner, H. (1964). Conditioning history and human fixed-interval performance. *Journal of the Experimental Analysis of Behavior, 7*, 383-385.

Weiner, H. (1977). An operant analysis of human altruistic responding. *Journal of the Experimental Analysis of Behavior, 27*, 515-528.

Weisberg, P., & Kennedy, D. B. (1969). Maintenance of children's behavior by accidental schedules of reinforcement. *Journal of Experimental Child Psychology, 8*, 222-233.

Weiss, B., Weisz, J. R., & Bromfield, R. (1986). Performance of retarded and nonretarded persons on information processing tasks: Further tests of the similar structure hypothesis. *Psychological Bulletin, 100*, 157-175.

Weiss, R. F., Lombardo, J. P., Warren, D. R., & Kelley, K. A. (1971). Reinforcing effects of speaking in reply. *Journal of Personality and Social Psychology, 20*, 186-199.

Weldon, E., & Gargano, G. M. (1985). Cognitive effort in additive task groups: The effects of shared responsibility on the quality of multiattribute judgments. *Organizational Behavior and Human Decision Processes, 36*, 348-361.

Wells, G. L., Petty, R. E., Harkins, S. G., Kagehiro, D., & Harvey, J. H. (1977). Anticipated discussion of interpretation eliminates actor-observer differences in the attribution of causality. *Sociometry, 40*, 247-253.

Wenrich, W. W. (1963). Response strength of an operant under stimulus control with satiated subjects. *Journal of the Experimental Analysis of Behavior, 6*, 247-248.

Wertsch, J. V. (1985). *Vygotsky and the social formation of mind*. Cambridge, MA: Harvard University Press.

Wetherall, M. (1986). Linguistic repertoires and literacy criticism: New directions for a social psychology of gender. In S. Wilkinson (Ed.), *Feminist social psychology* (pp. 77-95). Milton Keynes, England: Open University Press.

Wetherington, C. L. (1982). Is adjunctive behavior a third class of behavior? *Neuroscience and Biobehavioral Reviews, 6,* 329-350.

White, G. L. (1977). Counternormative behavior as influenced by deindividuating conditions and reference group salience. *Journal of Social Psychology, 103,* 75-90.

White, K. G. (1991). Psychophysics of direct remembering. In M. L. Commons, J. A. Nevin & M. C. Davison (Eds.), *Signal detection mechanisms, models, and applications* (pp. 221-237) Hillsdale, NJ: Erlbaum.

White, K. G., McCarthy, D. C., & Fantino, E. (Eds.). (1989). The experimental analysis of cognition [Special issue]. *Journal of the Experimental Analysis of Behavior, 52* (3).

White, M. J., & Gerstein, L. H. (1987). Helping: The influence of anticipated social sanctions and self-monitoring. *Journal of Personality, 55,* 41-54

White, P. A. (1988). Knowing more about what we can tell: 'Introspective access' and causal report accuracy 10 years later. *British Journal of Psychology, 79,* 13-45.

Whitman, W. (1855/1986). *Leaves of grass.* New York: Viking Penguin.

Wichman, H. (1970). Effects of isolation and communication on cooperation in a two-person game. *Journal of Personality and Social Psychology, 16,* 114-120.

Wike, E. L. (Ed.). (1966). *Secondary reinforcement: Selected experiments.* New York: Harper Row.

Wildavsky, A. (1972). The self-evaluating organization. *Public Administration Review, 32,* 509-520.

Wilkenfield, J., Nickel, M., Blakely, E., & Poling, A. (1992). Acquisition of lever-press responding in rats with delayed reinforcement: A comparison of three procedures. *Journal of the Experimental Analysis of Behavior, 58,* 431-443.

Willer, J. (1971). *The social determination of knowledge.* Englewood Cliffs, NJ: Prentice-Hall.

Williams, B. A. (1983). Revising the principle of reinforcement. *Behaviorism, 11,* 63-88.

Williams, B. A. (1984). Stimulus control and associative learning. *Journal of the Experimental Analysis of Behavior, 42,* 469-483.

Williams, K., Harkins, S., & Latané, B. (1981). Identifiability as a deterrent to social loafing: Two cheering experiments. *Journal of Personality and Social Psychology, 40,* 303-311.

Williams, K. D., & Karau, S. J. (1991). Social loafing and social compensation: The effects of expectations of co-worker performance. *Journal of Personality and Social Psychology, 61,* 570-581.

Williamson, P. N. (1986). Behavioral gerontology. In H. W. Reese and L. J. Parrott (Eds.), *Behavior science: Philosophical, methodological, and empirical advances* (pp. 185-205). Hillsdale, NJ: Erlbaum.

Winch, P. (1958). *The idea of a social science.* London: Routledge and Kegan Paul.

Winett, R. A., King, A. C., & Altman, D. G. (1989). *Health psychology and public health: An integrative approach.* New York: Pergamon Press.

Winkler, R. C. (1980). Behavioral economics, token economies, and applied behavior analysis. In J. E. R. Staddon (Ed.), *Limits to action: The allocation of individual behavior* (pp. 269-297). New York: Academic Press.

Winokur, S. (1976). *A primer of verbal behavior.* Englewood Cliffs, NJ: Prentice Hall.

Winston, A. S., & Baker, J. E. (1985). Behavior analytic studies of creativity: A critical review. *The Behavior Analyst, 8,* 191-205.

Wirth, W. (1986). Control in public administration: Plurality, selectivity and redundancy. In F. X. Kaufmann, G. Majone & V. Ostrom (Eds.), *Guidance, control, and evaluation in the public sector* (pp. 595-624). Berlin: De Gruyter.

Wise, C. R. (1985). Liability of federal officials: An analysis of alternatives. *Public Administration Review, 45,* 746-753.

Wisocki, P. A. (1984). Behavioral approaches to gerontology. In M. Hersen, R. M. Eisler, & P. M. Miller (Eds.), *Progress in behavior modification* (Vol. 16, pp. 121-157). New York: Academic Press.

Wittgenstein, L. (1953) *Philosophical investigations.* Oxford: Basil Blackwell.

Wittig, M. A. (1985). Metatheoretical dilemmas in the psychology of gender. *American Psychologist, 40,* 800-811.

Wober, J. M. (1990). Language and television. In H. Giles & W. P. Robinson (Eds.), *Handbook of language and social psychology* (pp. 561-582). New York: John Wiley.

Wolf, M. M. (1978). Social validity: The case for subjective measurement or how behavior analysis is finding its heart. *Journal of Applied Behavior Analysis, 11,* 203-214.

Wolf, M.M., Braukmann, C.J., & Ramp, K.A. (1987). Serious delinquent behavior as part of a significantly handicapping condition: Cues and supportive environments. *Journal of Applied Behavior Analysis, 20,* 347-359.

Wolf, M.M., Risley, T.R., & Mees, H.L. (1964). Application of operant conditioning procedures to the behavior problems of an autistic child. *Behavior Research and Therapy, 1,* 305-312.

Wolfe, V.V., Boyd, L.A., & Wolfe, D.A. (1983). Teaching cooperative play to behavior-problem preschool children. *Education and Treatment of Children, 6,* 1-9.

Wolff, P.C., Burnstein, D.D., & Cannon, D.L. (1964). The use of schedules of reinforcement to regulate a collective team response rate. *The Psychological Record, 14,* 57-70.

Worchel, S., Coutant-Sassic, D., & Grossman, M. (1992). A developmental approach to group dynamics: A model and illustrative research. In S. Worchel, W. Wood, & J. A. Simpson (Eds.), *Group process and productivity* (pp. 181-202). London: Sage.

Worchel, S., Lind, E. A., & Kaufman, K. H. (1975). Evaluations of group products as a function of expectations of group longevity, outcome of competition, and publicity of evaluations. *Journal of Personality and Social Psychology, 31,* 1089-1097.

Wulfert, E., Dougher, M. J., & Greenway, D. E. (1991). Protocol analysis of the correspondence of verbal behavior and equivalence class formation. *Journal of the Experimental Analysis of Behavior, 56,* 489-504.

Wulfert, E., & Hayes, S. C. (1988). Transfer of a conditional ordering response through conditional equivalence classes. *Journal of the Experimental Analysis of Behavior, 50,* 125-144.

Wyckoff, L. B. (1952). The role of observing responses in discrimination learning. Part I. *Psychological Review, 59,* 431-442.

Yamagishi, T., & Sato, K. (1986). Motivational bases of the public goods problem. *Journal of Personality and Social Psychology, 50,* 67-73.

Yamamoto, J., & Mochizuki, A. (1988). Acquisition and functional analysis of manding with autistic students. *Journal of Applied Behavior Analysis, 21,* 57-64.

Yarkin, K. L., Harvey, J. H., & Bloxom, B. M. (1981). Cognitive sets, attribution, and social interaction. *Journal of Personality and Social Psychology, 41,* 243-252.

Yarkin-Levin, K. (1983). Anticipated interaction, attribution, and social interaction. *Social Psychology Quarterly, 46,* 302-311.

Yerbury, D. (1981). Employee relations and appraisal systems. In R. D. Lansbury (Ed.), *Performance appraisal* (pp. 202-221). South Melbourne: Macmillan Company.

Young-Eisendrath, P. (1988). The female person and how we talk about her. In M. M. Gergen (Ed.), *Feminist thought and the structure of knowledge* (pp. 152-172). New York: New York University Press.

Zaccaro, S. J. (1984). Social loafing: The role of task attractiveness. *Personality and Social Psychology Bulletin, 10,* 99-106.

Zajonc, R. B. (1960). The process of cognitive tuning in communication. *Journal of Abnormal and Social Psychology, 61,* 159-167.

Zajonc, R. B. (1962). The effects of feedback and probability of group success on individual and group performance. *Human Relations, 15,* 149-163.

Zajonc, R. B. (1965). Social facilitation. *Science, 149,* 269-274.

Zajonc, R. B. (1980). Compresence. In P. B. Paulus (Ed.), *Psychology of group influence* (pp. 35-60). Hillsdale, NJ: Erlbaum.

Zalenska, M., & Kogan, N. (1971). Level of risk selected by individuals and groups when deciding for self and for others. *Sociometry, 34,* 198-213.

Zander, A., & Forward, J. (1968). Position in group, achievement motivation and group aspiration. *Journal of Personality and Social Psychology, 8,* 282-288.

Zeiler, M. (1977). Schedules of reinforcement: The controlling variables. In W. K. Honig and J. E. R. Staddon (Eds.), *Handbook of operant behavior* (pp. 210-232). Englewood Cliffs, NJ: Prentice Hall.

Zeiler, M. D. (1972). Superstitious behavior in children: An experimental analysis. In H. W. Reese (Ed.), *Advances in child development and behavior* (Vol. 7, pp. 1-29). New York: Academic Press.

Zeiler, M. D. (1984). The sleeping giant: Reinforcement schedules. *Journal of the Experimental Analysis of Behavior, 42,* 485-493.

Zettle, R. D., & Hayes, S. C. (1980). Conceptual and empirical status of rational-emotive therapy. In M. Hersen, R. M. Eisler & P. M. Miller (Eds.), *Progress in behavior modification* (Vol. 9). New York: Academic Press.

Zettle, R. D., & Hayes, S. C. (1982). Rule-governed behavior: A potential framework for cognitive-behavioral therapy. In P. C. Kendall (Ed.), *Advances in cognitive-behavioral research and therapy* (Vol. 1, pp. 73-118). New York: Academic Press.

Zettle, R. D., & Hayes, S. C. (1986). Dysfunctional control by client verbal behavior: The context of reason-giving. *The Analysis of Verbal Behavior, 4,* 30-38.

Zimbardo, P. G. (1970). The human choice: Individuation, reason, and order versus deindividuation, impulse and chaos. In W. J. Arnold & D. Levine (Eds), *Nebraska Symposium on Motivation 1969* (pp. 237-307). Lincoln, Nebraska: University of Nebraska Press.

Zimmerman, E. H., & Zimmerman, J. (1962). The alteration of behavior in a special classroom situation. *Journal of the Experimental Analysis of Behavior, 5,* 59-60.

Zimmerman, J. (1963). Technique for sustaining behavior with conditioned reinforcement. *Science, 142,* 682-684.

Zucker, L. G. (1986). Production of trust: Institutional sources of economic structure, 1840-1920. *Research in Organizational Behavior, 8,* 53-111.

Zuriff, G. E. (1972). A behavioral interpretation of psychophysical scaling. *Behaviorism, 1,* 118-133.

Zuriff, G. E. (1976). Stimulus equivalence, grammar, and internal structure. *Behaviorism, 4,* 43-52.

Zuriff, G. E. (1979). Ten inner causes. *Behaviorism, 7,* 1-8.

Subject Index

absenteeism, 293
accents, 202
accountability, 111, 115, 215, 219, 223, 293-294
adjunctive behaviors, 77
affect, 187, 236
affection, 101
affordances, 45, 217
aged persons, 290-292
aggression, 24, 75, 77, 79, 88, 99, 110, 136, 262, 290
ambiguous situations, 97, 175, 251
amount of reinforcement, 57, 69-70, 71, 191
analyzing human behavior, 18-19, 43, 44, 48, 49, 52, 57, 58, 61, 66, 67, 78, 80, 85, 88, 99-100, 101, 120, 122, 168-175, 210-211, 222, 261 (*also see* behavioral methodology)
anchoring and adjustment, 174, 193
animal foraging, 70, 135, 177, 193
animal training, 281
animal welfare, 70
animal-human differences, 18, 25, 28, 48, 61, 65, 70, 127, 131, 132, 143, 155, 156, 161, 180-181, 195, 198, 235
anonymity, 111, 114, 118
antecedent conditions, 23
anthropology, 197-198, 210, 215, 221, 225, 246
anticipation, 38, 176
arbitrary relations, 66, 91, 129, 144, 160, 206, 210, 214, 222, 227, 235, 276 (*also see* detached control)
associations, 64-66
attending, 26, 92, 289
attention, withholding, 265
attitude change, 241-243
attitudes, 236-241
attributions, 116, 159, 165, 186, 222-226; causality, 201, 225; responsibility, 232, 234
audience, 145, 149, 151-153, 182, 197, 240, 249
auditing, 96, 100, 130, 251
authority, 138, 198, 213, 220, 270

autism, 164, 290
autoclitics, 91, 147, 148, 203, 204, 212, 238-239, 241, 254, 296
automatic consequences, 44, 45, 127, 146, 262, 272, 289
automatic processing, 172, 235
availability heuristic and biases, 193
avoidance, 48, 53, 118, 180, 214-215, 253, 263, 267, 297
awareness, 26 (*also see* self-awareness)
basic units of psychology, 32, 60
behavior, definition, 31
behavioral methodology, 20-21, 196, 204, 281, 283, 286-287
behavioral model of choice, 190-191
behavioral momentum, 33
behavioral pharmacology, 281
beliefs, 236, 239
bonus, 38
brainstorming, 301
breakdown of tradition, 216 (*also see* self-regulation)
bribery, 263
bureaucracies, 222-224
bursts of behavior, 36
buzzwords, 202
bystander intervention, 132, 162
causality, 201
caution, 299 (*also see* safety, but be careful)
chains, 55, 61, 63, 67, 71
changing behavior, 259-260; ethics, 259, 264, 266, 267-268, 273, 276; generalization, 270-271; individuals, 260-268; maintenance, 217-273; side-effects, 293-302; verbal communities, 293-302; verbal control, 268-270 (*also see* intervention)
children, 76, 151, 218, 287-289
choice, 68-71, 103, 189, 193, 225
chunking, 174
circularity of the reinforcement concept, 39
classical conditioning, 27, 32
cliché phrases, 52
clinical psychology, 282
cognitive processing; environment, 169; time-frame, 170

cognitive psychology, 165-168, 171, 187
cognitive reframing, 269
cognitive science, 173, 178
cognitive tuning, 116, 152
cognitive unconscious, 173
collateral behavior change, 76
community interventions, 207 (*also see* changing behavior)
community psychology, 207, 246
community, 198, 199
competition, 97, 106, 125, 126, 130-131; group, 202
computer analogies, 166
computers, 86; computer communication, 254-255
concepts, 24, 170, 172
conditional discrimination, 62-63, 104
conditioned consequences, 42, 60
conscious cognition, 172
consequences, 37, 41; role of, 17
conservation model, 73
consistency of behavior, attitudes, beliefs, 157, 240, 243
constant ratio rule, 74
contextual control, 62
contingencies, 31
contingency history, 26, 36, 53, 80, 85, 87, 89, 92, 101, 167, 169, 177, 193, 244
contingency layers, 27, 55, 61, 63, 71, 80, 103
contingency space analysis, 159
contrived consequences, 46, 263, 264
control, 259, 283 (*also see* countercontrol)
controlled processing (*also see* verbally controlled behavior), 172, 187
conversation, (*see* social interaction)
cooperation, 116, 118, 125, 126-130, 136, 261
correspondence, 157; training, 158, 183
countercontrol, 157, 223, 293-302
creativity, 189, 298-299, 300
crowds, 109, 110
cultural practices, 137, 138, 154, 159, 174, 197, 213, 233, 269
cultural relativism, 225-226
culture shock, 209
cumulative consequences, 49
danger, 214

decision making, 68, 70, 116, 167, 189-194, 255-256, 295
deindividuation, 110-111, 116, 120
demonstration rather than postulation, 31, 39, 40, 196, 288
dependency, 113
depression, 291
deprivation, 29, 45, 57, 102, 160
depth metaphor in psychology, 186
desires, 17, 34
detached control, 19, 145, 157, 222, 223, 224, 235, 252, 254
diffusion of responsibility, 120
discrimination, 25-26, 58, 180; social objects, 86
discriminative stimulus contexts, 23, 42, 58, 85, 99
disembedding of experience, (*see* detached control)
disinhibition, 77
distraction, 92, 111, 296, 301
division of labour, 199-200, 201, 219, 228-229, 282
dominance, 88, 284
dreaming, 27
drives, 17, 34, 207
driving cars, 20, 137, 157, 266, 275, 279
dynamic social contingencies, 103, 130
echoics, 147
economic behavior, 281
education, 281
effort, 33, 93, 295, 296
EMail, 254-255
emotion, 35, 187, 201, 291
empiricism (*see* demonstration rather than postulation)
empowerment, 207-208, 280, 283-285
energy conservation, 281
environmental protection, 281
equal redistribution rule, 74
equilibrium theory, 47, 73
equivalence classes (*see* stimulus equivalence classes)
escape, 48, 266, 267
establishing operations and stimuli, 26-27, 29-30, 31, 42, 45, 46, 75, 76, 85, 102, 204, 278, 288
ethnolinguistic vitality, 204
evaluation apprehension, 93, 296, 301

evaluation, 49, 85, 92, 107, 114, 120, 223, 293-294, 297
evasive goals, 51
evolution of verbal behavior, 143, 227-229
evolutionary theory analogy, 34, 99, 176
exchange, 217, 219-222, (also see reciprocity)
expectancy-value, 112
experts, 156, 192
explanations, 113, 232-233
explicit knowledge, 172
extinction, 52, 74-75, 189, 264
facial gestures, 98-99, 103, 250
family, 198, 216, 218-219, 246
farm animal preferences, 41, 70
feedback, 42, 97, 108, 292, 293, 295-296
feelings, 18, 175
feminist psychology, 283-287
folk society, 201
following response, 94
food and eating, 217-218
four-term contingencies, 62, 80, 89, 104, 152
functional consequences, 41
Gemeinschaft, 198
generalized consequences, 44, 61, 120
generalized imitation, 95-97, 262
generalized social consequences (also see loose consequences), 44, 100, 103, 116
generativity of language, 66-67, 189
Gesellschaft, 198
gestures, 80, 88, 91, 97, 109, 144, 146, 212, 254
gifts, 220
goal-setting, 293
graduated prompts, 263
grammar, 144, 148, 164, 178
grass, 61, 73
greetings, 55, 211
group behavior, 105, 109, 112, 120, 125, 162, 228; advantages, 126, 185
group cohesiveness, 205, 213
group conflict, 202, 216, 221, 229, 251 (also see social unrest)
group contingencies, 105, 109, 120
group membership, 90, 110-111, 120, 126, 234 (also see social identity)
group structure, 105

health and illness, 182, 247, 273
hedonic relevance, 17, 112
helping, 116, 125, 132-133, 162, 164
hermeneutics, 287
hierarchical rule, 74
hypnosis, 102, 104, 175, 262, 270, 276
identifiability, 107
identity relation of stimulus equivalence, 63-64
imagery, 27, 168, 269
imitation, 94, 249, 261
impersonal relations, 164, 221, 245-246, 252-253
impression management (see self-presentation)
incentives, 37, 292
indirect consequences, 42, 50
individualism, 17, 19, 125, 221
inducing operants, 35
information, 30-31, 87, 166, 169
informational influences, 89
ingroup, 202, 203
innate, 32, 34, 40, 45, 65, 85, 88, 92, 96, 98, 99, 126, 132, 213, 284, 287-288
inner determination, 161, 184, 187, 188
innovation, 278
insight, 189
instructional control, 38, 104, 153, 218, 224, 262, 270
intellectual disabilities, 289-290
intention, 176
interests, 26
intergroup discrimination, 205
interlocking social behaviors, 136
intervention, 295-302; negative effects, 296-299; positive effects, 295-296
intraverbals, 49, 147, 233, 239, 241, 242
intrinsic motivation, 187, 299
intuition, 26, 192, 235
irrational behavior (see rationality)
keystone behaviors, 75, 77, 288, 290
know your animal, 40, 260
knowing that, 62, 172
knowing, 43, 62
language acquisition, 95
language, (also see verbal behavior, linguistic), 143, 144
Law of Effect, 39
law, 20, 224, 277-278

lawyer's syndrome, 297
layers, (see contingency layers)
leadership, 293
lifestyles, 199, 201, 215, 217, 222, 272-273
linguistic communities, 202
listeners (see audience)
long term social interactions, 136
long-term consequences, 49
loose consequences, 18, 19, 66, 102, 134, 139, 146, 197, 199, 204, 206, 219, 227, 235, 245, 283, 301
lumpy contingencies, 115-116
macro consequences, 41, 86, 188
maintenance (see changing behavior)
mands, 147, 150, 158, 159, 205, 238-239, 254
mass media, 20, 253-254, 278-279 (also see television)
Matching Law, 51, 58, 69, 71, 106, 135, 191, 193, 244
mathematical models, 47, 58, 69, 73-74, 191, 192, 244
meaning, 16, 63, 87, 99, 144, 148, 212-213, 250
mechanical solidarity, 199
media (see mass media)
memory (see remembering)
mental representations, 28, 95, 166, 170
mere presence, 93
metacognition, 181-182, 248
metacontingencies, 136, 210, 247, 275
mindfulness, 172
minority groups, 90, 280
modeling, 94, 134, 261
modernity, 199, 201, 224, 246, 252-253
money, 43, 44, 60, 61, 79, 164, 197-198, 201, 216, 219-222, 224, 245, 249, 252, 281, 282, 292
monotony, 45
motivative variables, 29
multiple causation, 51, 153
multiple contingencies, 47, 52, 58, 61, 67, 71, 74, 80, 135, 136, 155, 158, 177, 180, 187, 190, 194, 216, 244, 260, 273, 275, 284, 291, 294, 298
multiples selves, 153, 179
music, 36, 37, 63, 93, 129, 143, 200, 231, 249-251
mutual shaping, 130, 301

naming, effects of, 25, 28, 58, 66, 167-168, 171, 175, 187, 206-207, 233
natural consequences, 46, 95, 263, 264, 271, 272
natural sciences, 81, 170, 197, 213, 235
needs, 17, 34, 43, 89, 188, 207, 242
negative reinforcement, 40, 48, 102, 136, 215, 263
nirvana, 194
nonsocial behavior, 79, 125
nonverbal behavior (see gestures)
normative influences, 89, 111
novel behaviors, 25, 35, 61, 92, 189, 298-299
obedience, 89, 90, 104
observational learning, 94-95
observing responses (also see establishing operations), 26
obvious consequences, (also see macro consequences), 41, 86, 94, 95, 96, 112, 128, 186, 211
operant class, 32
organic solidarity, 199
organizational behavior management, 292-293, 294-302
organizational culture, 293
overcorrection, 267
pain, 39, 103, 176, 180-181, 182, 233
paralanguages, 212
past experience, effects of, (Also see contingency history), 169, 170, 192-193
pause after reinforcement, 71
perception, 25, 44, 60
performance appraisal, 295
philosophy of behaviorism, 16, 21, 143, 197, 226, 286
phobias, 214-215
physical guidance, 262-263
plans for behavior, 61, 68, 71, 74, 166, 179, 181-182
pleasure, 39
pliance, 91, 154, 156, 236, 241, 262, 280
politeness, 211
politics, 218-219, 277-278, 281, 282-283
porpoises, 35
positive reinforcement, 40
postmodernism, 225-226
praise, 102, 128, 293
precurrent verbal operants, 248

predicting reinforcement effectiveness, 40
prediction of behavior from context alone, 90, 112, 120-122
Premack's Principle, 46, 68, 72
primary groups, 201
private events, 28, 42, 145, 165, 175, 179, 186, 233, 290
private languages, 153
probability of response (*see* response probability)
problem-solving, 44-45, 177
processing environment, 169-170
program evaluation, 293
pronunciation, 203, 205
Prospect Theory, 191
protocol analysis, 183
prototypes, 172
psychological instability, 76, 209
psychological sense of community, 207-208
psychophysics, 25, 60
public opinion, 251
public policy, 277-278
punishment, 37, 40, 92, 102, 118, 213, 267-268, 300
purpose, 35
pushing, grabbing and shoving, 80, 101, 102, 218
quasi social stimuli, 79
rapport, 274, 276 (*also see* trust)
rate of reinforcement, 69-70, 71, 183, 191
rationality, 198 ,200, 210, 215, 222, 225-226
rationalization, 200
reality, 226, 235, 286-287
reciprocity, 206-207, 209, 220, 246; generalized, 206, 218
recruiting natural consequences, 46
reference groups, 90, 205
reflex reserve, 33
reframing, 259
rehearsal, 262, 263-264
reinforcement (*also see* amount, consequences, rate, strengtheners), 37, 40
reinforcement, delay, 42, 50, 57, 69, 70, 71, 96, 97, 108, 126, 155, 185, 191
relative deprivation, 46
remembering, 31, 57, 58, 160, 167, 169, 219, 224, 247-248, 289, 291

remote consequences, 50, 105, 108, 125, 126, 155, 160, 216, 222, 228
repetition, 107, 107, 250-251, 262, 263-264
representative heuristic and biases, 193
response classes, 31, 76
response cost, 266
response force, 33
response probability, 33, 36, 43, 47, 66
response rate as social cue, 86, 96
response restriction, 73
response strength, definitions, 33
response-induced responses, 36
responsibility, 114
restricting contingencies, 73, 215
resurgence, 74
reversibility of consequences, 115
reward interdependence, 202
rewards, 38, 125, 188, 292
rituals, 19, 104-105, 138, 143, 163, 197, 200, 201, 202, 211, 221, 237, 254, 282; changing behavior, 276-277; group maintenance, 210-211, 215-219
role obligations, 114, 228, 284
rudeness, 159
rule-governed behavior (*also see* verbally governed behavior), 42, 153, 178, 200
rumours, 251, 254
safety, 281, 293
satiation (*also see* deprivation), 44, 106
satisfaction, 39
saying and doing (*also see* correspondence), 157
schedules of reinforcement, 51, 52, 55, 69; adjusting , 52, 103, 130; complex, 71; concurrent, 69; DRL, 106, 108, 265; DRH, 108; DRI, 265, 267; DRO, 265, 267; interval, 52, 55, 77; OT, 265; progressive, 52; random time, 50; ratio, 52, 55; social, 103 (*also see* extinction)
schema, 24, 167, 170, 172
science, 61, 146, 156, 226, 253, 283, 286; and politics, 226
screaming, 47
scrutiny, 223, 233, 293, 295, 301-302
secondary consequences, 43, 219
secrecy, 201
selection model of behavior, 34, 59, 176, 189

selection substitution rule, 74
self talk (*also see* thinking), 79, 179, 192
self-attribution, 186, 232
self-awareness, 93, 111, 118
self-categorization, 205-207
self-control, 58, 97, 145, 185-186, 194, 237, 248
self-determination (*see* inner determination)
self-editing, 153
self-events, 178-180, 184, 272
self-identity, 252
self-perception, 232, 242
    self-presentation, 93, 239, 241, 297, 298
self-reference, 186
self-regulation, 111, 126, 135, 145, 155, 157, 159, 160-164, 192, 200, 237, 264, 291; conflict with social compliance, 161-164, 199, 216
self-reinforcement, 48, 184-185, 195, 248
self-reporting, 180-184, 203, 204, 232, 237, 272, 286
sensory consequences, 45, 249, 253, 291
sequential dependence rule, 74
setting events (*see* establishing operations)
sex, 61, 213
sexist language, 280
shaping, 261
sharing, 133-134
shyness, 134
signal detection models, 26, 183
signals, 30-31, 43, 87, 100
signs, 30-31, 97
silence, 150, 237
single-channel processing, 144, 171
size of behavior repertoire, 76, 157, 240, 264, 268, 288-289
smiling, 88, 89, 98, 129
smoking, 137, 146, 236, 273, 276, 278
social approval, 89, 101, 184, 264
social atomism, 245
social behavior, 42, 78, 125; properties, 49, 78, 80, 86, 106
social comparison theory (*see* auditing)
social compliance, 89, 104, 111, 121, 128, 132, 156, 161-164, 205, 214, 215
social consequences, 46, 49, 101, 103, 105, 111, 112, 113, 255

social construction of knowledge, (*see* social knowledge)
social cues (*see* social discriminative stimuli)
social discriminative stimuli, 86-88, 97, 109, 134, 151, 210, 217, 262
social facilitation, 92, 101
social holism, 245
social identity theories, 205-207
social identity, 198, 205, 212
social influence, 89-90, 104, 109, 280
social interaction, 44, 55, 78, 97, 135, 147, 150-151, 164, 202, 204, 210, 218-219, 222, 228, 237, 252, 254-255, 272
social knowledge, 179, 181, 182, 186, 187, 199, 201, 232-234, 235-236, 238-239, 251, 279, 282, 285-287
social loafing, 106-107, 116, 120, 249
social marketing, 279-280
social negotiation, 90, 104, 116, 202, 224, 239
social networks, 202, 208, 246-247, 280
social power, 80, 138, 283, 284, 293
social psychology, 89, 112, 121; manipulation of consequences, 113
social remembering, 247
social representations, 16
social sciences, 16, 81, 197, 198, 211, 213, 253
social skills, 52, 103, 125, 134-135
social support, 246-247, 280
social unrest, 209, 220, 221, 229, 245, 251
social validity, 260
social work, 281, 298
sociolinguistics, 202-205
sociology, 197-198, 207, 209, 225, 246
speech accommodation, 204-205
speech communities, 202
spelling, 164
status, 114, 138, 270
stimulus contexts, 23-24, 31, 58-59
stimulus control, 23, 55, 76, 247, 291
stimulus equivalence classes, 27, 63, 145, 152, 184, 189, 260, 289-290
stimulus generalization, 24, 85, 152, 270-271
stimulus induction, 24
Stimulus-Response behaviorism, 23, 36, 66, 96, 165

stoperants, 41
strangers, 49, 85, 92, 97, 135, 150, 209
straw-person behaviorism, 16, 188, 283
(*also see* Stimulus-Response behaviorism)
strengtheners, 37
strengthening behavior, 263-264
structures, 31, 55, 105, 107-108, 116, 146
subcultures, 89, 162, 203, 212, 254
subjectivity, 17, 244, 284, 286, 287
successive approximations, 261
suicide, 200
superego, 265
superficiality, 296-297
superstitious consequences, 50, 215
symbolic behavior, 19, 101, 210, 213, 220
symmetry relation of stimulus equivalence, 63-64
taboos, 201, 214-215
tacts, 147, 150, 159, 168, 205, 232, 237, 290
technology, 251-255
telephone, 248
television, 77, 253-254
textuals, 147
Theory of Reasoned Action, 243-245
therapy, 269, 270, 282
thick description, 212
thinking, 18, 19, 23, 87, 177, 201, 215, 242, 285
three-term contingencies, 58
timeout, 266-267
token economies, 276, 298
TOTE unit, 166
totems, 213-214
touching, 80, 102
    tracking, 91, 95, 111, 129, 154, 156, 173, 182, 222, 236, 262
training new behaviors, 75, 261-263, 299, 300
transitivity relation of stimulus equivalence, 63-64
trust, 114, 154, 245-246, 276
truth, 19, 21, 226, 240
two-term contingencies, 55, 60-61
unconscious, 26, 172, 173-174, 186, 187, 235
value averaging model, 73
variability in behavior (*see* novel behaviors)

verbal behavior, 29, 42, 65-66, 80, 90, 104, 143, 168, 172, 121; attitudes, 236-239, 241-242; changing, 268-270; functions of, 28, 66, 197, 212; linguistic, 143, 212-213
verbal communities, 18, 79-80, 127, 130, 134, 136, 138, 144, 154, 181-182, 197-210, 219, 231, 234, 237, 246, 259, 272, 282; changing, 236, 274-280; and decision making, 191-194; group breakdown, 161-164, 216, 236, 276; group development, 136, 138, 228-229, 275, 282; historical development, 227-228; individual breakdown, 265, 266, 268, 269, 275; individual development, 134, 162, 275; linguistic, 138, 151, 162, 164, 208, 269, 280, 285
verbal conditioning (*see* verbal consequences)
verbal consequences, 49, 108, 149-150, 220
verbal control of verbal behavior, 173-174, 274-280, 282, 287
verbal labels, (*see* naming)
verbal probabilities, 173, 178, 190; and delay, 193
verbal slips, 51, 153
verbalizable knowledge, 172
verbalizing, (*see* naming)
verbally controlled behavior, 112, 130, 153-157, 158, 168, 174, 194, 199, 206, 222, 233, 241, 243-244, 250, 253, 269, 294; advantages, 28, 66, 98, 144, 146, 155-156, 172, 228; disadvantages, 93, 102, 146, 155, 156-157, 172, 194; increased role with groups, 112, 130 (*also see* bureaucracies, law, rationality)
voluntary behavior, 32, 243
wanting, 34, 43, 122
weak ties, 199, 201, 251
weakening behavior, 2640268
women and society, 280, 283-287
word associations, 64-66
workplace communities, 208, 246, 277
writing, 45, 155-156, 199, 200, 224, 231, 247, 248-249, 259, 262, 300
Zen Buddhism, 194-196
zoo behavior, 281

Author Index

Aach, S. R. 281
Abel, D. M. 292
Abelson, R. P. 68
Abrams, D. 89-90, 205-207, 280
Abramson, P. R. 238
Achebe, C. 163, 219
Acker, J. 286
Adams, J. S. 124
Adelberg, S. 119, 122-123
Adelbratt, T. 192
Ader, R. 92
Aeschleman, S. R. 47
Agras, S. 268
Ainlay, S. L. 247
Ajzen, I. 31, 240-241, 243-245, 279
Alberto, P. A. 281
Alford, B. A. 164
Alicke, M. D. 119, 123
Allansdottir, A. 236
Allison, J. 47, 73
Allport, G. W. 251
Allyon, T. 276
Altman, D. G. 277
Amabile, T. M. 298
Amato, P. R. 246
Anderson, B. A. 238
Anderson, D. C. 292
Anderson, J. R. 167
Anderson, N. H. 191
Anderson, P. A. 299
Anderson, S. R. 66, 151-152
Andrasik, F. 119, 123, 290, 292
Andronis, P. T. 164
Anjoh, Y. 262
Arbuthnot, J. 119, 123
Arias, M. F. 35
Arkes, H. R. 122
Aronson, E. 121-124
Arrow, K. J. 299
Asano, T. 191
Asch, S. E. 89
Ash, R. A. 121-124, 298
Ashford, S. J. 296
Atak, J. R. 33
Atkinson, L. 164

Atkinson, P. 235
Augelli, R. W. 134
Austin, J. 143
Austin-Broos, D. J. 235
Averbach, R. 277
Azrin, N. H. 49, 75, 129, 149, 267, 276
Bâ, M. 219
Back, K. 198, 251
Baer, D. M. 32, 46, 66, 78, 96, 102, 107, 133-134, 151-154, 158-159, 161, 184, 189, 240, 248, 260, 261, 271, 287-288
Baer, J. S. 122-124, 247
Baer, R. A. 158
Baker, D. 285-286
Baker, J. E. 189
Baker, W. A. 294
Balcazar, F. E. 207, 277, 280
Baldwin, J. D. 198, 202
Baldwin, J. I. 198, 202
Baldwin, M. W. 180
Balsam, P. D. 297
Bandura, A. 95
Banerji, N. 251
Barber, B. 246
Bargad, A. 285
Barker, R. G. 208
Barnes, D. 90
Barnett, K. 164
Baron, A. 53
Baron, R. S. 296
Barrera, M. 246
Barrett, D. H. 35, 92
Barrett, J. E. 281
Barrett, R. A. 210
Barry, A. 131
Barry, K. 286
Bartis, S. 107, 298-299
Bartlett, F. C. 31
Barton, E. J. 129, 133-134
Bartunek, J. M. 124
Basho. 196
Bass, B. M. 108
Bassett, J. E. 298
Bateman, S. 47
Bateson, N. 123

Batson, C. D. 119, 122-123
Battalio, R. C. 74
Bauermeister, J. J. 47, 239
Baum, W. M. 23, 70
Bauman, A. 279
Bauman, R. 247
Baumeister, R. F. 107
Baxter, J. C. 121-124
Beach, L. R. 121, 123-124, 295
Beaman, A. L. 114, 119, 123
Beardsley, S. D. 26, 70
Beattie, A. E. 253
Beattie, J. H. M. 225
Beckhouse, L. 121-122, 124
Beckman, L. J. 247
Behr, R. L. 253
Belfiore, P. 33
Bell, J. C. 133-134
Bellettirie, G. 119, 123
Bem, D. J. 124, 178-179, 186, 232, 236-237
Benét, J. 285
Benjumea, S. 35
Bennett, R. H. 52
Bentall, R. P. 154
Bentley, A. F. 170, 175, 186
Benton, A. A. 121, 123-124
Benton, R. G. 27
Ben-Yoav, O. 122-124, 298
Berg, W. K. 263
Berger, P. L. 50, 178, 235
Berkman, L. F. 247
Berkowitz, L. 113, 119, 123
Bernard, H. R. 246
Bernstein, D. J. 47, 71-74, 136, 183, 188,
    244-245
Bernstein, G. S. 277
Berry, D. C. 172
Berscheid, E. 122-123
Bertram, B. C. R. 126, 128
Bhatt, R. S. 52, 135
Bhavnani, K-K. 286
Bickel, W. K. 29, 53, 63
Bigelow, G. E. 136
Biglan, A. 137, 210
Bijou S. W. 102, 164, 287-289
Billig, M. 266
Binion, A. F. 292
Bitetto, V. E. 26, 29

Bixenstine, V. E. 119, 123
Bjorkman, M. 190
Black, S. A. 158
Blaine, B. 251
Blake, R. R. 119, 123
Blakely, E. 51, 156
Blanchard, E. B. 298
Blatz, C. V. 294
Blau, P. 217
Blau, P. M. 299
Blevans, S. A. 122
Bloch, M. 215, 219-221
Block, R. A. 175
Blough, D. S. 36
Bloxom, B. M. 122
Blumer, C. 122
Bochner, S. 209
Boer, D. P. 47, 73
Bolt, M. 122
Bonacich, P. 119, 123
Bondy, A. S. 297
Booth, M. 279
Borck-Jameson, L. 280
Bordo, S. 285
Boren, J. J. 132
Borgida, E. 122
Borland, R. 277-278
Bourhis, R. Y. 204
Bowdery, B. K. 80
Bowie, M. 173, 178
Bowman, E. D. 292-293
Boyd, L.A. 128
Braam, S. J. 149
Brady, J. V. 43, 73, 136, 162
Branch, M. N. 31, 41, 169
Brandt, J. R. 122-123
Brannon, M. E. 293
Braukmann, C. J. 281
Brawley, E. R. 102
Breakwell, G. M. 236, 285
Breaugh, J. A. 121, 124
Breckler, S. J. 112, 118, 237
Breen, C. G. 78, 134
Brehmer, B. 123, 295
Bremner, K. J. 70
Brethower, D. M. 292
Brickner, M. A. 119, 123
Brigham, T. A. 185

Brilmayer, A. G. 90
Britton, S. D. 121, 123-124, 298
Broadbent, D. E. 172, 191
Broadbent, M. H. P. 172, 192
Brock, T. C. 122, 124
Bromfield, R. 289
Bron, M. 164
Brown, B. R. 121-122, 124
Brown, D. K. 33
Brown, S. W. 135
Brownell, A. 247
Brownell, K. D. 273
Brownstein, A. J. 155, 175, 192
Bruner, J. S. 235, 237, 242
Bruun, S. E. 119, 123-124
Bryant, L. E. 133
Buck, R. 187
Budd, K. S. 133
Buell, J. 78
Bullock, D. 94
Bundy, R. P. 206
Burgio, K. L. 290
Burgio, L. D. 290
Burke, A. 277
Burkhard, B. 74
Burns, C. E. S. 164
Burns, R. 80
Burns, T. F. 208, 274
Burnstein, D. D. 108
Burt, R. S. 278
Buskist, W. F. 125, 130-131, 155, 281
Butterworth, E. 85
Buzsaki, G. 29
Cacioppo, J. T. 132, 240-243
Cairns, E. 90
Callan, V. J. 203
Camarata, S. 134
Cameron, D. 202-203, 285
Campbell, D. T. 110, 189
Campbell, K. E. 208
Cannon, D.L. 108
Cantor, G. 172
Caplan, N. 298
Capriotti, R. M. 73, 136
Carello, C. 29
Carlsmith, J. M. 121-122, 124
Carlton, P. L. 281
Carment, D. W. 131

Carnevale, P. J. D. 121, 123-124, 298
Carr, E. G. 134, 290
Carroll, J. D. 294
Carstensen, L. L. 290
Carter, N. 293
Carterette, E. C. 191
Carver, C. S. 111, 114, 166
Case, D. A. 27, 29
Castrogiovanni, A. 191
Catania, A. C. 32, 41, 52, 55, 67, 74, 80,
    143-144, 146, 148, 154-155, 158-159,
    164, 184, 192, 228
Cavanaugh, K. L. 277
Center for Human Information Processing.
    247
Cerutti, D. T. 52, 67, 153, 155, 158
Cervone, D. 175
Chaiken, S. 121-122, 124, 295
Chang, J. 157
Chao, C-C. 164
Chapman, S. 277-278
Charters, W. W. 265
Chase, P. N. 30, 53, 146, 153, 164
Chavis, D. M. 207
Cheney, C. D. 73-74
Cherek, D. R. 136
Cherpas, C. 30
Chesnick, E. I. 192
Chiesa, M. 23, 36
Chippendale, P. R. 294
Chomsky, N. 42, 66, 100, 202
Chon, K-K. 187, 235
Christensen, C. 122
Christensen, J. 191
Christenson, G. M. 277
Cialdini, R. B. 104
Citera, M. 108
Clark, N. K. 247-248
Clark, N. T. 296
Clark, R. D. 132
Coates, J. 202, 285
Cobb, S. 247
Cobern, M. K. 281
Cochrane, S. 280
Cohen, A. R. 122, 124
Cohen, C. B. 285
Cohen, D. 96
Cohen, J. 192

Cohen, N. J. 172
Cohen, S. 247
Cohen, Y. A. 246
Cohn, E. S. 119, 123
Colavecchia, B. 104
Coleman, A. 292
Coleman, L. M. 151
Collier, G. H. 32, 73
Collins, B. E. 119, 122-124
Collins, R. L. 292
Colman, A. D. 132
Commons, M. L. 41, 51, 69, 70, 135, 178, 185
Condor, S. 285
Cone, J. D. 281
Connor, W. H. 123
Connerton, P. 247
Conolley, E. S. 97, 131
Conway, M. 119, 123, 298
Cook, F. L. 253, 279
Cook, M. S. 129
Cook, T. D. 114, 122, 124, 242
Cooley, C H. 201
Cooper, J. 122, 123
Cooper, J. O. 261, 274
Cooper, R. L. 280
Corbin, L. H. 122
Costall, A. P. 29
Cotton, J. L. 129
Cottrell, N. B. 93, 296
Coupland, J. 204
Coupland, N. 203-205
Coutant-Sassic, D. 228-229
Coyle, C. 294
Cramer, R. E. 131
Crano, W. D. 112-113
Crawford, M. 283, 285
Creed, T. 86, 96
Crisp, S. 164
Critchfield, T. S. 183
Crocker, J. 238
Croll, W. L. 47
Crosbie, J. 73
Cross, D. 191
Croteau, D. 235, 253-254
Crow, R. S. 277
Crowell, C. R. 47, 292
Culler, J. 202

Cumming, W. W. 29
Cummings, L. L. 296
Cushman, P. 179-180, 252
Cvetkovich, G. 123
Cybulski, K. A. 73
Czerlinsky, T. 124
Czyzewska, M. 172
Czyzewski, M. J. 277
D'Aunno, T. A. 209, 277
Dake, K. 235
Dalton, G. 220
Damasio, A. R. 171
Damasio, H. 171
Daniel, W. J. 132
Daniels, A. K. 285
Daniels, L. R. 119, 123
Danson, C. 86, 96
Darcheville, J. C. 185
Darley, J. M. 96, 107, 114, 122-123, 132, 153, 162
Darwin, C. 35-36, 176
Dattilo, J. 143
Davenport, D. G. 131
Davey, G. 52
David, J. H. 47
Davidson, I. 228
Davis, H. 50
Davis, H. L. 175
Davis, J. H. 121-124, 247
Davis, K. E. 232
Davison, M. 26, 57, 58, 69, 187
Dawes, R. M. 130
Day, W. F. 175, 178-179
Deacon, J. R. 158
Deaux, K. 285
DeBaca, P. C. 47
DeBono, K. G. 122, 237
Deci, E. L. 187
Deen, E. 122
DeGrandpre, R. J. 63, 155, 281
Deguchi, H. 96
Deitz, S. M. 24, 35, 92
Deleuze, G. 186
Della-Piana, G. 189
Delprato, D. J. 16, 32
Delquadri, J. 112
DePaulo, B. M. 151
Derby, S. L. 192

Dermer, M. 122-123
Desselles, M. L. 292-293
Deterline, W. A. 294
Detrich, R. 158
Deutsch, M. 89-90, 122
Devany, J. M. 65, 289
Devine, J. V. 47
DeVore, I. 217
Dickinson, A. M. 38, 108, 146-147, 149,
    188, 292, 299
DiClemente, C. C. 279
Diener, C. 123
Diener, E. 111, 114, 119, 122-123
Dineen, J. 114, 123
Dinsmoor, J. A. 27, 29
Ditrichs, R. 119, 123
Doise, W. 124, 235-236
Doms, M. 280
Donahoe, J. W. 53, 173
Donaldson, S. 92
Donaldson, T. 86-87
Donnerstein, E. 119, 121, 123
Donnerstein, M. 119, 121, 123
Donovan, R. J. 279
Doob, A. N. 122, 253
Dornbusch, S. M. 178
Dougher, M. J. 66, 184, 282
Douglas, M. 214-215, 217, 219
Douglas, R. L. 122
Dovidio, J. F. 132
Downing, L. L. 119, 123
Downing, N. E. 285
Druckman, D. 123-124
Dubnick, M. J. 294
Dubrovsky, V. 255
Dugdale, N. 65
Dulany, D. E. 172
Dumas, J. E. 289
Duncan, B. L. 234
Dunham, P. J. 41, 74
Dunlap, G. 271
Durand, V. M. 134, 290
Durkheim, E. 199-201, 211, 213-214, 220,
    223, 225, 228-229, 246
Duveen, G. 235
Dwyer, W. O. 281
Eagly, A. 285
Ebbesen, E. E. 47, 71-72, 74, 136, 183

Echabe, A. E. 235
Eckenrode, J. 247
Eckert, P. 202, 280
Edelstein, B. A. 271
Edland, A. 192
Edwards, K. A. 282
Edwards, W. 190
Egel, A. L. 164
Egerman, K. 108
Eifert, G. H. 149
Eikenberry, K. O. 294
Einhorn, H. J. 175, 192
Einzig, P. 220
Eisenberger, R. 33, 41, 47
Eiser, J. R. 122, 237-238
Elkine, D. 247
Ellen, P. S. 243
Elling, R. C. 294
Elliott, B. 278
Ellis, J. 34, 36, 139, 154, 275, 281
Embry, J. E. 292
Emerson, J. H. 268
Emurian, C. S. 136, 162
Emurian, H. H. 136, 162
Endo, G. T. 189
Endresen, K. 114, 123
Engelstad, P. H. 280
England, G. 294
Engram, P. 121, 124
Epling, W. F. 47, 70, 73
Epstein, A. L. 251
Epstein, R. 35, 74, 95, 185, 189
Epstein, Y. 122
Erber, R. 124
Erickson, B. H. 201, 238
Erickson, M. H. 194, 260, 262, 269, 276
Ericsson, K. A. 183
Espinosa, J. M. 33
Esposito, J. L. 251
Esseveld, J. 286
Etzel, B. C. 29
Eubanks, J. L. 292-293
Evans, G. 122
Evans, I. M. 75-77, 282
Evans-Pritchard, E. E. 217, 219, 225
Everett, P. B. 281
Fairhurst, S. K. 279
Falk, J. L. 77, 102

Fantino, E. 27, 29, 41, 52, 167
Farber, I. E. 149
Farh, J-L. 188
Farmer-Dougan, V. A. 40, 47
Farr, R. M. 235-236
Faucheux, C. 122
Favero, J. 108
Fawcett, S. B. 207, 260, 277-278, 280
Fazio, R. H. 241
Feallock, R. 136
Feil, D. K. 217
Feinberg, R. A. 131
Feingold, B. D. 188, 299
Fellner, D. J. 293
Felner, R. D. 276, 280
Felton, B. J. 280
Fentress, J. 247
Fenza, K. M. 75
Ferster, C. B. 15, 46, 52, 57, 101-102, 104, 112
Festinger, L. 96, 198, 251
Field, T. M. 96
Fielding, J. E. 277
Finch, M. L. 119, 121, 123-124
Findley, J. D. 43, 69, 71-72, 136, 174
Fine, G. A. 212
Firth, R. 251
Fischhoff, B. 192
Fischman, M. W. 73, 136
Fishbein, M. 31, 240-241, 243-245, 279
Fisher, G. A. 187, 235
Fiske, S. T. 124, 238
FitzGerald, P. 172, 191
Flament, C. 206
Flanders, J. P. 95
Flay, B. 242
Flay, B. R. 278
Fleishman, J. A. 123
Fleming, J. H. 153
Fletcher, R. K. 277-278
Flora, J. A. 278
Flora, S. R. 185, 188
Foltin, R. W. 73, 136
Fondacaro, R. 122, 124
Forcey, B. 121, 124
Ford, J. D. 293
Ford, J. K. 122, 295
Forehand, R. 281

Forward, J. 124
Foster, D. 205
Foster, T. M. 11, 70, 187
Foucault, M. 178-179
Fowler, S. A. 46, 112, 133, 271, 281
Fox, J. 119, 123
Fox, J. J. 30
Fox, R. 219
Foxx, R. M. 267
Fraley, L. E. 237, 240
Frankel, M. 190-193
Fraser, C. 205, 235-236
Fraser, S. C. 114, 119, 123-124
Frazer, E. 203, 285
Frazier, G. L. 277, 279
Frazier, T. W. 26, 29
Frederiksen, L. W. 77, 292
Freud, S. 153, 173-174, 180
Frey, D. 124
Frey, R. L. 124
Friedman, J. 210
Friedman, M. P. 191
Fromkin, H. L. 122, 124
Fuerst, J. 134
Fujita, T. 96
Fung, H. 235
Funk, S. G. 122
Furnham, A. 209
Fushimi, T. 86
Gaertner, S. L. 132
Gainer, P. 132
Galanter, E. 68, 165-168
Galbicka, G. 32
Galizio, M. 52, 154
Gallego, J. 172
Galli, I. 235
Gallo, P. S. 122
Gallois, C. 203-204
Gamson, W. A. 235, 253-254
Gange, J. J. 273
Gargano, G. M. 119, 123-124
Gaskell, G. 235-236
Gaydos, G. R. 35, 92
Gaylord-Ross, R. 78
Geen, R. G. 93, 107
Geer, J. H. 123
Geertz, C. 212-213, 216
Geesey, S. 112

Gelfand, D. M. 287-288
Geller, E. S. 281
Gellner, E. 226
Gelman, R. 87
Gentry, M. 285
Genung, V. 122
Gerard, H. B. 89-90, 96, 122, 131
Gergen, K. J. 122, 179, 197, 235
Gergen, M. M. 179, 286
Gersick, C. J. G. 228
Gerstein, L. H. 132-133
Geva, N. 168
Gewirtz, J. L. 287
Ghezzi, P. M. 164
Giacalone, R. A. 297
Gibbon, J. 190-193
Gibney, L. 251
Gibson, E. J. 27
Gibson, J. J. 27, 45
Giddens, A. 214, 252-254, 285
Giles, H. 203, 207
Gilovich, T. 192
Ginter, M. 276, 280
Gintner, G. G. 185
Gist, N. P. 251
Glanz, K. 277
Glaser, R. 108
Glasgow, R. E. 137, 210, 277
Glass, D. C. 93
Gleeson, S. 51
Glenn, S. S. 34, 36, 134, 137-139, 143, 154,
     164, 210, 247, 259, 281
Glow, P. H. 45
Gluckman, M. 138, 215, 219
Glynn, T. J. 208
Gniech, G. 124
Gō, S. 208
Goethals, G. R. 96, 107, 122
Goetz, E. L. 189
Goldberg, M. 119, 123
Goldiamond, I. 29, 184
Goldring, J. 294
Goldstein, R. S. 248
Golinkoff, R. M. 87
Gollub, L. R. 42
Goltz, S. M. 108
Goody, J. 224, 247
Goranson, R. E. 123

Gordon, J. R. 273
Gottlieb, A. 121, 124
Gottlieb, B. H. 247
Gould, J. L. 288
Grabowski, J. G. 52
Graham, W. K. 122
Granovetter, M. 199, 246
Graft, D. A. 106
Grant, D. L. 86
Grantmyre, J. 74
Grassia, J. 192
Graves, J. 123
Gray, M. J. 129
Graziano, W. 122, 123
Green, G. 63, 67, 73-74, 77
Green, L. 186
Green, L. W. 277
Greenberg, J. 122-124
Greenberg, R. 96
Greene, B. F. 277
Greene, S. 299
Greenglass, E. R. 123
Greenspoon, J. 34, 36, 139, 282
Greenwald, A. G. 112, 118, 172, 173, 179,
     237
Greenway, D. E. 66, 184, 192
Greenwood, C. R. 46, 112
Greer, R. D. 149, 153
Griffin, J. C. 268
Grosch, J. 188
Gross, A. M. 184
Grossman, M. 228-229
Grott, R. 105-106
Gruder, C. L. 119, 121-124
Gruzen, J. 118-119, 123
Guattari, F. 186
Guerin, B. 27-29, 45, 49, 77-78, 92-93, 112,
     114, 118, 120, 148, 152, 187, 202, 204-
     206, 211-212, 235-236, 239, 242-243,
     249, 251, 286-287, 296
Guess, D. 152
Guest, T. A. 119, 123-124
Guevremont, D. C. 158-159
Guild, J. 112
Gumpert, P. 122
Gunthorpe, W. 11, 78
Gusfield, J. R. 198
Gustavsen, B. 280

Guyer, M. 119, 123
Haack, S. 286
Haag, R. 35, 189
Haaren, F. van 186
Haas, J. R. 192
Haccoun, R. R. 121, 124
Hagafors, R. 123, 295
Hake, D. F. 75, 79-80, 86-87, 96, 125, 129, 131, 133-134, 282
Halbwachs, M. 247
Hale, S. 193
Haley, J. 194, 260, 269
Haley, N. 278
Hall, G. A. 30, 148, 151
Hall, R. L. 108
Halperin, S. 69
Hamilton, M. C. 203, 280, 285
Hamm, R. M. 192
Hammer, C. 102
Hammond, K. R. 192
Haneda, F. 290
Hannah, G. T. 277
Hansen, A. 253-254
Hansen, R. D. 285
Hanson, S. J. 47
Haran, D. 192
Harari, O. 122
Harding, C. G. 86
Hare-Mustin, R. T. 283
Haring, T. G. 78, 134
Harkins, S. G. 49, 92, 107, 114, 118-119, 122-124, 296, 298-299
Harkness, A. R. 122
Harman, L. D. 209
Harper, D. R. 175
Harris, F. R. 78, 102
Harris, M. 210, 216-217
Harris, R. 123
Harris, S. 158-159
Harrison, S. 216
Hart, B. M. 102
Hart, K. 220-221, 252
Hartje, J. C. 47
Hartmann, D. P. 287-288
Hartwick, J. 243, 247
Harvey, J. H. 122, 124
Hastings, G. 279
Hayes, L. A. 96, 112

Hayes, L. J. 63, 67, 143, 145, 164, 227
Hayes, N. A. 172
Hayes, S. C. 16, 63, 65, 67, 91, 94, 143, 145, 153-154, 164, 175, 181-182, 184-186, 191-192, 194, 200, 227, 233, 269, 281-282, 289
Haywood, A. 279
Heath, J. L. 23
Hebdige, D. 89, 163, 212
Heiby, E. M. 164
Heider, F. 232
Heimberg, J. S. 292
Heller, J. F. 122
Helmreich, R. 119, 122-123
Henchy, T. 93
Hendy, E. 58, 66
Henige, D. 247
Henley, N. M. 203, 280
Hennigan, K. M. 122, 124
Herbert, F. 76
Herek, G. M. 237
Hermann, M. 124
Heron, T. E. 261, 274
Herrnstein, R. J. 44, 50, 58, 69-70
Herzlich, C. 165, 182
Hest, A. van 186
Heward, W. L. 261, 274
Hewstone, M. 234
Hickman, C. 290
Hieser, R. A. 129
Higgins, E. T. 112, 122, 124
Higgins, S. T. 53, 63
Hill, D. 277-278
Hill, T. 172
Hilton, J. L. 153
Himle, J. 282
Hineline, P. N. 16, 48, 52, 234, 289
Hirota, T. T. 27
Hirsch, E. 32
Hoberman, H. M. 247
Hoch, S. J. 175
Hock, M. L. 33
Hodkin, B. 131
Hoffman, C. 122-124
Hogarth, R. M. 175
Hogg, M. A. 89-90, 205-207, 280
Holland, J. G. 26-27, 148, 227
Holmes, J. G. 180

Holmstrom, A. 293
Holt, L. E. 122-124
Holt, R. W. 121-124
Holz, W. C. 49, 149, 267
Homme, L. E. 47
Honig, W. K. 24
Hoogstra, L. 235
Hopkins, W. D. 131
Hops, H. 112
Horcones. 136
Horne, P. 154
Horner, R. D. 263
Horner, R. H. 134, 271
Howard, J. A. 234
Howard, M. L. 95
Hoynes, W. 235, 253-254
Hoyt, M. F. 122, 124
Hrydowy, E. R. 46
Hubbard, J. 50
Huff, C. 255
Hull, C. L. 23, 36, 45, 165-167, 283
Humphrey, C. 220
Hurlbut, B. 263
Hursh, D. E. 287-288
Hurst, P. M. 122
Hussian, R. A. 290-291
Husted, J. R. 86
Hutchinson, R. R. 75
Hyde, J. S. 285
Hymovitch, B. 251
Hyten, C. 30, 80, 86-87, 153
Ichheiser, G. 234
Ikemoto, T. 195
Ingham, A. G. 123
Ingram, R. E. 134
Innes, J. M. 119, 121-124, 152, 242-243
Insko, C. A. 119, 123
Irle, M. 124
Israel, A. C. 158
Iversen, I. H. 23, 165
Iverson, D. C. 277
Iwata, B. A. 30, 277
Iyengar, S. 253
Jacklin, C. N. 286
Jackson, D. A. 34
Jackson, G. M. 290
Jackson, J. M. 119, 282
Jackson, K. 210, 282

Jackson, R. L. 261, 171
Jacobson, D. E. 247
Jacobson, N. S. 273, 282
Jaffe, Y. 119, 123
Janis, I. L. 299
Jaques, E. 294
Jarmecky, L. 123
Jarrett, R. B. 184, 186
Jason, L. A. 277
Jaspars, J. M. F. 234
Jeffery, R. W. 275
Jenkins, H. 254
Jensen, M. 108
Jerdee, T. H. 119, 123
Johnson, D. F. 73
Johnson, K. R. 146
Johnson, L. M. 33, 53
Johnson, M. R. 47
Johnson, P. 203-204, 206
Johnson, R. D. 119, 123
Johnson-Laird, P. N. 178
Johnston, J. M. 164, 177-178, 241
Johnstone, M. 203
Jones, E. E. 232, 234, 297
Jones, R. T. 46, 263
Jones, S. C. 121-124
Jordan, R. C. 273
Jorgenson, D. O. 119, 123
Jovchelovitch, S. 236
Joyce, J. H. 53
Joyce, T. M. 248
Kacelnik, A. 70, 135, 178
Kachanoff, R. 77
Kagehiro, D. K. 122, 124
Kagel, J. H. 74
Kahan, J. P. 119, 123
Kahneman, D. 174-175, 190-193
Kamarck, T. 247
Kamil, A. C. 135
Kanak, N. J. 131
Kanarek, R. 32
Kantor, J. R. 24
Kaplan, S. J. 96, 131
Karau, S. J. 107
Karpman, M. 47
Kassin, S. M. 172
Kasture, H. S. 277
Katz, D. 237, 277

Katz, E. 251, 275, 278
Katz, J. 235
Kaufman, H. 295, 301
Kaufman, K. H. 119, 122-123
Kaufman, R. A. 294
Kaufmann, F. X. 294
Kazdin, A. E. 46, 74, 112, 263
Keating, J. P. 253
Keel, R. 122
Keenan, M. 90, 95
Keeney, R. L. 192
Keesing, R. M. 210
Keilitz, I. 263
Keithly, L. 122, 124
Kelem, R. T. 119, 123
Kelleher, R. T. 42
Keller, F. S. 127, 178
Kelley, H. H. 122, 125, 232, 251
Kelley, K. A. 150
Kelly, J. G. 277
Kelly, T. H. 73, 136
Kemper, T. D. 187
Kendon, A. 228
Kendzierski, D. A. 253
Kennedy, D. B. 50
Kent, S. 134, 217
Keren, G. 192
Kerker, R. M. 253
Kerr, N. L. 119, 123-124
Ketchen, C. M. 119, 123
Keys, C. B. 124
Kidder, L. H. 119, 123
Kiecolt, K. J. 238
Kiesler, C. A. 122
Kiesler, S. 255
Kilgour, R. 70
Killeen, P. R. 33
Killen, J. 277
Killian, L. M. 205
Killworth, P. D. 246
Kilpatrick, D. 69
Kim, J. I. 112, 119, 121-124
Kimmel, M. J. 121, 124
King, A. C. 277
King, G. R. 70, 185
Kinnaird, V. 284
Kish, G. B. 45
Kitzinger, C. 286-287

Klanderman, S. 123
Klaus, D. J. 108
Klee, P. 107
Klein, K. J. 209, 277
Kleinke, C. 122
Kleinke, C. L. 233
Kleinman, S. 212
Kleiter, G. D. 190
Klentz, B. 119, 123
Klimoski, R. J. 121-124, 298
Kline, T. 97, 131
Knapp, T. J. 47
Knox, R. E. 122
Koegel, R. L. 25, 263, 270-271
Koestner, R. 188
Kogan, N. 121, 123-124
Kohlenberg, B. S. 269
Kohlenberg, R. J. 282
Kohler, F. W. 46, 133
Kojetin, B. A. 153
Komaki, J. L. 108, 125, 292-293
Konarski, E. A. 47, 158
Korn, Z. 185
Kotler, P. 279
Kottak, C. P. 210
Kramarae, C. 203, 285
Krantz, P. J. 281
Krapfl, J. E. 294
Krauthammer, C. 294
Krebs, D. L. 132
Krige, E. G. 217
Krige, J. D. 217
Kruglanski, A. W. 96
Kumpf, M. 124
Kurkjian, J. A. 76
Kushi, G. S. 76
Kymissis, E. 95
Labov, W. 203
Lacan, J. 173-174, 178, 180, 235
Lai, C. 122
Lalli, J.S. 33
Lalljee, M. 234
Lamal, P. A. 112, 281-282
Lamarre, J. 148
Lambek, M. 214
Lamm, H. 121-124
Landers, C. 278
Langford, G. 80

Lanzetta, J. T. 122
Lao Tzu. 194
Latané, B. 107, 114, 119, 123-124, 132, 162, 253
Lather, P. 283, 286
Lattal, K. A. 51
Layng, T. V. J. 164
Lazarsfeld, P. F. 251, 275, 278
Le Guin, U. K. 283
Lea, M. 255
Lea, S. E. G. 106, 281
Lee, M. 78
Lee, R. B. 217
Lee, S. 255
Lee, V. L. 16, 23, 32, 41, 80, 144-145, 148-149, 152, 156, 164
Leeming, F. C. 281
LeFrancois, J. R. 53
Leigland, S. 30
Leont'ev, A. N. 235
Lepper, M. R. 299
Leveille, R. 77
Leventhal, G. S. 119, 123
Leventhal, H. 124
Levi, A. 232
Levin, M. 280
Levine, J. R. 122
Levinger, G. 123
Levitt, C. A. 119, 123
Levy, M. R. 253
Lewicki, P. 172
Lewinsohn, P. M. 47
Lewis, F. M. 277
Lewis, J. D. 245-246
Lewis, L. L. 285
Lewis, S. 172
Lévi-Strauss, C. 174, 214, 218
Lévy-Bruhl, L. 214
Libet, J. 268
Lichtenstein, E. 247, 273
Lichtenstein, S. 123, 192
Liebold, K. 65
Liebold, K. E. 132
Lin, N. 246
Lind, E. A. 119, 122-123
Lindskold, S. 119, 121, 123-124
Lindsley, O. R. 127, 129, 290-292
Lingle, J. H. 168

Linke, R. 294
Litow, L. 112
Litwak, E. 200, 246
Livingstone, S. M. 253
Lloyd, B. 235
Lloyd, K. E. 158, 177, 210, 240, 292-293
Lockwood, K. 70
Lodhi, S. 149, 153
Logan, C. A. 52
Logue, A. W. 70, 185-186, 190-193
Lombardo, J. P. 150
Longino, H. E. 286
Lopes, L. L. 191-193
Losch, M. E. 132
Loud, R. E. 122-123
Lovaas, O. I. 290
Lowe, C. F. 66, 154
Lubinski, D. 33, 181
Lucas, G. A. 50
Luce, R. D. 74
Luckmann, T. 50, 178, 235
Luhmann, N. 246
Luria, A. R. 161
Luthans, F. 292-293
Lyons, C. A. 73-74
Mabel, S. 152
Macaskill, P. 279
Maccoby, N. 253, 277-278
MacCorquodale, K. 143
Macdonald, G. E. 253
Mace, F. C. 33, 71
Machado, A. 53, 189
Machina, M. J. 190
Mackay, H. A. 29
MacKenzie, J. G. 70
MacKenzie-Keating, S. E. 104, 267
Madden, T. J. 240, 243
Magenau, J. M. 121, 124
Mageo, J. M. 180
Magnus, P. 279
Mahoney, M. J. 185, 188, 299
Maibach, E. W. 278
Majone, G. 294, 300
Malagodi, E. F. 139, 210, 282
Malcolm, T. 122
Malinowski, B. 221
Malone, L. W. 24
Malott, R. W. 15, 29, 42, 51, 210

Mandell, C. 33
Mann, L. 119, 121-124
Manning, M. R. 273
Mansfield, H. C. 297, 299
Manstead, A. S. R. 114, 232, 294
Mantyla, T. 31
Marcucella, H. 86, 132
Marcus, B. H. 279
Marecek, J. 283
Marin, G. 259, 275
Markowitz, H. 281
Markus, H. 179-180
Marlatt, G. A. 273
Marler, P. 288
Marlowe, D. 122
Marsden, P. V. 246
Marshall, A. M. 66, 151-152
Marshall, H. 285
Martens, B. K. 69
Martin, G. L. 46
Maruyama, G. 124
Marwell, G. 109, 127, 129
Mascia-Lees, F. E. 285
Maslach, C. 122
Massermann, J. H. 132
Mathes, E. W. 119, 123-124
Mathews, R. M. 207, 277-278, 280
Matson, J. L. 290
Matthews, B. A. 129, 154-155, 158-159, 192
Matthews, L. R. 70
Matthews, M. W. 123
Mauss, M. 174, 217, 220
Mawhinney, T. C. 188, 292-293
May, E. 250
Mayer G. R. 261
Mayseless, O. 96
Mazis, M. B. 122, 124
Mazur, J. E. 51-52, 70, 73, 185-186
McAdie, T. M. 70
McAdoo, W. G. 273
McAllister, D. A. 273
McAllister, D. W. 121, 123-124, 295
McCann, C. D. 122, 124
McCarthy, D. C. 26, 57-58, 69, 167
McCarty, C. 246
McClannahan, L. E. 281
McClelland, J. P. 77
McConnell-Ginet, S. 203, 280

McDonald, L. 267
McDowell, J. J. 26, 70, 193
McFarland, C. 119, 123, 298
McGee, G. G. 281
McGinnies, E. 15, 104
McGuire, T. W. 255
McHale, C. A. 73
McKenna, F. S. 86
McKnight, D. L. 184, 186
McLaughlin, B. 15, 104
McMillan, D. W. 207
McNamara, J. R. 292
McNeill, D. 97
McPherson, A. 30
McReynolds, W. T. 112
Mead, G. H. 144, 178, 235
Mednick, M. T. 285
Medow, H. 124
Meeker, R. J. 122
Mees, H.L. 289
Mefferd, R. B. 27
Meichenbaum, D. H. 189
Meisch, R. A. 281
Melancon, S. M. 269
Melin, L. 293
Mellgren, R. L. 135
Meltzoff, A. N. 96
Mermelstein, R. 247
Merton, R. K. 205
Messe, L. A. 122
Meyer, L. M. 75-77
Meyerhoff, J. L. 136
Michael, J. L. 27, 29-30, 41-42, 44, 143, 146, 151
Michael, R. L. 136, 183, 244-245
Michaels, J. W. 119, 123
Michela, J. L. 232
Michelini, R. L. 119, 121-124
Middleton, J. 138
Midgley, B. D. 16, 32
Milan, M. A. 276
Milardo, R. M. 246
Milgram, S. 89
Milio, N. 277
Millar, W. S. 102, 288
Millard, W. J. 86
Miller, D. T. 122, 132
Miller, F. G. 119, 123

Miller, G. A. 68, 165-168
Miller, H. L. 48
Miller, J. G. 233-234
Miller, L. K. 136
Miller, N. 123
Miller, P. J. 235
Milroy, L. 203, 208
Milton, K. 286
Mims, V. 188
Minkler, M. 280
Mintz, D. E. 33
Mintz, J. 235
Mischel, W. 122-124, 185
Mitchell, J. C. 246
Mitchell, T. R. 121, 123-124, 295
Mitchell, W. S. 47
Miyamoto, S. F. 178
Mladinic, A. 285
Mochizuki, A. 149, 164, 290
Momsen, J. H. 284
Monson, T. 122-123
Monson, T. C. 122
Montgomery, H. 192
Mooney, S. E. 53
Moore, D. 296
Moore. D. L. 129
Moore, J. 175
Moore, M. K. 96
Moore, S. F. 224
Morgan, C. J. 124
Morgan, D. 125, 130-131
Morgan, D. B. 291
Morris, C. J. 35
Morris, E. K. 16, 29, 32-33, 53, 57, 75, 102,
    165, 277, 281, 287-288
Morse, S. J. 119, 123
Morse, W. H. 52
Moscovici, S. 109, 122, 173-174, 235-236,
    253, 275
Mosher, F. C. 299
Mostofsky, D. I. 24
Mougey, E. H. 136
Mountjoy, P. 15, 104
Mouton, J. S. 119, 123
Moxley, R. A. 23, 36
Mueller, K. L. 27, 29
Mugny, G. 235-236, 275
Mullen, B. 107

Munoz, R. F. 277
Munro, C. 294
Munt, E. D. 185
Murdock, G. 252-253
Murphy, C. M. 282
Murray, D. C. 150, 237
Murray, P. 191
Myerson, J. 193
Nadler, A. 119, 123
Naficy, A. 122
Nakajima, S. 189
Nation, J. R. 272
Nau, P. A. 104
Naughton, K. A. 288
Neale, M. A. 175
Neef, N. A. 71
Nel, E. 122-123
Nellis, M. J. 73, 136
Nelson, R. O. 65, 184, 186, 289
Nemeth, C. 90
Neuringer, A. 35, 94, 105-106, 186, 189,
    298
Nevin, J. A. 33, 44, 51, 65, 70, 104, 185, 193
NewBrough, J. R. 207
Newby, T. J. 108
Newcomb, T. M. 205, 234
Newman, E. 294
Newsom, C. 290
Newston, D. 124
Newton, J. W. 119, 121-124
Nezu, A. M. 273
Ng, S. H. 203, 280
Nicassio, P. M. 208
Nickel, M. 51
Nielson, K. P. 208, 274
Nigro, G. 235
Nilsson, L-G. 31
Ninness, H. A. C. 134
Nisbett, R. E. 179, 182, 232, 234
Noble, W. 228
Nolan, R. J. 47
Nordquist, V. M. 76, 282
Norman, S. A. 122
Northcraft, G. B. 175
Notterman, J. M. 33
Novelli, W. D. 279
Nurius, P. 179-180
Nuttin, J. M. 122

Oah, S. 146-147, 149
Oakes, P. J. 205-207
O'Brien, R. M. 292
Ochsmann, R. 122
O'Dell, S. 281
Ogden, J. K. 122
Oldenburg, B. 279
O'Leary, V. E. 285
Olmstead, J. S. 119, 123
Olson, T. W. 184
Olvera, D. 125, 129, 133-134
O'Mara, H. 66
Ono, K. 50
Orbell, J. M. 130
O'Reilly, J. 35, 189
Orlandi, M. A. 278
Ormel, J. 246
Orne, M. T. 89
Osborne, J. G. 30
Oskamp, S. 122, 253
Osland, A. 273
Osland, J. S. 273
Osnes, P. G. 158-159, 271
Ostrom, T. M. 119, 123, 168
Ostrom, V. 294
Otis-Wilborn, A. 277
Overskeid, G. 77
Owen, N. 271, 273, 277-279
Owens, K. 86, 132
Page, S. 35, 189, 298
Paine, A. L. 207, 277, 280
Paisey, T. J. 267
Pallak, M. S. 122
Palmer, D. C. 31, 52, 169, 173
Paloutzian, R. F. 119, 123
Pandey, J. 234
Paniagua, F. A. 158, 161
Papciak, A. S. 119, 123
Parke, R. D. 96
Parrott, L. J. 30, 80-81, 125, 145, 164, 282
Parry, J. 219-221
Parsons, J. A. 248
Parsonson, B. S. 288
Patterson, C. J. 185
Patterson, G. R. 125
Patterson, M. L. 212
Patterson, R. L. 290
Paulus, P. B. 107

Pavlik, W. B. 185
Pavlov, I. 165
Peake, P. K. 175
Pearson, T. 192
Peckham, V. 123
Peel, J. L. 27
Peele, D. B. 102
Pegler, A. M. 164
Peláez-Nogueras, M. 287
Penn, P. 292
Peragallo, J. 121, 124
Pérez, J. A. 275
Perkins, D. V. 208, 274
Perone, M. 53, 183
Perri, M. G. 273
Perrott, M. C. 101
Perruchet, P. 172
Perry, C. L. 277
Perry, J. C. 208, 274
Peters, T. J. 300, 302
Peterson, G. L. 77
Peterson, N. 42
Peterson, R. F. 95
Peterson, W. A. 251
Petty, R. E. 119, 122-124, 132, 240-243
Pickens, R. 281
Pierce, W. D. 47, 70, 73
Piliavin, J. A. 132, 286
Pinter, E. 33
Pittam, J. 204
Pittman, T. S. 297
Ploog, B. O. 27, 29
Plous, S. 175
Podsakoff, P. M. 188
Poling, A. 51, 281, 292
Poll, N. E. van de 186
Poppen, R. L. 194, 269
Poret, M. K. 185
Porter, B. E. 281
Postman, L. 251
Potts, R. 235
Poulson, C. L. 95
Powell, F. A. 122, 124
Powers, W. T. 42
Prakash, A. 234
Prasad, J. 251
Pratkanis, A. R. 112, 179, 237
Premack, A. 47

Premack, D. 46-47
Prentice-Dunn, S. 111, 119, 121-124
Pribram, K. H. 68, 165-168
Price, V. 207
Primavera, J. 276, 280
Prochaska, J. O. 279
Pruitt, D. G. 121-124, 298
Pryer, M. W. 108
Pryor, J. 168
Pryor, K. W. 35, 189, 281
Pumariega, A. J. 158
Pumroy, D. K. 112
Purdy, J. E. 27
Quinn, P. C. 35, 92
Rabbie, J. M. 122
Rabbit, P. 251
Rachlin, H. 51, 69-70, 74, 185-186, 190-193
Radcliffe-Brown, A. R. 218
Radlow, R. 122
Ragsdale, E. K. E. 175
Ralph, A. 135
Ramp, K.A. 281
Randolph, J. 102
Rao, R. K. 293
Rapoport, A. 190
Rappaport, J. 207
Rappaport, R. A. 211, 217
Ray, B. A. 26, 29, 36
Reber, A. S. 172
Reberg, D. 50
Redfield, R. 201
Redman, S. 277-280
Redmon, W. K. 70
Reese, H. W. 287-288
Reicher, S. D. 205-207
Reid, A. K. 77
Reid, D. H. 263, 293
Reid, J. B. 125
Reis, H. T. 118-119, 123
Reps, P. 195-196
Reser, J. P. 42
Reynolds, N. J. 102
Ribeiro, A de F. 158-159
Rice, G. E. 132
Rich, M. 122, 124
Rickert, E. J. 47
Ridgway, V. F. 297, 300
Riegler, H. C. 153-154, 158-159, 240

Riger, S. 283, 286
Riley, D. 247
Rimer, B. K. 277
Rincover, A. 25, 263, 270
Risley, T. R. 260, 289
Riviére, V. 185
Robert, M. 95
Roberto, E. L. 279
Roberts, A. E. 47
Roberts, B. 235
Roberts, D. F. 253
Roberts, R. N. 184
Roberts, S. 224
Robinson, D. 277
Robinson, J. C. 47
Robinson, J. P. 253
Robinson, P. W. 108
Roering, K. J. 122-124
Roger, B. 78
Rogers, E. M. 275, 278
Rogers, R. W. 111, 119, 121-124
Rogers-Warren, A. 133-134, 158
Romaine, S. 203
Romzek, B. S. 294
Rook, K. S. 247
Roper, T. J. 77
Rorty, R. 226
Rosaldo, M. Z. 143
Rosch, M. 124
Rose, G. L. 122-124
Rosen, B. 119, 123
Rosen, N. A. 119, 121-124
Rosenbaum, M. E. 129
Rosenberg, M. J. 296
Rosenberg, S. 108, 152
Rosenfarb, I. 185
Rosenfeld, H. M. 151
Rosenfeld, P. 297
Rosenthal, D. 204
Rosenthal, T. L. 290
Rosnow, M. P. 292
Rosnow, R. L. 251
Ross, E. B. 210
Ross, M. 119, 123, 298
Rossi, E. L. 276
Rossi, J. S. 279
Rossi, M. 131
Rossi, S. I. 276

Rothenberg, S. 277
Rothschild, M. L. 275, 280
Rotter, J. B. 187
Roush, K. L. 285
Rovira, D. P. 235
Rowold, K. L. 119, 123
Rozelle, R. M. 121-124
Rumbaugh, D. M. 131
Rummel, J. E. 69
Russell, B. 143
Russo, D. C. 66
Rutherford, R. D. 134
Rutter, D. R. 247
Ryan, R. M. 187-188
Ryle, G. 62, 212
Sá, C. P. de. 235
Sahlins, M. D. 206, 217-218, 220, 246
Sajwaj, T. 268
Sameoto, D. 104
Sampson, E. E. 178, 180, 252
Samson, H. H. 52
Sanchez, H. 296
Sandberg, K. 31
Sanders, G. S. 92, 296
Sanderson, G. M. 164
Sanderson, P. M. 172
Sanford, C. 119, 123
Sanger, D. J. 281
Sanson-Fisher, R. W. 277-280
Santamaria, M. C. de. 293
Santi, A. 65
Sarason, S. B. 207
Sasson, T. 235, 253-254
Sato, K. 122
Sato, M. 96, 189
Saunders, R. R. 35, 63
Saussure, F. de. 144, 202, 235
Savy, I. 172
Sawin, L. L. 285
Sawyer, J. 122
Schachter, S. 198, 251
Schaeffer, R. W. 47
Schank, R. C. 68
Scheier, M. F. 111, 114, 166
Scherl, L. M. 42
Schlenker, B. R. 122
Schlenker, P. A. 122
Schlinger, H. D. 156, 168-169, 204, 287

Schmid, T. L. 133
Schmitt, D. R. 70, 125-127, 129-130
Schneider, R. H. 277
Schneider, S. M. 29
Schnelle, J. F. 291
Schoenfeld, W. N. 29, 32, 39, 41, 80, 127, 164, 178
Schoenrade, P. A. 122-123
Schofield, M. J. 277, 280
Schoneberger, T. 145
Schooler, R. D. 122
Schopler, J. 123
Schreibe, K. E. 89
Schreibman, L. 290
Schroeder, S. R. 26
Schuh-Wear, C. L. 293
Schumaker, J. B. 134
Schwartz, B. 35, 189
Schwartz, I. S. 260
Schwartz, S. H. 121-124
Schweitzer, J. B. 186
Schwimmer, E. 217
Scott, W. E. 188
Searle, J. 143
Secan, K. E. 164
Seekins, T. 207, 277-278, 280
Segal, E. F. 32, 35, 112, 189, 282
Seidman, E. 207
Seilheimer, S. D. 121, 123-124
Semin, G. R. 294
Sergio, J. P 292
Serna, L. A. 134
Seta, C. E. 92
Seta, J. J. 92
Shade, D. 71
Shaffer, D. R. 122
Shapiro, E. G. 122
Shapiro, S. P. 245
Shapiro, S. T. 267
Sharpe, P. 285
Shaw, J. I. 122
Shea, M. C. 71
Sheldon, S. B. 134
Sheldrake, P. 294
Sheppard, B. H. 243, 247
Shepperd, J. A. 108-109
Sherman, S. 122
Sherman, S. A. 134

Sherman, S. J. 238
Sherrington, C. 165
Sheth, J. N. 277, 279
Shettleworth, S. J. 70, 135, 178
Shimamura, J. W. 112
Shimoff, E. 53, 154-155, 158-159, 192
Shinn, M. 280
Shovar, M. N. 129
Shull, R. L. 155
Shumaker, S. A. 247
Shure, G. 122
Shure, G. H. 122
Sidman, M. 20, 36, 48, 55, 62-63, 65, 67,
    101-102, 112, 204, 263, 266, 268, 300
Siegel, J. 255
Silberberg, A. 191
Silver, B. D. 238
Silverman, K. 66, 151-152
Silverstone, R. 253
Simmel, G. 131, 164, 201, 209, 219-223,
    246
Simmelhag, V. L. 50
Simon, H. A. 174, 183
Simon, S. 119, 123
Simpanen, M. 293
Singer, G. 137, 210
Sinha, D. 251
Sinha, Y. 234
Sisson, L. A. 281
Skevington, S. 285-286
Skinner, B. F. 16, 20-21, 23-24, 31-34, 36,
    38, 44-46, 49-50, 52, 56-59, 62, 69, 74,
    76, 80, 96, 102-102, 110, 112, 127, 143-
    146, 148-153, 160, 168, 170, 175-178,
    181, 196, 205, 207, 227, 232, 237, 248-
    249, 252-253, 268, 287, 290-292, 294
Slavin, R. E. 112, 125
Sloane, H. N. 189
Slovic, P. 122-123, 192
Slusher, E. A. 122-124
Slyck, M. V. 121, 124
Smith, B. L. R. 294
Smith, J. F. 207, 277, 280
Smith, K. 41
Smith, K. H. 108
Smith, L. K. C. 112, 281
Smith, M. 285
Smith, M. B. 237, 242

Smith, P. M. 206
Smith, R. F. I. 294
Smith, R. H. 119, 123
Smith, T. 290
Smith, T. L. 146
Smith, T. W. 134
Sniezek, J. A. 175
Snowden, L. R. 277
Snyder, C. R. 134
Snyder, M. 237
Society for the Experimental Analysis of
    Behavior. 207, 261, 274, 281
Solomon, L. 123
Sorrentino, R. M. 112
Sotirakopoulou, K. P. 236
Spann, R. D. 301
Spears, R. 255
Spelke, E. 87
Speltz, M. L. 112
Spence, J. T. 285
Spence, K. W. 165-166
Spencer, E. A. 278-279
Spiga, R. 136
Spitzer, C. E. 121-124
Spong, R. T. 184, 186
Spradlin, J. E. 35, 151-153
Sproull, L. 255
Squire, C. 283
Squire, L. R. 172
Staats, A. W. 39
Staats, E. B. 299
Staddon, J. E. R. 33, 50, 77
Stafford, M. W. 149
Stammbach, E. 88
Stark, M. T. 268
Stasser, G. 121-124
Stathopoulou, A. 236
Steensma, H. 122
Steigleder, M. K. 131
Steinberg, J. L. 136
Steiner, F. 214, 217
Steinhorst, R. 47
Steinman, W. M. 95
Stephens, D. 122
Stephenson, G. M. 247-248
Stoddard, P. 78
Stoffelmayr, B. E. 47
Stokes, T. F. 46, 158-159, 261, 271

Stolz, S. B. 260, 278
Stoneman, K. G. 108
Storey, K. 134
Street, R. L. 204, 212
Street, W. R. 93, 111, 172, 233
Striefel, S. 73-74, 77
Stromer, R. 67
Stryk, L. 195
Suarez-Balcazar, Y. 207, 277, 280
Suls, J. 96-97
Sulzer-Azeroff, B. 146, 186, 261, 271, 293
Sundberg, M. L. 30, 143, 149
Svanum, S. 119, 123
Svartdal, F. 232
Svenson, O. 192
Swindell, A. 119, 122-124
Switzer, F. S. 175
Szelenyi, I. 200, 246
Szymanski, K. 49, 92, 107, 118, 296, 298-299
Tait, D. 138
Tajfel, H. 205-207, 229
Tanizaki, J. 219
Tanur, J. 121-122, 124
Tarpy, R. M. 281
Tatham, T. A. 52-53
Tatum, R. 92
Taylor, C. J. 132
Taylor, D. C. 248
Taylor, L. A. 188
Taylor, S. 119, 123
Taylor, S. E. 122, 238
Taylor, S. J. 122
Tedeschi, J. T. 239
Teitelbaum, P. 33
Telch, M. J. 277
Temple, W. 70
Terborg, J. R. 277
Terrell, D. J. 164, 177-178, 241
Terris, W. 132
Tetlock, P. E. 112, 114-115, 119, 121-124, 232, 294-295, 298-299
Tharp, R. G. 164
Thibaut, J. W. 122, 125, 251
Thoits, P. A. 76, 179-180
Thomas, S. V. 253
Thompson, J. B. 253
Thompson, K. R. 292-293

Thompson, S. 63
Thompson, T. 33, 52, 55, 181, 281
Thorensen, C. E. 185
Thorslund, C. 122
Thyer, B. A. 281-282
Thynne, I. 294
Tilley, C. S. 164
Tilley, K. J. 63
Timberlake, W. 40, 47, 50, 86
Titchener, E. B. 196
Todd, J. T. 16, 75
Tolman, E. C. 69
Tonkin, E. 247
Tönnies, F. 198-201, 228
Trattner, J. 47
Traughber, B. 291
Tripathi, R. C. 234
Trommsdorff, G. 121, 124
Troutman, A. C. 281
Trudgill, P. 203
Tsai, M. 282
Tuchman, G. 285
Tuckman, B. 228
Turem, J. 294
Turner, J. C. 205-207, 229, 280
Turner, J. H. 199
Turner, P. J. 206
Turvey, M. T. 29
Tustin, R. D. 26
Tversky, A. 174, 190-193
Tyler, T. R. 253, 279
Ulman, J. D. 146
Ulrich, R. 15, 104
Umbreit, J. 164
Unger, R. K. 283, 286
Urcuioli, P. J. 24
Van Avermaet, E. 275, 280
Van Hasselt, V. B. 281
Van Houten, R. 104
van der Kragt, A. J. C. 130
van der Pligt, J. 237-238
van Sonderen, E. 246
van Tilburg, T. 246
Vargas, E. A. 49, 146, 153, 157, 210
Vatmanidis, P. C. 164
Vaughan, M. E. 27, 44, 290-292
Vaughan, W. 48
Veblen, T. 154

Velasquez, M. M. 279
Velicer, W. F. 279
Verplank, W. S. 238
Vidmar, N. 123-124
Voeltz, L. M. 282
Volger, R. E. 68
Vollmer, T. R. 30
von Cranach, M. 235-236
von Grumbkow, J. 122
von Winterfeldt, D. 190
Vukelich, R. 79, 96, 125, 129, 131, 133-134
Vygotsky, L. S. 235
Wacker, D. P. 263
Wade, G. S. 247-248
Wade, J. 119, 123
Wagenaar, W. A. 192
Wahler, R. G. 30, 282, 289
Walker, C. J. 251
Walker, I. 285
Wall, J. A. 121, 124
Wallace, I. 248
Wallace, R. F. 34
Wallace, R. K. 277
Wallach, M. A. 124
Wallack, L. 278
Walster, E. 232, 234
Wanchisen, B. A. 52-53
Ward, C. 234
Ward, J. M. 294
Warren, D. R. 150
Warren, S. F. 133-134
Warshaw, P. R. 243
Washburn, D. A. 131
Wasik, B. H. 47
Wasserman, E. A. 52, 134
Waterman, R. H. 300, 302
Watson, J. S. 96
Watson, J. B. 23, 36
Watt, A. 90
Watts, A. W. 194-195
Watts, W. A. 122, 124
Wayner, M. J. 77
Weardon, J. H. 185
Weber, M. 200-201, 222-223, 249
Weber, S. J. 114
Webley, P. 281
Wechkin, S. 132
Wegner, D. M. 247-248, 253

Weick, K. E. 275
Weidner, M. F. 122
Weigert, A. 245-246
Weiler, J. 121-122, 124
Weiner, H. 53, 133
Weinstein, E. 121-122, 124
Weinstein, M. S. 123
Weisberg, P. 50
Weiss, B. 289
Weiss, R. F. 131, 150
Weisz, J. R. 289
Weldon, E. 119, 122-124, 295
Weller, P. 294
Wells, G. L. 122
Weninger, J. M. 158
Wenrich, W. W. 44, 104
Wenzlaff, R. 253
Wertsch, J. V. 235
West, B. J. 33
Westford, K. L. 123
Weston, R. 278
Wetherall, M. 205-207, 280, 285
Wetherington, C. L. 77
White, G. L. 119, 121, 123-124
White, G. W. 207, 277, 280
White, K. G. 31, 57, 167
White, M. J. 132-133
White, P. A. 182
White, R. W. 237, 242
Whitehurst, G. J. 95
Whitman, T. L. 47
Whitman, W. 61, 240
Whitworth, T. L. 106
Wichman, H. 119, 123
Wickham, C. 247
Wiemann, J. M. 203
Wike, E. L. 42
Wildavsky, A. 301
Wilke, H. 122
Wilkenfield, J. 51
Wilkes, A. L. 206
Wilkes, P. V. 294
Willemyns, M. 204
Willer, J. 235
Williams, B. A. 29, 41
Williams, D. M. 136
Williams, K. D. 107, 114, 119, 123-124
Williams, M. L. 47

Williamson, P. N. 290
Wills, T. A. 96-97, 247
Wilson, G. T. 273
Wilson, K. G. 269, 282
Wilson, K. V. 119, 123
Wilson, T. D. 179, 182
Winch, P. 197, 225
Winett, R. A. 277, 281
Winkler, R. C. 136, 276
Winokur, S. 143, 151
Winston, A. S. 189, 287-288
Wirth, W. 294
Wise, C. R. 294
Wisocki, P. A. 290-291
Wittgenstein, L. 79, 153, 178, 181
Wittig, M. A. 283, 286
Wixted, J. 29
Wober, J. M. 253
Wojnilower, D. A. 184
Wolf, M. M. 46, 260, 281, 289
Wolfe, D. A. 128
Wolfe, V. V. 128
Wolff, P.C. 108
Woods, D. J. 272
Woodson, R. 96

Worchel, S. 119, 122-123, 228-229
Wright, E. 122
Wu, C. 122
Wulfert, E. 66-67, 184-185
Wyckoff, L. B. 27
Yamagishi, T. 122
Yamamoto, J. 149, 164, 262, 290
Yarkin, K. L. 122
Yarkin-Levin, K. 122
Yerbury, D. 295
Young, L. 164
Young-Eisendrath, P. 285
Zaccaro, S. J. 124
Zajonc, R. B. 85, 93, 108, 122, 124, 187
Zalenska, M. 123-124
Zander, A. 124
Zanna, M. P. 240-241
Zeiler, M. D. 33, 50, 52, 55
Zettle, R. D. 91, 94, 154, 185, 233, 269, 282
Zimbardo, P. G. 110, 119
Zimmerman, E. H. 102
Zimmerman, J. 43, 102
Zucker, L. G. 245
Zuriff, G. E. 25, 164, 175

Other Books from CONTEXT PRESS

Ethical Issues in Developmental Disabilities
  Linda J. Hayes, Gregory J. Hayes, Stephen L. Moore, and
  Patrick M. Ghezzi (Eds.) (208 pp.)

Behavior Analysis of Language and Cognition
  Steven C. Hayes, Linda J. Hayes, Masaya Sato, and
  Koichi Ono (Eds.)

Outline of J. R. Kantor's Psychological Linguistics
  Sidney W. Bijou and Patrick M. Ghezzi (79 pp.)

Varieties of Scientific Contextualism
  Steven C. Hayes, Linda J. Hayes, Hayne W. Reese,
  Theodore R. Sarbin (Eds.) (320 pp.)

Behavior Analysis of Child Development (3rd edition)
  Sidney W. Bijou (224 pp.)

Radical Behaviorism: Willard Day on Psychology and Philosophy
  S. Leigland (Ed.) (208 pp.)

Understanding Verbal Relations
  Steven C. Hayes and Linda J. Hayes (Eds.) (224 pp.)

Dialogues on Verbal Behavior
  Linda J. Hayes and Philip N. Chase (Eds.) (349 pp.)

To order write to:

CONTEXT PRESS
933 Gear St.
Reno, NV 89502-2729